Czech Republic

the Bradt Travel Guide

Marc Di Duca

edition
I

www.bradtguides.com

Bradt Travel Guides Ltd, UK
The Globe Pequot Press Inc, USA

Czech
Republic
Don't
miss...

The bustling capital, Prague
Old Town Square
(LC) pages 73–126

Perfectly preserved castles and mansions
Jaroměřice nad Rokytnou
(PCL) pages 255–6

The wines of south Moravia
(PCL)

Hiking in the countryside
Mochtín, Šumava
(JV) pages 227–30

Medieval towns
Český Krumlov
(PCL) pages 217–22

top **Vineyards in south Moravia**
(PCL)

centre **Buskers in Prague** (PCL)

left **Tram in Prague**
(PCL) page 78

above **Workers in Petřín Park, Prague** (CE)

below left **Castle guard at Prague Castle** (PCL) pages 92–7

below right **Café menu, Prague** (PCL)

top **Northern geese roosting at Nové Mlýny at dawn, south Moravia** (JC)
above left **Red deer** *Cervus elephus* (SS)
above right **Hiking trails in south Bohemia** (MD)
below **Lake Lipno** (JV)

Author/Acknowledgements

AUTHOR

Born in the UK, Marc Di Duca left for rural central Bohemia for three months' work experience in 1991 and returned a decade later! Initially going there to tutor Czechs in English, he was fascinated with all aspects of the country, leading him to become proficient in the language and enabling him to teach it to foreigners and work as a translator. In 2000 Marc returned to Great Britain to work for the Czech Tourist Authority in London where he spent four years. He now works as a freelance travel writer and translator based in sunny Eastbourne.

ACKNOWLEDGEMENTS

Many thanks go to the many local people around the Czech Republic whose expertise and local knowledge were an immense help and useful tool when I was writing this book. Special thanks belong to Tricia Hayne and Hilary Bradt for giving me the chance to write this guide; Radka Pomikálková of Czech Tourism for her support and practical assistance throughout; the Rouček family of Rakovník for their support and use of their apartment in Prague; Iveta Schoppová, head of Czech Tourism in London for her encouragement; Martina Kalinová and family for their invaluable assistance in south Bohemia; Ms Olga Stavělová of Slavonice information centre; Mr Zdeněk Přibyl of Prachatice information centre; Mrs Pojarová of the Jewish Museum in Prague; the staff of the Prague Information Service; Gerard Gorman for checking the natural history section; Jan Kaplan for his encouragement and contributions; Ondřes Krátký for inspiring me to travel; and most of all to my beloved wife, Tanya, for giving me the space to work.

FEEDBACK REQUEST

The Czech Republic seems to be in a constant state of flux and every time I visit I am staggered at what has changed, appeared, disappeared, been abolished, increased in price or banned. Therefore, your visit is a vital source of information for future editions of this book so if you come across something in the country which you think I should follow up (a particularly good restaurant or hotel, especially outside of Prague, a new museum, or a closed gallery for instance), or if you would like to tell me where you found the guide useful, interesting or lacking, or what you liked or disliked about the country and its people, then send your thoughts and observations to me c/o Bradt Travel Guides, 23 High Street, Chalfont St Peter, Bucks SL9 9QE, England. I will acknowledge all helpful contributions in future editions.

First published March 2006

Bradt Travel Guides Ltd
23 High Street, Chalfont St Peter, Bucks SL9 9QE, England
www.bradtguides.com
Published in the USA by The Globe Pequot Press Inc, 246 Goose Lane,
PO Box 480, Guilford, Connecticut 06437-0480

British Library Cataloguing in Publication Data
A catalogue record for this book is available from the British Library

ISBN-10: 1 84162 150 1
ISBN-13: 978 1 84162 150 0

Photographs

Front cover: Roof tops of Prague's Old Town and Charles Bridge
(Pictures Colour Library)
Text: Chad Ehlers/Tips (CE), Humberto Olarte Cupas/Tips (HC), Josef Chytil (JC),
Joanna Vaughan (JV), Luis Castaneda/Tips (LC), Marc Di Duca (MD), Pictures Colour
Library (PCL), Stephen Street/Tips (SS)
Back cover: Golden Lane, Prague (PCL), Lake Lipno (JV)
Title page: Tram (PCL), Castle guard (PCL), Jaroměřice nad Rokytnou (PCL)

Illustrations Carole Vincer
Maps Terence Crump, Steve Munns

Typeset from the author's disc by Wakewing, High Wycombe
Printed and bound in Italy by Legoprint SpA, Trento

PUBLISHER'S FOREWORD

The first Bradt travel guide was written in 1974 by George and Hilary Bradt on a river barge floating down a tributary of the Amazon. In the 1980s and '90s the focus shifted away from hiking to broader-based guides covering new destinations – usually the first to be published about these places. In the 21st century Bradt continues to publish such ground-breaking guides, as well as others to established holiday destinations, incorporating in-depth information on culture and natural history with the nuts and bolts of where to stay and what to see.

Bradt authors support responsible travel, and provide advice not only on minimum impact but also on how to give something back through local charities. In this way a true synergy is achieved between the traveller and local communities.

* * *

The forerunner of this guide was published in 1987. *The Bradt Guide to Czechoslovakia* was the first in English to cover this austere, Soviet-dominated country which nevertheless had one of the most beautiful capitals in Europe and some of the most courageous, hospitable people. The guide was our bestseller for several years, its life cut short by the division of Czechoslovakia into two countries. I am therefore particularly pleased to be publishing this sequel, written by Marc Di Duca with such love and enthusiasm. It's impossible to read it without longing to see the place for yourself.

Hilary Bradt

23 High Street, Chalfont St Peter, Bucks SL9 9QE, England
☏ 01753 893444   f 01753 892333
e info@bradtguides.com   www.bradtguides.com

Contents

LIST OF MAPS

For key to map symbols, see page VI.

KEY TO SYMBOLS

·—·—	International boundary	⊞	Chateau
------	District boundary	☆	Night club
National park boundary		†	Church or cathedral
✈	Airport	✡	Synagogue
▬▬	Railway	🐘	Zoo
----------	Footpath	*i*	Tourist information
⛽	Petrol station or garage	$	Bank
🅿	Car park	♟	Statue or monument
🚌	Bus station etc	∴	Archaeological or historic site
🚲	Cycle hire	⚑	Golf course
M	Underground station	🏃	Stadium
⌂	Hotel, inn etc	✳	Scenic viewpoint
Δ	Campsite	❀	Botanical site
⚲	Wine bar	⌣	City wall
✕	Restaurant, caf etc	▲	Summit
⊠	Post office	⌂	Rock shelter
ℭ	Telephone	⌑—⌑	Cable car, funicular
e	Internet caf	⊨	Mountain pass
✚	Hospital	≈	Marsh
✛	Health centre		
⚱	Museum/gallery		
🏰	Historic building		

Bradt

Introduction

Friday 17 November was Children in Need day in Britain in 1989. As I walked up Penny Lane in Liverpool to my hall of residence that crisp autumn afternoon I passed red-nosed students rattling buckets full of change, messing around in front of cameras from local TV. Unbeknown to me, across Europe in Prague another group of students were gathering, but theirs was a less jolly appeal. That evening they clashed with police in central Prague kicking off a series of events which would see the communist regime swept from power. Little did I know that November day how these events would affect my life.

Uninspired by university and longing to see the world and find adventure I found myself 15 months later on the midnight Nuremberg–Prague express heading to a teaching post in a country I knew nothing of, with a language I could not speak and on the other side of a border virtually out of bounds for the last 40 years. At the frontier my compartment emptied, and as the train moved off and the darkness began to lift, a mysterious new country revealed itself to me, a place which would be home for the next decade, though I did not know it then. Drab, grey buildings, dark wooded hills, a smell of coal smoke in the air, a dusting of snow in late April, Škoda cars everywhere, curious marks above letters in place names; all these things I saw from the compartment window as the Czech lands began to bombard my senses and my inquisitive young mind lapped it up. From that first morning in the hazy, cold light of an April Monday in 1991 I was hooked and have been fascinated with this mysterious country ever since.

My teaching post took me to a small district town in central Bohemia, 50km west of Prague. The air was thick with brown coal smoke, the cars belched fumes, the shops, whilst not empty, did not seem to sell anything you needed and the buildings were stained a uniform shade of ochre. People stared at my shoes, wondered with incredulity at how I could be vegetarian (which I very soon no longer was) and questioned why I was not rich. A beer was 8p, a ticket to the cinema 16p and a meal in a restaurant cost the same as a Mars bar back home. When it rained the pot-holes in the roads turned into lakes, when the sun shone it highlighted the dilapidated state of the town and when darkness fell, the street lamps took turns to shine to save energy. No-one spoke English, everyone presumed I would speak German and most students invited me home and stuffed me with food. The days got longer and hotter, I discovered real beer, roasted sausages over open fires, explored the hills and castles of the region, drank more beer and decided to stay in this odd place which I was slowly beginning to decipher and adore.

How times have changed since those bizarre days following the fall of communism in central and eastern Europe. Over the decade I spent in the Czech lands, I watched the country change from a dreary place to a renovated, renewed, colourful central European state, now a member of the EU and back in the fold of the European family of nations. I watched the town I lived in develop as its inhabitants started businesses, renovated their houses, bought Western goods and began to travel. And I saw myself change from a 19 year old enveloped by a foreign culture to a fluent Czech-speaking employee of the Czech Tourist Authority in London, advising others on a place where once I was a stranger. I linked my life with the fortunes of the Czech lands, a decision I have yet to regret.

In all likelihood you will not spend ten years in the Czech Republic, but however long you stay, you will find a country steeped in history, its people friendly, its architecture lovingly restored and countryside as relaxing as it is inspiring. It is the most user-friendly of the former communist countries with excellent public transport and a high standard of accommodation and other services. Enjoy Prague with its fine architecture, vibrant culture and historical sights, but to experience the Czech lands for real, break out of the capital to the mountains, a chateau, a historical town or a hiking trail through the woods. There is more to the Czech Republic than Prague and it is just waiting to be discovered.

Part One

General Information

THE CZECH REPUBLIC AT A GLANCE

Location Central Europe, 49°N and 15°E. Borders Poland, Germany, Austria and Slovakia

Size 78,866km²

Geography Rolling plains and hills encircled by low mountains

Climate Continental with cold winters and hot summers. Average temperature January –3°C, July 18°C. Mountain areas are colder in winter and cooler in summer.

Status Republic

Administrative divisions 13 regions and Prague

Capital Prague

Other major cities Brno, Ostrava, Pilsen, České Budějovice, Hradec Králové, Olomouc

Population 10.2 million

People Czech 81%, Moravian 13%, Slovak 3%. Remaining 3% includes Poles, Germans, Romany and Hungarians

Life expectancy 79 years for females, 72 years for males

Languages Czech, Slovak, Roma

Religion Officially Roman Catholic

Currency Czech crown, Kč occasionally CZK

Exchange rate €1 = 29Kč, £1 = 42Kč, US$1 = 24Kč (January 2006)

National airline Czech Airlines, international flight code OK

International dialling code +420

Time GMT + 1 hour (6 hours ahead of New York City)

Electricity AC is 220 volts and frequency is 50 hertz

Flag Two equal horizontal bands of white and red with a blue isosceles triangle on the left

National anthem 'Kde domov můj' (Where is my home), words by Tyl put to music by Škroup

National tree Linden tree

National sport Ice hockey, soccer

Public holidays 1 January (New Year's Day), Easter Monday, 1 May (May Day – Workers' Day), 8 May (Liberation Day), 5 July (Slavic Apostles St Cyril and St Methodius), 6 July (Burning of Jan Hus), 28 September (Czech Statehood Day), 28 October (Independence Day), 17 November (Freedom and Democracy Day), 24 December (Christmas Eve), 25 December (Christmas Holiday), 26 December (St Stephen's Day)

Background Information

GEOGRAPHY AND CLIMATE

If Shakespeare is to be believed, Bohemia is 'a desert country near the sea' (*A Winter's Tale*). The bard had evidently never visited this part of central Europe as the Czech Republic is in fact situated in the very heart of the European continent at 49°N and 15°E, and in the complicated jigsaw which is central Europe, fits snugly between Poland, Germany, Austria and Slovakia. It has almost 2,000km of borders shared exclusively with other EU members, and is one of only two landlocked EU countries to enjoy such neighbours (Luxembourg being the other). The Czech lands cover an area of 78,866km² making them slightly smaller than South Carolina, about the same size as Austria, and the 21st-largest country in Europe, which, in fact, is not very large at all.

The Czech Republic is divided into Bohemia in the west and Moravia in the east. Bohemia is largely made up of rolling plains and low, wooded hills, while Moravia is hillier and crisscrossed with broad flood plains. The whole country is framed by a ring of mountains creating natural borders, thus making the Czech Republic the only landlocked country you could in theory pick out from space. Thanks to these natural borders the Czechs have virtually no territorial disputes with their neighbours, rare in this neck of the woods. A slang name for Germans even means 'those over the hills'.

The country sits on the division between the half of Europe drained by the Elbe (or Labe in Czech) and the other half drained by the Danube. Interestingly, this division also roughly divides Bohemia from Moravia. Despite what many may assume, the Danube at no point flows through the territory of the Czech Republic, but *is* fed by Moravia's major river, the Morava. Bohemia's main river is the Vltava (Moldau) whose tributaries swell it into a substantial waterway en route from the Šumava in the south to Prague. North of Prague, even the mighty Vltava has to give way to an infant Elbe, which drains the mountainous areas in the north, meets the Vltava in Mělník before making a beeline for the German border, and on to the North Sea. With all this water sloshing around the republic, it can come as no surprise that the only natural hazard comes in the form of regular flooding.

The highest peak is Sněžka in the Krkonoše Mountains at 1,602m above sea level. The country's lowest point at 115m above sea level is on the river Elbe in east Bohemia.

Climate

The Czech Republic has a continental climate meaning bitterly cold, snowy winters and sweltering summers. Spring tends to come later the higher the elevation, and autumns are mild. The average January temperature is −3°C, and July sees an average of 18°C. At elevations over 1,000m temperatures are lower year round, something to bear in mind when heading into the mountains.

MADE IN CZECH?

It may seem odd but the Czech Republic is not actually the official name of any country in Europe! When the old Czechoslovakia broke up in 1993, the name began to be used without anyone really sitting down and agreeing that this was going to be the country's title. Since then a messy, inconclusive debate has gone on sporadically about the name. Many would agree that there is nothing wrong with Czech Republic, but the problem is that certain Czechs seem to consider it too long for foreigners to say, never mind remember.

The debate divides the nation with politicians, government bodies, celebrities, linguists and pub philosophers all putting their oar in. Various think tanks and PR and marketing gurus have come up with names including Czecho and Czechia and even just Czech. In Czech, Czechia translates as *Česko* about which former president Václav Havel proclaimed: 'When I hear *Česko* it is as if I have slugs crawling all over me', from which it can be seen how passionate the debate can become. Two camps seem to have formed. Those with enough faith in the intelligence of the human race to use *Česká republika* (Czech Republic) versus those who think the name is bad for the country as a brand, and would like to use a dumbed-down shorter version, namely *Česko* (untranslatable, Czecho, Czechia). 'Made in Czech' found on some products is a result of this confusion.

NATURAL HISTORY AND CONSERVATION

Protected areas, nature reserves and national parks cover an impressive 16% of the total territory of the Czech Republic, double the European average. The largest national park is the 685km^2 Šumava National Park in the very southwest, bordering Germany and Austria. Other particularly scenic areas are the Krkonoše National Park in the northeast, the Czech 'Switzerland' area in north Bohemia, and the Podyjí National Park in south Moravia. Apart from these large protected areas, the country is literally peppered with hundreds of small nature and biosphere reserves. Six biosphere reserves are under UNESCO protection. These are the White Carpathians (Bílé Karpaty) in north Moravia, the Křivoklát region in central Bohemia, the Krkonoše mountains in the northeast, the Pálava area in south Moravia, Šumava and the Třeboň Basin 'lakeland' in south Bohemia.

When the Iron Curtain was swept back in 1989 some landscapes damaged by acid rain and opencast mining were revealed. In some towns, especially in north Bohemia and north Moravia, the air was sometimes so toxic children had to wear gas masks to school and the elderly were advised to stay indoors. But Czech conservationists have been very active since the early 1990s and much has improved with, for example, a reduction in the amount of low grade brown coal being burnt by households and industry. Today threats to the environment come from different quarters with economic pressure to build more motorways drawing ever more cars and lorries onto the roads to deliver goods to mammoth out-of-town shopping centres. The dangers of nuclear power are still high on the agenda, too, with the Czechs' decision to activate the Temelín nuclear power station in south Bohemia, much to the dismay of neighbouring Austria.

Mountains, foothills, valleys, plains, rivers and lakes create a very diverse environment in the Czech Republic where wildlife flourishes, often without the intervention of man. One-third of the country is woodland, usually pine, spruce, beech and birch. Such places are home to woodpeckers, owls, red and roe deer, wild boar and pine marten. There are lynx, too, though some luck is needed to see these. In spring hares can be seen scampering across fields and foxes, badgers and otters are fairly common in the appropriate habitat. A few wolves and brown bears occupy the Beskydy Mountains and White Carpathians in the east of the country bordering Slovakia. In spring and summer nesting white storks are a feature in many rural villages, too.

HISTORY

If a visit to such a historically and culturally rich land as the Czech Republic is not to become a pointless tour of meaningless places, the visitor should be acquainted with a minimum of knowledge of what has gone on there prior to him or her getting off the plane. If you are eager to find out exactly which Charles built Charles Bridge or who exactly *was* Good King Wenceslas then read on.

With some notorious exceptions (the 1938 Munich agreement according to which Hitler was handed the Sudetenlands and the 1968 Warsaw Pact invasion to suppress the Prague Spring, for instance) not a great deal is commonly known about Czech history outside of central Europe. However, this country's often unfortunate geographical position, its one-time ambitious and intrusive neighbours and the Czechs' almost fatally daring breaks with European religious power make this an absorbing story; a cliffhanger the nation itself almost did not survive. Czech history is the tale of a small nation which once had glimpses of greatness as an independent country but which has mostly had to accommodate domination from Moscow, Vienna or Berlin while trying to hold on to some form of national identity without offending foreign overlords.

History surrounds you in the Czech Republic. It peers down at you from every hilltop castle, it echoes in every place name and is etched into the features of the population. From the earliest Slav rulers to Bohemia's golden age under Emperor Charles IV, from the Hussites to the Habsburgs and from the classy 1920s first republic to the bleak days of communism, all have left their mark. And remember, this is only the story so far. The Czech Republic's recent entry into the EU was just another chapter in its eventful history which has given hope and new opportunity to many, but also stirred old fears and prejudices.

For clarity it should be added that although the Czechs existed for over 70 years alongside the Slovaks in a single state, namely Czechoslovakia, the two nations followed a common path *only* for that period. The history of the two countries have touched only briefly over the centuries.

Prehistory to the arrival of the Slavs

The oldest human remains discovered in the Czech Republic date back to the late Stone Age 600,000–700,000 years ago. More important evidence of prehistoric human life dates from 26,000–22,000 years ago, and was discovered around Předmostí u Přerova, Pavlov and Dolní Věstonice in Moravia. The most significant and best-known find belonging to these mammoth hunters is the so-called Venus of Věstonice, a small clay figure of a woman with exaggerated hips and breasts, although many other ceramic artefacts were unearthed at the Věstonice burial site near Mikulov in south Moravia. From that time onwards there is proof of uninterrupted human activity in the Czech lands.

Thanks to the authors of antiquity the Celts became the first named inhabitants of the region. Indeed the very name Bohemia is derived from the Latin name *Boii*, a Celtic tribe. The Celts arrived in low-lying fertile areas in the first half of the 4th century BC and left behind standing stones which pepper the country to this day. The Celts were eventually driven out principally by the Germanic Markoman tribe who may have waged war against the Romans in AD17. The Czech lands remained outside the Roman Empire which naturally had a significant effect on their subsequent development.

In the 5th and 6th centuries the Germanic tribes including those with such well-known names as the Goths, Vandals, Burgunds and Langobards were slowly replaced or absorbed by the ethnic group that would come to dominate: the Slavs. The Czechs belong to the western Slavs along with the Poles, Slovaks and Lusatian Sorbs, all of whom gradually moved into central Europe from the east, themselves under pressure to migrate west from central Asia. Most of the Germanic tribes left apart from the Langobards who stayed for some time in southern Moravia before migrating to Italy in AD568, which in turn opened up even more territory for the Slavs to migrate to from the north and south. By the beginning of the 7th century the Slavs had occupied most of the territory east of an imaginary line from Lübeck on the Baltic coast to Trieste on the Adriatic.

The Samo Empire

Relatively little is known about the first centuries of Slav domination and there are very few archaeological finds. The Slav and German tribes probably lived side by side for a certain time in places but this co-existence was disturbed by the Avars, a nomadic people who had taken control of the territory of what is now Hungary west of the Danube. As a result of these attacks Samo, a foreigner thought to be a merchant from central France, united some of the Slavic tribes and successfully rose up against the Avars. In the year 625 the Samo Empire was established, sometimes cited as the first coherent western Slav empire. The actual extent of Samo's empire is not precisely known though it is safe to say that it covered most of today's Czech Republic and some of Slovakia. The capital, Vogastisburg, which Samo successfully defended against the Frankish King Dagobert in 631, was situated somewhere in west Bohemia. Meanwhile a new state was being created with its centre in what is now south Moravia.

The Great Moravian Empire

This state would come to be known as the Great Moravian Empire though contemporary sources speak only of Moravia and the Moravians. Byzantine Emperor Porfyrogennetos first mentioned 'distant Moravia' as opposed to Serbian Moravia which is closer to Byzantium. Centres of cultural, political and religious life were the south Moravian walled settlements of Mikulčice and Staré Město near Uherské Hradiště.

The first notable ruler of the empire was Prince Mojmír I whose most noteworthy achievement was the defeat of an awkward rival Prince Pribina and the integration of his territory, Nitransko in Slovakia, into the empire. The greatest extent of the empire came under Mojmír's successors, covering present-day Bohemia, Moravia, parts of Poland, Slovakia and Hungary. Prince Mojmír was probably a Christian and during his reign missionaries from Bavaria and Salzburg were active in the region. The ruling classes were adopting the new religion; the rest of the population, however, retained their pagan beliefs. Mojmír's nephew Rostislav, ruler from 846, had the greatest impact on the spread of Christianity in Moravia. In order to offset the influence of the Frankish Empire of Ludwig II, Rostislav turned his attention towards Byzantium and asked the Byzantine emperor to send missionaries to Moravia.

Cyril and Methodius

These two brothers, the so-called 'Apostles of the Slavs' were missionaries from present-day Thessaloniki in northern Greece. They arrived in Moravia in around 863, were both familiar with Slavic dialects and had already worked as missionaries to Ukraine and Russia. Fluent in Old Slavic they developed the Glagolitic alphabet which later became the Cyrillic alphabet used in Russia, Ukraine and parts of the Balkans (hence the similarity between Cyrillic and Greek letters) and began to conduct services and translate religious texts. There is no evidence that they managed to translate the whole Bible, however. In 867 their activities were approved by Rome and the Great Moravian Church was for a time free from Frankish influence. Cyril spent a mere $4^1/2$ years in Moravia promoting the Slavonic liturgy but Methodius was later made archbishop of Moravia and Pannonia and resided at Velehrad where he died in 885. The significance of Cyril and Methodius for Moravia and for the entire Slavic world cannot be overstressed. Later declared saints, these missionaries, producers of the first Slavic literature and creators of a liturgical language still used in the Russian Orthodox Church, are celebrated each year in the Czech Republic with a national holiday (5 July).

Fall of the empire

Several factors led to the fall of the Great Moravian Empire. Internal strife, conflict with the East Frankish Empire and constant attacks by nomadic Hungarians considerably weakened the Moravian state. Under pressure from the Franks Svatopluk handed over his uncle Rostislav to Moravia's powerful western neighbour, reverted back to the Latin mass and banished Methodius's disciples. Svatopluk's death in 894, however, caused even greater instability and with nomadic Hungarians raiding from the east the Czech nobles used the situation to free themselves from Moravian subjugation. Czech princes began to pay tribute to the East Frankish King Arnulf and in 907 Moravia was defeated by the Hungarians at the Battle of Bratislava marking the end of its existence. The Hungarians never settled in Moravia but withdrew to the Danube and Tisa river plains. Moravia became dependent on the Czech princes and the Hungarians took Slovakia which stayed under Hungarian control as 'Upper Hungary' until the creation of Czechoslovakia in 1918.

With the demise of Moravia focus switches to the Czech lands, naturally better protected from potential enemies than the open plains of Moravia.

The Přemyslid dynasty

Czech legend has it that Libuše, the mythical Czech princess and prophetess, sent out her nobles to follow her horse who would lead them to her future husband and ruler of the Czechs. The horse led them to a village where they found Přemysl ploughing a field. Přemysl returned to Vyšehrad with the nobles, married Libuše and ruled over the Czechs from then on. Bořivoj, the first recorded member of the Přemyslid dynasty, derived his power from this old Slavic myth. The Přemyslid dynasty ruled the Czech lands for 400 years and many symbols, traditions and even the idea of a Czech state with Prague as its capital have their origin in the Přemyslid era.

Early Přemyslid rulers

Before his death Methodius managed to christen Bořivoj and his mother Ludmila. Bořivoj's most important act as ruler was to move his capital from Levý Hradec to Prague, a decision which made practical sense as Prague was the site of a major ford over the river Vltava. Bořivoj's successor was his son Spitihněv (895–905) who took Bohemia out of the Great Moravian Empire and began to pay tribute to the Frankish King Arnulf. He gave preference to the Latin mass though both Latin and Old Slavonic strains existed side by side for two centuries. Spitihněv's brother Vratislav I (915–21) was next to take the reins of power. He resisted several Hungarian attacks, consolidated the Czech state and was responsible for the foundation of the Basilica of St George at Prague Castle.

Vratislav had two sons, Boleslav and Václav (Wenceslas) (921–29 or 35) the celebrated 'Good King Wenceslas' of the 19th-century Christmas carol by John Mason Neale. He was indeed Good King Wenceslas, an enlightened and educated ruler for his time who stuck firmly to his Christian beliefs. The beginning of his reign was a turbulent one. He was too young to rule on his own and came under the influence of his mother Drahomíra and grandmother Ludmila who instilled deep Christianity in the boy prince. A dispute broke out between the two women over Václav resulting in Drahomíra having Ludmila murdered. Ludmila was later canonised, becoming a patron saint of the Czech lands. During his reign Václav founded the Cathedral of St Vitus at Prague Castle which later grew into the Gothic place of worship we see today commanding the Prague skyline. Václav was himself assassinated by his envious brother Boleslav on 28 September 929 (or 935 according to some sources). This date was recently promoted to a national holiday in the Czech Republic.

Václav plays a unique role in the Czech Republic, being regarded a symbol of Czech statehood, its continuity and the ideal ruler. He was canonised later in the 10th century and is the patron saint of the Czech lands. The cult of St Václav continues to this day and is a very important aspect of the Czech national identity.

Boleslav's rule came to an end with his death in 972 and his son Boleslav II (973–99) replaced him on the throne. The Prague bishopric was established in 973 and placed under the archbishopric in Mainz. The first bishop was a Saxon called Thietmar but of much greater historical significance was Vojtěch (Adalbert), the second bishop to take up office. An educated, well-travelled man, Vojtěch came into conflict with Boleslav II for two reasons. First of all he attempted to strengthen the Church's prestige and develop a deeper understanding of the principles of Christian belief. Secondly he was of the Slavník house, a dynasty which controlled much of east and southeast Bohemia and rivals to the Přemyslid dynasty. Following in his father's footsteps, Boleslav rid himself of this troublesome family by murdering every single member except Vojtěch who himself was later martyred while a missionary in Prussia. After Ludmila and Václav he is the third patron saint of the Czech Republic, the quartet being completed by St Procopius, an abbot and the founder of the Sázava Monastery (see page 142). St Vojtěch's greatest legacy is the Břevnov Monastery, founded in 993.

Later Přemyslid rulers

At the turn of the 9th and 10th centuries the Czech kingdom found itself in crisis. New powerful neighbours, Poland and Hungary, were emerging on its borders and disputes between Boleslav's sons weakened the seat of power. The powerful King of Poland, Boleslav the Bold, in a bid to create a Slav empire occupied Moravia, and in 1002 got his man Vladivoj on to the Czech throne. Vladivoj's most significant achievement was to have freehold of the Czech realm given to him by Holy Roman Emperor Henry II in exchange for a pledge of service, in essence placing the Czech lands under Rome. Břetislav I (1034–55) set out to restore Bohemian pride. With his father Oldřich he retook Moravia from the Poles and even launched an attack on Poland itself. Away from the battlefield Břetislav issued the first book of laws in the Czech lands and declared that from that moment on the eldest member of the Přemyslid dynasty should automatically become Czech ruler; the cause of later conflict.

The most famous of Břetislav's sons was undoubtedly Vratislav II, best known to every Czech schoolboy as the first Czech king. He gained this title with support from the Holy Roman Emperor Henry IV though it was only for his lifetime. Nevertheless it confirmed Bohemia's importance in the Holy Roman Empire.

During the 12th century a series of rulers came to the throne and many a dispute raged over who should hold power. While authority changed hands many times, away from the court the Romanesque architectural style was taking hold. The Judith Bridge, the predecessor of the famous Charles Bridge constructed after the Judith Bridge collapsed in 1342, was built to span the Vltava. Examples of Romanesque architecture are the Rotunda of St Catherine in Znojmo (south Moravia) with its wall paintings depicting members of the Přemyslid dynasty, and several rotundas in Prague.

The end of the 12th century saw stability and prosperity return to the Czech lands. A major factor in this was the arrival of German colonisers, who settled agricultural land in difficult-to-reach places and established towns. They brought with them more advanced agricultural technology and a legal framework which defined the relationship between feudal overlords and serfs. From then until 1946 the Czech lands were a country of two ethnicities, a state of affairs which came to an end only when the Czechs ethnically cleansed the Germans for supporting Hitler. Several new towns were established either around existing castles (Hradec Králové, Brno, Olomouc) or as completely new settlements (České Budějovice, Nymburk). Some towns were given royal status allowing them to hold a market or brew beer. Taxes from this economic activity went straight to the royal coffers. Important mining towns emerged, the most significant of which was Kutná Hora. The vast amounts of silver ore extracted from the mines there were a vital source of revenue and were used to strike new coins in 1300. This economic rise, combined with a weakening of Rome's position, was used to good effect by Přemysl I Otakar (1197–1230) who succeeded in making the title of king hereditary and in winning many other privileges from Emperor Friedrich II in the Golden Bull of Sicily, a key document in Czech history which not only created a hereditary kingship but also gave the king the right to defend the borders of the Czech lands and name bishops. With the Czech king also holding the post of one of the electors of the Holy Roman Emperor, the Czech lands were on the road to regional superpower status.

Perhaps the weightiest Přemysl of all was King Přemysl II Otakar who some compare to the later Charles IV. Dubbed the 'king of iron and gold' for his military might and wealth, he was an ambitious king who won territory for his kingdom and saw himself as the Holy Roman Emperor. He failed in his bid, with Rudolf von Habsburg gaining the title. Conflict between Přemysl II Otakar and the new emperor was inevitable and the former was eventually killed in 1278 at the Battle of Marchfeld.

Gothic architecture took hold in the 13th century, examples of which can be seen across the country.

End of the Přemyslid dynasty

Václav II (1278–1305), the son of Přemysl II Otakar, followed in his father's military footsteps, turning his attention northwards and becoming king of

Poland. His son Václav III (1305–06) was murdered in Olomouc leaving no male heir. Václav III had four sisters, but as female succession was not recognised, his demise brought to a close 400 years of Přemyslid rule which could trace its roots back to the earliest Czech state and beyond to a mythical Slav past.

The Luxembourg kings – Bohemia's golden age

In 1310, after a messy and uncertain period of struggle for the Czech throne, John of Luxembourg (1310–46), husband of Elizabeth Přemysl, one of Václav III's four sisters, emerged as the Czech king. John, the son of Emperor Henry VII and raised at the French royal court, never adjusted to the Czech court and concentrated primarily on foreign policy, adding Silesia, the Cheb region and Upper Lusatia to the realm.

It was John's son Charles IV (1346–78) who became not only the most famous of the Luxembourg kings, but the most influential and celebrated ruler the Czech lands have ever had. Unlike his father, Charles concentrated on domestic matters and resided in Prague. He had also spent his early years at the French royal court, was highly educated and could speak several languages including Czech. Already crowned King of Rome, he assumed the Czech throne in 1346 when his father was killed at the Battle of Crécy. He was made Holy Roman Emperor in 1355, thus making the Czech kingdom one of the most important places in Christendom. Prague had to reflect its position as the capital of the Holy Roman Empire and Charles set about changing the face of the city. He founded the New Town, the university (today's Charles University), the first in central Europe, ordered the Gothic reconstruction of the Royal Palace at Prague Castle and Vyšehrad and reunited the banks of the river Vltava with a new bridge to replace the Judith Bridge which had collapsed in 1342. The soaring Old Town Bridge Tower is the work of Charles's architect Petr Parléř who also worked on the Gothic reconstruction of St Vitus Cathedral. Outside the capital Charles had Karlštejn Castle built specially as a place of safekeeping for the crown jewels. He greatly raised the status of the Church in the Czech lands by elevating the Prague bishopric to archbishopric and creating a new bishopric in Litomyšl in east Bohemia. He encouraged trade and manufacture which contributed significantly to the prosperity and stability of the country. When Charles IV passed away in 1378, he bequeathed to his heir one of the most powerful kingdoms in Europe. The Czechs hail him as the 'father of the nation' and his legacy is on show everywhere in Prague and around the Czech Republic to this day. He was aware and proud of his Přemyslid ancestry, dedicated to the land of his mother but was also one of the most important pan-European statesmen of his time.

Decline of the Czech lands after Charles's death

Alas, Charles's son Václav IV (1378–1419) did not inherit his father's intelligence, statesmanship or his diplomatic skills. This violent drunkard was more interested in his private pastimes than affairs of state. In 1400 he was deposed as Holy Roman Emperor by the electors. Soon after Charles IV's death the Czech lands were knocked reeling by a devastating plague which obliterated 10–15% of the population. There were further outbreaks in the ensuing 40 years which naturally had a negative effect on the economy. In desperation people turned to crime, organised mobs began to rob and murder and outlaws roamed the country, often in the pay of desperate noblemen. The kingdom became a place merchants feared to transit and it was a time of poverty and instability, a far cry from the pleasant land of Charles IV.

Medieval society perceived these setbacks as God's wrath and punishment for disobeying the Bible. The Church, which had begun to bask in riches from the sale of indulgences, was seen as the main culprit. People believed that only a return to the principles laid down in the Bible could cure society's ills.

The Hussites

A group of intellectuals from Prague University with Jan Hus at their head became the main advocates of this opinion. Jan Hus, one of the most important figures of Czech history, was born in Husinec in south Bohemia. He became a priest in 1400 and preached at the Bethlehem Chapel in Prague. He was an advocate of the teachings of John Wyclif, the English reformer and writer and even translated some of his work. Hus's preaching soon became popular among the nobility, the general public and at the royal court. His opponents were naturally the Church prelates and the Catholic German burghers. The German minority was beginning to fear growing Czech influence in the towns which had come about as a result of the Black Death. The German teachers at Prague University vehemently disagreed with Hus and his followers and things came to a head when Václav IV issued the Decree of Kutná Hora which more or less handed over the university to Hus. The Germans consequently left Prague and founded a university in Leipzig.

In 1414, Hus was invited to Constance to attend the Church Council and given safe passage there by Zikmund, son of Charles IV and heir to the Bohemian throne. He considered this an opportunity to convince the Church of the necessity of reform. Instead he was arrested, tried as a heretic and burnt at the stake on 6 July 1415, now a national holiday in the Czech Republic (conveniently the day after the national holiday celebrating Cyril and Methodius).

Hus's martyrdom heightened the tension between the Catholics and the Hussites as they were now called. On 30 July 1419, the so-called first Prague defenestration, a Czech historical speciality, took place. For those not familiar with the practice it entails ejecting someone you are not pleased with from an upper-floor window. The defenestration would appear again in Czech history, hence the title 'first' Prague defenestration. Those thrown from the window of the New Town Hall by the Hussites were members of the despised town council. When Václav IV died just a few days later the Hussite revolution could not be halted.

Soon after the beginning of the revolution the Hussites came forward with the so-called Four Prague Articles, a list of aims they hoped to achieve. Equality between the clergy and congregations during services (by which they meant that both must receive Holy Communion under both forms – bread and wine *sub utraque specie* from which comes the term Utraquism), freedom to spread God's word, confiscation of Church property and punishment for sins which prevent Christians from reaching redemption were their demands.

Although all Hussites were united on the programme set out above, they were divided when it came to the force they were prepared to use, from the moderate nobility and university professors, to the slightly more extreme inhabitants of Prague through to the radical Hussite groups in east Bohemia and Tábor. The town of Tábor in south Bohemia was in fact founded by the Hussite radicals in 1420.

The heir to the Czech throne on Václav IV's death was the fourth and final Luxembourg king, Václav's brother Zikmund. The Hussites refused to recognise his accession to the throne so with the pope behind him Zikmund led five crusades against the Hussites, considered heretics by most of Europe. All ended in failure thanks to the efforts of Jan Žižka of Trocnov, a fearless and crafty Hussite warlord. One of his greatest achievements was to defend Prague against Zikmund, hence the name of the Prague quarter Žižkov where the battle took place. He is also said to have employed a kind of medieval tank in battle and used various other ingenious new tactics.

End of the revolution
After many defeats Zikmund had little choice but to enter into negotiations with the Hussites. The slow progress of these talks and the desperate economic situation in the country turned the population against the position of the uncompromising Táborites and east Bohemian radicals who were eventually defeated by a coalition of Catholics and moderate Hussites at the Battle of Lipany. Their defeat opened the way for a peace deal between the Catholics and Hussites. The *Compactata* declared in Jihlava in 1436 meant in essence victory for the Hussites, but also for Zikmund who could now take up the throne which was rightfully his. Ominously the pope never recognised this agreement.

Jiří of Poděbrady and the Jagiellon dynasty
Inevitable problems between the Hussites and Catholics continued after the *Compactata* and in 1458 the nobleman Jiří of Poděbrady was elected king, the so-called Hussite king. He was the first who did not belong to a ruling dynasty and was regarded by most of Europe as a heretic. He strived to be a ruler who would unite both sides of the religious divide and even suggested the creation of a kind of medieval United Nations to resolve problems through diplomacy, not war. He was far ahead of his time and when the pope declared the *Compactata* null and void and the Catholics and the Hungarian King Matyáš Korvín occupied parts of the country, Jiří's position became somewhat isolated. Matyáš Korvín was pronounced king by the Catholics in 1469. When Jiří died in 1471 Vladislav Jagiellon, the King of Poland, gained the Czech throne and when Matyáš Korvín passed away in 1490, the Jagiellon dynasty again united the country under one ruler. In 1485 the Catholics had recognised the *Compactata*, opening the way for unprecedented religious freedom in the Czech lands.

The estates and the Thirty Years War
No sooner had peace broken out between the Hussites and the Catholics than a new conflict began between the nobility and the royal towns. The result of this struggle was the Treaty of St Wenceslas of 1517, whereby the royal towns surrendered some of their privileges (the right to hold a market, to brew beer etc) and the nobility agreed to the towns' representation in the assembly. So came into being a system whereby the ruler shared power with the nobility and the royal towns, the so-called Bohemian estates.

After the demise of the last Jagiellon King Ludwig in 1526 when battling against the Turks, the Bohemian estates elected Ferdinand I, a Habsburg, as ruler. Ferdinand was already ruler of Austria and soon added the Hungarian crown to his list of titles. With his brother Charles on the Spanish throne and Holy Roman Emperor, the Habsburgs had established themselves as the most powerful dynasty in Europe. Ferdinand immediately set about centralising power and weakening the political influence of the Bohemian estates. He also began systematic support for the Catholic Church against the Protestants. He attempted to extend the influence of Catholicism by forming the Jesuit Academy in Prague and by naming a new archbishop of Prague in 1561, an office unoccupied since the 15th century. None of this was to the liking of the Bohemian estates who rightly considered the Habsburgs a threat to their political influence and religious freedom. Ferdinand successfully put down a rebellion by the estates in 1547 and severely persecuted those involved.

Prelude to the Thirty Years War

The eccentric, depressive and paranoid Rudolf II (1576–1611) is one of the best-known and most colourful characters of Czech history. He was the last Habsburg to reside in Prague (from then on they ruled from Vienna) and is famous for his patronage of the arts, alchemy, astronomy, physicians and literature. He was an avid collector of antiques, wild animals and works of art, including paintings by Da Vinci, Michelangelo, and Raphael. The generosity of this rich patron was very often misused by fraudsters. One of the myths which grew up around the Golden lane at Prague Castle is that Rudolf's alchemists lived there. The houses date from that period but the alchemists never resided there. The architectural style of the time was Renaissance, which had spread to the Czech lands from Italy, magnificent examples of which can be seen at Prague Castle and in south Bohemia.

Away from his pastimes Rudolf's most notable act was to issue a Letter of Majesty that promised toleration of the Czech Reformed Church, gave control of Charles University to the Czech estates, and made other concessions. The Catholics saw this as a defeat and an obstacle to the creation of a centralised Habsburg state in central Europe. Tension between the two groups came to a head when Rudolf was forced to abdicate by his family, and his successor Matthias (1611–19) attempted to rescind these concessions. The blue touch paper was lit with the second Prague defenestration in 1618 when a group of Protestant nobles threw two representatives of the Habsburg king from the window of Prague Castle. Conflict between the Catholic royalists and Protestant Bohemian estates was unstoppable, a conflict which escalated into a Europe-wide conflict known as the Thirty Years War (1618–48) which devastated many towns and cities across the Czech lands. The last decade of the war saw the Czech lands become a battleground between the Protestant Swedes and the imperial Catholic forces. The Swedes looted, ransacked and laid siege to any town or monastery that stood in their way, and many were left devastated in their wake. They even took Prague's Malá Strana district, but not the Old Town.

IN THE FOOTSTEPS OF EDWARD KELLEY

One of the most colourful figures to arrive in Rudolf II's Prague was the English alchemist Edward Kelley. Not a lot is known about his early life in England: he was possibly born in Worcester in 1555, possibly educated at Oxford. What is known is that he arrived in Prague in 1584 with John Dee, a fortune teller, and in 1586 found favour with Count Vilém z Rožmberka and settled in Třeboň. Under this patronage, Kelley grew wealthy though his attempts at turning ordinary metals into gold were, naturally, fruitless. Believing his promises, Ro žmberk gave him lands and money, while Rudolf II made him a baron. However, the emperor's patience ran out in 1591 and he had Kelley arrested for duelling and jailed at Křivoklát to force him to produce results. He was crippled trying to escape and released for medical treatment. Imprisoned again in Most and injured in yet another escape attempt, he committed suicide by taking poison.

Battle of the White Mountain

In 1620, the Bohemian estates levied an army, decreed the expulsion of the Jesuits, and proclaimed the Bohemian throne to be elective. They chose a Calvinist, Frederick of the Palatinate (sometimes dubbed the Winter King as his reign lasted a mere two months), the son-in-law of King James I of England, for the Bohemian throne and Bohemian troops began to confront the Habsburg forces. In 1620, however, came a turning point in Czech history which would influence its course for the next 300 years. The Bohemian armies were soundly defeated at the Battle of the White Mountain to the west of Prague. Frederick fled the country and the commanders of the Bohemian army elected not to defend the capital. The Habsburgs took Prague and put down the uprising. Ferdinand II (1620–37) then set about punishing the rebels and creating an absolute Catholic Habsburg monarchy. Those Protestant nobles who did not manage to flee the country were arrested and on 21 June 1621, some 27 were executed in the Old Town Square in a show of strength. The Bohemian estates were at an end, Protestantism was crushed and the fate of the Czech lands was sealed for the next 300 years.

The Counter-Reformation

The Habsburgs launched a systematic campaign to pacify or get rid of anyone who stood in their way and secure imperial authority and the dominance of the Roman Catholic Church. All rebel noblemen had their property confiscated, a campaign of recatholicisation was commenced and a new constitution called the Revised Ordinance of the Land was drawn up in 1627, putting the Habsburgs' ambitions into law. All members of the Bohemian estates who wished to belong to a non-Catholic Church were forced into exile, and the peasants were given no choice but to revert to Catholicism. To fully understand what this meant it has to be taken into account that approximately two-thirds of the population of the Czech lands were Protestants. The new constitution also declared the Habsburg dynasty hereditary heirs to the Czech throne, they would rule by decree, and the German language was given the same status as Czech in official business. The upshot of these measures was the emigration of tens of thousands of people, perhaps the most famous of them Jan Amos Comenius, the thinker, philosopher, writer and educator who emigrated to Poland (though he later travelled extensively around Europe), often referred to as the 'teacher of nations' and the father of modern education. Many estates fell into the ownership of foreign nobility, mostly Germans, which would have a marked effect on the cultural and political development of the Czech lands in the following centuries.

Recovery and Baroque

The Treaty of Westphalia which officially ended the Thirty Years War formally handed over the Czech lands to the Habsburg Empire. The war left behind a devastated economy and reduced the population of the Czech lands by a third. An uncompromising feudal system left the peasants paying high taxes and tied to the land. The peasants revolted several times, most notably in 1680. This miserable state of affairs lasted until the beginning of the 18th century when signs of recovery began to appear. At the time of the economic upturn and when the Catholic Church had the opportunity to rebuild many of its devastated buildings under the recatholicisation process, Baroque was in fashion in central Europe, and the many palaces, houses, parks and church buildings constructed at the time can still be enjoyed today. Baroque changed the face of the Czech lands for several centuries, though it was linked to recatholicisation, the Counter-

ARCHITECTURAL STYLES – A CRASH COURSE

Romanesque 10th–13th centuries. Typical characteristics: thick walls, rounded arches, closely spaced columns, rotundas. Examples: Basilica of St George, Prague Castle; Rotunda of St Catherine, Znojmo.

Gothic 13th–mid 15th centuries. Typical characteristics: vaulted ceilings, flying buttresses, pointed arches, long slender windows, bare stonework, arcading. Examples: Cathedral of St Barbora, Kutná Hora; Charles Bridge, Prague.

Renaissance Mid 15th–early 17th centuries. Typical characteristics: sgraffito, frescoes, symmetry, brickwork. Examples: Summer Palace, Prague Castle; Schwarzenberg Palace, Prague Castle.

Baroque and Rococo 17th and 18th centuries. Typical characteristics: curves, stucco, onion domes, over-the-top decoration, symmetry. Examples: Church of St Nicholas, Prague (Malá Strana), Loreta, Prague (Hradčany).

Classicism and Empire 18th–mid 19th centuries. Typical characteristics: return to Classical lines, Doric columns, huge symmetrical buildings, simplicity. Example: Estates Theatre, Prague.

'Neo' styles Second half of 19th century. Typical characteristics: return to styles of the past – neo-Gothic, neo-Renaissance, neo-Baroque. Examples: Cathedral of St Vitus, Prague Castle; National Theatre, Prague.

Modern styles Early 20th century. Typical characteristics: Art Nouveau, Cubism (unique to the Czech Republic), Functionalism, Constructivism. Examples: Municipal House, Prague; Villa Tugendhat, Brno.

Reformation and all the other negative aspects of the post–white-mountain era. The best-known architects of the day were undoubtedly the Dientzenhofers (Church of St Nicholas on Prague's Malostranské Square, the Loreta near Prague Castle) and Santini-Aichel (Chapel of St John of Nepomuk at Zelená hora near Zďár nad Sázavou and many other churches and monasteries). Brokof and Braun were Baroque sculptors who worked on the statues that line Charles Bridge, and the most famous Baroque painter was Karel Škréta, whose work can be seen hanging in churches and galleries across the country.

Enlightened absolutism

At the beginning of the 18th century the absolutist Habsburg Empire had emerged as a European superpower encompassing the Czech lands, Hungary and Austria. The most noteworthy ruler in the 18th century was Empress Maria Theresa (1740–80). Having lost the industrially important area of Silesia to Prussia in the wars of 1741–48 and the Seven Years War (1756–63), she recognised that absolutism had had its day and that reform was urgently needed in order to bring the empire up to the standard of France or England. Ask any Czech what Maria Theresa's greatest legacy was and the vast majority will cite the introduction of compulsory schooling begun in 1774, a step which would eventually lead to the national revival of Czech culture. While this was undoubtedly a step in the right direction, more centralisation, bureaucratisation and the declaration of German as the official state language were not. The enlightened rule of Maria Theresa and her son Joseph II (1780–90), who legalised Protestantism and abolished serfdom in 1781, played an essential role in the development of the modern Czech nation, but one that was full of contradictions. The policy of centralisation whittled down further any vestiges of a separate Bohemian kingdom and resulted in the Germanisation of the administration and nobility. On the other hand, by removing the worst features of the Counter-Reformation and by introducing social and educational reforms, they enabled economic progress and social mobility. The consequences for Bohemia were of widespread significance. The nobility turned its attention to industrial enterprise, many subletting their lands and investing profits in the development of textile, coal and glass manufacture. Czech peasants, free to leave the land, moved to cities and manufacturing centres. Urban areas, formerly populated by Germans, became increasingly Czech in character. The sons of Czech peasants were sent to school; some attended university, and a new Czech intellectual elite emerged. During this period the population of the Czech lands increased fourfold. Joseph II's successor Leopold (1790–92) reversed some of these measures but nevertheless the stage was set for the Czech National Revival.

Austro-Hungary and the Czech National Revival

At the end of the 18th century, as a reaction to the measures implemented by an empire at best insensitive to, at worst hostile towards the wishes and needs of the individual nations it encompassed (the empire-wide imposition of German being one of the most obvious examples) but also an empire that gave the oxygen of education to its subjects, a new sense of national awareness began to appear in the Czech lands. A process had begun which would continue until the 1860s and would come to be known as the Czech National Revival. The cards were certainly stacked against nationalists whose aim was to revive Czech language and culture, the first step on the road to a Czech state. The Austrians were aware of the movements in Europe towards the creation of nation states based on linguistic and cultural affinity and were vigilant in systematically blocking attempts at national emancipation which would spell the demise of an empire based solely on the hereditary right of the ruling dynasty.

Key to the national revival was the Czech language. Once spoken by Emperor Charles IV himself, over two centuries Czech had been demoted to an unfashionable language spoken by uneducated peasants. Now that peasant children were receiving an education and then moving off the land to look for work in the increasingly industrialised towns, Czech began to increase in importance. The scientist, historian and linguist Josef Dobrovský and the linguist and translator Josef Jungmann through their various works played an important part in getting Czech into the state schools and transforming and codifying Czech into a literary language. The result was a Czech reading public hungry for literature and curious about their glorious past. This hunger was satisfied by the many Czech nationalist writers who followed: poets such as Jan Kollar, F L Čelakovský, Karel Erben and Karel H Mácha, the dramatists V K Klicpera and J K Tyl, and journalist Karel Havlíček Borovský. The most famous woman writer of the period was Božena Němcová, whose most loved work *Babička* (Grandmother) has since been translated into many languages. In 1818 the Czechs opened their first national museum and in 1831 the *Matice Česká*, a society of Czech intellectuals devoted to the publication of scholarly and popular books, was founded.

A key figure in the Czech National Revival was the politician and historian František Palacký (1798–1876). As a founding member of the *Matice Česká*, a

THE SOKOL MOVEMENT

Founded by Miroslav Tyrš and Jindřich Fügner in 1862, the Sokol Movement promoted the principle that a healthy body makes a healthy mind, based on the teachings of Comenius. The idea behind it was to forge a sense of nationhood through collective physical exercise and was an integral part of the Czech National Revival. Tyrš's pamphlet entitled *Tělocvičová soustava* (A PE Guide) describes sets of exercises for various ages and sexes. The imperial authorities were always suspicious of the movement and banned its activities during World War I. The movement flourished during the First Republic but in 1948 the communists took it over, banned the name Sokol and transformed it into a communist national physical education organisation. The huge Sokol rallies transmuted into the famous *Spartakiáda*, one of the most enduring images of eastern European communism, with tens of thousands of gymnasts all performing in unison at the monster Strahov Stadium. The Sokol Movement has been revived since the revolution but attracts few young people. The most visible legacy of the Sokols is the *sokolovna* building in almost every town and village, with some still used as exercise halls, others hosting discos, council meetings and dances.

member of the Czech Academy of Science and the editor of the National Museum's own magazine, Palacký began work on his epic *History of the Czech Nation*. He moved into politics after the 1848 revolutionary fervour which swept across Europe and put forward a proposal for a federal Habsburg state which would acknowledge the existence of the individual Slav nations. The empire's reaction to 1848, its measures against the nationalist movements and the neo-absolutism of Franz Joseph I pushed Palacký back to his academic pursuits. He returned to politics in 1861 as an MP but became disappointed with the Czechs' fruitless strive for recognition in the empire, especially when under so-called dualism Hungary pushed the Habsburgs into recognising the Hungarian crown, leading to the creation of the Austro-Hungarian Empire in 1867, but subsequently blocked a three-way split put forward by the Czechs. He is often rightly referred to as one of the 'Fathers of the nation'. His son-in-law F L Rieger followed in his footsteps, becoming one of the most important figures in Czech politics.

The frustration and disillusionment which the Czechs experienced from 1867 onwards was also because their position in the empire did not reflect the level of development in the Czech lands. Bohemia had three-quarters of Austro-Hungary's industry, a well-developed political scene, flourishing arts and great writers. It was becoming obvious that the Czechs would not be content with their status as mere servants to Vienna for very much longer.

World War I and independence

World War I was the final step on the road to the creation of nation states in central Europe, making it possible for the Czech lands and many other countries in the region to either break free from stifling empires altogether, or come together to form new entities. Following the assassination of Franz Ferdinand d'Este, the successor to the Austrian throne in Sarajevo in 1914, war was inevitable. From 1914 to 1918 conflict raged across the continent, but the Czech lands got off very lightly with no military operations on their territory. However, life was by no means pleasant as prices soared, shortages of food and basic materials bit hard and fear spread of a quick German victory. The Austrian authorities cracked down hard on dissent and opposition during the war in which many Czech soldiers were sent to fight. On the front lines in Russia, Serbia and Italy many deserted and united with prisoners captured by the enemy to create legions which then turned around and fought against the Austrians. The death of Franz Joseph I in 1916 and the accession of Charles I brought about a relaxation of Austrian suppression which gave impetus to leading Czech politicians opposed to Austrian rule and dreaming of an independent Czech state.

The First Republic

The new democratic republic immediately faced numerous problems, not least aggression from some of its neighbours and ethnic minorities within its own borders. The Sudeten Germans were hostile to the new Czechoslovakia and tried to secede to Germany, Hungarian troops occupied large parts of Slovakia and the Poles occupied the Těšínsko region. Czechoslovakia dealt successfully with these problems though the treaty to divide Czechoslovakia and Hungary along the Danube left many Hungarians cut off from their homeland, a problem which simmers to this day. The Treaty of Versailles put an official diplomatic end to the problems by defining the legal borders of the country. According to a census carried out in 1921, just over 50% of Czechoslovakia's inhabitants were Czech, 23% German, a mere 15% Slovak, 5% Hungarian and 3% Ruthenian. The state languages were to be Czech and Slovak though widespread use of other languages was granted in regions where the minority language was spoken by more than 20% of the population, part of the new constitution adopted in 1920. All state bureaucrats had to pass an exam in either Czech or Slovak which was a hard pill to swallow for non-Slavs. Ethnic tensions would torment the newborn republic throughout its entire short life and would ultimately lead to its demise.

Left with the Habsburgs' industry, Czechoslovakia found itself one of the ten most industrialised countries in the world. Companies such as Baťa (shoes) and Škoda (heavy industry and cars) flourished and exported to the whole world. Bohemia and Moravia, which had inherited most of the heavy industry, experienced an economic boom but there was a wide economic gap between these regions and Slovakia and Ruthenia. Following the Wall Street Crash in 1929 the latter suffered most and the increasing economic difficulties only fuelled more ethnic tension, especially in the Sudetenlands and Slovakia. Unemployment rocketed between 1930 and 1933 to almost 1 million. The Nationalist Party in Slovakia led by Hlinka wanted autonomy for Slovakia and objected to Prague's obsession with centralisation. More ominously, in the Sudetenlands, dissatisfaction was leading people to peer over the border into Germany and listen to Adolf Hitler, the new leader there from 1933, who was already promising to unite all Germans in one state. By the mid 1930s Czechoslovakia was slowly becoming an ever more threatened oasis of democracy in a desert of fascism.

As Britain had the swinging '60s, Czechoslovakia had the 1920s, a kind of golden age which has been etched into the national conscience. It was a time of decadence and luxury and many grew rich. When the country broke free of Soviet communism in 1989, many of the symbols, imagery and style which were chosen to depict capitalism and sound economics, freedom and choice were echoes of the 1920s, the last time the Czechs had experienced prosperity. Of course much architecture remains from this period, some of the finest examples being the Cubist House of the Black Madonna in Prague and the Villa Tugendhat in Brno. The period also produced one of the best-known Czech writers, Karel Čapek, who gave the world the word 'robot', as well as German-language author Franz Kafka and the composer Bohuslav Martinů.

World War II
Peace in our time – Munich

A fateful day and one that still sticks in the throat of many Czechs is 29 September 1938, the day that Neville Chamberlain, British prime minister, Edouard Daladier of France and Italian fascist dictator Benito Mussolini handed over the Sudetenlands to Adolf Hitler in Munich in a gesture of appeasement. The new Czechoslovak president, Edvard Beneš, was not invited to attend. In the face of fascism the Czechoslovak state was abandoned by its allies and the door into central and eastern Europe had been swung open for Hitler to walk in. Not the finest hour for the west, which perhaps some older Czechs will not be hesitant to remind you of, given the chance. By winter 1938, the Czechoslovak government had handed over Těšínsko to Poland and southeast Slovakia to Hungary, demands which Hitler had blackmailed Chamberlain into accepting by threatening to declare war on Czechoslovakia. Slovakia and Ruthenia were granted autonomy, to all intents and purposes marking the end of the First Republic. President Beneš was left with no choice but to accept the ill-fated Munich agreement. The Czechoslovak army of $1^1/_2$ million was completely outnumbered by Germany's $3^1/_2$ million men, the border defences were still under construction and the country would have in all likelihood faced simultaneous attack from Poland and Hungary, stretching the Czechoslovak forces in three directions. Beneš abdicated in October 1938 and left for Great Britain. Emil Hácha took the unenviable position of Czech president.

Nazi occupation and the resistance

Hitler did not wait long to complete what he had intended to do from the outset and on 15 March 1939 German units began to occupy Bohemia and Moravia. Hitler did not occupy Slovakia as he had secured their loyalty days earlier by threatening to hand the country over to Hungary, who did invade Ruthenia. The Nazis seized the Czech lands with hardly a shot being fired though they did meet some resistance in the Moravian town of Místek, but it was too little too late. Hitler declared the Czech lands an autonomous part of the German Reich and the Protectorate of Bohemia and Moravia was born. Emil Hácha remained president and at first Czech politicians thought they would be able to share power with the Germans. These illusions were gradually dashed as the Nazis set about creating a state along their lines. Many institutions such as the police and courts were in the hands of the Nazi representatives and true power lay with the *Reichsprotektor*, the first being von Neurath, Hitler's man in Prague. The Nazis' long-term plans for the Czechs involved Germanisation of some of the population and deportation for the rest. However, more immediate use of the population was required for the war effort and most long-term ideological aims were sacrificed. Nothing can deflect from the fact that Hitler had plans for the complete liquidation of the Czech nation. Right from the beginning of the protectorate Jews were forced to wear a yellow Star of David, their movements were restricted, they received smaller food rations and Jewish children were barred from schools. Later their possessions were seized and many were sent to the Terezín camp in north Bohemia before transportation to the death camps in the east.

Life in Nazi-occupied Czechoslovakia was at best humiliating and at worst horrific. Propaganda, the promotion of German as the official language, rationing, air raids (Prague and Pilsen were worst hit), fuel shortages, disappearances and deportation to work in the Reich or to a concentration camp were just a few of the things people endured. As far as the general population was concerned there were three attitudes to the occupation. The majority, while against the Germans, remained passive but some collaborated with the Nazis while others joined the resistance. Beneš, who was now recognised as president in exile, co-ordinated the resistance from the safety of London. The Czech resistance's greatest success was the assassination of *Reichsprotektor* Reinhard Heydrich on 27 May 1942 in Prague. Heydrich had arrived in Prague in September 1941 and had overseen the introduction of martial law, the mass arrest of hundreds of members of the resistance including the Prime Minister Alois Eliáš and the executions of many of those arrested. He was assassinated in his car in a Prague street by members of the resistance who had been trained and parachuted in by the British. Heydrich's death raised the profile of the Czech resistance around the world but also led to Nazi reprisals in which 1,600 people died. The worst of these reprisals was the razing to the ground of the villages of Lidice near Kladno and Lešáky near Chrudim and the slaughter or deportation of all their inhabitants. The assassins themselves were betrayed and eventually cornered in the Church of Cyril and Methodius in Prague's Resslova Street on 18 June 1942. The bullet holes can still be seen around a slit in the wall through which the Germans fired. They all committed suicide. The assassination of Heydrich was a success but the Czech population paid a heavy price, as did the resistance which never really got on its feet again under the repression of Heydrich's successor K H Frank.

The Czech contribution abroad

While the Czech resistance was reasonably successful at home, Czechs played an important role elsewhere in the war against Nazi Germany. Czech and Slovak pilots shot down around 70 enemy planes in the Battle of Britain, Czechoslovak units fought in North Africa, the Middle East, Yugoslavia, the USSR and Italy. When war broke out between Germany and the USSR in 1941, Czechoslovak units were formed under Colonel Ludvík Svoboda. These units fought alongside the Soviet Red Army as they liberated vast swathes of eastern Europe, eventually ending up in the Czech lands themselves in 1945.

Liberation

If the Cold War was a piece of music then the liberation of central Europe was the opening bars. In 1943, an agreement was signed in Moscow promising to restore the Czechoslovak state to its pre-war borders. Stalin did not hide the fact that the Soviet Union was looking to spread its influence into central Europe, and the presence of the Red Army anywhere played a political as well as a liberating role. A taste of things to come was the annexation of Ruthenia and repression of those who were for Ruthenia remaining in Czechoslovakia. The Czechs had to accept this as a fait accompli but it was now clear that Czechoslovakia had become reliant on the USSR. Czechoslovakia was finally liberated on 8 May 1945. The Soviets occupied Prague while the Americans stopped at a line between Carlsbad and České Budějovice. Around 144,000 Soviet troops died while liberating the country. On 5 May 1945, Prague had risen against the Nazis, opening the way for the Soviets to enter. The last shots of World War II in Europe were fired in the Czech lands.

Communism until 1968

Following the liberation of Czechoslovakia, Edvard Beneš, who had seen out the war in London, returned to Prague and became president once again. In October

1945 Beneš issued decrees which are still controversial and the subject of political debate to this day. These decrees nationalised vast swathes of the Czechoslovak economy including the banks and mines. They also placed certain groups, including anyone who had collaborated with the Germans and certain ethnic minorities, outside of the law. The result was the expulsion of over two million Sudeten Germans (the expulsion of Hungarians from southern Slovakia never went ahead). In 1950 only 1.8% of the German population remained. Some towns in Moravia lost over 90% of their inhabitants. In one fell swoop the ethnic problem had been solved. This remains a political hot potato. Ask anyone in the Czech Republic what the worst thing President Havel did during his years in office and most will cite his apology to the Sudeten Germans for their expulsion after World War II. The Czech government refuses to rescind the Beneš decrees and the events of 1945–46 were even an obstacle in the Czech Republic's negotiations to join the EU. The majority of Czechs will admit the horror of what happened to the German population but ask them whether they would like the Sudetenlanders back and an awkward silence will follow.

In 1946, the Communist Party won a general election by a large margin which set the direction the country was going to take, ie: closer ties with the Soviet Union and the implementation of Stalinist ideology and repression. What is often forgotten is that as a reaction to the events of World War II many people saw the communists as the only option and they enjoyed great popularity. In February 1948 they cooked up a government crisis and forced President Beneš to accept the resignation of the ministers of all the democratic parties and entrust the creation of a new government to the communist leader Klement Gottwald. The Communist Party had come to power by legal means and with the support of the population which very often goes unmentioned. When President Beneš refused to sign an undemocratic constitution and resigned, the communists capped their success in June 1946 with the election of Klement Gottwald as the first workers' president.

Communists consolidate power

The communist putsch at the end of the 1940s spelt the end of democracy in Czechoslovakia for four decades. The parliamentary system was not wholly dismantled but elections became a fiasco with the population choosing from a list of communist candidates. During the 1950s dissent was quashed, employing Stalinist methods such as show trials, political executions, concentration camps, torture, forced labour in the uranium mines, forced collectivisation and nationalisation, confiscation of property and the suppression of religious freedom (especially targeting the Catholic Church). Much of this repression was targeted at members of non-communist parties, members of the World War II resistance movement and those who served in the Czechoslovak legions in the West including significantly those pilots who played such an essential role in the Battle of Britain. The trial and execution of Milada Horáková is probably the best-known Stalinist crime of the 1950s in Czechoslovakia. Horáková was initially a member of Prague City Council until World War II broke out. She was active in the resistance until 1940 when she was captured and spent the rest of the war in a concentration camp. After the war she entered politics until the communist putsch and then became involved in the resistance movement against the regime. Her arrest was inevitable but her execution in 1950 shocked the world.

In the field of economics the 1950s saw the complete dismantling of the private sector, central planning, a focus on heavy industry and military production and collectivisation of agriculture. The USSR was now dictating

**THE CZECH REPUBLIC'S TOP FIVE MOST OUT OF PLACE
COMMUNIST-ERA BUILDINGS**
1 **Nová scéna** Národní třída, Prague
2 **Prior Department Store** Masarykovo náměstí, Jihlava
3 **Communist-era supermarket** Masarykovo náměstí, Znojmo
4 **Prior Department Store** ulice 8. května, Olomouc
5 **Former Czechoslovak parliament building** Wilsonova, Prague

what would be produced in Czechoslovakia and what the country would import
and export and to whom. On top of all this, monetary reforms in 1953 consigned
whole swathes of the population to poverty.

In 1953, eastern Europe and indeed the whole world gasped a sigh of relief
when Stalin died. Coincidentally, President Gottwald of Czechoslovakia also
passed away in the same year. Both of these events opened the way for a slight
relaxation in conditions in Czechoslovakia under Presidents Zápotocký
(1953–57) and Novotný (1957–68) and in the Soviet Union under Khrushchev
until 1964 when neo-Stalinist Brezhnev came to power. Czechoslovakia
meanwhile continued on the path of liberalisation throughout the 1960s which
set it on a collision course with its Soviet overlords.

The grey years 1968–89
1968 invasion
In January 1968, Alexandr Dubček became head of the Communist Party, and
two months later Ludvík Svoboda became Czechoslovak president. Dubček was
an advocate of economic and political reforms and a policy of 'Socialism with a
human face'. He also set about making changes at the top of the Communist
Party. The result was the Prague Spring, a short period of freedom when many
Czechs and Slovaks engaged in activities unthinkable for three decades (religion,
green shoots of new political parties, listening to Western pop music etc). These
policies and the social changes they were bringing about were disturbing the
Kremlin who saw any moves towards liberalisation in their sphere of influence as
a threat. On 21 August 1968, a joint Warsaw Pact force invaded Czechoslovakia
to put down this threat to communism. Some 750,000 troops and 6,000 tanks
occupied a peaceful country where not a shot had been fired. The international
community was taken aback by these events but limited itself to expressions of
solidarity. On 23 August 1968, a Czechoslovak delegation began talks in
Moscow, the upshot of which being that with one exception all the delegates
agreed to the presence of Soviet troops in Czechoslovakia for an indefinite
period.

Dubček was removed as party leader, a direct result of the protests by students
in Prague. Two students in particular decided to vent their anger in an extreme
way which shocked not only Czechoslovak society but the world too. Jan Palach
and Jan Zajíc set fire to themselves in protest at the Warsaw Pact occupation of
their country. Jan Palach is remembered in the name of a Prague Square (in front
of the Rudolfinum by the river).

Normalisation
There followed a period known as normalisation, basically 20 years of watered-
down Stalinism. The personification of this period is the Slovak Gustav Husák,
head of the Communist Party and president from 1975. To ensure political

stability, the standard of living was artificially raised. People began to buy cars (the famous Škoda products so derided in the West) and weekend cottages. It was also a time when many intellectuals and professionals were forced to leave their jobs and many could not study at university or had their studies terminated because they would not join the Communist Party or a member of their family was out of favour with the state or had emigrated. Between 700,000 and 800,000 such people emigrated following the Soviet invasion. Most people existed in a grey zone, not suffering great material hardships (though there were shortages of some basic products) but not sticking their head above the parapet. Passivity was the only way the vast majority of the population could ensure a peaceful existence and political apathy was the norm. The political elite, however, enjoyed luxury goods from the West for symbolic prices and lifestyles which most could only dream of. Corruption, bureaucracy and the grey economy were rife. People withdrew from public life and family meals around kitchen tables were the only times the truth could be spoken and even then with schizophrenic concern that the children would repeat what was being said at school. It was a time of environmental damage especially in north Bohemia through opencast mining and coal-burning power stations and pollution became a problem in most large cities. Criticism of the environmental and ecological state of the country was seen as political dissent. Censorship bit hard in the 1970s and even well-known writers such as Bohumil Hrabal were forced to publish their books in so-called *samizdat* editions (photocopied or illegally printed) or abroad.

At the beginning of 1977 the Charter 77 movement, which included the writer and future president Václav Havel, called on the communist regime to enter into an open debate. The movement's main task was to monitor human rights in Czechoslovakia, bring attention to abuses of the legal constitution and attempt to inform the outside world of any excesses it found. It grouped together a wide spectrum of Czechoslovaks from those thrown out of the party on the one hand to sworn anti-communists on the other. Charter 77 gained worldwide recognition though many in Czechoslovakia itself knew nothing of its activities or even of its existence.

Even though changes took place in the Soviet Union under Gorbachev (the new policies of *glasnost* and *perestroika*) there was only a mild thaw in Czechoslovakia. As events began to gather pace around eastern Europe at the end of 1989 with the fall of the Berlin Wall, it was only a matter of time before the wind of change blew into Czechoslovakia.

November 1989 and the so-called Velvet Revolution

On 17 November 1989, the students of Prague were set to take part in an officially sanctioned demonstration to mark the 50th anniversary of the murder of nine students and the closure of the universities by the Nazis in 1939. Around 50,000 people took part in a march which took them along Národní třída. Here they were brutally attacked by the state security forces, many were beaten (though reports that one student had been killed were later found to be false) and around 100 were arrested. Whether or not this was a preconceived series of events planned either by those who wanted to see the end of the hard-line regime or by the hard-line communists themselves seeing dark clouds on the horizon and fearing a violent revolution (a thing Ceaucescu in Romania failed to predict) and looking for a way to leave the scene quietly (with their amassed wealth), is now academic. The demonstrations of the evening of 17 November 1989 set in motion a chain of events which would lead the country away from a totalitarian state and towards freedom, democracy and capitalism. This was dubbed the 'Velvet Revolution' by Western journalists but in the Czech Republic it is simply known as the revolution. Comparisons were naturally drawn between the reaction of the communist state and the actions of the Nazis 50 years earlier. On 19 November, the Civic Forum (*Občanské forum,* OF) was created, an umbrella movement for anyone who wanted change. In the following days many more demonstrations were organised and students went on strike and began to travel around the country informing the populace of what was happening in Prague. On 24 November Miloš Jakeš, the head of the communist Party, resigned which in essence meant the end of one-party rule despite attempts by the communists to form another government with OF with a communist majority. President Husák resigned on 10 December 1989, after naming a new government of national reconciliation in which members of OF and the Slovak equivalent enjoyed a majority. Václav Havel was elected president on 29 December 1989. Politically, Soviet-style communism had come to an end but it left a legacy which the now-free state is still grappling with to this day.

The division of Czechoslovakia and the new Czech state
At the beginning of the 1990s the now-free Czechoslovakia faced a myriad of problems. Pollution and the devastation of the environment by acid rain and opencast mining, economic problems as markets in the East went bankrupt and stopped importing Czechoslovak goods, increases in crime, growing unemployment as the state began to sell off industries, crumbling infrastructure and political uncertainty were just some of the ills the new state faced. The overriding priority for the new government was to organise free elections, the first since 1946, which were held over 8 and 9 June 1990. These were not so much elections as a referendum to provide the population with a formal opportunity to give a resounding 'no' to the Communist Party. OF emerged victorious in Bohemia and Moravia whilst in Slovakia the Slovak equivalent *Verejnost' proti násiliu* (Public against Violence) won the most votes. Václav Havel was once again elected president by the parliament of a newly renamed Czechoslovak Federal Republic.

The division of Czechoslovakia
It should have been obvious to anyone that OF and *Verejnost' proti násiliu* were each far too broad political movements to last very long without splintering into many different parties, which is exactly what occurred. These movements had served their purpose and delivered the country through the precarious transformation from totalitarian regime to democratic state. The main two parties to emerge from the break-up of OF and *Verejnost' proti násiliu* were *Občanská demokratická strana* (ODS, Civic Democrats) with the finance minister Václav Klaus at the helm in Bohemia and Moravia and *Hnutí za demokratické Slovensko* (HZDS, Movement for a Democratic Slovakia) led by Vladimír Mečiar in Slovakia. Fresh elections were held over 5 and 6 June 1992 which decided the fate of Czechoslovakia. Vladimír Mečiar in Slovakia became the personification of disillusionment with Klaus's free-market economic reforms and so-called *Pragocentrismus*, Prague's domination as the capital. ODS gained most votes in the Czech lands and HZDS did likewise in Slovakia. The two victors were unable to form a stable federal government as their disagreements were just too great. The Slovak deputies refused to re-elect Václav Havel as president and after much discussion it was finally decided on 25 November 1992 to split the country in two. On 1 January 1993, two new countries appeared on the map of Europe, the Czech and Slovak republics.

The new Czech state

Klaus's economic policies seemed to be working as the Czech Republic got to its feet. Foreign investment flowed into the country, small and medium-sized businesses were privatised either through auction, restitution to former owners and their descendants or through so-called coupon privatisation whereby ordinary citizens were able to purchase shares in companies. Environmental issues were addressed, people renovated their houses, started businesses, travelled abroad for the first time, bought new cars and mobile phones and generally things began to improve. Politically, however, the Czech Republic has not been quite as stable. Elections were held in 1996, 1998 and 2002 and always produced precarious coalitions and unpopular power deals between the parties, a situation which continues to this day. In 1998 the Social Democrats (ČSSD) were asked to form a government by President Václav Havel, the only permanent political fixture throughout the 1990s and only replaced in 2003 by Václav Klaus. At the last count the Social Democrats have had four prime ministers, the incumbent being Jiří Paroubek. The Social Democrats have become deeply unpopular mainly because of their social and economic reforms and not assisted by general apathy and dissatisfaction with politics as a whole and by the time you read this book will most likely have been replaced by the Civic Democrats (ODS).

Despite weak political leadership the Czech Republic has made enormous progress on the international scene. In 1999 the country became part of NATO (despite Russian objections) and a long-term aim of every Czech government was fulfilled in 2004 when the Czechs were finally admitted to the European Union, opening up a whole new chapter in the country's history. Despite a current economic downturn the long-term future for the Czechs is promising.

GOVERNMENT AND POLITICS

The Czech Republic is a bi-cameral parliamentary democracy. The lower house is called the *sněmovna*, and the upper house the *senát*. The main political parties are the Civic Democrats (ODS, *Občanská demokratická strana*), the Social Democrats (ČSSD, *Česká strana sociálně-demokratická*) and the communists (KSČM, *Komunistická strana Čech a Moravy*). It may come as a surprise to many

WHAT THE CZECHS HAVE GIVEN THE WORLD

Did you know, that whenever you put your soft contact lenses in, drop a sugar cube in your tea, say the word 'robot' or drink a pils beer, you are using something thought up in the Czech lands? The Czech Republic has given the world much for its small size. There are the overachievers of the sports world such as Martina Navrátilová (tennis), Emil Zátopek (athletics: distance running), Roman Šebrle (athletics: decathlon), Jaromír Jágr (ice hockey) and Pavel Nedvěd (football). In the arts and culture we could mention Alphons Mucha (Art Nouveau painter), Václav Havel (dissident playwright), Antonín Dvořák and Bedřich Smetana (composers), Miloš Forman (film director), Karel Čapek, Milan Kundera and Franz Kafka (writers) who have all achieved world recognition. Škoda cars are a thing we see daily on our streets. Once ridiculed, they have been transformed into attractive, desirable and reliable vehicles, a far cry from their predecessors. Even Czech beers have appeared in our bars, pubs and supermarkets so now we can all enjoy the best of the Czech Republic at home.

to see the communists still on the political scene more than 15 years after the revolution. In fact their popularity is on the increase. In local elections in 2004 they took 20% of the vote nationally, and this figure was even higher in some regions. The Social Democrats are the current ruling party, and have been since 1997. In that time they have gone through four prime ministers and tens of ministers. Due to the seemingly endless reforms they have implemented, and their evident incompetence, they are deeply unpopular, and will almost certainly be unceremoniously thrown out of office by the Czech electorate at the next election. Social Democrat prime minister number four is Jiří Paroubek who has experienced a suspiciously meteoric rise from Prague municipal official to Czech premier in less than a year. The vast majority of Czechs had never heard of him until he became Minister for Regional Development in 2004. The Civic Democrats are the firm favourites to take over at the helm, though they are very likely to need the help of a smaller party to gain a majority in parliament. This will not be the communists who have been purposefully sidelined since the revolution by all the other parties when forming coalitions, but who will, in all likelihood, form the main opposition in the next parliament.

Czech politics is a never-ending saga of scandal, intrigue, widespread corruption, accusations, resignations, infantile fall-outs, weak coalitions, voter indifference, nepotism, cronyism, lies and general ineptitude. Yet the country ticks along regardless, has joined NATO and the EU without major problems, and continues to gradually improve the lives of its citizens. This all seems to happen *despite* Czech politicians rather than as a result of their efforts.

The Czech president is elected by parliament and from 1990 until 2003 this post was held by the world famous playwright and former dissident, Václav Havel (from 1990–93 he was Czechoslovakian president). You may be surprised to hear that during his term in office he was rather unpopular among the populace. A

TOMÁŠ GARRIGUE MASARYK

The single most important Czech politician of the time and without doubt the most influencial Czech of the 20th century was Tomáš Garrigue Masaryk. Born in 1850 in Hodonín in south Moravia in humble circumstances, Tomáš Masaryk completed his university education in Vienna graduating in philology. He met his wife, an American named Charlotte Garrigue, while undertaking further studies in Leipzig (hence the middle name which he took from her). In 1882 he accepted a post at the university in Prague where he also worked as an editor. Soon he was drawn into politics and took his seat in the imperial assembly in 1891. Apart from a very successful political career he was a prolific writer. In 1914 he went into exile on the advice of a friend. Whilst in America he managed to persuade President Woodrow Wilson to support the break-up of the Austro-Hungarian Empire and the creation of a new state, Czechoslovakia, an idea Masaryk had promoted throughout the war with support of Edvard Beneš and Slovak astronomer Milan Štefánik. As the Habsburg Empire collapsed and World War I drew to a close, the new state of Czechoslovakia was declared on 28 October 1918 (still, incidentally, the Czech National Day), and Masaryk rightly returned as its first president, holding office until 1935. The new state consisted of the Czech lands, Slovakia and the Ruthenia region, today part of Ukraine.

president can only serve for two five-year terms, and in early 2003 Havel handed over the reins to the former Civic Democrat prime minister and post-revolution Thatcherite finance minister, Václav Klaus. Often described as a Euro-sceptic, Klaus's speeches are never dull and always controversial. He is a very popular figure who speaks his mind. Fortunately, or perhaps unfortunately, the president has very limited political power.

In 2001, new administrative regions came into being, the first changes since the 1960s. Previously the country had been divided into approximately 50 tidy administrative blocks called *okresy* based around a town or city. In 2001, these were effectively replaced by 13 larger regions called *kráje* based around larger cities such as Pilsen and Hradec Králové. The *okres* system is still in place, but has little administrative meaning. I have kept to the traditional division of the country into central, north, south, east and west Bohemia and north and south Moravia, with one exception, the newly created Czech-Moravian Highlands *kráj* around the town of Jihlava.

ECONOMY

Bohemia and Moravia were the real workhorses of the industrial revolution in central Europe under the Austro-Hungarian Empire, and thanks to the liberal capitalism of the First Republic from 1918 to 1938, Czechoslovakia became one of the most economically advanced and industrialised countries in the world, some rating it at seventh or eighth overall, which would have made it a member of the G8, had it existed at the time; unimaginable today. Engineering was the country's particular strength. The communist takeover in 1948 put paid to all that, as the country switched to an inflexible command economy geared towards heavy engineering, military production and the needs and whims of the Soviet Union. Industries were nationalised, farms collectivised and private enterprise smothered. Absurd five-year plans were completed in record time with scant regard for the environment or the economic needs and wishes of the population. Throughout the communist era, however, Czechoslovak trams, trolleybuses, motorcycles and various other vehicles were exported to every corner of the communist world, and their reliability can still be seen today in every town and city from Germany to the Pacific.

With the dismantling of the Soviet Union and the ensuing economic and social chaos at the beginning of the 1990s, Czech manufacturers lost their traditional markets and had no option other than to begin to compete in the aggressive Western markets. The country embarked on a lengthy and painful series of economic reforms, spearheaded by finance minister, and current president, Václav Klaus. Privatisation was the watchword of the 1990s and was carried out in three stages. Restitution, whereby property was returned to its former owners on condition that it had been confiscated after 1948, was the first stage. The 1948 cut-off date prevented Sudeten Germans claiming back property seized at the end of World War II. The second stage was the auctioning off of thousands of shops and other premises. The third and perhaps most controversial stage was Klaus's coupon privatisation, whereby every adult in the country was permitted to buy 1,000Kč worth of bargain-basement shares, which would then hopefully grow in value as the Czech economy grew.

Up until 1997 the Czech Republic was seen as the economic success story of the former communist bloc. People began to set up small businesses, foreign investors poured millions of dollars into the country to take advantage of the low wages and educated workforce, and tourism began to bring in much-needed revenue. An economic downturn in the late 1990s, however, was a setback the country has gradually been coming to terms with ever since. Unemployment continues to dog the economy running at around 10% in the last few years, and the country is operating an ever-increasing budget deficit, partly because of an overgenerous social benefit system, which some say does little to motivate the unemployed to work. Red tape, low workforce mobility and recession in neighbouring countries have not helped.

Today the Czech Republic produces machinery and vehicles, beer, chemicals, glass and cement, with agriculture accounting for only a small proportion of the economy (unlike neighbouring Poland). Main produce are sugar-beet, wheat, potatoes, corn and hops. Its largest trading partners are Germany, Slovakia and Austria but many new markets have opened up since the Czechs' entry into the EU. Cars, beer and tourism constitute the success stories of the Czech economy. Škoda cars, produced in Mladá Boleslav in central Bohemia, and once ridiculed in the West, have become a desirable consumer durable under the company's new owners, Volkswagen. Numerous brands of unrivalled Czech beer are exported to all corners of the globe, and tourists in their millions fill Prague's streets and cash registers, spending an average 3,500Kč a day.

The Czechs current per capita GDP is approximately US$16,000, placing it in 60th place in the world and putting it on a par with Barbados and the Bahamas and ahead of its neighbours Slovakia and Poland. The average wage is in the region of 15,000Kč a month, of which roughly 20% is paid to the government in income tax.

PEOPLE

Approximately 10.2 million people call the Czech Republic home, the overwhelming majority of whom are Czechs. Some minor ethnic groups live alongside them such as Slovaks, Gypsies, Vietnamese, Germans, Poles and Hungarians, but collectively make up less than 6% of the total population. The Czech lands were a melting pot of German, Czech and Jewish ethnicities until the Holocaust and the expulsion of the Sudeten Germans after World War II, creating one of the most ethnically homogeneous regions in Europe. Around 13% of Czechs would call themselves Moravians, though for the outsider there is virtually no difference between the two groups except perhaps in the types of alcohol they drink. Bohemian Czechs like their beer while the favoured tipple of Moravians is wine. As far as its people are concerned, the Czech Republic is about as un-diverse as it could be.

So who exactly *are* the Czechs? A mix of Slavs, Germans and a mixed bag of those who remained after invasions by various armies (Swedes, French, Italians, Russians) is how many would sum up. In many areas previously inhabited by the Sudeten Germans, many Czechs can also trace their genes to Ukraine. I have heard it said that Czechs are eternally pulled between a tender, romantic Slavic heart and a hard, logical Germanic brain, a perfect way to describe the Czech character.

Having lived among the Czechs for over a decade, I am loath to make many broad guidebook-style generalisations about them. While some might say Czechs live closely to the earth, love nature, food, traditions and family, those who know the country and its people well know this is a stereotype, and alas, see these characteristics being steadily eroded by the forces of globalisation. What is true, however, is that Czechs have quite tight-knit families depending on parents well into adulthood; Czechs like to drink beer surrounded by friends and are a hospitable nation when it comes to foreigners (though nowhere near as much as a decade ago); Czechs love to read, sing, play musical instruments and pass this knowledge on to the next generation; and they are certainly not a God-fearing

TEN GREATEST CZECHS (ACCORDING TO CZECH TV VIEWERS)

Charles IV (1316–1378)	Czech king and Holy Roman Emperor
Tomáš Garrigue Masaryk (1850–1937)	First Czechoslovak president
Václav Havel (1936–)	Dramatist, communist-era dissident and post-communist president
Jan Amos Komenský (1592–1670)	Historian, linguist, writer, pedagogue
Jan Žižka (1360–1424)	Hussite warlord
Jan Werich (1905–1980)	Actor, dramatist and writer
Jan Hus (1371–1415)	Priest, instigator of the Hussite movement
Antonín Dvořák (1841–1904)	Composer
Karel Čapek (1890–1938)	Inter-war writer and journalist
Božena Němcová (1820–1862)	Most famous Czech woman writer

nation, most of them never setting foot in a church for religious reasons in their lives. They also tend to be very knowledgeable on a wide range of subjects thanks to the excellent education system. Factory workers may be surprised to learn you have never heard of that 18th-century German novelist, or the teachings of Comenius. Czechs do suffer slightly from a sense that the whole world revolves around the Czech lands, and are occasionally surprised that foreigners are not acquainted with figures from Czech literature or the 1970s dissident movement. They are sometimes guilty of regarding Anglo-Saxons as rather uninformed.

Positive thinking and confidence in themselves as a nation are sometimes seen as their weakest traits. Self-criticism and dark forecasts of a bleak future accompany almost every change the country encounters. Islands of optimism and pride come with every world championship victory in ice hockey and soccer success, though defeat is usually followed by more introspection and finger pointing. Czechs see themselves as both the victims of history and too weak to have altered the course of that history.

LANGUAGE

Spoken by approximately 11 million people, Czech belongs to the western Slav group of languages along with Polish, Slovak and Lusatian, and uses the Roman alphabet as opposed to the Cyrillic employed by eastern Slavic and some southern Slavic tongues. Czech and Slovak are mutually comprehensible, though interestingly enough, Czech children who have grown up since the division of Czechoslovakia may have problems with Slovak TV programmes. Czech is a highly complex language with seven cases, three genders and a whole range of other mind-bending grammatical features, making it one of the most troublesome languages in Europe, if not the world, for non-Slavs to learn.

Many who embark on the long road to speaking Czech gasp in disbelief at some of the tongue-twisting feats they are called upon to perform. Vowelless words which look like spelling mistakes such as *prst* (finger), *strž* (ravine), *smrk* (spruce), *hlt* (gulp), *smršť* (cyclone), *smrt* (death) or *krk* (neck) are perhaps the most astounding. In fact there is a rather nonsensical, but all the same remarkable sentence, which can be created, completely lacking in vowels: *Strč prst skrz krk*, which literally means 'push your finger through your neck'. Nonsense indeed, but it demonstrates Czech's apparent lack of need for vowels. Another stumbling block as far as pronunciation is concerned is the innocent letter *ř*. There is no real equivalent in any other European language (though some come close) and its pronunciation may seem nigh on impossible at first. Some Czechs have difficulties with this letter as children, and there is a tongue twister *třitisícetřista stříbrných stříkaček* ... (the spitting continues for several more lines) which helps learners master this tricky sound. See *Appendix 1, Language* for at least an attempt at an explanation on how to pronounce this letter. If it is any consolation Czechs have exactly the same problems with the *th* sound in English. Despite all of the above Czech pronunciation is very regular, words are pronounced to a large extent as they are written, and having mastered the pronunciation of each individual letter you should, in theory, be able to make a reasonable attempt at any word in the Czech dictionary with a few exceptions.

The Czechs are aware that the whole world is not learning Czech, and therefore *they* have to make the effort to learn other nations' languages, namely the so-called 'world languages'. The jury is most definitely out on how successful this is going. Throughout the communist era almost all Czechs were forced to endure Russian lessons at school and university, but because of the existence and proximity of the former GDR, German was also taught. Only a chosen few had the opportunity to learn English. This all changed after the fall of communism in 1989, and now it seems everyone is attempting to acquire knowledge of a foreign language in their spare time. It is now the norm that office workers are given language courses free of charge. Educated and travelled people in Prague now speak English, but when you are trying to get through to a hotel receptionist or shop assistant with the most basic of requests, you might question the Czechs' linguistic ability somewhat. Outside of Prague the situation is even worse except around the border areas where German and Polish are widely spoken.

As far as your attempts to utter some words of Czech are concerned, go for it. Your friends around the pub table will be amused and appreciative, even your hotel receptionist or ticket taker at a tourist sight may crack a smile.

CULTURE
Symbols
All public buildings, policemen's shoulders and footballers' shirts in the Czech lands bear the Czech Republic's coat of arms. Divided into four fields, the top left and bottom right sections show a silver double-tailed lion rampant on a red background sporting a golden crown, the symbol of Bohemia dating back to the Přemyslid dynasty. In the top right-hand field is a red and silver chequered eagle on a blue background also with golden crown, representing Moravia, and the symbol of Silesia is also an eagle, this time black on a yellow field with a half moon emblazoned across its chest in the last field. The state colours of the republic are a white, red and blue tricolour (in that order).

Another important symbol is the linden tree, especially its leaves and branches which can be seen in many important places such as on banknotes and on the president's coat of arms.

National costume
Each region of Bohemia and Moravia has slightly different traditional folk costume. Some are elaborately decorated affairs with thick embroidery, lace and

ICE HOCKEY
While the Czechs enjoy relative success in football (World Cup finalists in 1934 and 1962 and winners of the European Championships in 1976), they excel most at their other national sport, ice hockey. For a country of just ten million people their dominance of the sport is astonishing. Since 1920 they have won 11 world championships (six as Czechoslovakia) including three in a row from 1999 to 2001 and have lost 12 times in the final. However, Czech ice hockey celebrated its greatest moment in Japan in 1998 when the team overcame Russia to win Olympic gold. The country continues to supply the NHL (the National Hockey League) with some of its top names, the most famous being Jaromír Jágr from Kladno.

ribbons, while others are simpler and more modest. Regional dress differences played a double role in the not so distant past. Firstly, they were a status symbol illustrating wealth of the region, and secondly they limited inbreeding, as potential partners could be confident from the differences in their dress they were not marrying a distant cousin from the same village!

Red, white and black dominate, though other colours do make an appearance from region to region. White is the prevailing colour symbolising freshness and cleanliness. A rich blend of cotton, brocade, silk, felt, lace, wool and velvet all feature in the costumes which were mainly worn for special occasions such as weddings, pilgrimages and rural celebrations. Women typically wore (and wear) an embroidered headscarf or lace bonnet, a white blouse with seemingly inflated sleeves, a pleated skirt, a dark laced-up bodice, a lace embroidered pinafore, stockings and black leather shoes. For men the costume is usually simpler, consisting of felt cap or hat, a white tunic, dark waistcoat, dark trousers with a high waistline and black leather boots. Of course there are many different variations and styles which change from region to region.

Czechs tend to see national costume as somehow associated with the communist regime which did have a tendency to pull out costumed youngsters at special occasions to underline the Czechs' Slavic ethnic roots (and therefore their naturally close relationship with big brother Russia). You are far more likely to see national dress in Moravia where a greater number of folk traditions are kept alive in general, and where national costume is still regarded as an integral part of the country's rich heritage.

Arts
Literature
The 10th-century *Legends of St Wenceslas* are regarded as the first literature in Czech though until the 15th century Czech literature consisted mostly of chronicles (most notably by Cosmas who wrote in the 12th century), hymns and chivalrous poems. Things really took off after Jan Hus helped Czech become a codified literary language and the climax of the Renaissance period was the Kralice Bible translated by the Protestant Czech brethren at the end of the 16th century. Comenius wrote in Czech in exile otherwise the language was demoted to a peasant tongue after the Thirty Years War and very little literature was produced. Czech rose from the ashes in the late 18th century with writers such as Dobrovský and Kollár and literature was at the forefront of the Czech National Revival, without doubt its golden age. Writers such as Božena Němcová and Jan Neruda, poets Karel Hynek Mácha and Karel Erben, and later František Palacký

ŠVEJK
John Burke

None of the personages who have studded the pages of Prague's kaleidoscopic history have left such a mark as that fictitious rotund dog-fancier called Švejk (or Schweik as his name is sometimes transcribed). The fatuous fame of this moon-faced bumpkin, who was wont to quaff Pilsner plus cherry-brandy at the tavern U Kalicha, has spread so far and wide that the restaurant on Na Bojišti Street now heaves with tourists. It remained a plain pub (the name translates as The Flagon) under the communist regime that saw Švejk as an anti-Germanic peacenik from the proletariat, while wary of his appeal to anarchists and nationalists.

The hilarious adventures of this anti-hero in *The Good Soldier Schweik*, an anti-war book, summed up a particular patriotism in the old Bohemian capital that became the chaotic cockpit of central Europe. And the reluctant recruit to the imperial Austro-Hungarian army became a model for Czech insubordination during two later occupations by foreign powers.

The author, Jaroslav Hašek, was himself a Bohemian, both literally and figuratively, for he quit his job in a bank for freelance journalism, leading an eccentric and wandering life that took him into many a tavern. Švejk's garrulous anecdotes and gargantuan adventures are drawn from life, for Hašek too was conscripted and then captured by the Russians during World War I. He died in 1923, with the masterpiece unfinished, but it is still a rollicking tale packed with martinets and other oddballs whose portraits adorn the walls of U Kalicha.

Even though Švejk never suffered the fate meted out to real heroes in Prague's past – defenestration from Prague castle, drowning in the Vltava, execution on the Old Town Square – he got into scrapes galore. His biggest triumph, however, was doing something so terrible that he could not even be told what it was. Ordered to distribute a two-part novel to the officer corps, he reasons that they should read the first volume before getting the second. Actually, the whole thing was to work as a codebook, so Švejk's typical bungling means that the entire army is without secret communications!

Things like that inspired the Czechs in 1968, when the Red Army moved in to halt the Prague Spring, to turn round signposts and snarl up tanks. But Švejk really survived the absurdity of World War I by deliberately playing the fool. Hašek's books are a satire on army life of the time but also on the Czechs' attitude to their Austrian overlords and to absurd, bureaucratic regimes in general. Švejk's actions have spawned the verb Švejkovat (literally 'to do a Schweik'), a common activity throughout the communist era. Yet, perhaps understandably, many Czechs now find the whole Švejk image a touch uncomfortable.

and Alois Jirásek (Old Czech Myths) rose to prominence and fed a nation hungry for patriotic, romantic literature. The most influential writer of the early 20th century was Karel Čapek (he gave the world the word 'robot' which first appeared in his play *RUR*) and of course there was Hašek with his Good Soldier Švejk. Kafka was around at that time in Prague too, though he wrote in German. Communism saw the rise of writers such as Bohumil Hrabal, Milan Kundera and

Václav Havel who have gained worldwide recognition. The 15 years since the fall of communism have seen very few writers of note come to the fore.

Music

Co Čech, to muzikant (Every Czech is a musician) goes the Czech saying and unlike the world of literature, the Czechs have produced numerous composers of world renown with Dvořák, Smetana, Martinů, Janáček, Suk and Fibich the best known. Many will know Dvořák's *New World Symphony*, Smetana's opera *The Bartered Bride* and Janáček has become popular in recent years.

Thankfully Czech popular music has hardly ever crossed the borders of the Czech Republic and it is easy to hear why. One exception is the evergreen Karel Gott, the Czech Tom Jones of minor fame among older generations in Germany and across the former USSR. Otherwise rock and pop is all much of a sameness and may seem jaded and out of date to Western ears.

Cinema

The Czech Republic is the powerhouse of central and eastern Europe when it comes to film. From decadent First Republic black-and-white pictures, to Voskovec and Werich's slapstick of the 1930s, from optimistic 1950s communist propaganda, to the New Wave of the 1960s, from hilarious comedies of the 1970s, to the critical works of the 1980s and 1990s, coming to terms with the trauma of the 20th century, all have produced wonderful films of the highest quality. The Czechs have also given the world Miloš Forman, director of *One Flew over the Cuckoo's Nest* and *Amadeus* and Czech directors Jiří Menzel and Zdeněk Svěrák junior won Oscars for *Closely Observed Trains* in 1966 and *Kolya* in 1997 respectively. Since the revolution Prague has provided the backdrop to films such as *Mission Impossible* and *Bad Company* and the Barrandov Studios now churn out countless ads and films for foreign film companies.

RELIGION

While the 1990s saw ethnic religious strife raging in the Balkans, the Catholic Church reasserting its power in Poland and the Eastern Orthodox Church rebuilding gigantic churches across the former Soviet Union and attracting ever greater congregations, the Czech Republic remained and remains an island of atheism. This seems hard to believe when looking back at the 14th and 15th

UNESCO-LISTED SITES IN THE CZECH REPUBLIC

Site	Year listed
Český Krumlov historical centre	1992
Prague historical centre	1992
Telč historical centre	1992
Church of St John of Nepomuk, Žďár nad Sázavou	1994
Sites in Kutná Hora and Sedlec	1995
Lednice and Valtice region	1996
Holašovice village green	1998
Kroměříž chateau and gardens	1998
Litomyšl chateau	1999
Holy Trinity column in Olomouc	2000
Tugendhat Villa in Brno	2001
Jewish Quarter and Basilica of St Prokop in Třebíč	2003

centuries when the Hussites in the Czech lands shook the very foundations of the Catholic Church and the Protestant estates defied the mighty Catholic Habsburgs at the beginning of the Thirty Years War. Congregations are slightly larger in Moravia than in Bohemia but across the country the Church is viewed with suspicion and even ridicule.

The country is officially Roman Catholic but the Hussite Church is still going strong and claims to have over 400,000 worshippers. Hussite churches are very often former synagogues. The Czech Brethren (*Jednota bratrská*) are another Protestant group with 200,000 members. There are tiny pockets of Jews around the country but nothing to compare to the pre-war communities. The largest group of Jews is in Prague. The Eastern Orthodox Church also has a large following.

EDUCATION

Most citizens of former eastern bloc countries would agree that the communist system did get the odd aspect of society right. Possibly the greatest success of socialism in the Czech Republic is, with the possible exception of its universities, the education system. No-one can deny that syllabuses were laced with communist indoctrination until 1989, but the new democratic state inherited a system it could work with. However, problems soon arose as teachers' wages shrivelled into a pittance, and a dearth of qualified pedagogues affected the quality of teaching, as graduates flocked into the private sector for higher pay and status in society. These problems seem to have been successfully addressed in the last few years, and with investment in new technology and infrastructure, the future again looks rosy for the Czech Republic's state education system, with one exception. Czech universities are in crisis and have been since the revolution. There is a severe lack of university places, courses are too long, the universities themselves are threadbare institutions, their facilities decidedly chipped around the edges and textbooks and other materials well thumbed or photocopied. Ageing professors, low wages and morale, underfunding and talk of tuition fees in parliament drive brighter Czech students abroad to learn. There does not seem to be any improvement on the horizon either.

Education is compulsory from age six to 15. Children up to three years of age may start their education at a *jesle* or nursery. At age three, parents can send them to one of the many *Mateřská školas* or kindergartens. *Základní škola* or infant school is where the serious business starts. Classes 1–9 prepare Czech children for *Střední škola* or secondary school. These are divided into grammar schools (*gymnázium*, nothing to do with a gymnasium), *ekonomická škola* (schools focused on business, accounting, economics and the like) and various vocational institutions. At 19 students can apply to go to one of the universities, but competition verges on the ridiculous with sometimes tens of students chasing one place. The major universities are in Prague (Charles University), Brno (Masaryk University) and Olomouc (Palacký University) and there less prestigious establishments in Pilsen, České Budějovice and Ústí nad Labem.

Practical Information

WHEN TO VISIT (AND WHY)

Prague is a year-round destination and ever increasing numbers of people are coming at times generally regarded as out of season. The tourist season is from June until August but the shoulder seasons, spring and autumn, are increasingly popular too. Winter, with the exception of Christmas and New Year, is quieter, but not by much. Outside of Prague many tourist attractions close over winter and there are fewer services available such as tour guides. Do not automatically assume that Prague is best in summer. Most city-dwellers flee the sweltering heat and package tour crowds and in my opinion spring and autumn are much more agreeable times to visit.

Spring

Spring must be one of the best times to visit as the country awakes from its long winter slumber. Museums, galleries, castles and chateaux reopen, the weather warms up, the last snows disappear from mountain trails and trees buckle under the weight of pink and white blossom. Easter is a much more significant celebration in Slavic countries (see *Public holidays and festivals*, page 38) and many towns and villages hold Easter fairs and special events to mark the arrival of spring. The weather is quite unpredictable though it can be surprisingly warm even in mid May.

Summer

Obviously summer is the season most tourists descend on Prague and the Czech Republic in general. Summers are hotter than many imagine with the mercury in the thermometer regularly pushing 30°C, though humidity remains low. The mountains experience temperatures around 10°C lower than Prague, and are quite often a more pleasant destination. Summer is a time for activity holidays, and wherever you go in the country, you will see people cycling, hiking, canoeing down rivers and enjoying the beautiful countryside. A warm, pleasant evening spent roasting *buřty* (big fat pork sausages) over a crackling pine log fire listening to the grasshoppers and catching the scent of the pine forests on the warm summer breeze is an essential Czech experience. Meanwhile Prague's cobbles and stone buildings echo to the sound of languages from all corners of the globe and the balmy summer nightlife is second to none in the region. Prague's churches host classical music concerts and after-show diners cruise on the Vltava. Prague Castle stands illuminated and shimmering in the warm night air.

Autumn

Personally I like the Czech Republic best in September. The weather is not as hot as in July and August, the days are still long and it rains less. Everything is still

CZECH MONTHS AND THEIR MEANING

While most languages in Europe have taken on some form of the Roman names for the months of the year, the Czechs have retained the old Slavic versions. Rather than being the names of irrelevant Roman gods or out-of-sync Latin numerals, the months describe the time of year, or traditional activities associated with the season.

English	Czech	Root and meaning
January	leden	Led = ice, month of ice
February	únor	Nora = fox's den, or nořit = to sink (ice in rivers)
March	březen	Bříza = birch tree, month when birches bud
April	duben	Dub = oak, month when oaks bud
May	květen	Květ = blossom, month of blossoming trees
June	červen	Červ = worm, used for making red dye
July	červenec	See červen
August	srpen	Srp = sickle, month of the harvest
September	září	Zářit = to shine, last days of summer
October	říjen	Říje = rut, month when deer rut
November	listopad	List = leaves, pád = fall, month of falling leaves
December	prosinec	From an old Czech word meaning grey, washed out

open but the tourist crowds have gone home and you feel as though you have the country all to yourself. In late September and early October the forests burst into colour in the soft hazy sunshine and it is an ideal time to mountain bike deserted trails or hike the Šumava. Life in small Czech towns reverts to normality; bright-faced schoolchildren gabble away to each other in Czech on the buses and trains, farmers gather in the last of the crops and wine festivals are held in south Moravia and central Bohemia. Finally the nights close in, and an evening in a cosy traditional Czech pub with friends, some hearty Czech food and a few pints of superb Czech beer is perfect entertainment.

Winter

Winters are much colder than many people, especially from Britain, anticipate; if the cold bothers you, choose another time of year to travel. In late December, January and February the temperature can sink to as low as −20°C. While snow is never guaranteed in the mountains, Czechs are avid skiers and make regular weekend trips to the Krkonoše Mountains, the Šumava or the Beskydy range. Christmas is one of the best times to visit Prague which holds Christmas markets, ideal for unusual gifts. In winter, Prague is an atmospheric place especially when snow covers the rooftops of Malá strana and the Vltava freezes over. February can be bright and crisp.

HIGHLIGHTS AND ITINERARIES

A long weekend Sandwich a day trip out into central Bohemia between two days exploring Prague. Karlštejn or Křivoklát castles to the west, Kutná Hora to the east or Mělník to the north are all within easy reach of the capital. There are companies in Prague who even run day trips down to Český Krumlov and out to the west Bohemian spa towns.

1 week Seven days is enough time to fully explore Prague, take in a central Bohemian castle or two, make it down to Český Krumlov for a day and still have time for a west Bohemian spa.

2 weeks 14 days would allow you to explore Prague to a fuller extent than most manage. After three or four days in the capital, head west for the spas via Křivoklát Castle. After a day in Carlsbad and a day in Marienbad head down to Český Krumlov via Pilsen for a short stop-off at the Prazdroj Brewery. From Krumlov gently make your way east across the tranquil south via České Budějovice, Třeboň, Jindřichův Hradec and Telč to Brno. After a day or two exploring the capital of Moravia take a train back to Prague stopping off at historical Olomouc and Kutná Hora if time allows.

3 weeks The luxury of a full 21 days would allow you to manage all the above as well as taking in Domažlice and Prachatice en route from Pilsen to Český Krumlov and adding the perfectly preserved Renaissance town of Slavonice after Telč. Basing yourself in Brno you could take trips to the Moravský kras and Kroměříž before making your way slowly back into Bohemia via Litomyšl, Pardubice and Hradec Králové. End your stay with some leisurely walking in the Czech Paradise region and among the Teplice and Adršpach 'rock towns'.

PUBLIC HOLIDAYS AND FESTIVALS
National holidays have been in a state of flux since the 1989 revolution and every year witnesses a tweaking of the calendar. As with the names of streets and squares, many holidays had to be altered after the demise of communism, some were scrapped altogether and some were retained, just like the countless Revolution Streets around the country, now celebrating a different revolution. The Czechs 'celebrate' their liberation from fascism on 8 May, unlike in the former Soviet Union where it is observed on 9 May. The Czech patron saint, St Wenceslas (*svatý Václav*) is honoured on 28 September, a relatively new holiday introduced in 2000. Czechs also celebrated 17 November for the first time in 2000, which recalls two events: the persecution of students under the Nazis and the 1989 protests which sparked off the Velvet Revolution.

Public holidays
1 January	New Year's Day and Day of the Renewal of Czech Statehood
March or April	Easter (Monday only)
1 May	May Day
8 May	Liberation Day or Victory Day
5 July	Day of the Slavic Missionaries Cyril and Methodius
6 July	Death of Jan Hus
28 September	Day of Czech Statehood
28 October	Declaration of Independent Czechoslovakia in 1918
17 November	Struggle for Freedom and Democracy Day
24 December	Christmas Eve (Czech Christmas Day)
25 December	Christmas Holiday
26 December	St Stephen's Day

Christmas
The word for Christmas in Czech, '*Vánoce*', is most likely derived from the words '*o dvanácti nocích*' meaning 'during the 12 nights', betraying its pre-Christian Slavic pagan origins as the 12-day festival to celebrate the return of the sun. Czechs call Christmas Eve '*Štědrý den*', the theory being that '*Štědrý*' originates

from the word '*čtvrtý*' meaning 'fourth', the fourth day of the pagan festival, celebrated with particular gusto. The Christian festival was conveniently superimposed on the original pagan celebration.

The festive season begins in the Czech lands on 5 December, on the eve of St Nicholas's Day. Students attired as angels, devils and St Nick with flowing white beard, bishop's robes and crook, visit children in their homes, asking if they have been well behaved during the year, and rewarding them for good conduct with a small gift. Children often recite a poem as proof of their good behaviour. Naughty children receive ashes or potatoes. Small children are understandably petrified by the devil, and some claim the tradition may have mild negative psychological effects on the wee ones. It continues stronger than ever, nonetheless.

The days leading up to Christmas are a hectic time. Churches display their carved nativity scenes and echo to the Christmas mass by Jan Jakub Ryba. Mothers bake vast quantities of *vánoční pečivo*, Christmas biscuits, at least ten types, so many in fact that it is not uncommon to be offered them still in March. Christmas markets fill the streets with townspeople hunting down presents for loved ones. Czechs eat carp, not turkey, at Christmas and huge plastic tanks, overflowing with gargantuan live carp, appear on the streets of all Czech towns, their writhing fishy contents destined for festive dinner tables. The fish are netted out of hundreds of drained ponds in south Bohemia, and distributed to every corner of the republic. Fewer people nowadays kill the oversize murky goldfish themselves, which rather inconveniently have to be kept in the bath until the big day, preferring instead to have it bludgeoned to death on the street by the fishmonger. Czech streets can be a freezing bloodbath just prior to Christmas, the pavement and gutters splattered with carp brain to instil one with yuletide cheer!

Christmas really gets going on 24 December and Czechs traditionally leave everything until the last minute, managing to put up decorations, erect the tree, fry the carp and usually two other dishes (usually chicken and pork), while keeping the children away from the presents. On top of everything, there is also a surprisingly well-observed tradition of fasting until evening. In the early evening, at the tinkle of a small bell, the children burst into the room where they discover the gifts under the tree left by *Ježíšek* (literally 'Little Jesus'). No-one actually ever sees *Ježíšek*, which is just as well, as how the infant Jesus would get a new racing bike through the window unaided, remains unexplained. The family then sit down to Christmas dinner. According to superstition an odd number of guests around the table brings bad luck. Then comes after-dinner fun, in the form of telling the future, using candle-bearing walnut shells floating in water, and pouring hot lead into water. An ever decreasing number of families indulge in these curious traditions these days, usually opting for the TV instead.

The next two days are set aside for visiting relatives, eating, drinking and general merry-making. Traditional foods consumed are goose, duck or turkey served with sauerkraut and dumplings. Czechs rarely go to work between Christmas and New Year and many offices, shops and businesses are closed, especially in small towns. Inevitably, every year sees Christmas become increasingly more commercial in the Czech Republic.

Easter

Somewhere between 22 March and 25 April, the Czechs celebrate Easter along with the rest of the Christian world. Good Friday is not a holiday in the Czech lands but Easter Monday is. On this day, local boys weave a *pomlázka*, a kind of whip of braided willow twigs. They then seek out young girls and, having whipped their behinds, receive a painted egg or a shot of alcohol as a reward. The custom has little to do with Christian Easter and is the remnant of a pagan fertility ritual, making the girls fresh and young and rejuvenating older women as nature rejuvenates itself in spring. Love it or hate it, it is usually a lot of fun until the boys get drunk, and start marauding through the streets armed with their whips. To describe the custom as sexist or humiliating for the women illustrates ignorance of its origins.

Egg painting has a particularly strong tradition in the Czech Republic and around Easter time you will see stalls laden with amazing, intricately decorated eggs called *kraslice*, coming from the old Slav word for red, the colour which once dominated the decoration. They make a first-rate souvenir. Traditional foods at this time are sweetbreads in the shape of rams and wreathes, lamb with Easter stuffing, and pork with sauerkraut and dumplings.

Festivals and other events

You may want to plan your trip to the Czech Republic to coincide with a special event such as a music festival, sports event or a holiday like Christmas or Easter. The following is an overview of some of the main events around the country and various others of interest to visitors. Ask the local information centres for more details.

Prague

Prague Spring Music Festival May–June. Best-known classical music festival in the Czech Republic held for over 60 years.
Prague Autumn Music Festival September–October. A more recent addition to the cultural calendar but still a classical music festival of the highest quality.
The Khamoro Festival May. Celebrates Romany culture and traditions.
Prague International Jazz Festival October. The capital's foremost jazz festival.
Christmas Markets December–January. Bizarre gifts and mulled wine in Prague's historical centre.
Prague Opera Festival January–February. Held every two years. The last was in 2005.
Prague International Marathon May. One of the most beautiful marathon courses in the world.

Bohemia

Český Krumlov Music Festival August. International jazz and alternative music festival.
Český Krumlov Cinquefoil Rose Celebrations June. A Renaissance celebration during which the town returns to the time of knights, damsels in distress and court jesters.
Carlsbad International Film Festival July. One of Europe's most important film festivals attended by film stars from around the world.
Carlsbad Jazzfest October. A festival of traditional and modern jazz running for over 20 years.
Karlštejn Wine Festival September. Traditional wine festival held at the Gothic castle and in the village below.
Kutná Hora Royal Silver Festival June. Celebrates Kutná Hora's illustrious past.
Kutná Hora Music Festival September. Music from the Gothic period to the 20th century in the stunning surroundings of UNESCO sites.

Smetana's Litomyšl June–July. An international opera festival, held in the courtyard of Litomyšl's Renaissance chateau for almost 50 years.
Marienbad Chopin Festival August. International music festival dedicated to the music of Frédéric Chopin.
Beroun Autumn Potters' Market September. The Autumn Potters' Market is part of the celebrations to mark the Days of European Heritage.
Rock For People (Český Brod) July. One of the largest open-air rock festivals in the Czech Republic. Acts from the Czech Republic and abroad.
Holašovice Rustic Celebrations June. Festival of folk traditions, folklore and handicrafts. Takes place on the village green
Annual re-enactment of the Battle of Hradec Králové July. Period uniforms and weapons at the annual re-enactment of the Battle of Hradec Králové in 1866 between Austrian and Prussian forces.
Folklore Festival Pardubice and Hradec Králové June. The largest folklore festival in the country.
Festival in the Heart of Europe – Mitte Europa June–August. A Czech–German cross-border cultural project, the main focus being classical music. Takes place in more than 60 towns on both sides of the northwest border (Cheb).
International Festival of Records and Curiosities (Pelhřimov) June. A marathon of attempts to get into the *Guinness Book of Records*.
Pilsner Fest September–October. Pilsen's beer festival.
Strakonice Bagpipe Festival August. The country's largest bagpipe festival.
Velká pardubická steeplechase October. The Czech Republic's most famous horserace. Takes place annually in Pardubice.

Moravia
Olomouc Summer of Culture, June–September. Open-air shows, concerts, exhibitions, literary evenings and theatre performances in the historical city centre.
Easter and Christmas in the Valašsko Region – Rožnov pod Radhoštěm December and Easter time. Traditional Easter and Christmas folk customs at the open-air museum in Rožnov pod Radhoštěm.
Strážnice Folk Festival June. The oldest folklore festival in the country.
Znojmo Wine Festival September. A traditional festival in the Czech Republic's major wine-producing region.
Vlčnov Celebrations and the Ride of the Kings May. Folk celebrations in the Slovácko region.
Janáček's Hukvaldy June–August. Music festival at the medieval Hukvaldy Castle.

TOURIST INFORMATION
Czech Tourism 131 Harley St, London W7G 9QG; ↘ 020 7631 0427; f 020 7631 0419; www:czechtourism.com. Czech Tourism does not accept callers at its office.
Czech Tourism 1109 Madison Av, New York, NY 10028; ↘ 2112 288 0830 Ext 105, 101; f 212 288 0971; www.czechtourism.com

TOUR OPERATORS
UK
Čedok Morley House, 320 Regent St, London W1B 3BG; ↘ 020 7580 3778; f 020 7580 3779; www.cedok.co.uk. The former Czechoslovak state-run travel company still offering the most comprehensive range of holidays to Prague and many other destinations in the Czech Republic.

Czech Travel Ltd 16 Albermarle Gardens, Braintree, Essex CM7 9UQ; ℃ 01376
560592; f 01376 560593; www.czechtravel.freeuk.com
Czech-It-Out Ltd 111 Bell St, London NW1 6TL; ℃ 020 7258 7800; fax; 020 7724
6694; www.goaway.co.uk
Erna Low 9 Reece Mews, London SW7 3HE; ℃ 020 7594 0290; f 020 7823 9774;
www.bodyandsoulholidays.info. Spa holidays to Marienbad.
Prague Tours The Coach House, Coopers Hill, Ongar, Essex CM5 9EG; ℃ 01277
366599; www.prague-tours.co.uk
Regent Holidays 15 John St, Bristol BS1 2HR; ℃ 0117 921 1711; f 0117 925 4866;
www.regent-holidays.co.uk
Thermalia Travel Ltd 1a Stanmore Hill, Stanmore, Middx HA7 4BL; ℃ 0870 165
9420; f 0870 165 9430; www.thermalia.co.uk. Spa breaks in Marienbad.

US
American Travel Abroad 505 8th Av, Suite 801, New York, NY 10018;
℃ 800 228 0877; f 212 581 7925; www.amta.com
Continental Journeys 5249 Leghorn Av, Sherman Oaks, CA 91401; ℃ 800 601 4343;
f 818 995 8673; www.continentaljourneys.com

Canada
Carlson Wagonlit Travel – Voyages Paradis 8875 boul Henri Bourrassa,
Charlesbourg, Quebec G1G 4E4; ℃ 418 627 0911; f 418 627 4499;
www.voyagesparadis.com. Breaks to Prague and other towns including Český Krumlov,
Olomouc and Carlsbad.
Rhapsody Tours 8424–174 St, Edmonton, Alberta T5T 2B9; ℃ 780 444 2763; f 780
484 6352; www.rhapsodytours.com. Prague and tours of the Czech Republic.

In the Czech Republic
Čedok Na Příkopě 18, 111 35, Prague 1; ℃ 224 197 641; www.cedok.cz. Čedok is still
the best travel agent in the country after 85 years in the business. Almost every town has
a branch providing local services for foreigners and holidays abroad for Czechs. Their
long experience makes them the best people to contact wherever you want to go and
whatever you want to do there.

RED TAPE
Praise be, that the days when most people needed a visa to enter the Czech
Republic (or Czechoslovakia) are over, hopefully for ever. Czech EU
membership since May 2004 means restriction-free travel for citizens of the
other 24 member countries. US citizens can enter the Czech Republic for 90
days without a visa. After much consultation, the ridiculous visa restrictions on
Canadian and Australian citizens were also lifted in 2004. Citizens of China,
India, Russia, Ukraine and various other countries should apply for a visa. The
Czech embassy website in your country should include a list of countries whose
citizens require a visa and the length of time certain nationals can be in the
country. Czech visas are straightforward and inexpensive to obtain, and are
issued without fuss and usually quite promptly and you should not encounter
too many problems.
Immigration and customs are now virtually non-existent for EU citizens. You
can even travel to the Czech Republic carrying just your national identity card
(sorry Brits, you still need your passport). If and when the Czechs become part
of the Schengen Agreement borderless travel between most countries of the EU
will become a reality. Things have certainly come a long way since 1989.

Non-EU citizens still need to show a passport and visa if required. Luggage searches at Prague Ruzyně Airport are rare.

Embassies and consulates

Australia Culgoa Circuit, O'Malley, Canberra ACT 2606; ✆ +61 262 901386; f +61 262 900006; e canberra@embassy.mzv.cz; www.mzv.cz/canberra; General Consulate in Sydney, 169 Military Rd, Dover Heights, Sydney NSW 2030; ✆ +61 293 718878; f +61 293 719635; e sydney@embassy.mzv.cz; www.mzv.cz/sydney

Austria Penzingerstrasse 11–13, Vienna 1140; ✆ +43 1 894 2125–6; f +43 1 894 1200; e vienna@embassy.mzv.cz; www.mzv.cz/vienna

Canada 251 Cooper St, Ottawa, Ontario, K2P 0G2; ✆ +1 613 562 3875; f +1 613 562 3878; e ottawa@embassy.mzv.cz; www.mzv.cz/ottawa; General Consulate in Montreal, 1305 Av des Pins Ouest, Montréal, Québec H3G 1B2; ✆ +1 514 849 4495; f +1 514 849 4117; e montreal@embassy.mzv.cz; www.mzv.cz/montreal

France 75 Bd Haussmann, Paris 75008; ✆ +33 1 72 76 13 00; f +33 1 72 76 13 13; e paris@embassy.mzv.cz; www.mzv.cz/paris

Germany Wilhelmstrasse 44, Berlin-Mitte, 10117; ✆ +49 30 226 380; f +49 30 229 4033; e berlin@embassy.mzv.cz; www.mzv.cz/berlin; General Consulate in Dresden, Erna-Berger-Strasse 1, Dresden-Neustadt, 01097; ✆ +49 351 655 670; f +49 351 803 2500; e dresden@embassy.mzv.cz; www.mzv.cz/dresden; General Consulate in Munich, Libellenstrasse 1, München-Freimann, 80939; ✆ +49 89 95 837 232; f +49 89 95 03 688; e munich@embassy.mzv.cz; www.mzv.cz/munich

Hungary Rózsa utca 61, Budapest VI. 1064; ✆ +36 1 351 05 39; f +36 1 351 91 89; e budapest@embassy.mzv.cz; www.mzv.cz/budapest

Ireland 57 Northumberland Rd, Ballsbridge, Dublin 4; ✆ +353 1 668 1135; f +353 1 668 1660; e dublin@embassy.mzv.cz; www.mzv.cz/dublin

Israel Zeitlin St 23, Tel Aviv, PO Box 16361, 64 955; ✆ +972 3 691 8282–3; f +972 3 691 8286; e telaviv@embassy.mzv.cz; www.mzv.cz/telaviv

Japan 16–14, Hiroo 2-chome, Shibuya-ku, Tokyo 150-0012; ✆ +813 3400 8122–3; f +813 3400 8124; e tokyo@embassy.mzv.cz; www.mzv.cz/tokyo

Netherlands Paleisstraat 4, 2514 JA Den Haag; ✆ +31 70 34 69 712; f +31 70 35 63 349; e hague@embassy.mzv.cz; www.mzv.cz/hague

New Zealand See *Australia*

Poland ul. Koszykowa 18, Warsaw, 00-555; ✆ +48 22 628 7221-5; f +48 22 629 8045; e warsaw@embassy.mzv.cz; www.mzv.cz/warsaw

Russia ul J Fučika 12/14, Moscow 123 056; ✆ +7 095 251 0540–5; f +7 095 250 1523; e moscow@embassy.mzv.cz; www.mzv.cz/moscow

Slovakia Hviezdoslavovo nám 8, Bratislava 810 00; ✆ +421 2 5920 3303–4; f +421 2 5920 3330; e bratislava@embassy.mzv.cz; www.mzv.cz/bratislava; General Consulate in Košice, Rázusova 13, Košice, PO Box E-10, 042 40; ✆ +421 55 623 1801–2; f +421 55 623 1799; e kosice@embassy.mzv.cz; www.mzv.cz/kosice

South Africa 936 Pretorius St, Arcadia, Pretoria; ✆ +27 12 431 2380; f +27 12 4302033; e pretoria@embassy.mzv.cz; www.mzv.cz/pretoria

Spain Avda. Pío XII, 22–24, Madrid 28016; ✆ +34 91 353 1880; f +34 91 353 1885; e madrid@embassy.mzv.cz; www.mzv.cz/madrid

Switzerland Burgernzielweg, Bern, PO Box 170, 3006; ✆ +41 31 350 4070; f +41 31 350 4098; e bern@embassy.mzv.cz; www.mzv.cz/bern

UK 26 Kensington Palace Gardens, London W8 4QY; ✆ +44 20 7243 1115; f +44 20 7727 9654; e london@embassy.mzv.cz; www.mzv.cz/london

Ukraine Jaroslaviv Val 34-A, Kiev, 019 01; ✆ +38 044 212 2110; f +38 044 229 7469; e kiev@embassy.mzv.cz; www.mzv.cz/kiev

US 3900 Spring of Freedom St, NW, Washington, DC 20008; ✆ +1 202 274 9100; f +1 202 966 8540; e amb_washington@embassy.mzv.cz; www.mzv.cz/washington; General Consulate in New York, 1109–1111 Madison Av, New York, NY 10028; ✆ +1 212 717 5643; f +1 212 717 5064; e newyork@embassy.mzv.cz; www.mzv.cz/newyork; General Consulate in Los Angeles, 10990 Wilshire Bd, Suite 1100, Los Angeles, CA 90024; ✆ +1 310 473 0889; f +1 310 473 9813; e losangeles@embassy.mzv.cz; www.mzv.cz/losangeles

GETTING THERE AND AWAY
Air
From/to Europe
In the not too distant past the air travel options to the Czech Republic were pretty much limited to national carriers. Czech Airlines (ČSA) provided the best service with other national carriers perhaps providing a daily flight to Prague. How times have changed! The now defunct GO was the first low-cost airline to link Prague with London but this was just the lighting of the blue touch paper which set off an explosion of budget carriers now linking Prague with the whole of Europe. This has meant that national carriers have had to slash prices and increase and improve services, all good news for the traveller. The low-cost airlines have meant that central and eastern Europe have become more accessible than at any time in history. It is, however, important to realise exactly what you are getting when you fly with a budget carrier. They are an excellent option when the sun is shining, runways are clear and baggage handlers are not striking. When things go wrong, however, they lack the infrastructure to deal with problems the national carriers are used to.

From Britain there are now numerous flights from regional airports making a change of flight in say Amsterdam or Paris a thing of the past. British Airways has up to four scheduled flights a day from Heathrow and Gatwick with Czech Airlines flying from Heathrow, Stansted, Gatwick, Edinburgh, Manchester, Birmingham, Dublin and Cork; easyJet are easily the best low-cost option with services from Gatwick, Stansted, Edinburgh, Newcastle, Bristol and East Midlands airports. Ryanair have also started flights from Stansted to Brno. Other low-cost airlines flying from the UK are BMI Baby, FlyBE, and Jet2 who have scheduled departures from regional airports. ČSA offer services from almost all other major airports in Europe and are usually in direct competition with the national carrier. Since the Czech Republic joined the EU in May 2004 a Czech budget airline has appeared in Europe's skies. Bearing a typical budget airline name, Smartwings offers services to and from London Gatwick, Dublin and eight other popular European destinations for very low fares indeed. Book online at www.smartwings.net.

Flying further east will also transport you back in time to when low fares and budget airlines were unthinkable. It is by and large all national carriers with heavy pumped-up long-haul fares from here onwards to places like Moscow, Kiev, Minsk, Belgrade, Bucharest and further afield. Warsaw, Krakow and Bratislava are now served by local budget airlines.

From/to North America
ČSA has four direct flights a week to and from New York (JFK), Montreal two or three times a week and Toronto three times a week. Czech Airlines is part of the Skyteam group of airlines along with the likes of Air France, Alitalia, Delta and KLM. Booking a flight via Paris or Amsterdam to Prague using these airlines via their respective hubs should have cost benefits. Otherwise flying via London is your best option.

Other routes

Heading east, Czech Airlines has direct flights to and from Dubai, Colombo, Cairo, Istanbul, Kiev, St Petersburg, Samara (Russia), Moscow, Baku, Yerevan, Riga, Tallinn, Vilnius and Tel Aviv. Other airlines flying from Prague to long-haul destinations include Korean Air to Seoul and Tunis Air to Tunis. Qantas have flights to and from Frankfurt, just a short hop from Prague on a ČSA flight.

Overland

The Czech Republic lies at the geographical centre of Europe, equidistant give or take a few hundred kilometres from the extremities of the continent. Travelling overland is, therefore, a realistic alternative when coming from most places in Europe, and cheap especially when coming from the east where air fares tend to be higher. Bus is a good option from western Europe; train is probably better from eastern Europe. The quickest way to travel overland is by car or motorcycle of course, although a direct journey from say London to Prague is just a series of different motorways, autobahns and *dálnice* and not greatly inspiring.

By bus

Prague is linked by coach to almost every corner of eastern and western Europe. Coach travel, particularly in summer, represents by far the cheapest option. The bus journey from London to Prague takes approximately 18 hours. Eurolines (*www.nationalexpress.com*), Capital Express (*www.capitalexpress.cz*) and Kingscourt (*www.kce.cz*) are well-established companies operating luxury coaches on this route for at least the last decade. Prices range from £60–100 return.

By rail

These days travelling by rail only makes sense if you are travelling to Prague from eastern Europe where there are precious few budget flight options. The Czech capital still has excellent links to all points east and travelling in an overnight sleeper train to somewhere like Budapest or Kiev is an experience you will never forget. It gives a taste of travel further east, of the trans-Siberian or other long-distance routes across the former USSR and beyond. Trains or direct carriages run daily between Prague's main railway station and Vienna (4¹/₂ hours), Berlin (5 hours), Budapest (7¹/₂ hours), Krakow (8 hours), Warsaw (9 hours), Minsk (20 hours), Bucharest (24 hours), Moscow (30 hours) and Kiev (36 hours). There are also regular direct services to many large towns in Slovakia.

Borders

Gone are the days of queues, visas, unpleasant border officials, intrusive luggage searches and long delays at the borders with Germany, Austria, Poland and Slovakia. The Czech Republic is surrounded exclusively by other members of the EU making crossing its borders incredibly straightforward. The situation is likely to get even better with the Czechs' intention to sign up to the Schengen Agreement, which would effectively do away with most borders altogether. Getting in and out of the Czech Republic could not be simpler, especially when arriving at Prague Ruzyně Airport where EU citizens simply flash the photo page of their passport at the official. How times have changed. Non-EU citizens may still have to queue up to get their passports stamped, but this should not take more than a few minutes.

The main road border crossings into the country are Rozvadov, Pomezí and Folmava when coming from Bavaria; Vojtanov, Cínovec and Boží Dar in the north when entering from eastern Germany; Náchod, Dolní Lipka, Bohumín and Český Těšín when travelling from Poland; Lanžhot, Starý Hrozenkov and Hodonín on the border with Slovakia; and Dolní Dvořiště, České Velenice, Mikulov, Halámky and Hatě when travelling from Austria. When driving from Britain you are very likely to enter the country at Rozvadov. The D5 motorway continues from there via Pilsen to Prague. The Czech Republic has countless further crossings. The vast majority are open 24 hours a day. There are tens of small border crossings for pedestrians only. These tend to be open from early morning until 18.00 or 20.00 and many cannot be used by citizens of states who need a visa to enter the Czech Republic.

HEALTH

No immunisations are necessary before departure and the vast majority of visits are trouble free. One of the health matters which may cause concern is **tick-born encephalitis**, a viral infection transmitted to humans when bitten by an infected tick, common in forests in certain regions of the country. Encephalitis is an infection of the brain which starts with a flu-like illness followed a few days later with headache, neck stiffness, confusion and occasionally coma. Brain damage and death have been known.

If you intend to spend more than a month in the country in spring or summer in mostly forested areas, consider pre-departure immunisation. Vaccination against tick-borne encephalitis (TBE) may be available in the UK (on a named-patient basis) and comprises a series of three injections that can be done over three to four weeks. Take advice from your doctor or a reputable travel clinic. Whether you are immunised or not you should make sure that you wear suitable clothing, such as long trousers tucked into boots, and a hat. Also use tick repellents and at the end of the walk check yourself for ticks or better still get someone to do it for you. If you are travelling with young children you need to be especially careful to check their hair as ticks have a habit of dropping from overhanging branches. If you discover a tick then it is important to remove it slowly and carefully to avoid damaging the mouthpiece. Take some hand cream, suntan lotion or similar, cover the tick depriving it of oxygen, wait a few minutes then gently work it out with a circular rubbing motion using tweezers or failing that your thumb and forefinger wrapped in tissue paper. Medical advice should be sought locally, as treatment following exposure may be available. Tell the doctor whether or not you have been immunised.

For stays of a month or more, vaccination against **hepatitis A** is recommended. A single dose of vaccine (eg: Havrix Monodose, Avaxim) lasts for one year and a booster dose taken 6–12 months later (or longer if not travelling in high-risk areas) will then last for 20 years.

Salmonella rears its head every summer somewhere in the country and precautions should be taken to avoid this nasty condition. Watch out for refrozen ice cream and egg dishes. **Mushroom poisoning** is rare but potentially fatal, so never eat or even touch anything you are instructed not to

The Czech healthcare system

The Czech Republic is now a member of the EU so take your EHIC (which has replaced the old E111) entitling you to free basic health treatment. Of course your own private health insurance is always a good idea. Every town has a *poliklinika* full of doctors and appointments are not necessary. You may have to pay a few crowns to get a prescription. Wherever you travel, as a precaution carry a **travel first aid kit** with you. These can be purchased from any good travel equipment shop and can solve numerous minor problems (cuts and bruises, headaches) on the road.

CRIME, SAFETY AND SCAMS

While the Czech Republic still has relatively low levels of crime there are things to be aware of when travelling in the country. Prague can sometimes be that very incompatible marriage of rich Western tourists and less affluent locals where drug use is on the rise and tourists are still seen as dollars (or perhaps now euro) on legs and easy targets for petty crime. While random attacks on foreigners are extremely rare, theft is a big issue, not only for you, but for every citizen of the country, in Prague and elsewhere. Prague's public transport system, or to be more exact, those who police it, can leave a nasty taste in the mouth and various scams, some ingenious in their simplicity and sensitivity to the preconceptions and vulnerability of Western tourists, also need to be highlighted. The vast majority of tourist visits to the country are without incident.

Theft is probably the aspect of travel the visitor should be most aware of and travel insurance is recommended when travelling in the Czech Republic. Bag snatching, camera swiping, pickpocketing and (extremely rarely) mugging are all unwanted travel experiences you can prevent. Forewarned is forearmed and there are basic steps one can take to avoid being parted from valuable items. Never leave items such as your passport, air tickets and money in hotel rooms; always put them in the hotel safe; never put your wallet in your back pocket; never leave cameras or video equipment lying on pub or café tables; always keep an eye on your bags; on busy trams and town buses never keep a daypack on your back but hold it in front of you; do not flash large sums of money or expensive equipment in public places; in general use common sense and take the same precautions as you would at home.

Pickpockets operate frequently on tram 22, Wenceslas Square, Charles Bridge and basically anywhere there are large crowds of people. Car crime is a growing problem in Prague too with foreign vehicles being the target of special attention. Take the same precautions as you would at home, never leave anything on display in your car and use manned car parks (*hlídané parkoviště*) and hotel parking facilities. Cars are rarely stolen in the Czech Republic by joy riders but more often by professional gangs who sell them on to garages, spare parts dealers and to countries further east. In the unlikely event you do experience a theft, go straight to the police who will issue you with Protokol (police report) for your insurance company. This will be in Czech which you will have to have translated if your insurance company requires such a document. The police are generally regarded as a bad lot in the Czech Republic. All in all, however, they do their job – just do not expect cups of tea and sympathy.

Prior to the 1989 revolution and then for much of the 1990s illegal money changers (*vekslák* in Czech from the German *wechseln*, to exchange) operated in Prague's historical centre. At first changing money with them was advantageous though it always came with a risk. Now there is absolutely no need to change money this way and doing so puts visitors at risk of becoming victims of crime. The latest scam these money changers pull on unsuspecting tourists is to hand over virtually worthless Bulgarian currency instead of 5,000Kč banknotes. Another involves the tourist being led into some backstreet where he is robbed. Anyone who does not heed this warning cannot complain of the consequences. Another scam involves two people. The first approaches the visitor with a request which immediately gets the attention of the tourist. A second then runs up claiming to be a policeman and accuses both the tourist and passer by of money changing. He then asks to see the tourist's wallet which the tourist, believing that the policeman has the right to see it, hands over. The false policeman then either flees with the wallet or cleverly extracts credit cards and cash. There have been reports of this at

Vyšehrad and other slightly less crowded tourist spots in Prague. If approached by a policeman like this, ask to be taken to the nearest police station.

Approximately 90% of complaints Czech Tourism in London receives from tourists on returning from Prague concern the public transport system. All of these could be avoided if tourists were armed with one very simple piece of information before they travelled. Whether you are going by tram, bus or metro you *must* buy a ticket beforehand which you *must* stamp in the large yellow machines at the entrance to the metro or inside the bus or tram (see *Prague* chapter for details). If you do not follow these rules, you will be liable to pay a fine. Those caught protest that they have paid for the ticket so why should they pay a fine. Using this logic it would be possible to buy a 14Kč ticket and ride the system for ever! The above is now explained in English on all the ticket machines. Fare dodgers do have reason to complain when it comes to the behaviour of the *revizoři* (ticket inspectors). Rude, surly behaviour, marching terrified British pensioners to cash machines and generally making a genuinely innocent mistake seem like a crime against humanity do nothing for the reputation of Prague's otherwise excellent public transport system. Whatever happens, they must produce a red badge proving they are ticket inspectors although how foreigners are supposed to know what a real badge looks like I am not sure. It goes without saying that false *revizoři* have been known to operate on the system.

False theatre tickets and overcharging in restaurants and pubs are other niggling scams visitors occasionally encounter.

Women travellers
In general the Czech Republic is safer than most of western Europe for women though crime against females has risen considerably since 1989 with Prague particularly affected. Handbag snatching is the most common offence. At night use common sense; avoid parks, deserted bus stations, Prague backstreets outside the city centre, and do not accept lifts. Prague's public transport system is very safe indeed. One sad development in the capital is the hordes of British men who will wolf whistle and harass any woman, Czech or foreign. Pubs away from tourist areas can be slightly daunting as some tend to be male-only haunts, though Czech males tend to be more courteous to women, opening doors, helping with bags etc, than their Western counterparts. The Czech Republic has a long way to go, however, when it comes to tackling exploitative female nudity in advertising, rampant male chauvinism on TV, sex discrimination at work and widely available pornography.

WHAT TO PACK
What you take to the Czech Republic depends a lot on what you intend to do there and when you are arriving. Do not forget that Czech shops are bursting at the seams with Western goods, and 99% of basics you can buy at home are obtainable throughout the country.

Travel equipment
When travelling, carrying a few basic pieces of equipment can solve an infinite number of problems on the road. Recommended gear:

- Torch and spare batteries
- Insect repellent
- Penknife (with bottle opener for liberating the contents of beer bottles)

- Basic first aid kit (at least painkillers and plasters)
- Water bottle
- Sewing kit (strange how your clothes mutiny when you are on holiday)
- Duct tape (for repairing damaged backpacks)
- Sunglasses (even in winter)
- Pocket Czech dictionary (for decoding menus and timetables)

Clothing

It may seem blindingly obvious but central European summers are hot and stormy and winters bitterly cold and dry. Temperatures above 30°C are nothing strange nor are winter temperatures well below zero. Dressing accordingly is a question of common sense. In summer light cotton garments and shorts can be worn without drawing attention. Carry a light sweater with you for visits to caves, catacombs and churches and for summer evenings by lakes and outdoor restaurants. Comfortable shoes are essential for Prague's scorching cobbles and trail shoes are ideal for most situations.

Thick socks, a hat, a waterproof lined jacket, gloves, a scarf, sturdy waterproof shoes (preferably walking boots) and as many layers of clothing as is humanly possible to wear at once are imperative in the winter months. Forget them at your peril. Brits are particularly guilty of underestimating the weather in winter.

Do not forget to take something slightly more formal to wear for visits to the opera, concerts or just to someone's house for dinner.

Luggage

The size and type of your luggage depends on the length and nature of your stay. For Prague city breaks, a suitcase on wheels is fine, though pulling it through the capital's cobbled streets can be awkward and loud. If travelling around Bohemia and Moravia, a medium-sized backpack is the luggage of choice, compact enough to be wedged into luggage racks and stored away in bus luggage compartments, but large enough to take everything you need. Huge wheeled suitcases in small rural towns turn heads, and medieval cobbles and flagstones gnash away the wheels.

ELECTRICITY

The Czech Republic works on 220V AC, 50Hz. To use electrical appliances from home you will need a simple adapter to fit standard continental two-pin sockets. These are available from travel shops, electrical goods' retailers and these days your local supermarket. The electricity supply is very reliable and power failures rare. Batteries are widely available and cheap.

MONEY AND COSTS

Since 1993 the Czech currency has been the Czech crown (Kč or occasionally CZK). No other currency can be officially used with the exception of the euro in some places in Prague and perhaps in the areas bordering on Germany and Austria. The crown has been freely convertible since 1996, and is simple to obtain abroad. Most banks in Britain will be able to order it and Thomas Cook usually has the best rates. Alternatively take pounds sterling and exchange them there. If changing money on arrival, there are several reputable exchange offices at Prague Ruzyně Airport. Avoid the small exchange booths scattered around Prague's historical centre and squeezed into nooks and crannies of Baroque and Gothic buildings. They boast 0% commission but their rates are worse. They also run a few mini-scams such as handing you what you assume is a complimentary map but one look at the receipt will tell you it cost 50 or 100Kč. Go to any bank where there are better rates and minimum commission. Scottish banknotes cannot be exchanged in the Czech Republic. Travellers' cheques in these days of ATMs on every street corner across the globe are not worth the hassle for the security they give. If you do insist on using them most banks will charge 3% commission to exchange them for cash. Anyone who changes money unofficially on the street is asking for serious trouble.

By far the most convenient way to get crowns nowadays is at an ATM (cash machine, *bankomat*) using a debit or credit card. ATMs are widespread in Prague and larger centres, though smaller towns may have only a handful, generally situated near or in banks or at popular supermarkets. Your bank or credit card company will charge a fee for card transactions abroad so ask before you leave home. Czech ATMs accept all major credit and debit cards and give users the option of seeing instructions in English. Paying with plastic is a very convenient way of settling the bill at your hotel, the vast majority of which now accept most cards. Paying for other things in other places may not be as straightforward, particularly outside of Prague, though every day more and more places introduce the technology necessary for card transactions. Cash, however, still rules in the Czech Republic and occasionally pulling out plastic causes a slight fuss, grumbles from people in the queue behind you, huffy behaviour from shop assistants, or can result in your being sent to another part of the shop. It may take an age for your card to be cleared and expect your signature to be scrutinised with unabashed post-communist distrust. Some supermarkets have only one checkout where cards can be used. You cannot at present use plastic at railway station ticket offices (unless buying international tickets at a special window), at bus stations, in some supermarket chains, the vast majority of small privately owned supermarkets outside of Prague, at newsagents, post offices, ticket offices at tourist sights, in the Prague transport system ticket offices and machines, in small pubs and bars in the countryside, in village shops and basically anywhere else you cannot use them at home (eg: McDonald's). Credit card fraud is nothing new in this part of the world (some of the scams you may have seen in your own country were probably devised in this region of Europe) so be on your guard as you would be on your local high street. Keep all receipts just in case, as adding zeros to transactions is a common scam especially in places heavily frequented by foreigners.

The crown

One crown (*koruna*) is made up of 100 hellers (*haléřů*). Notes come in denominations of 5,000, 2,000, 1,000, 500, 200, 100 and 50Kč and 20, 10, 5, 2 and 1Kč and aluminium 50 heller coins are also in circulation. Until summer 2003, 20 and 10 heller pieces were in use but their value had become less than the metal they were made of, so they were withdrawn. Prices are still, however, in units of ten hellers, but totals at checkouts are rounded up or down to the nearest 50h. Czech bills are colourful and distinct from one another. The blue 5,000Kč bill depicts a stern- looking Masaryk, first president of Czechoslovakia; the green 2,000Kč note is dedicated to the Czech opera singer Ema Destinnová; František Palacký, the 19th-century Czech politician peers out from the purple 1,000Kč banknote. The beautiful 19th-century Czech writer Božena Němcová adorns the brown 500Kč bill; the pedagogue Jan Amos Comenius the orange 200Kč note; a merry Charles IV dominates the very common green 100Kč note, and bringing up the rear is St Agnes on the red 50Kč banknote. Whilst small change is not a significant problem, it is sometimes difficult to pay for certain things with large-denomination banknotes. Always try to keep a supply of coins for toilets and metro tickets and 50–200Kč notes for fares and admission fees.

The Czech currency has enjoyed relative stability over the last decade and seems to have settled at an exchange rate of approximately 45Kč to the British pound, approximately 30Kč to the euro and 25Kč to the US dollar. For the latest exchange rates visit www.xe.com. Despite fears following EU accession, inflation has remained steady at around 1.5%. The Czech Republic remains a relatively cheap country though this cannot last much longer.

The best way to handle your money on say a week's stay in the country is to make one or two withdrawals from ATMs keeping a stash of money in your hotel safe and carrying around with you what you will need for that day (see *Budgeting* below). Never carry all your money and cards around with you in the same place and for longer periods of travel consider buying a money belt.

Budgeting
After 16 years of frenzied, unchecked capitalism it is now possible to spend as much as you want in the Czech Republic: the sky is the limit. Numerous four- and five-star establishments will gladly relieve you of large amounts of cash to sleep and eat in their plush surroundings. Top brands fill Prague's shop windows and exclusive emporiums to bursting point and private taxi and chauffeur companies will happily take you to any corner of the country for 50 times the train fare. At the other end of the scale you could stay in hostels, campsites and dormitories for migrant workers, eat in pubs and from supermarkets and travel by bus or train with a budget of around 500Kč a day at a stretch. Outside of Prague a more realistic and comfortable budget is around 1,000–1,500Kč a day, staying in sound three-star accommodation, eating at average restaurants and taking in two or three sights a day. In Prague, budget for 1,500Kč upwards as accommodation in the capital is not cheap.

Getting around is still very reasonable, especially by bus. Even the trains are still amazing value for money despite fare rises in the last few years, and 100km of travel by train costs just 120Kč. Public transport in cities generally costs just a few crowns. Eating out is still relatively cheap and in an average restaurant outside of Prague expect to pay around 200–300Kč a head for a starter, a main course and dessert. Prices are considerably higher in Prague though not astronomically so. Beer itself is probably the most pleasantly priced (and the best) in Europe at 20–30Kč a pint.

Tipping
Tipping in the classic sense of giving a porter or door boy a few pennies is an activity most Czechs have only seen in foreign films and movies from the decadent First Republic. There is not a tipping culture to speak of, though there is a handful of occasions when a tip is expected or welcome. In restaurants or bars when the waiter brings the bill, round the total up to the nearest 10Kč or the nearest 100Kč if that seems too little. I am a big fan of showing gratitude to tour guides in museums and galleries; a 50Kč note will suffice. Tipping with foreign currency (unless you are tipping in euro or handing out large amounts) is a bit pointless.

GETTING AROUND
Air
The Czech Republic is a relatively small country, and can be traversed in an afternoon by road. However, domestic air services link Prague with Ostrava and

Karlovy Vary aimed primarily at business travellers, and in the case of Karlovy Vary, those going to take the waters at the spas. Popular with Russians, the west Bohemian spa town also has a direct air connection with Moscow. Maps and timetables show a connection to Brno which is in fact a ČSA coach service departing Prague Ruzyně Airport up to six times throughout the day and night. There are up to four flights a day to Ostrava in north Moravia, a great enough distance away from the capital to take to the skies, as the flight time is a mere one hour, a good three hours faster than the fastest SuperCity rail service. One-way fares are from 1,000Kč before taxes etc.

Bus

Travel by bus is now cheaper than by train, and usually faster, the only disadvantage being the greatly reduced service on Saturdays and Sunday mornings when rail is definitely the better option. Another slight disadvantage is the question of supply and demand, especially Monday mornings, Fridays, and Sunday evenings when reservations are recommended.

Buses depart from Prague Florenc central coach station (metro lines C and B) to every corner of the Czech Republic and destinations abroad. In recent years, however, in a move to rid Prague's streets of buses in order to make room for even more cars, various departures have been transferred to metro stations outside the city centre. The most common metro stations for bus departures are Zličín (western end of line B), Dejvická (line A), Nádraží Holešovice (line C), Roztyly (line C) and Želivského (line A). When travelling to destinations with less frequent connections and further away, tickets sometimes, but not always, must be purchased in advance. They are available up to half an hour before departure, after which you just have to hope there are sufficient seats for passengers without reservations. Buses fill up on Fridays and Sunday evenings. Tickets can be bought at any office sporting the AMS reservation system sign. AMS is a centralised booking system subscribed to by almost all transport companies in the Czech Republic. Book online at www.jizdenky.amsbus.cz. For shorter journeys or between smaller towns and villages buy your ticket from the driver.

Many buses and coaches in the Czech Republic are still the old Czech Karosa type or newer Renault versions of the same, more often than not without most facilities, but still very comfortable. On the popular Prague–Brno and Prague–Carlsbad routes you may get something more luxurious with more in the way of conveniences. Pack a snack and a bottle of mineral water and enjoy the countryside flying by your window. Coaches on longer hauls make stops for toilet breaks. Look out for the decorated inside front windscreens of some buses adorned by drivers with plastic flowers, lucky charms, pictures of wives and children and sometimes little Christmas trees and other seasonal decorations.

Complicated is not the word for Czech bus timetables and by the time you work out whether a bus goes or not, one will probably have turned up anyway. On weekdays the task of deciphering timetables is fairly simple, as most buses will run, though definitely not all of them. Basically two hammers crossed signify that the service runs on working days. It is all the other letters and symbols scattered around the flimsy piece of paper pasted to the inside of the bus shelter and now flapping in the wind (but surprisingly almost never vandalised) which cause the most concern, the vast majority of which indicating how the bus runs at weekends, school holidays, bank holidays, weekends after bank holidays, working days after bank holidays, weekends after weekends, solar eclipses … the list goes on. Asking the locals is often not much use. Departure boards at major coach stations show a list of services according to destination. This simplifies matters somewhat, but there is still the problem of deciphering the various symbols on this too. Avoid confusion by visiting the www.vlak.cz online timetable (in English) beforehand.

Even the smallest communities are served by bus and timetables are designed to meet the needs of schoolchildren and factory workers and not the Sunday morning day tripper. Plan your travels to coincide with the start of the school day (08.00), the end of the school day (around 14.00–16.00 pm) or the beginning and end of the factory shifts (06.00, 14.00 or 22.00) and you will have no difficulty getting to and from even the remotest of places. There also tend to be more buses on Sunday evenings.

Sample fares
Prague–Brno: 130–160Kč, Prague–Pilsen 80Kč, Prague–Ostrava 260Kč, Prague České Budějovice 120Kč, Brno–Ostrava 140–170Kč, České Budějovice–Brno 180Kč, Prague–Carlsbad 130Kč.

Train
The Czech railways are one of those quaint aspects of the country which seem to have escaped the attentions of the economists and reformers – up until now that is. They are an absolute joy to ride presuming you have a soft spot for trains and you are not in a particular hurry to get anywhere urgently. Sixties' retro waiting rooms, tiny rural Austro-Hungarian stations, station masters in smart uniforms, rooms just off the platforms full of tinkling bells, buzzers and whirring machinery, tracks that disappear in the long summer grass creating the impression that the train is floating along on air, a spider's web of branch lines with quite often several uneconomical ways of getting from A to B, tiny stations lost in the mountains – all in all an unmissable part of the Czech Republic and one of the very few aspects of the country to remain virtually untouched since the revolution.

That said, darkish clouds are gathering over the idyllic scene. In 2003, the government offloaded the railways on to a new 'private' company still heavily subsidised by the state. Within a year the company had sacked a significant chunk of the railway workers but had not closed any of the hugely unprofitable branch lines. The EU then compounded the problems with its competition laws preventing freight profits from keeping the passenger service afloat, as had been the case throughout the 1990s. A Beeching-style decimation is not anticipated, but the fear is that something along the lines of the disaster which befell British Rail is being cooked up by car-driving bureaucrats in Prague. So go now and ride the train! It is cheap and thanks to the sometimes unambitious timetable, always on time.

Train types
A total of 99% of rail services running on the 9,500km of track are operated by České dráhy (Czech Railways, ČD). There is a handful of other tiny private operators such as the romantic little narrow-gauge lines around Jindřichův Hradec in south Bohemia. There are various types of train trundling along Czech rails. The first and slowest is the osobní vlak (personal trains) that run between most towns and villages and on all branch lines, stopping at every station along the way and taking an eternity to do so. A journey by osobní vlak can, however, be a great way to see the country and meet its people, but a bad way of getting from A to B in a hurry. Such journeys are ideal on long summer evenings with time to kill, when you can just sit back and watch the forests, hills and picturesque villages crawl past your window. It is no cheaper to travel by osobní

vlak than by the next two faster types of train, but in remote places there may be no other option. The next and slightly faster train type is the *spěšný vlak* (fast train). They make fewer stops, run on the same routes as the slower trains but tickets cost the same. Next is the *rychlík* (express). These services call at large towns only, are the much quicker option, and again are no more expensive. They tend to be made up of around ten carriages of the corridor type with compartments for eight passengers. Luggage is stored overhead. Recently ČD has introduced refreshment trolleys and there is usually a restaurant car. Many of these express services have interesting names such as 'Smetana', 'Vyšehrad', 'Ostravan' and 'Silesia', to reflect the places they pass through or to honour a famous Czech figure. The last and least common types of train are the SC (SuperCity) EC (EuroCity) and IC (InterCity) services which run on main lines and link major centres in the Czech Republic with places abroad. These trains are of international standard with air-conditioned carriages, clean comfortable seats and higher ticket prices. They call at major cities only and are an excellent way of getting from say Prague to Brno or Ostrava in a hurry. Of course they really come into their own when travelling to places like Bratislava, Berlin, Budapest or Vienna, and are sometimes a better option than flying.

Tickets and timetables

Tickets for all journeys are purchased before boarding the train. As far as prices are concerned, the most expensive way to travel is to buy single tickets, as a

CZECH RAILWAY STATIONS

First impressions last and your first impression of any place in the Czech Republic may be of its railway station or *nádraží*. It is hard to talk about the hustle and bustle of rail travel in this country; words such as sleepy, drowsy and forgotten come to mind. Only the larger stations in Prague and Brno are constantly busy. Most are village halts, manned by a handful of staff where the loudest noise in the heat of a sleepy afternoon may be the ticking of the station clock. The architecture of rail facilities tends to be Austro-Hungarian as most lines were built in the 19th or early 20th century and pure, untouched 1960s interiors are also not uncommon.

One aspect of the platform which may surprise you is its absence. In many smaller places you board the train from ground level, clambering over the other rails to reach your carriage. Only at stations used by very fast expresses are there signs forbidding passengers to cross the lines, advice habitually ignored. Locals know the movements of the trains etc; you do not, so care should be taken when walking on any line.

You will find all the facilities you would expect at a railway station including waiting rooms (*čekárna*), refreshment (*občerstvení*) and news kiosks (*trafika*), perhaps a restaurant (*restaurace*) or a pub (*hospoda*), an information office (*informace*), ticket offices (*výdejna jízdenek*) and left luggage (*úschovna zavazadel*). At small rural stations just one member of staff will provide all these services. Have no fear of handing over your luggage to the nice lady at the left-luggage office. The service is ridiculously cheap (in Prague 15Kč for an average piece of luggage) and theft is unheard of. *Never* use the self-service lockers at Prague's main station or anywhere else for that matter. You may as well leave your bags on a park bench there are so many thefts from these lockers.

CZECH STREET NAMES AND NUMBERS

While strolling around Prague you may notice that each building has two numbers, red and blue. The red are chronological numbers showing the order in which the houses were built. The blue numbers, which came into use in 1878, are the order in the street. The nearer the house is to the Vltava, the lower the number. Some addresses are written using both numbers, ie: Plzeňská 1234/32.

Czech street names are a history and geography lesson in themselves, and a knowledge of the background to all the names in an average Czech town would make you an expert on the country. Streets are named after famous people, places, historical events, and features of the surrounding land or townscape. Almost every medium-sized town in the country will have a Masaryk Square or Street, a Beneš Embankment or Avenue, a Lidice Road or Lane. When one looks at the turbulent history of the Czech lands over the last century one can imagine how linking place names to people and events has, on some occasions, been a sensitive issue. With every political change, countless roads, gates, bridges and squares have had to be renamed. At the beginning of the 1990s all places bearing the names Lenin, Marx, Red Army, Gottwald, Victorious February and Julius Fučík had to be swiftly erased and new ones thought up to replace them. However, Revolution Streets etc (referring originally to the 1917 Russian Revolution) stayed, as their meaning transferred to a different revolution, the Velvet Revolution.

return will cost you only a fraction more. Returns are the best option for those making perhaps one or two day trips from Prague. However, a Zákaznická karta (literally a 'customer card') entitles you to a large chunk off the single fare. It costs only 200Kč, anyone can get one and it is valid for a year. Simply take your passport and a passport-size photograph to any ticket office. As mentioned above, tickets for international expresses are more expensive. This comes in the form of a surcharge so before boarding one of these trains, tell the employee at the ticket-office window your destination and the time of the train. All tickets are inspected on all trains. As ticket prices are so low, consider travelling in first class. First-class compartments are carpeted, have soft seats, individual reading lights and curtains, but apart from the increased comfort, the main advantage is that you will probably have the compartment to yourself. This can be an excellent option on popular routes in summer, or if you have a lot of luggage (or just want some peace and quiet). First-class tickets cost around 50% more than second class though not all trains have first-class carriages.

Timetables are sometimes complicated, though nowhere near as mind-boggling as the bus schedules, and are simplified a great deal by the fact that the service is not decimated at the weekend. Timetables from smaller branch line stations are usually very simple. At the station you will find a board with *odjezdy* (departures) and *příjezdy* (arrivals). Above the departures board there will be the *směr* (direction). The full Czech railway timetable is available at www.cd.cz, or paper or CD versions are available at most stations.

Sample fares

The following are some sample fares for second-class travel without a *Zákaznická karta*:

Prague–Brno: 130–160Kč, Prague–Pilsen 140Kč, Prague–Ostrava 424–484Kč, Prague–České Budějovice 204Kč, Brno–Ostrava 204Kč, České Budějovice–Brno 274Kč, Pilsen–České Budějovice 162Kč, Prague–Carlsbad 274Kč, Cheb–Ostrava 640–698Kč.

Sleeper trains
If you intend travelling to somewhere like Kiev, Bucharest or Moscow you will usually have no other option than to travel in a sleeper compartment. Tickets for these can in theory be bought up to departure time but booking in advance is advisable. Fares are calculated according to international tariffs plus the sleeper surcharge. A compartment has three berths, a washbasin, luggage storage and a small table. Each carriage has its own conductor who supplies passengers with bedding and sometimes drinks, or at least hot water for tea. Many travellers love this way of travel as sometimes the compartment and occasionally the whole carriage is transformed into an informal get-together on wheels with people from various nations sharing food, alcohol and stories. Others find being cooped up for 36 hours with strangers in the increasingly stale air of a claustrophobic compartment unbearable.

Hitching
Hitching is still relatively common in the Czech Republic and unlike in many other former eastern bloc countries drivers do not demand money for petrol. You will always see hitchhikers on the roads out of Prague holding a piece of cardboard with their destination daubed in black marker, extending a hopeful thumb and praying that the next car to stop is not a Trabant going to the next village! Hitchers never wait long, drivers still seem willing to take them and long may this mode of transport thrive. It is a great way of meeting people, hearing their story, picking up the language and getting a real feel for life in the country. An invitation home for food and to meet the family is a bonus unhurried travellers should rarely turn down.

Guidebooks warn of the dangers involved in hitching and the Czech Republic is no exception. Women travellers should avoid hitching alone, men should also be careful whose car they get into. Hitching couples should make sure the female gets into the vehicle last and out first. Always make sure your luggage does not continue on its way without you and use common sense when accepting any invitations to homes etc. Also beware of theft and suspicious activity at motorway service stations and in general anywhere lorries congregate. Hitching in winter in the mountains is not a good idea.

ACCOMMODATION
There are 8,000 places to stay in the Czech Republic with a total of 171,000 rooms and almost 450,000 beds, making finding a place to stay, even in high season in Prague, relatively trouble free.

Types and standards
The country possesses a wide spectrum of accommodation, from campsites next to rivers for a few crowns a night, to standard three-star hotels in cities across the country for a few hundred crowns, to some of the most beautiful hotels in the region with all the facilities you could imagine in a four- or five-star establishment for a few thousand crowns. Standards are high whatever you choose, and most hotels are either newly built or recently renovated. The only part of the market with room for improvement is the budget sector outside of

the capital, but cheap family-run pensions usually fill the gap and some student hostels open their doors for tourists in summer. So-called *ubytovna* dormitories should be avoided as they are usually occupied by armies of *gastarbeiter* from Ukraine, Poland and Slovakia, and perhaps not the most comfortable places to spend the night unless you are desperate. They are usually booked static year-round anyway and for a few hundred crowns extra there will be a nice, spotless, quiet private room somewhere in town. Other cheap accommodation options include some 478 campsites where the average price for erecting your tent is a mere 95Kč. Typically open April–September, facilities can vary from very rough and ready to semi-luxurious. Some have chalets for a few hundred crowns. Unless you are walking or skiing in the Krkonoše Mountain range, you will not encounter the mountain chalet (*horská bouda*). These vary enormously from huts to huge complexes with all mod cons and prices to match. This sort of accommodation in the mountains should be booked ahead. Some will allow you to erect your tent in the vicinity and use their facilities when they are full.

Cost and payment
You will not spend as much on anything else during your stay in the Czech Republic as on accommodation. Prices across the country vary little, except in Prague and to a lesser extent, Brno, where rooms cost more across the board. On average expect to pay upwards of 4,000Kč a night in five-star hotels, 2,000Kč in four-star establishments and anything up to 2,000Kč in three-star places. The average price of bed and breakfast in the Czech Republic is 500–1,000Kč a night. Sometimes I have quoted the price in euro as the hotels often do, especially the more upmarket establishments in Prague. The vast majority of hotel rooms have en-suite facilities, and the price includes breakfast, normally a buffet affair of rolls, cheese, ham, salami, cereals and tea and coffee. Many offer half and full board which generally works out very good value for money when compared with eating in restaurants.

In the vast majority of accommodation (except campsites) the bill is settled on departure. As mentioned in the *Money and costs* section (see page 49), paying with plastic has its drawbacks, but should not be a problem in more upmarket places.

Checking in
When checking in, reception staff will request to see your passport, and you will be required to fill in a form with some basic personal details. This in theory is then shown to the police in order for them to register foreign nationals. In low season ask to see the room before you take it. Most hotels have a safe for valuables.

Internet bookings
Booking over the internet is not a risk but contact details for the hotel concerned may not be easy to find should you have a query.

EATING AND DRINKING
If it tastes good it is probably bad for you – this statement just about covers the whole Czech diet and since a Czech menu reads like a list of all that the doctor recommended you not to eat in order to stay alive past 45, you can be sure that on Czech dinner tables naughty means nice and that you are in for a stodgy, creamy, succulent, filling culinary experience like nowhere else in Europe. Wash your meal down with some of the best (and cheapest) beer in the world and you

ZABIJAČKA

Should you be a vegetarian for any of the usual reasons of health, cruelty to animals or just squeamishness, beware the *zabijačka*. Sometime in late winter or early spring a pig is bought or taken from a relative's sty and slaughtered in the back garden. This is just the beginning of a process which sees almost every part of the animal used to make some traditional dish or other. Friends are invited, spirits are served and special *zabijačka* dishes are eaten. Each guest is given a task to perform such as stirring blood, stuffing sausages or chopping garlic and herbs. Though not as common as during the self-sufficient communist period, the *zabijačka* is alive and kicking (unlike the pigs) and even Prague tower-block dwellers will head out to the countryside to their home town or village to perform it once a year.

will be looking forward to your next meal before you have put down your glass. Vegetarians, however, beware, as outside of Prague your diet of fried bread-crumbed cheese and chips may become slightly monotonous.

For a nation that lives to eat, however, breakfast can be a somewhat disappointing affair. Czechs usually limit themselves to rye bread or a white roll and cheese or ham, perhaps a pastry with poppy seed paste or cottage cheese and a cup of tea or coffee. The only explanation for this is that they are still full from the evening before or are saving themselves for what is yet to come. Those expecting a full English breakfast will, however, be disappointed – breakfast is small.

That said, the Czechs are then used to supplementing their small breakfast with the ten o'clock *svačina* which usually consists of the same type of food eaten at breakfast. *Svačina* is a national obsession with time being made for it in school timetables and work rotas.

Although quite often a hurried affair, lunch can be quite substantial. Thick spicy goulash, creamy potato soup, greasy potato cakes, various mayonnaise-soaked salads, baked pasta in creamy sauce and of course a heavy dessert are just some of what is on offer. Perhaps a half of beer then quickly back to work – you see beer is not really alcohol as such, as many a Czech man will inform you.

The longest break between meals then follows but around 19.00 the Czechs really make up for it. Meat is what every man, woman and child expects for their evening meal and Czech meat dishes are superb. This is also where the inevitable dumplings make their appearance – not round small dumplings we find in soup but large circular flat cakes, sometimes fluffy and light, other times heavy and dense. Vegetables are rare, sauerkraut is a firm favourite and in some restaurants you may get a few token slices of cucumber or tomato more for decorative purposes than anything else. The Czech national food is pork with dumplings and sauerkraut washed down with a first-rate, golden Pilsner beer. Other favourites include duck, sirloin in a creamy spicy sauce, crispy schnitzel (bread-crumbed pork or chicken, fried and served with potatoes and gherkins) tasty meatballs, various liver dishes and beef goulash with dumplings. Chicken has become increasingly popular since the revolution, as have turkey and fish, whilst wild boar and venison are traditional specialities found usually on restaurant menus only. Traditional desserts include fruit-filled dumplings, pancakes, ice cream and pastries.

As touched upon earlier, Czech beer can be spoken of only in superlatives. The best brands are Pilsner Urquell, Staropramen from Prague, Gambrinus,

Krušovice and Budvar (the original Budweiser). There are numerous smaller breweries scattered across the country but despite high consumption, many of these have gone bankrupt or seem constantly to be on the verge of doing so. With such high quality and from only 15Kč a pint, it can come as no surprise that the Czechs have the largest per-capita consumption of beer in the world. They are intensely proud of their favourite brew and it is safe to say that most foreign brands have no chance of ever getting a foothold on the Czech market. Other alcoholic drinks worthy of mention are Becherovka, a herbal liqueur brewed in Carlsbad and Slivovice, plum brandy distilled in Moravia. Moravia produces some reasonable wines and a visit to a Moravian wine cellar is a must for visitors to the region. As far as soft drinks go, the Czech Republic has some excellent mineral waters from the numerous spas which pepper the country. Try Mattoni and Magnesia from Carlsbad both at around 15Kč a bottle.

Eating out

The vast majority of visitors to the Czech Republic find themselves at some point or other in a restaurant or other eatery. Here are a few definitions of places you may wander into, and what you can expect to find there.

Restaurace

As in most places, restaurant can mean five-star service, white tablecloths and attentive waiters or something not so good. Czech restaurants can also be a kind of pub with food and waiters. In tourist spots the menu is usually in English and the waiting staff should at least understand the menu. Restaurants tend to be either wholly Czech or have a selection of international and Czech mains. When ordering, you must also order the side dish separately, unless stated otherwise on the menu. Throughout the guide I state the price of the main meal only. Side dishes usually cost from 15–30Kč. Restaurants generally have a selection of wines, Czech and international and perhaps three types of beer but only one on tap.

Hospoda

Czech pubs differ from pubs and bars in Britain and the US. Firstly, everyone is seated. If the pub is full, you can rarely stand to drink your beer, though you may be able to sit at a few bar stools. Find a place to sit and wait for the waiter who will place a piece of paper on the table, on which he will mark whatever you order. Beer is marked with an inch-long line and everything else according to price. Pub food is always available and generally much cheaper than the same dishes in restaurants. The waiter will return to your table at regular intervals to offer you more beer. In some places it is the custom for the waiter to plonk a beer in front of you the minute your empty glass leaves your lips. There may be only one type of beer on offer, and you will probably be asked whether you would like 10° or 12° (see boxed text on beer, page 153). At the end of the evening the bill is reckoned up according to the number of lines on the piece of paper, plus anything else you have ordered.

You could cut the air with a knife in Czech pubs it gets so heavy with cigarette smoke, and there is little debate about passive smoking there yet. Pubs are rowdy, noisy but merry places, and drunken Czechs tend to sing and hug each other, rather than becoming boisterous or even violent. Binge drinking is unheard of.

Pivnice

Beer halls are not as common as the *hospoda*. The main differences are that there is not much food on offer, the beer is cheaper, the company more inebriated and the décor a shade shabbier. They can be quite 'spit and sawdust' kind of establishments, and vary from old, traditional institutions to newer but dirtier and much less pleasant dives with slot machines and staring locals.

Cukrárna
The *cukrárna* is a Czech institution. The name comes from the Czech for sugar – *cukr* and is a cross between a cake shop and a café. These places serve up a wide selection of sumptuous cream cakes, freshly baked pastries, Czech sweets and chocolate and sometimes open sandwiches, and the staff can make you any sort of tea or coffee you could wish for. Viennese and Turkish coffee are the most popular choices, but there are always soft drinks as well. Prices can be absurd in these places, with most items on the menu costing just a few crowns. Everything must be ordered at the counter and paid for immediately. They are great places to kill time between trains and to people-watch, and every town has several.

SHOPPING
A few short years ago the idea of travelling anywhere east of the Iron Curtain to shop would have been absurd. Czech shops were by no means empty but their dour assortment of foodstuffs, low-quality clothing, recycled paper goods and bulky electrical appliances was not exactly souvenir material, with perhaps the exception of some alcohol. How times have changed. Now groups of housewives fly in for the day from Newcastle and Southampton to peruse Prague's boutiques looking for that item which nobody back home will have, or an original Christmas present. Germans and Austrians flock over the border to buy up palettes of cheap mineral water, salami and meat, and tourists can choose from a wide selection of traditional souvenirs. It is now possible to buy anything you want or need in Prague and larger centres and while the range of goods elsewhere may be more limited you are never far away from a giant branch of some hypermarket chain or other.

The best place for shopping without doubt is Prague city centre. Wenceslas Square and surrounding streets, Na Příkopě, Na Poříčí, Republic Square (*náměstí republiky*), Národní Street, the Old Town Square and surrounding streets are all good places to start. If you are a fan of out-of-town mall-style shopping, Prague now has some mammoth shopping complexes in Zličín (end of metro line B heading west), Stodůlky (metro line B westbound), and Hostivař in southern Prague and Černý Most (eastern end of yellow line B).

Opening hours in Prague are by and large like in the West, though more shops may be closed on Sundays than you are used to. There is no hard and fast rule about when shops open and close in the capital anymore and most are open seven days a week in the centre. They are perhaps open longer in the evening than in Britain. Outside of Prague the situation could not be more different. Small shops tend to open early, between 07.00 and 08.00 and close at around 17.00. Set off on a shopping trip on a Saturday afternoon and you will return empty-handed as 99% of the shops will have closed at around 12.00. Sunday opening is as yet still in its infancy and only a handful of the larger supermarkets will be open, and that may be only for a few hours. Some of the giant hypermarkets, however, have Western opening times such as 8 till 8, seven days a week.

Souvenirs
The Czech Republic has a wealth of souvenirs, the vast majority of which are authentic traditional products which have been around for decades, if not centuries. Of course in every street in Prague city centre there are the ubiquitous

gift shops with T-shirts, key rings and various other items with 'Prague' or 'Czech Republic' daubed on them. After the fall of communism many Soviet soldiers facing an uncertain future back home and desperate to raise cash sold off a lot of Red Army paraphernalia to Czechs who then sold it on the streets to tourists. When you imagine that was 16 years ago, not much of the Soviet memorabilia you see on the streets today can be genuine. Some of the Czech items may be, the rest will be imports from China. You will also see brightly painted Russian dolls and other seemingly eastern Slav objects which have no relation to very much in the Czech lands and just play to the perceived ignorance of Western tourists about where they actually are.

Bohemia is traditionally a beer-brewing region and elaborate beer tankards or glasses or the beer itself make good gifts. Another alcohol produced in Bohemia is Becherovka which must be one of the most popular items visitors take home. Look out for the tall green bottles with yellow labels in every supermarket in the country or in Carlsbad where it is made. Carlsbad is the major source of souvenirs from the Czech Republic as circular chocolate, nut- or cream-filled spa wafers, crystal, glass, porcelain and the peculiar spouted drinking cups used for sipping mineral water all hail from that region. Crystal is very popular among visitors and most take at least a small piece home. Cut crystal in every form, shape and size can be exceedingly beautiful and a long-lasting reminder of your visit. Some of the coloured painted crystal can be stunning. It is very reasonably priced and available across the country. Central Bohemia has its wine available in Mělník and Karlštejn and east Bohemia gingerbread, which is traditionally made in Pardubice. Prague is the best place to pick up coffee-table books on the capital and the country as a whole (printed here in abundance), local brass band or other traditional music, garnet costume jewellery, large chunky amber jewellery with whole prehistoric insects trapped inside (beware of imitations), traditional wooden puppets, wooden toys, traditional wooden kitchen utensils, cloth, linen and lace. At Christmas, Prague holds traditional Christmas markets on the Old Town Square, Wenceslas Square and various other smaller sites around the city. This is a great time to pick up simple traditional folk Christmas decorations made of straw or corn leaves, Czech mead, candles, freshly minted Prague groschen coins ... the list goes on. At Easter you will find elaborately decorated hollow eggs called *kraslice* though getting them home in one piece poses a slight problem.

Botanicus is a chain of outlets across the country selling locally produced natural soaps, oils, herbs and spices, pot-pourri, candles and the like. Botanicus produces everything it sells in the small village of Ostrá near Lysá nad Labem east of Prague, using the knowledge of the eminent botanist Dr Malcolm Stuart. Items from their 16 shops make excellent gifts.

Moravia has a few different items such as *slivovice* (plum brandy) and many other spirits ending in -*ovice* (eg: *hruškovice*, pear brandy) but is best known for its wines. The whites are crisp and light but the reds lack body. Handmade paper from Velké Losiny is also an original souvenir especially when bought where it is produced after a tour of the museum and small factory.

Czech art is freely available and as long as it is not a national treasure you should have no problem taking it out of the country. If you do want to buy a valuable piece of art or anything that may belong in a museum, seek advice at the National Museum or a customs office. Prague has some lovely little antique shops (*starožitnictví*) and second-hand bookshops (*antikvariát*) where you can find all sorts of ancient bric-a-brac. The bookshops can be fascinating places full of weighty dusty tomes in Czech and German but also maps new and old, dictionaries, some books in English, First Republic, Nazi and communist propaganda posters, old coffee-table books and sometimes original prints by lesser-known Czech artists for just a few hundred crowns. I would recommend the two shops in Dlážděná Street near Masarykovo railway station, the *antikvariát* in Bělehradská Street near the crossroads with Rumunská Street and the shop in Valentinská Street near the Staroměstská metro station (line A) popular with students.

ARTS AND ENTERTAINMENT
Classical music and opera

Prague is slowly becoming a Mecca for classical music and opera lovers with tens of concerts happening every day at all kinds of venues such as churches, libraries, gardens and of course the Prague State Opera, the National Theatre, the Estates Theatre and many more. Ticket prices are a fraction of what they are back home but some complain of the casual dress code and ignorant, badly behaved audiences.

Galleries and museums

Prague has some outstanding museums and galleries such as the assorted National Gallery venues, the Museum of Prague and the Technical Museum. Alas, museums and galleries across the country are in general sorely underfunded, dusty, threadbare affairs, though there are some real gems out there. Most are guarded by overbearing pensioners whose knowledge of the exhibits varies wildly from place to place. Some museums and galleries are not heated in winter and in many lights will be turned on especially for you, perhaps the only visitor that day.

Cinema

As the Czechs do not dub their films for the cinema, you can go to see any film in English anywhere in the country. The dubbing process takes place afterwards to prepare the film for TV audiences too lazy to read subtitles. Dubbing is a Czech speciality and it is quite amusing to see characters from your favourite TV series speaking in a Slavic tongue. Prague cinemas are a mix of spanking new 30- screen complexes run by international chains and old, cosy pre-revolution picture houses with plush seats and dark interiors run by pensioners in their free time. There can be quite a large difference in ticket prices between the two, but none of Prague's cinemas could be described as cheap. In smaller towns, pre-revolution cinemas have survived for the most part and ticket prices are considerably lower than in the capital. Almost every town in the country has an open-air or 'summer' cinema. They operate from May to September only and due to the long daylight hours, showings can begin as late as 21.30. Take a blanket, a cushion to sit on, waterproofs and an umbrella. Occasionally the weather plays along with the film providing a curious interactive, multimedia experience!

Sport

There is no language problem when it comes to sport. Football and ice hockey matches are exciting, passionate and unbelievably cheap to attend. You can even still enjoy a beer on the terraces in this country. Sparta Prague's stadium and matches are the best in the capital and most large towns in the sticks have a team. Every town has an ice hockey stadium.

Theatre

Theatre is generally out of bounds for foreign visitors due to the language barrier. Ask at the Celetná Theatre about English-language theatre for Prague's expatriate community.

A note on admission to tourist sights: where two prices are quoted, the higher represents the full fee, the lower the concessionary fee (unless otherwise stated).

MEDIA AND COMMUNICATIONS
Newspapers
The *Prague Post* (*www.praguepost.com*) is Prague's most widely read and longest-running English-language publication. It has appeared on Prague's news-stands since October 1991 and has a readership of 40,000. Apart from stories of journalists being ripped off by taxi drivers, articles slating the government for its treatment of the Roma and expat businessmen grumbling about Czech absenteeism, it does print acres of information on new restaurants, cultural events, current goings-on in the Czech Republic, flats for rent, jobs, sport, business, cinema listings and loads more.

Telephone
The international dialling code for the Czech Republic is +420 followed by the whole number. In September 2002 regional prefixes became part of telephone numbers and all numbers became nine-digit, all of which must be dialled even if calling within the same town. The old numbers no longer work so beware of old listings. Mobile phone use is comparable to anywhere in Europe, and there is now one handset for every person in the country. The mobile networks are operated by Eurotel, T-Mobile and Oskar, landlines by Český Telecom. Some 86% of exchanges are now digital and the whole system has improved immensely in the last 15 years.

Public phone boxes are relatively widespread and easy to use. All coins are accepted bar the 50 heller piece. Phonecards (*telefonní karta*) can be bought at newsagents. You can call direct to anywhere in the world from a Czech phone box but the minute rate is astronomical.

Post
The Czechs have as reliable a postal service as you will find anywhere in Europe. Look out for the sign of the *Česká pošta*, a black post horn on a bright yellow background, in every town and village across the country. Local post offices are used for a range of transactions such as paying bills and collecting benefits. Tourists, however, usually just want to send a few postcards. Not all the windows will provide the service you need so make sure you are standing in the queue at the window marked *Listovní služby* (Letters). Hand what you want to send to the clerk, who will weigh it and put it through a stamping machine. If you really want stamps, say *Prosím, známky* when handing over the letter or postcard. The Czechs have a long tradition of producing interesting and very colourful postage stamps. The Czech for parcel is *balík*. All post sent abroad goes by airmail. Letters and postcards generally take three to five days to reach anywhere in Europe and a week to North America.

Internet
Although the Czechs were sluggish to get on the World Wide Web, they have now caught up, with an estimated three million internet users and widespread public access. Even small towns have several internet cafés and many of the larger hotels provide internet connection. Tourist information centres sometimes have a couple of PCs for public use. Charges everywhere usually work out at 1Kč per minute, but there may be a minimum charge of 15–30Kč.

The Czech keyboard differs slightly from the English and American versions. Firstly, the *Y* and *Z* are switched around. Secondly, the numbers across the top of

Anglo Saxon keyboards have been replaced by all the letters in the Czech alphabet with diacritical marks such as ž, š, and ě. Press shift and the relevant key to get the number. As these keys are already serving two functions, all of the other symbols such as &, % and ! have been relocated to other parts of the keyboard.

Czech web domains end in .cz and Czech companies and organisations tend to use it with very few exceptions. Many Czech sites have been translated into English but one can never rely on this being the case.

Radio

The BBC World Service broadcasts in English in Prague on 101.1 FM, in Brno on 101.3 FM, in Ostrava on 106.3 FM, in Carlsbad on 94.7 FM and in České Budějovice on 89.8 FM, as well as in eight further towns and cities across the republic. Broadcasts somewhat irritatingly cut between Czech and English for several hours at a time. There is no shortage of FM pop music stations in every corner of the land. Should you yearn for something gentler, tune into Classic FM on 98.7 FM, or Český rozhlas 3 Vltava specialising in classical music, jazz and plays (in Czech) on 105.0 FM in Prague.

Television

The foursome of ČT1, ČT2, Nova and Prima constitute the Czech Republic's selection of terrestrial television stations. ČT1 and ČT2 are state owned and funded from licence fees. ČT1 broadcasts a mixed bag of general-interest programming, news, current affairs and sport. ČT2 is not dissimilar to BBC2 in Britain broadcasting highbrow culture, foreign films and occasionally sport. Nova is a commercial channel which beams out recycled US series dubbed into Czech, blockbuster films and tabloid-style news. Prima is a slightly more upmarket, privately owned channel.

SPECIAL INTERESTS
Walking and cycling

A walking or cycling holiday is one of the best ways of seeing the Czech Republic in all its glory. You will discover parts of the country not accessible any other way, see countless places of outstanding natural beauty and meet friendly unhurried locals in far-flung mountain outposts. Well-marked walking trails will take you from city centres to mountain tops, wooded hillsides to tiny village pubs and icy mountain streams to dewy meadows and it is all free. Well-maintained cycle tracks, many created only recently, connect towns and villages with tourist sites and national parks and the network is being added to every year. Walking gear and cycle equipment is widely available and generally at lower prices than at home, and almost every town has a couple of cycle repair shops where they will fix your two-wheeled friend for a few crowns. It is relatively easy to get your bicycle on Czech trains and some services in summer even have special carriages for this purpose. Cycling, especially mountain biking, is far more popular than in say Britain, and you will certainly not be alone on the trails in summer. Accommodation out on the trails is easy to find, and naturally prices are considerably lower than in Prague.

If you intend hitting the Czech Republic's dense network of walking and cycling trails, you would be well advised to buy a **map** of the area you are heading for. The VKÚ–KČT (Vojenský Kartografický ústav–Klub Českých turistů), a joint effort by the Military Cartographic Institute and the Czech Hiking Club, have been publishing unbelievably excellent 1:50,000 maps covering the entire country since 1991. These are former secret military maps

HINTS ON PHOTOGRAPHY
Nick Garbutt and John Jones
All sorts of photographic opportunities present themselves in the Czech Republic, from simple holiday snaps to that atmospheric shot of Prague Castle. For the best results, give some thought to the following tips.

As a general rule, if it doesn't look good through the viewfinder, it will never look good as a picture. Don't take photographs for the sake of taking them; be patient and wait until the image looks right.

Photographing people is never easy and more often than not it requires a fair share of luck. If you want to take a portrait shot of a stranger, it is always best to ask first. Focus on the eyes of your subject since they are the most powerful ingredient of any portrait, and be prepared for the unexpected.

There is no mystique to good wildlife photography. The secret is getting into the right place at the right time and then knowing what to do when you are there. Look for striking poses, aspects of behaviour and distinctive features. Try not only to take pictures of the species itself, but also to illustrate it within the context of its environment. Alternatively, focus in close on a characteristic which can be emphasised.

- Photographically, the eyes are the most important part of an animal – focus on these, make sure they are sharp and try to ensure they contain a highlight.
- Look at the surroundings – there is nothing worse than a distracting twig or highlighted leaf lurking in the background. Getting this right is often the difference between a mediocre and a memorable image.
- A powerful flashgun adds the option of punching in extra light to

making them extremely accurate and superbly detailed and they are regularly updated to show all walking trails and cycle tracks plus every hill, castle ruin, campsite and railway line in the given area. A total of 93 maps cover every inch of the country and Czech walkers and cyclists swear by them. They try to cover a whole area of interest in one map and do not cut national parks etc in half if at all possible. The VKÚ–KČT maps are widely available at bookshops, and information centres around the country and cost no more than 80Kč. They are obtainable by post from Freytag & Berndt, in Prague (\ +420 221 732 62). You can find a full list of maps and the areas they cover at www.klubturistu.cz.

Walking is a very popular pastime in the Czech Republic which has one of the densest networks of **walking trails** in Europe. They are well marked, superbly maintained, cover the whole country and are widely considered to be the best in Europe. The *Klub Českých Turistů*, the Czech Hiking Club, founded in 1888 and boasting an incredible 45,000 members, is responsible for the upkeep of the 38,500km of walking trails as well as the maintenance of similar trails for cyclists and skiers. Walking trails are marked blue, red, yellow or green with a strip of the colour between two white strips for visibility. Look for them at eye level on trees, fences, bridges, rocks, bus shelters and walls. The colours have no meaning and do not give an indication of the level of difficulty of the terrain ahead. Trails usually start on town squares or at significant places such as castles or hilltops. At certain places along the way and at locations where several trails meet there are sign posts, usually on trees, giving distances to various places on those trails. Long transform an otherwise dreary picture. Artificial light is no substitute for natural light, though, so use it judiciously.

- Getting close to the subject correspondingly reduces the depth of field. At camera-to-subject distances of less than a metre, apertures between f16 and f32 are necessary to ensure adequate depth of field. This means using flash to provide enough light. If possible, use one or two small flashguns to illuminate the subject from the side.

Landscapes are forever changing, even on a daily basis. Good landscape photography is all about good light and capturing mood. Generally the first and last two hours of daylight are best, or when peculiar climatic conditions add drama or emphasise distinctive features. Never place the horizon in the centre – in your mind's eye divide the frame into thirds and either exaggerate the land or the sky.

Film
If you're using conventional film (as against a digital camera), select the right film for your needs. Film speed (ISO number) indicates the sensitivity of the film to light. The lower the number, the less sensitive the film, but the better quality the final image. For general print film, ISO 100 or 200 fit the bill perfectly. If you are using transparencies for home use or for lectures, then again ISO 100 or 200 film is fine. However, if you want to get your work published, the superior quality of ISO 25 to 100 film is best.

- Try to keep your film cool. Never leave it in direct sunlight.
- Don't allow fast film (ISO 800 and above) to pass through X-ray machines.
- Under weak light conditions use a faster film (ISO 200 or 400).

distance European trails are marked on maps with an 'E' then a number.

Cycling trails use four colours, blue, red, white and green with a strip of the colour between two yellow strips for visibility and easy recognition. All trails are numbered and are marked on the VKÚ-KČT maps with a small cyclist. There are 19,000km of marked cycle trails in the Czech Republic and more are added every year.

Climbing and mountaineering
The most popular destinations for climbers in the Czech Republic are the Czech Switzerland area in the north, the Teplice and Adršpach 'Rock Towns' and the Czech Paradise (Český ráj) in the east of the country. There are many other smaller sites scattered around the country and even in Prague it is possible to climb at Divoká Šárka on the road out to the airport. Specialist gear is available in Prague though may be harder to get out in the provinces. Various limitations exist on climbing in protected areas and it is always best to check before climbing in such places.

One of the biggest annual climbing events is the International Mountaineering Film Festival held in late August in Teplice nad Metují. Apart from a film competition with entries from the Czech Republic and other countries there are also exhibitions, discussions, skiing on artificial snow, mountain bike races and a run through the 'rock towns'. For more information see the website at www.teplicenadmetuji.cz/filmovyfestival.htm.

The Czech Mountaineering Association (Český horolezecký svaz) can be contacted at info@horosvaz.cz but their website (*www.horosvaz.cz*) is in Czech only. A better and more exciting source of information is the website www.czechclimbing.com (in English) which has heaps of detailed information on all possible aspects of climbing in the country.

Winter sports

The Czechs are big skiing fans and most weekends from December until March see the icy approach roads to the mountains across the country clogged with Škodas, each bearing a roof rack of skis. Children even have to undergo skiing lessons as part of their primary education and a Czech who cannot ski is a rare occurrence. Downhill is just one form of skiing and cross-country is just as popular, especially among the older generation, while snowboarding is as fashionable in the Czech mountains as anywhere else among young people. Even though most Czechs now see the local mountain ranges as tame practice for the real deal in the Alps, this does not stop the resorts becoming overcrowded at weekends, so expect long queues at ski lifts and accommodation to be quite hard to come by. Germans coming over the border for the cheaper facilities only make things worse. It is also worth bearing in mind that there is no guarantee of snowfall at any time anywhere in the Czech mountains though artificial snow is produced in some places.

The Krkonoše Mountains in the north boast the best downhill skiing in the country and their relative proximity to Prague means they receive the most visitors. Head for the resorts of Harrachov, Pec pod Sněžkou and Špindlerův Mlýn and you cannot go wrong. Other good ski resorts can be found in the Šumava Region, the Jeseníky Mountains, the Jizerské Mountains and the Beskydy range in the northeast.

Caving

The Moravian Karst, the best known cave network in the country, can be found just north of Brno (*www.moravskykras.net*). There are less spectacular caves in the Czech Karst (Český kras) just west of Prague, the best of which are the Koněprusy Caves 7km south of Beroun (*www.gweb.cz/jeskyne/english.asp*).

Outdoor practicalities

Camping is officially prohibited outside of camping grounds but this rule is generally ignored. If you do camp wild just be careful about lighting fires. Never make a fire in the forest especially in summer when highly flammable pine and spruce catch light at the slightest spark. The only people who may disturb wild campers are gamekeepers who patrol forests across the Czech Republic but even they will leave you in peace as long as you are not doing anything very naughty like setting fire to trees or poaching. Always remember to take all your rubbish with you after a night in the open and generally leave the place in the same condition as you found it.

Getting your bicycle on Czech trains is relatively easy but never free. On the smaller branch line *osobní* trains you can take your bike on with you. On express trains they have to be registered and put in the guard's van. Ask at the ticket office when you buy your ticket.

Most hiking in the Czech Republic is along well-worn trails in hilly, wooded sometimes reasonably rugged terrain which should pose no real danger to the experienced walker or even a complete novice. There are some trails, however, that take in the more mountainous and remote areas of the country such as the

Krkonoše mountains or the Šumava. In winter these places should not be underestimated, though problems are rare. When heading into the Czech mountains in winter, use common sense, take plenty of warm clothing, a colourful windproof and waterproof outer shell, extra food and water and some form of shelter. Sturdy waterproof walking boots are a must as are a whistle and a torch. Always tell someone where you are going and when you expect to be back. Never be ashamed to turn back if the weather turns nasty.

Another annoyance for outdoor enthusiasts, especially in humid summer forests, is biting insects. Take insect repellent, a hat, long trousers and a long-sleeved T-shirt if you are going to be spending time in wooded areas or around lakes in south Bohemia. Another (potentially fatal) danger is tick-borne encephalitis, a viral infection transmitted to humans when bitten by an infected tick (see *Health*, page 45)

Bears are extremely rare in the Czech mountains and are only found in the far east of the country in the Beskydy or White Carpathians. They wander over the border from Slovakia but you would be extremely lucky (or unlucky) to see one.

BUYING PROPERTY IN THE CZECH REPUBLIC

Up until June 2004 foreign nationals were officially not permitted to buy real estate in the Czech Republic. If truth be told, this was a good thing for the Czechs as it safeguarded them from Germans and Austrians pricing them out of their own property market (and perhaps from repopulating the Sudetenlands with German speakers). That all changed shortly after the Czechs' accession to the EU and all that foreigners now require is a Czech resident's permit (getting one is not the Byzantine paperchase it once was) and the services of a very competent lawyer, preferably one with local knowledge of the area where you intend to purchase. Finding a good lawyer should be your first step, then get the resident's permit and only after that should you start a property search. A translator/interpreter to accompany you at all times is also advisable. Never sign anything without consulting your lawyer first as property scams are all the rage. Ask any Czech to tell you the famous interwar case of the man who sold Karlštejn Castle to a rich American, and you will understand.

You will find at least one estate agent in every small town in the republic offering a wide choice of properties in the immediate area. These will range from crumbling garages behind communist era tower blocks to 18th-century Baroque chateaux in nearby villages, from gross 1990s villas with swimming pools on the edge of town to cramped medieval townhouses on picturesque central squares. Potential buyers from Britain will be astounded by the absurdly low asking prices of property in the Czech lands, especially outside the major population centres, except in Prague, where the market is overheated, overpriced and not great value for money. Even properties in popular tourist spots such as Carlsbad and Český Krumlov are surprisingly affordable.

To give some idea of the prices you can expect to pay, at present (spring 2006) a studio flat in a dreary Prague suburb costs around 1–1¹/₂ million Czech crowns (£23,000–34,000) and expect to pay in the region of 2–3 million (£45,000–69,000) for a one-bedroom flat. A remotely historical appearance sends the price soaring to Western levels as does proximity to the historical centre, especially the Old Town and Malá Strana. A typical house in Prague costs anywhere between 5–10 million crowns (£115,000–230,000). Outside of Prague the situation improves dramatically with a large house in a village with a large plot of land included costing 1–2 million (£23,000–45,000) and town houses going for 2–6 million (£45,000–138,000). There are often real bargains to be had in villages where you can find huge properties in need of renovation for as little as 500,000Kč (around £11,500). 15 million crowns (£350,000) will buy you a modest chateau in the Czech lands and the occasional derelict Baroque mansion comes onto the market for as little a four million crowns (£90,000). 20 million crowns (£460,000) will almost buy you a national treasure complete with parklands, lakes, fountains and more rooms than you can count. At the other end of the scale, if it is just a basic weekend cottage or cabin you are after, these can be found for as little as 200,000Kč, around £4,500. Now what can you buy for that back home?

The question you have to ask yourself is 'Do I really want to buy property in the Czech Republic?' If you do set your heart on that log cabin in the Berounka Valley or Gothic town house in Kutná Hora, be sure to take advice and know what you are buying. Buyers are sometimes shocked to learn that many villages have no sewerage system and rely on wells for water, as well as perhaps lacking other pieces of infrastructure. Buying a historical property can bring its own specific problems as you may be very limited with what you can do with it and the town hall, the ministry of culture and the president may have to rubberstamp a new door knob. Renovating a property may cost three times as much as you paid for it and getting planning permission may entail a brush with malevolent local officials, oligarchic village mayors, and the Kafkaesque machinery of Czech bureaucracy.

The joys of paperwork aside, the advantages of buying Czech are the prices, locations and most of all the opportunity to acquire properties of a size, historical value and character well out of the range of most ordinary people back home. So exchange your semi for a Bohemian palace – it's not as absurd as it sounds.

CULTURAL ETIQUETTE

Though only roughly 1,000km from London it is surprising how different some aspects of society can be in the Czech Republic. Armed with the following information you should not go wrong.

Make sure you do not have holes in your socks when you are invited to a Czech household as the first thing you do on entering the hall is to take off your shoes. You will normally be handed a pair of slippers (*bačkory* or *pantofle*) which you should don immediately. There may be a slight fuss around this as the whole family hunts around for a pair of slippers that will fit your size 12 foot. Having squeezed your oversized feet into slippers three sizes too small, just try to keep them on until you reach a table where you can quietly slip them off. Occasionally your host will implore you not to remove your footwear as the floor is cold, they do not have slippers in your size, or it is inconvenient for you. Your host is probably only being polite and not removing your shoes and marching into someone's flat will not go down very well. In winter it is especially important to comply with this Czech custom when the roads and pavements are layered with mud and slush. Eighteen-hole Dr Martens boots are not the best footwear for a visit to a Czech household.

When visiting a Czech family, take a small gift such as a bottle of wine, a box of chocolates or similar neutral gift as a small token of friendship. Czechs would never go visiting without something to hand over just before or after the shoe-removal ritual. Gone are the days when Westerners would be expected to bring something not available or very expensive in Czechoslovakia, and these days you would be hard pushed to really impress with a gift after 16 years of foreign travel and shops bursting at the seams with Western goods, but bringing something from home always goes down well. Single malt whisky, shortbread, local English

EARLY BIRD FRANZ JOSEF

You do not have to be in the Czech Republic long to learn that the working day there begins early. Some university students are yawning at lectures at 07.30, children and teachers arrive at school at 07.40, and most office workers are brandishing rubber stamps before 08.00. What is behind this extreme, bleary-eyed tradition, which sees schoolchildren take a 'mid morning break' at 09.40, a time when their British counterparts are just beginning lessons? Look no further than Austrian Emperor Franz Josef I (1830–1916) who, in typically bureaucratic Habsburg style, declared himself 'First Official' of the empire, and who was accustomed to rising in the early hours. The empire was encouraged to follow his example, as it was not the done thing for subjects to slumber in their beds while the chirpy emperor was already at his desk.

beers and ales, real curry, Californian wine, anything with Harrods written on it, football paraphernalia, books in English, English dictionaries and any local produce from where you live are things which cannot be had in the Czech Republic. Failing that, a slightly pricier bottle of local Czech wine is usually the best solution.

Czechs are incredibly hospitable so do not eat for the previous 12 hours before entering a Czech household. Vast quantities of food and drink will be placed before you, and your plate and glass will be refilled immediately you finish. Usually waving your hands in the air and rubbing your stomach as though you are fit to burst will halt the avalanche of food. Even now most people will think there is something wrong with you if you do not finish a meal. It is virtually unheard of for a Czech to say he or she does not eat this or does not like that. Such behaviour will draw great attention and may even lead to you being given that very thing to try so you see how nice it really is. Fussy Brits especially often become victims of this. When you sit down to your food you should never start eating before anyone else and the Czechs will always say '*dobrou chuť*' (bon appétit) before starting. '*Na zdraví*' (cheers) is said before drinking alcohol. This is not Russia or Ukraine with endless toasts and bottles drunk dry. The Czechs are more modest in their intake of spirits and refusing strong alcohol is accepted.

Everywhere you go in the Czech lands you will here '*dobrý den*' (hello, good day, good morning) and '*na shledanou*' (goodbye). The Czechs use these greetings a lot and every time one enters or leaves an office, a classroom, a shop, a railway carriage compartment, the barbers or any other confined public space those already present will expect to hear it. This can be quite strange for some foreigners and takes getting used to. Old people uttering '*na shledanou*' on their way out of an enormous hypermarket to nobody in particular out of habit is a curious sight. Foreigners occasionally may get a frosty reception and bad service because they simply blurt out what they want without the obligatory '*dobrý den*'.

Giving up your seat on public transport can also be a prickly area for foreigners. On the metro, trains and buses it tends not to be much of an issue but Prague's trams are where you will witness it most perhaps because more old people use them. Basically give up your seat for the obviously old and invalids. If you are male, giving up your seat to a girl or woman will meet with anything from a scowl to a flirtatious batting of the eyelashes. Standing avoids the problem altogether.

Black cats mean bad luck in the Czech Republic as in most of eastern Europe. Good luck cards from Britain with black cats emblazoned on the front receive interesting reactions.

GIVING SOMETHING BACK

In the rush to introduce a market economy, privatise and reform, sometimes the focus of Czech post-communist governments has not been on the weakest members of society or the environment. The following are just a few of the many hundreds of Czech charities and foundations trying to address the social and environmental legacy of communism and its aftermath. Contributions of any kind are always welcome.

Fond ohrožených dětí Na Poříčí 6, 110 00, Praha 1 (New Town); ℩ 224 221 137; e fodeti@volny.cz; www.fod.cz (in Czech); account no: 3055103/0300. Helps abused and neglected children in orphanages, children's homes and in problem families; runs foster homes. Branches across the country. Money, toys, children's clothes all welcome. **Nadační fond Verda** Bratislavská 41, 602 00, Brno; ℩ 545 211 576; e dubska@erag.cz; www.verda.cz (in Czech); account no: 2027315319/0800. Aids young members of the Romany community to gain desperately needed education and training. Financial contributions welcome.
Hnutí duha Bratislavská 31, 602 00, Brno; ℩ 545 214 431; e skupiny@hnutiduha.cz; www.hnutiduha.cz (in Czech). One of the largest organisations working to protect the environment in the Czech Republic. Financial contributions are welcome but you could also ask about practical help on projects they organise across the country.

Part Two

The Guide

Prague: Old Town Square

Prague

Golden Prague, Stone Prague, Praga caput regni, a
city of a thousand spires, Mother of all Cities,
Rome of the North – these are just some of
the ways Prague has been depicted over the
centuries, and all of them describe a city which
is stunningly beautiful. History has bequeathed a
wealth of architecture unrivalled in central Europe and
Prague is certainly up there with Rome when it comes to sheer numbers of
historical sites. Heaps to see and do, relatively low prices, a remarkably efficient
public transport system and a geographical position in the very heart of Europe
make Prague one of the best city-break destinations in Europe, if not the
world. Some of its sights such as Charles Bridge and Prague Castle are on the
verge of becoming as instantly recognisable as the Eiffel Tower or Big Ben as
millions of tourists a year flock to its narrow medieval streets, Gothic and
Baroque churches, majestic squares, leafy parks, smoky beer halls, stylish
restaurants and bars and ever improving museums and galleries. Prague seems
to have universal appeal, and must be one of a handful of cities in Europe able
to attract opera-goers, marauding stag-night groups, pensioners on weekend
city breaks, honeymoon couples, families with children, backpackers from all
corners of the globe, art and architecture lovers and classical-music enthusiasts
to its few square kilometres.

As far as tracks go, Prague has become one of the most relentlessly beaten,
featuring year after year in the top ten European city-break destinations. You
will never be alone in Prague city centre and in summer Italian, Spanish and
German tour groups clog the narrow streets (and sometimes the wide ones
too) religiously following their umbrella- or flag-wielding guide. Cheap flights
from Britain pack Prague's streets with British holidaymakers, and Saturday
nights in the Old Town can sometimes feel like a strange kind of Baroque
Brighton or neo-Classical Newcastle. Spring and autumn are gradually going
the same way, and Christmas and New Year see Prague sold out. Come in late
October and November or January to early March to avoid the worst of the
crowds.

That said, the number of foreign tourists visiting the Czech Republic grew
126% from 1992 to 1999 to over 7 million, but has levelled off since then to
around 6½ million a year, though the number of actual bona fide tourists (as
opposed to German bargain hunters and Polish businessmen etc) may be lower.
The capital receives around 3½ million visitors, and perhaps surprisingly the
British come top in the Prague visitor league table with 17%. The Brits have
found their way to Prague in the last few years, largely thanks to the boom in
budget air travel from the UK.

HISTORY

'I see a city whose glory will touch the stars' are the words of the mythical Slav prophetess Libuše as she stood high atop the Vyšehrad cliff, the Vltava swirling below. The city she saw in her trance-like state was Prague, *Praha* in Czech, supposedly derived from the word *práh* meaning doorstep or threshold as Libuše also predicted that the great city would sprout up where her subjects found a man fashioning a doorstep for his house. The spot was Hradčany, and the rest is history … well, perhaps not quite.

The strategic Hradčany promontory and the surrounding area were in fact inhabited by hunter-gatherers probably as far back as 250000BC with the first farmers arriving around 4000BC. The first Slav settlers came here sometime in the 6th century AD, choosing Prague for its position at a shallow ford across the slow-moving Vltava in preference to the fertile but vulnerable Labe (Elbe) plain. The Přemyslid dynasty really put Prague on the map when Bořivoj I founded Prague Castle in 870, and the city began to grow rich thanks to its position on major trans-European trade routes. The Prague bishopric was created in 973, and Vratislav II founded a palace and church at Vyšehrad in 1070. Merchants and tradesmen moved into the city to benefit from its wealth and relative safety, and the Old Town was established in 1234. The Malá Strana followed in 1257, created by King Otakar Přemysl II for German merchants and confusingly called the New Town (nova civitas sub castro Pragensi, the new town under Prague Castle). What we know today as the New Town was the brainchild of Emperor Charles IV who needed to upgrade Prague to a capital worthy of the Holy Roman Empire. His reign marked Prague's golden age when many of its Gothic buildings were constructed, the population swelled, new streets and squares were added and the entire city was encased in bulky town walls. It would be hard to imagine Prague without Charles Bridge, the Cathedral of St Vitus or Wenceslas Square, all the legacy of one inspired emperor. A few decades after his death the Hussites did their best to destroy many of Charles's creations, most effectively at Vyšehrad where only fragments remain. The Hussite wars were a dark time for Prague, divided between the radical New Town and moderate Old Town, though they did leave us the Bethlehem Chapel and the suburb of Žižkov, named after the ruthless Hussite warlord Jan Žižka who thrashed the Catholic crusaders there at the Battle of Vítkov in 1420.

Many call the reign of Habsburg Emperor Rudolf II Prague's second golden age, but the insane ruler, withdrawn and occasionally suicidal, bequeathed hardly any architecture to the city, and even his huge collection of art and scientific curiosities was steadily carted away over the centuries by invading armies. He did attract countless scientists and artists to Prague, most infamously scores of iffy alchemists. After his death the scene was set for a showdown between the Catholics and the Bohemian estates. The Battle of the White Mountain at Bílá Hora to the east of the city ended in debacle for the estates and they relinquished Prague without a fight. However, the Thirty Years War rumbled on until 1648, during which time the left bank was occupied by the Swedish.

Czechs call the three centuries from 1620 to 1918 the dark ages as political power was shifted from Prague to Vienna, thousands of Protestant families were forced into exile and Czech language and culture were suppressed in favour of German. However, as far as architecture goes, Prague flourished in the 17th and 18th centuries. Loyal Catholic noblemen received land confiscated from Protestants in Prague, especially in Malá Strana, where they built exquisite Baroque palaces. The Church of St Nicholas, the Valdštejn Palace and the Loreta were all added during this period. Prague was saved from complete obscurity in the late 18th and 19th centuries by the Habsburg policy of educating the (Czech-speaking) masses, then drawing them into the city to work in new industries. This sparked off the Czech National Revival that led to the building of such symbols of Czech national identity as the National Theatre, the National Museum and the Municipal House at the end of the 19th century. Alas, at this time Prague also witnessed the clearing of the Jewish Town and development of the New Town, causing the loss of countless historical buildings. During the ill-fated First Republic the population reached one million and Prague was the booming capital of a country extending from Cheb in the west to Ruthenia in the east. The examples of functionalist and unique Cubist architecture which dot the city are the legacy of this swish, confident era.

Prague escaped major damage during World War II, though the city's ethnic face following the Holocaust and the expulsion of the Germans was unrecognisable. Liberated by the Red Army, Prague was the scene of the 1948 coup which brought a Stalinist regime to power. The horrors of the 1950s show trials gave way to a thaw in the 1960s known as the Prague Spring, a time when many of Prague's historical buildings were listed as such. The Warsaw Pact marched in to 'liberate' Prague once again in 1968, and the dim days of normalisation followed. During the 1970s and 1980s, Prague gained much of its infrastructure such as the metro and the acres of soulless tower blocks, 'rabbit hutches' as Czechs call them, in the southern reaches. The 1989 revolution spread from Prague, and crime, unbridled capitalism, rampant development and mass tourism followed predictably in its wake. In 1993, Prague became the capital of the new Czech Republic and May 2004 saw the city celebrate the Czech's long-awaited entry into the EU.

GETTING THERE AND AWAY
By air
As the Czech Republic has only one real international airport, Ruzyně just west of Prague, see *Getting there and away*, page 43, for details of how to reach Prague from destinations around the world.

Airline offices in Prague
Aeroflot Truhlářská 5; ℑ 224 812 682
Air France Václavské náměstí 57; ℑ 221 662 662
American Airlines Železná 14; ℑ 224 234 985
Austrian Airlines Aviatická 12; ℑ 220 116 272–4
British Airways Ruzyně Airport, Departure Hall; ℑ 239 000 299
Czech Airlines V Celnici 5; ℑ 239 007 007
KLM Ruzyně Airport, Departure Hall; ℑ 233 090 933
Lufthansa Aviatická 12; ℑ 220 114 456
Malév Na Příkopě 15; ℑ 224 224 471
Swiss International Airlines Lazarská 8/13; ℑ 221 990 444

Prague Ruzyně Airport
Prague Ruzyně Airport is the Czech Republic's only true international airport. Situated 11km west of the city, it is cheap and simple to get to and from by public transport. Buy a 20Kč ticket from the machines at the stop in front of the terminal and board bus 119 alighting at Dejvická metro station at the end of green line A, from where trains can be taken to the city centre. Should your flight arrive after midnight, there are hourly buses to Divoká Šárka tram terminus from where night trams run to the city centre. A taxi from the airport to the centre costs around 500Kč, perhaps a better option after midnight.

By rail
Prague's railway stations
Unfortunately Prague's main railway station, **Hlavní nádraží** (metro station Hlavní nádraží), very often provides overland travellers with their first taste of the country. Once a proud, attractive, bustling First Republic station built in 1871 in the neo-Renaissance style and given an Art Nouveau restyling in the early 20th century, a communist-era parasite of a main hall and 15 years of deterioration and social upheaval have made this a place to avoid. While it possesses all the facilities you would expect to find in a station of this size, it is a mildly unsanitary place, invaded at night and in the winter months by down and outs, drug addicts, beggars, pickpockets and the equally unpleasant private security officers and Czech policemen sent to play cat and mouse with them until sunrise. Thankfully the station is earmarked for reconstruction. Where the roughly 300 homeless people, who call this place home, will be relocated remains unknown.

Services run from here to destinations all over the European continent as well as to most towns in the Czech lands.

Holešovice station (metro station Nádraží Holešovice) is situated north of the Old Town on the opposite bank of the Vltava. Trains heading north and the occasional international express call here.

Masarykovo station (metro station Náměstí republiky) is the large old terminus, a stone's throw from the Renaissance Hotel and Na poříčí Street. The main entrance is on Havlíčkova Street but the ticket windows are round the corner on Hybernská. Trains leave Prague's oldest station mostly for the north and west.

Smíchov station (metro station Smíchovské nádraží) deals in trains heading west to Beroun and Pilsen. Some expresses heading east start or call here.

By bus
Florenc coach station (metro station Florenc) can be found at the end of Na poříčí Street behind the Museum of the City of Prague. The entrance to the ticket office and other facilities is on Křižíkova Street, and the open platforms spread out behind. Not a lot has changed here since the revolution, and it can be a slightly daunting and confusing experience for first timers. Do not forget, that not all services leave from Florenc, and a bus to your destination may depart from some far-flung metro station in the suburbs (see *Chapter 2, Getting around*, page 51). Most international coaches arrive at Florenc.

GETTING AROUND
Prague must have one of the most efficient public transport systems in Europe with metro, buses and trams running at frequent intervals to every part of the city even in the middle of the night. Up until July 2005 it was also one of the cheapest, but long-anticipated fare increases put paid to that. The service is operated by the *Dopravní podnik hlavního města Prahy* (Prague Transport Company) who also run the funicular railway up to Petřín.

Tickets, available from yellow machines at stops and stations and from many newsstands, can cause problems as visitors frequently discover. Remember, it is not sufficient simply to buy a ticket. At the entrance to the metro there are large, highly visible yellow boxes with a slit with an illuminated arrow above it. You must punch your ticket in one of these before taking another step. Once you are in the system you must have a punched ticket or pay a fine. The same machines are on board the buses and trams and the same rules apply.

There are two types of ticket. The first costs 14Kč and is for short journeys of 20 minutes on the trams and buses and for journeys of five stations and no longer than 30 minutes on the metro. With this ticket you cannot change from one mode of transport to another, but changing lines on the metro is permitted. The second type costs 20Kč and allows unlimited travel for 75 minutes during the day and for 90 minutes from 20.00 to 05.00 and at weekends. These are the best tickets to purchase as you can chop and change as you like. Tickets for children between the ages of six and 15 cost 7Kč and 10Kč respectively. Children under six travel free of charge. Day tickets giving unlimited travel on the whole network are also available from ticket machines for 80Kč. Tickets valid for three days (220Kč), seven days (280Kč) and 15 days (320Kč) are also available. Children under six, skis, bicycles (metro only), prams, pushchairs and luggage (up to 50kg) are all carried free of charge.

Metro

There are three lines in total: A (green), B (yellow) and C (red), with a tidy round number of 50 stations. Changing lines is possible at Muzeum at the top of Wenceslas Square (A+C), Můstek at the bottom of Wenceslas Square (A+B) and Florenc at the main coach station (B+C).

The system is clean, modern, safe and easy to use. Much of the old Soviet-built rolling stock is being replaced by shiny new carriages. Two new stations on line C at Kobylisy and Ládví opened in 2004 and there is constant talk of extending line A west to the airport.

There is disabled access at the majority of stations and the newer stations are quite wheelchair friendly. According to EU regulations the whole system will soon have to be made accessible.

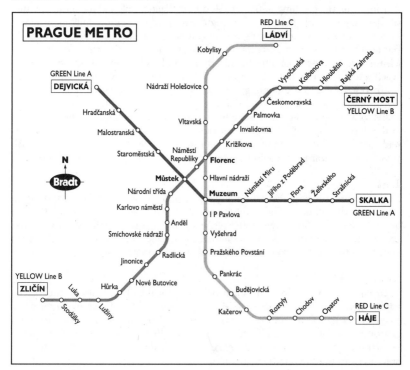

UNMISSABLE PRAGUE
- Prague Castle with the regal Cathedral of St Vitus dominating the Prague skyline
- Hradčany – the Loreta plus numerous Baroque and Renaissance palaces
- Malá Strana – the overpowering Baroque interior of the Church of St Nicholas
- Gothic Charles Bridge with its gallery of Baroque statues and stunning views
- The Old Town Square and the medieval streets of the Old Town and Jewish Quarter
- Bustling Wenceslas Square, the city's principal commercial and shopping hub
- A stroll around leafy Vyšehrad, the mythical seat of the first Czech rulers
- An evening in a rowdy Prague beer hall over a tankard of the world's finest beer
- A visit to the opera or a classical music performance in a Baroque church

Tram

Trams have been trundling through Prague's cobbled streets since 1897 and there is no sign of this ever changing. While trams in other parts of the world have had their ups and downs, Prague's have served the city faithfully, and are an integral part of the city. Prague would not be the same without the ring of the trams' warning bell, the grinding of the wheels on the shallow rails and the distinct whine of their huge electric motors propelling them up and down the hilly cityscape.

A total of 25 tram routes crisscross Prague in all directions. There is a route 26 but no 13. All routes originate in the suburbs, head for the centre, and mill around a bit before heading back into the suburbs in another direction. Trams hardly ever reach the city limits but do serve districts that the metro does not, especially northwest areas and south along the Vltava. Most have few seats and tend to fill up the nearer the centre they get and vice versa. Trams are most certainly off-limits to wheelchair users and those with walking difficulties due to the steep steps at the doors. Prague also has an excellent system of night trams (different numbers and routes) which run every half an hour from midnight until around 05.00. All pass through Lazarská, the central interchange stop during the hours of darkness.

Bus

Prague's buses today link every far-flung part of the city with the tram and Metro stations in the suburbs. This is the principal purpose they serve, and their routes are not designed for longer journeys. As buses hardly touch the city centre, tourists are very unlikely to need their services. One exception is bus 119 which shuttles between the airport and Dejvická metro station.

Taxi

Many visitors who arrive in Prague have probably heard about the Czech capital's unscrupulous taxi drivers. Many subsequently avoid taxis like a medieval plague, and get along fine using the city's excellent public transport network. Astronomical fares for non-Czech speakers are the taxi drivers' most common misdemeanour. The situation is improving gradually, but just to be on the safe side, here are a few rules to follow:

- If you can use public transport, do. The substantial fare difference is worth a few more minutes on a bus or tram.
- Agree a price before you get into the taxi.
- Never get into an unmarked car.
- Tariffs should be stated on the outside and inside of the car. The basic fee is 35Kč, the fare per km is 25Kč, and you will be charged five crowns for every minute the taxi waits.
- Use a reliable company such as AAA Taxi; ⤢ 140 14, or City Taxi; ⤢ 233 103 310.

Car rental

Europcar Pařížská 28; ⤢ 224 811 290; f 224 810 039; www.europcar.cz. Discounts for those flying with easyJet. Branch at Ruzyně Airport.
Czechocar Ul 5. května 65, Prague 4; ⤢ 261 222 079; f 261 172 432; www.czechocar.cz
Renocar Pivovarská 3, Prague 5; ⤢ 257 313 798; f 257 315 858; www.renocar-praha.cz
Hertz Dědinská 29, Prague 6; ⤢ 220 102 424; f 220 102 464; www.hertz.cz

WHERE TO STAY

The Czech capital has literally hundreds of hotels, pensions and hostels (601 to be precise) of all shapes, sizes, standards and locations reflecting the city's status as a major European tourist destination. The following is a mix of the best, most conveniently located and traditional, well-known Prague institutions. If booking through an agency in your home country or via the internet, check that your hotel is near the city centre.

Luxury (5-star)

Ambassador–Zlatá Husa Václavské náměstí 5–7; ⤢ 224 193 111; f 224 226 167; www.ambassador.cz. The Ambassador offers 5-star luxury right in the thick of things at the lower end of Wenceslas Square. The Art Nouveau building from 1920 somehow conceals 162 exquisite, air-conditioned rooms with jacuzzi. Expect to pay a wallet-busting 174–300 whatever and whenever you book.
Aria Tržiště 368/9; ⤢ 225 334 111; f 225 334 666; www.ariahotel.net. Situated in Malá

ALL CHANGE

Following the fall of communism across eastern and central Europe, hundreds of streets, squares, embankments, stations and bridges had to be renamed. Here are a few interesting examples of how post-revolution Prague quickly cleansed itself of the communist past:

Old name	New name
Moskevská Metro Station	Anděl
Leninova Metro Station	Dejvická
Gottwaldova Metro Station	Vyšehrad
náměstí Krásnoarmejců (Red Army Square)	náměstí Jana Palacha
náměstí Maxima Gorkého	Senovážné náměstí
Klement Gottwald Bridge	Nuselský Bridge
Leninova Street	Evropská
Lidových milicií Street (People's Militia Street)	Legerova
Nábřeží Karla Marxe (Karl Marx Embankment)	Podolské

Strana, the Aria sells itself as Prague's first 5-star de luxe boutique hotel. It has a musical theme with each floor dedicated to a certain genre, and each of the 52 rooms containing books, music and an in-room flat-screen computer with the biography of a particular artist or composer of the genre. It really is the last word in hotel luxury, full of little touches making guests feel they are being taken good care of. The views from the roof garden are some of the most breathtaking in the capital. 325–975 a night may also leave you breathless.

Carlo IV Senovážné náměstí 991/13; ↘ 224 593 111; f 224 593 000; www.boscolohotels.com. Carlo IV is Charles IV in Italian but even the Father of the Homeland himself might have found this place too luxurious after all those draughty Gothic hunting lodges. Housed in a neo-Classical palazzo 10 mins' walk from Wenceslas Square, this 5-star establishment offers exclusive Italian-style hospitality and ranks as one of Prague's best hotels. The 152 ever-so-slightly over-the-top rooms start at around 189. Check out that pool!

Four Seasons Hotel Prague Veleslavínova 2a/1098; ↘ 221 427 000; f 221 426 666; www.fourseasons.com/prague. On the banks of the Vltava River, 5 mins' walk from the Old Town Square, the Prague branch of the well-known chain does not disappoint. Some of the 161 rooms and the Allegro Restaurant have striking views over the water to Charles Bridge and the castle. Beautiful, fully equipped rooms start at 260.

InterContinental Náměstí Curieových 43/5; ↘ 296 631 111; f 224 811 216; www.prague.intercontinental.com. Housed in a modern building looking out over the Vltava between the river and the Jewish Quarter it has an amazing 372 modern rooms. The roof space is occupied by what many consider as Prague's finest restaurant, the Zlatá Praha, the views from which are as good as its cuisine. Room rates start at around 160.

Jalta Václavské náměstí 45/818; ↘ 222 822 111; f 222 822 833; www.hoteljalta.cz. Apart from its sumptuous atmosphere and first-rate service, the Jalta's biggest plus point is its location at the top of Wenceslas Square. The 94 guestrooms are truly classy with real attention to detail. Dbls start at 300.

Hotel Paříž U Obecního domu 1080/1; ↘ 222 195 195; f 224 225 475; www.hotel-pariz.cz. Experience the style of the Art Nouveau era at a Prague institution situated in the thick of the action next to the Municipal House. Purpose built in 1904 as a hotel, there is a wide range of lavish 5-star rooms to choose from, all light, airy and modern, but with Art Nouveau touches. Room rates start at around 160 a night.

Savoy Keplerova 6; ↘ 224 302 430; f 224 302 128; www.hotel-savoy.cz. One of the Savoy's many attributes is its location near Prague Castle. Inside you will certainly appreciate the elegant décor of the 61 spacious, pristine rooms and the first-class service. Room rates start at 320, which includes among other things an à la carte breakfast and complimentary shoe-shine.

The Iron Gate Michalská 436/19; ↘ 225 777 777; f 225 777 778; www.irongate.cz. Situated between the Old Town Square and Národní třída, this is a relative newcomer to the Prague 5-star hotel scene and one of the most exquisite and distinctive hotels in the capital. All rooms are furnished with real antiques and some have 14th–16th-century murals on the ceilings! Room rates start at 290 but, dare I say it, it is worth it.

Luxury (4-star)

Andel's Hotel Prague Radlická 857/40; ↘ 251 171 310; f 251 171 390; www.hotelandel.cz. This popular 4-star hotel is situated in Prague's Smíchov district on the opposite side of the river from Vyšehrad. Choose one of the 31 comfortable, well-furnished rooms which are a relative bargain at 1,800–3,100Kč for a sgl and 2,400–3,900Kč for a dbl, though the location is not the hotel's most appealing attribute.

Casa Marcello Rašnovka 783; ↘ 222 310 260; f 222 313 323; www.casa-marcello.cz. Housed in a former convent dormitory in a tiny lane just off Haštalské Square in the

Old Town this hotel describes itself as an aristocratic residence. Some of the historical, irregular-shaped rooms are a bit on the poky side, but the price starting at 95 and the location are perfect.

Corinthia Panorama Milevská 7; ↘261 161 111; f 261 164 141; www.corinthia.cz. The Panorama is the giant 24-storey modern tower block with a mega 450 rooms near Pankrác metro station south of Vyšehrad. The rooms themselves are modern, standard, spotless affairs with better views the higher up you stay. Despite its location, the metro means Museum station is only around 5 minutes away. Rates start at around 100 rising to around 170 in summer.

Diplomat Evropská 15; ↘296 559 213; f 296 559 207; www.diplomatpraha.cz. The Diplomat is a modern hotel next to Dejvická metro station in the Dejvice part of the city and one of the best located for getting to and from the airport. It has 398 pristine rooms and a standard sgl is 210, a standard dbl 235, somewhat pricey for a 4-star establishment.

Duo Teplická 492/19; ↘266 133 011; f 283 880 142; www.hotelduo.cz. The Duo is in Prague's ninth district, a little way from the action but easy enough to get to and from by public transport. From the outside the Duo may look like the worst kind of communist tower block imaginable, but the interior does not disappoint. It has an enormous swimming pool, a huge sports centre and a whopping 562 immaculate, modern rooms. Sgls go for 46–106 and dbls for 63–134; tremendous value, despite its appearance.

Holiday Inn Prague Congress Centre, Na Pankráci 15/1684; ↘296 895 000; f 296 895 010; www.holidayinn.cz. The Holiday Inn's 251 rooms can be booked up if there happens to be a large conference going on in the adjoining conference centre, the main venue for such events in the Czech Republic. It won the award for best 4-star hotel in the Czech Republic in 2002. It is located in the Pankrác district around 200m from Pankrác metro station. There is a flat rate of 215 for sgls and dbls, at any time of year.

Josef Rybná 693/20; ↘221 700 111; f 221 700 120; www.hoteljosef.com. Situated in the Old Town on the edge of the Jewish Quarter this sophisticated hotel was designed by top Czech architect Eva Jiřičná. Modern design is the watchword here with lots of glass, steel and spotlights. The 110 contemporary rooms contain design features such as bathrooms and furniture made entirely of glass and IKEA-style in-built storage. Perhaps not everyone's cup of tea, but a good location and room rates starting at 129 make this one of the best options in this category.

Mövenpick Mozartova 261/1; ↘257 151 111; f 257 153 131; www.movenpick-prague.com. The Mövenpick is actually 2 giant hotels on 2 hills connected by a cable car, a feature possibly no other hotel can boast. This all goes on in Prague's Smíchov district virtually at the mouth of the Smíchov Tunnel. Together the 2 complexes house 436 guestrooms, some a bit on the basic side for the price which starts at 100.

Questenberk Úvoz 15; ↘220 407 600; f 220 407 601; www.questenberk.cz. Housed in a Baroque church building just off Pohořelec in Prague's Hradčany district near the Strahov Monastery, the Questenberk is a relative new kid on the block. Most people passing think at first glance that the building is another tourist sight. The guestrooms are modest, but tastefully furnished, and the whole place has an air of clean simplicity. Sgls can be booked here for 160–190, dbls for 230–270.

Top Hotel Praha Blažimská 1781/4; ↘267 284 111; f 272 765 854; www.tophotel.cz. The mammoth Top Hotel has a mind-boggling 1,020 rooms and 3,000 beds! Though rarely completely booked up, its main downside is its location among the dreary tower blocks of Prague's depressing southern outreaches, not the usual haunt of foreign tourists. That said, the rooms are faultless and a relative bargain at 109 for a sgl in high season and 150 for a dbl, with rates falling by around a third in winter.

U Zlaté Studny Karlova 175/3; ↘222 220 262; f 222 220 262; www.uzlatestudny.cz.

One of my own personal favourites, though some may not like its location on the main tourist drag through town, the Royal Way, halfway between the Old Town Square and Charles Bridge. This tiny hotel in a narrow, 16th-century house has 8 absolutely wonderful historical rooms with antique furniture and oriental carpets. Expect to pay around 5,000Kč a night for a room, if one is free.

Middle range (3-star)

Albatros Botel Nábřeží Ludvíka Svobody; ☎ 224 810 541; f 224 811 214; www.botelalbatros.cz. If staying on moored boats is your thing try the ubiquitous botel docked just past the Štefáníkův most north of the Old Town. The cabins are definitely on the cramped side and rather expensive at 62 for a sgl and 76 for a dbl in high season. The location is this hotel's saving grace, and it does have a decent restaurant.

Andante Ve Smečkách 1408/4; ☎ 222 210 021; f 222 210 591; www.andante.cz. Ve Smečkách Street leads off Wenceslas Square, though this hotel is a good 5 mins' walk from there. A hotel since 1995, the Andante has 32 modern rooms with a newly decorated feel to them and some are 4-star standard. Sgls in high season are 110 and dbls 135.

Antik Dlouhá 22; ☎ 222 322 288; f 222 328 540; www.hotelantik.cz. The Antik is a tiny, 12-room hotel in Dlouhá Street around 2 mins' walk from the Old Town Square. There are not many antics going on at this quiet, family-run affair in the very centre of the city with immaculate dbl rooms for around 4,000Kč a night with breakfast outside in the secluded courtyard. Perhaps a bit steep, but the location is worth it.

Apostolic Residence Staroměstské náměstí 26; ☎ 221 632 222; f 221 632 204; www.prague-residence.cz. This is an absolutely superb place to reside with some of the 15 rooms looking directly out at the Old Town Hall and the *orloj*. The fully equipped rooms are traditionally furnished, and kept in an immaculate state. For such a location the prices are relatively good with dbls with a view for 132–218 and sgls from 97–218. Breakfast is served in the Gothic restaurant downstairs.

Cloister Inn Konviktská 14; ☎ 224 211 020; f 224 210 800; www.cloister-inn.com. This large, newly refurbished hotel in the unfashionable part of the Old Town has 75 comfortable, immaculately maintained en-suite rooms. Expect to pay 3,000–4,000Kč for a sgl or dbl with breakfast whatever the season.

Haštal Haštalská 16; ☎ 222 314 335; f 222 314 336; www.hastal.com. The Haštal has certainly had a colourful history. The building started life as a brewery and served as the Mačeka Hotel occasionally frequented by Hašek and Mucha, the headquarters of the occupying Warsaw Pact forces in 1968, and a proletariat tourist hotel until it was returned to the original owners in 1991. There are Art Nouveau features throughout, the location on quiet Haštalské Square is excellent and there is a good restaurant. However the rooms are slightly pricey for 3-star standard at 119–132 for a standard dbl and 75–97 for a sgl.

Ibis Praha City Kateřinská 36–38 ☎ 222 865 777; f 222 865 666; www.hotelibis.cz. The ultra-modern Ibis Praha City, just one of 3 hotels in Prague belonging to the Accor-Ibis group is situated in the New Town near I P Pavlova Square. The 181 business-standard rooms have all the basics, and dbls and sgls can be had for as little as 67–79 respectively in low season. Breakfast is an absurd 9 extra.

Novoměstský Hotel Řeznická 4; ☎ 222 231 498; f 222 233 052; www.novomestskyhotel.cz. The 'New Town Hotel' can be found just east of Karlovo náměstí. For the location the 34 very decent 3-star-standard rooms are quite a bargain at 2,800Kč for a sgl and 3,500Kč for a dbl in high season including breakfast in the hotel restaurant.

Prague Expres Hotel Skořepka 5; ☎ 224 211 801; f 224 223 309; www.pragueexpreshotel.cz. The 31-room Prague Expres is situated right in the thick of

WHERE TO STAY **83**

things near the Bethlehem Chapel in the Old Town. The spanking new rooms are a bargain in this part of town with sgls with shared facilities costing a mere 800Kč in winter and large en-suite dbls for around 3,000Kč in high season. The management offer various ways of cutting the bill by 10% (paying with cash, booking direct).

Ungelt Malá Štupartská 1; ☎ 22482 8686; f 22482 8181; www.ungelt.cz. The 10 spacious stylish apartments at the Hotel Ungelt are outstanding value for say 2 families travelling together. A large suite measuring 150m² with 2 bedrooms and a living room with breakfast costs as little as 8,350Kč for 4 people sharing in low season. The Old Town location makes it even better value.

U Mušketýra Mezibranská 13; ☎/f 296 220 000; www.umusketyra.cz. The 54-bed U Mušketýra has a great location at the top of Wenceslas Square near the National Museum and is probably one of the cheapest places to stay in the city centre with sgls in low season for as little as 1,620Kč and dbls in summer for 2,760Kč. Rooms are of a good standard and there is an interesting cellar restaurant.

Budget (2-star or less) and hostels

A Plus Hostel Na Florenci 1413/33; ☎ 222 314 272; f 222 314 263; www.aplus-hostel.cz. A newcomer to Prague's hostel scene in 2005, the A Plus looks promising. A dorm bed goes for as little as 220Kč in low season and even at the peak of summer an en-suite dbl costs only around 800Kč. Breakfast is included and there is internet access, guests' kitchens, a common room and lots more. Situated a stone's throw from Florenc coach station.

Art Prison Hostel Bartolomějská 9; ☎ 224 221 802; f 224 217 555; www.unitas.cz. A bed in a 6-bed dorm costs from 400–550Kč per night in this convent which used to be the StB cell block in the dark days of communist rule. The rooms are actually the cells where dissidents and other enemies of the state were imprisoned!

Evropa Václavské náměstí 25; ☎ 224 228 117; f 224 224 544. One never hears anything good about the Evropa, one of Prague's best situated and from the outside at least, most attractive hotels. The original Art Deco façade is a pretty front for overpriced rooms and, by all accounts, very bad service. A common source of complaints and probably best avoided though the location is one of the best in the New Town. Sgls are 1,600–3,000Kč, dbls 2,200–4,000Kč.

Travellers' Hostel Dlouhá Dlouhá 33; ☎ 224 826 662–3; f 224 826 665; www.travellers.cz. Prague's best-known and most popular hostel is situated 3 mins' walk off the Old Town Square along Dlouhá Street. Prices per night range from 280Kč for a dormitory bed off season to 1,300Kč for a sgl room with its own facilities in summer. There are 4 other Travellers' Hostels in Prague on Střelecký Island, 2 in Malá Strana and in Husova Street in the Old Town.

Renting apartments
The following agencies rent apartments in Prague's Old Town and in other areas. Otherwise ask at the Prague Information Service.

Old Town Apartments Zubatého 11; ☎ 257 316 662; f 257 313 441; www.stay-prague.com

Praga Magica Masná 9; ☎ 224 819 218–19; f 222 320 605; www.pragamagica.cz

Camping
Džbán Nad Lávkou 672/5, Prague 6 – Veleslavín (trams 20 and 26, stop Nádraží Veleslavín); ☎ 235 358 554; f 235 351 365. Open year round.

Sokol Troja Trojská 171a, Prague 7 – Troja (trams 14 and 17, stop Trojská, bus 112 from Nádraží Holešovice metro station, stop Čechova škola); ☎ 228 542 908; www.camp-sokol-troja.cz. Open year round.

Sunny Camp Praha Smichovska 1989, Prague 5 – Stodůlky (Luka metro station 500m, bus 174, stop Píškova); ❜ 251 625 774; f 251 625 774; www.sunny-camp.cz. Open year round.

Sokol Praha Národních hrdinů 290, Prague – Dolní Počernice (bus 168 from Palmovka metro station, stop Dolní Počernice); ❜/f 281 931 112; www.campingsokol.cz. Open Apr–Oct.

WHERE TO EAT

The restaurant guide to Prague is almost as thick as this guidebook, proving the capital has a superb choice of dining options for every pallet and pocket, from simple Czech eateries to luxurious French restaurants and exotic Bulgarian and Afghan places to the ubiquitous McDonald's. To my mind, when in Prague, eat as the locals do and give the cuisine a try. However, should you have your fill of dumplings, Prague has hundreds of other places waiting to please the taste buds. Here is just a selection of unmissable Prague institutions and the city's more interesting eateries.

Czech

Novoměstský pivovar Vodičkova 20; ❜ 222 232 448; f 222 232 448; www.npivovar.cz. When in the vicinity of Karlovo or Wenceslas Square, hungry and thirsty visitors could do worse than head for the huge, 10-room 'New Town Brewery'. A whopping 340 can enjoy Czech dishes (100–300Kč) in its timber spit-and-sawdust old Prague tavern environment. The brewer's goulash stewed in black beer comes highly recommended. Beer brewed on the premises is an opaque unfiltered ale (*kvasnicový ležák*) high in vitamin B and not pumped full of CO_2; a refreshing change. The service is swift and the atmosphere more raucous as the evening progresses.

Kolkovna V Kolkovně 8; ❜ 224 819 701; f 224 819 700; www.kolkovna.cz. The mothership of the Kolkovna group of restaurants (along with the Olympia and Celnice below) has the best location right opposite the Spanish Synagogue in the Jewish Quarter. The beer and goulash menu, the scampering waiters, the brass and dark wood interior and the simple, uncluttered ambience is the hallmark of this and the other restaurants in the chain. The superlative Pilsner Urquell beer complements mains for 100–300Kč.

Celnice náměstí Republiky – V Celnici; ❜ 224 212 240; f 224 212 253; www.celnice.com. Part of the same group as Kolkovna and Olympia, the Celnice is very similar, offering standard Czech fare and Pilsen beer in a stylised Czech pub environment. One difference is the brewery theme with a huge copper brewing kettle hood over the bar and polished copper piping and other (fake) brewing equipment throughout. Same food, same prices as the others.

Olympia Vítězná 7; ❜ 251 511 080; f 251 511 079; www.olympia-restaurant.cz. Another in the Kolkovna group, this huge, stylised, traditional Czech beer hall full of dark timber benches and wood panelling is a hop across the Vltava from the National Theatre.

U Fleků Křemencova 11; ❜ 224 934 019; f 224 934 805; www.ufleku.cz. The brewery and restaurant U Fleků is both a place to eat and a tourist sight. With a history going back to 1499, Napoleon is just one of the illustrious guests to have dined here. Its 8 beer halls seat up to 1,200, and thanks to its status as a firm tour bus favourite, at times it is packed to the rafters. The menu is limited to Czech meat and stodge such as goulash and bacon dumplings, beef in cream sauce, pork, cabbage and dumplings, roast duck and other substantial fare to put hairs on your chest. Just the entrées would fill most mortals' bellies. All mains cost around 200Kč. No visit to U Fleků is complete without tasting the *Flekovský ležák 13°* at 49Kč per tankard, brewed on the premises.

U Kalicha Na Bojišti 12–14; ❜ 296 189 600–1; www.ukalicha.cz. This is not just another Švejk theme restaurant, this is the Švejk theme restaurant actually mentioned in

Hašek's *The Good Soldier Švejk* (see box on page 32) which brought a run-of-the-mill Prague pub unprecedented attention and probably led to its survival to this day as one of Prague's most popular eateries. The proud friendly owner (the brother of a well-known Czech actor who also owns a share) is always on hand to welcome diners and talk of the 11 presidents and countless other dignitaries who have eaten here. The menu is in an unprecedented 23 languages plus Czech, the 3 rooms are full of references to Švejk and World War I and there is live Czech umpah music every evening. The walls of the tiny adjoining pub are thick with signatures of the rich and famous. Look out for Václav Havel's signature on the right. However, the no-nonsense Czech food here is not cheap at 250–300Kč but the service is excellent. Reservations are recommended as this is most certainly a tour bus favourite.

Klub architektů Betlémské nám 5a; ↘ 224 401 214; f 271 770 184; www.klubarchitektu.com. You do not have to be an architect to eat in this cellar restaurant opposite the Bethlehem Chapel. Enjoy mammoth portions of steak, pasta, chicken and salad at this popular eatery for a reasonable 100–300Kč washed down with Slovak Zlatý Bažant beer.

Plzeňská restaurace Obecní dům, náměstí Republiky 5; ↘ 222 002 780; f 222 002 778; www.obecnidum.cz. The cheaper and most Czech of the restaurants in the Municipal House is downstairs in the wonderful Art Nouveau tiled cellar. By no stretch of the imagination could this be called a typical beer hall, and the place has an overly clean, somewhat sterile ambience. The food is a touch overpriced, but the service is impeccable and the location and beer could not be better. Mains are 250–350Kč.

Sovovy mlýny U Sovových mlýnů 2; ↘ 257 535 900; f 257 535 906; www.sovovymlyny.com. Located in a former mill, this very accessible eatery has a great location on the bank of Kampa Island. Excellent food (275–400Kč) comes with great views of Charles Bridge from the riverside terrace and there is Staropramen on tap.

U Mecenáše Malostranské náměstí 10; ↘/f 257 531 631. You will find this tourist favourite in the shadow of the Church of St Nicholas at the upper end of Malostranské Square hidden under Gothic arcading. The best of a bunch of restaurants in this street offers diners Czech dishes (200–350Kč) and Moravian wine in 2 intimate rooms with knightly and other medieval regalia. I would describe the service here as 'tourist standard'.

U Golema Maislova 8; ↘/f 222 328 165. One of the Jewish Quarter's better options, the Golem is still a touch touristy, which is reflected slightly in the service. A huge golem greets diners in the first room. The menu features Czech dishes all for around 200–300Kč and portions are large. The food is not kosher despite the location.

Švejk restaurace Široká 20; ↘/f 224 813 964; www.svejk.cz. This large fake traditional timber beer hall, popular with tourists thanks to its Old Town location, has Czech and old Bohemian cuisine on the menu, with a few international standards and fried-cheese veggie option thrown in just in case. The tourists' favourite, Švejk, is plastered everywhere around the interior. Main courses come for a reasonable 100–300Kč, but the service is questionable.

U Sedmi švábů Jánský vršek 14; ↘ 257 531 455; f 257 531 454; www.viacarolina.cz. The 'Restaurant at the Seven Cockroaches' can be found in the middle of steps leading down from Nerudova Street in Malá Strana. The medieval interior is lit by candle and oil lamp only, which, along with the thick timber benches, waiters in medieval costume, knightly décor and old Bohemian dishes on the menu (in English), create a unique dining experience. Mains come for anything between 100Kč and 700Kč or you could try Hodokvas, as much as you can eat and drink for 1,500Kč! (excludes wines and spirits).

U Vladaře Maltézské náměstí 10; ↘ 257 534 121; f 257 532 926; www.uvladare.cz. Hidden on out-of-the-way Maltézské náměstí this restaurant has been going since 1776!

3 spaces (wine cellar, restaurant and club room) all have a distinct character and are great places to dine. The outdoor space is heated in winter. Mains, including a large selection of venison, come for roughly 240–450Kč though some specialities are more. Reservations are recommended.

U Provaznice Provaznická 3; ℅ 224 232 528; www.uprovaznice.cz. Hidden behind Můstek metro station this is a superb place for a beer and quick bite to eat. The menu offers no great selection but the 'Old Prague Plate for Two', almost 1½ kg of meat for 333Kč is good value. Everything else costs around 150–200Kč. Enjoy Gambrinus, Urquell and black Kozel beers in the bench-lined brightly painted rooms. The outdoor seating is in an unattractive location. More a pub than a restaurant but cheap, very conveniently located and generally overlooked by tourists who pass the end of the street unawares.

Restaurant 7 Angels Jilská 20; ℅ 224 238 489; f 224 234 381; www.7angels.cz. Dinner reservations are strongly recommended at the tiny 7 Angels, a few steps off the Royal Way where Jilská and Karlova streets meet. The 2 cosy vaulted dining rooms envelop diners in historical atmosphere and the service is impeccable. The upmarket menu features old Bohemian as well as very un-Czech dishes all for 200–400Kč.

U Dlabače V Tůních 1; ℅ 296 200 296. A short walk from the metro station I P Pavlova, this small standard Czech eatery with almost countryside prices (50–200Kč), Krušovice beer on tap, and a large selection of Czech and international dishes is the place for a cheap eat in the New Town.

U Krkavců Dlouhá 25; ℅ 224 817 264; f 222 329 121; www.u-krkavcu.cz. The 'Restaurant at the Ravens' has one of the most intriguing interiors of any eatery in the capital with diners seated close together under 13th-century rough stone arches of a Romanesque cellar and surrounded by murals. The menu is heavy with Bohemian favourites such as rabbit and duck and there is a good selection of seafood. All main courses come for around 200–400Kč. Reservations are recommended because of size and location.

Restaurace M D Rettigové Truhlářská 4; ℅ 222 314 483. Magdalena Dobromila Rettigová was the author of a famous 19th-century Czech cookbook, hence the name of this modest eatery just off náměstí Republiky. The menu (in English) features many of her patriotic specialities, superbly prepared by the chefs remaining true to her original recipes. Needless to say meat, cabbage and dumplings feature heavily. Mains come for 75–400Kč, there is Pilsen beer on tap and the service is agreeable.

Others

Hergetova cihelna Cihelná 2b; ℅ 257 535 534; f 257 535 820; www.cihelna.com. Moving statues of two men peeing into a pool greet you in the courtyard but there the bad taste ends at the Cihelna (which means brickworks). The terrace providing a panoramic view of the full span of Charles Bridge is one of the best vantage points in the city. The Italian-style interior is modern and cutting edge, and there is a dark intimate lounge upstairs. At 300–600Kč for main courses it is not cheap, but the view from the terrace makes it worth that little bit extra. Highly recommended

Rybí trh Týn 5, Týnský dvůr; ℅ 224 895 447; f 224 895 449; www.rybitrh.cz. The expert chefs at Prague's top seafood restaurant can prepare fresh fish, flown in from around the world, any way you like for 300–1,000Kč.

Reykjavik Karlova 20; ℅ 222 221 218; f 222 221 419; www.reykjavik.cz. Very conveniently located on the Royal Way between Charles Bridge and the Old Town Square, Reykjavik is, as the name suggests, an Icelandic restaurant (it even doubled up as the Icelandic embassy once upon a time). It does, however, have a quite British feel to it, and fish and chips feature on the menu more than once. Otherwise the food is a real mixed bag interspersed with few Icelandic dishes. The interior is large and plain, the outdoor seating is the place to watch the tourists funnel into Karlova as it narrows towards Charles Bridge. Mains are somewhat pricey at 200–500Kč. There is Krušovice beer on tap.

Restaurant Agnes Hotel Casa Marcello, Řásnovka 783; ↘ 222 311 230; f 222 313 323; www.casa-marcello.cz. The restaurant at the Hotel Casa Marcello, a few steps off quiet Haštalské Square in the Old Town has a small, intimate dining room with a slightly upmarket ambience, but reasonable prices and flawless service. The international menu features fish, pasta and Czech dishes, there is Velvet beer on tap and a wide choice of Moravian and foreign wines.

Don Giovanni Karolíny Světlé 34; ↘ 222 222 060; f 222 221 495; www.dongiovanni.cz. Prague's first and best Italian restaurant uses only the freshest ingredients shipped in directly from Italy. The ambience is most certainly snooty northern Italian with Venetian masques adorning the walls, northern specialities on the menu and not a rustic Italian item in sight. The prices are also directly from northern Italy with no starter under 120Kč, fish for around 400Kč, pasta for 170–500Kč and other main courses for 400–700Kč. The walls are lined with potraits of illustrious Czech diners including Karel Gott and Tomáš Baťa. The location provides pleasant views of the Vltava waterfront.

Ariana Rámová 6; ↘/f 222 323 438; www.ariana.dreamworx.cz. The name of this restaurant, tucked away in a side street off Dlouhá Street, means Afghanistan in Latin, and it is the cuisine of that country you can enjoy here. The Ariana is very accessible with simple décor (woven Afghan rugs, water pipes), Afghan music (CD), Czech waiters and very reasonably priced rice dishes, kebabs and plenty of vegetarian fare for 130–250Kč as well as other regional specialities. Come for the relaxing atmosphere and something a bit different.

Thrakia Rubešova 12; ↘ 603 388 860. This Czech-owned Bulgarian restaurant at the corner of Rubešova and Římská behind the National Museum serves up a selection of Bulgarian, Czech and Balkan food for 150–300Kč. The rooms have a folksy Balkan feel and southern European music lilts from the CD player.

King Solomon Široká 8; ↘ 224 818 752; f 274 864 664; www.kosher.cz. Prague's finest and oldest kosher restaurant is situated in the heart of Josefov across the road from the Old Jewish Cemetery. The delightful interior is divided into a temple with a stone statue of King Solomon looking down on diners and a conservatory at the rear. The limited menu has Jewish and Middle Eastern main courses from 450–800Kč.

TV Tower Restaurant TV Tower, Mahlerovy sady 1; ↘ 267 005 778; f 222 724 014; www.tower.cz. You will find Prague's highest-situated restaurant 66m up the Žižkov TV Tower. Expect to pay 200–500Kč for well prepared Czech and international food. The breathtaking views of the city are free.

Cafés, bars and pubs

U Zlatého tygra Husova 17; ↘ 222 221 111. The 'Golden Tiger' is not a Chinese restaurant but one of Prague's most renowned pubs mainly because writer Bohumil Hrabal regularly held court here. His bust can be found above his favourite drinking spot. A real down-to-earth Czech *pivnice* complete with *výčep* (where the beer is drawn) swimming in beer, it has a limited menu of pub food all under 100Kč and superlative Pilsner Urquell for 30Kč per communist-era thick glass tankard-full. The benches and seats are so close together that after a few pints you will soon know your fellow drinkers. However, this is not exactly Prague's friendliest establishment and at times the locals can be prickly about foreigners taking up space.

Slavia Smetanovo nábřeží 2; ↘ 224 218 493. Come to the stylish Slavia to sip a coffee at one of the many small café tables. They also serve snacks, sandwiches, pancakes, ice cream, and a small range of meals for 200–300Kc. Enjoy the 1930s décor and the ambience of one of Prague's most famous meeting places.

U Pinkasů Jungmannovo náměstí 16; ℄ 221 111 150; f 221 111 153; www.upinkasu.cz. One of Prague's best-known pubs, they have been serving Pilsen beer here since 1843. A restaurant, a lively bar, a cellar and 2 outdoor spaces front and rear offer real choice. The rear terrace is tight up against the Gothic buttresses of the Church of St Mary of the Snows. It is all hearty Bohemian fare here (mains 100–200Kč) and not for those on diets.

U Krále Brabantského Thunovská 15. At the foot of Zámecké schody you will find this great little *pivnice* frequented chiefly by local residents, which claims to be the oldest in Prague. The small beer hall with painted vaulted ceiling and tightly packed benches is a great place to down some Pilsen beer accompanied by unbelievably cheap soak-up material (meatloaf, goulash, pickled sausages, 40–80Kč) and get to know the locals.

Louvre Národní 20; ℄ 224 930 949. The busy Louvre is a great place to enjoy a relaxing coffee, a snack or breakfast, watch the trams and people pass along Národní Street below and admire the high ceilings and 1920s and '30s posters lining the walls. Prices are reasonable and the clientele mostly Czech. Open daily until 23.30.

Kavárna Lucerna Lucerna Palace, Štěpánská 61. Hidden away on the first floor of the Lucerna Palace this authentic, unaltered Art Nouveau café is an atmospheric place to enjoy a coffee or beer in the company of Czechs waiting for the cinema to begin or Bohemian types, actors and the odd celebrity discussing arty matters of the day. There is no food on the menu but the drinks are cheap.

Šenk Vrbovec Václavské náměstí 10. How this simple little place has survived so long amidst cut-throat competition on Wenceslas Square is anyone's guess. This small, basic, cosy, very popular wine bar serves wine from the Znojmo region straight from the barrel, no food and a limited selection of other drinks, nuts etc. A glass of wine is 28Kč, 70cl costs from 125Kč upwards. They do superb mulled wine in winter.

Kavárna Imperiál Na Poříčí 15. The grandly named Imperiál does not look much from the outside but inside one sees the reason for coming to this huge kavárna on the corner of Zlatnická and Na Poříčí. The amazing, shiny, tiled interior, the wood panelling, the numerous small wooden tables and the hurrying waiters transport one back to Prague's early 20th-century café society. However, the doughnut-lined counter is the first hint that not all is well here. The food is awful, the service criminal and the free doughnut with every coffee invariably stale.

ENTERTAINMENT AND NIGHTLIFE

Prague is not just about highbrow classical music and opera, though that is what it does best. You will also find an array of pubs, rock clubs, discos, nightclubs and jazz joints to suit every taste. Cinema is also an option as hardly any films are dubbed into Czech for the silver screen (alas, not true for TV). Cinema ticket prices start at 100Kč.

Opera and classical music

The Estates Theatre Ovocný trh 1; ℄ 224 215 001. What better place to experience Mozart's *Don Giovanni* than in the theatre where it was premiered. Tickets cost in the region of 500–1,000Kč and smart dress is appreciated.

Prague State Opera Wilsonova 4; ℄ 224 227 266; www.opera.cz. Nightly servings of Mozart, Verdi, Puccini and Bizet for the masses. Tickets from 200–1,200Kč. Smart, casual dress though jeans and trainers (even shorts!) are, alas, commonplace.

The National Theatre Národní 2; ℄ 224 901 377; www.nd.cz. Opera, ballet and drama in Czech. More variety than the previous 2 venues. Czechs dress very smartly for performances here so do likewise. Tickets 600–1,000Kč.

Municipal House náměstí Republiky 5; ℄ 222 002 101; www.obecnidum.cz. Classical music concerts held in the Smetana Hall (Smetanova síň). Smart attire. Tickets from 130Kč.

Rudolfinum Alšovo nábřeží 12; ⟍ 227 059 270. The Dvořák Hall is the home of the Czech Philharmonic Orchestra. Smart attire essential. Cheapest tickets for as little as 100Kč.
Bertramka Mozartova 169; ⟍ 257 317 465; www.bertramka.cz. Mozart is not the only composer to feature on the programme of the Bertramka. Smart dress advised. Tickets around 400–500Kč.
Church concerts Many churches now host classical music concerts and there is always someone around the Old Town handing out programme flyers. Daily performances are now the norm in summer and around Christmas. In winter make sure the church is heated and if not, wrap up warm! For some of the best concerts head to the Church of St Nicholas in Malá Strana. The programme for these can be found at www.psalterium.cz and tickets cost around 400Kč.

Ticket agencies
Bohemia Ticket International Malé náměstí 13, Old Town; ⟍ 224 227 832; f 224 218 167; www.ticketsbti.cz. Online booking.
Ticketpro Pasáž Rokoko Václavské náměstí 38; ⟍ 296 333 333; www.ticketpro.cz. Online booking.

Cinemas
Palace Cinemas Slovanský dům Na Příkopě 22, New Town. 10 screens, the only one of its kind in the city centre.
Kino Lucerna Lucerna Palace, Štěpánská 61, New Town. Prague's most glorious cinema, the Art Nouveau décor making a change from all those soulless multiscreens.
Kino Blaník Václavské náměstí 54, New Town. Located conveniently on Wenceslas Square.
Světozor Vodičkova 41, New Town. Good old-fashioned communist-era cinema a few steps off Wenceslas Square.
Village Cinemas Anděl Radlická 3179, Prague 5 – Smíchov (Metro Station Anděl). Talk of the town when it opened and one of the biggest multiplexes in the country.

Discothèques, nightclubs, jazz and rock
Nightclub to some, brothel to others, so be careful where that helpful taxi driver takes you as they receive commission for each person they deliver. Stick to the following and you cannot go wrong.

Karlovy Lázně Smetanovo nábřeží 198 (Old Town near Charles Bridge). 5 floors of music and every one different in this, the largest disco complex in central Europe.
Radost FX Bělehradská 120, Prague 2 (just off I P Pavlova Square). Established in the early 1990s, Radost is possibly the best-known dance club in town. It also houses a vegetarian restaurant.
Reduta Národní 20, New Town. Prague's premier jazz club.
Futurum Zborovská 7, Prague 5 – Smíchov. One of Prague's favourite nightspots with regular '80s and '90s parties.
Malostranská beseda Malostranské náměstí 21, Malá Strana. You will hear mainly local rock bands at this club, popular with students and housed in the former Malá Strana town hall.
Lucerna Music Bar Lucerna Palace, Štěpánská 61, New Town. Check out local Czech bands in the Lucerna.

OTHER PRACTICALITIES
Tourist information offices
Prague Information Service (Pražské informační služba – PIS) Comprehensive tourist information on Prague is provided by the outstanding PIS. The range of services they

provide is too long to list here, but includes leaflets and brochures on the city in numerous languages, tickets for virtually any cultural event happening in Prague, guides, trips out to Karlštejn, Terezín and the like, and they also sell maps, guides, postcards and metro tickets. The PIS general information line is a special short number – 12 444, and their 4 offices are located as follows:

Staroměstské 1 (Old Town Hall) Open daily, year round.

Na příkopě 20 Open Mon–Sat, year round.

Main railway station (main hall) Open Apr–Oct daily, Nov–Mar Mon–Sat.

Malostranská mostecká věž (Bridge tower on the Malá Strana side of Charles Bridge) Open daily Apr–Oct, closed Oct–Mar.

CzechTourism (Czech state tourist board) This is the other organisation in Prague providing authoritative tourist information. Their office on the Old Town Square closed down recently, but they still run a large office at Vinohradská 46 (❧ *221 580 611;* f *221 580 711–2*), around 15 minutes' walk from the National Museum.

Around Prague Celetná 14, Národní 4, Karlova 1, Nerudova 4; www.aroundprague.com. The Around Prague agency is a trustworthy private company providing tourist information and selling bus and theatre tickets, as well as facilitating a myriad of other tourist services. They also produce a free glossy monthly magazine for tourists in Czech and English called *Tim.*

Prague Card

The Prague Card (*www.praguecard.biz*) is an all-inclusive ticket to 40 of the city's sights and the entire public transport system, valid for three consecutive days. It comes with a 100-page colour guide to the city, and can be purchased at American Express, Čedok, the PIS, some hotels and a couple of travel agents. The cost is 790Kč or 590Kč without public transport.

Local travel companies

Čedok Na Příkopě 18; ❧ 224 197 632; www.cedok.cz/incoming
AVE Pod Barvířkou 6/747, Prague 5; ❧ 251 091 111; f 251 556 005–6; www.avetravel.cz
Prague International Senovážné náměstí 23; ❧ 224 142 431; f 224 142 000; www.pragueinternational.cz

City tours and walks

Martin Tour Praha Štěpánská 61, palác Lucerna; ❧ 224 212 473; f 224 239 752; www.martintour.cz. Martin Tour have been in the business of bussing tourists around the city for 16 years. Convenient kiosks at 4 sights in the city centre (*Old Town Square, náměstí Republiky, Melantrichova Street and Na Příkopě Street*) sell tickets for hourly buses. A sightseeing tour of Prague costs 250–350Kč and they also run walking tours, boat trips, tours of Jewish Prague and day trips to places like Terezín, Hluboká Castle, Carlsbad and Karlštejn. On longer trips the ticket price usually includes lunch.

Walks of Prague Dobratická 523; ❧ 737 884 745 or 723 158 804. The departure point for these interesting themed walks is the Astronomical Clock on the Old Town Square. Tickets are bought from the guides up to 10 mins before departure. Try their 'Hidden Pubs' tour or the 'Dinner on the River' evening cruise (book in advance on above numbers).

City Walks ❧ 608 200 912; www.praguer.com. Prague's most respected walking-tour company operate a wide selection of excellent themed walks and comprehensive sightseeing tours which, with some exceptions, leave from the Astronomical Clock (tickets from guides). Their daily evening Ghost Tour is said to be superb and they also run 'Prague by Bike' and 'Prague by Historic Tram' tours.

Internet cafés

Inetpoint.cz Jungmannova 32, New Town; ✆ 296 245 962
KávaKávaKáva Národní 37, New Town; ✆ 224 228 862
Batalion (24 hours) 28 října 3, New Town; ✆ 220 108 147
Netc@fe.info Na Poříčí 8, New Town; ✆ 222 310 947

Post

Prague's main post office is in Jindřišská Street just off Wenceslas Square, and is conveniently open 24 hours a day, seven days a week. In the Old Town there is a post office at Kaprova 12, and across the river you can get those postcards off at Josefská 4 or at the post office at Prague Castle (third courtyard).

Banking

There is now a bank or an ATM or both in virtually every street. The most convenient bank in the city centre (and one of the most attractive) is the Česká spořitelna just south of Můstek.

WHAT TO SEE AND DO

Your main problem in Prague may in fact be what not to see – that is, deciding what to leave out. The city has an incredible number of sights crammed into the historical centre and in the suburbs and outskirts. However, there is a definite list of 'must-sees' (Prague Castle, the Old Town, Charles Bridge) and the rest is up to you.

The historical city centre is divided into five distinct areas – Hradčany including Prague Castle, Malá Strana on the left bank of the Vltava, the Old Town and Josefov, Vyšehrad and the New Town. Of course Prague has numerous other districts but these five are of most interest to visitors.

NATIONAL GALLERY IN PRAGUE

Unlike London or Paris, Prague never quite got round to putting a single roof over its art treasures. The National Gallery (*Národní galerie, www.ngprague.cz*) is scattered around the city in various historical buildings:

1 Šternberk Palace, European Art from Antiquity to Baroque – Hradčanské Square a few paces from the gates of Prague Castle
2 Monastery of St George, Mannerist and Baroque Art in the Czech Lands – Jiřské Square within the grounds of Prague Castle
3 Convent of St Agnes, Medieval Art in the Czech Lands and Central Europe – U Milosrdných Street in Josefov
4 Veletržní palác, Modern Art of the 19th, 20th and 21st centuries – Dukelských hrdinů Street, Prague 7
5 Zbraslav Chateau, Asian Art – Bartoňova 2, Prague 5
6 Kinský Palace, Czech Landscapes – Old Town Square
7 Wallenstein Riding School, temporary exhibitions – opposite the Royal Gardens at Prague Castle
8 House of the Black Madonna, Museum of Czech Cubist Art – Ovocný trh 19 in the city centre

All of the above exhibitions have different opening hours and entrance fees. Admission is free every first Wednesday in the month 15.00–20.00.

Prague Castle and Hradčany

According to the *Guinness Book of Records* Prague Castle is the largest castle complex in the world. *Pražský hrad* (or just *hrad*) as it is known in Czech dominates the skyline from the banks of the Vltava and Malá Strana perched high on a strategic promontory watching over the city. Its most striking feature is without doubt the Gothic Cathedral of St Vitus, the largest and most important place of worship in the Czech Republic, whose tower and flying buttresses protrude above the acres of buildings. No visit to Prague is complete without a walk through arguably the most significant historical site in the country, the seat of Czech kings and presidents down the centuries and steeped in history, from Romanesque structures to 20th-century improvements.

Empress Maria Theresa is responsible for much of the huge façade we see today. Her architect Nicolo Pacassi placed buildings between the protective walls creating hundreds of rooms and acres of floor space. Some of the interiors were given an Art Deco facelift in the 1920s under the first Czechoslovak President Tomáš Garrigue Masaryk by the Slovene architect Josip Plečnik, though his alterations are not obvious to the tourist.

Tickets

Tickets can be purchased at the main ticket office or at the individual sights. A route A ticket is an access-all-areas pass for all parts of the castle open to the public. Tickets are valid for two days but you can visit each place only once. Allow at least half a day to see the castle properly, but if you are pressed for time, go for route B. Many of the exhibition spaces have separate opening times and admission fees. Allow a whole day or more to see everything.

Ticket type	Full price	Concessions	Family ticket
Route A	350Kč	175Kč	520Kč
Route B	220Kč	110Kč	330Kč
Route C	50Kč	–	100Kč
Route D	50Kč	25Kč	100Kč
Route E	50Kč	25Kč	100Kč
Route F	100Kč	50Kč	150Kč

Route A Cathedral of St Vitus including the Great Tower, Old Royal Palace including the Story of Prague Castle exhibition, Basilica of St George, Prašná Tower, Golden Lane, Daliborka Tower
Route B Cathedral of St Vitus including the Great Tower, Old Royal Palace, Golden Lane, Daliborka Tower
Route C Golden Lane, Daliborka Tower
Route D Basilica of St George
Route E Prašná Tower
Route F Convent of St George

Audioguides can be hired for 300/250Kč for three hours and 250/200Kč for two hours.

First courtyard

Arriving at Prague Castle from Hradčanské náměstí, the entrance is through a gate topped with two mammoth, gruesome statues called the **Battling Titans**, one with raised dagger, the other wielding a club, and both about to mutilate their unfortunate victims. The gate is also guarded by two sentries standing motionless and expressionless in front of their pillboxes while tourists from around the world pose for photographs next to them. The changing of the guard

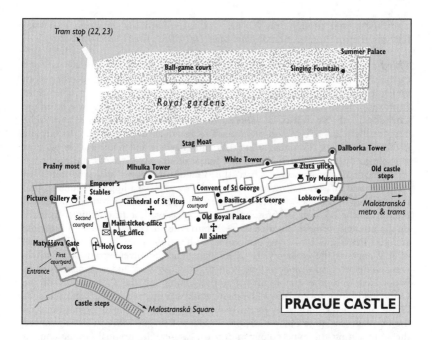

Tram stop (22, 23)

Ball-game court

Summer Palace

Singing Fountain

Royal gardens

Stag Moat

White Tower

Dallborka Tower

Prašný most

Mlhulka Tower

Zlatá ulička

Old castle steps

Emperor's Stables

Convent of St George

Toy Museum

Picture Gallery

Cathedral of St Vitus

Third courtyard

Basilica of St George

Lobkovicz Palace

Malostranská metro & trams

Second courtyard

Main ticket office

Old Royal Palace

Post office

All Saints

Matyášova Gate

Holy Cross

First courtyard

Entrance

Castle steps

Malostranská Square

PRAGUE CASTLE

is an unspectacular affair and not worth hanging around for even at midday when it is performed with slightly more pomp and ceremony. Having entered the courtyard, notice the two huge flagpoles which taper off to a needle-thin point guarding the entrance to the larger second courtyard, the **Matyášova Gate**. The early Baroque entrance from the 17th century named after Emperor Matyáš II used to stand on its own in front of a moat, long since filled in, and formed the main entrance to the castle.

Second courtyard
Flights of stairs lead up from the Matyášova Gate to some of the grandest halls in the castle, the **Spanish Hall** (Španělský sál) and the **Rudolf Gallery** (Rudolfova galerie), both inaccessible to the public. Blank façades close off every side of the second courtyard, and the only real place of interest is the **Chapel of the Holy Cross** (kaple Svatého Kříže) from 1763 protruding into the courtyard on the right. The building houses a ticket office and a gift shop, but in between is the pretty chapel with marble and gold décor, now demoted to an elaborate corridor. Notice the porch next to the chapel on the main building, one of Plečnik's few exterior additions hinting at his controversial interiors. At the opposite end of the courtyard there are two art galleries; the **Emperor's Stables** (Císařská konírna) house temporary exhibitions while next door the **Prague Castle Picture Gallery** (Obrazárna Pražského hradu) contains the imperial art collection begun by eccentric Emperor Rudolf II. His original collection was gradually moved to Vienna by subsequent rulers and much of the remainder was plundered by the Swedish during the Thirty Years War, though some works remain. The collection was re-established in 1650 when the brother of Emperor Ferdinand III purchased over 500 paintings from the Duke of Buckingham. Some of these were later carted off to Vienna, but some stayed. It was significantly added to after 1918, and was opened to the public in 1965. The castle possesses over 4,000

paintings in total, though only 107 are on display. Look out for works by Titian, Rubens, Tintoretto and Brandl (*admission 100/50Kč, family ticket 150Kč*).

Third courtyard and Cathedral of St Vitus

On the right as you enter there is the main ticket office and a post office from which postcards can be sent bearing the Prague Castle postmark. The third courtyard is hardly large enough to allow visitors to get far enough away from the **Cathedral of St Vitus** to appreciate its Gothic magnificence and some occasionally resort to lying on the ground to get a half-decent picture. Its full title is the Cathedral of SS Vitus, Wenceslas and Adalbert and is the largest place of worship in the Czech lands as well as a burial site for Czech kings and noblemen and place of coronation. When the Prague bishopric was promoted to archbishopric in 1344, Charles IV ordered the building of a huge cathedral around the tomb of St Wenceslas which had itself replaced an earlier rotunda housing a bone from the body of St Vitus. Matthias of Arras was the first architect to work on the immense project, but died six years into construction. Charles IV's preferred architect Petr Parléř took over, but on his death in 1399 only the choir, the Chapel of St Wenceslas, the Golden Gate (Zlatá brána) and the lower section of the tower were complete. It took another 650 years to finish the work and nothing substantial was added until the establishment of the Union for the Completion of the Cathedral of St Vitus in 1859. The main work was finished in 1929 and the neo-Gothic nave was fashioned by Josef Mocker among others. The difference between the two halves is quite obvious, despite decades of Prague's foul air having stained the stone almost the same colour in equal measure. The original Gothic choir is more elaborate while the 19th-century additions are more conservative in appearance. The 96m-tall **Great Tower** (Hlavní věž) also documents the various stages of building work over the centuries with a somewhat incongruous green Baroque steeple sitting on the lighter stone of the Renaissance-era viewing gallery, which in turn contrasts with the blackened Gothic stonework. The tower in particular gives the impression of a rushed, improvised solution, a compromise to the ambitious plans of Charles IV and his builders. The oldest bell in the tower is the 18-tonne *Zikmund* which has pealed out over Prague Castle since 1549. Climb the 287 steps for truly striking views (*Apr–Oct only*). Beneath the Great Tower notice the Golden Gate with its unique Gothic mosaic made up of one million glass tiles of 30 different shades. Its creator is not known.

Anyone can wander into the 19th-century nave for free to admire the amazing 33m-high vaulting, sometimes barely visible in the haze. Above the entrance stop to admire the **Rose Window** as well as the 19th- and 20th-century stained-glass windows which inundate the nave with a myriad colours. The window in the third chapel to the right (New Archbishop's chapel) was designed by Alfons Mucha in 1931. The highlight of the nave and the focal point of the whole cathedral is the ornate **Chapel of St Wenceslas**, its importance evident from its Byzantine-like decoration. Semi-precious stones and murals depicting Wenceslas's life surround the tomb itself containing the 1,000-year-old remains of the Czech patron saint. Stealing a peek through the narrow doorway into the chapel can be hard when the cathedral is heaving with tour groups. A door in the corner of the chapel leads to the coronation chamber where the crown jewels are kept. The centrepiece is the priceless Crown of St Wenceslas, created for Charles IV in 1346 and inlaid with some of the largest sapphires on earth. Seven keys held by the president, the prime minister, the archbishop, the speakers of parliament and the senate, the metropolitan chapter of the cathedral and the mayor of Prague are needed to unlock the coronation chamber.

With a ticket you can pass into the more ornate Gothic choir. In the centre notice the cherub-adorned **Imperial Mausoleum** surrounded by a fancy grille and containing the remains of Ferdinand I, Anna Jagiellon and Maxmilian I dating from 1589. Opposite is the very modest altar. Walking around the ambulatory the traffic jam of tourists is caused by the strangely located, over-the-top Baroque **Tomb of St John of Nepomuk** from 1736. The silver tomb which almost blocks the ambulatory is protected by a canopy held up by angels who appear to be actually floating above it. From there descend to the **Royal Crypt** (Královská hrobka), the final resting place of many kings of Bohemia. However, the tomb of the great Charles IV was created only in the 1930s, and his actual burial site under the main altar was rediscovered in 2005 after 130 years.

Old Royal Palace (Starý královský palác)

Across from the Golden Gate is the entrance to the palace of Czech rulers from the 11th to the 16th century. The lower, older floors dating from the rule of Soběslav I and founded in 1135 lie below Gothic rooms and halls built by Charles IV which since 2004 have housed the definitive permanent exhibition on the *hrad* entitled the **Story of Prague Castle** (*www.pribeh-hradu.cz*). Fascinating artefacts, interactive screens and informative English explanations bring the history of the castle as well as the dim Gothic spaces to life. The main route traces the development of the strategic promontory and the life of its occupants from prehistory to the 20th century, while side rooms focus on particular topics such as the story of burials, disasters to have hit the castle or the Czech patron saints.

The upper floors of the Old Royal Palace are dominated by the cavernous **Vladislav Hall** (Vladislavský sál). Commissioned by Vladislav Jagiellon and built over a decade from 1492 to 1502, it was the largest secular indoor space at the time and provided the backdrop for balls, trials, markets, feasts and jousting when the weather was bad outside. The sloping Riders' stairs (Jezdecké schodiště), now the exit, were built as a special entrance for the horses. The Vladislav Hall still has great significance for the modern Czech state as presidents are elected and sworn in here and occasional state functions and events take place under the swirling Gothic vaulting reaching almost to the floor. To the right of the entrance enter the doorway into the Ludvík Wing, famous for the second Prague defenestration of 1618. Czech governors Vilém Slavata z Chlumu and Jaroslav Bořita z Martinic plus an unfortunate secretary, who was just in the wrong place at the wrong time, were ejected from a window in the last room by Protestant nobles, kicking off the revolt against the Catholic Habsburg monarchy which developed into the Thirty Years War. From the Ludvík Wing along the outside of the hall runs a terrace providing great views down across Malá Strana. Further up the hall on the left is the old Czech parliament (sněmovna). Until 1847 this grand room was the meeting place for the Council of the Estates, and served as the Supreme Court. The portraits hanging on the walls are of Empress Maria Theresa and Emperors Joseph II and Leopold II. At the end of the hall visitors can peer down into the **Church of All Saints** (Kostel všech svatých) built in 1370 by Petr Parléř on the site of an earlier Romanesque chapel and virtually destroyed by fire in 1541, after which it was lengthened and united with the Vladislav Hall.

Basilica of St George

Leaving the Old Royal Palace one finds oneself on St George's Square (náměstí sv Jiří). Do not be fooled by the red Baroque façade glued on to the Basilica of St George (Bazilika sv Jiří). Inside you will find one of the purest examples of

Romanesque heritage in the Czech Republic and the second-oldest church in Prague, founded in 920 by Vratislav I. St Ludmila, the murdered grandmother of St Wenceslas, was laid to rest here in 925 and the basilica served as the burial site for the Přemyslid dynasty until the Church of St Vitus was begun. To the right the Baroque Chapel of St John of Nepomuk was tacked on to the basilica in 1718, though the Baroque additions are tasteful, by no means over the top, and do not detract from the simple Romanesque stonework. Tight against the basilica stands the **Convent of St George** (Jiřský klášter), part of the National Gallery housing an exhibition of Mannerist and Baroque art with works by Brandl and Škréta.

Zlatá ulička and the towers

From the Square of St George double back to the other side of St Vitus (*Vikářská Street*) to find the **Mihulka Tower**, sometimes known as the **Prašná věž**. The 44m-high round tower was built to fortify the northern side of the castle in the 15th century. It has been put to many uses over the centuries such as a workshop for bell maker Tomáš Jaroš who also created the singing fountain and the *Zikmund* bell, a laboratory for Rudolf II's famous alchemists, a prison, a gunpowder store (hence the name '*prašná*' from the Czech '*střelný prach*' meaning gunpowder) and as the verger's living quarters. Now it contains a rather poor military history exhibition on the first level but upstairs is a slightly more engaging display of historical uniforms and weapons of the castle guards.

Behind the Monastery of St George, tucked away down an alley leading off Jiřská Street is the **Golden Lane** (Zlatá ulička), a fairy-tale row of miniature houses. The higgledy-piggledy, one-room, originally 16th-century cottages evolved between the Romanesque and late Gothic fortifications, and the lane derives its name from the goldsmiths who once inhabited it. Kafka had a study at No 22 and various artists and craftsmen found this slummy part of the castle a stimulating place to work until 1951 when the authorities moved them out. The cramped spaces are now occupied by tiny shops and galleries. Some of the cottages are linked by a kind of common attic, the **Obranná chodba**, which runs across the top linking the **White Tower** (Bílá věž) with the **Daliborka Tower** at the ends of the Golden Lane. The White Tower served as a prison until the mid 18th century and there is not much to see there now. The Daliborka Tower built by Benedikt Ried in 1496 is the more interesting of the two and is famous for the story around its name. The first prisoner to be incarcerated in the tower, roughly two years after it was built, was Dalibor z Kozojed for the crime of giving refuge to peasants from a neighbouring estate who had revolted against the lord of the manor. With so much time on his hands he learnt to play the violin, his music attracting the attention of passers-by who passed food through the bars. It did not save him from execution but did inspire Bedřich Smetana's opera *Dalibor*.

Along Jiřská

The vast **Lobkovicz Palace** in Jiřská Lane houses a museum (*admission 40/20Kč, free first Wednesday in the month*) tracing the history of the region from the Celts to the mid 19th century. The principal reason for visiting used to be to admire the replica of the Czech crown jewels, which have unfortunately been removed, leaving an ageing, communist-era, somewhat disappointing exhibition which makes vague attempts to give class struggle and Czechoslovak unity a firm place in the history of the region. The highlight of the collection must be the impressive carving of the last supper from the Bethlehem Chapel. Head downhill and leave the castle via the Black Tower, guarded by more unflinching sentries, and you will arrive at the **Old Castle steps** (Staré zámecké schody) whose shallow, stall-lined gradient eventually descends you to Malostranská metro station or trams 18, 22 and 23 to the right bank.

The gardens

From the second courtyard pass between the Emperor's Stables and the Picture Gallery, cross the Prašný Bridge across the Stag Moat (Jelení příkop), and locate the entrance to the **Royal Gardens** (*Královská zahrada, open Apr–Oct*) on the right. Guarding the way in is the Lion Court (Lví dvůr) where Rudolf II kept wild animals including lions, tigers and bears in heated cages, now a restaurant. The 3.6ha of exquisite gardens were founded by Ferdinand I in 1534 on the site of a former vineyard, and extend the entire length of the north flank of the castle, separated from it by Jelení příkop. Work on the Renaissance gardens was begun by Italian architects and gardeners and was the first large-scale Renaissance project in the capital. The **Ball Game Court** (Míčovna) on the right as one strolls through the gardens was, as its name portrays, purpose built in 1567–69 for ball games such as six-a-side tennis and others we would not recognise today, but hugely popular among the nobility at the time. The Míčovna represented the pinnacle of Renaissance architecture, but was hit by a shell in 1945 and burnt to the ground. Restoration work took almost 30 years to complete. The interior is open for exhibitions and state functions only. At the far end of the Royal Gardens you will discover the **Summer Palace** (Královský letohrádek, sometimes mistakenly called Belvedere) begun in 1538 by Ferdinand I for his wife Anna Jagiellon, a kind of Prague Taj Mahal. Unfortunately neither of them saw it finished. The building must be one of the purest examples of Italian Renaissance north of the Alps. Next to the Summer Palace hums the **Singing Fountain** (Zpívající fontána) cast by Tomáš Jaroš in the mid 1560s and Prague's oldest water feature. See if you can hear the tones the fountain is said to produce when the water drips into the lower bowl.

Hradčanské náměstí

To the southeast of the castle spreads the cobbled expanse of Hradčanské náměstí with a small park gathered around a **plague column** erected on the site of services held during the plague of 1713–14. A more recent addition to the square is the bronze **Masaryk** looking back at the castle, put in place to mark the 150th anniversary of the birth of the Czechs' unerring first president in 2000.

Immediately to your right you cannot fail to notice the **Archbishop's Palace** (Arcibiskupský palác) which has served as the official residence of the archbishop from the 16th century to the present day. It was given to the archbishop in 1561 by Ferdinand I who acquired it half-finished after the great fire of 1541 which destroyed much of Hradčanské Square. A well-signposted entrance in the Archbishop's Palace leads visitors down a narrow lane to the **Šternberk Palace** (Šternberský palác) dating from 1698, housing the National Gallery's European Art from Antiquity to Baroque exhibition (*admission 150/70Kč*) including 16th–18th-century German and Austrian works on the ground floor, 14th–16th-century art from the Konopiště collection of Duke Ferdinand d'Este of Sarajevo fame on the first floor and 16th–18th-century works by Italian, French and Flemish painters on the second floor. Highlights are works by Dürer, Goya, Rubens, Van Dyck and Rembrandt. Across the square looms the ageing sgraffitoed hulk of the **Schwarzenberg Palace** (Švarcenberský palác) which stands on the site of three houses burnt down in 1541 and originally belonging to the Lobkovicz family. Until 2000 it housed the Military History Museum but is now closed for reconstruction. The National Gallery will move in when work finishes. Directly opposite Prague Castle stands the stern-looking, mainly bare sandstone façade of the late 17th-century **Toskánský Palace**, now part of the Foreign Ministry.

Loretánské náměstí

From Hradčanské náměstí there are two routes to Loretánské náměstí. Either follow Loretánská Street straight up or from the far right-hand corner take the more interesting winding streets of the so-called Nový Svět (New World) via the Military Church of John of Nepomuk. The irregular pretty houses of the Nový Svět contrast with Hradčany's palaces and give one an idea of how things looked before the blaze of 1541. Loretánské Square is dominated on the western side by Prague's longest Baroque structure (150m), the **Černín Palace** dating from 1669–82, built by the Černín family. Some of the High Baroque work was carried out by the prolific Santini. The Černíns followed the fashion among the nobility and left for Vienna in the late 18th century, abandoning the palace to be used as a hospital, a card factory and a hop store. It is now the Czech Foreign Ministry and most Czechs associate the palace with the death of post-war foreign minister, Jan Masaryk, the son of President Masaryk. On 10 March 1948, just two weeks after the communists came to power, Jan Masaryk was found dead after allegedly falling from his bathroom window. The communists claimed he had committed suicide, but despite having kept his post, the fervent democrat was not popular with Gottwald's new regime, and to this day there is speculation that he was murdered by the secret service. It remains one of the most famous unsolved cases of the communist era, and the truth may never be known.

Across the square visitors are welcomed by a statue-lined balustrade to the beautiful Baroque Loreta (*admission 90/70Kč, family ticket 160Kč, open Tue–Sun*) begun in 1626 and financed by the Lobkowicz family. Passing through the main gate under the clock tower visitors find themselves in a perfectly preserved Baroque courtyard dominated by the **Santa Casa**, the *raison d'être* of the Loreta. The original Santa Casa in Italy is the authentic Nazareth house of the Virgin Mary where she was visited by the Angel Gabriel. Miraculously transported by angels from the Holy Land to a laurel grove in Italy (hence the name Loreta) in 1291, it is an important place of pilgrimage. The pope probably had bits of the building transported to Italy in a more conventional way, but news of the miracle led to copies of the shrine being erected across Europe. Fifty were built in the Czech lands alone. The Prague Santa Casa has stucco reliefs of the house's miraculous journey, though the detail can be hard to pick out. The plain brick interior hides a traditional black limewood Madonna in a silver cage. The buildings enclosing the Santa Casa were added later and are the work of both Dientzenhofers. The magnificent Baroque **Church of the Nativity of Our Lord** (kostel Narození Páně) with its incredibly ornate Rococo interior stands immediately behind the Santa Casa with over-the-top dark marble and gold décor, extremely lifelike cherubs and crowds of angels and other figures bombarding the senses. Notice the organ at the rear laden with cherubs each playing a different musical instrument. From the church ascend to the first floor to the **Treasury** (Klenotnice) the highlight of which is the **Prague Sun** (Pražské slunce) from 1699, a solid silver monstrance encrusted with 6,222 diamonds from the wedding dress of Countess Kolovrat who bequeathed her fortune to the Loreta. The impressive hoard includes numerous other gem-adorned pieces. Outside on the hour, listen out for the 27 bells which chime out the hymn *We*

Greet Thee a Thousand Times. The large yellow building adjacent to the Loreta is a Capuchin Monastery.

Strahov Monastery

From Loretánské Square head west along Pohořelec, more of an oval square than a street, and access the Strahov Monastery (Strahovský klášter) through a well-signposted doorway on the left. One of the most significant religious sites in the country, founded in 1140 by Vladislav II and the Bishop of Olomouc, Jindřich Zdík, it was the first Premonstratensian monastery on Bohemian soil. Originally the largest Romanesque building in the capital it was rebuilt in the Gothic style after a fire in 1258. Having fallen into disuse during the Hussite wars the monastery rose from the ashes in the 16th and 17th centuries during which time the remains of St Norbert, the founder of the Premonstratensian order (named after the Premontré valley in France), were brought from Magdeburg. The 17th century also saw the monastery ransacked by marauding Protestant Swedish forces in the Thirty Years War. The monastery received a full Baroque makeover during the Counter-Reformation with numerous illustrious Baroque-era builders and sculptors such as Kilián Ignác Dientzenhofer and František Platzer leaving their mark. Thanks to its libraries it survived the abolition of the monasteries during the reign of Josef II in the late 18th century, but 1950 saw the monks evicted by the communist authorities. As so often in its almost 900-year history, this stubborn survivor performed another comeback in the early 1990s when the monks returned. The current abbot is the 70th to hold the post.

In front of the monastery the substantial Baroque **Church of the Assumption** (kostel Nanebevzetí Panny Marie) has a cavernous Baroque interior and is worth a peek inside. Originally a Romanesque basilica it is the final resting place of the monastery's two founders, though the exact whereabouts of their graves are not known. The first of two areas of the monastery open to the public is the **library** (*admission 80/50Kč*) consisting of two halls, the ornate **Philosophy Hall** (Filozofický sál) with its grand walnut bookcases and the smaller, plainer **Theology Hall** (Teologický sál) boasting stucco decoration and frescoes. A total of 200,000 books and manuscripts make this the largest monastery library in the Czech Republic (the second largest can be found at the Premonstratensian Monastery in Teplá in west Bohemia). Unlike in Teplá, visitors cannot actually get into the halls, and the admission fee seems slightly steep for ten minutes in a packed corridor lined with a curious assortment of stuffed fish, giant crabs and other objects not found in central Europe, fighting off fellow tourists to get a peek through a narrow doorway. Fewer visitors bother with the **Strahov Gallery** (Strahovská obrazárna, *admission 50/20Kč*) housing the monastery's art collection, reassembled in the early 1990s after being broken up by the authorities 50 years earlier. Some of the works on display originate from the collection of Rudolf II, and there are also paintings by Baroque masters Brandl and Škréta. Below the monastery you will find the **Strahov Gardens** which provide a sweeping view of the valley between the Petřín Hill and Prague Castle.

Malá Strana

Squeezed between the Vltava, Petřín Hill and the Prague Castle promontory, Malá Strana (the name literally means 'small side' and is sometimes translated as Lesser Town or Quarter) is less than 1km² of picturesque, narrow, sloping streets, secluded yards and tranquil parks little changed since the 18th century. Founded by Přemysl Otakar II in 1257 and until 1348 called the New Town (as opposed to the Old Town across the river), there had been a settlement here since the 9th century. The district's appearance was greatly influenced by the fire of 1541 which cleared the way for many of the palaces we see today. After the Battle of the White Mountain and the exile of much of the Protestant nobility, Malá Strana was settled by rich Catholics who added many Baroque façades. Numerous foreign embassies now occupy these palaces making Malá Strana the city's unofficial diplomatic district.

The focal point of Malá Strana is **Malostranské Square** (Malostranské náměstí), the district's main marketplace which has had several names over the centuries, finishing up with its current title in 1869. The square boasts one palace next to another, yet some Gothic houses with typical arcading but neo-Classical façades have survived along the south side. This swathe of old cobbles is cut in two by Malá Strana's centrepiece and one of Europe's finest Baroque churches, the **Church of St Nicholas** (Chrám sv Mikuláše, *admission 50/25Kč, children 10Kč*) begun in 1704. The simplicity of the sparklingly clean, gold and sandstone exterior, and the tower and green dome do nothing to prepare the visitor for the spectacular, almost overwhelming Baroque interior. The place is a riot of cherubs, angels, gilding, marble, paintings, frescoes and church decoration the eye cannot quite take in all at once. The pulpit drips with gilt figures, an army of angels clamber over the organ, four Church Fathers look sternly down at the visitor and the ceiling is covered in a fresco by Johann Luis Kracker depicting the life of St Nicholas (look out for him as Father Christmas). No surface is left unadorned and the list of its creators reads like a roll-call of the best of Baroque top ten. The Dientzenhofers, the builder Anselmo Lurago, painters Škréta and Palko, and the sculptor Platzer all did their bit to fashion this Baroque masterpiece. The elder Dientzenhofer, Kryštof, began construction, but on his death in 1722 his son, Kilián Ignác, and Lurago took over. Škréta supplied paintings which now hang upstairs in the church and Palko adorned the dome with his work. Platzer is responsible for the Church Fathers and the statue of St Nicholas above the altar. This was all for the benefit of the Jesuits who were subsequently told their time was up by Maria Theresa in 1773, just 20 years after the church's completion.

The church tower (*admission 50/40Kč, Apr–Oct*) has a story all of its own. At 70m high it was Prague's last fire watchtower. From the early 1950s until 1989 it served as a different kind of lookout point, this time for the secret police who would spy on Western embassies from above. Climb the 299 steps to the viewing platform (65m) for views over the red-tiled roofs of Malá Strana.

From the lower end of Malostranské náměstí take Tomášská to the left to reach the intimate **Valdštejnské náměstí**, dominated across one whole side by the Baroque **Valdštejnský Palace**, Prague's largest, built in 1624–30 by one of the most powerful nobles of the post White Mountain era and general of the imperial forces in the Thirty Years War, Albrecht von Wallenstein. The ambitious noble grew rich on property confiscated from Protestant nobles and on just such a plot he built his main residence. Since 1945 the palace has been state-owned and since 1996 has served as the upper house of the Czech parliament, the Senate. A part of the exquisite interior is open to the public (*admission free, open Sat and Sun only*) with excellent English explanations in every room.

Climbing steeply west from Malostranské Square is **Nerudova Street**, the main tourist thoroughfare up to the castle. At first sight it appears to be another street lined with the usual souvenir shops and tourist-trap restaurants, but look closer and you will discover that many of the buildings have preserved their original Baroque façades, windows and huge barn doors plus their original house

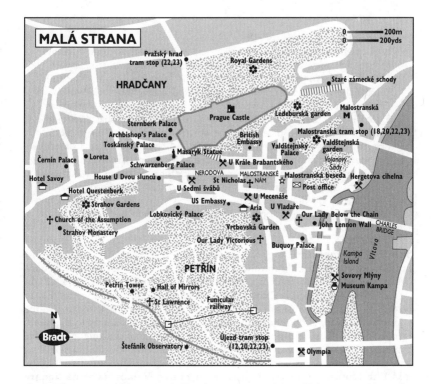

MALÁ STRANA

HRADČANY

Pražský hrad tram stop (22,23)

Royal Gardens

0 ——— 200m
0 ——— 200yds

Staré zámecké schody

Sternberk Palace

Prague Castle

Ledeburská garden

Malostranská
M

Archbishop's Palace

Toskánský Palace

British Embassy

Malostranská tram stop (18,20,22,23)

Valdštejnský Palace

Valdštejnská garden

Černín Palace
Loreta

Masaryk Statue

Schwarzenberg Palace

U Krále Brabantského

Vojanovy Sady

Hotel Savoy

House U Dvou slunců

NERODOVA
St Nicholas NÁM

MALOSTRANSKÉ
Malostranská beseda

Hergetova cihelna

Hotel Questenberk

U Sedmi švábů

Post office

Strahov Gardens

US Embassy

U Mecenáše

Church of the Assumption

Lobkovický Palace

Aria
U Vladaře

Our Lady Below the Chain

John Lennon Wall

CHARLES BRIDGE

Strahov Monastery

Vrtbovská Garden

Our Lady Victorious

Buquoy Palace

Kampa Island

Vltava

PETŘÍN

Petřín Tower
Hall of Mirrors

St Lawrence

Funicular railway

Sovovy Mlýny
Museum Kampa

N

Bradt

Štefánik Observatory

Újezd tram stop (12,20,22,23)

Olympia

signs. The street itself is named after the most prominent 19th-century journalist and writer Jan Neruda, born in 1834 in the house **U Dvou slunců** (the two suns) right at the top on the left. He also lived for ten years (1863–73) across the street at No 44, now the aptly named Hotel Neruda. His best-known work is the *Povídky malostranské* (Tales from Malá Strana) which paints a realistic picture of the life of Malá Strana's ordinary folk in the mid 19th century. Leave Nerodova along any street running south and enter a different world of secluded, narrow, winding streets with attractive houses and secluded courtyards such as Jánská and Šporkova. Running parallel to Nerodova is Vlašská on which towers the grand **Lobkovický Palace**, now the German embassy. Vlašská then runs up to Petřín and in the other direction down to the Tržiště where the American embassy is housed in the slightly less elaborate **Schönbornský Palace**. Several narrow alleyways link Tržiště back to Malostranské Square or follow it down to Karmelitská to the **Church of Our Lady Victorious** (Kostel Panny Marie Vítězné) built by German Lutherans in 1611 and given to the Carmelites by Ferdinand II in 1624. The reason for visiting this somewhat unremarkable church is the *Pražské Jezulátko* or, as it is sometimes known, the **Bambino di Praga**, a miracle-working 45cm wax effigy of Jesus as a three year old brought from Spain in 1628, and kept in an ornate glass box on the second altar to the right as you enter. The museum upstairs exhibits some of the *Jezulátko*'s 60 ornate little robes, some dating back to the 18th century and one sewn by Empress Maria Theresa herself. The church is a popular place of pilgrimage and is usually heaving with Italian and Spanish schoolchildren. The whole place plus the gift shop with its 30,000Kč gold replicas of the Bambino may perhaps leave non-pilgrims rather bewildered.

THE DIENTZENHOFERS

It is hard to imagine Czech towns and villages without the instantly recognisable fingerprint of Baroque architecture, the greatest exponents of which were the father-and-son duo of Christoph (Kryštof) Dientzenhofer (1655–1722) and Kilián Ignác Dientzenhofer (1689–1751). Christoph arrived in Prague from Bavaria in the 1780s, initially working as a fort builder before turning his hand to churches, monasteries and houses. Some of his most admired structures are the Church of St Margaret at Břevnov and the Church of St Nicholas in Malá Strana almost finished by his son Kilián Ignác. Dientzenhofer junior is perhaps better known and the more prolific, leaving an indelible mark on townscapes across the country. Regarded as the architect of the Czech Baroque style, every one of his buildings is different and his style influenced architects across Europe. Strangely enough he never grew rich from his work.

South of Karmelitská

From busy Karmelitská cut down Prokopská to quiet **Maltézské Square** (Maltézské náměstí) to find the **Church of Our Lady Below the Chain** (kostel Panny Maria pod řetězem). Dating from 1169 and the first institution to belong to the Knights of the Maltese Cross, its former title used to be the Church of St Mary at the End of the Bridge thanks to its proximity to the Judith Bridge and later Charles Bridge, and because of the role of the knights as bridge guardians. A Gothic reconstruction was interrupted by the Hussite wars, leaving only the towers and the chancel complete. Carlo Lugano Baroque-ified it in the mid 17th century. From the church turn right into **Velkopřevorské Square** (Velkopřevorské náměstí), another pleasingly tranquil piazza with the Rococo **Buquoy Palace** on the right, now serving as the French embassy. This square has not always been so peaceful, as the **John Lennon Wall** will testify. The graffiti-covered wall on the left is not originally the work of Prague's incessant and enraging graffiti-crazed kids (Prague has more graffiti than any city I have ever seen). Following the former Beatle's death in 1980 young people, for whom Lennon was a symbol of peace and freedom, began to gather at a graffiti image of him on the wall every year on 8 December to mark the day he was murdered. The authorities painted over the graffiti and raided the meetings, but people kept coming. From a real place of protest where ideas, philosophy and the odd LP were exchanged, the wall has become a tourist attraction daubed in 'Luigi or Carlos woz 'ere' in 20 languages and repulsive tags. A bespectacled John is just visible through the layers of tourist scrawl and the 8 December anniversary is still observed.

From Velkopřevorské Square cross the footbridge next to the large mill wheel on to **Kampa Island**, the largest of the city's islands, and divided from Malá Strana by the Čertovka Stream, altered over the centuries to drive the islands' many erstwhile mill wheels. This area is occasionally dubbed the 'Prague Venice' though usually only by tour companies. The island itself is divided into the Na Kampě Square in the shadow of Charles Bridge and the park to the south. The pleasant, tree-lined, oval square, where shops, restaurants and the odd embassy face each other across the cobbles, is accessible via steps from the bridge. The sleepy parkland to the south is one of the many tranquil spots on this side of the Vltava and a great place for urban picnicking and soaking in the views of the Old Town across the water. It is also the site of the **Museum Kampa** (*admission*

120/60Kč), not a museum but a modern art gallery housing the private collection of the Mládek family (*www.museumkampa.cz*).

The gardens of Malá Strana

One of the highlights of Malá Strana is its tranquil, secluded gardens, refuges of peace and quiet from the bustling city all around. In cramped Malá Strana, added to by every generation, it is surprising these open green spaces have survived. The terraced Ledeburská Garden (*admission 69/39Kč*) is located just off Valdštejnská Street, and is made up of various smaller gardens linked together and extending up to the castle. The gardens are a pleasing system of steps and terraces, dotted with statues and pavilions and fun to explore. Prague's oldest park is **Vojanovy sady**, just off nearby U Lužického semináře Street. Here the sounds of the city fade away behind the walls of this English-style park with its mature trees, rows of white benches and roaming peacocks. It is the ideal place to enjoy a picnic or a long warm afternoon in the company of a good book. Unquestionably the capital's grandest green spot is the **Valdštejnská Garden** (*admission free*) off Letenská Street. The geometrically perfect early Baroque gardens were created at the same time as the palace by Albrecht von Wallenstein in 1623–30, and feature a huge *sala terrena*, a strange 'dripstone wall' (*krápníková stěna*) and a large false lake. The whole immaculately pruned space is peppered with stone benches and statues among which struts the odd peacock, proudly ignoring the attentions of the tourists. The last of Malá Strana's exquisite green spaces is the **Vrtbovská Garden** (*admission 40/25Kč, open Apr–Oct*) just off busy Karmelitská Street. These stylish, immaculate Italian gardens were created in 1715–20, and are UNESCO listed.

Petřín

Above Malá Strana looms the wooded **Petřín Hill**, a traditional spot for lovers, dog walkers and those escaping the crowded streets below. You can walk to the cluster of tourist sights at the top, but the lazy way to reach them is by **funicular railway**, part of the Prague transport system, which leaves Újezd station every 15 minutes taking roughly five minutes to labour up the side of the hill. The main pull is the 60m-high miniature Eiffel Tower, the **Petřín Tower** (Petřínská rozhledna, *admission 50/40Kč*), a must for all visitors to the city. Inspired by the Eiffel Tower during the 1889 World Exhibition in Paris, members of the Czech hiking and walking club (*Klub českých turistů*), decided to build their own version. The tower, which is one-fifth the size of its more illustrious counterpart in Paris, was erected in a mere six months and opened in August 1891. From 1953 until the opening of the Žižkov Tower, Petřín served as the city's TV mast. From the ticket office you will be shown to the 299 steps to the top (or you can take the lift). The view from the top is incredible and even on a misty day virtually all the city's historical sights can be picked out.

A few strides to the right of the tower stands the curious little **Hall of Mirrors** (Bludiště, *admission 50/40Kč*), a copy of the former Gothic Špička gate at Vyšehrad. Inside you will find the hall of mirrors with 31 ordinary and 14 distorting mirrors though after all that beer and *knedlíky* just the non-distorting mirrors may have you in stitches. There is also an 80m² panorama of the inhabitants of Prague fending off the Swedes on Charles Bridge in 1648. Opposite the Hall of Mirrors stands the much-ignored Baroque **Church of St Lawrence** (Chrám sv Vavřince). Running across Petřín Hill one cannot fail to notice the crenellations of the 8m-high **Hunger Wall** (Hladová zeď) which dates from the reign of Charles IV, built to protect Malá Strana from potential

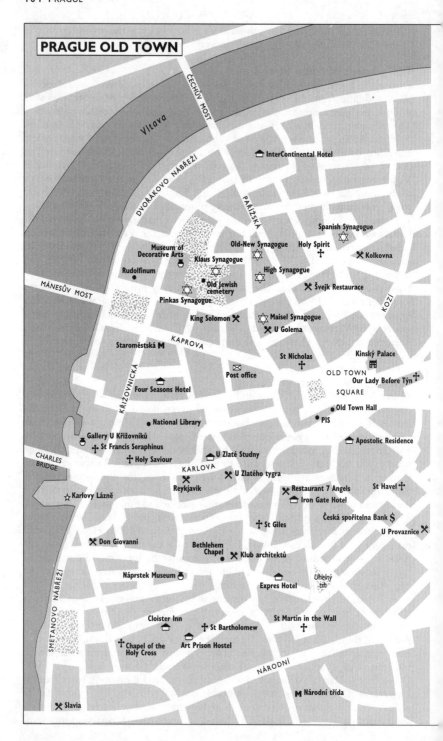

PRAGUE OLD TOWN

Vltava

ČECHŮV MOST

DVOŘÁKOVO NÁBŘEŽÍ

PAŘÍŽSKÁ

InterContinental Hotel

Spanish Synagogue

Old-New Synagogue   Holy Spirit

Museum of
Decorative Arts   Kolkovna

Klaus Synagogue

Rudolfinum   High Synagogue

MÁNESŮV MOST   Old Jewish
cemetery   Švejk Restaurace

Pinkas Synagogue

King Solomon   Maisel Synagogue

U Golema

KOZÍ

KAPROVA

Staroměstská M

Kinský Palace

St Nicholas

KŘIŽOVNICKÁ

Post office   OLD TOWN
Our Lady Before Týn

Four Seasons Hotel   SQUARE

National Library   Old Town Hall

PIS

Gallery U Křižovníků   Apostolic Residence

St Francis Seraphinus

CHARLES
BRIDGE   Holy Saviour   U Zlaté Studny

KARLOVA

U Zlatého tygra

Reykjavik   Restaurant 7 Angels   St Havel

Karlovy Lázně   Iron Gate Hotel

Česká spořitelna Bank $

St Giles   U Provaznice

Don Giovanni
Bethlehem
Chapel   Klub architektů

Náprstek Museum   Uhelný
trh

Expres Hotel

SMETANOVO NÁBŘEŽÍ

Cloister Inn   St Bartholomew   St Martin in the Wall

Chapel of the   Art Prison Hostel
Holy Cross

NÁRODNÍ

Slavia   M Národní třída

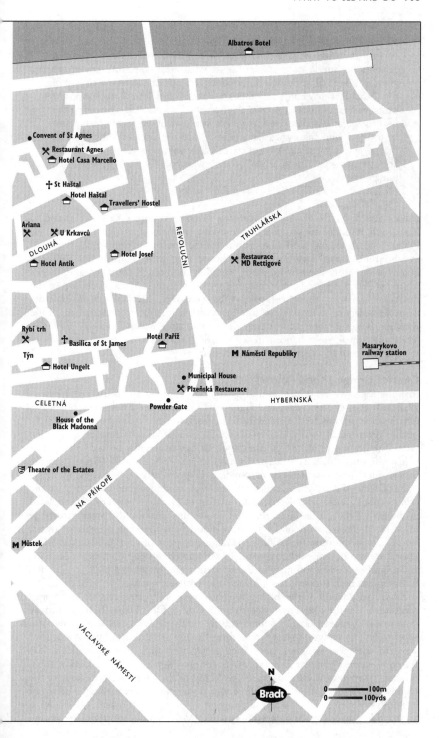

Albatros Botel

Convent of St Agnes
Restaurant Agnes
Hotel Casa Marcello

St Haštal
Hotel Haštal
Travellers' Hostel

Ariana
U Krkavců
DLOUHÁ
Hotel Antik
Hotel Josef

REVOLUČNÍ

TRUHLÁŘSKÁ

Restaurace
MD Rettigové

Rybí trh
Basilica of St James
Hotel Paříž

Týn
Hotel Ungelt

Náměstí Republiky

Masarykovo
railway station

Municipal House
Plzeňská Restaurace

CELETNÁ
HYBERNSKÁ

Powder Gate
House of the
Black Madonna

Theatre of the Estates

NA PŘÍKOPĚ

Můstek

VÁCLAVSKÉ NÁMĚSTÍ

N

Bradt

0 ——— 100m
0 ——— 100yds

BLUE DANUBE IN GOLDEN PRAGUE?

Apart from some misguided individuals who may think the Czech Republic borders on Siberia, or is part of Russia, what must constitute one of the greatest pieces of ignorance about central Europe concerns the course of the Danube. It may come as a shock to many, but neither Prague, nor any other part of the Czech Republic lies on the Danube. It is astounding the percentage of even seasoned travellers who think it does, and the number of tourists who think they have peered into the Danube from Charles Bridge, or the sheer numbers of cruise passengers who were disappointed at not viewing the Czech capital on their way from Germany to Vienna or Budapest!

enemy attack. Myths abound concerning its construction. Charles IV is said to have built it partly to provide employment (ergo food, hence the name) to Prague's destitute, and worked incognito on the site several hours a day disguised in labourer's attire. Starvation actually broke out during construction, and the image of the Holy Roman Emperor, raised at the French court, lugging bits of stone up Petřín is pure fantasy, but one which has stuck. Back at the top of the funicular railway the **Štefánik Observatory** (Štefánikova hvězdárna, *www.observatory.cz, admission 30/20Kč*) is worth half an hour for stargazing if the weather is good. The observatory is named after Milan Rastislav Štefánik, Masaryk's Slovak right-hand man who made his name as an astronomer before turning his hand to political and military matters.

Charles Bridge (Karlův most)

Imagine there were no bridges uniting the two banks of the broad river Vltava. That was the state of affairs in Prague in 1342 after the forerunner of today's Charles Bridge, the Judith Bridge (Juditin most), was demolished by ice. At 05.31 on the morning of 9 July 1357, Charles IV himself laid the first stone in what would be known until 1870 as the Stone Bridge (Kamenný most); 1357 (year), 9 (day), 7 (month), 5.31 (time) creating the palindrome 1357-9-7531, was the first magical step on the way to building Prague's most enchanting medieval sight. Charles IV's architect, Petr Parléř, was commissioned to construct the 0.5km-long, almost 10m-wide sandstone feat of Gothic engineering, completed in the early 1400s. It has since survived floods, the Hussites, the Swedish barrage in 1648, the revolution of 1848, more floods, the grinding wheels of trams, lorries, cars, communism, pollution, millions of pairs of tourists' feet and more floods to become one of the most celebrated and cherished sights in the country, and a symbol of the continuity of Czech identity and statehood itself. Legend has it that its strength is down to eggs mixed in with the mortar.

Slightly crooked Charles Bridge weighs down on 16 irregular arches to span the Vltava. On the Old Town side rises the Gothic **Old Town Bridge Tower** (Staroměstská mostecká věž), which can be climbed (*daily, year round, admission 40/30Kč*). The views of Malá Strana from the top are stunning, and it is a great place to take photos. The bridge itself is adorned with 30 soot-black, mostly Baroque statues. The first, the statue of St John of Nepomuk, was added in 1683, the last, Cyril and Methodius, in 1938. Many of the originals, now kept in the Lapidarium of the National Museum and in Vyšehrad's casemates, were damaged in floods or worn away by wind and rain, and replaced with copies. On the Malá Strana side the bridge ends in **two towers** (Malostranské mostecké věže), the higher of which is also open to the public (*admission 50/40Kč, open daily Apr–Nov*). The shorter tower stood guard over the original Judith Bridge.

Today's pedestrianised bridge is a sea of tourists, tiny stalls selling various trinkets, artwork, souvenirs and the like, buskers, hawkers, pickpockets and the odd Czech using the bridge for the purpose it was built for over 600 years ago. Come shortly after sunrise, at night or at quieter times when the bridge is covered in a fresh layer of snow to capture the magic of the best-known legacy of Prague's golden era.

The Old Town and Josefov

The Staré město or Old Town is an enchanting web of medieval streets and alleyways defined by Národní, Na příkopě and Revoluční streets, the line of the former town walls. All roads in the Old Town lead to the Old Town Square, Prague's true heart, the oldest square in town and one of the great European medieval marketplaces.

A settlement for merchants and craftsmen from the 10th century, the Old Town was granted town status in the 13th century by Wenceslas I permitting it to erect town walls and oversee its own administration. It did not fare badly under Charles IV either, gaining Charles Bridge and the university which still retains many of its departments in this part of town. The Old Town saw less development than Malá Strana and Hradčany after the Thirty Years War, as the 1541 fire which opened up land on the left bank, did not touch the Old Town, leaving the medieval street layout virtually intact. The Jewish Quarter was slum cleared in the late 19th century at the same time as the Old Town Square was given a facelift and newly created Pařížská Street was driven straight through Josefov to the Vltava.

Despite its mainly Baroque appearance, the original Gothic houses remained buried underneath when the ground level was raised to stop the Vltava spilling its muddy waters into the town. The new buildings were simply added on top from the new street level. This has created hundreds of Gothic cellars, some of which are used today as restaurants and bars. The extent of this ground raising can be seen on the banks of the Vltava which rise to almost 10m in some places.

The Old Town is a Mecca for tourists who clog its narrow lanes and swarm disorientated across the Old Town Square which draws modern-day visitors as it once drew merchants and market-goers. The square is, nonetheless, a pleasant place to sit in an open-air café, browse Christmas and Easter markets, watch the astronomical clock chime the hour and soak up the atmosphere of the very heart of the medieval city.

Old Town Square

The Old Town Square has been a stage for numerous events in the country's history. From the execution of the Hussite preacher Jan Želivský to the first communist president Klement Gottwald proclaiming communist rule, the square has witnessed countless events which have fundamentally changed the course of Czech history. However, recently the Czechs have gathered here to celebrate their sporting successes, especially in ice hockey. Political demonstrations have now shifted to the larger Wenceslas Square.

Almost 100 years old but the most recent addition to the square is the Art Nouveau **Monument to Jan Hus** by Ladislav Šaloun, unveiled in 1915 to mark the 500th anniversary of Hus's death. Like other similar monuments of this period, the stone and greening bronze is not aesthetically pleasing, and does not fit well into the general background of the square. However, the Czechs lend

PRAGUE'S HOUSE SYMBOLS

Before houses had numbers, the inhabitants of Prague needed some way of naming them. Thus house symbols came into existence, the principle being like that of pub names in Britain. Nobody really knows why certain houses have certain symbols. Perhaps in some cases they reflect the original use of the premises, shoes for example for a cobbler or candles for a chandler. Stone clocks and white Indians are harder to explain. It is known, however, that a snake represented a pharmacy as it does today.

Prague's townsfolk began to differentiate their houses in this way at the beginning of the 15th century. Sometimes the signs can be found more than once due to Prague originally being made up of four separate towns: the Old Town, the New Town, Hradčany and Malá Strana. Animals feature heavily in the signs: lions, donkeys, camels, tigers, foxes, bears, swallows, carp, emus and peacocks all make an appearance. Perhaps more closely linked to the original use of the building are horseshoes, violins, keys, bells and grapes. We can only wonder what went on in houses with symbols such as a fig leaf, a donkey in the cradle or seven deadly sins.

great patriotic significance to the monument, which was draped in a black shroud during the 1968 Warsaw Pact invasion.

The Old Town came into existence in the early 13th century, but the town councillors had to wait another 100 years to acquire a town hall. King John of Luxembourg granted them the right to build the **Old Town Hall** (Staroměstská radnice, *admission 50/40Kč, open daily, year round*) in 1338. Over the next century the council gradually bought up the adjacent houses until they reached the Dům U Minuty on the corner which still has a proud sgraffito façade, hence the jumble of house fronts but a united interior behind them. The houses purchased behind the tower were demolished in the early 19th century and from 1838 to 1848 a neo-Gothic wing appeared. Nothing remains of the 19th-century additions, a casualty of the Prague uprising when it came under tank fire on the last day of World War II. The neo-Gothic arches which end in mid air on the north side are testament to the events of that day. The entrance to the town hall is through the pink façade occupied by the Prague Information Service (PIS) Information Centre. There is a rather long and uninspiring tour of the maze of Gothic and Romanesque cellars and representative halls of the town hall, so instead head straight for the lift to the top of the tower. The views may not be as spectacular as from Petřín or the Žižkov Tower, but give a more intimate perspective of the Old Town. The best views of the Týn church and down into the secluded terraces and courtyards of the Old Town can be had from the tower's sometimes rather crowded viewing platform. Come on a spring or summer Saturday and you may witness a wedding party in and around the building. This is a favourite venue for tying the knot, especially among foreign grooms and Czech brides.

The crowds that gather in anticipation in front of the Old Town Hall just before the hour have come to witness the ornate *orloj* (astronomical clock) in action on the south-facing side of the tower, crafted in 1410 by Mikuláš z Kadaně and perfected by Hanuš z Růže in the late 15th century. According to popular fable, Hanuš was the original creator, subsequently blinded by the Prague councillors to prevent him from repeating the feat in another city. Hanuš's revenge was to bring the clock to a standstill. The mechanism did indeed grind to a halt in 1865 and the *orloj* was threatened with removal until a Prague clockmaker, Ludvík Hainz, managed to repair and save it from the scrapheap. Just before the hour, the complex mechanism, still incorporating some of the original components, sets in motion an assortment of figures. A skeleton representing death pulls a cord, a bell rings, and two small doors above the astronomical dial open to allow a parade of 12 apostles to jerkily greet the expectant crowds, six on each side. Next to the dial a Turk shakes his head, a miser (originally a Jewish moneylender) nods and shakes his stick, a figure representing Vanity glances into a mirror, a cock crows and the bell rings out to mark the hour. The Turk, the Jew, vanity and death represent the main medieval threats to the city, while the motionless figures next to the lower dial are a chronicler, an angel, an astronomer and a philosopher. The 1945 fire destroyed all the figures, though thankfully the early Baroque originals are kept in the Museum of the City of Prague, as is the original lower disc, painted by Josef Mánes in 1865 with Czech name days around the perimeter (Czechs have birthdays and name days). Unlike in Olomouc the devastated *orloj* was not given a post-war proletariat makeover and the figures we see today were carved in 1948.

Plaques on the eastern face of the tower recall two significant events in Czech history. The large plaque is a roll-call of the 27 Czech Protestant nobles beheaded following the Battle of the White Mountain in 1621. The white crosses on the ground mark the spot where the executions took place. The smaller plaque commemorates the Red Army and Czechoslovak victory at the Dukla Pass in Slovakia.

Dominating the square's northwest corner is the elegant Baroque façade of the **Church of St Nicholas** (Chrám sv Mikuláše), not to be confused with its big brother and namesake across the Vltava. The two churches share a common architect, Kilián Ignác Dientzenhofer, who built it for the Benedictines on the site of an earlier Gothic structure. The interior is disappointingly plain having lost many of its treasures when used as a store in the 19th century and does not live up to its exterior. It was hidden from the square until 1945 by the north wing of the town hall. Immediately to the left of the church is the site of the house where Franz Kafka was born in 1883. The current building dates from 1902 and houses the touristy Franz Kafka Museum.

The eastern flank of the square is dominated by two resplendent buildings. The Gothic **Church of Our Lady Before Týn** is accessed via a narrow passageway by the Caffé Italia. A church has stood on this site since the 11th century, but the present building dates from the mid 14th century, and bears the hallmarks of Petr Parléř, especially the northern portal (*in Týnská Street*) with reliefs depicting the Crucifixion. Once a breeding ground of Hussite ideas, the majestic 80m-high double spires are now one of the most recognisable features of the Prague skyline. The church would be an even more impressive sight were it not partially obscured by houses, and can only be fully appreciated from a distance. The interior is a riot of black and gold Baroque cluttering the simple Gothic design. You will also find paintings by Karel Škréta, the tomb of Rudolf II's Danish court astronomer Tycho de Brahe and the oldest organ in Prague dating from 1673. Notice the small blue plaque on a house opposite in narrow, stall-lined Týnská Street, indicating the birthplace of Karel Škréta.

The **Kinský Palace**, completed in 1765 and bought by the Kinský family in 1768, possesses Prague's finest Rococo façade and is the work of Kilián Ignác Dientzenhofer and his son-in-law Anselmo Lurago. Put to many uses over the centuries (Kafka went to school there and first communist president Klement Gottwald launched 40 years of totalitarian rule from the balcony in 1948) it now serves as the Old Town Square branch of the National Gallery specialising in

---

KAREL ŠKRÉTA (1610–74)

The prized possession of many churches and monasteries across the Czech Republic is a painting by Karel Škréta, the greatest Czech painter of the Baroque period. Born in Prague in the shadow of the Týn church, he was trained by Rudolf II's artists but as a Protestant was forced to flee abroad in 1628. After almost a decade in Italy he converted to Catholicism, allowing him to return home in 1638 after which he painted prolifically. His dark, powerful works influenced generations of Czech painters and can be admired in countless places around the country, most notably the Church of St Nicholas in Malá Strana.

---

landscapes in Czech art from the 17th–20th centuries. Look out for paintings by Josef Mánes, Toyen, Lada and Havel's green head surrounded by mushrooms, a curious work by National Gallery director Milan Knížák. Behind the church the picturesque cobbled Ungelt or Týn courtyard, originally a kind of fort where merchants stayed and kept their goods safe, opens out before ending in a low gateway leading to the Gothic, triple-nave **Basilica of St James** (bazilika sv Jakuba). Established next to a Minorite monastery in 1232, it was rebuilt during the reign of the Luxemburg kings in the 14th century, and was the longest church in Prague at the time. The swirling stucco work on the façade is the work of Italian Ottavio Mosto and dates from the early 18th century as does the imposing Baroque interior. The gruesome, shrivelled human arm is that of a robber who tried to steal some pearls from the statue of the Virgin. The statue is said to have caught him by his hand and held him there until he was apprehended. His arm was lopped off and strung up as a warning to others with similar intents.

West of the Old Town Square

Let yourself be swept along with the hordes of tourists, your feet hardly touching the ground, southwest out of the Old Town Square across Malé Square and into narrow, zigzagging **Karlova Street**, unquestionably Prague's busiest, tackiest, most touristy thoroughfare, a great place for getting that Borussia Dortmund away strip or a fake Russian Army cap made in China, but not so good for getting from A to B. As you near Charles Bridge the secluded **Klementinum** complex hides off to the right. The Jesuits began construction in 1578 on the Renaissance **Church of the Holy Saviour** which now dominates the end of Karlova and Křižovnické Square, and from 1653 to 1727 gradually built up the area north of Charles Bridge. This vast complex of Jesuit college buildings, chapels and churches later became part of the university after the suppression of the order in 1773. The students moved out during the First Republic, and it now houses the **National Library**, the largest in the Czech Republic, the Library of the Technical University and the Slavonic Library. The Klementinum **meteorological observatory** boasts a world record as the weather has been monitored here uninterrupted since 1775, longer than anywhere else. At the end of Karlova cross traffic-choked Křižovnická Street on to Křižovnické Square, which generally goes unnoticed by tourists as they cross on to or off Charles Bridge. Here you will find the Baroque **Church of St Francis Seraphinus**, established by the Knights of the Cross with a Red Star, guardians of the Judith Bridge, the precursor to Charles Bridge. Next door is the **Galerie U Křižovníků** (*www.guk-prague.cz, admission 120/70Kč*) housing generally intriguing temporary exhibitions and bits of the original Judith Bridge. Outside the gallery towers the neo-Gothic statue of Charles IV, leaning cheerfully on his sword. It was erected in 1848 to mark the 500th anniversary of the founding of the university but was unveiled in 1849 because of the revolutionary events of the previous year when the statue had to be boarded up to protect it from the fighting.

North of the Old Town Square

Pařížská Street, running dead straight north out of the square to the Vltava, was created when the Jewish Quarter was cleared in the late 19th century. Lined with tall early 20th-century Art Nouveau tenements and shady trees lending it a Parisian air, this is Prague's most stylish shopping avenue with exclusive brand names vying for the attention of passers-by. The surrounding streets are very much in the same style, interrupted by pretty little squares where streets converge. At one such place east of Pařížská you will find the Gothic, single-nave **Church of the Holy Spirit** (kostel sv Ducha) opposite the Spanish Synagogue. The original structure dates from 1346, and used to occupy a narrow sliver of Christian territory which separated Prague's two Jewish communities. The freshly renovated **Church of St Haštal** (kostel sv Haštala) can be found on tranquil, almost rural Haštalské Square further east. A Gothic church was built here on the foundations of its Romanesque predecessor, and contains 14th-century murals. Head out of the square north down cobbled Anežská to the **Convent of St Agnes** (Anežský klášter), Prague's oldest Gothic building founded in 1231. It bears the name of his sister Anežka Přemyslovna, who after several attempts to marry her off to various European nobles, entered the Order of the Poor Clares becoming the first abbess of the new convent built for her by her brother, Václav I. The reward for giving up a life of luxury at Prague Castle to live as a poor nun in a damp and draughty convent by the river was her canonisation in November 1989. St Agnes is buried in the convent church along with Václav I and Kunhuta, the second wife of King Přemysl Otakar II. The convent itself bit the dust under Emperor Joseph II's reforms of 1782, lying derelict for almost two centuries before undergoing extensive restoration in the 1980s. The low-lying complex was completely submerged in the floods of August 2002 and the high-water mark is still clearly visible on the interior bare red brick and stone walls. A large portion now fittingly houses the National Gallery's large collection of medieval art including Madonnas, altarpieces and paintings from churches and monasteries across the Czech lands. Some of Master Theodoricus's decorative panel paintings from the Chapel of the Holy Cross at Karlštejn are on display, as well as altarpieces from Třeboň and Vyšší Brod. Allow a good one to two hours to explore the whole convent.

Josefov – the synagogues and Old Jewish Cemetery

The tangle of streets north of the Old Town Square is known as Josefov, Prague's Jewish Quarter. A handful of synagogues, a cemetery and a town hall are all that remain of a once thriving Jewish community, which existed here from the 12th century (Jews originally settled in Malá Strana at least 200 years earlier). In the late 19th century the tight web of dark streets, alleyways, hovels, shops and religious buildings was demolished to make way for the four- and five-storey Art Nouveau tenements intended to lend Prague a more Parisian feel. To a certain extent, this was achieved, but in so doing, the Prague municipal authorities wiped out a community and an integral part of life in the city for 1,000 years. Most of the few thousand Jews who did remain in Josefov did not survive the

Holocaust, and only a handful lived here during the communist decades. Since 1989, there has been a mini-renaissance, though in all probability the number of Jews in Prague today does not exceed 2,000.

Prague's Jewish heritage is one of the highlights of any visit to Prague and should be on every visitor's itinerary. Five synagogues and the Old Jewish Cemetery are open to the public. All except the Staronová synagoga (Old–New Synagogue) are in the care of the Jewish Museum (*www.jewishmuseum.cz*) and a 300/200Kč ticket covers everything. A separate 200/140Kč ticket must be bought at the Old–New Synagogue. Men are supplied with a blue paper *kippa* or skullcap to be worn in most places.

Prague's Jewish Museum holds one of the largest collections of Jewish art, religious items, documents and everyday objects in the world. Geographically limited to Bohemia and Moravia, the collection provides an undiluted picture of all aspects of the life of a vanished community. The **Maisel Synagogue** (Maiselova synagoga) in Maiselova Street, built in 1590–92 as the private place of worship for the Jewish mayor Mordechai Maisel, should be your starting point. There are displays on the Jews in the medieval Czech state and their fate up until 1780. The original synagogue endured a neo-Gothic overhaul in 1895–1905 explaining its bare whitewashed interior and façade. The exhibition continues a couple of streets east at the most elaborate of the five buildings, the **Spanish Synagogue** (Španělská synagoga) built in 1868 and sporting a peaches-and-cream façade. The frankly breathtaking, intricately decorated interior packed with symmetrical patterns in dull shades of gold, red, green and brown along with the stained-glass windows, create a dim mysterious setting. The clearance of the ghetto, Jewish writers (including Kafka), artists, the Holocaust, ceremonial silverware and Jews in post-war Czechoslovakia are the subjects of the glass exhibition cases here, located on two floors. Next on your itinerary should be the **Pinkas Synagogue** (Pinkasova synagoga) back along Široká Street, dating from 1535 and the most moving of Prague's Jewish sites. After World War II it was turned into a memorial to Czech Jews murdered during the Holocaust, with the names of the 80,000 victims covering the walls. The infamous death camps are listed behind the *bimah*, every place a horror story of pain and suffering. Upstairs you will find an exhibition of drawings by children of the Terezín ghetto (see *North Bohemia* chapter, page 182), the most harrowing story of wartime Bohemia. The Pinkas Synagogue also serves as the entrance to the **Old Jewish Cemetery**, in use from the mid 15th century until 1787. The people, laid to rest here in several layers, far outnumber the 12,000 headstones, each with fading Hebrew inscriptions. Both Rabbi Loew, creator of the Golem legend, and Mordechai Maisel, influential 16th-century Jewish mayor who considerably extended the Jewish town, are buried here. The rows of crooked, slightly overgrown headstones, crammed into the uneven walled space shaded by trees, is quite a sight. The one-way system in the cemetery leads visitors efficiently to the **Klaus Synagogue** (Klausova synagoga), built in the late 17th century on the site of three small prayer rooms founded by Mordechai Maisel. The Baroque interior houses religious exhibits such as prayer books, Torah scrolls, Hanukkah lamps, skullcaps and other items connected with birth, circumcision, bar mitzvahs, weddings, home life and death. Next door is the neo-Romanesque **Ceremonial Hall** (Obřadní síň) from 1912, now housing the last part of the exhibition dealing with death and funerals.

Last stop is the **Old–New Synagogue** (Staronová synagoga) 100m east on Červená Street. Completed sometime between 1270 and 1280, this is the second-oldest synagogue, and the oldest *working* synagogue in Europe, as well as one of Prague's earliest Gothic structures. The steps down into the building confirm the original ground level before the Old Town was raised. Josef Mocker of Karlštejn fame gave it a probably uncalled-for neo-Gothic facelift in the late 19th century. The atmosphere of its poky interior with dark wooden pews and large *bimah* behind an iron grille is difficult to appreciate in the tourist crush, so get here early for the best experience. The last of Josefov's synagogues is the closed **High Synagogue** (Vysoká synagoga) opposite, which the Jewish community keeps for services only.

South of the Old Town Square

At the far southeast corner of the Old Town at the end of Na Příkopě Street stands the **Obecní dům** (Municipal House, *www.obecnidum.cz*), one of the Czech Republic's finest Art Nouveau buildings. Built in 1905–11 and originally called the Prague Representative House, it replaced the Old Royal Palace which had stood on the site since the late 14th century. With typical early 20th-century patriotic zeal this was pulled down to make way for a representative building for the city where Czech cultural life could thrive. The Municipal House is a truly remarkable and unique building, pure Art Nouveau inside and out. At the time it was not only attractive, but technically ahead of its time too with 28 lifts, a telephone exchange and linoleum. The building houses two large restaurants, a café, numerous salons including the Mayor's Salon decorated by Alfons Mucha, a gallery, and the Smetana Concert Hall, the largest in Prague, where a performance of Smetana's *Má vlast* traditionally kicks off the celebrated Prague Spring Music Festival. Prague's favourite piece of Art Nouveau has inevitably played its part in history. Czechoslovak independence was declared here on 28 October 1918, and in 1989 Havel and student leaders met here with the communist government. Tours of the building (*150/100Kč*) leave at least twice daily, though times vary. Check with the ticket office.

Next to the Municipal House stands the somewhat redundant **Prašná brána** (Powder Gate), one of the finest examples of late Gothic architecture in the capital. It was begun in 1475 by builder Matěj Rejsek during the reign of the Jagiellon King Vladislav II, and was not finished until Josef Mocker completed it in the neo-Gothic style in 1875–86. Originally called the *Nová brána*, the name was changed at the beginning of the 18th century when it was used to store gunpowder ('prašná' coming from the word '*prach*' meaning powder). It used to stand next to the Royal Palace, marking the starting point of the Royal Way to Prague Castle. The decoration includes statues of the Czech patron saints, the great kings Jiří of Poděbrady, Vladislav II, Přemysl Otakar II and Charles IV. Visitors can climb up to the viewing platform, 44m up the 65m tower (*admission 50/40Kč*). Pass through the Prašná brána and continue along Celetná Street for around 400m to the Cubist **Dům U černé Matky boží** (House of the Black Madonna) on the corner at Ovocný trh 19, built in 1911–12 by the architect who so influenced the townscape of Hradec Králové, Josef Gočár. Replacing a Baroque house of the same name the original house symbol was retained, and can be seen on the corner of the building behind gold bars. It is the oldest Cubist structure in Prague and the original wine bar, coffee house and offices were once fitted out with Cubist interiors, furniture, crockery and countless other everyday items. Though a modern building, it blends in well with the historical cityscape, a fact which must have inspired architect Karel Prager (of Nová scéna and parliament notoriety) to redeem himself when restoring the building in 1993–94. The House of the Black Madonna now houses the National Gallery's exhibition of Czech Cubism from 1911–19 (*admission 100/50Kč*) including works by Czech

THE ROYAL WAY

A good way to see almost all of Prague's main sights is to follow the so-called Royal Way, from the Prašná brána in the city centre through the Old Town, across Charles Bridge and up to the castle. It is called the Royal Way as it traces the route Czech kings used to take from their palace to the castle. Until the end of the 19th century the palace stood next to the Prašná brána but was pulled down to make way for today's Municipal House, a decision you may find rather odd.

artists Emil Filla, Bohumil Kubišta, Otto Gutfreund and Josef Čapek, brother of the famous inter-war writer Karel Čapek, as well as superb Cubist furniture by Gočár himself. End your visit with a coffee at the Grand Café Orient on the first floor (notice the Cubist menu!).

From the House of the Black Madonna head up the cobbled expanse of the **Ovocný trh**, the site of the former fruit market, at the end of which stands the proud neo-Classical **Stavovské divadlo** (Theatre of the Estates) dating from 1781. Originally called the Nostitz Theatre after its builder Count Franz Anton von Nostitz-Rieneck, a German nobleman, it was the venue for the 1787 world premiere of Mozart's *Don Giovanni*. The Czech national anthem 'Kde domov můj' (Where is my Home) also received its first performance here in 1834.

Continue along Havelská to the **Church of St Havel**, originally from 1232 and established at the same time as the surrounding Havelské Město (St Gall's Town). Gothic inside, its Baroque façade is probably the work of Santini from 1722–29. Early Church reformers Konrád Walderhauser and Jan Milíč of Kroměříž preached here in the late 14th century as well as Jan Hus himself. Karel Škréta is buried in the church. Still in Havelské Město, straight ahead of you is Prague's best open-air market, the **Havelský market** (Havelský trh). Held daily, it is a great place to buy fresh produce as well as souvenirs and gifts.

The Havelský market ends at another former market, the triangular **Uhelný trh**, the erstwhile coal market (*uhlí* means 'coal'). A few steps along Martinská bring you to the ancient-looking **Church of St Martin in the Wall** (kostel sv Martina ve zdi) founded as early as the 12th century as a parish church for the then village of Újezd. It was separated from the settlement when it found itself part of the Gothic town fortifications, hence the name. The church is a regular classical music concert venue, the only way to get inside. Take a right into Na Perštýně Street to reach **Betlémské náměstí**, the site of the original **Bethlehem Chapel** (*admission 40/20Kč*). I say original as the present building is a 1950s mock-up of the 14th-century chapel where Jan Hus preached, which was demolished in 1786. The **Náprstek Museum** can also be found on the square (see *Museums* section, page 124).

MOZART IN PRAGUE

'The Prague people understand me,' proclaimed Mozart during a visit to Prague. The composer fell in love with a city that celebrated his work, his operas playing to packed theatres. Mozart visited Prague three times. *The Wedding of Figaro* was a huge success in 1786 and *Don Giovanni* was premiered at the Estates Theatre in 1787. His last sojourn was in 1791 for the premiere of *La Clemenza di Tito*.

There are three other churches in the vicinity of Betlémské náměstí. The giant **Church of St Giles** (kostel sv Jiljí) in Husova Street was another church popular with the early reformers before the building of the Bethlehem Chapel. The usual Baroque flourishes were added in the 1730s. Apart from rows of dreary police offices, grim **Bartolomějská Street** also has the **Church of St Bartholomew** and a convent, part of which used to be the cells of the hated StB (the Czechoslovak equivalent of the KGB). The block was returned to the Franciscans in the 1990s, and the enterprising nuns have turned the cells into a budget hostel (Art Prison Hostel, see *Where to stay*, page 83) so you can sleep in Havel's former cell if you so wish! On the corner of Konviktská and Karoliny Světlé streets sits the **Chapel of the Holy Cross** (kaple sv Kříže), a squat Romanesque rotunda and one of Prague's oldest structures dating from the late 11th century. Strange to imagine that this modest building has watched the Old Town rise around it for over 900 years.

New Town
Many first-time visitors to Prague prior to their departure imagine the New Town as all high-rise blocks and other delights of modern city architecture, and express a wish to stay in the 'old' part of town. The New Town was most definitely 'new' when it was founded over 650 years ago by Charles IV and, while not possessing the tightly knit web of irregular streets like the Old Town, its medieval origins are still evident despite 19th- and 20th-century additions. Charles IV was eager to transform Prague into a city worthy of its status as the capital of the Holy Roman Empire and he planned streets and squares to join up the Old Town with Vyšehrad to the south. However, the Old and New towns remained separate entities and rivals and there existed a clear boundary between the two – a moat which ran roughly along today's Národní, Na Příkopě and Revoluční streets. They were officially united into one city only in 1784.

This is the commercial heart of the city with wide boulevards, bustling squares, restaurants, cinemas, department stores and numerous places of culture such as the National Theatre and Museum, as well as medieval churches, some pre-dating the streets they stand on.

Wenceslas Square
The focal point of the New Town, Prague and possibly the entire Czech Republic is Wenceslas Square or *Václavské náměstí* as it is known in Czech, named after the patron saint of the Czech lands, St Wenceslas (*svatý Václav*). Created as part of the New Town in 1348 it is 750m long, tapering down from 63m wide at the top near the National Museum to 48m at the bottom near Můstek. Originally called *Koňský trh* meaning 'horse market', the name was changed in 1848 on the suggestion of Czech journalist and poet Karel Havlíček Borovský after a meeting around a statue of St Wenceslas which stood on the square until 1879. Today the square is a centre for shopping, business and entertainment with acres of passages, shops and offices behind the tall façades in almost every architectural style from the last 200 years lining both sides. This is the very heart of the country, a place of protest and celebration throughout history where Czechs gather, and will gather, to vent their anger and joy at events in the country. Czechoslovakia's much longed-for independence from the Austrian Empire was announced here, a large crowd welcomed the communist takeover in 1948 on the square, Jan Palach and Jan Zajíc set themselves alight in protest against the 1968 Soviet invasion (near the statue of St Wenceslas) and mass demonstrations on the anniversary of the occupation were brutally dispersed here

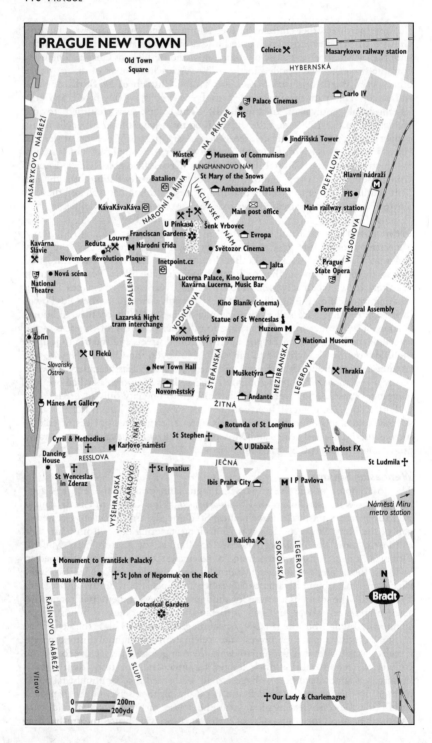

PRAGUE NEW TOWN

Old Town Square

Celnice ✕

Masarykovo railway station

HYBERNSKÁ

MASARYKOVO NÁBŘEŽÍ

NA PŘÍKOPĚ

🏠 Carlo IV

🏛 Palace Cinemas

PIS

● Jindřišská Tower

Můstek Ⓜ 🏛 Museum of Communism

JUNGMANNOVO NÁM

Batalion ⓔ

OPLETALOVA

Hlavní nádraží

St Mary of the Snows

NÁRODNÍ 28 ŘÍJNA

🏛 Ambassador-Zlatá Husa

PIS ● Ⓜ

VÁCLAVSKÉ

KávaKávaKáva ⓔ

Main railway station

✕ † † ✕

Main post office ✉

U Pinkasů

Šenk Vrbovec

WILSONOVA

Franciscan Gardens ❀

🏛 Evropa

NÁM

Kavárna Slávie ✕

Reduta ☆ ✕✕

Louvre Ⓜ Národní třída

● Světozor Cinema

Prague State Opera

November Revolution Plaque

Inetpoint.cz ⓔ

🏛 Jalta

SPÁLENÁ

🎭 ● Nová scéna

National Theatre

Lucerna Palace, Kino Lucerna, Kavárna Lucerna, Music Bar

VODIČKOVA

Kino Blaník (cinema)

● Former Federal Assembly

Lazarská Night tram interchange

Statue of St Wenceslas ⚑

Muzeum Ⓜ

🏛 National Museum

● Žofín

✕ U Fleků

✕ Novoměstský pivovar

ŠTĚPÁNSKÁ

MEZIBRÁNSKÁ

LEGEROVA

✕ Thrakia

Slovanský Ostrov

● New Town Hall

U Mušketýra

Novoměstský

Máneš Art Gallery

🏛 Andante

ŽITNÁ

NÁM

● Rotunda of St Longinus

Cyril & Methodius †

Ⓜ Karlovo náměstí

St Stephen †

Dancing House ●

RESSLOVA

KARLOVO

✕ U Dlabače

☆ Radost FX

St Ludmila †

St Wenceslas in Zderaz †

† St Ignatius

JEČNÁ

VYŠEHRADSKÁ

Ibis Praha City 🏠

Ⓜ I P Pavlova

Náměstí Míru metro station

U Kalicha ✕

SOKOLSKÁ

LEGEROVA

N

Bradt

⚑ Monument to František Palacký

Emmaus Monastery ●

† St John of Nepomuk on the Rock

RAŠÍNOVO NÁBŘEŽÍ

Botanical Gardens ❀

NA SLUPI

VLTAVA

0 ___ 200m
0 ___ 200yds

† Our Lady & Charlemagne

in 1969. The 1989 revolution saw demonstration after demonstration here and speeches by Havel and other dissidents from the balcony of the Melantrich Building. Without doubt the square will play a similar role in any future historical upheavals the Czechs experience.

Wenceslas Square top end

At the upper end stands the **Statue of St Wenceslas**, begun by the great Czech sculptor Josef Václav Myslbek in 1887 and completed in 1924. St Wenceslas sits proudly upon a mighty steed brandishing a spear reaching almost 8m in height. Smaller representations of the Czech patron saints surround the main statue. The declaration of Czechoslovak independence was symbolically read out in front of the statue on 28 October 1918, the date set in stone at the foot of the base. Wenceslas Square is the place for outpourings of Czech national pride and protest and St Wenceslas is the focal point of the square itself. The statue is also a favourite everyday rendezvous point, and meeting '*pod koněm*' (below the horse) is part of Prague life, hence the gathering of individuals you may see loitering expectantly below St Wenceslas.

Looking down the square from the statue Jindřišská Street races off to the right where Prague's main post office is located and further along the very prominent **Jindřišská Tower**, which has stood on this site since 1472. Like the Powder Tower by the Municipal House, it was given a neo-Gothic facelift in the late 1870s by Josef Mocker. At 67.7m it is the tallest free-standing bell tower in Prague, and visitors can scale its height or take the lift to the top where superb views of the New Town can be taken in from the viewing platform and the recently opened restaurant on the 8th floor. The tower also houses the Museum of Prague Towers (*admission 60/30Kč*). Head in the other direction from Wenceslas Square along Vodičkova Street to enter the **Lucerna Palace**, spread between Vodičkova and Štěpánská streets. Built by Václav Havel, the grandfather of ex-President Havel, and now owned by his sister-in-law Dagmar Havlová, the palace dates from 1906 and is one of the largest examples of Art Nouveau architecture in Prague. The palace is in fact a complex of shops, cafés, restaurants, bars and a cinema plus a huge underground concert hall, a frequent venue for performances by world-famous artists, balls and other grand occasions, which once echoed to the ranting of communist congress delegates. There is also a famous rock club called the Lucerna Music Bar. Look out for the take-off of the statue of St Wenceslas hanging from the ceiling of the main passage.

Glowering down on Wenceslas Square and proudly dominating the skyline is the **National Museum**. The stern neo-Renaissance edifice, purpose built in 1885–90, came into existence to accommodate the growing collection of the National Museum then spread around numerous sites in the city. It is one of the great 19th-century symbols of the Czech National Revival alongside the National Theatre, with which it shares a common architect, Josef Schulz. Just as Prager's Nová scéna stands inharmoniously next to the National Theatre, another of his glass-and-steel monsters, the **Former Federal Assembly**, keeps the National Museum company. One of Prague's ugliest communist-era buildings, the former communist parliament now rather paradoxically houses Radio Free Europe, moved from Munich in the mid 1990s. Many would like to see the heavily guarded, US-funded radio station and potential terrorist target (thanks to controversial broadcasts to the Middle East) banished as far from the city centre as possible. Next to the former parliament further along Wilsonova Street, a dangerous dual carriageway at the best of times, hides the neo-Renaissance **Prague State Opera**. Constructed by the prolific Viennese theatre-building company Fellner and Helmer, it was opened in 1888 as the *Neues Deutsches Theater* (New German Theatre) to compete with the 'new Czech theatre' opened five years earlier beside the Vltava. Opera has always dominated the programme, and in 1910 the theatre saw the premiere of Strauss's *Electra*.

Wenceslas Square lower end

Můstek is the focal point of the lower end of Prague's main square, and is also the name of the **metro station**, one of the busiest thanks to its central location. This whole area is a pedestrian zone, forever alive with shoppers, tourists, street performers and beggars. During December it is clogged up with the Wenceslas Square Christmas markets. Heading from Můstek to Národní třída one passes through **Jungmannovo náměstí** (Jungmann Square) dominated by the bronze seated figure of a meditative Josef Jungmann, the Czech translator, writer and leading figure of the Czech National Revival. The statue was erected in 1873 to commemorate the centenary of his birth. One of this district's best-kept secrets is the **Franciscan Gardens** (Františkánská zahrada) lying just off Jungmannovo náměstí. An antidote to the hustle and bustle of the busy streets and passages, these well-kept, tranquil gardens have row upon row of white wooden benches, ideal for summer picnics. Within view of the gardens and once a dominant feature, but now all but hidden behind soaring commercial buildings, is the curious, unfinished **kostel Panny Marie Sněžné** (Church of St Mary of the Snows). In 1347, Charles IV founded a Carmelite monastery and a coronation church, meant to surpass the Cathedral of St Vitus in size and grandeur. By 1397, the chancel had been completed, but the Hussite wars halted all further work. In the early Hussite days, Jan Želivský, leader of the Prague radicals preached here, after which the church was abandoned. Restored by the Franciscan order who acquired the church and monastery in the 16th century, this peculiar, almost secret church, seemingly as long as it is tall, boasts the highest vaulting in Prague (34m) and also the highest altar in the capital (29m).

Walking in the opposite direction from Můstek you will find yourself on the swish pedestrianised shopping precinct called **Na příkopě** which ends at the Municipal House. *Příkop* means ditch or moat, exactly what you would have found here 150 years ago. The vile, stinking open sewer dividing the Old and New towns was thankfully paved over in the late 18th century.

Národní třída

Národní třída extends from Můstek to the Vltava ending at the National Theatre. Busy with all kinds of shops, bars and offices near Můstek it becomes progressively quieter as it nears the river. This wide street provided the backdrop to the violent confrontation between students and riot police which set in motion the 1989 November Revolution. The momentous events of that cold night are marked by a very simple **plaque** with hands making the V for victory sign and the date 17.11.1989 hidden in the arcading halfway along. Every year on that date the space is illuminated by thousands of candles lit by politicians, famous personalities and ordinary people alike (hence the waxy floor).

At the end of Národní stands the **National Theatre** dating from 1883. Czech National Revivalists had been clamouring for a national Czech theatre for over a decade when Czech playwright and fervent nationalist, Josef Kajetán Tyl, suggested a nationwide whip-round to raise the capital to construct one. From peasants to noblemen, many contributed, and within two years enough had been amassed to purchase a plot of land by the Vltava, where a temporary theatre was built. The construction of the real thing was entrusted to architect Josef Zítek and the foundation stone was laid on 16 May 1868, an event which turned into the largest 19th-century demonstration for recognition of Czech national identity. A total of 26 symbolic stones were hauled in from all corners of the Czech lands (plus one from Czechs in America) and placed in the foundations. The theatre was opened on 11 June 1881, but was destroyed by fire two months later. More money was raised in yet another collection for the rebuilding work, completed in 1883 and carried out by Zítek's assistant, Josef Schulz. Smetana's opera *Libuše*, specially composed for the occasion, was performed at the reopening on 18 November 1883. The glass blob obscuring one side of the National Theatre is the widely unloved **Nová scéna**, a showcase example of insensitive communist-era architecture from 1983. The architect (or culprit) is Karel Prager, one of the country's top communist-period architects who left his mark throughout the city. On the corner, across Národní is the **Kavárna Slávie**, the capital's oldest coffee house and a Prague institution which has been serving guests since 1881. Still a stylish place to sip a drink, watch the trams swerving into Narodní, and rub shoulders with famous personalities from the theatre opposite, it is traditionally seen as a prestigious place to come and nonchalantly intellectualise, and everyone from avant-garde writers to 1970s dissidents have met here.

Karlovo náměstí and around

Karlovo náměstí (Charles Square), established as part of Charles IV's New Town in 1348, is the largest square in the Czech Republic measuring over 7ha and by all accounts could effortlessly accommodate almost half a million people. Due to the size and layout of the square, with its unkempt parkland and noisy Ječná Street carving it in two, it does not feel like a square at all. After numerous name changes including *Dobytčí trh* (Cattle Market), it gained its current title in 1848 half a millennium after its foundation, and as far as Prague squares go, this is most definitely second division. Unlike the Old Town and Wenceslas squares, Charles Square hardly gets a mention in Czech history and most of the historical architecture has long gone, replaced by modern structures. It is also ever-so-slightly off the tourist trail, making its shambolic parkland packed with benches an ideal spot for a quiet picnic or a snooze in the shade.

Undoubtedly the most noteworthy building, the **New Town Hall** (Novoměstská radnice, *admission 20/10Kč*) stands at the northern end. This fine example of Gothic architecture was built soon after the New Town was laid out and served as the town hall until the unification of Prague's towns in 1784. Visitors can climb its tower and visit the scene of the 1419 defenestration of the town councillors by radical Hussite leader Jan Želivský and his followers livid at the imprisonment of some of the brethren, an event which marked the eruption of the Hussite conflict. Halfway along the square on the left be sure to call in at the fine Jesuit **Church of St Ignatius** (kostel sv Ignáce), begun in 1665 by Carlo Lurago. Admire its wonderful wedding-cake stucco interior, giant altar and gold and salmon marble before continuing along the square.

Leaving Charles Square at the southwest corner, walk along Vyšehradská Street to the **Church of St John of Nepomuk on the Rock** (kostel sv Jan Nepomucký na skalce) which, as its name suggests, was built on a cliff by Kilián Ignác Dientzenhofer in 1739. Alas, its lavish Baroque interior is not open to the public. Across the street is the **Emmaus Monastery**, originally (and very often still) called Na Slovanech. Though there is not a great deal to see here, the history of the place is interesting. Many state with confidence that the Slavic liturgy was last carried out in the Czech lands in 1097 at the Sázava Monastery east of Prague. However, Charles IV, ever aware of his Slavic roots and desiring to link his Přemyslid origins with the arrival of Christianity from the East, founded a monastery where monks from Croatia would practise the Slavic liturgy and write in a version of the Glagolitic alphabet. The Hussites used it as their sole monastery, but in 1636 it returned to the hands of the Catholics. Closed by the Nazis in 1941, it was damaged by American bombers in 1945. The modern sweeping roof of the Church of St Mary replaced the bomb damage in the 1960s.

Some 100m south of the monastery visitors will find Prague's **Botanical Gardens** (admission 15/10Kč, trams 18 and 24, stop Botanická zahrada), belonging to Charles University. It costs nothing to wander the uneven plant beds, rockeries and gardens dotted with benches or pay the entry fee to visit the sweltering greenhouses crammed full of exotic plants. Roughly 500m southeast of the gardens stands one of Prague's least visited churches. Anyone who crosses the span of the Nuselský Bridge from the south cannot fail to notice the peach façade and triple black domes of the **Church of Our Lady and Charlemagne** (chrám Nanebevzetí Panny Marie a svatého Karla Velikého). Begun by Charles IV in 1350 and intended to recall the octagonal burial church of Charlemagne in Aachen, it was not roofed until 1575. The span of the unsupported dome is so large that the builders were suspected of being in league with the devil when it did not collapse in on itself. Visitors can inspect the interior only as part of Sunday afternoon guided tours. The building is a typical mix of solid Gothic shell and Baroque icing and the vaulting has to be seen to be believed. Do not miss the views over the Nusle valley across to Vyšehrad behind the church.

Back on Charles Square head west along traffic-plagued Resslova Street to the orthodox **Church of Cyril and Methodius** (chrám sv Cyrila a Metoděje), the setting for the last stand of *Reichsprotektor* Heydrich's assassins (see *History*, page 20). Apart from the slit in the façade facing the street, still chipped and riddled with bullet holes, another reminder of the events of that day (18 June 1942) is the memorial to the valiant members of the resistance in the crypt (admission 50/20Kč). There are photographs, uniforms and weapons and beneath the slit on the inside you can see the hole the men dug in a desperate attempt to escape into the sewers.

Further down Resslova, elevated above the street rises the **Church of St Wenceslas in Zderaz** (kostel sv Václava na Zderaze) whose most interesting feature is the original 12th-century Romanesque windows in the western façade. The village of Zderaz was consumed by the New Town in 1348.

Štěpánská Street, running east from Charles Square to Wenceslas Square, has two noteworthy churches. The **Church of St Stephen** (kostel sv Štěpána) was established in 1351 as the parish church for the upper part of the New Town. The sober façade received the Mocker treatment during the 1870s, though the interior has kept some of its Baroque decoration including a work by Škréta. Behind that in Na Rybníčku Street squats the **Rotunda of St Longinus** (Rotunda sv Longina), the second-oldest of Prague's Romanesque rotundas from the early 12th century, and the parish church of the village of Rybníček, wiped off the map by the New Town. Originally dedicated to St Stephen, Charles IV renamed it after St Longin, a Roman soldier who took part in the Crucifixion of Christ, and whose remains were brought to Prague by Charles IV.

The embankment

Heading south from the National Theatre along Masarykovo Embankment lined with high, elegant Art Nouveau apartment blocks with superb views across the Vltava at its broadest, you soon arrive at **Slovanský ostrov**, a drowsy island park named 'Slav Island' after the pan-Slavic congress held here in 1848. The shady silt bank is a pleasant refuge from the mad traffic of the embankment and the bridges across the Vltava. Berlioz, Schubert, Liszt, Tchaikovsky, Wagner, Dvořák and Smetana all held performances here and the island also witnessed the first steam locomotive demonstration in 1841. At the northern end you will find the statue of Czech 19th-century writer Božena Němcová. The 19th-century **Žofín** is the capital's most prestigious ball venue whose neo-Classical decoration contrasts with the functionalist white blocks of the 1930 **Mánes art gallery** spanning the channel between the island and the embankment. The 16th-century onion-domed Šítek water tower next door has certainly seen better days.

Continuing southwards, the busy crossroads at once-elegant Jiráskovo náměstí, is now dominated by the so-called **Dancing House**, Prague's best-known work of contemporary architecture bolted together in the mid 1990s. Some may like this cutting-edge piece of wavy glass and steel, others may say it resembles a squashed plastic bottle someone has neglected to throw into the recycling bin. Critics argue it has no place in the architectural landscape of such a well-preserved city and hope this sort of intrusion into Prague's architectural treasure trove is not repeated. The same was probably said of Gočár's House of the Black Madonna and the Municipal House but somehow I doubt the Dancing House will ever be in the same league. On the square a bronze of old Jirásek, the Czech writer and First Republic senator, seems to be just turning his head to look at the glass-and-steel intruder. What would he have to say on the subject?

Some 300m further south on Palackého náměstí is a curious **Monument to František Palacký**, created by Stanislav Sucharda from 1898 to 1912 to mark the centenary of the historian and politician's birth in 1798. A granite Frankenstein-esque Palacký looks sternly across the bridge bearing his name while greening bronzes representing the suffering and awakening of the Czech nation writhe behind him. The Nazis intended to destroy the monument but it was taken apart, hidden and restored in 1948. In the vein of the Hus monument on the Old Town Square from the same period, it is not very pleasing to the eye.

Vyšehrad

South of the New Town on a strategic cliff above the Vltava rises Vyšehrad, a complex of fortifications, churches, cemeteries and ruins, and the original mythical Slavic settlement where chieftain Krok, descendent of Čech, the leader of the first Slavic tribe to arrive in the region, ruled, followed by his daughter the prophetess Libuše. The popularity of the stories is largely down to writer Alois Jirásek and his *Staré pověsti české* (Old Czech Myths) but as yet no archaeologist has unearthed concrete evidence of any such rulers though it is almost certain that the very prominent cliff was a pagan worship site. King Vratislav II built a royal palace and churches here around 1070, and Soběslav I was the last ruler of Bohemia to reside here, moving the court back to Prague Castle in 1140. Ever eager to preserve the umbilical cord to the early Přemyslid rulers, Charles IV recognised Vyšehrad's significance and roped it into the New Town with protective walls, built a Gothic palace, a church and the Špička Gate, only for the Hussites to lay waste to the lot several decades later. For over 200 years Vyšehrad was a dangerous slum area inhabited by the poor and artists until the Austrians beefed it up into a Baroque fortress with typical red-brick earthworks and moats in the mid 17th century. The 19th century saw the rebuilding of the Church of SS Peter and Paul by the prolific neo-Gothic fanatic Josef Mocker and the establishment of the Slavín, a cemetery whose headstones read like a who's who of Czech artistic and literary life of the past 150 years. Vyšehrad is always a peaceful, pleasant place away from the crowds and for light sightseeing and relaxation on summer afternoons.

Vyšehrad is divided from the New Town by the wide Nusle valley, spanned by the impressive 485m-long and 40m-high Nuselský Bridge, a feat of communist-era engineering opened in 1973. Until the revolution it was named after Czechoslovakia's first proletariat president, Klement Gottwald. It carries six lanes of incessant traffic and a tunnel for the metro is suspended below. To the chagrin of those who dwell beneath, it has the gory reputation as Prague's choice suicide spot. The best way to reach Vyšehrad is to alight at the metro station of the same name (red line C) and walk via the unattractive Prague Congress Centre, following the signs to the bulky outer fortress walls. Enter through the hefty **Tábor Gate** and continue on to the **information centre** which provides maps and guides, and where you can also see the remnants of the Gothic **Špička Gate**, destroyed by the Hussites. Further up the road stands the mighty arch of the Baroque **Leopold Gate** from 1670. A couple of hundred metres further brings you to the **Rotunda of St Martin**, the oldest Romanesque rotunda in the capital dating from the reign of Vratislav II. The thickset little building has been used as a storehouse and as a dwelling for the poor but has survived this as well as invading armies and town planners for more than nine centuries.

The twin towers of the **Church of SS Peter and Paul** (*admission 20/10Kč, open winter Sat and Sun only, summer closed Fri*), the centrepiece of the Vyšehrad complex, are one of the most prominent and instantly recognisable sights on the Prague skyline. This church has undergone many transformations from Vratislav II's Romanesque basilica, to Charles IV's Gothic church, to a Baroque place of worship and finally the neo-Gothic remodelling in the late 19th century. The interior sports beautifully painted columns and vaulting added in the 1920s. Next to the church be sure not to overlook the leafy **Vyšehrad Cemetery**, the final resting place of such Czech greats as footballer Josef Bican, writers Karel Čapek, Božena Němcová and Jan Neruda, poet Karel Hynek Mácha, composers Dvořák and Smetana, artist Alfons Mucha, architect Josef Gočár, opera singer Ema Destinnová and even Josef Mocker himself. Many are buried in the **Slavín monument**, from 1893 topped with a sarcophagus and a statue representing Genius. Incredibly no communist bigwig was ever buried here; in fact there are no politicians at all. Come here on your last day in the republic to pay homage to many of those behind the sights you have admired on your travels.

The **Casemates** (*admission 30/20Kč*) at the **Brick Gate** (Cihelná brána) to the north keep six original statues from Charles Bridge safe from vandals and smog. The **foundations of Charles IV's palace** are just visible to the south of the Church of SS Peter and Paul, and nearby visitors can look down from the cliff at **Libuše's Bath** where legend has it that the prophetess bathed with her lovers before casting them to their death in the Vltava. Watch the trams rumbling along the embankment down below and the cruiseboats turning in the tranquil waters of the Vltava.

Museums
National Museum (Národní museum)
The neo-Classical architecture, stern exhibition cases, creaky floorboards and dusty lifeless exhibits make this the classic, archetypal museum. Highlights include the Pantheon, 48 busts of important figures from Czech history, the neo-Classical interiors and the views of Wenceslas Square. Children will love the thousands of stuffed animals and insects on the top floor. Top-notch temporary exhibitions.

www.nm.cz. Admission 100/50Kč, family ticket 120Kč. Open daily except first Tuesday in the month. Free entry every first Monday in the month.

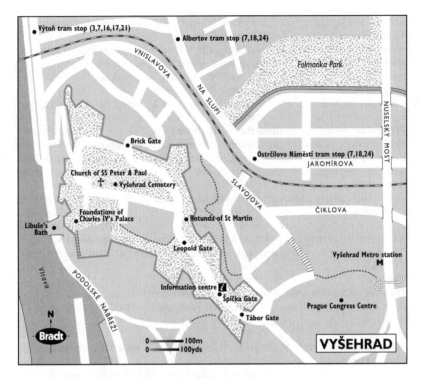

On the map:
- Výtoň tram stop (3,7,16,17,21)
- Albertov tram stop (7,18,24)
- VNISLAVOVA
- NA SLUPI
- Folimanka Park
- NUSELSKÝ MOST
- Brick Gate
- Ostrčilovo Náměstí tram stop (7,18,24)
- JAROMÍROVA
- Church of SS Peter & Paul
- Vyšehrad Cemetery
- SLAVOJOVA
- ČIKLOVA
- Foundations of Charles IV's Palace
- Rotunda of St Martin
- Libuše's Bath
- Vltava
- PODOLSKÉ NÁBŘEŽÍ
- Leopold Gate
- Vyšehrad Metro station M
- N
- Bradt
- Information centre
- Špička Gate
- Prague Congress Centre
- Tábor Gate
- 0 — 100m
- 0 — 100yds
- VYŠEHRAD

Museum of Communism (Muzeum komunismu)

The exhibition takes the visitor on a journey through communism in Czechoslovakia, beginning with the dream (statues of Karl Marx and Lenin, the liberation of Czechoslovakia by the Red Army), moving on to the reality of daily life (mock-up of classroom and austere shop, propaganda posters) and ending with the nightmare (interrogation room, border guards) and the eventual fall of the regime in November 1989. One symbolically leaves through a hole in the Berlin wall! All the artefacts are the real thing.

www.muzeumkomunismu.cz. Admission 180/140Kč. Open daily. Seek out this entertaining museum on the first floor of Na Příkopě 10.

Museum of the City of Prague (Muzeum hlavního města Prahy)

Housed in a specially constructed building dating from 1896, this is one of Prague's better museums. The collection on two floors traces the history of Prague from prehistoric times to the end of the 19th century. Explanations are in English and highlights include the amazingly detailed *Langweilův model Prahy*, a paper scale model of the city from the early 19th century, and the original lower dial from the *orloj* by Josef Mánes as well as numerous other fascinating exhibits throughout.

www.muzeumprahy.cz (in Czech only). Admission 80/30Kč, family ticket 160Kč. Open daily except Mondays.

National Technical Museum (Národní technické muzeum)

Situated a short walk from Letenské náměstí in Prague's Letná district (tram 1, Letenské náměstí stop) stands the huge building of the popular Technical

Museum. The collection includes old bicycles, cars, motorcycles, locomotives and aircraft as well as a huge dusty exhibition on cameras and a mock-up of a mine (guided tour, 45 minutes). Highlights are the huge steam locomotives, the Klement and Laurin cars and motorcycles and the Albatros training jet, widely used around the world. The museum has an outdated early 1980s 'isn't technology wonderful' feel to it, interesting in itself.
www.ntm.cz. Admission 70/30Kč, family ticket 150Kč. Open daily except Mondays.

Náprstek Museum (Náprstkovo muzeum)
With its poor permanent exhibitions on the Americas, Australasia and Oceania this is Prague's dullest museum, and is more designed for Czechs to come and gaze at the exotic. It does occasionally hold some interesting temporary exhibitions.
www.aconet.cz/npm. Admission 60/30Kč, family ticket 100Kč. Open daily except Mondays.

Museum of Decorative Arts (Uměleckoprůmyslové muzeum)
17 listopadu 2, Old Town; www.upm.cz. Admission 120/60Kč, family ticket 120Kč. Open daily.

Dvořák Museum (Muzeum Antonína Dvořáka)
Ke Karlovu 20, New Town; www.nm.cz. Admission 40/20Kč. Open daily except Mondays.

Bertramka (Mozart Museum) (Muzeum W A Mozarta a manželů Duškových)
Mozartova 169, Prague 5; www.bertramka.cz. Admission 110/50Kč. Open daily.

Prague Transport Museum (Muzeum MHD)
Patočkova 4, Prague 6; www.dp-praha.cz. Admission 25/10Kč. Open weekends and holidays, April–November.

Other places in and around Prague
Along Vinohradská třída
Vinohradská Avenue runs from behind the National Museum out into the Vinohrady district east of the city centre named after the vineyards which once grew here. Some parts have a decidedly Parisian feel to them with tree-lined boulevards and high 19th-century apartment blocks. To the north is the Žižkov district with its bars, cemeteries and run-down housing. Tram 11 runs the length of Vinohradská.

The first place of interest south of Vinohradská is **Náměstí Míru** (green metro line A, Prague's deepest metro station), translatable as 'Peace Square', the ideal place to find some peace away from the tourist throngs, and to picnic on a park bench. The square is dominated by the double clock towers of the pleasing, neo-Gothic, brick **Church of St Ludmila** concealing an attractive painted neo-Gothic interior and bright, colourful stained-glass windows.

One stop east by metro from Náměstí Míru is **náměstí Jiřího z Poděbrad**, a rectangular park dedicated to one of the Czechs' favourite rulers, the so-called Hussite King George of Poděbrady and home to one of the Czech Republic's most bizarre churches. Built in 1928–32 by the Slovenian architect Josip Plečnik who oversaw the functionalist additions to Prague Castle under President Masaryk, the **Kostel Nejsvětějšího Srdce Páně** (Church of the Most Sacred

Heart of Our Lord) is a daring but beautiful piece of architecture. The most striking feature is the oversized transparent clock, meant to mimic a Gothic rose window, which looks as if it would fit a building twice the size. The exterior is a mix of imitated architectural styles, but as with the majority of functionalist churches the interior is disappointingly plain.

A few streets north of the square and clearly visible above the rooftops rises the sci-fi **Žižkov TV Tower** (*admission 150/75Kč*). The first thing you will notice are the babies crawling up and down the steel tubing, a recent addition by Czech sculptor David Černý. Erected in 1985–91 it is the highest building in the Czech Republic at 216m. Having paid the extortionate entrance fee visitors are whisked via the ultra-fast lift to the 93m-high viewing platform in around a minute. On a clear day Ještěd, a mountain near Liberec in north Bohemia 100km away, is visible on the horizon, as are peaks in the České středhoří range. Prague in its entirety lies at your feet and apart from picking out the city's famous landmarks, this may be the only time tourists get to see Prague's other face, the acres of grey, drab, depressing, communist-era tower blocks to the south where most of the population dwells.

Three more stops on tram 11 brings you to the huge **Olšany Cemetery** (Olšanské hřbitovy) the Old Town's municipal burial grounds since 1679 when it was used for plague victims. An estimated two million people have been buried here over the centuries including World War II victims (Red Army soldiers, Czech resistance fighters), Klement Gottwald (first communist president), Josef Jungmann (linguist and leading figure in the Czech National Revival), Josef Lada (painter), Josef Mánes (painter), Jan Palach (student who burnt himself to death in protest at the 1968 invasion) and hundreds of others who did not make it into the Vyšehrad Cemetery. Next to the Olšany Cemetery is the **New Jewish Cemetery** (Nový židovský hřbitov) with the grave of Franz Kafka.

Výstaviště
Prague's exhibition grounds (Výstaviště) occupy a huge space near Holešovice railway station with the even larger Stromovka Park right next door. Apart from trade fairs and the like, this is also the venue for the popular **Matějská Fair** (Matějská pouť) in February and March with rides, attractions and candyfloss. The exhibition grounds are also the site of the **Křižík Fountain** (Křižíkova Fontána) which puts on watery shows to music for audiences of up to 6,000 at a time. The dramatic, over-the-top performances including a light show, dancers and film projection will not be to everyone's taste, but are quite a spectacle, if slightly kitsch. Tickets can usually be bought prior to the performances. Check out the fountain's website (*www.krizikovafontana.cz*) for the programme. Visitors can also visit the National Museum's **Lapidarium** (*admission 40/20Kč*), a repository for 400 Prague statues from the 11th to the 19th century including original statues from Charles Bridge. To reach the exhibition grounds take the metro north to Nádraží Holešovice and walk, or trams 5, 12, 14, 15 or 17, alighting at the Výstaviště stop.

West to western suburbs
Břevnov Monastery
The Břevnov Monastery (Břevnovský klášter, *admission 50/30Kč, open Sat and Sun year round, tours in Czech only*) is the oldest in the country founded in 993 by rivals Boleslav II of the Přemyslid dynasty and Bishop Vojtěch a Slavníkovec (later St Vojtěch). In true medieval fashion both had a dream about a place to found a monastery and met next day at a beam across the Vojtěška Stream

(břevno means beam in Czech, hence Břevnov). Its Baroque appearance dates from the early 18th century, the work of Krištof Dientzenhofer. Take trams 15, 22 or 25, alighting at the Břevnovský klášter stop.

Letohrádek Hvězda (Star Summer Palace)

A short distance west of the Břevnov Monastery stands the attractive Letohrádek Hvězda, set in the midst of a hunting reserve covering an entire hill. This curious Renaissance building in the shape of a six-pointed star was the pride and joy of Archduke Ferdinand of Tyrol who had it constructed in 1556. The grounds witnessed clashes during the Battle of the White Mountain in 1620. There is a small museum inside open May to September.

Bílá Hora (White Mountain)

As tram 22 reaches the site of the Battle of the White Mountain (*Bitva na Bílé Hoře*), the automatic voice announces 'Bílá Hora, terminus …'. This always reminds me that Bílá Hora almost was the end of the line – for Czech language and culture that is. The battle on 8 November 1620 saw the Protestant estates' forces routed by the army of the Catholic Habsburgs, marking the beginning of 300 years of Austrian dominance in the Czech lands and the relegation of Czech to the language of the uneducated peasant classes.

The monument to the battle itself is a simple pile of stones on a mound in the middle of a muddy field, but the significance of the place makes up for that. It is also the best place to get photos of Letohrádek Hvězda in all its glory, and a great vantage point to watch jumbo jets gliding just above the rooftops on their descent into nearby Ruzyně Airport. From the tram terminus head round the back of the large Baroque Church of St Mary and then take a right. The site of the battle is easy to spot.

Průhonice

The picturesque chateau with its magnificent landscaped park (*admission 20/10Kč*) is the reason to make the short trip to the village of Průhonice just outside the city limits. Visitors are rewarded with the peace and quiet of the 240ha of exotic surroundings, a home for hundreds of species of flora and fauna, making up one of the largest manmade natural environments in Europe. The landscape with its varied micro-environments gives plants from all corners of the globe the chance to thrive, some the only examples to be found in the Czech Republic. The park is now in the care of the State Botanical Institute and is open to the public year round. Although the park is the main attraction in Průhonice, the chateau originally dating from the 13th century cannot be overlooked. Reconstructed and added to over the centuries, its current appearance dates from the end of the 19th century when it was renovated in the neo-Renaissance style by Count Arnošt Emmanuel Sylva-Taroucca. The chateau and the grounds were bought by the Czechoslovak state in 1920 and remain state property to this day. Sadly, as the interiors are used by the State Botanical Institute and other scientific organisations, the public cannot enter though there is a permanent exhibition on Sylva-Taroucca, the chateau and the park, which can be viewed by prior arrangement by telephoning 271 015 234.

Průhonice lies just outside Prague and is therefore part of the Prague Integrated Transport System. Take red metro line C south to Opatov, from where buses depart several times an hour.

Central Bohemia

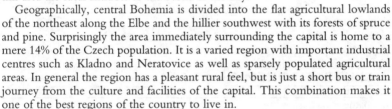

Central Bohemia, the area encircling Prague in a 50–70km radius, is a place for relaxing day trips for those weary of Prague's crowds and traffic. Despite the capital's popularity, not a great many people venture beyond the end of the metro lines making the castles, wooded hills, sleepy provincial towns and villages and tranquil riverbanks of this area the ideal antidote to the bustle of the city.

Geographically, central Bohemia is divided into the flat agricultural lowlands of the northeast along the Elbe and the hillier southwest with its forests of spruce and pine. Surprisingly the area immediately surrounding the capital is home to a mere 14% of the Czech population. It is a varied region with important industrial centres such as Kladno and Neratovice as well as sparsely populated agricultural areas. In general the region has a pleasant rural feel, but is just a short bus or train journey from the culture and facilities of the capital. This combination makes it one of the best regions of the country to live in.

Certain locations in the region are closely linked to important events in Czech history such as the once affluent historical silver-mining town of Kutná Hora, and from the more recent tragic past, Lidice. Central Bohemia gave history the Hussite King Jiří of Poděbrady, the final battle for the Hussite extremists at Lipany, and many places along the Berounka and around Kladno are linked to the original Czech myths on which the Přemyslid dynasty based its right to rule. The castles of Křivoklát, Karlštejn and Konopiště are also situated in the region, as are the pleasant and interesting towns of Beroun and Mělník, excellent day trips from Prague. Many important transport arteries pass through the region facilitating carefree travel, and four of the country's main rivers, the Berounka, Vltava, Elbe and Sázava flow through at the beginning of their long journey to the North Sea.

GETTING AROUND

It goes without saying that Prague, as the transport hub of the whole of Bohemia, fulfils the same role as far as central Bohemia is concerned. Every town and village has a direct bus and/or train service to Prague, but some of the less inhabited areas of the west and southwest have fewer connections. Prague radiates roads and railway tracks in every possible direction, and central Bohemia has by far the most kilometres of motorway of any of the Czech regions, a fact which also makes getting around simple.

KUTNÁ HORA

Stepping off the train at the somewhat dilapidated railway station in Kutná Hora there is little to suggest that this small town with its 21,000 inhabitants 70km east

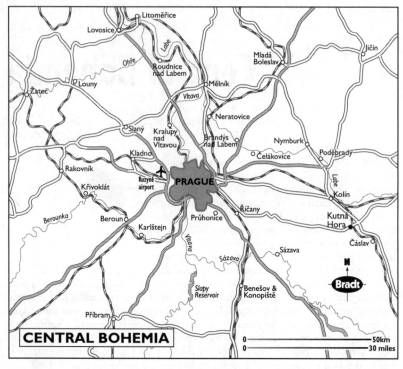

of Prague was once one of the most prominent towns in the Czech lands, if not in Europe. The town enjoyed a golden era which bequeathed a wealth of architecture, a fact recognised by UNESCO in 1996. Perhaps that should really read 'silver era' as silver mining is what gave Kutná Hora its significance. The silver extracted from beneath the town for around 200 years from the late 13th century was the principal source of revenue for medieval Bohemia and provided the raw material for the minting of the Prague groschen, one of Europe's most stable currencies at the time. Alas, when the flow of silver ore ran dry, the town was pensioned off and became a sleepy regional centre.

Kutná Hora is a kind of miniature Prague with its Gothic and Baroque architecture. Walking along Husova Street in the town's historic quarter you could be in Prague's Malá Strana district; the similarity is astounding. The likeness with Prague ends when you see the lower prices, friendlier locals and noticeable absence of tourist crowds and tacky paraphernalia. It is most certainly the best day trip visitors can make from Prague with good connections from the capital, and is an excellent combination of a tourist-savvy town that does not try to empty your wallet or go for the hard sell. It is also compact enough to be toured on foot. One of the main attractions in the area, the famous ossuary, is located in Sedlec. Once a separate village it is now virtually a suburb of Kutná Hora.

Most people make a day trip to Kutná Hora but there is sufficient in the town to warrant an overnight stay. It is a tourist-friendly place with an excellent and helpful **information centre** (*Palackého nám 377;* ⅄/f *327 512 378*), good-quality hotels and restaurants and signposts to the various attractions seemingly on every corner.

History

Sedlec was the original settlement where a Cistercian monastery was founded in 1142, the first in the Czech lands. Silver mining in the area dates back to the 13th century, though metal mined here may have been used to mint coins even earlier. Silver was discovered in 1260 and German miners from Jihlava to the southeast were the first to settle in what is now Kutná Hora. There are at least three versions of how the town got its name. It may be from the Czech verb *kutat*, meaning 'to mine', but a more imaginative version is that the name is derived from the Czech word for a monk's habit, *kutna*. The story goes that a monk, on finding some silver in the grass, concealed it with his habit to prevent anyone else finding it.

At the end of the 13th century the town experienced what can only be called a 'silver rush'. Many prospectors moved into the area, mines were opened, foundries set up, houses built and very rapidly a town shot up. In 1300, King Wenceslas II introduced a mining law which regulated the mines, and set up the central Bohemian mint in the town. The Prague groschen struck at the Italian Court (Vlašský dvůr) had a guaranteed and very high silver content, making it a particularly stable currency, and not only in the Czech lands. Over the course of the 14th century the town grew in importance and town walls, churches and many other buildings were added despite several sieges. In 1388, the foundations of the Cathedral of St Barbora, the patron saint of miners, were laid.

During the Hussite revolution Kutná Hora was on the side of the anti-Hussites. Many Hussites met their death by being cast into the mine shafts, and

BOHEMIA, MORAVIA AND SILESIA

The Czech Republic is made up of three historical territories, namely Bohemia, Moravia and Silesia. Bohemia is the largest and occupies most of the west and centre, Moravia is situated in the east along the border with Slovakia and Silesia is a tiny strip of land across the top of Moravia. Prague is obviously the capital of Bohemia; Brno is the main city in Moravia, and Opava is the historical capital of Silesia though Ostrava is larger, but not entirely in Silesia. The differences between the three are not at all evident to the first time visitor, though one major distinction is the fact that Bohemians drink beer while Moravians prefer wine. There are of course hundreds of subtle features which differentiate Bohemians from Moravians and Silesians such as accent, food, folk costume and religion. Many say that Moravians (and Silesians) are a warmer, more easy-going and god-fearing people than their Bohemian neighbours and generally more aware of their folk heritage and traditions. It is no coincidence that most of the major folk festivals in the Czech Republic take place in Moravia.

For many the word 'Bohemia' has other connotations, evoking visions of arty types in black polo necks sipping coffee in Parisian street cafés. The word 'Bohemia' is in fact derived from the Latin name of a Celtic tribe, the Boii, who inhabited the Czech lands in the 4th century BC. In the mid 19th century the French began to call gypsies *bohémiens* as it was thought they had come from central Europe. Later the term began to be used for anyone with unconventional social habits. Interestingly, the concept of a bohemian lifestyle is now filtering back to Prague from the west. The Czechs have never called themselves 'Bohemians' though most will know that the name exists.

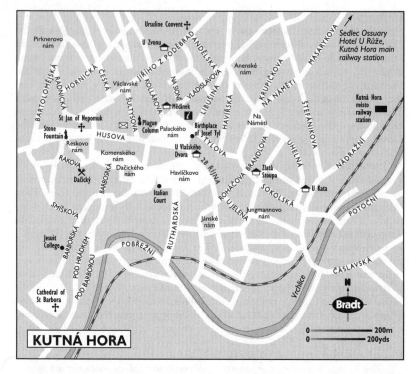

Emperor Zikmund used Kutná Hora silver to finance his crusades against them. The Hussites in turn burnt the monastery in Sedlec to the ground and Kutná Hora, including the mines, emerged from the Hussite period in general bad shape. Thanks to the declaration of the *Compactata* in 1436 (see page 12), the ethnic make-up of the town was altered when the disgruntled Germans uprooted and were replaced by Czechs.

In 1471, Vladislav Jagiellon was elected Czech king at the Italian Court in Kutná Hora and during his reign and the reign of his son Ludwig, Kutná Hora acquired its Gothic architectural treasures.

As ever, all good things must come to an end, and by the 16th century the mines had become too deep (one boasting the title of deepest in the world at the time) for the technology of the day to cope, and they fell out of use.

During the reign of Habsburg Ferdinand I, Jesuits arrived in the town after it had sustained considerable damage in the Thirty Years War, and the Counter-Reformation saw Baroque take a firm hold. Following unsuccessful attempts to revive the silver-mining industry, Kutná Hora became a sleepy provincial town.

Getting there and away

The most straightforward way to reach Kutná Hora from Prague is by hopping on one of the many **trains** that run east from Prague's main railway station to the Czech Republic's second city, Brno, and other destinations in Slovakia and further, which call at the town. As this is one of the principal lines in the country, services are relatively frequent and fast. There are eight direct services to Kutná Hora from the main railway station, but should there be none when you want to travel, a simple change in Kolín is necessary (112Kč return, 1 hour). Kutná Hora

Hl. nádraží (main railway station) is, confusingly enough, in Sedlec. You can reach Kutná Hora's historical centre by rail on a connecting service to Kutná Hora město (municipal station) which takes around ten minutes, you can take a local bus for 8Kč (tickets from the driver) or walk to the ossuary en route to the centre and catch a bus from there. Walking the 3km into the centre is perhaps not the best preparation for all the walking you are going to do *in* the centre, and the route along a busy road lined with quite unattractive *paneláky* is time wasted. You can also reach Kutná Hora by **bus** from Prague's Florenc coach station (at quite irregular intervals on weekdays) (1¼ hours, 60Kč one way). Brno is another 2½ hours away by train.

Where to stay and eat
Kutná Hora has a good selection of hotels and pensions and visitors should have no trouble finding a bed even at the height of the season. The information centre can supply you with a comprehensive list on request.

Top end located in the historical centre
Hotel Mědínek Palackého nám 316; ☎ 327 512 741–2; f 327 512 7843; www.medinek.cz. The centrally located, 50-room, 3-star Mědínek is a modern establishment near the information centre. The spick and span rooms are excellent value at 700–900Kč for a sgl with breakfast and 1,100–1,500Kč for a dbl.
Hotel Zlatá Stoupa Tylova 426; ☎ 327 511 540–3; f 327 513 808; www.web.telecom.cz/zlatastoupa. Equally well situated but slightly more expensive is this stylish, 4-star establishment. The 25 immaculate rooms come for around 1,800Kč with breakfast.
Hotel U Vlašského dvora 28 října 511; ☎ 327 514 618; f 327 514 627. As the name suggests it is situated near the Italian Court. Cosy, newly renovated rooms start at 1,400Kč.
Hotel U Zvonu Zvonářská 286; tel 327 511 516; f 327 516 571; www.uzvonu.cz. Near the Ursuline Convent, this is a tiny, 7-room pension and a sound option at 900–1,200Kč for a basic but comfortable room with bathroom and breakfast.

Tighter budgets
Hotel U Kata Uhelná 596; ☎ 327 515 096. Near Kutná Hora město railway station and recommended for its location and cheapness, this is a very reasonable option at 400Kč for a dbl with breakfast, though its 2-star rating is about right, so do not expect much luxury.

In Sedlec
Hotel U Růže Zámecká 52; ☎ 327 524 115; f 327 563 202; www.ruzehotel.cz. Literally a skull's throw away from the ossuary, the Rose has 14 beautiful dbl rooms, if sometimes slightly over-furnished. Prices hover around 900–1,300Kč for a room with breakfast.

Places to eat
Dačický Rakova 8; ☎ 327 512 248. A medieval beer hall with mural-covered walls, this is an unmissable Kutná Hora institution. There are 6 beers on tap from the Budvar and Kutná Hora breweries and almost 1,000m² of space for downing Czech medieval-style specialities for 100–200Kč to the sound of live music. Just a superb place to enjoy beer and *knedlíky*, and chill out.

What to see and do
Sedlec Ossuary Chapel of All Saints
Thanks to its relative proximity to the railway station the ossuary is very likely to be your first stop on a day trip from Prague. It is around ten minutes' walk from

the railway station along Vítězná Street. Follow the signs for the *Historické jádro* (historical centre). The ossuary is down a side street called Zámecká, which is opposite the Church of the Ascension of the Virgin Mary. Entry costs 35Kč, 20Kč for students; to take photographs will cost you 65/50Kč and to film inside the chapel will set you back 95/80Kč. Texts in English are provided and you can wander the ossuary at will.

Originally the cemetery of the Cistercian monastery in Sedlec, it became fashionable to be buried here after earth brought back from the Holy Land by the abbot of Sedlec was sprinkled on the cemetery ground. The grounds were enlarged to accommodate plague victims and again during the Hussite wars. So where did all the bones come from which are now inside? The bones were stacked up outside and then inside the small Chapel of All Saints when the cemetery was reduced in size. The chapel was then restyled into an ossuary. The building we see today is the work of the prolific Baroque architect Santini, and dates from 1710. The present arrangement of bones dates from 1870 and is the achievement of one František Rint, a woodcarver, whose name you can see written in bones at the foot of the steps on the right looking down. It is incredible to think that the bones of an estimated 40,000 people were used to create this creepy decoration. You cannot miss the chandelier in the middle of the ossuary containing at least one of every bone in the human body, or the coat of arms in bones of the Schwarzenberg family who purchased the abbey and the land around in 1784.

This is an eerie, thought-provoking place and not one you would not want to visit alone after dark. The intention, however, is not to frighten but to remind us of the transience of life and the inevitability of death. Each skull represents a whole life lived and reminds visitors of the short period we have to roam the planet.

Near by you will find the Church of the Ascension of the Virgin Mary and the old monastery now part of the tobacco factory (closed to visitors). The church was closed at the time of writing.

Cathedral of St Barbora

To locate the cathedral follow the signs for Chrám sv Barbory (*admission 30/15Kč*). En route you pass the huge former Jesuit College from the late 17th century on the right. St Barbora is the patron saint of miners and it was employees from the town's silver mines who were responsible for the creation of this masterpiece of Gothic architecture, one of the finest in the republic. It was begun in 1388 by Jan Parléř, the son of Charles IV's architect, Petr Parléř, followed by architects Matyáš Rejsek (who worked on Prague's Powder Tower – Prašná brána) and Benedikt Ried (Vladislav Hall in Prague Castle), but was not completed until 1905, 500 years later. Comparisons with Prague's Cathedral of St Vitus are inevitable. Look out for the Baroque organ overhead, the black and gold Baroque altars and the abundant reminders of Kutná Hora's mining past.

Italian Court (Vlašský dvůr)

The Italian Court is situated on Havlíčkovo Square not far from the main Palackého Square (*admission 40/20Kč in Czech, 70/50Kč in English*). The building served as the royal Bohemian mint until 1727 and it was here that the famous Prague groschen were hammered out at a rate of 2,000 per 12-hour shift at the height of production. They were called 'Prague' groschen as they were first minted in the capital. The tour leads visitors through the treasury with a fascinating exhibition on the minting of the silver coins. It continues to the Royal Audience Hall with its murals depicting the election of Czech King Vladislav Jagiellon and the decree of Kutná Hora in 1409, and the Chapel of SS Wenceslas and Vladislav decorated in Art Nouveau style rather like the Church of SS Peter and Paul at Vyšehrad in Prague. The remainder of the building is used as the town hall with council meetings, weddings etc still conducted in the Royal Audience Hall.

Other places of interest

Apart from Kutná Hora's 'big three', there are several other sites scattered around the historical centre worthy of mention. The **Ursuline Convent** (klášter Voršilek) in Jiřího z Poděbrad Street, built by Dientzenhofer in the 18th century, was returned to the order in 1989 after the communists had closed it in 1950. The oversize **plague column** on Šultysova Street reminds us of the town's 6,000 plague victims. In the subsequently named Tylova Street leading off Palackého Square you will find the **birthplace of Josef Tyl**, composer of the Czech national anthem. The beautiful **Church of St Jan of Nepomuk** in Husova Street should be visited on summer mornings when a mysterious light passes over the picture of the saint. And thirsty tourists can seek out the again rather oversize circular Gothic **Stone Fountain** (Kammená kašna) which has a gargoyle water tap.

MĚLNÍK

High above the confluence of Bohemia's two great rivers, the Elbe (Labe) and the Vltava, stands the 1,000-year-old picturesque town of Mělník, an ideal, relaxing day trip from Prague. A strategically important position since the arrival of the Slavs, the town's history is dominated by whatever fort or castle has stood on the site of today's chateau, a place which witnessed the lives of some of the most revered figures in Czech history such as St Ludmila and St Václav who spent his boyhood there. The wooden fort originally called Pšov was replaced by a Romanesque stone castle which served as a royal widows' residence, spawning a town which was given the name Mělník after the chalky, crumbly stone of the surrounding area (*mel* being an old Slavic word for chalk). At the beginning of the 13th century Otakar II Přemysl granted the town royal status, and Charles IV introduced Burgundian vines to the area in 1365. Mělník was a staunch Hussite town due to its predominantly Czech population, and enjoyed economic prosperity under Jiří of Poděbrady and the Jagiellon kings. The chateau was added to over the centuries, and in 1753 came into the possession of the Lobkowicz family, the owners today, though it was only returned to them in 1992, the communists having seized it in 1948. Today Mělník is a significant port because of its position on the Elbe.

Plan your visit to coincide with the wine festival (*vinobraní*) held annually in mid to late September. Failing that you can always buy a bottle of the famous wine year round.

Getting there and away

By far the simplest way to reach Mělník from Prague is by **bus**. A regular half-hourly to hourly service departs Prague's Holešovice station (red metro line C, nádraží Holešovice station) on weekdays (32Kč or 40Kč, 40 minutes). On weekends a less frequent service runs from Florenc coach station. From Mělník bus station climb the hill to the historic centre up Kpt Jaroše or Krombholcova Street.

Tourist information

The information centre (*nám Míru 11;* ⟍/f *315 627 503*) has lots of free info, but do not expect a smile.

Where to stay

Hotel U Rytířů Svatováclavská 17; ⟍ 315 621 440; f 315 621 439; www.urytiru.cz. This small, newly renovated hotel opposite the chateau is a sound option. Prices start at 1,900Kč for a suite with all mod cons accommodating up to 4 people. The hotel has a restaurant with covered terrace in summer serving Czech and international staples for 130–230Kč and Czech Budweiser.

Hotel Jaro 17 listopadu; ⟍ 315 626 852; f 315 626 851; www.hoteljaro.cz. This similarly newly renovated 50-bed place is 5 mins' walk south of the central square and has decent dbls for 1,000–1,700Kč, as well as a restaurant where you can eat well for 70–150Kč.

Hotel Ludmila Prašská 2639; ⟍ 315 622 419; f 315 623 390; www.ludmila.cz. The tower block-like Ludmila has 200 beds so is hardly ever full, but has the slight disadvantage of being about 1km south of the historical centre along Pražská Street. Prices start at 980Kč for a sgl room in low season.

Where to eat

Zámecká restaurace ⟍ 315 622 121. The best place to taste the local wines is the touristy and occasionally quite raucous Chateau Restaurant, which has great views of the river. The entrance is in the courtyard of the chateau, and prices range from 80–130Kč. Wash your food down with a delicious locally produced wine.

Restaurace na Hradbách nám Míru 9; ⟍ 315 625 825; f 315 621 630. A nice little place on the main square where you can enjoy generous portions for 80–220Kč, and which has a shady garden and children's play area.

What to see and do
The chateau

The entrance to the chateau (*admission 60Kč*) at the end of Svatováclavská Street south of Míru Square, is through an inconspicuous archway beneath the Lobkowicz coat of arms. Traditionally the residence of Czech queens and royal widows the chateau underwent a major Gothic restyling during the reign of the last Přemyslid kings. The last wife of Charles IV, Eliška of Pomerania, lived here, and the last Czech queens to reside here were the wives of Jiří of Poděbrady. In 1542, the castle was renovated in the Renaissance style, but fell into disrepair during the Thirty Years War. An early Baroque southern wing was added at the end of the 17th century. In 1753, through marriage, the chateau and the surrounding estates found themselves in the ownership of the Lobkowicz family. The communists confiscated the estate in 1948, but the chateau was returned to the family in 1992, since which time it has been in a constant state of renovation.

The self-guided tour leads you through the former living quarters of the Lobkowicz family and to the Great Hall and the Chapel of St Ludmila. Highlights include the Baroque altar in the Chapel of St Ludmila, a fascinating collection of maps (find Prague and see what you recognise) in the Great Hall and paintings by Škréta throughout. Some of the rooms were closed at the time of writing. Wine tasting takes place in the 14th-century wine cellars beneath the chateau.

The ossuary and Church of SS Peter and Paul

Entry to the ossuary is 20Kč, which is about right for the size of the place. Notice the 16th-century graffiti on the columns and the skulls turned inwards, curiously identified as German owing to their wrinkled surface. Unfortunately only groups of ten are given tours of the Church of SS Peter and Paul. If you cannot leave Mělník without seeing its interior, try twisting arms back in town at the information centre or bribery.

Other places of interest

One of the best features of Mělník is the **view** from the pathway running under the chateau and the church. From this vantage point look out for the confluence of the Elbe and Vltava rivers, the vineyards and on a clear day the extinct volcanoes which form the low mountain range known as the České středohoří. The strange bump as you look right is **Říp**, a mountain of great significance for the Czechs. Legend has it that the leader of the Czech clan, *Čech*, stood on the summit and proclaimed that all he saw around would be their new homeland. The **Prague Gate** (Pražská brána) is worth ascending for superb views of the town and surroundings (*open year round, afternoons only, admission 20Kč*). The **District Museum** situated next to the Baroque **town hall** has interesting exhibitions on winemaking and historical prams and both are located on the delightful **town square** (náměstí Míru) with its arcades and fine architecture.

LIDICE

The assassination of *Reichsprotektor* Reinhard Heydrich on 27 May 1942 in Prague by Czechs trained in Britain was the greatest success of the Czech resistance movement, but it came at a price. The Nazis were enraged at the assassination and sought to take their revenge on the Czech population. Under pressure from Berlin to come up with the perpetrators, Heydrich's successor Karl Frank was desperate for any shred of evidence of the assassins or anybody who may have known about the plot, or assisted in its execution.

Up until June 1942 Lidice was just an ordinary quiet Czech village with 500 inhabitants, a school and a church. The men of the village worked mostly in the foundries and mines of nearby Kladno. Whilst investigating the assassination of Heydrich, the Kladno Gestapo chanced upon a letter addressed to a woman in the nearby town of Slaný. The text of the letter makes no mention of the plot, but the Gestapo became suspicious because of its vague wording. Even after interrogating the two people involved, the Nazis still had no evidence, but this flimsiest of links, plus the fact that the Nazis were aware that the parents of two Czechs serving in Great Britain lived in Lidice, was sufficient for them to deem the community guilty, despite a lack of concrete facts.

The Nazis arrived on the morning of 10 June 1942, and set about murdering every male over the age of 15 and razing the village to the ground. Some of the children were sent to Germany for Germanisation, the rest of the children and all the women to concentration camps. Of the 500 inhabitants a mere 143 women and 17 children returned after the war. One can only imagine the emotional and physical torture these innocent, peaceful people went through at the hands of the dehumanised fascist regime. This crime against humanity sent shockwaves around the world and the horror of Lidice is etched into the Czech national identity; every Czech knows the story behind it, and almost every town has a Lidická Street in honour of the village. In 1947, work was begun on a new Lidice, 300m from the original site.

The story above is told in much greater detail by the exhibits and 18-minute film at the Lidice Museum (*admission 50/20Kč, open year round*). When enough speakers of a common language are present, the film is projected in a small cinema beneath the museum and includes SS footage of the destruction of the village used as evidence at the Nuremberg trials. On the ground floor an exhibition remembers the dead of Lidice with photographs of the men folk, artefacts from the village and lots of other information. A recorded commentary (available in English) is played while you peruse.

Following a visit to the museum walk down the hill to where the village once stood. On the right you will see a moving bronze cast of a group of children representing not only the children of Lidice, but all child victims of World War II. The fate of the children of Lidice is particularly disturbing. Continue down the hill to the Red Army monument, and below that is the site of Horák's farm where the Nazi firing squads shot the men. There is also a memorial and beautiful rose garden with a fountain called the 'Park of Peace and Friendship' back at the top of the hill adjacent to the museum. The rose bushes were gifted to Lidice from all around the world. A stroll around these places gives you a chance to contemplate what you have seen. Lidice should never be forgotten.

Getting there and away

Half a day is sufficient to visit the site 20km west of Prague just short of Kladno. **Bus** is the only option, and because half the population of the nearby former industrial town of Kladno commute to Prague (especially to Ruzyně Airport) the service is swift and regular. Buses depart from Dejvická metro station, on the opposite side of the road from the Hotel Diplomat (21–25Kč, 25 minutes). You would be unlucky to wait half an hour for a bus on weekdays, and at the weekend the service runs approximately every hour or half-hour depending on the time of day. Other services leave from Zličín metro station. This can be irritating on the return journey, as the bus you hop on back might take you to Zličín, a long metro ride from the centre of Prague.

KARLŠTEJN

Picturesque Karlštejn, with its hefty cream Gothic towers rising boldly out of the wooded hills of the Berounka valley, occupies a unique place among castles and chateaux in the Czech Republic. Karlštejn was a prestigious residence and seat of power but its principal *raison d'être* was as an oversize safe for the imperial crown jewels and other treasures, and was purpose built by Charles IV in the mid 14th century. The foundation stone was laid in 1348 by Archbishop of Prague Arnošt z Pardubic, Charles's friend and adviser, and the huge, impregnable Gothic strongbox was named after the emperor himself (the village had been called Budy up until that point). It is not known for sure who actually oversaw construction of the castle, though one possible candidate is Matthias of Arras, the architect who worked on St Vitus Cathedral. Whoever designed Karlštejn did a good job, as the Great Tower housing the most precious objects was never taken, despite the best efforts of the Hussites and the Swedes.

After Charles's death his son King Václav IV resided there for a while (the last king to do so), but later shunned his father's creation in favour of Točník further up the Berounka River. Under his brother Zikmund the crown jewels were moved to Prague during the Hussite wars, never to return. From then until the grand restoration in the 19th century, the building had a bumpy ride, suffering at the hands of the Swedish during the Thirty Years War, eager for anything of value they may find inside, then left in a state of virtual ruin and subsequently used as a convent and storehouse with little attention paid to its maintenance. At the beginning of the 19th century, thanks to the renaissance of Czech national identity, Karlštejn's historical significance was realised again, and in 1886 funds were released by the imperial authorities for its restoration, carried out by Josef Mocker, the great 'neo-Gothiciser'. The intention was to revert the castle to its original 14th-century Gothic glory, but many have since criticised Mocker's efforts, especially for the shape of the roofs, never part of the original, and for the demolition of numerous buildings.

The castle today is a tourist magnet and the most popular castle in the country after Prague Castle. In summer the courtyard heaves with tour bus groups, the approaches to the castle are lined with tacky crystal shops and snack bars, and the tours are sickeningly overpriced. That said, in contrast to the busy area around the castle, the dark wooded hills, so typical for this part of Bohemia, offer peace and serenity, only interrupted by birdsong, the breeze in the tree tops and the fall of your shoes on the carpet of pine needles underfoot.

Getting there and away

Karlštejn lies conveniently on the main railway artery west making **rail** by far the best mode of transport. International expresses do not stop here, but all other slow services to Beroun do. These leave either Prague Smíchov or the main station approximately every hour and the journey to Karlštejn takes around 35 minutes. The views of the delightfully picturesque Berounka valley from the carriage window are well worth the 46Kč fare on their own (do not be so taken with the views that you forget to get off!). The castle is 20–25 minutes on foot from the railway station and most of the walk is uphill. Follow the signs saying '*hrad*', though you will know you are heading in the right direction from the gift shops and snack bars lining the route

Where to stay

Trains run back to Prague until 23.00 at night so becoming stranded in Karlštejn would take some doing. Accommodation in the village is marginally overpriced, but if you desperately must, need or want to stay the night, the best options are the **Pension U Královny Dagmar** just below the castle (*Karlštejn 2;* `\/f 311 681 383`) which has comfortable rooms for around 1,000Kč, and the 14-room **Hotel Koruna** (*Karlštejn 13;* `\ 311 681 465; f 311 681 341`) which has similarly priced rooms and an excellent restaurant.

Where to eat

Karlštejn is not lacking in places to eat and in general prices are not as inflated as they first appear. At the bottom of the hill next to the coach park try **U Elišky**, a renovated communist-era eatery with Czech and international staples. It is always chock-a-block at meal times. Heading further up the road to the castle on the right there is the restaurant in the **Hotel Koruna**, a very safe option with mains for

REICHSPROTEKTOR HEYDRICH AND THE CROWN OF ST WENCESLAS

In a show of unbridled arrogance and disregard for Czech history, *Reichsprotektor* Heydrich once placed the crown of St Wenceslas on his head, and in jest proclaimed himself King of *Böhmen und Mähren*. Perhaps he had not been informed of the superstition, which says that whoever wears the crown without rightful claim to the Czech throne, will die within a year. Heydrich was assassinated not long afterwards.

50–200Kč and lots of outdoor seating. Almost opposite is the **Restaurace U Janů** with slightly cheaper meals and again a lot of tables in the sun.

What to see and do
The castle
There are two tours available. Tickets for standard **tour I**, which runs year round, are bought on the day (*120/60Kč in Czech, 200/100Kč in English*), and groups leave at least once an hour. As a maximum of 12 people per hour may enter the highlight of **tour II**, the Chapel of the Holy Cross, this must be booked in advance, but *not* with the castle directly. Bookings for these tours (*Jul–Nov only*) can only be made by contacting Národní památkový ústav, Územní odborné pracoviště Středních Čech v Praze, Sabinova 5, 130 11 Praha 3; ❨ 274 008 154–6; f 274 008 152; e reservace@stc.npu.cz.

Reserving months (or even a year) in advance is strongly recommended, as the tours are hopelessly booked up during the summer. Tickets cost 300/100Kč in Czech and English and there is a booking fee of 20Kč. The chapel containing precious panel paintings by Master Theodoricus and amazing walls decorated with a stunning combination of gold, precious stones and Venetian glass is protected by limiting visitor numbers, as moisture created by large groups could cause damage. Very occasionally at the end of the tourist season these restrictions are lifted for a short period of time.

The vast majority of visitors settle for tour I (50 minutes) which explores the **Imperial Palace**, including the Knights' Hall (Rytířská síň) with portraits of Charles's actual and fictitious Přemyslid ancestors from mythical Čech to Václav III, the Dining Hall (Hodovní síň), Charles's bedroom, the recently restored Audience Hall (Audienční síň) and the guards' quarters. It then moves on to the **Marian Tower** (Mariánská věž), under extensive renovation at the time of research, but nevertheless housing a tour-stopping exact replica of the Bohemian crown jewels, previously on display in the Lobkovicz Palace in Prague, a truly awe-inspiring piece of medieval royal regalia, especially the crown of St Wenceslas with its rubies and sapphires as big as pebbles from the banks of the Berounka. Having shaken off the guide (and disconcerting private security guard) you are free to explore the Gothic **Bell Tower** and the **Well Tower** where you can look down into the yawning, 80m-deep well shaft.

Walks around Karlštejn
The hills, forests and valleys surrounding Karlštejn are invigorating places for walking and hiking. In stark contrast to the busy tourist area below the castle, the tree-covered hills created by millennia of the Berounka's flowing waters are as peaceful and serene as anywhere in the Czech countryside. The combination of the picturesque train ride, the castle tour, a picnic by the river and a gentle walk in the beautiful landscape is an ideal lazy day out from the capital.

A simple, unambitious walk could be in any direction along the river to the next railway station. However, various marked trails provide more interesting rambles. VKÚ-KČT map 36 *Okolí Prahy–západ* covers the area. Those who seek more of a challenge could take the green trail to the Koněprusy caves and Tetín to the northwest ending in Beroun. Alternatively there is the red trail through the forest to the Church of St John under the Rock (kostel sv Jana pod skalou) switching to a blue trail to Vráž where you can catch a bus or train to Beroun. Or take the red trail to Mořinka where you can pick up a blue trail into the Karlík valley, a nature reserve with the ruins of a 15th-century castle, ending in Dobřichovice on the Beroun–Prague railway line.

KŘIVOKLÁT

A Czech fairy-tale castle perched high on a promontory towering above a sleepy village and rising out of a sea of forested hills – Křivoklát is that typical Czech blend of striking architecture set in ancient woodland and is a perfect place to wander along walking trails, observe the wildlife and feel the eternal forest all around you. This is timeless Bohemia where events move as slowly as the Rakovnický stream flows through the valley, and life is still very much in tune with the gradual changing of the seasons. Visitors to Prague with a day to kill and a craving to break out of the cramped, tourist-choked confines of the city's historical centre, find a day trip out into the wooded valleys of central Bohemia's countryside a fascinating and romantic experience. Whilst most find their way to Karlštejn Castle, a few extra miles by train would deliver them to Křivoklát and its dramatic surroundings which have retained more of the ambience visitors expect from a medieval castle.

Getting there and away

Two hours or so by train (the only option) from the capital, the journey up the picturesque Berounka valley alone is worth leaving Prague for. There are two ways to reach Křivoklát by train and both involve a change unless you take the only direct train which departs Prague Smíchov station at 09.00 arriving two hours later. Otherwise take any train to Beroun from Prague's main railway station, and change on to services heading north to Rakovník (1 hour 40 minutes, 98Kč). If you are feeling adventurous you could instead board one of the trains which leave Prague Masaryk station every two hours to Rakovník, and then head south towards Beroun, though this takes a lot longer and you miss the views of the Berounka valley.

Where to stay and eat

After your tour and stroll through the forest, what better way to end your trip than with a hearty Czech meal at one of the two nearby restaurants? **Hotel U Sýkory** serves traditional Czech fare and excellent beer whilst you can choose local specialities, including venison and wild boar, at the **Restaurant U Jelena** before your train trundles you back down the Berounka valley and to Prague. If you do decide to stay in Křivoklát the Hotel U Sýkory has basic rooms for 1,000Kč a night, or alternatively you could make the short 16km trip north by train to Rakovník where there is more choice.

What to see
The castle

From Křivoklát station follow the steep cobbled road ascending to the castle ticket office and the main entrance. Entry into the castle is permitted with a guide only and groups are usually small. Entry is 80/40Kč for a tour in Czech, 150/80Kč in a foreign language and the castle is open weekends only March, November and December and every day except Mondays April–October.

Křivoklát originally served as a hunting lodge for Czech kings and princes and the original structure dates back to the 13th century. Though built by kings Wenceslas I and Přemysl Otakar II, evidence has been unearthed of a much older structure on this site. Unlike its more illustrious cousin Karlštejn, Křivoklát played a less glamorous role in Czech history, but it is associated with Charles IV who was imprisoned here as a boy by his suspicious father. By 1487, the castle had undergone reconstruction and suffered a major fire and in that year King Vladislav of the Jagiellon dynasty instigated a complete reconstruction, adding the chapel and transforming the castle into a fine example of Jagiellon-era Gothic architecture. Yet more renovation was begun in 1856 by the Fürstenberg family, who owned the castle at the time, but it was not until 1920, under state ownership, that it gained its current appearance. Every age and owner have left their mark on the castle, which explains its perplexing muddle of architectural styles. The castle remains the property of the Czech state to this day.

A tour of the castle not only gives visitors the opportunity to admire the architecture of the Gothic chapel and the Royal Hall, but also provides glimpses of everyday life. In the Royal Hall look for the graffiti and doodles on the wall opposite the throne, left by children whose playful laughter once echoed here. Do not miss the castle's collection of historical sleighs with their heated seats and ornate runners and the library which contains some 53,000 volumes. Horrific instruments of torture and the dungeon confirm the darker purposes the castle served, often being used as a prison owing to its location. The castle courtyard regularly hosts medieval markets, festivals, concerts and other events with a historical theme.

KONOPIŠTĚ

The neo-Gothic chateau of Konopiště, 40km southeast of the capital is one of the most interesting day trips visitors can make from Prague. Of central Bohemia's three 'K's (the other two being Karlštejn and Křivoklát), Konopiště may be the least imposing from the outside, but certainly rises above the other two as far as interiors are concerned with room after room crammed with hunting trophies, historical firearms, priceless furniture and works of art.

Founded in the 13th century by Bishop Tobiáš of Benešov, its best-known owner (and its last) was Archduke Franz Ferdinand d'Este, heir to the Austro-Hungarian throne, famously assassinated along with his wife Žofie Chotková in Sarajevo in 1914, an event which lit the blue touch paper of World War I. The archduke bought Konopiště from the Lobkovicz family in 1887 and set about transforming it into the neo-Gothic residence we see today. He was also a fanatical huntsman and some of his hunt statistics are almost beyond belief. It is documented that over the course of his life, abruptly ended by the gun of Serb student Gavro Princip, the trigger-happy archduke bagged some 300,000 birds and animals and could easily down 1,000 pheasants in a day's shooting. A mere 1.5% of his trophies are displayed in the chateau. The man was obsessed with guns and shooting, hence the mechanical shooting range in a wing of the chateau where he would hone his skills, and the huge armoury, the third largest in Europe. Live by the sword, die by the sword some might say, and gun-crazy Franz had certainly accumulated some bad karma by the time he arrived in Bosnia!

Getting there and away

The chateau lies approximately 2½km west of the town of Benešov which is well served by road and rail from Prague and the south. **Buses** leave Florenc coach station and Roztyly metro station in southern Prague at very regular intervals, and the journey takes only 30–50 minutes. The fare is around 35Kč. **Trains** depart Prague's main railway station at least once an hour with slow trains ending in Benešov and expresses continuing south to České Budějovice (50 minutes to 1¼ hours, 64Kč).

On alighting in Benešov, turn left out of the railway station (right out of the bus station opposite), cross the bridge over the tracks and follow the road signs to Konopiště. You will not see the chateau until you are right underneath it. At

Benešov station notice the *Císářský salónek*, the Imperial Waiting Room built specially for Ferdinand d'Este to avoid waiting with the plebs.

Where to stay
Nová myslivna Konopiště 22; ℐ 317 722 496; f 317 723 017; www.e-stranka.cz/novamyslivna. Thanks to its proximity to Prague few visitors would choose to stay over in Konopiště. If you must or simply get the urge to, the best place near the chateau itself is the Nová myslivna at the coach park. The 40 rooms under the crazy slanting roof which reaches right down to the ground are plain but bearable, and the price is good at 275–500Kč a night. There is also a tour bus restaurant.

Benešov has a few reasonable hotels. Ask at the information centre (*Malé náměstí 1700;* ℐ/f *317 726 004*) for details.

Where to eat
Stará myslivna Konopiště 2; ℐ/f 317 721 148; www.staramyslivnakonopiste.cz. By a long way the best place to get your dose of meat, dumplings and beer is the Old Hunting Lodge, a short walk downhill from the chateau. Hunting trophies like Franz Ferdinand d'Este's back in the chateau line the walls, a huge hearth crackles in the middle of the long dining room and the tables are beautifully laid and decorated with fresh flowers. Though mostly frequented by foreigners, the main dishes of wild boar, venison, pheasant and other game cost a reasonable 100–250Kč and the superb local 12° Ferdinand beer flows freely.

What to see
The chateau
The only way to see the inside of the chateau is on a guided tour (*Tours I and II 100/50Kč in Czech, 150/80Kč in English, tour III 140Kč in Czech and 250Kč in English (no concessions), open Mar–Oct*). Tour I takes in the hunting trophies, the chateau's Meissen porcelain collection and rooms used by Kaiser Wilhelm II during a visit in 1914. Tour II is perhaps the most diverting of the trio as it explores the armoury, Franz Ferdinand's bedroom and the beautiful Chapel of St Hubert in addition to the trophies. Tour III is limited to eight people at a time, and examines the early 20th-century living quarters of the d'Este family providing the best insight into the everyday life of the chateau's most distinguished owners. Of everything on display, the highlight must be the armoury containing row upon row of hunting rifles, powder pouches, hunting knives and other hunt regalia, as well as swords, spears, suits of armour, cannons and crossbows, all reflecting the archduke's passion for slaughtering anything that moved on the estate.

When Franz Ferdinand d'Este was not hunting in the surrounding forests, one would probably have found him in his own private **shooting range** (*střelnice, admission 25/10Kč*) just off the courtyard, a mechanical contraption more at home in an English seaside resort than a Bohemian chateau. Put together in Vienna it arrived in Konopiště in 1900. There is a short film showing the thing in action but unfortunately you are not permitted to shoot off a few rounds at it!

Another focus of the Archduke's obsessive mind was St George, a fact which can be seen in the **Gallery of St George** (Galerie sv Jiří) behind the chateau (*admission 25/10Kč*). The large space is packed to the rafters with statues and paintings of the saint spearing the dragon from all eras and in all shapes, sizes and styles which he collected throughout his life. The scene becomes monotonous after a while, but is an interesting sight, especially for the English. Only around 10% of the total collection is displayed.

SÁZAVA MONASTERY

Towering above the river Sázava and set against a backdrop of rounded, tree-covered hills, the Sázava Monastery (Sázavský klášter) is a suitable day trip for visitors staying for longer periods, or for those with a deeper interest in the country's past. There are undoubtedly grander and more engaging places in central Bohemia, but Sázava should be visited for its significance rather than its tourist value.

As legend would have it, in 1032 during a chance meeting in the woods, a local monk called Prokop persuaded Prince Oldřich to found a monastery on a hilltop overlooking the river Sázava. In reality Prokop probably financed it himself. From the outset the monastery leant towards eastern Christianity, and is widely considered the last place in the Czech lands to preach the Slavic liturgy and produce religious texts in the Glagolitic alphabet brought to the region by Cyril and Methodius. Prokop was later canonised and is one of the country's four patron saints. In 1097 Latin arrived in Sázava along with monks from the Benedictine monastery in Břevnov (Prague), though the Slavic past was resurrected for a short period during the reign of Charles IV. His kingship also witnessed the beginning of construction by the monks of an ambitious Gothic basilica, whose dark red sandstone skeleton dominates the courtyard next to the monastery, never finished due to a lack of funds. Despite a major Baroque restyling in the 18th century, the monastery never reclaimed its former glory, and was eventually abolished in 1782 by Austrian Emperor Josef II, and transformed into a private residence. It rather surprisingly remains in private hands to this day.

The hour-long tour in Czech (*50/25Kč; open Apr and Sep weekends; May–Aug Tue–Sun*) seems slightly superfluous as an explanatory text would suffice. English texts are available, and I was assured that calling ahead could secure an English-speaking guide (\ *327 321 177*). The tour begins in the museum with exhibits on the Great Moravian Empire, the arrival of Christianity in the Czech lands under the Přemyslid dynasty and the founding of the monastery. It then moves on to the Gothic Chapter Hall where you should look out for the Sázava Madonna portrayed ticking off a naughty three-year-old Jesus, possibly the only representation of the Virgin of this kind. The tour ends in the beautiful Rococo Church of St Prokop.

After the long train journey and tour of the monastery, why not enjoy a hearty Czech meal and a beer at the **Perla Restaurant and wine bar** (*Klášterní 19;* \ *327 320 757, mains 50–120Kč*) roughly 100m down the hill heading towards the river before the ride back to Prague.

Getting there and away

The Sázava Monastery lies around 50km southeast of Prague. Direct hourly **buses** run from Skalka metro station (end of green line A) to Sázava Černé Budy where you should alight for the monastery (1 hour 20 minutes, 88Kč). A change in Čerčany is necessary when travelling by **train**. Board any train from Prague's main station heading for Benešov and change in Čerčany on to services heading along the Sázava River, alighting at Sázava Černé Budy. The whole wonderfully picturesque journey takes 1¾ hours and single tickets cost 88Kč. On arrival at Sázava Černé Budy cross the tracks, pick your way through the *paneláky* downhill to the footbridge over the river. You cannot miss the monastery on the opposite bank.

BEROUN

Beroun, it must be stated, is slightly off the beaten track, but has enough to warrant half a day's exploration. Most visitors to the Czech Republic passing through the area will only see the town flash by beneath them from the viaduct, which hurls the D5 motorway over the outskirts, or the railway station from the window of an express train heading west. However, a few may find themselves with time to kill between trains on their way elsewhere.

The town sprang up in the 13th century alongside the river Mže, now called the Berounka, at the site of a natural ford on an important medieval trade route from Prague to Pilsen and on to Bavaria. After being abandoned sometime towards the end of the 13th century, Beroun was rebuilt during the reign of Václav II, and a Dominican monastery was founded. The town experienced great prosperity during the golden era of the reign of Charles IV, excelling in winemaking, beer brewing and pottery production. During the Hussite revolution the town was divided along ethnic lines until Jan Žižka arrived to put the Germans to the sword and burn down the monastery. Beroun was again prosperous under the Jagiellon kings. The town also suffered many fires, floods, pillaging and epidemics, but always seems to have risen again from the ashes of history.

Beroun today has around 18,000 souls and prospers from jobs in easily reachable Prague and in local light industry. The town took the brunt of the terrible floods which hit the region in 2002, but there is little evidence of the devastation, and in effect the deluge gave the town a unique opportunity to renovate.

A huge, very popular pottery fair invades Hus Square and the surrounding streets each year in mid September to coincide with the Days of European Heritage, most definitely the most exciting time to visit.

Getting there and away
Beroun enjoys excellent rail connections as it is a halt on the main international route west to Germany. A **train** leaves either Prague Smíchov or Prague's main station for Beroun approximately every half an hour. Beroun is the last stop for many slow trains, but expresses continue on to places such as Františkovy Lázně, Cheb and Pilsen. The 22km journey takes approximately 50 minutes and a return ticket costs 76Kč. Beroun has become a dormitory town, reflected by the regularity of the **bus** service seven days a week from Zličín metro station (last stop on yellow line B) or Nové Butovice (same line). The bus works out slightly cheaper and is quicker, but without the views of the Berounka.

Tourist information
The information centre (*Husovo nám 69;* \ *311 654 321*) has relatively informative brochures on Beroun's attractions and the staff will be pleased to see you.

Where to stay
Hotel Český dvůr Husovo nám 86; \/f 311 621 411; www.cesky-dvur.cz. This is a centrally located, friendly place with basic sgl rooms with shower and TV for an extremely reasonable 350Kč, and dbls for 600Kč.
Hotel na Ostrově na Ostrově 816; \ 311 713 100; f 311 713 199. Many go for the bright, colourful more upmarket option which seems to belong to the ice hockey stadium nearby. Prices start at 1,240Kč for a very decent sgl room, 1,860Kč for a dbl.

Where to eat
U Madly na Ostrově 3; \ 311 625 103; www.umadly.cz. Just east of the main square and across a small bridge over the Berounka is one of the best places in central Bohemia to empty some half-litre glasses of golden Czech brew, and fill up on tasty giant helpings

of Bohemian food. This popular place has a superb atmosphere with frequent live music, an intimate tavern ambience and an imaginative menu with mains for 100–220Kč. Back from the dead after the floods it is as good as ever.

What to see and do
The main **Husovo náměstí** (Hus Square) has three of the town's main sights, namely the town hall and the two Gothic gates which guard two of the access roads. The square itself was badly damaged in the 2002 flood and has since undergone a complete restoration, improving its appearance considerably. The **town hall**, while not exactly dominating the square, is an example of pseudo-Baroque architecture from 1903, fully renovated in 1998. The **Prague or Lower Gate** (Pražská or Dolní brána) looks practically the same as when it was built in the 14th century, as does the **Pilsen or Upper Gate** (Plzeňská or Horní brána) which can be climbed for bird's-eye views of the town. The **Church of St Jacob** stands at the opposite end of the square to the town hall. Unfortunately the church is not open to the public as such, but you can peer through the grill at the fabulous Baroque altar, or sneak in after the daily service. Above the church looms the **'Town Mountain'** with its viewing tower, open year round. Again the views are excellent. The mountain is also the site of the *Medvědárium* or **bear enclosure**. Beroun has a bear in its coat of arms which is apt, with a family of real bears living just outside the town centre! Follow the signs from Husovo náměstí for the bear enclosure. The original, bulky medieval town walls which almost encircle the main square are also worth a look.

THE RAKOVNÍK REGION
Few would consider the Rakovník region, 50km west of Prague, a tourist destination, save for Křivoklát Castle (see page 139) and the Berounka valley. But while the town of Rakovník itself has few historical monuments of note, the surrounding area is ideal for mountain biking and leisurely hiking. It is also well off the beaten track meaning low prices, friendlier locals and unspoilt beauty. A lattice of marked walking trails leads hikers over dark wooded hills, through secret valleys, to tiny villages and romantic castle ruins. Not a day trip destination, but two to three days discovering the area on foot will leave you feeling refreshed and inspired.

The area is famed for its hops, and in the not too distant past three breweries in Rakovník, Krušovice and Křivoklát prospered here, cooking up the Czech 'golden nectar'. While two of these met their demise, Krušovice brewery has gone on to become one of the major players on the Czech beer market. The north of the region is a mesh of wired hop fields, and hops from this area are an essential and prized ingredient of beers brewed across Bohemia and Moravia.

Getting there and away
Rakovník is an hour away from Prague by **bus**. Services depart Hradčanská metro station (green line A) around once an hour (1 hour, 50Kč). As is generally the rule, there are fewer buses at the weekends when you could try the **train** from Masarykovo station. The somewhat tedious journey via Kladno takes up to two hours and the single fare is 98Kč. An alternative and more picturesque option is to jump on any train to Beroun, and change on to services heading north via Křivoklát. This can be a slightly shorter journey with considerably prettier views from the window.

The bus and railway stations are next to one another five minutes south of the main square on the opposite side of the stream.

A MUSHROOMING PASTIME

Obsession, sport, pastime – I am not sure which to use, but probably all three describe the Czechs' relationship to mushroom picking. *Houbaření* (mushrooming) is science, adventure, competition and a topic of endless conversation and newspaper articles on giant examples found here or there, or the latest person to die from mushroom poisoning. Your fellow passengers on branch-line trains dressed in old sports clothes and bearing two covered wicker baskets brimming with fungi know exactly what to look for, when and where and never return home empty handed. There are three types of mushrooms – edible, inedible but not poisonous, and poisonous. Mushrooms can be found in the forests on cool mornings after light rain. Look at the foot of tree trunks to find them. If you know nothing about mushrooms, always go with someone who does, and never pick or even touch anything you are instructed not to. Czechs have 101 mushroom recipes including mushroom omelette, pickled mushrooms, fried breadcrumbed mushrooms, dried mushrooms and mushroom sauce for dumplings, common dishes in Czech households – especially in early autumn.

Where to stay

Hotel Sole Tyršova 157; ⊠ 313 250 111; f 313 517 047; www.hotelsole.cz. This small, family-run pension has modern, comfortable rooms for around 1,000Kč and is the nearest accommodation to the bus and railway stations just off the main square.

Pension Bezděkov Soukupova 1530; ⊠ 313 514 151; www.sweb.cz/penzion.bezdekov. This pension perched on the hillside around 15 minutes' walk north of the bus and railway stations, is probably the best option in town. The friendly owner will accommodate you in one of the 7 modern, clean rooms, some with views over Rakovník, for 400Kč for a sgl and 800Kč for a dbl. There is a restaurant on the ground floor and seating outside in the large garden, weather permitting (mains 60–150Kč).

Where to eat

Slávia Husovo náměstí 53; ⊠ 313 519 030. Slávia is a Rakovník institution and has been serving food and drink on the main square for as long as anyone cares to remember. Given a major facelift in the early 1990s, it could now do with a lick of paint here and there, but still serves decent Czech and international dishes for 70–200Kč and Pilsen beers.

What to see and do
Rakovník

Rakovník derives its name from '*rak*', the Czech for crayfish, which once used to revel in numbers in the muddy waters of the local stream. Legend has it that a poor woman, having nothing to give her children to eat, decided to end their suffering by feeding them crayfish, generally believed to be poisonous. Of course the children lived to tell the tale, and when word got round of the tasty treat at the bottom of the stream, people began to move to the banks, and a settlement formed, hence the name. The red crayfish appears in the town's coat of arms, and in the names of many local companies including Rakona, a giant detergents' manufacturer, one of the town's major employers, and, ironically, until recently the biggest polluter of the stream!

The town occupies a steep-sided valley with the Rakovnický Stream (now sadly minus the crayfish) dribbling its way to Křivoklát at the bottom. The centre of Rakovník is dominated by **Husovo náměstí**, one of the largest squares in central Bohemia with the Gothic **Church of St Bartholomew** at the eastern end where you will also find a small **museum** (*admission 20/10Kč*) with exhibitions on the town and the writer Zikmund Winter who taught at the secondary school opposite in the late 19th century. However, Rakovník's most interesting architectural sites are its perfectly preserved Gothic **gates**, some of the best examples in the country. Two of the original four have survived, the stocky **Prague Gate** (Pražská brána) built in 1516 next to the museum and housing part of the exhibition, and the taller, leaner **High Gate** (Vysoká brána) north of Husovo Square, which replaced a wooden structure in 1517–23. There are breathtaking views across the valley from the top of the latter.

Lužná Railway Museum
A short train ride north through the forest brings you to the run-down village of Lužná, a grimy rural railway junction, but with a great little railway museum (*admission 50/30Kč, open May–Sep*). Numerous old steam engines and rolling stock as well as scale models and other railway paraphernalia are housed in a former locomotive shed opposite the station.

Walks in the region
The Rakovník region is covered comprehensively by VKÚ-KČT map 33 *Křivoklátsko a Rakovnicko*.

West to Rabštejn
Should you have two days to kill and some stout walking boots, this route is a great way to see a large chunk of the region on foot. Starting in Rakovník take the Bečov nad Teplou train west to the small village of Blatno. From there take the red trail up into the hills which will lead you the 11km or so to Rabštejn through thick forest strewn with odd giant boulders which are fun to climb. Tiny Rabštejn, officially the smallest town in the Czech Republic, perched on a hill above the fast-flowing river Střela is one of the quaintest places in central Bohemia. It has a Renaissance palace, part of which is a hotel where you can stay the night and have a meal in the beautiful restaurant. Next day, head south along the green trail which will take you through the Střela protected area and through the Střela valley to Mladotice, or futher south to Plasy. Both have railway stations, from which there are services to Pilsen, back to Rakovník or to towns in north Bohemia. Alternatively, head west for the small town of Manětín with its Baroque chateau, rebuilt according to plans by Santini in 1712. The whole area is sparsely populated and public transport options are few and far between.

West to Jesenice
A scenic green marked trail and cycle path head west from Rakovník 20km over wooded hills and through tiny forgotten villages to Jesenice, a small town surrounded by picturesque lakes and woods. Trains run several times a day back to Rakovník.

South to the Berounka River
A gentle walk heading south from Rakovník takes hikers to the castle ruins at Krakovec, where Jan Hus resided before his fateful departure to Constance, through a shady valley, wooded hills and gurgling streams to Kostelík, from there continuing along the Berounka River to Křivoklát. The route is approximately

55km long, but can be broken in two by camping in Skryje, from where a short, dead-end yellow trail leads to the dramatic ruins of Týřov Castle.

Other places of interest

The village of **Lány**, around 20km east of Rakovník, is the Czech equivalent to Chequers in the UK or Camp David in America. All Czech presidents since Masaryk have come here to take a well-deserved weekend break from hectic Prague Castle, and the interior of the chateau is not open to the public. However, visitors can pay their respects to Masaryk and his wife who are buried in the village cemetery along with their children Jan and Alice, as well as wander the large English park. The nearest railway station is in nearby Stochov which has a special presidential waiting room.

A close second to Lány in the best-known village in the Rakovník region competition is **Krušovice** 12km to the north of Rakovník. Krušovice beer is one of the biggest brand names in the Czech Republic, and the huge brewery in the village is where perhaps one of the best beers in the world is produced. Rudolf II liked it so much he bought the brewery in 1583, and during his reign exclusively Krušovice beer was consumed at Prague Castle. The brewery has been known as 'Royal Krušovice' ever since. Tours and beer tasting can be organised by calling ahead (❧ *313 569 226*).

West Bohemia

No other province of the Czech Republic receives more income from tourism than the West and it is not difficult to see why. West Bohemia has many faces, from snow- dusted mountains, deep mysterious forests, pine-covered hills and fast-flowing rivers that run warm with mineral-laden water, to industrial centres, half-forgotten border villages and elegant spa towns. Some of the most popular and characteristic Czech produce such as glass, crystal, porcelain, mineral water, Becherovka, and of course Pilsen beer hark from this area and the spa towns in particular are great places for picking up souvenirs. As one of the most appealing and diverse regions in the country it should be on the itinerary of every traveller who ventures from the capital.

Under the Přemyslid rulers this last outpost of Slavdom was colonised by German miners, glassmakers and other craftsmen from the 12th century onwards, encouraged to settle in empty areas rich in minerals. Thanks to these medieval *Gasterbeiter* many towns in the region became completely German speaking, a reasonably peaceful arrangement until three factors combined to turn the ethnic Germans against the Czechs. The rise of Czech nationalism in the 19th century, the declaration of an independent Czechoslovakia in 1918 and the subsequent rise of Hitler across the border put the two ethnically irreconcilable groups on collision course. The Sudetenlanders paid a high price for supporting the Nazis when they were expelled to Germany after World War II, leaving many parts of west Bohemia underpopulated, a situation which continues today, the Czechs perhaps subconsciously reluctant to quit their original Labe Basin cradle.

A pint of authentic Pils beer in Pilsen, a stroll along the colonnade sipping mineral water in Carlsbad (Karlovy Vary) or Marienbad, a visit to the perfectly preserved medieval towns of Domažlice and Cheb and a hike in the Slavkovský Forest are the essence of the west and the highlights of any visit to the region.

GETTING AROUND
Thanks to major transport arteries from Prague into Germany which dissect the region, bus and rail services between major towns are frequent and swift. Difficulties sometimes arise when you leave the major centres and travel into sparsely populated areas, but the majority of towns and villages are surprisingly well served by bus or train or both.

PILSEN (PLZEŇ)
An industrial city and the administrative capital of the region of the same name, Pilsen (*Plzeň* in Czech) may not be the most glamorous place in the Czech Republic, but could be described as one of the most remarkable. The fourth-

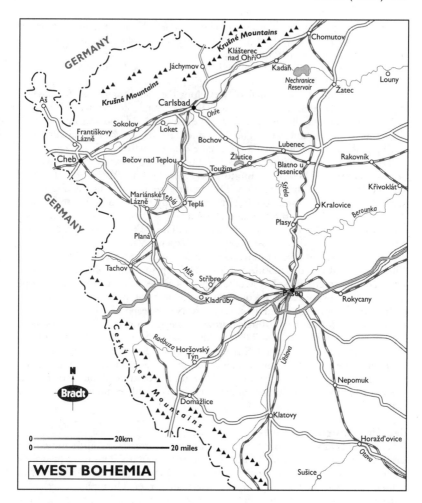

WEST BOHEMIA

largest city in the country is a pulsating, vibrant centre with a new, up and coming university, the Škoda engineering works and, of course, the legendary brewery that gave the world Pils beer. The main square, náměstí Republiky, is as handsome as any in the land and the Renaissance town hall and Church of St Bartholomew, boasting the highest church steeple in the country, are must-sees. A tour of the brewery and the brewery museum in town is also unmissable. Drop in on Pilsen's 167,000 inhabitants on your way from Prague to the spas in the west, if only to taste some of the best beer in the world, Pilsen's Urquell, or *Prazdroj* as it is known in Czech.

History

Pilsen was founded by King Václav II in 1295 where the Radbuza, Mže and Úhlava rivers unite to form the Berounka. The town immediately became a significant trading post on the way to Bavaria, and by the 14th century was the third-largest settlement in the Czech lands after Prague and Kutná Hora. There is evidence of beer being brewed in the town as early as 1307.

Unwaveringly Catholic during the Hussite wars, Pilsen came under siege in 1421 from the Hussite warlord, Jan Žižka. The town walls held out, as they did under further assailment from the Hussites in 1431 and 1433–34. Pilsen was so loyal to Rome it would not recognise Jiří of Poděbrady as Czech king, preferring Matyáš Korvín instead.

Pilsen was briefly the capital of the Holy Roman Empire in 1599, when Emperor and Bohemian King Rudolf II fled Prague to escape the plague. Catholic Pilsen naturally sided against the estates in 1618 and was occupied by their forces in the same year. The 17th and 18th centuries saw the advent of Baroque, the first example being the plague column of 1681.

The 19th century witnessed Pilsen's boom time, shown by the swell in population from 5,000 in 1786 to over 100,000 in 1918 when the First Czechoslovak Republic was born. During that period the engineering works were founded in 1859 and bought ten years later by Emil Škoda, whose surname has become possibly the most spoken word in Czech outside the Czech Republic (the word actually means *pity* or *damage!*). The *Měšťanský pivovar* or Civic Brewery began its activities in 1842 when pub owner Václav Mirvald, dissatisfied with the standard of beer produced by the tiny breweries scattered throughout Pilsen, grouped together 250 brewers to cook up something drinkable using a more complex technique. The beer they produced became known across Europe and was being exported to 34 countries by the outbreak of World War I.

Industrial complexes in Pilsen, used as Nazi weapons' plants during the occupation of Bohemia and Moravia, attracted the attention of American bombers. Almost 1,000 people died and 7,000 buildings were damaged in 11 air raids from 1942–45. Ironically it was the US army that liberated Pilsen on 6 May 1945.

Pilsen's population continued to grow during the communist era and the city was a key centre of heavy industry. After the revolution, Pope John Paul II created the bishopric of Pilsen, and the Church of St Bartholomew became a cathedral.

Getting there and away

Thanks to its location on two main transport arteries in and out of the country, Pilsen is straightforward to reach from Prague. The town is on the main railway line to Cheb and beyond into Bavaria, and the D5 motorway which runs west to Rozvadov and the German border. Until recently, the D5 used to plunge straight into Pilsen city centre, making it one of the most polluted places in the Czech Republic. Nearly all heavy-goods traffic en route to and from Germany was pounding through the middle of the city. The bypass took many years to build but was finally completed in 2003 meaning the city could breathe once again.

Trains (1¾ hours, 86Kč) run regularly from Prague's main railway station including some international expresses. **Buses** leave Florenc coach station at up to half-hourly intervals (1½ hours, 80Kč). There are also buses to places in west Bohemia and train connections to Klatovy (11 per day), Hradec Králové (3 per day), Cheb (16 per day, many of which continue on into Germany), Domažlice (1 an hour), České Budějovice (every 2–3 hours) and Františkovy Lázně (2 per day).

The main railway station in Pilsen is southeast of the historical centre. To get to the main square (náměstí Republiky) negotiate the series of underpasses to get on to Americká Street, from which the centre is along any street to the right. The bus station is on the opposite side of the historical centre to the railway station. Turn right out of the station and follow the main road until it meets sady

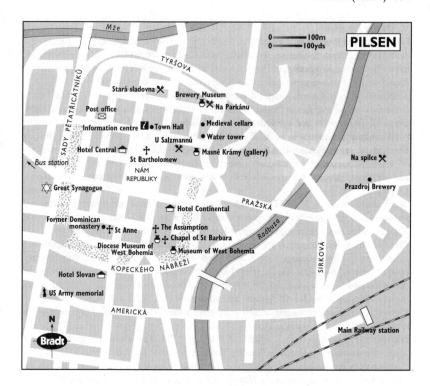

Pětatřicátníků. The historical centre is on the other side of the road. Pilsen has trams and trolleybuses but you are unlikely to need them.

Tourist information
The information centre (*nám Republiky 41;* ✆ *378 035 330;* f *378 035 332*) provides a comprehensive information service on the city and sells tickets for cultural events.

Where to stay
Hotel Slovan Smetanovy sady 1; ✆ 377 227 256; f 377 227 012; http://hotelslovan.pilsen.cz. The huge, old-world Slovan has 96 rooms and is set in its own park just off the main square. It has rooms of varying standards, some renovated, some slightly chipped around the edges. Sgls with breakfast cost around 1,450Kč, dbls 2,100Kč.

Hotel Central nám Republiky 33; ✆ 377 226 757; f 377 226 064. By far the best-situated hotel in Pilsen, sitting right in front of the Church of St Bartholomew on the main square, but definitely not the most attractive. It is the only modern building on Republic Square and looks like a wooden spoon among silver cutlery. A sgl with breakfast in this 130-bed piece of incongruity can be had for 1,550Kč, a dbl for around 2,400Kč.

Hotel Continental Zbojnická 8; ✆ 377 236 477; f 377 221 746; www.hotelcontinental.cz. The Continental has served as a hotel since 1929 and despite being damaged in an American air raid in World War II, it survived and has been accommodating visitors ever since. A large, tastefully decorated sgl costs 1,580Kč, a dbl 2,150Kč, and there is a restaurant and bar in the building.

Where to eat

U Salzmannů Pražská 8; 377 235 855; f 377 235 476; www.usalzmannu.cz. Often described as a Pilsen institution, at U Salzmannů they have been serving the hungry and thirsty for almost 370 years and the first barrel of the new Pilsen beer left here for Prague in 1842. It has a traditional Czech beer-hall ambience with lots of wood panelling and light-footed, smartly dressed waiters. Main courses are 60–250Kč and there are numerous vegetarian options on the menu. Velkopopovický kozel and Urquell beers are an obvious part of the U Salzmannů experience.

Na Parkánu Veleslavínova 6; ℄ 377 324 485. This is the slightly touristy pub at the Brewery Museum situated in the authentic surroundings of the tap house of the original brewery. Main courses arrive on your table for 60–160Kč and they have many salty savoury thirst-inducing Czech specialities as well to make you imbibe even more of the Urquell.

Stará sladovna Malá 3; ℄ 377 225 151. Housed in the original malt house (the beams are decorated with wreaths of dried hops) this is a real gem of a restaurant and the best place to eat in town. Everything about it is medieval, from the exterior to the menu. The first thing that hits you is the darkness, as most of the dining area is lit solely by candles and the fire in a large hearth. The smell of the wax and the log fire enhance the taste of the medieval-style food costing 100–250Kč. There are some interesting dishes on the menu such as 'remains from the executioner', apparently a huge pan of various kinds of meat, enough to feed a whole table and costing 800Kč. Wash it all down with either Urquell, Gambrinus, Radegast or Kelt beer. Kelt is the Czech version of Guinness and is not bad at all.

Na spilce U Prazdroje 7; ℄ 377 062 755; f 377 062 703. This is the very touristy cavernous mock beer hall at the Prazdroj Brewery opposite the visitor centre. It has 'German tour bus groups' written all over it, though reports of it being overpriced proved incorrect. Take one of the 600 places and enjoy main courses for 60–200Kč, naturally accompanied by the local fermented hop drink.

What to see and do
Prazdroj Brewery and Brewery Museum
On leaving the railway station, fight your way north over the busy roads to one of Pilsen's highlights and its *raison d'être*, the Prazdroj (Urquell in German) Brewery. You cannot miss the double-arched gate on U Prazdroje Street. Follow the signs to the visitors' centre where tickets for the tour can be purchased (*120Kč, concessions 60Kč*). Tours with an English-speaking guide leave year round at 12.30 and 14.00 and additionally at 10.30 and 15.30 in summer. The tour starts with a ten-minute film on the history of brewing and the brewery, and continues to the brewing house, the cellars, transformed into a skanzen-type exhibition, and the coopers' workshops. One can also sample Pilsen's finest product direct from the barrels. Across town at Veleslavinova 6 is the Brewery Museum (*admission 60/30Kč with text in 18 languages (!), 120/60Kč with guide, open year round*) housed in a Renaissance malt house, unchanged over the centuries. The tour includes well-organised exhibits on the history of the museum itself, beer brewing in Mesopotamia and Egypt, reconstructed pubs from the turn of the 19th and 20th centuries and the 1930s, the malting process, the history of the Prazdroj Brewery and many more fascinating beer-related topics.

Náměstí Republiky
Commanding the square is the enormous Gothic **Cathedral of St Bartholomew**, begun in 1297, but not completed until the late 15th century. Its tower (*admission 30Kč*) is the highest in the Czech Republic at 102m, and

BEER

Every country in the world excels at one thing or another: France has wine, Italy has pasta and pizzas, Russia has vodka and the Czech Republic has its delicious, refreshing, bitter, ice cool, golden beer (*pivo*). It is truly unsurpassed by the beverages of other countries, and is an aspect of the country it would be a sin not to sample at least once. There is no more beautiful sight in the Czech lands on a balmy summer eve than a dewy half-litre tankard, the creamy head still spilling over the brim and the icy, deep amber contents just waiting to be gulped down.

The vast majority of beer comes in two strengths: 10° and 12°; 10° has around 3.5% alcohol content, while 12° has around 5%. Stronger beers are occasionally available. Beer is further divided into light (*světlé*), lager (*ležák*) and dark (*tmavé*). Most pubs will have only one or two types on tap and only a couple of brands. Krušovice, Prazdroj/Urquell, Gambrinus, Staropramen, Velkopopovický kozel and Budvar are the most common. Other brands you may encounter on you travels are Bernard, Regent, Samson, Ježek, Braník, Primus and Radegast. Czechs have the highest per capita consumption of beer in the world (160 litres per person per year!) and are rightly proud of their famous brews. Their consumption may have a lot to do with the price. Expect to pay around 20–25Kč in a pub and 10–25Kč in a supermarket for the Czechs' most celebrated product. Czech *pivo* is also generally regarded as healthy, as it contains no chemicals, only locally grown hops, barley and crystal-clear water from Bohemia's thousands of springs are used in the process. It may also come as a surprise to learn that it contains fewer calories than orange juice and has large amounts of vitamin B!

visitors can climb 301 steps to more than halfway up, from where the Šumava Mountains can be seen on a clear day. From April until December the church is open to the public (*admission 20Kč*). The square's other architectural treasure is the **town hall**, which is one of the finest examples of Renaissance-style architecture in the country. Built between 1554 and 1559, it is richly decorated with intricate sgraffito. The **plague column** from 1681 stands in front of the information centre and is in need of a thorough sandblasting.

North of Republic Square

To the northeast of the square on Pražská Street stands the late Gothic **Water Tower** dating from 1530, which supplied the town's water until the early 20th century. Immediately opposite is the turreted gable of the **Masné krámy** from 1392, which served as a meat market until the 1950s. It now houses temporary exhibitions of the West Bohemian Gallery. Turn the corner from Pražská into Perlová where house No 8 constitutes the modest entrance to **Historical Underground Pilsen** (*admission 45Kč, open Apr–Nov*) a kilometre or so of dusty, clammy passageways and cellars created between the 13th and 19th centuries for storing food, producing beer and recently for running cables and pipes under the town. Tours are in Czech, but an informative English text is available. Take a sweater!

South of Republic Square

Head south along Bedřicha Smetany Street to the **Church of St Anne** and the **former Dominican Monastery**. The monastery was built in 1711 and the attractive, double-towered Baroque church was added later. Alas, both are under lock and key. One block east is a complex of buildings housing the **Church of the Assumption** and **Diocese Museum of West Bohemia** (*admission 30Kč, Apr–Oct*). A tour of the quiet and undervisited museum includes the Gothic **Chapel of St Barbara** with its frescoes depicting the martyrdom of St Barbara, which have miraculously survived from the 1460s. The **Museum of West Bohemia** (*admission 20/10Kč, open year round*) is housed in the impressive neo-Renaissance complex on the corner of Kopeckého sady. The huge building contains an Art Nouveau library, the beautiful, recently opened Art Nouveau Jubilee Hall and the museum collections with some interesting permanent exhibits including a complete and original armoury.

Other places of interest
Pilsen's **Great Synagogue** on Pětatřicátníků Street, dating from the turn of the 20th century, is the second largest in Europe, and the world's third largest after those in Jerusalem and Budapest. It is one of the most impressive sights in Pilsen. An inspection of the interior costs 35Kč (*15Kč concessions, 30Kč family ticket*).

At the top of Americká Street where it meets Klatovská třída and Pětatřicátníků Street, you will find the **US Army Memorial** commemorating the liberation of the town. Two granite pillars bear the words 'Thank you America' and a large circular plaque on the ground shows the division of Europe in May 1945. Many in Pilsen perhaps wish it had stayed that way. Pilsen gets mileage out of the fact that it was liberated by the Americans and not the Red Army, a fact effectively denied by the communists for 40 years.

Around Pilsen
Kladruby
Fans of the extraordinary Gothic Baroque work of architect Giovanni Santini should make a beeline for the Benedictine monastery in Kladruby, 30km as the crow flies west of Pilsen near the town of Stříbro. One of the oldest monasteries in the Czech lands, it was founded by Přemyslid King Vladislav I in 1144 who was laid to rest here in 1172, the only Czech ruler to be buried outside of Prague. After a period of prosperity in the 15th century the usual trials and tribulations all monasteries endured (Hussites, fires) spelt ruin for Kladruby. After a slow recovery following the Thirty Years War, an inspired abbot, Maurus Finzgut, commissioned reconstruction work in the early 18th century and hired the best two architects of the Baroque period, Kilián Ignác Dientzenhofer to work on the monastery and Giovanni Santini to transform the Church of the Assumption. Whilst perhaps not as revolutionary or flamboyant as Santini's most prized work, the Church of St John of Nepomuk in Žďár nad Sázavou, it is still a splendid example of his idiosyncratic Gothic Baroque style. Guided tours including the church (*admission 40/30Kč*) take around an hour.

There are no direct connections from Pilsen to Kladruby. Take a train or bus to Stříbro and change on to a local bus for the final 6km south to Kladruby. The whole journey takes about an hour.

Plasy
Plasy lies 23km northeast of Pilsen on the main Pilsen–Rakovník road. The main reason to visit is to view the Baroque monastery dating originally from 1146 and rebuilt in the early 18th century by Giovanni Santini and Kilián Ignác Dientzenhofer. It underwent another makeover in 1826 when it was transformed into a residence for the Metternich family. As part of the various tours on offer,

visitors can see the interiors of the monastery, the Metternich family tomb, the granary and the gallery. Admission varies from 20–40Kč for each tour.

Plasy is simple to reach from Pilsen with direct regular buses (45 minutes, 34Kč) and trains (45 minutes, 46Kč) throughout the day. The quickest method of reaching Plasy from Rakovník is by bus and requires a change in Kralovice (weekdays only, 1½ hours, 40Kč). Alternatively board a train heading west to Bečov nad Teplou from Rakovník and change at Blatno on to a service headed south to Pilsen; the journey can take anything from 1½ to three hours! This is the only option from Rakovník at weekends.

DOMAŽLICE

Lying a mere 20km from the border with Germany, Domažlice is a truly charming little town and not to be missed if you find yourself in this extremity of Bohemia. It has one of the most attractive main squares in the country with flowing Baroque gables of houses, renovated, but not overdone, and not a Day-Glo Austrian façade or plastic window in sight. Two fascinating regional museums, the beautiful Baroque church on the square, medieval streets and friendly locals make Domažlice one of my personal favourites. Domažlice is also the centre of the proud and colourful Chodsko region.

One feels good in and around Domažlice's arcades, low-ceilinged shops and passageways as everything is still on a human scale. The enemies of urban beauty, namely glass and steel, have been halted at the gates of Domažlice's unique Baroque square sporting preserved arcading along its length, interrupted only by the town hall and the church. There are no gaping empty expanses; just stone, wood and plaster, each house a work of art by a proud master builder of 18th-century Chodsko.

Attractive as the square may be, the authorities should, however, consider measures to limit the countless Vietnamese traders on the square to the *interior* of their premises, the one blight on what is otherwise a very picturesque town. Some towns have taken this step or pushed the unsightly shops out of town where Bavarians can purchase oversized garden gnomes and other peculiar objects to their hearts content. Anyone who has spent time around the Czech–German border will have witnessed this rather curious post-communist phenomenon.

There is evidence that trade routes traversed this area in prehistoric times and by the 10th century a large share of goods passing from the Czech lands into Bavaria transited Domažlice, making it an excellent place to set up a customs point and from which to guard the border. The citizens of the surrounding villages were entrusted with patrolling the frontier. This state of affairs was exploited by Czech King Přemysl Otakar II in the 13th century who beefed up the town's fortifications and granted it royal town status. Throughout the Middle Ages the Chods were granted special privileges for the service they provided, a status they lost when the border's location became stable.

One of the best times to visit the town is mid August when the **Chod Folklore Festival** is held. This is a celebration of Chod folk traditions featuring bagpipes, folk costumes, a market of traditional produce and much hearty Chod song, dance and merry-making.

Getting there and away

There are three direct **buses** (3 hours, 120Kč) and two **trains** (2½ hours, 204Kč) a day to Domažlice from the capital. Otherwise change in Pilsen on to regular bus and rail connections, both taking around 1 hour 20 minutes to cover the

CHODS AND CHODSKO

From the 14th century the Chod ethnic group of the 11 villages of the Chodsko region were granted certain privileges by Czech rulers for guarding the border with Bavaria. One of these privileges was that in feudal terms they were subordinate directly to the king, a guarantee of good treatment. Never very many in number, fiercely proud and independent, they kept these privileges until the Counter-Reformation when Ferdinand II sold them to a local noble called Laminger. The Chods were not too enamoured with Laminger's feudal ways and took their case to the highest courts in Vienna and Prague. A delegation was sent to Prague but Laminger had one of the leaders, Jan Sladký Kozina, imprisoned and later executed in Pilsen. Kozina put a curse on Laminger saying he would die a year and a day after his execution. Laminger died of a stroke as Kozina predicted but the Chods' revolt had failed.

Proud of their past, the Chods keep alive many of their traditions. The typical folk costumes of the Chod women consists of black, white or red headscarf, white blouse, black and red bodice and a flowery black and red long skirt with red tights and black shoes. The men wear a simple cap, white shirt, black waistcoat, yellow trousers, white knee socks and black shoes. Small bagpipes are the traditional instrument of the region.

60km. There are seven trains a day to Klatovy (1 hour, 52Kč) and up to five buses (1 hour, 36Kč). For those in no particular hurry, a scenic 90km branch line runs northwest from Domažlice up to Planá u Mariánských Lázní taking over three hours to make the journey.

When arriving by train, turn left out of the station and follow Masarykova Street, then Husova to the Lower Gate and Míru Square. The walk should take you no more than ten minutes. The bus station is a stone's throw north of the main square.

Where to stay

Penzion Konšelský šenk; Vodní 33; ℡ 379 720 200; www.konselskysenk.cz. This cosy pension is conveniently situated 2 mins off the square down Branská Street behind the town hall. Its 10 immaculate, tastefully furnished en-suite rooms behind the metre-thick walls of a medieval town house, are a bargain at 580Kč per person, with the per-person price based on the number of people staying in the room. A buffet breakfast is included in the room price.

Sokolský dům náměstí Míru 121; ℡ 379 720 084; e info@sokolskydum.cz. The only hotel on the square is located at the eastern end next to the house once inhabited by Božena Němcová. The 13 pleasant en-suite rooms can be a touch cramped and some are even on 2 levels to create more space. The price is just right at 800–1,100Kč for a sgl and 960–1,200Kč for a dbl including breakfast.

Where to eat

Chodská rychta Msgre B Staška 66; ℡ 379 722 524. Heading out of the square in the opposite direction to the Lower Gate you will see the Chodská rychta on your right. This is the most traditional place to eat and drink in Domažlice with its large historical interior, traditional wooden furniture, exposed beams and menu heavy with Czech and local specialities. The staff are pleasant, the food is good (if a touch on the overpriced side at 90–270Kč per main course) and tankards of Czech Budvar beer round it all off.

Konšelský šenk Vodní 33; ↘ 379 720 222. Beneath the pension of the same name the medieval interior of this restaurant is an atmospheric place to enjoy a meal. It advertises itself as a pizzeria but is more like a medieval tavern. Main courses cost 90–200Kč.
Restaurace Chodský hrad Chodské náměstí 96; ↘ 379 776 010; www.chodskyhrad.cz. Adjacent to the museum on Chodské Square, this is a great place to satisfy your hunger after working up an appetite next door. They serve Czech fare for 90–200Kč in a historical dining room, originally part of the castle.

What to see and do

All of Domažlice's sights, hotels and restaurants are to be found in or around **Náměstí Míru**, one of the Czech Republic's most attractive Baroque squares. Visitors can wander the long arcaded square, browsing the snug interiors of the small shops imagining what wares used to be sold here and what the bustling arcades would have looked like 300 years ago. When coming on foot from the railway station the first sight of note you will see is the **Lower Gate**. Dating originally from the 13th century it has a Gothic lower half and Renaissance upper section. Note that because of the layout of this end of the square traffic still uses the gate after more than 700 years. Heading down the square you cannot fail to notice the **Church of the Nativity of the Virgin Mary and Tower**, the sole building to interrupt the arcading on the right-hand side.

At the end of the square stands the plain Gothic **Church of the Assumption**. A bust on the first house on the square next to the church reminds us that the 19th-century Czech writer Božena Němcová lived in the town from 1845 to 1847, a fact evident in her work.

Chod Castle and Museum

Chod Castle was founded in the middle of the 13th century by the prolific town-builder, King Přemysl Otakar II. The building we see today dates from the 1720s and is the work of the equally prolific Kilián Ignác Dientzenhofer. It now houses the Chodsko Museum (*admission 35/15Kč*), opened in 1999 and one of the best museums in the region, if not the country. The various rooms house exhibitions on the region from prehistory to the 19th century including a scale model of Domažlice complete with town walls, and a lifesize Chod wedding scene in full folk costume. Unfortunately none of the explanations is in English but it is still worth a look. Included in the admission fee is the climb up the 100 rather creaky steps to the top of the 52m tower for views across the town.

Jindřich Jindřich Museum

This is a fascinating collection with an intriguing story behind it. Born in 1876, Jindřich Jindřich was a composer, respected Domažlice citizen and local celebrity who specialised in Chod music and compiled the largest collection of regional songs ever put together. In 1918, he began to collect art from the region and by the outbreak of World War II had transformed the rooms of his large apartment into a private museum with literally thousands of exhibits stacked from floor to ceiling. He handed over the unique collection to the municipal authorities in 1945 and virtually ignored by the communists, continued to show visitors round until his death in 1967. The museum was created in 1972 and shows part of Jindřich's collection including furniture, Chod folk costumes, glass paintings and hundreds of books, busts, photos and pieces of artwork. A couple of rooms of the original apartment museum have been left in their original state (*admission 15/10Kč, open Mon–Fri 10.00–12.00 and 13.00–15.00, Apr–Oct and 09.00–12.00, Oct–Apr*).

Souvenirs from Domažlice

The Chodsko region is rightly proud of its folk art traditions and items produced in the surrounding villages and in town can be bought in numerous shops on the square. Chod ceramics in all shapes and sizes (either white base decorated with flowers or black base decorated with poppies), folk costumes, chequered cloth and collage work are all traditional items. Mainly thanks to the hordes of Bavarian tourists milling around in Domažlice, there are several fascinating antique shops dotted around town, where genuine articles and artwork from the surrounding villages can be had for a few crowns.

KLATOVY

Klatovy may not have the pretty façades and arcaded square of Domažlice, but this small town, famous for its carnations if nothing else, has quite a lot to see for its size including the ghostly mummies under the church and the unique UNESCO-protected Baroque pharmacy. Visit the town on your way to the Šumava Mountains or Domažlice 40km to the northeast, or as a day trip from Pilsen.

The most colourful time to visit is during the Klatovy International Folklore Festival in early July, when the main square is chock-a-block with Czechs and other nationalities in folk costume, performing for the crowds. Ask at Klatovy's superb **information centre** (*náměstí Míru 63;* \ *376 347 240;* f *376 347 390; www.klatovy.cz*) for more details.

Getting there and away

Two direct **buses** (3 hours, 95Kč) and two **trains** (2½ hours, 204Kč) make the journey to Klatovy from Prague daily. The other way is to change in Pilsen on to one of the frequent buses (1 hour, 32Kč) or trains (1 hour, 64Kč) to Klatovy. (See page 156 for connections to Domažlice)

The bus and train stations are 15 minutes' walk out of town. Nádražní Street leads from the railway station, passes the bus station then follows the river and stops just short of the historical centre. If arriving by bus from Domažlice, alight at the first stop in town near the Plus supermarket, considerably closer to the centre.

Where to stay

Hotel Ennius Randova 111; \ 376 320 567; f 376 320 564; www.sweb.cz/ennius. This pleasant, recently renovated 3-star hotel is situated a stone's throw from the main square along Randova Street. Its 26 rooms are on the basic side, but are comfortable enough. All have bathroom and TV and are very reasonable at around 700Kč for a sgl and 1,000Kč for a dbl.

Hotel Centrál Masarykova 300; \ 376 314 571; f 376 314 745; www.centralkt.cz. The popular Hotel Centrál is around 10 min' walk from the historical centre heading towards the railway station. It was founded in 1929, hence the functionalist architecture. The building was renovated in 1994 and has 47 very comfortable rooms. A sgl costs no more than 870Kč, a dbl around 1,200Kč depending on the standard of the room. The hotel has a restaurant and a bar which takes guests back to the decadent days of the First Republic.

Where to eat

Restaurant Tep náměstí Míru 151; \/f 376 311 958; www.mybox.cz/tep. Klatovy's top dining establishment is situated on the second floor of a building on the opposite side of the square to the town hall. The staff are extremely proud of the fact that the current president Václav Klaus has eaten there 3 times, and they have the photographs to prove it. It has an upmarket air, main courses for 65–300Kč, including Czech and various other cuisines (such as Argentine) and very attentive waiters. It may be slightly mutton dressed as lamb, but such a standard of service is rare outside of Prague.

Beseda náměstí Míru 191; ↘ 376 311 075. The modern Beseda can be found next to the church on Míru Square. This basic eatery has Czech and international staples for 100–250Kč and Urquell and Gambrinus beers on tap. The outdoor seating on the square in summer is a great place to eat and people-watch.

U Švejka Denisova 90; ↘ 376 321 419. Situated in a Renaissance house along Balbínova by the side of the Jesuit College is the omnipresent restaurant named after Hašek's most famous literary character. Anyone who has visited a few of these places might assume it was a franchise, and that a Švejk pub may one day appear in your neighbourhood. This is not the case. This is the best place in Klatovy to have some typical Czech fare and a beer. Main courses are 100–250Kč with some vegetarian dishes around 60Kč.

What to see and do

The imposing **Jesuit Church of the Immaculate Conception and St Ignatius** which dominates Míru Square was begun by the Jesuit order in 1656 and is, needless to say, built in the Baroque style. It was renovated by Kilián Ignác Dientzenhofer in 1722 after a fire. Open year round for visitors to peek inside it must be one of the most impressive buildings in the area. The foundations of the church hide Klatovy's eerie **catacombs** (*closed Nov–Mar*), where 200 members of the local Jesuit order and other town dignitaries were laid to rest between 1676 and 1783 when Austrian Emperor Joseph II put a stop to burials in churches. Burial is perhaps not the right word, as the bodies were mummified by a clever natural ventilation system which keeps the underground chamber at a humidity and temperature at which the bodies do not rot. Around 30 mummies are on display (*admission 40/20Kč*). A few steps away from the church is the 81m-tall **Black Tower** dating from the mid 16th century which served for centuries as a lookout tower to warn the townsfolk of fires and enemies on the horizon. The views from the top make climbing the 226 steps worthwhile. Directly adjacent to the tower to the right sits the solid **former Jesuit College**, now a rather curious Baroque shopping mall, evidently not too popular with local shoppers judging by the numerous vacant lots. To the left of the tower stands the neo-Renaissance **town hall**, originally dating from 1557, but rebuilt several times over the centuries.

Back on the square, along from the church, is another Baroque commercial premises, this time an original, the UNESCO-protected **White Unicorn Pharmacy**, which quite unbelievably dispensed medicines uninterrupted from 1776 until 1966. Its rich Baroque interior now houses an exhibition of historical pharmacy artefacts (*admission 30/20Kč*). Contact the information centre first if you want to visit between November and April.

From the northeast corner of the square head out along Křížová Street to the 13th-century **Church of the Virgin Mary**, housing a miraculous picture of the Virgin Mary which was said to have bled several times in the 17th century. Guarding over the church is the 60m-tall **White Tower** dating from 1581. Behind it are the remnants of the town walls surrounded by a park. Five minutes' walk southwest of the square in Hostašova Street is situated the **Dr Hostaše Museum** (*admission 20/10Kč, closed Mon*) which has exhibitions on regional history, carnation growing and other local industries.

CARLSBAD (KARLOVY VARY)

No other place in the Czech lands outside Prague has so much to see and do, so much history or such a magical atmosphere as the spa town of Carlsbad. The largest of the big three towns forming the west Bohemian spa triangle, Carlsbad is a must-see for anyone spending more than a few days in the Czech Republic, and should be second on every tourist's and traveller's list of places to go. A day trip from Prague is possible, though you should give yourself two to three days to fully explore this fairy-tale spa town.

Carlsbad sits around the confluence of two rivers, the Teplá and the Ohře. *Teplá* means warm in Czech, and the source of the river's warm water is the hot mineral springs which rise in the town, and which possess curative properties, drawing thousands of visitors a year in search of treatments. There are 13 springs in Carlsbad: 12 of them come gurgling and spitting out of taps on the street, but one comes oozing out of green bottles. The liqueur Becherovka, often dubbed the 13th Carlsbad spring, is produced in the commercial district.

The town centre is divided into the commercial district where the two rivers meet, and the spa district, which follows the twists and turns of the river Teplá up the valley surrounded by the Slavkovský Forest. The wooded hills can be easily explored on foot and there is even a funicular railway to take you high above the town for striking views.

One special aspect of the town concerns its inhabitants. There is no other town in the Czech Republic dominated to such an extent by an ethnic group other than the Czechs. Thanks to the Russians' love of anything spa-like, they have settled in large numbers here, and thousands come as tourists. In the spa district you are more likely to hear Russian spoken than Czech, the Cyrillic alphabet is much in evidence, and many shops, hotels and other businesses are owned and run by Russia's nouveaux riches. The Russians have made the place their own, bringing their inimitable style, panache and exclusivity. Alas, they have also pushed prices sky high.

History

Karlovy Vary, the Czech for Carlsbad, means 'Charles's Spa' and is named after Charles IV (who else?), said to have discovered the hot springs while out hunting when his dogs leapt into the hot water chasing down a stag. This is probably just the customary legend which always seems to surround the origin of Czech spas, and it is more likely that Charles IV's own doctors discovered the water's curative properties without the medieval drama.

Over the next three centuries a growing number of Europe's elite found their way to the miraculous springs. Carlsbad hit hard times from 1582 until 1664 when in a historically short period the town suffered a catastrophic flood, was almost completely destroyed by fire and was plundered by several armies including the Swedes in the Thirty Years War. The 18th and 19th centuries saw Carlsbad become well known again for its cures, and was visited by anyone who was anyone (Goethe, Beethoven, Marx, Tsar Peter the Great, Bismarck, Chopin to name just a few).

Apart from a small community of Czechs who settled there in 1860, the population of Carlsbad was exclusively German. After the declaration of an independent Czechoslovakia in 1918 a short armed conflict broke out between Czechoslovak soldiers and Carlsbad's Germans. Tensions continued to simmer throughout the 1920s and '30s, and many began to sympathise with the expansionist intentions of Adolf Hitler across the border. In 1935 the Sudeten German Party was founded, represented in Carlsbad by Konrád Henlein and Karl

WHAT THE SPAS ARE FOR
Spas have become trendy in the last decade with tourists seeking out ever more exotic locations in which to be pounded and pampered. Wellness programmes, fitness training, massage, relaxation by the swimming pool and a myriad pleasant light mud packs and bubbly jacuzzi mineral baths are what the average Anglo-Saxon spa-worshipper expects to find at his or her chosen destination. While the Czech spas are striving to provide this sort of experience, it is essential to understand that eastern European spas are places where people come to cure, or at least ease a whole host of medical conditions, or convalesce after operations. They are not the pampering centres many expect, and can at times resemble hospitals complete with white-coated doctors and shuffling pensioners in dressing gowns. The spa towns are doing their utmost to accommodate both kinds of spa guest, but visitors should always respect the more practical role spas play in Czech life.

Hermann Frank. Frank, born and bred in Carlsbad, would go on to become *Reichsprotektor* in 1942 after the assassination of Reinhard Heydrich, and gave the order for the annihilation of Lidice. Hitler visited the town in 1938 during the euphoria following the Nazi occupation of the Sudetenlands. World War II saw the bombing of both railway stations by Allied planes and the death of several hundred people. After liberation, the overwhelming majority of German speakers were driven out of the town.

Getting there and away
Bus is the best option from Prague with services departing Florenc coach station every couple of hours. The best service is operated by Asiana, who run luxury air-conditioned coaches from Florenc to Ruzyně Airport, and then non stop to Carlsbad. A ticket costs 130Kč, 100Kč for those lucky enough to have an ISIC card. The journey takes around 2¼ hours and reserving a seat is recommended, as these coaches fill up even on winter Wednesdays. In Carlsbad get off at the first stop located nearer the town centre and spa district. On the return journey to Prague coaches leave from the main coach station only. There is an AMS sales point in the railway station. Bus is also the best way of reaching Carlsbad from Pilsen (hourly, 1 hour 40 minutes, 60Kč).

Carlsbad has two railway stations, *Horní nádraží* (Upper station) and *Dolní nádraží* (Lower station). Some **trains** call at both. There are direct services from Carlsbad to Cheb (Upper station, hourly, 1 hour, 76Kč), Marienbad (both stations, 9 daily, 1½ hours, 76Kč) and Johanngeorgenstadt just across the German border to the north (both stations, 7 daily, 1½ hours, 50Kč).

The main bus and lower railway stations are adjacent to one another. On leaving both, cross the main road and turn left. Keep going until you see the giant green Becherovka bottle at the end of T G Masaryka Street. This is the beginning of the commercial district. Follow T G Masaryka until you see the awful, megalomanic, 1970s Thermal Hotel, the rather woeful beginning of the spa district lining the meandering valley of the Teplá River.

Getting around
Carlsbad has its own local bus service run by the *Dopravní podnik Karlovy Vary* (DPKV). Tickets cost 10Kč, and can be bought at news kiosks. A useful route is

bus 11 which runs from the Upper station to Tržnice and then on to Divadelní náměstí. The DPKV also run a sightseeing bus (91) from Divadelní náměstí which leaves three times a day in the afternoon during the high season. Tickets cost 50Kč.

Where to stay

Carlsbad has more hotels than you can shake a stick at. Some of the top-end establishments are stunning places which exude luxury and opulence with prices to match. What Carlsbad lacks are real budget options, though it is possible to find a room for around 1,200–1,500Kč with luck. Otherwise you could try **Čedok travel agency** (*Dr Davida Bechera 21–23;* ☎ *353 234 249;* f *353 222 226*) who arrange private rooms for 500–700Kč per room. The **information centre** (*Lázeňská 1;* ☎ *353 224 097;* f *353 232 858*) can also help with accommodation. A 15Kč per night spa tax is added everywhere. Many of the hotels offer spa treatments, but this is not always on the premises.

Top end

Pupp Mírové náměstí 2; ☎ 353 109 111; f 353 224 032; fax number for reservations: 353 226 638; www.pupp.cz. The Pupp is one of the most celebrated hotels in the Czech Republic, famous among Czechs as the venue for the Miss Czech Republic contest. Carlsbad's top hotel has been putting up guests since 1701, and is the last word in luxury with prices to match. Bach, Empress Maria Theresa, Wagner, Bismarck, Whoopi Goldberg, Michael Douglas and King Juan Carlos are just some of the variety of guests to have graced the Pupp's plush rooms. Divided into the Grandhotel (5 stars, 112 rooms) and the Parkhotel (4 stars, 116 rooms), sgls cost 95–230, and dbls 120–290.
Bristol Sadová 19; ☎ 353 344 444; f 353 341 801; www.bristol.cz. While appearing huge, the modern, 4-star Bristol has only 36 rooms. Modern, luxurious sgls with bathroom and breakfast in high season start at 101, dbls at 86. This is a spa hotel and the full range of treatments and procedures is available.
Central Divadelní náměstí 17; ☎ 353 182 111; f 353 182 631; www.interhotel-central.cz. This 4-star 83-room hotel is mainly used by guests looking for spa treatments but does accept tourists. Impeccable modern rooms are 40 for a sgl out of season rising to 118 for a luxury dbl in high season.
Dvořák Nová Louka 11; ☎ 353 102 111; f 353 102 119; www.hotel-dvorak.cz. The Dvořák is one of Carlsbad's most prominent hotels and has 126 immaculate, comfortable, stylish, state-of-the-art rooms for corresponding prices. A sgl out of season will set you back 80, a dbl in high season 165. However, this price does include breakfast and unlimited use of the indoor swimming pool, fitness centre, sauna and steam bath. Sorry, no children under 12 are allowed in the Dvořák.

Mid range

Petr Vřídelní 13–15; ☎ 353 169 401; www.hotelpetr.com. The Petr is situated in the house where Tsar Peter I stayed, with the conspicuous maroon carved-wood façade opposite the *Mlýnská kolonáda*. A night in one of its very tastefully furnished rooms costs ˙45 for a sgl and 90 for a dbl. Seasonal price difference is minimal. Some rooms are in the new building behind. If you have just won the lottery you could try the king suite at 500 a night.
Astoria Vřídelní 92; ☎ 353 335 111; f 353 224 368; www.astoria-spa.cz. The Astoria is a spa hotel but accepts tourists who have not come to take the waters. Situated directly opposite the *Mlýnská kolonáda* it has 100 standard rooms for reasonable prices. Without spa treatments a sgl will set you back around 40 in low season and a dbl in high season costs around the same per person including breakfast.

Romance Tržiště 37; ☎ 353 222 646; f 353 224 134; www.hotelromance.cz. This charming 4-star hotel offers real value for money. Situated right in the middle of the spa district in an Art Deco building dating from 1899, an attractively furnished sgl in low season comes for 1,600Kč, a dbl in high season for 3,200Kč. All of the 37 rooms are en suite.

Elwa Zahradní 29; ☎ 353 228 472–5; f 353 228 473; www.hotelelwa.com. Sgls in low season come for 2,300Kč, dbls in high season for 3,800Kč. You can probably find better than the Elwa for this price and apparently it is almost permanently full in high season.

Cordoba Zahradní 37; ☎ 353 230 473; f 353 230 758; www.hotel-cordoba.com. Just along from the Elwa, the 12-room Cordoba is a shade overpriced but has decent rooms with bathroom and satellite TV. The hotel has only dbls and suites costing from   45 per night.

Embassy Nová Louka 21; ☎ 353 221 161–5; f 353 223 146; www.embassy.cz. This attractive 20-room hotel offers 4-star luxury in the heart of the spa district, but for a reasonable price. As little as 1,800Kč will get you a beautiful sgl out of season. A dbl in high season costs around 3,000Kč. Needless to say, breakfast is included.

Good value

Kosmos Zahradní 39; ☎ 353 225 476; f 353 223 168; www.hotelkosmos.cz. The Kosmos is next to the Cordoba and is quite similar, a bit larger and cheaper. A sgl in one of its 40 newly renovated rooms in low season is 960Kč, a dbl in high season 1,750Kč including breakfast.

Hotel Kavalerie T G Masaryka 43; ☎ 353 229 613; f 353 236 171; www.kavalerie.cz. You will find the Kavalerie in the commercial district, just along from the Becherovka Museum. It has 16 standard rooms on the basic side. Dbls with bathroom start at around   50, and apartments at around   60 a night including breakfast.

Hotel Jizera Krále Jiřího 40; ☎ 353 235 577; f 353 235 578. This hotel has 22 rooms and is one of the cheapest options in town, situated in the commercial district. A basic sgl costs a mere 700Kč, a dbl 1,400Kč. Breakfast costs an extra 100Kč.

Pension Villa Basileia Mariánskolázeňská 4; ☎ 353 224 132; f 353 227 804; www.villabasileia.cz. This is a small cosy pension right at the end of the spa district on the opposite bank of the Teplá to the Pupp. Its quiet immaculate rooms with all mod cons are excellent value. Sgls with breakfast are 1,400Kč high season, dbls 1,750Kč.

Where to eat

As mentioned, Carlsbad is divided into the commercial district, and the spa area. Restaurants in the spa district (especially some of the hotel restaurants) have inflated prices, but the food is of international standard made with ingredients imported at great cost into the Czech Republic, and prepared by master chefs. Photographs of celebrities who dined there during a recent film festival take pride of place on the walls of some establishments, and some boast very elegant premises indeed. For cheaper, less star-studded Czech options, head for the commercial district where you will find cosy Czech inns and cellars with normal Czech menus and prices.

Charleston Bulharská 1; ☎ 353 230 797. This is an Anglo-American style bar with lots of dark wood and polished brass. The service is faultless, the food is excellent and the place has a snug but stylish ambience. A real gem of a place (though quite un-Czech) with excellent mains for 130–340Kč. Open until midnight every day.

Kavalerie T G Masaryka 43; ☎ 353 229 613; f 353 236 171. This is the restaurant at the hotel of the same name. Small and cosy, it serves up a limited selection of dishes for less than 150Kč.

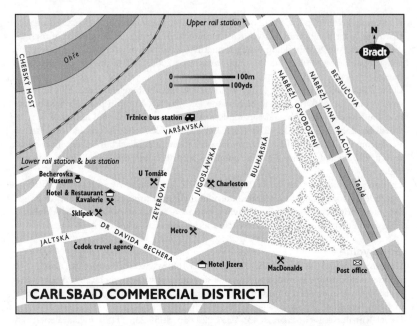

CARLSBAD COMMERCIAL DISTRICT

Metro T G Masaryka 27; ✆ 353 229 555. If you are looking for a bite to eat in the commercial district with Czech surroundings, good food and reasonable prices, Metro is the place to go. Mains are served up for 100–160Kč with some specialities costing a bit more.
U Tomáše Zeyerova 3; ✆ 777 120 030. Why the Czechs love eating underground so much I have yet to fathom. This Czech restaurant in a cellar off one of the main thoroughfares in the commercial district has a selection of beers and main courses for 50–160Kč, a pleasant atmosphere and friendly staff.
Caffé Pizzeria Venezia Zahradní 43; ✆ 353 229 721. This pleasant pizza restaurant looks down on the dreary Hotel Thermal. Just look for the pink neon sign. A pleasant place to eat year round with an outdoor dining space and a light airy pink interior, diners can choose from a wide selection of pizzas and other Czech and international food for 100–200Kč.
Lázně III (spa building No 3) Mlýnské nábřeží 5. This is the dining room on the first floor of spa building No 3 just before the Mlýnská Colonnade heading from the commercial district. It is open to the public, serves Czech standards for 100–200Kč and is just about the best value you will find in the spa district. Next door is the Dvořák Concert Hall, venue for the November Dvořák Festival.
Elefant Café Stará louka 30. The most stylish coffee house in town and one of the best places to sample some Becherovka or just sip a coffee and people-watch. There is outdoor seating, weather permitting, though it would be a shame to miss the elegant interior.
Café Pupp Mírové náměstí 2. If you cannot afford to stay in one of its rooms, you can at least sample a bit of luxury at the Pupp's café on the corner of the hotel. It could be described as a posh *cukrárna*. Beethoven resided here in 1812 when it was still a spa-house.

What to see and do
The only place of interest in the commercial district, but also one of Carlsbad's unmissables, is the **Becherovka Museum** at the end of T G Masaryka Street. Admission is 100Kč (*concessions 50Kč*) and the tour is with an English speaking

guide, who will lead you through the museum and cellars of the Becherovka distillery explaining the production process and history of the most Czech of liqueurs along the way. Of interest to British visitors will be the fact that the whole Becherovka story starts with a mysterious Englishman who came up with the original recipe. The tour ends in the large tasting room where various types of Becherovka are set before you while you watch a kitschy film. Stumbling out of the museum you will be glad you came.

Heading towards the spa district, after passing the Hotel Thermal, the first of the **Colonnades**, the white wrought-iron **Park Colonnade** (Sadová kolonáda) is on the right. Once part of a much larger pavilion, it was built in 1880. The main **Mill Colonnade** (Mlýnská kolonáda) is further along Mlýnské nábřeží. Built in 1881 by Josef Zítek, the architect who worked on the National Theatre in Prague, it houses four hot springs, a forest of columns and is the pride and joy of Carlsbad. The **Castle Colonnade** (Zámecká kolonáda) is up the hill opposite the Hotel Romance and marks the site where Charles IV's hunting lodge stood until a fire destroyed it in 1604. Further along the Teplá you cannot fail to notice the intricate woodwork of the **Market Colonnade** (Tržní kolonáda) dating from 1883. The highlight of the colonnades should be the final **Geyser Colonnade** (Vřídelní kolonáda). However, this 1970s eyesore housing the geyser and five of the hot springs is a disappointment. How anyone could plonk such an ugly construction bang in the middle of pretty Carlsbad is beyond most people's comprehension. The geyser splutters and spurts an incredible three million litres of water per day to a height of around 12m and is fun to watch. As far as the water is concerned, anyone is free to take as much as they like of the slightly salty, mineral-laden water, whose temperature ranges from 40–70°C. Opposite the Geyser Colonnade is the Baroque **Church of Mary Magdalene**, a Kilián Ignác Dientzenhofer creation from the early 1730s. The other church worthy of mention is the compact little Russian Orthodox **Church of SS Peter and Paul**, built at the end of the 19th century at the top of the steep, villa-lined Sadová Street (see map). It is worth the climb to see the five typical gold onion-shaped domes and the beautifully painted interior. As Sadová turns towards the church you will see the **Karl Marx Monument** from 1988 commemorating his three sojourns here in the mid 1870s.

Other places of interest

The **Carlsbad Museum** with interesting exhibits on the history of the spas, glass and porcelain production is well worth the 30Kč admission. A five-minute walk up Mariánskolázeňská Street to Divadelní Square will bring you to the **Vítězslav Nezval Theatre**, an impressive building dating from 1886. High above the town in the surrounding wooded hills are two places with superb views of the town. **Jelení skok** (Stag's Leap) is an outcrop of rock topped with the statue of the deer which led Charles IV to the hot springs. Follow the yellow marked trail from behind the Švejk Restaurant on Stará Louka Street. The **Diana viewing tower** can be reached by funicular railway from behind the Grandhotel Pupp. The railway is open 09.00–18.00 and a ticket there and back costs 40Kč (*18Kč for children and 80Kč for a family of four*). Take note of the fact that the stop halfway up called Jelení skok is quite a walk through the forest to the place of the same name mentioned earlier.

Souvenirs from Carlsbad

Carlsbad is the source for many of the souvenirs visitors take home from a visit to the Czech Republic. Becherovka, the small cups used to drink it

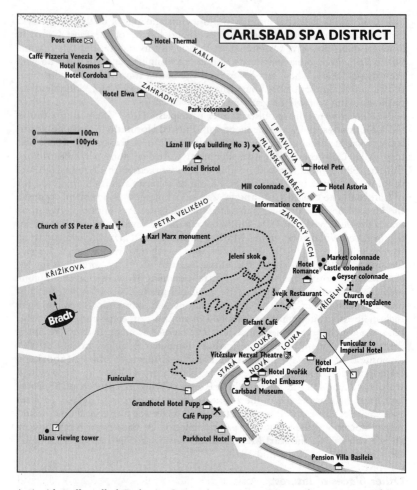

CARLSBAD SPA DISTRICT

Post office ⊠
Caffé Pizzeria Venezia ✕
Hotel Kosmos
Hotel Cordoba
Hotel Elwa
Hotel Thermal
KARLA IV
ZAHRADNÍ
Park colonnade ●
I P PAVLOVA
MLYNSKÉ NÁBŘEŽÍ
Lázně III (spa building No 3) ●
Hotel Bristol
Hotel Petr
Mill colonnade ●
Hotel Astoria
Information centre
ZÁMECKÝ VRCH
Church of SS Peter & Paul ✝
PETRA VELIKÉHO
Karl Marx monument
Jelení skok ●
Hotel Romance
Market colonnade
Castle colonnade
Geyser colonnade
KŘIŽÍKOVA
Švejk Restaurant ✕
VŘÍDELNÍ
Church of Mary Magdalene ✝
N
Bradt
Elefant Café ✕
STARÁ LOUKA
NOVÁ LOUKA
Vítězslav Nezval Theatre
Funicular to Imperial Hotel
Hotel Central
Hotel Dvořák
Hotel Embassy
Carlsbad Museum
Funicular
Grandhotel Hotel Pupp
Café Pupp ✕
Diana viewing tower ●
Parkhotel Hotel Pupp
Pension Villa Basileia

0 ▬▬▬ 100m
0 ▬▬▬ 100yds

(coincidentally called *Becher* in German), ceramics, Moser glassware, crystal in a myriad shapes and sizes, spa waters, petrified roses and other objects placed in the hot spring water and special drinking vessels with spout handles for sipping the *aqua mineralis* are some of the most popular items packed into suitcases at the end of a visit to Carlsbad and are available everywhere you look in the town.

Around Carlsbad
Loket
Some 12km southeast of Carlsbad sits the charming, peaceful little town of Loket whose foremost attraction is a magnificent hilltop 14th-century Gothic **castle** which towers over the town and the river Ohře. Loket gets its name, meaning 'elbow' in Czech, from its location on a sharp bend in the river. Vladislav II first built a castle at this strategic spot in the 12th century. King Přemysl Otakar II had it enlarged and beefed up in the 14th century. Charles IV was also a regular visitor, using the castle as a base for hunting in the surrounding forests. After a fire in 1725, part of the castle was rebuilt as a prison, a function it performed until 1949.

The interiors of the castle can be viewed alone or on a tour. Inside you will see exhibitions on the development of the castle over the centuries, porcelain, a Romanesque rotunda, the castle cells, the view from the tower and historical weapons. Rare in being open year round, an hour-long tour with a guide is 90/60Kč, with an English text 80/45Kč.

The early Baroque town hall on Masarykovo Square houses the **Book Binding Museum**. Run by the castle and focused on the development of book binding in the 20th century it has some exquisite examples of this dying art (*admission 30/15Kč, open year round*). Goethe certainly enjoyed his visits to Loket as it was in the building now housing the *Bílý kůň* (White Horse) restaurant on the square that the 72-year-old writer met his last love, the 16-year-old Ulrike von Lewetzow.

Buses leave Carlsbad every hour and call at Loket en route to Cheb and Sokolov (30 minutes, 20Kč). Services hardly tail off at all at weekends. Of course you could always walk the 17km to Loket following the sometimes spectacular blue trail from Diana via the Doubská hora viewing tower and the *Svatošské skály*, dramatic granite rock formations above the river Ohře, whose meanders the trail then hugs until it reaches Loket.

Andělská Hora

The ruins of another 14th-century mammoth hilltop castle can be visited at Andělská Hora, a village just off the busy Carlsbad–Prague road, 10km west of Carlsbad. The castle perches atop a gigantic hunk of rock which dwarfs the village below. It was abandoned in the 17th century after being destroyed by fire and marauding Swedes in the Thirty Years War and the villagers recycled much of the castle to build their houses. No tours or history lessons here, just the fun of clambering up to the top of the ruins for the great view from high above the tree tops of the village and the Krušné Mountains.

Buses call at Andělská Hora on their way to towns west of Carlsbad such as Toužim and Žlutice. A bus heads out in this direction approximately every half an hour on weekdays, with a reduced service at weekends. The journey takes around 15 minutes. It is a reasonably gentle and attractive 11km hike to Andělská Hora along a green walking trail that heads out of Carlsbad from the Hotel Thermal.

MARIENBAD (MARIÁNSKÉ LÁZNĚ)

Less than two centuries have passed since the small spa town of Marienbad (Mariánské Lázně in Czech) was founded by the abbot of the Teplá Monastery, Karel Kašpar Reitenberger, with a little help from his friends, doctor Jan Nehr and town planner Václav Skalník. Reitenberger got little thanks for his efforts, and, accused of sinking too much of the monastery's money into the town, he was banished to Austria. The town he created which belonged to the monastery and was in the end an important source of revenue, became one of *the* places to be seen in the 19th century, attracting royalty, nobility and celebrity alike. The spa addict Goethe came here three times and was even jilted here by the teenage Ulrike von Lewetzow. There is a strong British connection with the spa as it was a favourite stomping ground of King Edward VII. The British monarch made nine visits to Marienbad, an average of almost one visit per year of his reign. He stayed at the Weimar Hotel in the spa district at No 9 Goethovo Square. His visits to various sites in the town are commemorated with plaques and the like, but perhaps his most significant act was to found the royal golf course just outside of the town, the oldest in the country. This link to the glorious British past attracts a disproportionate number of visitors from the UK. Other illustrious visitors have included Kafka, Edison, Mark Twain, Dvořák, Strauss, Nobel, Freud, Ibsen, Chopin and Wagner.

You would be mistaken to think that Marienbad is just about the spa. The dark, wooded hills of the Slavkovský Forest provide great opportunities for gentle hill walking and cycling. At over 600m above sea level, Marienbad has a sub-alpine climate and the air is as good for you as the water. It is a place for improving health, fitness and for clearing the mind in a relaxing environment.

After 40 years of serving as a place of recuperation for particularly productive factory workers, Marienbad has experienced a Renaissance in the last decade, though from the neon signs, armies of German pensioners and the number of derelict and unused buildings, it is obvious that the exclusivity of the 19th century has not returned. This is one of the major attractions in the Czech lands, though larger, more exciting Carlsbad up the road gets my vote every time.

Getting there and away
Roughly halfway between Cheb and Pilsen, Marienbad is on the main Prague–Pilsen–Cheb rail route facilitating easy travel to the spa from Prague. A total of 13 **trains** a day cover the route in around three hours, and the ride costs 224Kč. As usual the **bus** is cheaper (130Kč), but takes longer. Marienbad is at the end of a branch line running north to Carlsbad via Teplá and 11 lazy stopping trains ply the scenic line daily in both directions.

Marienbad's bus and railway stations are next to one another on the southern side of the town about 2km from the spa district. Turn right out of the station past the bus stops. The road eventually becomes Hlavní třída which leads all the way to the spas. Alternatively take bus 5. The fare is 7Kč which is dropped into a ticket machine by the driver. Public transport peters out around 22.00.

Tourist information
The reasonably helpful municipal information centre (*Hlavní 47;* ⟍ *354 622 474;* f *354 625 892; www.marianskelazne.cz*) is housed in the Chopin House just outside the spa district. There you can pick up a copy of the monthly *Promenáda* magazine (10Kč) containing full listings as well as heaps of useful information and tips. Marienbad's signposting is the worst in the country and in dire need of renovation.

Where to stay
Every other building in Marienbad seems to be a hotel or pension. The town's 15,000 inhabitants are almost outnumbered by hotel guests at the height of the season. Prices are high, but so are standards. Private rooms with breakfast cost from 20–30. Ask at the information centre for details. The following is a selection of the interesting and reasonably priced. There is a spa tax of 17Kč a night.

Luxury
Villa Butterfly Hlavní 655; ⟍ 354 654 111; f 354 654 200; www.marienbad.cz. One of 9 hotels in Marienbad belonging to the Danubius group, the Villa Butterfly stands out with its inimitable modern but pleasant façade. The 96 4-star rooms with all possible facilities cost 2,500Kč in low season to 3,720Kč in high season for a dbl with breakfast.
Cristal Palace Hlavní 61; ⟍ 354 615 111; f 354 625 012; www.cristalpalace.cz. With so many attractive *fin de siècle* spa hotels to choose from, not everyone would plump for the ultra-modern Cristal Palace, built in 1996. Its 93 rooms are light and spacious but slightly characterless. Expect to pay 2,000–3,000Kč for a sgl and 3,000–4,500Kč for a dbl.
Nové Lázně Reitenbergerova 53; ⟍ 354 644 111; f 354 644 044; www.marienbad.cz. This is without doubt one of the town's most striking hotels and one of the largest. Built in 1898, King Edward VII was a regular and guests (and non-guests) can sample a

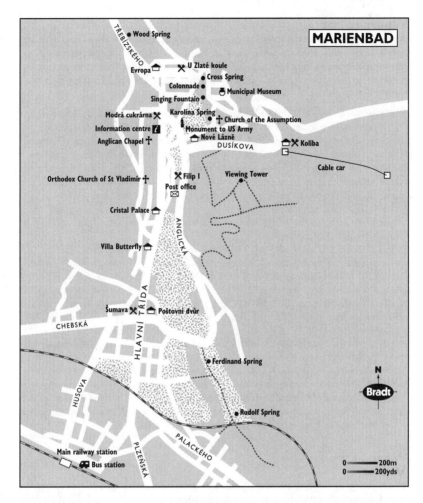

mineral bath in the royal cubicle. The inviting water of the ornate Roman baths is one of the highlights of a visit to Marienbad. A dbl in one of the 98 rooms costs a reasonable 2,000–3,000Kč for this standard of accommodation.

Tighter budgets

Poštovní dvůr Hlavní 622; ℡ 354 602 632; f 354 620 556; www.dexin.cz/posthof. Tucked away in a quiet yard just off Hlavní the Poštovní dvůr may look like a mock-Tudor Portakabin, but inside the 12 immaculate en-suite rooms are superb value at 950Kč year round for a sgl and 1,300Kč for a dbl. The caring staff serve up a hearty breakfast in the pleasant breakfast room whose walls are crammed with pictures of old Marienbad.

Koliba Dusíkova 592; ℡ 354 625 169; f 354 626 310; www.koliba.xercom.cz. The Koliba is just about the best option outside of the spa area. The 15 simple rooms all have shower and TV and are good value. A sgl out of season is 800Kč, a dbl in summer is 1,400Kč.

Evropa Třebízkého 101; ℡ 354 622 063–4; f 354 625 408; www.kosev.cz. The 2-star Evropa is a cheap but decent option in the spa district. Prices range from 800Kč for a sgl to roughly 1,400Kč for a dbl.

Where to eat

As in other spa towns in west Bohemia, there are countless four- and five-star hotels eager and able to serve non-guests food of the highest standards for astronomical prices. At the other end of the scale, Marienbad has an abundance of pizza places and other 'tourist' options. The following are solid Czech places with mostly Czech prices.

Šumava Hlavní 244; ✆ 723 913 574. Švejk is the theme of this traditional wood-panelled Czech pub-cum-restaurant at the corner of Chebská and Hlavní streets. No-nonsense cheap-and-cheerful Czech staples (80–180Kč) are the norm here and portions are large.

Koliba Dusíkova 592; ✆ 354 625 169. The mountain-chalet-style Koliba is located on the first floor of the hotel of the same name at the foot of the cable car and in winter within earshot of the swish of skis on the small adjacent slope. My personal favourite in Marienbad takes one back to the good old days of large eateries and low prices (75–190Kč, some game specialities more). Despite its size there is a cosy ambience enhanced by a roaring fire in the hearth. Urquell and Gambrinus are on tap and there is a large selection of Moravian wines.

Filip I Poštovní 96; ✆ 354 626 161. The Filip I is a safe option where local office workers come to exchange their luncheon vouchers for Czech and international standards (60–200Kč) in the afternoon and where the modern décor sounds to more leisurely diners and drinkers until midnight. The menu boasts several decent vegetarian options.

U Zlaté koule Nehrova 26; ✆ 354 624 455. Decorated with seemingly ancient toys and other mock antiques, the 'Golden Ball' is a jolly, lively place in the heart of the spa. It is also jolly overpriced (250–500Kč, cheaper vegetarian options), but it *was* named Restaurant of the Year in 2003 (though in which category is not clear). The dining room regularly echoes to live music.

Modrá cukrárna Hlavní 45; ✆ 354 622 657. On the corner of Ruská and Hlavní a few steps along from the information centre, the 'blue' *cukrárna* is the biggest, best located and most Czech of Marienbad's selection. It has a posh half with TV and a plastic garden chair section full of pensioners sipping Becherovka. With views of Hlavní and the park it is the ideal place to have coffee and cakes and watch the tourists.

What to see and do
The spa

The centrepiece and most eye-catching feature of the spa area is the wrought-iron **Colonnade**, moulded in Blansko in Moravia in 1889 and hauled to west Bohemia in sections. The structure reminds many of a kind of miniature Austro-Hungarian-era railway station, especially in the way it subtly curves away to the left. The delicate wrought-iron work and the dark wood ceiling are a work of art, though I am not quite sure about the slowly moulting lino floor (mind you do not trip) or the out-of-place 1970s frescoes overhead. At the north end of the Colonnade a faint whiff of rotten eggs greets the visitor on entering the **Cross Spring** (Křížový pramen), thanks to the presence of so much sulphur-laden mineral water in an enclosed space. This is Marienbad's oldest spring and in winter the small colonnade built in 1912 is the best place to sample the highly mineralised water, which manages to be salty and sweet at the same time, and is less agreeable than the *aqua mineralis* of Carlsbad. At the southern end of the Colonnade is the famous **Singing Fountain** (Zpívající fontána) which in the summer months puts on a watery performance to the accompaniment of pieces of classical music every two hours from 07.00 until 22.00. The best shows are in the evening after dark when the fountain is illuminated. The programme is posted by the fountain, or can be found in the *Promenáda* magazine. Just south of the fountain stands the simple white **Karolína Spring** (Karolínin pramen) where one can also test the water.

Still in the spa do not miss the **Municipal Museum** on Goethovo Square (*admission 60Kč*) occupying the town's oldest house dating from 1818 and the former pension where spa fanatic Goethe stayed in 1823. One of the most interesting and popular parts of the collection are Goethe's rooms containing period furniture and items related to his time at the spa and a picture of the writer's bronze which lazed on the lawn outside until it was melted down for the Nazi war effort. Other rooms have geology and minerals, the Marienbad Jewish community, the town's history and porcelain and pewter as their themes. Ask the staff to put on the rather protracted video in English on the history of the town, available in seven other languages. Should you be in town long enough, a visit to the **Nové Lázně spa**, the only one open to non-guests, is a must. The relaxing Roman baths are superb though you are unlikely to share them with the naked models from the spa brochures, your fellow bathers more likely being overweight Bavarians. In the municipal park on Hlavní visitors cannot fail to notice the rather hideous **Monument to the US Army** who liberated Marienbad at the end of World War II. The monument has a paradoxically communist-era feel to it and does little to enhance the spa district.

Marienbad's churches
Ruská Street runs parallel to Hlavní higher up the hillside and accommodates two fascinating little churches. The small prim **Orthodox Church of St Vladimír** (*admission 20/10Kč, open year round Mon–Sat, strictly no photography or filming*), built in 1901–02, harbours a dazzling **iconostasis** weighed down with over 9kg of gold and supposedly the largest piece of porcelain in the world. Crafted in Russia, it won first prize at the 1900 Grand Prix de France exhibition before being acquired for Marienbad. Each of the 11 colours had to be fired separately. The church itself was and is used by Ukrainian Czechs who replaced the German inhabitants of the town after World War II. Further up Ruská and in perfect contrast to its colourful orthodox neighbour, the squat, plain brick **Anglican Chapel** would look more at home on a windswept Scottish island than in a central European spa town. Built in 1878 according to plans by London architect William Burges, it hides a plaque commemorating the visits of King Edward VII and is used by the museum for temporary exhibitions. The hefty octagonal **Church of the Assumption** (*free entry*) can be found near the museum in the spa district. Built in 1848 in the neo-Byzantine style, it is well worth inspection for its striking interior, all housed under the span of a colossal painted dome. Byzantine-style icons of the saints adorn the walls.

Other places of interest
From Mírové Square it is a short gentle walk into the woods to the picturesque **Wood Spring** (*Lesní pramen, closed 12.00–16.00*) hemmed in by the Slavkovský Forest which seems to lurk, waiting to take back the valley. Southeast of Hlavní the waters can be taken in the carved wooden **Rudolf Spring** (Rudolfův pramen) and under the simple Classical columns of the **Ferdinand Spring** (Ferdinandův pramen) from which the Excelsior brand of mineral water originates.

Around Marienbad
Teplá
Some 15km east of Marienbad, and a short train journey away, rise the imposing, plain twin towers of the monastery at Teplá. Steeped in history and lost in a

sparsely populated area of west Bohemia it is a perfect day trip from Marienbad, but conceivably worth visiting on its own.

A Premonstratensian monastery was founded here between 1193 and 1197 by Hroznata z Ovence, a Czech nobleman, also responsible for the establishment of another monastery at Chotěšov. Built on land donated by Hroznata, the monastery became his home when he lost his son and wife, and entered the order. Kidnapped in 1217 by his enemies, the knights of Cheb, he was starved to death when no ransom was forthcoming. His remains lie in the church in the monastery, and the martyr was made a saint in 1897.

Since then Teplá has certainly seen its ups and downs over the centuries, withstanding six major fires, the Hussite wars, a plundering by local nobles in 1467 for supporting King George of Poděbrady, several thorough ransackings by the Swedish in the mid 17th century, the dissolution of the monasteries under Emperor Josef II, two world wars and use as a barracks by the Czechoslovak People's Army.

Lying 2km south of the unexciting village of the same name, the monastery is open year round except January, and can be visited only on a guided tour (*admission 90/60Kč, no photography*). However, should you turn up in the depths of winter as the only visitor that week, the guides, some of whom have been involved with Teplá for decades, will bend over backwards for you. The courtyards and buildings which served as stores and offices for the army are beautifully dilapidated, and do little to prepare visitors for the magnificence of the Romanesque–Gothic–Baroque mix of the Church of the Annunciation and the neo-Baroque libraries which compare well to those at the best-known Premonstratensian monastery in the Czech lands, the Strahov Monastery.

The monastery has converted a colossal Baroque barn into a three-star hotel and restaurant. The **Hotel Klášter Teplá** (sometimes known as Klášterní hospice; ℩ *353 392 264;* f *353 392 312; www.pmgastro.cz*) has a whopping 66 rooms which are very comfortable and well maintained. Singles cost 750–950Kč, doubles 1,250–1,650Kč with breakfast and a little extra gets you a bath. The outstanding, tastefully furnished restaurant downstairs serves up substantial Czech countryside portions (50–200Kč), just the thing after your walk from the railway station and tour of the monastery.

Teplá is on a branch line between Marienbad and Carlsbad. Eleven trains a day pass through Teplá in both directions. It takes an hour to get from Carlsbad and 25 minutes from Marienbad. On leaving the station, turn right and follow the road for approximately 20 minutes. You will have the double 12th-century towers of the monastery in sight most of the way.

Hiking in the Marienbad area

A swift way to get up into the wooded hills, crisscrossed with marked walking trails, is by using the **cable car** next to the Koliba Hotel. The fare is 35Kč one way and 50Kč return, 20/30Kč for children. Ask at the information centre for a map of the 12 walks in the environs of the town which range from 1½km to over 7km in length. For more serious walkers VKÚ-KČT map 2 covers the Slavkovský Forest and Marienbad. Recommended hikes from Marienbad:

1 Take the green trail which runs west through the uninhabited Český les protected area to Dyleň on the German border before looping back to Lázně Kynžvart (around 25km in total).

2 Go along the red trail north which joins a green trail after around 13km which runs through hilly terrain to Bečov nad Teplou (approximately 25km in total).

3 Follow a green trail which runs north all the way to Loket with the option of continuing along the Ohře along a blue trail to Carlsbad (roughly 50km).

4 Hike along the red trail which heads east to the Teplá Monastery (15km).

CHEB

With ten minutes of my journey to Cheb (pronounced *Khep*) remaining, I received a text message from my Czech mobile phone provider welcoming me to Germany! On entering the main Krále Jiřího z Poděbrad Square all became clear. Those who know the Czech Republic, or have visited just a handful of its towns, will immediately notice the difference in architecture, with colourful high-roofed burghers' houses letting you know that this is former German soil. Two cultures, Czech and German, clash in this border town (known as Eger in German) though nowadays the only Germans you are likely to meet are day trippers from Bavaria. Once the most westerly outpost of the communist bloc, and now the most westerly major settlement in the Czech Republic, it gives the slight feeling that this is still the end of the line. Cheb does not enjoy the best of reputations on account of prostitution and other organised crime associated with the town, but that is to do this beautifully preserved medieval town a great disservice. Visit Cheb as a day trip from Carlsbad or Marienbad along with Františkovy Lázně, a spa town a mere 6km to the north. Many will pass through the town on overland journeys.

History

There is evidence of a prehistoric settlement on the cliff above the Ohře at Cheb dating back to around 1800BC, but Cheb does not really appear on the historical map of central Europe until the 12th century and the rule of Friedrich I Barbarossa who beefed up the town against the Bohemian kingdom to the east. Cheb subsequently grew in importance as an imperial market town. Přemysl Otakar II occupied it in 1266 and the town had close links to the kingdom throughout the 13th century, but it did not come into the realm of the Czech kings proper until 1322. Perhaps the best-known event to take place in Cheb at the end of the Thirty Years War was the murder of the powerful Duke Albrecht von Wallenstein in 1634 by Emperor Ferdinand II. The house that witnessed the events of that day still stands on Cheb's main square.

In 1930, only one-tenth of Eger's population was Czech. The remaining nine-tenths, who always felt uneasy in the new Czechoslovakia, welcomed inclusion into Nazi Germany in 1938. The Czech name Cheb began to be used officially after 1945 when the German population was expelled, and the town became ethnically Czech for the first time in its long history.

Getting there and away

Cheb lies approximately 150km west of Prague and is the Czech Republic's most westerly town, a few kilometres shy of the border with Germany. From Prague **trains** run every two hours or so from the main railway station (3¼ hours, 250Kč). Cheb is on the main line out of the country so there are direct trains to and from Nürnberg (2 hours), Munich (5 hours), Frankfurt (5 hours), Zwickau (2½ hours) and Marktredwitz just over the border.

Should you prefer to travel to Cheb by **bus**, services take 3–3½ hours to get to the republic's western extremity and a ticket will set you back 144Kč. Coaches leave Florenc coach station approximately every two hours. There are regular bus services to Pilsen and Carlsbad from Cheb.

From the bus and railway stations follow Svobody Street all the way to the central square; ten minutes on foot.

Tourist information

The **information centre** (*nám Krále Jiřího z Poděbrad 33;* ☎ *354 440 302;* f *354 440 330; www.mestocheb.cz*) can find private rooms with prices from 300Kč. Hotels are on the pricier side thanks to the proximity of the border.

Where to stay

Hotel Barbarossa Jateční 7; ☎ 354 423 446; www.hotel-barbarossa.cz. Just off the main square and by far the best deal in town with 18 immaculate new rooms from 900Kč for a sgl with breakfast. The one slight downside to the hotel is its overpriced restaurant and they skimp on the breakfast a trifle.

Hotel Slávie Svobody 32; ☎ 354 433 216; f 354 433 494; www.hotelslavie.cz. The Slávie has 30 rather drab rooms for 1,000Kč for a sgl in high season with breakfast and dbls for 1,600Kč. Prices come down by around a third in winter. The Barbarossa is a much more pleasant option.

Hotel Hvězda Jiřího z Poděbrad 4–6; ☎ 354 422 549; f 354 422 546; www.hotel-hvezda.cz. A bit pre-revolution but cosy and friendly. Its big advantage is its location on the main square. A sgl with breakfast costs 900Kč with bathroom, 600Kč without. Dbls cost about a third more.

Where to eat

Kavárna Špalíček nám Krále Jiřího z Poděbrad 499/50; ☎ 354 422 568. This basic Czech eatery is actually in the Špalíček facing up the square. They serve decent Czech food for decent Czech prices (80–150Kč) and the location is both historical and convenient. There is Pilsner Urquell beer and a limited selection of main courses.

Restaurace U kata Židovská 17; ☎ 354 423 465. 3 mins' walk off the square going towards the castle, this is the merry restaurant at the Pension U kata (*kat* means executioner!) with Czech standards for 40–110Kč and Velkopopovický kozel beer.

Klára Dlouhá 18; ☎ 354 422 024. This Czech place just round the corner from the Pension U kata advertises itself as a healthfood restaurant and the menu does indeed feature an unusual selection of healthy options for a restaurant in a Czech provincial town. Prices range from 40–100Kč for main courses and Gambrinus beer is on tap. The interior is a bit dull, but there is a pleasant garden with a covered dining area.

Vinárna Kamenka Kamenná 11; ☎ 354 422 045. Like so many wine bars in the country this is a restaurant in disguise. You will find it next to the former Dominican monastery. It is a nice little cosy place with mains for 40–120Kč, pleasant staff and perhaps fewer tourists.

Cukrárna Fantazie Kamenná 3; ☎ 603 707 653. This is the most attractive place in town to enjoy coffee and cakes. Just up from the former Dominican monastery it has high ceilings, a wide selection of goodies and friendly staff.

What to see and do
Náměstí Krále Jiřího z Poděbrad and around

The focal point of Cheb's historical centre, the large elongated triangular 'square' is an architectural spectacle and one of the finest in Bohemia. The tallest building is the Baroque **New Town Hall** dating from 1728, now serving as an art gallery. At the far end of the square is a tottering jumble of 11 irregular-shaped half-timbered houses, not attached to the rest of the square, the so-called **Špalíček**, a collection of former Jewish merchants' houses dating from the mid 13th century and restored in 1965 (and, evidently, quite recently too). The **Regional**

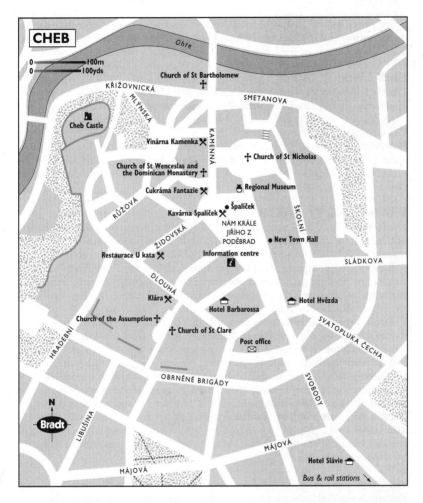

Museum is located in the pink Pachelbel's house at the end of the square behind the Špalíček, where it has been since its foundation in 1873. The building itself is one of Cheb's most noteworthy, as Albrecht von Wallenstein was murdered within its walls in 1634. It has exhibits on Wallenstein, including some of his personal items and the bedroom (not the actual place) where he was murdered, the history of Cheb, Gothic and Baroque sculpture, weapons, furniture and bicycles. The guided tour lasts around an hour (*admission 50Kč*).

Leave the square down by the side of the museum and you will arrive at the huge Romanesque and Gothic **Church of St Nicholas**, founded at the beginning of the 13th century. Though a bit chipped around the edges it is still a splendid sight. From there follow Kamenná Street almost to the river to the **Church of St Bartholomew**. A squat construction from 1414, it is one of the most interesting Gothic buildings of the Luxembourg period and now houses an exhibition of Gothic sculpture. Back up Kamenná Street is the **Church of St Wenceslas and the Dominican Monastery** founded by Wenceslas II in 1294. It is not accessible to the public. Back across the square and along Jatečni Street, facing one another across Františkánské Square are the **Church of the Assumption** and the Baroque **Church of St Clare** by Dientzenhofer senior, containing a newly opened gallery of Gothic sculpture (*admission 60/30Kč*).

Cheb Castle

Cheb's Romanesque castle ruins (*admission 30/15Kč, open Apr–Oct*) stand on a 30m-high cliff over the river Ohře. There has been a fort or castle at this strategic site since the 9th century. In the 12th century a stone fort appeared, built by Cheb's German rulers and extended by Cheb's most famous resident Emperor Friedrich I Barbarossa. Over the next five centuries it was added to and rebuilt several times. The only intact part of the castle is the exquisite Gothic Chapel of SS Erhard and Ursula. The castle is best seen from the outside from down by the river.

FRANTIŠKOVY LÁZNĚ

Františkovy Lázně, or Franzensbad as the Germans call it, lies just 6km northwest of Cheb, from which it can be reached by both bus and train. The smallest of the three spas in the West Bohemian Spa Triangle, it also has the least to see and do, and cannot be compared in any respect to Carlsbad or Marienbad. This is a serious functioning spa, where people come to cure various ailments, recuperate and relax. Relaxation is the reason you should travel there too, perhaps on a half-day trip from Cheb or one of the other spas in the region.

Františkovy Lázně has a strangely un-Czech feel to it. The symmetrical grid of streets making up the spa district has been completely renovated, all the neo-Classical buildings are painted the same colours (white and yellow), and the parks and gardens neatly pruned, all of which renders the place rather sterile and characterless. It is one of the few town centres in the country where little sign of 40 years of communism remain. The town is surrounded by acres of pleasant parks ideal for relaxing walks and dotted with statues and tepid salty mineral springs. The **information centre** is operated by the private travel agent FL Tours (*Americká 2;* ⤫ *354 543 162;* f *354 544 204; www.frantiskolazensko.cz*) and is housed in a hut at the bus stop. They can help with accommodation and offer private rooms for 350–500Kč.

History

As early as the 16th century water from the springs here was being carried in large ceramic jugs to Cheb, and sold as table water. In 1603, the main spring, now called Františkův pramen, attracted the interest of doctors from Cheb, who ascertained its curative properties. Cheb soon became a magnet for people wishing to take the waters, and the water itself began to be exported around Europe. In the 18th century tensions erupted between the Cheb authorities, who were profiting from spa guests using a spring 6km away, and local villagers. In 1785, to ensure hygienic use of the miraculous spring, a certain Dr Adler raised a barred pavilion around the spring, which was subsequently torn down by the women water carriers. Dr Adler went to Emperor Leopold II to ask him to protect the spring. The emperor sent a clergyman called Gruber to assess the situation, and in 1793 the village of Ves císaře Františka was founded, named after Austrian Emperor Franz I, and renamed Františkovy Lázně in 1807. It was officially part of Cheb until 1852.

During the 19th century the town grew, spa houses were built and parks laid out. Various famous personalities such as Goethe, Beethoven, Strauss, Nobel, and Czech writers Božena Němcová and Jan Neruda graced the prestigious spa with their presence. The spa area has remained unaltered since that time.

Getting there and away

Three direct **trains** a day (4 hours, 274Kč) make the 150km journey to Františkovy Lázně via Pilsen and Cheb. The five **buses** a day are no faster, but the fare is lower at 150Kč. Františkovy Lázně has excellent connections with Cheb, and there are several buses and at least one train an hour between the towns.

From the railway station head straight out across the Městské sady (Municipal Park) and look for the church where the spa area starts. The bus stop is on the corner of the Městské sady.

Where to stay

Hotel Kamenný Dům Ruská 6; ☎ 354 541 037; f 354 541 040; www.kamennydum.cz. This is a brand-new 14-room hotel across from the Church of the Holy Cross. A smart sgl with breakfast here costs around 1,100Kč in low season and a dbl in high season 1,900Kč.

Tři lilie Národní třída 10; ☎ 354 208 900; f 354 208 995; www.franzensbad.cz. The 35 air-conditioned rooms at the Tři lilie are about the most stylish you will find in Františkovy Lázně. The building dates from 1793 and was one of the first spa houses in the town. It underwent a complete renovation between 1993 and 1995 and the result is one of the best hotels in the region. With this in mind, the room prices are very good value. A sgl in low season is around 1,300Kč, a dbl in high season a mere 1,900Kč.

Hotel Slovan Národní třída 5; ☎ 354 542 841; f 354 542 843; www.slovan-hotel.cz. The 3-star Slovan on Františkovy Lázně's high street is a cheap option where sgls with bathroom and breakfast go for 1,000Kč in high season and dbls are 1,820Kč. For a few more crowns the Tři lilie is much better.

Where to eat

Other than slightly overpriced hotel restaurants, Františkovy Lázně has very few dining options.

Selská jizba Jiráskova 7; ☎ 354 204 250. This is the only real Czech pub/restaurant in the spa district. This merry place with wooden tables, tiled floor and occasional live music has Krušovice beer and sound Czech staples for 70–150Kč.

What to see and do

If you arrive by train in Františkovy Lázně, the first building of note you will see on crossing the Městské sady is the **Church of the Holy Cross**, one of the only churches in the country built in the Empire style and closed to the prying public. From the church, head down Národní třída, in which the Hotel Slovan and Tři lilie are situated. At the end you will notice the **Františkův pramen** (Franz's Spring) where you can test the water. It is closed in low season. Just to the left of the spring is a simple **Memorial to the US Army**, liberators of Františkovy Lázně on 25 April 1945. Two blocks away you will find Dr Pohoreckého Street, the home of the **Municipal Museum** (*admission 20/15Kč*) housing exhibits on the history of the town and development of the spas. Opposite the museum is the site of the house in which Božena Němcová stayed in 1846–47. The site is marked with a plaque on a large boulder. The green building at the top of the street is the Art Deco-style **Božena Němcová Theatre**, the only building painted a colour other than yellow.

North Bohemia

Potential visitors to the northern reaches of the Czech lands are often deterred by its poor reputation as an area of polluted factory towns, opencast mines, bad air quality due to inefficient coal-burning power stations, devastated environments and drab mountain settlements dogged by poverty, prostitution and cross-border organised crime. Throughout the 20th century the forests, hills, towns and mountains suffered horrific levels of pollution leading to increased instances of cancer and respiratory disease. Air quality was so bad during some winters in the 1980s and early 1990s that children and the elderly were advised to stay indoors, schools were closed and hospitals filled with the sick. Much has been done to remedy these problems such as the completion of Terezín nuclear power plant in south Bohemia (regarded by some as just creating a potentially even bigger problem somewhere else) which has meant the closure of some of the worst power stations. Some opencast mines have been turned into recreational lakes, and factories must now comply with EU regulations regarding emissions. While air quality is substantially better than ten to 15 years ago the main problem the province faces now is endemic unemployment, which has reached 50% in some rural communities. The region is also home to some large Romany communities and racial tensions simmer under the surface.

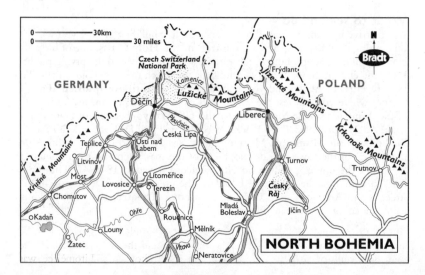

However, do not give up on north Bohemia as there is really so much more to the region than its depressed image. The České středohoří and Krušné Mountains, the ever improving spa town of Teplice, the Czech Switzerland National Park, pretty Litoměřice and sobering Terezín all draw visitors and services in these locations are now in place to accommodate foreign tourists. Říp Mountain in the southeast of the region is the original mythical settlement of the first Slavs to arrive here. Every year sees improvements in the ecological and environmental state of the north and the authorities like to promote the region as a place for outdoor pursuits. The region's now somewhat outdated image means fewer tourists, no crowds and a heartier welcome for those who do come here.

GETTING AROUND

North Bohemia has an excellent rail network with a major hub in Ústí nad Labem. Two main lines run north from Prague on either side of the Labe heading for Dresden via Děčín. There is also an east–west main line serving Teplice, Most, Chomutov and running all the way to Carlsbad in west Bohemia. To the west of the Labe around Liberec the bus is usually the better option.

LITOMĚŘICE

Ask anyone to name ten tourist attractions in the Czech Republic, and I doubt he or she would include the beautiful town of Litoměřice. Perhaps this is a good thing, as this atmospheric town of magnificent Baroque churches and town houses at the confluence of Ohře and Labe rivers remains reasonably undiscovered and unspoilt by mass tourism. Friendly locals, 'Czech' prices and numerous historical sites make this an appealing and very easy day trip from Prague, which could be combined with Terezín 3km away along the busy Ústí nad Labem–Prague highway (walking decidedly not recommended). The slight downside to Litoměřice's off-the-beaten-track status, is that none of the churches is open to the public, but it is the sort of place where someone with a key can always be found who will gladly let you in. Litoměřice is the seat of the bishop and the cathedral and residence are very much real working places.

History

The origin of the town's name comes from the Liutomerici Slav tribe who settled this fertile and strategic site at the confluence of two major rivers during the arrival of the Slavs in the area. The Dómský vrch (Dome Hill), the site of the present-day Cathedral of St Stephen, was the original centre, where Přemyslid Prince Spytihněv founded a chapter (a religious governing body) in 1057. The almost 1,000-year-old founding charter is one of the oldest-surviving documents in the country.

During the reign of Charles IV the Gothic town, which had grown up around the Dome Hill, increased in size, and town walls were added. The Hussites were persecuted in Litoměřice and Hus's friend and provost of the town Zdislav ze Zvířetic was forced out. The town subsequently felt the wrath of Jan Žižka, who laid siege to it in 1421. The burghers joined the less radical Prague Hussites to save the town.

Litoměřice thrived throughout the 15th century, proof of which are the many surviving grand Renaissance houses. The defeat of the Czech estates and the Thirty Years War resulted in over 200 Protestant families emigrating and the arrival of Jesuits in the town. The population fell and the town shrank. In the mid 17th century Baroque took hold, and the bishopric of Litoměřice was founded. Most of the town's churches date from this period, and are the work of the Italian architect Octavio Broggio who was born in Litoměřice.

Two of the most significant figures of the Czech National Revival, linguist and translator Josef Jungmann and Romantic poet Karel Hynek Mácha (who died here), resided in Litoměřice. The 19th century witnessed the arrival of the railway and steamboats on the Labe, but Litoměřice thankfully never developed into an industrial centre.

Litoměřice witnessed some of the worst horrors of World War II on Czech soil, not only because of its proximity to the infamous Terezín, but also because of the nearby camp Richard with its underground factory where thousands perished. Despite the construction of many *paneláky* (blocks of flats) on the outskirts during the communist period, today's 26,000 inhabitants can still be proud of the historical centre which has changed little in 300 years.

Getting there and away
The long and complicated rail journey to Litoměřice means that the **bus** is the best way to reach the area. Buses leave Florenc coach station approximately once every hour (1 hour, 60Kč) and pass through Terezín en route. Buses return to Holešovice metro station (red line C) in Prague, not to Florenc coach station. Services from Prague either end their journey in Litoměřice, or continue on to Ústí nad Labem, the regional capital. The bus and train stations are adjacent to each other, a short uphill walk to the main square and places of interest, all well signposted.

Tourist information
The town has an excellent information centre (*Mírové nám 15/7;* \ *416 732 440;* f *416 916 211*). The eager staff can arrange accommodation, visits to the underground cellars and to the 'Kalich' on the roof of the town hall, and generally make you feel welcome in the town.

Where to stay
Hotel Salva Guarda Mírové nám 12; \ 416 733 590; f 416 732 798; www.salva-guarda.cz. The place to stay in Litoměřice is the striking Salva Guarda, the sgrafitti-plastered building next to the information centre on the main square. It has been a hotel of some kind for centuries, and guests basically stay in a historical monument. The hotel has 16 rooms and sgls without breakfast go for 920Kč, doubles for 1,450Kč. The hotel also has an excellent restaurant.
Hotel Dejmalík Sovova 3; \ 416 733 685; A less luxurious option, the Dejmalík is just off the square up 5. května Street and across the main road. Sgls start at 610Kč, dbls at 920Kč, including breakfast. I am not sure how noisy the Saturday-night dances might be.

Where to eat
Radniční Sklípek Mírové nám 21; \ 416 734 306. The most interesting restaurant in the town must be the intimate Sklípek buried in the underground cellars, which also doubles up as the entrance to underground Litoměřice. They have a large selection of Czech and international food (100–170Kč) and Pilsen Urquell beer.

What to see and do
Mírové Square
The arcaded main square is the town's real centrepiece. Dominating the eastern end is the Gothic **Municipal tower** (Městská věž) attached to the All Saints' Church. Almost opposite, facing down the square, is the old town hall which

now houses the **Regional Museum** (Oblastní museum) which must be the best-value tourist sight in the country with its 8Kč admission fee. Exhibits map the Litoměřice area from the Stone Age to the present day. Walk down the middle of the square to the ubiquitous **plague column** (Morový sloup) dating from 1683. Level with the column is the current town hall and information centre with the enormous Hussite '**Kalich**' or chalice on the roof. Ask in the information centre to be taken up to the Kalich from which there are views of almost all the town's historical sites and which used to be used for council meetings. It is a good idea to do this first to know which direction everything is from the square. One house away from the town hall is the Renaissance **House at the Black Eagle** (Černý orel) which is now the Hotel Salva Guarda. At the far end of the square there is the Baroque **House at the Five Virgins** (Dům U Pěti panen) where the architect Broggio lived. In the corner there is the **Museum and Gallery of the Litoměřice Diocese** with treasures too precious to keep in the cathedral, including paintings by Škréta (*admission 20/10Kč*).

Litoměřice's churches
Just off the square is the **All Saints' Church** originally dating from 1235 but Baroque-ified by Octavio Broggio in 1718. In the same street is the former **Church of the Assumption of the Virgin Mary** (now a gallery) and the former Jesuit College. Said to be the most beautiful of Broggio's creations, the compact Eastern Orthodox **Church of St Wenceslas** built in 1716 is just off Dómská Street. The **Cathedral of St Stephen**, originally dating from the 11th century, was rebuilt in the 17th century, but has a distinctly Romanesque feel. Paintings by Škréta, black and gold Baroque altarpieces and the peculiar lamp-lined main aisle are just some of the things to look out for. In front of the cathedral is the Dómské Square, beautiful in its dilapidation, and behind that is the **Bishop's residence**, where the 18th Bishop of Litoměřice now lives.

Other places of interest
The uninspiring **Litoměřice Castle** is hardly worth the walk off the square and inexplicably has an ugly communist-era culture centre welded to it. Around 1.7km of the **town walls** remain to this day and can be seen as you leave the bus station. The house where **Karel Hynek Mácha** died aged just 25 is in Máchovy schody Street where you will also find a theatre bearing his name.

České středohoří
Litoměřice is the ideal gateway and base for exploring the curious peaks of the little-known České středohoří mountain range and protected area to the north

---

KAREL HYNEK MÁCHA (1810–1836)
Karel Hynek Mácha is regarded as the founder of modern Czech poetry and a leading 19th-century Romantic. Born the son of a poor Prague miller he studied at Prague University where he attended lectures in Czech by Josef Jungmann and was an amateur actor working under Tyl. Sometimes seen as the archetypal Romantic poet, he wandered the country on foot visiting castle ruins and even walked across the Alps to Italy. Shortly before he finished his law studies in Litoměřice he published *Máj*, his and the Czech language's greatest work of poetry. In true 19th-century Romantic poet's style, he died of flu shortly before his wedding day aged only 25.

and west. VKÚ-KČT maps 10 *České středohoří–východ* and 11 *České středohoří–východ* will guide you reliably along the tangle of marked trails which crisscross this area of extinct volcanoes, which rise up out of the plain and provide spectacular views in every direction. Most trails run north out of the town. Some of the best places to head for are **Milešovka Mountain** (837m) and the dramatic ruins of **Hazmburk** on the top of an extinct volcano.

TEREZÍN

Few places in the Czech Republic reveal the full extent of the horrific events of World War II like Terezín. This fortress town, built by Emperor Josef II in 1780 to defend the north of the empire against Prussian invasion and named after his mother, Empress Maria Theresa, was used by the Nazis as a ghetto, principally for Jews from Germany and the Czech lands, but also from Slovakia, Denmark, Holland and several other countries. The Nazis used Terezín as a propaganda tool to fool the world into thinking they were treating the Jews humanely and duped two delegations from the Red Cross into writing favourable reports about the conditions they found at the supposedly self-administered ghetto. The truth could not have been more different as cramped living conditions, epidemics and food shortages caused general misery and death. Under international pressure in autumn 1944 the Germans even shot a film showing the happy carefree life of the ghetto inhabitants which again had the desired propaganda effect. By the end of the war most of the people in the film had been murdered in the death camps of the east, mainly in Auschwitz. Prior to the Red Cross inspections the town underwent a 'beautification' process whereby houses were painted, people fed and the streets cleaned and given names (such as Lake Street, even though there is no lake in the vicinity of the fortress). This process also included vastly reducing the numbers of inmates by putting them on transports to death camps. Many Jews thought they could see out the war in Terezín, but these hopes slowly crumbled as more and more transports left for the east. For most Terezín simply became a halfway house between life and death. One-fifth of the ghetto's inhabitants died in Terezín itself.

This shocking place is all the more powerful owing to the vast amount of drawings, documents, poems, paintings, and other objects that survived to document life inside the ghetto and Gestapo prison in the Lesser Fortress. Many talented artists, musicians, actors and writers were brought here and allowed to work for propaganda purposes. The result is a disturbing first-hand picture of life in a Jewish ghetto created by people who within perhaps months had become victims of the Nazis' final solution in Auschwitz. Although this activity served Nazi propaganda purposes, more important by far is that it remains as a monument to brave and talented individuals and to their suffering.

Terezín lies just 3km south of Litoměřice, around 60km north of Prague, and can be visited as a day trip. It is divided into the octagonal Greater Fortress and the Lesser Fortress about a ten-minute walk along the busy Prague–Ústí nad Labem road from the main square (nám Československé armády) which used to serve as the parade ground for Austro-Hungarian troops. You do not really get a feel of the size of the Greater Fortress until you see it on a map or photograph. The town itself is quite an eerie place with its dusty empty streets and grid layout of neo-Classical blocks each with its own story of human misery. The particularly harrowing Lesser Fortress is probably the main attraction and takes a few hours to see.

Getting there and away

The only way to reach Terezín is by **bus**. These run from Prague and Ústí nad Labem (see *Litoměřice* section on page 180 for details) and stop on the central square in Terezín and near the Lesser Fortress. The bus drivers always assume tourists will want to alight at the Lesser Fortress but you may want to stay on the bus two minutes longer to get to the museum and the information centre.

Where to stay and eat
Because of its proximity both to Prague and Litoměřice few choose to stay in Terezín itself and after a tour of its sights you may not find the idea too appealing either. If you do want to stay here, or get stuck for any reason, Litoměřice has good accommodation options. As far as getting a bite to eat is concerned, the **Restaurace Atypik** (*Máchova 91;* \ *416 782 780*) is just behind the Ghetto Museum but is sometimes used by tour buses and can get full. Otherwise there are several small fast-food places around the coach park near the Lesser Fortress or try the restaurant inside the Lesser Fortress which used to be the Gestapo prison guards' canteen.

What to see and do
One ticket for everything can be purchased at any of the three main sites costing 180/140Kč (*family tickets 400Kč*). The information centre next to the museum belongs to the town of Terezín and has very little information, though they can help with bus timetables and accommodation.

Ghetto Museum
The Ghetto Museum was opened in a former school in 1991. It charts the course of events which led to the creation of the ghetto, the life of its inhabitants, the various propaganda uses it served and the fate of the Jews sent on transports to the east. Photographs, letters, children's drawings, official documents and everyday objects from the ghetto make up the disturbing exhibition. All explanations are in Czech, Hebrew, German and English as at all sites in Terezín. There is also a short 12-minute film shown in the museum cinema which uses footage from the Nazi propaganda film and art by ghetto inhabitants.

Magdeburg Barracks
The barracks along Tyršova Street from the main square was used as the seat of the Council of Elders and the Jewish self-administration. Now visitors can see a new reconstruction of a cramped ghetto dormitory created with assistance from former women inhabitants and various other exhibitions on the extraordinary cultural life of the ghetto, the talented individuals who created it and their fates.

Lesser Fortress
Ten minutes' walk from the main square is the Lesser Fortress. Near the road you will see the National Cemetery where 601 exhumed bodies of Nazi victims were buried in September 1945. Until 1918 the fortress had been used as a prison for those involved in activities against the Austro-Hungarian Empire. Its most famous inmate was Gavrilo Princip, the assassin of Archduke Franz Ferdinand d'Este in Sarajevo in 1914. From 1940, the Prague Gestapo used it as a prison mainly for Czechs, though there were also prisoners from the Soviet Union, Poland, Germany and Yugoslavia as well as some Jews. Some 2,600 prisoners died here, of whom 250–300 were executed. Typhoid hit the prison at the end of the war, after which the prison commanders were rounded up and many executed. The prison was then used for the internment of Germans.

A numbered map guides visitors around the various courtyards, solitary confinement cells, washrooms, stores, dormitories, workshops, hospital wards, execution grounds and other gruesome places within the walls. Daubed above a gate is the deriding Nazi slogan *Arbeit Macht Frei* (Work makes you free). There is also an interesting museum and separate exhibitions on the underground Nazi factory camp Richard in Litoměřice, the internment of the Germans and on the history of the fortress up to 1939.

TEPLICE

Although a reasonably well-known spa in the Czech Republic, and one of the oldest, many may write off Teplice immediately as a run-down north Bohemian industrial town with not much to offer. However, the town is clawing back some of its former glory – and what glory that once was. Teplice used to be nicknamed 'Little Paris' and a stroll through the streets lined with proud villas and spa houses will tell you why. Tsar Peter the Great, Goethe, Beethoven, Paganini, Chopin and many others came to the then-fashionable spa to take the waters. Today it is a town of leafy parks, forgotten statues, busy thoroughfares bursting with shops and shoppers and renovated spas, the main reason most visitors find themselves here. Visit Teplice as part of a hike into the Krušné Mountains, using it as a starting or finishing point. A day trip from Prague is easy but perhaps the town does not have enough to merit 1½ hours on the train.

Teplice is divided into the commercial area and the spa and park area, which also includes the chateau, although there is no clear dividing line. The Krušné Mountains loom in the background wherever you look. The town of almost 60,000 souls has both some beautiful architecture and some of the ugliest you will witness in the Czech Republic, not all of which dates from the communist era. An example of a new-ish construction which insults the senses is the glass-and-steel New Colonnade, the only function of which, as far as I could tell, is to be unattractive. The main sights in Teplice are centred around Zámecké náměstí (Chateau Square) with parks and gardens spreading out in virtually every direction from there.

The somewhat undignified origin of the town is linked to a legend of a pig falling into, and splashing around in, the hot springs, but this has no relation to any historical fact. However, the name of the town does come from the Czech word *teplý* meaning hot. The town's history begins in earnest in 1158 when a cloister of the Benedictine order was set up at the '*aquas calidas*' (hot water) by Queen Judita, wife of Břetislav II on the site of today's chateau. The town as a spa became well known in the 16th century. In 1643, the owner of Teplice was murdered along with Albrecht of Wallenstein in Cheb and the town came into the ownership of the Aldringen family. The Cláry-Aldringens held on to it until 1945. Teplice had its heyday in the 19th century when illustrious visitors came to take the waters. However, the 20th century brought pollution and decline, as the town found itself in the coal-mining area of north Bohemia, polluted heavily by coal-burning power stations. The spa now attracts an Arab clientele who caused controversy soon after 9/11 by submitting an application to build a mosque in the historical centre which was refused. You will notice the odd kebab place, water pipe and sign in Arabic as you stroll round, although the Arab presence is nothing like the current Russian 'occupation' of Carlsbad.

Getting there and away

The cheapest and swiftest way of reaching Teplice from the capital is by **bus** from Nádraží Holešovice metro station (red line C). Services leave once every two to three hours (1 hour 20 minutes, 80Kč). The bus station is directly in front of the railway station. The **train** is slightly slower and nearly twice as expensive.

There are three direct services a day from Prague's main railway station and one from Masarykovo station (1½ hours, 140Kč).

The railway station is worth seeing in itself. Two soot-coated members of the proletariat greet passengers at the entrance to an amazing ticket hall with church-like columns and an intricately painted vaulted ceiling, reminding you more of an Eastern Orthodox place of worship than a station. To get to the information centre on Benešovo Square turn right out of the station and then a left into 28 října street which leads you straight to it on foot in around ten minutes.

Tourist information
Teplice has a superb information centre (*Benešovo nám 840;* \ *417 459 97;* f *417 459 37; www.teplice.cz*) which can supply you with more information on the town that you can carry.

Where to stay
Hotel Prince de Ligne Zámecké nám 136; \ 417 537 733; f 417 537 727; www.princedeligne.cz. This is Teplice's top hotel opposite the plague column and adjacent to the chateau on Zámecké Square. It provides 4-star luxury with all the facilities one would expect. A night in one of the extremely comfortable 32 rooms will set you back 1,600Kč for a sgl and a whopping 3,500Kč for a dbl. If you have money to burn why not book the president's suite for 6,000Kč a night.
Penzion u Kozičky Rooseveltova 262; \ 417 816 411; www.ukozicky.cz. This newly built pension can be found on the hillside above Roosevelt Street opposite the Švejk Restaurant. A room costs 950Kč for sgl occupancy and 1,600Kč for a dbl, both including breakfast. It has a pleasant restaurant with mains from 100–180Kč and a summer terrace with picturesque views of the chateau.
Hotel Paradies Laubeho nám 4/258; \ 417 536 252–3; f 417 570 716; www.paradies.cz. This small hotel in the spa district has modern, fully equipped en-suite sgls for 1,500Kč and dbls for 2,100Kč including breakfast.

Where to eat
Restaurace Beethoven Lázeňská ulička (House at the Golden Harp); \ 417 550 153. Situated in the building where Beethoven stayed in 1811, this restaurant plays at being an upmarket affair but with ordinary Czech prices (130–200Kč). The service is excellent as is the food.
Švejk (U Petra) Rooseveltova 1; \ 417 538 337; f 417 537 727. I always have my doubts about restaurants with Švejk in the title. 'Tourist' prices and service to match are my worst fears but this place, just behind the chateau, is OK. Housed in a Renaissance building with a very distinctive double-spired roof it has a traditional Czech interior and a beer garden. They serve excellent goulash for 65Kč and other main courses cost up to 170Kč plus Pilsen beer.

What to see and do
Around Zámecké Square
The dominating feature of the square is the **chateau**, built between 1585 and 1634 on the site of a 12th-century Benedictine cloister founded by Queen Judita, wife of Břetislav II, and which now serves as the **Teplice Regional Museum**. Entry is with a guide only (*English-speaking guide available*) and admission costs a mere 15Kč, concessions 10Kč; excellent value when you see the exhibitions of ceramics, period furniture, clocks and the library. Behind the chateau the **Chateau Park** is centred around two picturesque lakes. Look out for the place where Beethoven and Goethe are said to have met just as you enter the park on

the right. Next to the chateau stands the neat little Orthodox **Church of the Exaltation of the Cross**, whitewashed from base to steeple. The original Renaissance structure got the neo-Gothic treatment in the late 19th century. It is closed to the public except during services. Behind that is the Roman Catholic **Church of John the Baptist**. Dating from the 12th century, it underwent a Baroque remodelling in 1700. The exquisite Baroque interior including paintings by Brandl and the particularly impressive altar can be viewed. Across from the chateau is the house where Austrian Emperor Franz I, Russian Tsar Alexander I and Prussian King William III met to form an alliance against Napoleon.

Spas and parks

Teplice has some wonderful neo-Classical **spa houses** dotted around the Šanov area south of the shopping district and set in relaxing parkland. The most appealing park is the **sady Československé armády** around the Vojenské lázně and Hadí lázně spa houses. A forlorn, neglected **Soviet War Memorial** still adorned with evocative hammer and sickle can be found in nearby Lázeňský Park.

DĚČÍN

Nestled among the majestic peaks of the *České středohoří* and the Czech Switzerland National Park, Děčín, which derives its name from the Slavic tribe called the *Děčané*, is an ideal base for discovering the whole of this extraordinary region along the border with Germany. While not perhaps a tourist destination in itself, it does have sufficient to keep visitors occupied for a day or so with its magnificent fortress-like chateau guarding the Labe as it hurries the combined waters of the Bohemia rivers to the border where it becomes the Elbe, bird's-eye views of the town and the surrounding rugged terrain from the Shepherd's Wall (Pastýřská stěna), and an interesting little district museum. With good accommodation options and some interesting eateries, more people should come to Děčín, if only to access the national park further north.

Having stood under a high-water mark on an archway in Děčín showing the extent of the 2002 floods I am surprised that the town is still there at all. Typically, there are hardly any signs of the devastation caused when the Labe burst its banks. When you see the width of the river and the steep mountains which encircle the town you can imagine how terrifying those days must have been.

Děčín is in fact made up of two communities, Děčín on the east bank of the Labe and Podmokly on the west bank, only united into one town called Tetschen–Bodenbach (the German names for the two communities) during the Nazi occupation in 1942. Since 1945, the town has been known simply as Děčín. The chateau is on the Děčín side while the railway and bus stations, the viewing point at the Shepherd's Wall and the district museum are in Podmokly.

History

The history of the town is essentially the history of the chateau. The settlement was probably formed around a fort built by the Děčan tribe on a strategic cliff above the confluence of the Labe and the Ploučnice Stream on the site of today's chateau. Přemysl King Václav III gave the castle and town to the Vartenberk family in 1305 and the Thun family acquired it in 1628, when the previous Protestant owner was forced to emigrate. The inevitable wars, fires and plague epidemics followed. The town prospered in the 19th century thanks to the textile industry and its position on a major European river and the main railway line to the north.

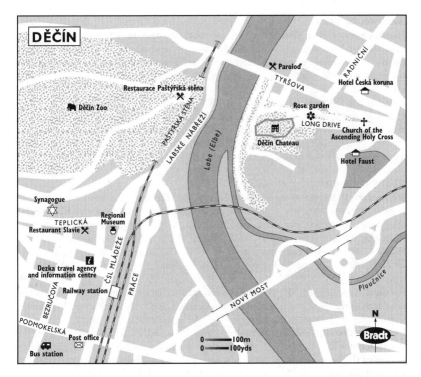

DĚČÍN

Restaurace Paštýřská stěna ✗

🦬 Děčín Zoo

✗ Paroloď

TYRŠOVA

RADNIČNÍ

Hotel Česká koruna 🏠

Rose garden
🌸
LONG DRIVE

Děčín Chateau 🏛

✝ Church of the
Ascending Holy Cross

Hotel Faust 🏠

Synagogue
✡
TEPLICKÁ
Restaurant Slavie ✗

Regional
Museum 🏛

ČSL MLÁDEŽE

PRACE

PAŠTÝŘSKÁ STĚNA

LABSKÉ NÁBŘEŽÍ

Labe (Elbe)

Ploučnice

NOVÝ MOST

ℹ
Dezka travel agency
and information centre

BEZRUČOVA

Railway station 🚉

PODMOKELSKÁ

Post office ✉
Bus station 🚌

0 ━━━━ 100m
0 ━━━━ 100yds

N

Bradt

Getting there and away

Děčín is relatively simple to reach from Prague, as it guards the major rail route and one of the road links to Dresden as they squeeze their way through the mountains and into Germany. Děčín could in theory be reached from Prague by boat along the Vltava then the Elbe, but as yet no-one has started such a service, although ferries do operate in the other direction to Pirna in Germany.

By **rail**, there are ten departures a day from Prague Masarykovo, the main station, and Holešovice station with spanking-new Pendolino trains plying the route (from Masarykovo). A quick and comfortable service is the EuroCity express which leaves the main railway station at just after 09.00 bound for Århus in faraway Denmark (1 hour 40 minutes, 162–222Kč). There are superb views of the Labe valley from the window as the train hugs every twist and turn of the river. More EuroCity trains will take you from Děčín to Dresden (1 hour) and beyond, and there are regular connections to Ústí nad Labem. The freshly refurbished station is on the Podmokly side of the Labe. To get to the Děčín side, take any town bus (12Kč) from the station and alight at Masaryk Square (Masarykovo nám).

Tourist information

The information centre (Prokopa Holého 808/8; ☎ 412 531 333; f 412 531 176) is limited to a desk in the Dezka travel agency which has the advantage of year-round Saturday-morning opening, but is somewhat limited in the brochures it provides. They can arrange accommodation, trips to the Czech Switzerland National Park and they do have town maps if precious little else.

Where to stay
Hotel Česká koruna Masarykovo nám 60; ℩ 412 516 104; f 412 519 086;
www.hotelceskakoruna.cz. The stunningly restored 'Czech Crown' with its stucco
exterior, 43 fresh, comfortable, modern rooms and pleasant restaurant is the plushest
option in town and is good value for money. A sgl with breakfast and bathroom goes for
around 900Kč in high season, a dbl for 1,200Kč.
Hotel Faust U Plovárny 43; ℩ 412 516 235; www.hotelfaust.cz. Adjacent to the
Chateau Lake (Zámecký rybník) this is a modern establishment in a good location for
the chateau and walks along the banks of the Labe. The 50 rooms are of a reasonable
standard though nothing special, but when everything is considered they represent a
good deal at 480–750Kč for a sgl and 960–1,200Kč for a dbl including breakfast.

Where to eat
Restaurace Paštýřská stěna Žižkov a 236/6; ℩ 412 532 198. If you make it up the hill
as far as the Shepherd's Wall you can relish the views from a table here with Czech
dishes from 90–200Kč. This modern pleasant place is in the tiny chateau, built on the
Podmokly side of the river to show that anything Děčín could do, Podmokly could
match it. They did not quite succeed. The restaurant is nicknamed '*Nebíčko*' which
means 'Little heaven', not because of it's celestial qualities but more as it is perched so
high up.
Paroloď Tyršova 30; ℩ 412 519 866. A recommended place to enjoy a pizza or pasta is
next door to the Tyrš Bridge. Enjoy the food for 60–180Kč, the rustic interior, friendly
staff and the great views of the Labe.
Restaurant Slavie Teplická 23; ℩ 412 532 258. Back on the Podmokly side just up
Teplická from the museum is this throwback to the cavernous eateries of the communist
days; all the more reason to go there. It is a great place for a beer and some real stodgy
Czech cuisine for 90–210Kč.

What to see and do
The chateau and surroundings
Under painstaking reconstruction for over a decade now, Děčín's photogenic
chateau is now partially open to the public. Since spring 2005 all but the west
wing have been echoing to the voices of the friendly and enthusiastic guides. The
first mention of a Přemyslid castle on this site dates from 1128. The Přemyslid
dynasty held the castle until 1305. Over the next 300 years it changed hands
several times until in 1628, when the Thun-Hohenstein family acquired it, the
owners until 1932, when they sold it to the Czechoslovak state because of the
unbearable financial burden of its upkeep. The Thun-Hohensteins had the
greatest influence on the chateau's appearance, rebuilding it several times from a
Renaissance chateau into a Baroque residence and subsequently into the neo-
Classical building we see today. The chateau's history from 1932 until 1991 was
one of military occupation and general misuse. It was used first by Czechoslovak
border soldiers as a barracks, from 1938 by the *Wehrmach* and again by the
Czechoslovak military after World War II until 1968, when it was occupied by
the Red Army who left it in a sorry state and in need of serious renovation. For
four days in spring 1991 the gates of the chateau were swung open for the first
time, allowing the residents of Děčín to have a look inside this dominant feature
of their town, in which the vast majority had never set foot. It was then closed
for over a decade for renovation.
   The approach to the castle is along the impressive and seemingly endless **Long
Drive** (Dlouhá jízda) dating from 1672. On the right as you approach the
chateau gates stretches the fragrant Baroque **Rose Garden** (*admission 24/12Kč*)

with views of the surrounding mountains and a concert venue on summer evenings. The **sala terrena** at the near end of the garden with its Baroque painted ceilings and walls depicting scenes from Greek mythology was apparently used by the Red Army as a gym. The tour of the chateau itself (*admission 36/18Kč*) includes the Chapel of St George, now used for exhibitions and concerts, the Baroque riding hall still complete with Cyrillic graffiti left by Soviet soldiers, and other parts of this huge building, still undergoing extensive renovation. The museum in the east wing (*admission 30/15Kč*) has displays of historical weapons, Baroque art including portraits of the apostles by Petr Brandl and interesting pictures charting the development of Děčín in the 19th century. The splendid Baroque **Kostel Povýšení sv Kříže** (the Church of the Ascending Holy Cross) dating from 1691 is accessible from the Long Drive. The church with its Baroque frescoes is still used for services as well as concerts of the Děčín Symphonic Orchestra.

Shepherd's Wall (Paštýřská stěna)
High above the Labe, opposite the chateau, towers a sandstone cliff called the Shepherd's Wall (Paštýřská stěna). The steep climb to the top is worth it for the views of the river, the chateau and the Děčín side. As you begin the ascent notice the beautifully restored synagogue from 1907, open to the public every day from 08.00 until 14.00. The Shepherd's Wall is not just about the views. There is a good restaurant (see page 188) and Děčín Zoo which, though one of the smallest in the Czech Republic, is certainly set in the nicest surroundings. The Shepherd's Wall is the starting point for several marked walking trails, including the red marked trail through the forest to Sněžník, where you will find a viewing tower, the oldest of its kind in the country and built by the Thun family in 1864, and offering views of the surrounding mountain ranges and over the border into Saxony. Interestingly, the first ever TV signal in Bohemia was received at Sněžník in 1936 from the Olympic Games in Berlin.

Regional Museum
Just along Csl Mládeže from the railway station is the District Museum (Okresní museum, *admission 30/15Kč*) based in an 18th-century palace. The exhibits include the history of Děčín Chateau, Gothic sculpture from the Děčín area and the development of water transport on the Labe.

CZECH SWITZERLAND NATIONAL PARK
Straddling the Czech–German border, this area of outstanding natural beauty is divided into the Czech and Saxon Switzerland. Only declared a national park on the Czech side of the border in 2000 (on the German side ten years earlier) it gets its name from the Swiss landscape painters who 'discovered' the region at the end of the 18th century. The main feature of the roughly 80km² park is the giant sandstone towers and cliffs which rise out of the forests, of which approximately 300 can be climbed. In the south the national park borders on the Labe sandstone 'rock town' protected area (CHKO Labské pískovce). The Czech Switzerland has almost 120km of marked walking trails and 50km of cycle tracks, and is very popular with Czech and German walkers and climbers alike. The summer months mean crowds, but come in the autumn when some of the trees begin to turn gold and yellow, the light becomes crisper and the temperatures cooler, and you may feel as though you have this magical place all to yourself. The park is virtually uninhabited, the only village being Mezná, just east of Hřensko, which lies outside its borders. Hřensko can be used as a base to explore the area but is

slightly overpriced. Go into the park to Mezná and Mezní Louka, or to the villages on its perimeter such as Vysoká Lípa or Jetřichovice for cheaper food and places to stay.

Getting there and away

Hřensko on the Labe is the gateway to the Czech Switzerland National Park and is a mere 16km by road north of Děčín. On the opposite side of the park is the village of Jetřichovice. There are four **buses** a day heading north to Hřensko and the same number making the return journey on weekdays. The first bus from Děčín is at 07.50, which goes all the way to Mezná via Hřensko stopping at the Pravčická brána on the way and the last bus from Hřensko is around 18.30. The journey takes 20 minutes. In total there are four buses a day between Hřensko and Mezná. At the weekends there are no connections at all, the only option being a taxi from Děčín. There are three buses a day between Děčín and Jetřichovice (1 hour).

Where to stay

Hřensko thrives on tourism and is the obvious option but can be relatively pricey and chock-a-block in summer. The beautifully reconstructed, 36-bed **Hotel Labe** (*Hřensko 13;* \ *412 554 088;* f *412 554 265*) is a comfortable option with 13 rooms at a flat rate of 440Kč. Said to be the best hotel in the region, the four-star **Hotel Praha** (*Hřensko;* \ *412 554 006;* f *412 554 162*) is a grand affair with beautiful rooms from 1,550Kč for a single with breakfast. The hotel has an interesting exhibition of old photographs of Hřensko. Inside the park at the crossroads village of Mezní Louka there is a **campsite** (*Mezní Louka 37;* \ *412 554 084*) which has bungalows. The pretty **Hotel Mezní Louka** (\ *412 554 220*) has small, modern single rooms with breakfast for 800Kč, doubles for 1,200Kč and sleeps a maximum of 67 guests. Because of the high number of visitors the park receives there are many private rooms and small pensions in the surrounding villages.

Highlights

The **Pravčická brána** is the largest natural stone bridge in Europe and the most frequented and best-known site in the Czech Switzerland. The natural arch is 21m high and however much you would like to, climbing is forbidden. The **Jetřichovické skály** (Jetřichovice cliffs) are just north of the village of the same name. A nature trail leads you round these extraordinary rock formations. Before joining the Labe in Hřensko the Kamenice River runs through the national park forming a deep gorge. Boats take visitors along two stretches of the gorge called **Tichá soutěska** (Silent Gorge) and **Divoká soutěska** (Wild Gorge).

Walking and cycling in the Czech Switzerland

The excellent VKÚ-KČT map 12 *Národní parky České a Saské Švýcarsko* will guide you along the marked trails which crisscross the area. For those who wish to get a taste of the area but have only a day to spend, the *naučná stezka* (nature trail) marked with green diagonal slashes will lead you from Hřensko to the Pravčická brána, Mezní Louka, Mezná and back to Hřensko via the Kamenice Gorge where you can take a boat part of the way in summer and autumn weekends. If there is no boat or you wish to miss it out take the yellow trail back to Tři prameny near the Pravčická brána. The long-distance red trail heads out from Hřensko along the same route as the nature trail as far as Mezní Louka then heads east to Jetřichovice via the Malá Pravčická brána and the Jetřichovické skály. From Mezní Louka another possibility is to take the green trail until it meets a blue trail which heads north to Brtníky which has a railway station, or south to yellow trails leading you to Jetřichovice.

If you are cycling, take the 3030 route from Hřensko to Mezní Louka then through the Hluboký důl and down to Mokrý důl where you can join route 3029 either to Vysoká Lípa or through more of the park and out to the village of Chřibská.

LIBEREC

While the town of Liberec (or Reichenberg as the Germans call it) could hardly be described as a particularly attractive place, it can serve as a base to explore the surrounding area such as Ještěd Mountain and is a gateway to the surrounding Jizerské Mountains. Regrettably the town itself has been the victim of various town planners and architects and has some downright hideous architecture from the communist era and the 1990s, 'enhanced' by constant traffic jams of vehicles squeezed onto tramline engraved roads by the pedestrianisation of much of the centre. Nevertheless, it is worth a few hours to see the town hall, the busy shopping streets and perhaps the famous Babylon Centre. Liberec is the capital of the Liberecký kraj (Liberec Region) and has around 100,000 inhabitants.

Known to some as the 'Manchester of Bohemia' Liberec was once the centre of the textile industry in the region and had been since the 14th century when German and Flemish weavers settled here. Rudolph II granted Reichenberg its charter in 1577 and the town grew rich on the export of cloth. This affluence was interrupted by the Thirty Years' War and the great plague of 1680, but the 18th and 19th centuries saw a return to prosperity and at one time Liberec was the second-largest town in the Czech lands after Prague.

Ferdinand Porsche, legendary creator of the Volkswagen Beetle and prolific automobile constructor was born in 1875 in the village of Vratislavice nad Nisou on the outskirts of Liberec. A celebrated Czech personality from the town was the interwar actor and comedian, Vlasta Burian.

Getting there and away

The only sane way to reach Liberec from Prague is by **bus** as travelling by train requires a change in Turnov and takes an age. Buses leave Prague's Černý most metro station (end of yellow line B) every two to three hours. The journey takes 1 hour 10 minutes and costs 78Kč one way. From Liberec there are direct trains to Zittau and Dresden in Germany and buses to Berlin and Slovakia. From the bus and railway stations take 1. máje Street to Soukenné náměstí then ascend Pražská up to the main square named after the wartime president of Czechoslovakia, Dr Edvard Beneš.

Tourist information

The information centre (*nám Dr E Beneše 1;* \ *485 101 709;* f *485 243 589; www.infolbc.cz*) is inside the town hall and provides information on the town's attractions, helps with accommodation and timetables and sells tickets for various events.

Where to stay

Grandhotel Zlatý lev (79 rooms) Gutenbergova 3; \ 485 104 086; f 482 710 270; www.zlatylev.cz. Opposite the chateau, this is Liberec's premier hotel with all the luxuries and services one expects from a 4-star establishment. A sumptuous sgl room with breakfast can be had for 1,560Kč, a dbl for 2,000Kč, not bad for such a high standard.

Hotel Praha (35 rooms) Železná 2; ✆ 485 102 655; f 485 113 138;
www.hotelpraha.net. One of Liberec's best situated hotels a few steps from the town
hall, this Art Nouveau building from 1905 is a joy to stay in for just the swish interior.
Its well-kept rooms also represent good value at around 1,200Kč for a sgl and 1,500Kč
for a dbl, both with breakfast. There is a restaurant on the first floor with mains for
80–220Kč. The hotel can apparently arrange horseriding trips into the surrounding
countryside.
Hotel Radnice (21 rooms) Moskevská 11; ✆ 485 100 562; f 485 100 578;
www.hotelradnice.cz. Just off the square is the attractive Hotel Radnice, boasting
immaculate modern sgls for 1,900Kč and dbls for 2,200Kč including breakfast.
Hotel Liberec (56 rooms low season, 84 high season) Nám F X Šaldy 1345; ✆ 482 710
028; f 482 710 605; www.hotel-liberec.cz. From the outside the Hotel Liberec is
possibly one of the least appealing hotels in the region. The interior is an improvement
on the exterior, although reminders of pre-revolution days (and the period immediately
afterwards) prevail. The room rates are the hotel's biggest plus with basic sgls costing just
650Kč, and dbls 990Kč including breakfast. There is also a cavernous restaurant with
mains for 100–150Kč. No luxury here but it serves its purpose.

Where to eat
Hotel Radnice Moskevská 11; ✆ 485 100 563. The bar/restaurant on the square
(seating outside in summer) is a convenient and lively place to eat. Enjoy the great
location, the large, newly renovated dining space and Czech and international standards
for 100–300Kč. Relax people-watching over a beer as Liberec bustles by.
Duli Moskevská 4; ✆ 485 100 738. There is an eatery on every floor of the Duli
opposite the Hotel Radnice. Downstairs you will find a great pizza place with pasta and
pizzas for 75–180Kč. The upper 2 floors are occupied by a restaurant with Czech and
international food for 60–200Kč.
Kavárna Pošta nám Dr E Beneše 24; ✆ 485 110 021. This stylish Viennese coffee
house/restaurant is opposite the theatre and is one of Liberec's must-sees. You can enjoy
food or just coffee and cakes in the amazing white and gold decorated interior with
huge mirrors and crystal chandeliers oozing with old world charm. You can eat here for
90–200Kč and on Fri evenings there are dances (entry 20Kč).
Café Praha Železná 2; ✆ 485 102 655. Directly to the left of the town hall looking
towards it is the Café Praha, part of the Hotel Praha in the same building. The friendly
staff will serve you a good selection of Czech fare for a very reasonable 70–200Kč. They
have Stella and Artois beer on tap and some vegetarian dishes on the menu.

What to see and do
Most certainly the pride of Liberec is the **town hall** which would dominate a
much larger square than the cosy one it occupies. Built between 1888 and 1893
in the neo-Renaissance style, its impressive tower rises 65m above the square.

The **Theatre of F X Šalda**, located behind the town hall, is named after
František Xaver Šalda, a critic, playwright and leading figure of the Czech avant-
garde, who was born in Liberec in 1867. The building itself dates from 1883, the
same year as the National Theatre in Prague reopened, hence the resemblance.
Liberec's churches are not much to write home about. The **Church of St
Anthony the Great** behind the Hotel Praha, founded in 1352 but completely
rebuilt in the neo-Gothic style in 1882, has seen better days. The interior is
spacious and plain but closed to the public. Slightly better is the other church in
the centre, the **Church of the Holy Cross**, five minutes' walk along the same
street. Dating from the end of the 17th century it houses the statue of the
Grieving Mary dating from 1506 and said to be carved from a piece of cedar

wood brought here from London. The **Renaissance chateau,** two minutes' walk from the main square along Felberova Street is unfortunately not open to the public. If and when it ever is, visitors will reputedly be able to see the largest collection of glass in the world, a superlative which may not stand up to much scrutiny.

The **Museum of North Bohemia** (*closed Mondays, admission 40/20Kč, family ticket 100Kč*) is about 500m out of the town centre along 5 Května Street which leads into Masarykova. The Museum is on the left at No 11. While not one of Bohemia's finest museums, it does contain some interesting exhibits on the history of the town and exquisite examples of glassware and porcelain. The **Regional Gallery** (*admission 30/10Kč*) at U Tiskárny 1, south of the chateau off Němcové Street, is one of Liberec's highlights with excellent collections of Dutch art from the 16th–18th centuries, French and German painting from the 19th century, and 20th-century Czech works. The gallery was built in 1871–72 for the Liebig family, who made their fortune in the Liberec textile boom of the 19th century, and most of the earlier works belonged to their own private collection.

For many Czechs, Liberec has recently become synonymous with the Babylon Centre a huge modern complex near the railway station, housing a shopping centre, hotel, restaurants, a disco, bowling alley and, most notably, the Aquapark. If you have been in the country for an extended period, it is not bad as an antidote to all the Baroque and Gothic architecture, if you like this sort of thing. For more detailed information have a look at the website at www.centrumbabylon.cz.

Around Liberec
Ještěd
The odd pointed mountain you can see to the southwest from various points in Liberec is Ještěd, a 1,000m-tall peak topped with an early 1970s Thunderbirds or James-Bond-style hotel. The building doubles up as a TV tower for which the architects were awarded the Perret prize by the International Union of Architects. You can get there by road, on foot and by cable car, which runs year round every hour on the hour, and which can be reached by taking tram 2 from the railway station to Dolní Hanychov and changing onto bus 33 to Horní Hanychov alighting at the last stop. The amazing panoramic views from the top of Ježtěd are worth the climb, and it is claimed that when the right conditions prevail, you can see as far as Prague, over 100km to the south.

The space age hotel is called **Horský Hotel Ještěd** (*Horní Hanychov 153;* ✆ *485 104 291;* f *485 104 295; www.hotel.jested.cz*) and has sometimes oddly shaped, futuristic but comfortable rooms with truly incredible views worth the 600–1,200Kč a night price tag on their own.

East Bohemia

From the broad Labe flood plain, the lowest and flattest part of the republic, to Sněžka, the highest mountain in the country, east Bohemia possesses some of the wildest and most beautiful areas in the Czech lands. The fittingly named Czech Paradise region (Český ráj), the Krkonoše mountain range and the Teplice and Adršpach 'rock towns' can be found here, as well as fascinating Renaissance towns such as proud Hradec Králové, quaint Pardubice and pretty Litomyšl. The province is also rich in dramatic hilltop castles such as Kost and Trosky. Many major towns are linked by the Labe, the main river artery which rises in the Krkonoše range, whose slopes and peaks form a natural border with Poland to the north.

Administratively, the area is divided into the Hradec Králové and Pardubice regions, the latter rather untidily straddling the historical divide between Bohemia and Moravia. The region's unrivalled variety and natural beauty do not as yet seem to have captured the imagination of tourists, with the Pardubice region receiving less than 1% of all foreign visitors to the Czech Republic. Skiing in the Krkonoše Mountains draws Škoda-loads of Czechs in winter, though many now treat the slopes as light training for the more challenging pistes of France and Italy.

GETTING AROUND

Pardubice and Hradec Králové act as transport hubs for the region and most visitors will find themselves in one of these towns sooner or later. Both have first-rate bus and rail connections to Prague and the rest of the country, and Pardubice sits handily on the principal rail artery linking Prague with Brno and beyond. The area north of the Labe has one of the densest webs of track on the Czech railway system, and therefore the train is generally an option, albeit a slow one. Even the foothills of the Krkonoše Mountains are well served. East Bohemia has not one kilometre of motorway, and roads in the north often follow a slow and snaking route.

HRADEC KRÁLOVÉ

The administrative capital of the newly formed region of the same name, Hradec Králové's 100,000 residents enjoy one of the most architecturally interesting towns in the republic. In the New Town visitors can admire early 20th-century modern architecture, mostly the work of the leading architects of the time, namely Josef Gočár, who built the famous Cubist House of the Black Madonna in Prague, and Jan Kotěra. The Old Town, squeezed between the Labe and the Orlice rivers which meet up here, is the historical centre with some impressive Gothic and Baroque sights. As with Pardubice, a short train or bus ride to the

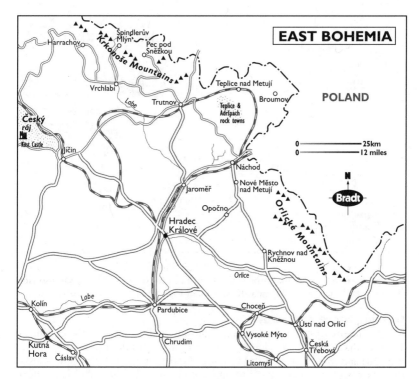

south, Hradec Králové can be visited as a day trip from Prague, or is a perfect place to break a journey to or from Moravia.

History

There is evidence that this piece of high ground at the confluence of the Orlice and Labe rivers has been inhabited since prehistoric times. Possibly because of its role as a centre of trade the Slavník dynasty regarded it as strategic enough to reside here in the 10th century. The castle and the surrounding community were elevated to royal town status in 1225, and the new Gothic castle, built in the 13th century, was often used by the Přemyslid dynasty. Václav II gave Hradec a special role as the dowry of the Czech queens, and their residence after the king's death, thus the name meaning 'queens' castle'. Hradec grew rich in the 14th century, and was second only to Prague in wealth and population. During the Hussite wars the town supported Jan Žižka who was later buried in the Church of the Holy Spirit (his remains were later moved). The Hussites destroyed the castle in 1423.

The Thirty Years War was a disaster for Hradec Králové as it lost many of its buildings, inhabitants and historical sites in Swedish raids. The town's importance then declined, though it was still important enough to be recatholicised by a Jesuit order who built a college and the Church of the Assumption of the Virgin Mary on the main square. In 1664, the bishopric of Hradec Králové was founded. Between 1766 and 1789 Empress Maria Theresa had thick defensive walls built around the town and demolished a large swathe of its suburbs. The Prussians did not even try to take Hradec Králové in the Austro-Prussian war of 1866, instead defeating the Austrians nearby in the famous Battle of Hradec Králové. The huge

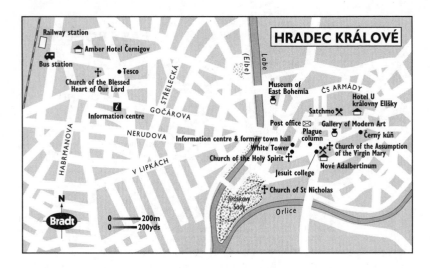

earthworks encircling the town were destroyed in 1884, enabling growth and allowing architects Josef Gočár and Jan Kotěra to create the New Town.

Getting there and away
Hourly **trains** leave Prague's main railway station and swiftly cover the 100km across the plain to Hradec Králové (1 hour 40 minutes, 140Kč). There is also a fairly regular service from Brno (3 hours) which costs the same as from Prague. There are hourly trains to and from Pardubice which shuttle between the two cities (30 minutes, 34Kč). **Bus** is also a good way of getting from the capital (1 hour 40 minutes, 80Kč) with services from Florenc coach station at frequent intervals. Buses also run between Pardubice and Hradec Králové (30 minutes, 28Kč).

The bus and train stations are around 15 minutes on foot from the historical centre. Follow Puškinova Street until it meets Gočárova Avenue. Continue as far as the Labe, on the other side of which you will find the main sights of the Old Town. The walk will take you through the less attractive New Town with its inter-war architecture and wide straight boulevards.

Tourist information
Hradec Králové has two information centres, one on the way from the railway station to the historical centre (*Gočárova 1225;* \ *495 534 485;* f *495 534 482; www.ic-hk.cz*) and the other on the main square (*Velké náměstí 165;* \/f *495 580 492*). Both have tons of information on the town and can help with accommodation, travel and tickets for cultural events.

Where to stay
Hotel U královny Elišky Malé náměstí 117; \ 495 518 052; f 495 518 872; www.euroagentur.cz. A 35-room upmarket hotel on the cosy, quiet Malé náměstí with all services you may require and prices to match. Sgls for 80 and dbls for 90.
Amber Hotel Černigov Riegrovo nám 1494; \ 495 814 111; f 495 521 998; www.legner.cz. This enormous hotel is the tower block you see directly in front of you as you leave the railway station. Despite its exterior, inside it is quite luxurious and charges accordingly for its rooms. A standard sgl with breakfast in high season costs

1,400Kč, an executive dbl around 2,700Kč. There is also a restaurant with surprisingly reasonable prices (100–200Kč for main courses).

Pension Nové Adalbertinum Velké nám 32; ☎ 495 063 111; f 495 063 405. This 30-room pension is in the former Jesuit College on the main square. Its pleasant rooms are an excellent deal at 825Kč for a sgl with shower and TV and dbls for 1,260Kč. For my money this is the best place to stay in Hradec Králové.

Where to eat

Restaurace Nové Adalbertinum Velké náměstí 32; ☎ 495 063 111; f 495 063 405. Inside the former Jesuit College on the main square. This is a no-smoking basement dining space under the pension of the same name with Czech food, Czech prices and friendly staff. Main courses cost 40–150Kč.

Černý kůň Malé náměstí 10; ☎ 495 511 804. The Black Horse has been a pub or restaurant since 1807, and is still serving up excellent Czech and international food for 75–220Kč in pleasant newly renovated historical surroundings. They also offer free meals for children at weekends, have a no-smoking area at lunchtime and no fewer than 5 types of beer.

Restaurant Satchmo Dlouhá 96–97; ☎ 495 514 590. The Satchmo is a vibrant place next to the Klicpera Theatre halfway along Dlouhá from Malé náměstí. They serve up very good un-Czech food (from 65Kč), and have a couple of excellent vegetarian options which can be washed down with Czech Budweiser. The building also houses a jazz club. Closed Sun.

What to see and do
Velké náměstí

Hradec Králové's elongated triangular 'square' is where visitors will find most of the town's heritage. On arriving from the railway station, the building immediately to your left with the two identical clock towers (yes, they do both show the same time!) is the **former town hall**. Now housing various offices the building was originally a Gothic structure, though no-one knows exactly when it was built. The late Classical-style building we see today dates from 1852, the clock towers from 1786. To the right of the former town hall stands the brick **Church of the Holy Spirit**. Founded in 1307 by the widow of King Wenceslas II, the church has had a turbulent history, having endured numerous fires, a ransacking by the Swedish and several reconstructions. The building we see today is from the mid 19th century when all late 18th-century Baroque features were scraped off, and the building restored in the neo-Gothic style. The Hussite warlord Jan Žižka was temporarily buried in the cathedral after dying in Hradec Králové from plague. Regrettably it is not generally open to the public though you can peek in through the gate. Behind the cathedral rises the **White Tower** (Bílá věž), which, as the name suggests, was evidently once white. The bell tower dating from 1574 can be climbed. The roof apparently contains a kind of time capsule (including coins from the reign of Charles IV amongst other things) which has been added to from time to time. Heading down the square you will notice the large former **Jesuit College**, now part of the university, a restaurant, housing and a pension. Beside that visitors cannot fail to notice the Baroque **Church of the Assumption of the Virgin Mary**, built by the Jesuits between 1654 and 1666 with its relatively plain exterior contrasting with an over-elaborate interior, rich even by Czech Baroque standards. There are more angels than you can count, but the colossal altar is false, painted on the back wall. Opposite the church the only modern building on the square houses the **Gallery of Modern Art**, open every day except Mondays. The gallery's four floors hold an extensive exhibition on the development of modern art at the turn of the 20th century. In the centre of the square stands the 19m-high **plague column** dating from 1717 and commemorating the fact that the plague spared the town in 1716. Continue down Velké náměstí to the end and arrive at the less picturesque but cosier **Malé náměstí** centred around a splashing fountain.

Museum of East Bohemia

The Museum of East Bohemia (Muzeum východních Čech, *admission 30/15Kč, family ticket 60Kč*) on the banks of the Labe where Palackého Street meets Eliščino nábřeží is worth seeing for the building's façade alone. Built in the years 1909–12 by celebrated Czech architect Jan Kotěra, the entrance is guarded by two glorious Art Deco figures representing art and industry. The building is as fine an example of Art Deco architecture as you will find in the Czech Republic. The museum itself has no permanent exhibits, but owing to its size and the amount of individual exhibitions it holds at once, always has something on to capture the imagination.

Other places of interest

Jiráskovy sady (Jirásek Gardens) are worth a visit for two reasons. Here you will find the curious wooden **Church of St Nicholas** brought here in 1935 from eastern Slovakia, and said to be almost 500 years old. A five-minute walk along either of the rivers which flow on both sides of the park will bring you to the **confluence of the Labe and Orlice**, a pleasant place to sit and watch the waters swirling together. Away from the historical centre, one of the highlights of Hradec Králové's New Town is the functionalist **Church of the Blessed Heart of Our Lord** (Kostel Božího Srdce páně, opposite Tesco), built in 1932. The interior is uninspiring but the exterior is straight out of Gotham City.

Around Hradec Králové
Opočno

One of the finest chateaux in the region can be found in the small town of Opočno, 20km northeast of Hradec Králové. Built as a Gothic stronghold it was transformed in the 16th century by the Trčka z Lípy family into a grand Renaissance chateau whose most prominent feature is the three tiers of typical Renaissance-period loggia. Subsequent Baroque additions and alterations were carried out by the last owners, the Colloredo family, who were handed the chateau in 1634 during the Counter-Reformation. Accused of collaboration with the Nazis, the Colloredos lost it in 1945 but after nine years in the Czech courts the family finally won it back in May 2005 to the chagrin of the authorities and sections of the Czech population. The full guided tour (*admission 60/30Kč, open Apr–Oct*) explores the noble interiors full of portraits, weapons from Europe and Asia, and hunting trophies and countless objects brought from Africa and America. Encircling the chateau is a shady park with a romantic summer palace (letohrádek).

Opočno is easily reachable by bus from Hradec Králové with a service at least once an hour on weekdays (30–50 minutes, 35Kč).

PARDUBICE

Horseracing, gingerbread and Semtex form the unusual trio that puts this pleasant town of 90,000 souls, 100km east of Prague, on the map. In the Czech Republic Pardubice is best known for the *Velká Pardubická* or Great Pardubice Steeplechase held in mid October, though Semtex, a very powerful plastic explosive used by miners, demolition experts and terrorists all over the world, comes a close second. While visitors will not see many explosions or racehorses in Pardubice's

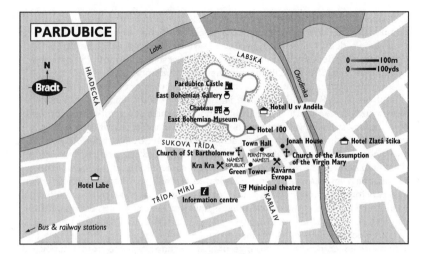

streets, gingerbread can be bought at many places, a great souvenir coming in many elaborately decorated shapes and sizes.

The town guards the confluence of the Elbe and Chrudimka rivers, and has a bustling modern centre encircling one of the most attractive historical cores in Bohemia. The old and the new are kept firmly apart creating the feeling that Pardubice is two towns in one. It is an easy day trip from Prague and Hradec Králové and an excellent place to break a journey from Moravia to Prague or vice versa.

History

First mentioned in 1295, Pardubice really came to the fore in 1340 when the powerful Arnošt of Pardubice, later to become the first Archbishop of Prague under Charles IV, bought the town. In 1491, it came into the possession of Vilém of Pernštejn, probably the most powerful nobleman in the kingdom at the time. The Pernštejns left an indelible mark on Pardubice and presided over its golden age. They transformed the Gothic castle into a Renaissance residence, built up the picturesque Renaissance square bearing their name and historical sights we see today, including the dominant feature of the town centre, the Green Tower. They sold the estate in 1560. The town suffered badly at the hands of the Swedish during the Thirty Years War, and lost many of its architectural treasures.

In 1845, the railway arrived in Pardubice heralding an era of industrialisation and trade, which brought wealth as well as a rich cultural and social life. At the beginning of the 20th century the chemical and electronics industry began to take hold. During World War II the town lost its Jewish inhabitants to the concentration camps in the east, and was bombed three times by American and British planes in 1944 with the loss of 250 lives.

Getting there and away

As Pardubice straddles the major rail artery heading east to Olomouc and Ostrava, **train** is quickest from Prague. Services leave the main railway station approximately once an hour (1–1½ hours, 130Kč). There are regular trains to and from Hradec Králové to the north which take 30 minutes to travel the 21km (34Kč). Looking at the departures board at Pardubice's cavernous 1960s main station will tell you it is possible to get virtually anywhere in the republic from

THE PARDUBICE STEEPLECHASE

The Pardubice Steeplechase (or the *Velká Pardubická*) is the biggest event on the Czech horseracing calendar, by far the most important annual event in Pardubice and the only horse race the Czechs get excited about. Equestrian sports were all the rage in the decadent days of the First Republic but have failed to capture the imagination much since the revolution. The Pardubice race claims to be the oldest cross-country steeplechase on the continent and is the Czechs' answer to the Grand National (which the Czechs logically call the *Velká Liverpoolská*). The 6.9km race, run almost every year in Pardubice since 1874, takes place annually in mid October and lasts a nail-biting ten minutes. The starting line-up is a snorting, head tossing mix of Czech and foreign chestnuts and greys, these days competing for a prize of 4¹/₂ million Czech crowns in one of the most gruelling steeplechases in Europe. Of the 30 fences, the fourth, known as *Taxis*, is particularly hard on horses and jockeys alike and sadly injuries and fatalities (among the horses) are relatively common. On average only about half of the starters actually cross the finishing line. The *Velká Pardubická* is the climax of a meet which sees races run on the flat on the Saturday followed by the big race on the Sunday afternoon. For information on the famous steeplechase, the racecourse and tickets see the course website at www.pardubice-racecourse.cz.

here. There are trains to north Moravia, south Moravia, the west Bohemian spa region and to destinations further afield such as Budapest, Warsaw, Bratislava, Vienna and Moscow. The **bus** service from Prague to Pardubice is virtually non-existent, but there are regular bus services to Hradec Králové (25 minutes, 28Kč). The bus station is almost opposite the railway station.

The historical centre is a ten- to 15-minute walk along Palackého třída and třída Míru. Buses and trolleybuses run as far as třída Míru. Tickets from machines at the railway station and from newsagents cost 9Kč, 15Kč from the driver.

Tourist information
Pardubice's busy modern information centre (*třída Míru 60;* ↘ *466 613 223;* e *info@pardubice.cz*) offers public internet access for 1Kč per minute and has a good supply of leaflets, maps and booklets.

Where to stay
Top end
Hotel Zlatá štika Štrossova 127; ↘ 466 052 100; f 466 052 130; www.zlatastika.cz. This large hotel lies just outside the historical centre. It is 5 mins' walk from Republic Square along Bubeníkova Street, then take the first street to the left after crossing the river. The complex houses a pub, restaurant and a 90-bed hotel. The restaurant is slightly overpriced, but the rooms are reasonably good value at 1,600–1,800Kč for a sgl with breakfast, and dbls at 1,800–2,000Kč.
Hotel Labe Masarykovo nám 2633; ↘ 466 717 111; f 466 535 358. This 12-storey tower block midway between the railway station and the historical centre has 160 rooms and 7 suites. It may not look too appealing, but represents reasonable value at 1,600Kč for a sgl and 1,900Kč for a dbl with breakfast. Ask for a room with a view of the historical town centre.

Tighter budgets
Hotel 100 Kostelní 100; ʼ\/f 466 511 179. This small, peaceful, 6-room hotel in the historical centre is very good value at 1,000Kč.
Hotel U sv Anděla Zámecká 25; ʼ\ 466 511 575. This charming little 17-room hotel right in the historical centre is an excellent place to stay at 1,200Kč for a dbl room.

Where to eat
Kra Kra (Underpass under náměstí Republiky). This cosy but lively place can be found in the subway that passes under the road which cuts through Republic Square. It also has some seating at street level in summer. An extensive menu offers Czech and international fare at 110–200Kč and a range of beers.
Kavárna Evropa Klášterní 54; ʼ\ 466 535 300; www.avekont.cz/evropa/. Located on the corner of Pernštýnské Square this high-ceilinged, grand, stylish, spacious coffee house is one of the best places in Pardubice to eat with vegetarian options from 45–80Kč, main courses from 75–200Kč and Staropramen beer.

What to see and do
Republic Square
Republic Square (náměstí Republiky) lies just in front of the Green Tower, the entrance to the historical centre at the end of Míru Avenue. When entering from Míru Avenue, to the right is the superbly renovated Art Nouveau **Municipal Theatre**, perhaps in better shape now than the day it opened. To the left is the **Church of St Bartholomew** dating originally from the 13th century and rebuilt in the 16th after having been destroyed by the Hussites. Directly in front of you is the entrance to the historical centre dominated by the 16th-century **Green Tower** (Zelená brána) with its copper roof tapering off into a spear-like point. Visitors can climb to the top for views of Pardubice and the surrounding countryside (*admission 15Kč, open Tue–Sun*).

Pernštýn Square
Having passed through the Green Tower one leaves the modern world behind and enters what must be one of Bohemia's finest squares, enclosed on all sides by majestic Renaissance town houses with curved gables and brightly painted façades. To the left stands the ornate neo-Renaissance **town hall**, built in the 1890s, in front of which rises the ubiquitous **plague column** dating from 1695 and decorated in 1775 with heraldic symbols, Czech lions and statues of the saints. At the far end of the square notice the conspicuous house No 50, the **Dům U Jonáše** (Jonah House) with its stucco relief of Jonah being swallowed by the whale sweeping across the whole façade and housing exhibitions of the East Bohemian Gallery. Just off the square and along from the Kavárna Evropa is the quite plain **Church of the Assumption of the Virgin Mary**.

Pardubice Castle
The narrow medieval streets and alleyways leading from Pernštýnské Square to the castle are packed with antique shops, clothes boutiques and places selling interesting souvenirs. From the square follow Pernštýnská Street, then Zámecká until you see the castle on the hill before you. The Renaissance chateau was created by the Pernštejn family in the 16th century from the original Gothic castle with its huge moat and earthworks. The chateau now houses the **East Bohemian Museum and Gallery** (*combined admission to the chateau, gallery including the Jonah House on Pernštýnské Square, and museum 70/35Kč*). The museum has permanent exhibitions of postcards (apparently the largest collection

in central Europe), coins, glass and weapons. The gallery has no permanent collections. The highlight of the chateau interior is the Renaissance murals, the oldest of their kind in the Czech Republic. Look out for the peacocks that roam the castle grounds.

LITOMYŠL

Some 50km southeast of Hradec Králové lies the plucky little town of Litomyšl. Famous as the birthplace of the Czech composer Bedřich Smetana, site of a stunning sgraffito-covered Renaissance chateau and recognised by UNESCO in 1999 as possessing treasures of European cultural heritage, Litomyšl is one of the most picturesque towns in east Bohemia and worthy of a day's exploration. With its long wide main square and almost uninterrupted arcading, its proud newly restored Renaissance and Baroque town houses, and the exquisite chateau on the hill above, it is a pleasant, relaxing town with a long and rich past, as well as an important place in the cultural and religious history of the Czech Republic.

History

The first written evidence of the existence of a settlement on a trade route linking Bohemia and Moravia comes from the 11th century when Břetislav II founded either a church or a Benedictine order here. In the mid 12th century the Bishop of Olomouc established a Premonstratensian order on the site of today's chateau. The monastery became an important centre in the region and the community which grew up nearby was elevated to a town by Přemysl Otakar II in 1259.

Charles IV promoted Prague to archbishopric and subsequently created the Litomyšl bishopric in 1344. Unfortunately for the town this state of affairs did not last very long. The bishop at the time of the Hussite revolution was an opponent of Hus's teachings and the town paid dearly for it. Although Litomyšl yielded to the Hussite armies without a fight, the bishop's residence and other buildings were burnt down, the bishop fled and the bishopric lapsed. Following the Hussite wars the town prospered under the Kostků z Postupim family, becoming an important centre of the Protestant *Jednota bratrská* and growing in size. The family and the *Jednota bratrská* both had to leave Litomyšl under Ferdinand I. In 1567, the new lord, Vratislav z Pernštejna, began the construction of the Renaissance chateau. Litomyšl was pillaged during the Thirty Years War after which a Piarist order was set up here. Their belief in education led to the building of a school and a Philosophy Institute which played an important role in the cultural development and reputation of the town.

Throughout the 18th century the town fought fire after fire and in the Czech lands the saying 'burn like Litomyšl' became widely used. The fires led to the rebuilding of the chateau and town houses. In 1830, the child prodigy Bedřich Smetana, born in the chateau brewery, had his first performance at the Philosophy Institute. In the first half of the 19th century the school and institute attracted many giants of the Czech cultural and scientific world. Writers such as Alois Jirásek and Božena Němcová arrived here partly because of a famous printing press being located in the town.

Following the creation of Czechoslovakia Litomyšl grew in size again, and many new buildings were added. The ethnic make-up of the area changed during and after World War II with the decimation of the Jewish community and the expulsion of the Sudeten Germans. In 1949, the first Smetana's Litomyšl opera festival was held, an important event in the Czech cultural calendar to this day.

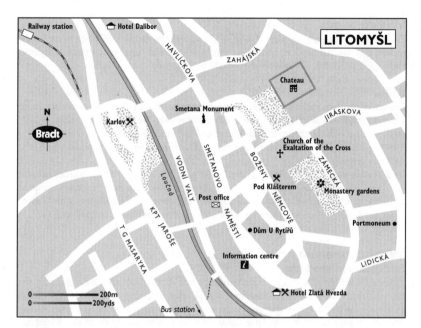

Getting there and away

There are up to six **coaches** a day from Prague, though the 170km journey is rather tedious (3 hours, 120Kč). Otherwise change in Hradec Králové on to one of the very frequent buses to Litomyšl (1 hour, 60Kč), the same being true for journeys to and from Brno. Travelling by **rail** from the capital, change at Choceň on to a little-used, winding branch line that ends in Litomyšl.

The bus station is five minutes' walk south of the main square and the railway station is roughly half a kilometre to the northwest.

Tourist information

The smart, professional information centre in Litomyšl is on Smetana Square (*Smetanovo nám 72;* ⅃/f *461 612 161; www.litomysl.cz*) and stocks an excellent supply of maps and general information. Visitors can also surf the internet for 1Kč per minute. Tickets for the Smetana's Litomyšl opera festival can be bought online at www.smetanovalitomysl.cz.

Where to stay

Hotel Zlatá Hvězda Smetanovo nám 84; ⅃ 461 615 338; f 461 615 091; www.zlatahvezda.com. Situated at the southern end of Smetana Square, the 30-room 'Golden Star' is undoubtedly the best place to stay in Litomyšl. The building was once a bank and during reconstruction it was discovered that the safes were too hefty to remove, so do not be surprised if your bathroom has a rather large bolt on the door. Excellent rooms cost 560–1,100Kč for a sgl and 920–1,550Kč for a dbl with breakfast.

Hotel Dalibor Komenského nám 1053; ⅃ 461 615 921; f 461 615 22; www.hotel-dalibor.cz. Named after Smetana's opera, the Dalibor stands at the northern end of town near the railway station. The unattractive tower block contains 50 reasonable rooms at 650Kč for a sgl and 990Kč for a dbl including buffet breakfast – about right for the standard.

Where to eat
Zlatá hvězda Smetanovo náměstí 84; ⟍ 461 615 338. By far the best place to eat on the square, this modern hotel restaurant has a huge selection of dishes including fish, Italian and vegetarian dishes all for around 100Kč. They also stock a large variety of Moravian and foreign wines. The service is impeccable.

Karlov Smetanův dům, Komenského 402; ⟍ 461 613 417. Housed in a wing of the Smetanův dům across the Loučná River, this is possibly the best dining option in Litomyšl. Dark wood panelling, stylish high ceilings and a tasteful First Republic ambience are complemented by flawless service and superior food. Mains come for 70–200Kč though some specialities cost more. The wine list features Moravia's best as well as foreign favourites.

Pod Klášterem Boženy Němcové 158; ⟍ 461 615 901. The décor of this small pension restaurant is a tasteful blend of modern and medieval. There is a very pleasant summer patio giving on to the cobbles of picturesque Toulovcovo Square complete with Gothic church. Main courses cost in the region of 100–150Kč, and Pilsner Urquell and Velkopopovický Kozel beers are on tap.

What to see and do
Renaissance chateau
A UNESCO-listed world cultural heritage site since 1999 and the venue for the annual Smetana's Litomyšl opera festival, the chateau is one of the finest Renaissance buildings in the land with triple-tiered loggia and a sgraffito exterior on which no two motifs are the same. It is in fact an example of the Moravian Renaissance style by the Italian architect Giovanni Battista Aostalli. Thirteen rooms of the chateau are open to the public, the highlight being the Baroque theatre in the west wing dating from 1797, one of the finest examples in the country. Performances occasionally take place there to this day.

There are two tours to choose from (*admission 80/40Kč, open May–Sep, Tue–Sun*). Tour I includes the theatre and representative rooms in the west wing, while tour II leads through the chapel and guest rooms of the east wing. In late June and early July the chateau echoes to the annual **Smetana's Litomyšl** opera festival on the temporarily roofed second courtyard. One of the surrounding outbuildings is the former chateau brewery where the composer Bedřich Smetana was born in 1824. The family's quarters (Rodný byt Smetany) can be visited (*admission 20/10Kč*). On the west side of the chateau are some relaxing gardens from where the grandeur and symmetry of the chateau's exterior sgrafitto, some of the finest in the Czech lands, can be fully appreciated.

On leaving the chateau be sure to head for the **Monastery Gardens** across the street. Brought back to life in 2000, this well-pruned open garden lying between two churches is centred around a fountain complete with modern bronzes of naked bathers, tentatively entering the water to the sound of classical music piped through speakers in adjacent walls. Relax with a coffee in the outdoor café and admire the view over old Litomyšl's rooftops.

Portmoneum
An unremarkable town house at No 75 Terezy Novákové Street contains the curious Portmoneum–Josef Váchala Museum (*admission 40/20Kč, open May–Sep*), a quite unexpected and peculiar place. It all started in 1920 when an art lover named Josef Portman invited his friend, artist and writer Josef Váchal, to decorate two rooms of his house. The result is an interior daubed from floor to ceiling with bright technicolour paintings. The motifs are a reflection of the artist's beliefs and opinions on art and every possible surface (bar the floor)

features Christian symbols and Hindu and oriental icons. This extraordinary place was lovingly restored in the early 1990s by the owners, the Paseka publishing house, whose premises on Smetanovo Square and J Váchala Street are adorned with modern sgraffito copies of some of Váchal's work.

Other places of interest

The impressive Baroque **Church of the Exaltation of the Cross** (Kostel Povýšení sv Kříže) below the chateau, and dating from 1714–22, underwent much renovation in the 1990s including the installation of an enormous organ. The truly remarkable, arcade-lined **Smetanovo Square** with pastel Baroque, Classical and Empire façades, is more of a long wide street than a classic square. The arcading had the simple function of protecting the townspeople from the rain and sun, a service it still provides today. It is fun to explore the nooks and crannies of its concealed shopfronts, carved stone doorways, dank passageways and secret windows extending the length of the square on both sides, only interrupted in places by 19th-century intrusions.

Dating from the mid 16th century the unplastered façade of the **Knights' House (Dům U Rytířů)** at No 110 stands out from the crowd. It is one of the finest houses in Litomyšl despite being damaged several times in the town's notoriously fire-prone history and gets its name from the two knights on either side of the middle window. It is currently used as a temporary exhibition space by the Litomyšl gallery and museum.

At the northern end of the square, the **Smetana Monument** by Czech sculptor Jan Štursa was erected to mark the centenary of the composer's birth in 1924. Oddly enough, the square acquired its current name only in 1989. A few steps from the statue is house No 27 where Czech writer Božena Němcová resided from 1839 to 1840, and the birthplace of her son, Karel.

JIČÍN

Lying around 90km northwest of Prague Jičín is not really a day-trip destination from the capital, but is often used as a gateway to the Czech Paradise protected area and especially the Prachovské skály 'rock town' to the north. There are a couple of interesting sights worthy of a few hours' exploration.

Jičín probably gets its name from Queen Jitka (Jitčino město – Jitka's town) and was granted town status at the end of the 13th century. The historical centre we see today was mostly built in the 1620s and 1630s when the powerful general Albrecht von Wallenstein (Valdštejn) transformed Jičín into his residence, added a Jesuit college and rebuilt the chateau (destroyed by fire in 1608) which occupies one whole side of the square bearing the Valdštejn name. He also began work on the adjacent Church of St James the Greater but did not live to see its completion after being assassinated in Cheb in 1634 on the orders of Ferdinand II. The town is also known for two other major events which took place in the 19th century: the meeting of representatives of Austria, Russia and Germany at which the Holy Alliance against Napoleon was formed, and the 1866 battle between the armies of Prussia and Austria.

Getting there and away

Bus is the quickest way to reach Jičín from Prague (1½ hours, 80Kč) with a regular service from Černý Most metro station (end of yellow line B). You can get there by **train** from Masarykovo station with a change in Nymburk (2½ hours, 120Kč). On arrival in Jičín the bus station is a five-minute walk from the historical centre up Pod Koštofránkem Street. From the railway station it is a 15-

minute walk north along Fügnerova then west along Husova. Jičín also has good bus connections to Hradec Králové and some services to Brno and destinations in Slovakia. Turnov is an easy train ride away on a branch line which traverses the Czech Paradise.

Tourist information

The information centre (*Valdštejnské nám 1;* \/f *93 534 390; www.jicin.org*) is situated on the square in a part of the chateau. It looks impressive, but has precious little information visitors can take away, although it does have lists of accommodation (in Jičín and the Czech Paradise area) and sells maps (including the tear-off map which is free in every other town in the republic!).

Where to stay

Hotel Jičín Havlíčkova 21; \ 493 544 250; f 493 544 251; www.hoteljicin.cz. This is a cosy little hotel in the centre of town with 16 new, airy, fully equipped immaculate rooms. Look for the green building just off Žižkovo Square. Sgls with breakfast go for 1,000Kč, dbls for 1,300Kč.

Hotel Paříž Žižkovo nám 3; \ 493 532 750. Undergoing renovation at the time of writing the Paříž had 29 rooms with prices from 300Kč for a sgl with no en-suite facilities, rising to 1,200Kč for a dbl with bathroom. It may become more expensive after the extensive makeover it was receiving.

Where to eat

U Piráta Husova 127; \ 493 532 190. An interesting little restaurant set back off the street serving Budvar beer and a large choice of main courses for 100–200Kč. Many of the dishes have a naval theme with names such as Captain Cook's purse and the like.

U Dělové koule Havlíčkova 21; \ 493 544 250; f 493 544 251. This is the slightly pricey restaurant at the Hotel Jičín with main courses from 100–300Kč. The dining room has a Prusso-Austrian war theme and is decorated with original period uniforms and weapons. This place has a general old-world feel and the food is good.

Zámecká vinárna Valdštejnské nám 1; \ 493 522 793. A cosy and convenient place to have a bite to eat and a glass of wine in the chateau. Walk from the information centre towards the Church of St James and you will see the wine bar at the corner of the chateau.

What to see and do

All of Jičín's sights are situated in and around **Valdštejnovo náměstí** (Valdštejn Square), the historical centre of the town. Not the most attractive square in Bohemia, it has arcading on all four sides, a **plague column** dating from 1702 and a fountain. One whole side is occupied by the **chateau**. Eight rooms of the chateau also house the **Regional Museum** which has interesting interactive exhibits on the history of Jičín and the surrounding area and is great fun for children. The museum won the Czech Ministry of Culture award for the best exhibition of 2002 and is well worth the 50Kč admission (*30Kč concessions, 100Kč family ticket*). Jičín has two churches of note, the Gothic **Church of St Ignatius of Loyola**, a crumbling shabby construction just off the square and desperately in need of repair, and the better cared-for **Church of St James the Greater** on Valdštejn Square, begun in 1627 and open to the public. It has an impressive Baroque interior and huge Baroque altar. Visitors can look down into the church from a gallery accessible from the museum next door. Most visitors will enter the square through the **Valdická Gate**, a 52m-high Gothic tower dating from 1568 which can be climbed for 15Kč from April until August.

Special events
Every year in mid September Jičín is transformed into the fairy-tale capital of the Czech Republic. The fairy-tale festival includes competitions, performances, workshops and other events for children. Ask the information centre for details.

ČESKÝ RÁJ
The increasingly popular Český ráj (*www.ceskyraj.cz*), which translates as 'Czech Paradise', is a small area of exceptional natural beauty with densely forested undulating hills, incredible sandstone 'rock towns', well-preserved folk architecture and a landscape dotted with castle ruins. It is not difficult to see why the region has been christened 'Paradise' and how it stirred writers, poets and painters of the romantic Czech National Revival of the 19th century. It is one of the most attractive and romantic places in the country and should not be missed if you are in the region.

The official nature reserve occupies only a small area and Český ráj is a term commonly used for the entire region between Jičín, Turnov and Mnichovo Hradiště. Jičín and Turnov are the usual starting points for hikes, though Jičín is by far the more appealing of the two.

Getting around
A scenic rail line runs for 30km between Jičín and Turnov via many of the area's places of interest. A ticket for the whole route costs 40Kč and the journey takes a mere 30 minutes. Distances are not great in the Czech Paradise, and most people come here to do some light, leisurely walking before returning to a hotel in the towns. The area has a veritable thicket of marked walking trails, all clearly illustrated on VKÚ-KČT map 19 *Český ráj*. Fit hikers could manage the whole 35km red Jičín–Turnov route in a long day, but would miss much along the way. Plan two or three days of gentle walking with short side walks off the major trails to get the most from the area.

What to see and do
Five kilometres northeast of Jičín stand the **Prachovské skály**, a warren of dramatic rock towers rising out of the woods like giant fingers reaching for the sky, some with trees growing on top like in a Japanese landscape painting. Declared a nature reserve in 1933 it is riddled with sandy hiking trails of all colours which lead walkers through deep gorges between the rocks as well as to viewing points above the pine trees. You could spend all day exploring the nooks and crannies of this place, but when the weather is favourable you will certainly not be alone. To get there from Jičín either walk (red trail, 4km) or take a local bus heading for the village of Sobotka, which run around every two hours and take five minutes (5Kč), alighting at the Holín-Prachovské skály stop.

On a rocky outcrop some 15km west of Jičín near the village of Sobotka stands stocky **Kost Castle** dating originally from the 14th century and one of the finest Gothic castles in the Czech lands. Now belonging to the Kinsky family, the interior is full of their treasures and can be explored with a guide (*90/50Kč, 1 hour, open daily May–Sep except Mon*). Lonely Kost can be reached by train from Jičín, though a change in Libuň is required and the nearest station is in Libošovice 2km away along a yellow marked trail. It is also 6½km along a red trail from Sobotka, served by bus from Jičín.

Another medieval castle, this time the ruins of **Trosky**, stands midway between Jičín and Turnov on the red marked trail. This is one of the country's most instantly recognisable ruins with its two remaining towers perched atop two tall outcrops of rock, the best-known sight in the Czech Paradise. Built in the 14th century it was left to the elements after becoming a victim of the Swedish Protestant forces during the Thirty Years War. The easiest way to reach the castle (*admission 40/25Kč, open Apr–Oct*) is by train, alighting at Ktová station near Rovensko around 2km away (35 minutes, 28Kč from Jičín)..

Just 4km to the south of Turnov is an area known as **Hruboskalsko** which has yet more bizarre rock formations all given amusing names such as Little Devil (Čertík), Cuckoo (Kukačka) and The Cigar (Doutník), as well as two castles. The first, **Valdštejn**, was the ancestral home of the Valdštejn (Wallenstein) family whose most illustrious member was Albrecht, the imperial generalissimo who grew rich on property confiscated from Protestant nobles following the Battle of the White Mountain. The Gothic ruins and later Baroque additions are now owned by the town of Turnov (*admission 30/10Kč, open Apr–Oct*). The castle of **Hrubá skála**, a 19th-century replica of the Gothic original built by the Valdštejns, is now an exquisite hotel with a superb medieval-style restaurant.

TRUTNOV AND THE KRKONOŠE MOUNTAINS

Most people venture to this extremity of the Czech lands, a mere 19km from the border with Poland and around 150km from Prague, to explore the curious rock formations at Adršpach and Teplice nad Metují to the east of Trutnov, reachable by train in 30 minutes from the town. This is to take nothing away from Trutnov itself, as this very pleasant town on the banks of the Úpa River, a tributary of the Elbe, warrants half a day's exploration, perhaps at the beginning of or to round off a trip to the surrounding countryside, or as a stop between Hradec Králové and the ski resorts in the Krkonoše Mountains to the northwest. Trutnov has a handsome arcaded main square lined with pretty Baroque and Renaissance façades and interestingly named after Krakonoš, the mythical bearded ruler of the Krkonoše Mountains.

The most significant event in the history of the town came in 1866 when the Austrians thrashed the Prussians at the Battle of Trutnov. Seven days later the Prussians returned the favour at Hradec Králové, effectively bringing to an end one of the shortest wars Europe has ever seen. One of Trutnov's major tourist sights is the battlefield, a brisk walk out of the town. Ex-president Havel has a cottage somewhere in the surrounding hills and during the repression of the 1970s was even forcibly employed as a worker in the local brewery.

Getting there and away

From Prague the best option is by **bus** from Černý Most metro station (end of yellow line B; 2½ hours, 120Kč). Services run about once an hour. The **train** journey is more expensive at 224Kč, quite tedious, and generally requires a change in Hradec Králové. From Trutnov there are coach connections to Pec pod Sněžkou (approximately every 30 minutes), Vrchlabí (hourly, around an hour), Špindlerův Mlýn (3 daily, 1½ hours) and several coaches a day to Brno. Train is the only option when heading out to Adršpach and Teplice nad Metují to the east. There are nine trains daily which trundle out along the branch line to the 'rock towns'.

From the bus station it is a five-minute walk to Krakonoš Square along Horská Street. The railway station is on the opposite bank of the Úpa River to the bus station.

Where to stay

For a busy town which receives more visitors than many others of a similar size, Trutnov does not have a great selection of accommodation. Should the following places be full, try the **information centre** (*Krakonošovo náměstí 72;* ↘ *499 818 245;* f *499 818 245; www.trutnov.cz*) where the staff can recommend private rooms for 200–300Kč per person per night including breakfast.

Penzion Pohoda Horská 7; ↘ 499 815 425; www.penzionpohoda.com. This is the large orange building halfway between the bus station and the main square on bustling Horská Street. There are 2 hotel-type rooms and 4 nicely furnished, attractive apartments, which are completely self-contained with fully equipped kitchen, bathroom, lounge and bedroom. The pension sleeps up to 27 people and houses a bar, restaurant and supermarket. Prices start at 1,200Kč for sgl occupancy rising to 1,600Kč for 2 people. 6 people sharing costs 2,500Kč.

Hotel Adam Havlíčkova 10/11; ↘ 499 811 955; f 499 811 957; www.hotel-adam.cz. A few steps off the main square you will find probably Trutnov's best place to stay. It has 27 pleasant, quiet rooms and downstairs there is a restaurant and café. All rooms are en suite with satellite TV which cost around 1,000Kč for a sgl and 1,500Kč for a dbl. There is a considerable discount at weekends.

Hotel Grand Krakonošovo náměstí 120; ↘/f 499 819 144. The 80-bed Grand is the main square's only hotel. The rooms are light, airy and conservatively furnished and are a relative bargain at 630Kč per person in summer and 480Kč in winter not including breakfast.

Where to eat

Restaurant Radnice Krakonošovo náměstí 72; ↘ 499 810 470. You will find this conveniently situated place round the corner from the information centre under the large Renaissance building of the town hall. Diners can choose from a variety of Czech and international main courses for 100–260Kč in the cosy cellars which arch over one's head or in summer on the street above, the perfect place to enjoy a Bernard beer after a day's exploring in the surrounding countryside. There is an internet café in the same building.

Restaurant Pod Hradem Školní 9; ↘ 499 810 189. The name of this quiet wine bar near the Church of the Nativity of the Virgin Mary means 'Under the castle' though all that remains of the castle are the cellars in which the wine bar is located. There is more exposed stonework, low lighting and very reasonable prices with main dishes from 80Kč.

Restaurace U kostela Kostelní ulice; ↘ 777 605 150. Not far from the previous restaurant, a few metres down from the church, this is a no-nonsense Czech eatery with a pleasant café downstairs and a restaurant on the first floor. The friendly staff serve Czech and international standards for a very reasonable 60–200Kč and Urquell and Gambrinus beers.

What to see and do

All of Trutnov's places of interest are centred around the pleasing **Krakonošovo Square** and the streets leading off it. Proud town houses line the square, propped up on thick columns which form arcading hiding the town's many shops and businesses. Many buildings gained their current appearance in the 18th and 19th centuries but rest on much older foundations. The square's cobbles are only interrupted by the **Trinity Column** dating from 1704 and **Krakonoš Fountain** topped by a statue of the mythical ruler of the Krkonoše Mountains himself complete with long flowing beard and brandishing a staff. While strolling around the square one cannot fail to notice the curious **town hall** building with its turrets and clock tower ending in a needle-thin spire. Originally built in the Renaissance period it was reconstructed in the neo-Gothic style after a fire in 1861. Behind the main façade one can still see the original Renaissance building

TEPLICE AND ADRŠPACH ROCK TOWNS

When the tourist bumf uses the phrase 'rock towns' (a direct translation from the Czech – *skalní města*), this a not a comment on the sort of music the locals listen to but a way of describing these curious colonies of stone towers rising high above the treetops. East Bohemia has more than its fair share of these geologically fascinating sites but one of the best is the 20km² Adršpach and Teplice rocks (Adršpašsko-Teplické skály) 15km northeast of Trutnov. Two wonderful masses of tall grey rock towers (the highest in the Czech Republic) rising among the pine trees hide a maze of sandy trails, deep clefts one can hardly squeeze through, waterfalls and a lake.

The rocks are ideal for climbing (which many do) but most content themselves with rambling, exploring and picnicking. The trip can be managed in a long day from Trutnov, but if you do get stuck, Teplice has a few cheap pensions and a hotel with a restaurant. VKÚ-KČT map 26 *Broumovsko, Góry kamienne a Stołowe* covers this area as well as the Broumov cliffs to the east.

As mentioned previously, nine trains a day make the journey out along a branch line to the rocks. To Adršpach allow one hour (40Kč) and to Teplice it takes the train a further 20 minutes (46Kč), though for the rocks one should alight at the Teplice nad Metují-skály stop just before the village. The last train from Teplice back to Trutnov departs at 20.00 calling at Adršpach at 20.11.

with typical sgraffito panels. Dating from 1782, the large, late Baroque **Church of the Nativity of the Virgin Mary**, a few hundred metres northeast of the square, dominates the Trutnov skyline and is a majestic sight against the backdrop of the surrounding wooded hills.

Museum of the Podkrkonoší region

Next to the church on the site of the former castle is situated the small regional museum (*admission 12/4Kč*). Temporary exhibitions occupy the ground floor with a permanent exhibition on the 1866 Battle of Trutnov and ethnographical exhibits taking up the first floor. The museum also has a curious collection of unique 18th-century beehives carved from whole tree trunks. During your visit, the museum staff will undoubtedly direct you to the **1866 battlefield**, signposted from the main square (Bitva 1866). This is spread along the whole southern flank of the town, the various monuments and graves peppering a pleasant forest park. Every year to mark the anniversary of the battle on 27 June, military history enthusiasts re-enact the Austrian victory over the Prussians.

Krkonoše Mountains

Trutnov is as good a launch pad as any to explore the Czech Republic's highest mountains, the Krkonoše, sometimes called the Giant Mountains in English. The 548km² **Krkonoše National Park** extends from Harrachov in the west and almost to Trutnov in the east with some pretty rugged alpine terrain in between. A lot more mountain country can be found over the border in Poland where a larger national park exists. The blight of the Krkonoše is acid rain caused by industry in nearby Polish cities. The situation has improved immensely in the last decade, but the damage is still visible in many places.

The Krkonoše are great hiking country but most Czechs come here for the skiing. In winter and early spring Škoda-loads of Czechs invade places like Pec pod Sněžkou, Špindlerův Mlýn and Harrachov loaded down with skis and boots on skiing day trips, many from the capital just 100km away. In summer walkers take over though the weather can sometimes be erratic (at least 10°C cooler than the rest of the country). VKÚ-KČT map 22 *Krkonoše* covers the park in detail and enables walkers to plan itineraries as it shows all the *bouda*, mountain huts where hikers can stay the night. Some are basic affairs with just a few facilities, others have turned into three-star-standard accommodation. Accommodation in the mountains should be booked ahead to avoid being left out in the cold though many will let you erect a tent in the grounds and use their facilities. Make sure you have all the necessary gear before you set out and take warm clothes even if it is a sweltering 30°C in Trutnov.

The highest peak in the Czech Republic is Sněžka (1,602m) and one of the most popular activities in the national park in summer is scaling the 6km trail to the top. If you do not fancy the walk there is a chairlift, but however you make the summit, you are rewarded with tremendous views from above the treeline.

Information centres in the Krkonoše

Pec pod Sněžkou Pec pod Sněžkou 188; ☎ 499 736 280; f 499 736 410; www.turistapec.cz
Harrachov Harrachov 150; ☎ 481 529 600; f 481 529 064; www.harrachov.cz
Vrchlabí Krkonošská 8; ☎ 499 422 136; f 499 421 121
Krkonoše National Park – Vrchlabí náměstí Míru 223; ☎ 499 421 474; www.krnap.cz

Mountain cottage

South Bohemia

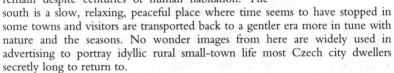

For centuries it seems the southern Czechs have been intent on creating a region in complete accord with nature. Pretty towns have grown against a stunning backdrop of dark wooded hills; lakes and ponds teeming with fish spread out in harmony with the land; and areas of virgin forest remain despite centuries of human habitation. The south is a slow, relaxing, peaceful place where time seems to have stopped in some towns and visitors are transported back to a gentler era more in tune with nature and the seasons. No wonder images from here are widely used in advertising to portray idyllic rural small-town life most Czech city dwellers secretly long to return to.

The south is the source of many things quintessentially Czech. Christmas carp comes from its lakes, many beers are brewed here, it was the birthplace of Jan Hus and Jan Žižka and the Vltava rises here. It has also given the world a brand name known universally as Budweiser, the original home of which is the south's largest city, České Budějovice.

Many towns in the region are called Rose Towns after their coats of arms featuring a five-petalled rose. Once the property of one family, the Rožmberks, their most famous contribution to Czech myth is the White Lady who roams their castles, including the largest in Český Krumlov. This incredibly beautiful town nestled in a bend of the Vltava is one of the most popular tourist attractions in the country and the only place in the south you will experience a crush of tourists. Many places still sport 16th-century Renaissance architecture created by Italian masters commissioned by inspired nobility with taste and style.

GETTING AROUND

České Budějovice is the region's transport hub. Rail and bus connections are OK but off-the-beaten-track public transport may be non-existent. The trans-Šumava rail line is one of the most scenic in the country and the narrow-gauge railway around Jindřichův Hradec is also enjoyable.

ČESKÉ BUDĚJOVICE

Laid-back České Budějovice (or just Budějovice to its friends) spreads out from the confluence of the Malše and Vltava rivers, and with its 100,000 inhabitants forms the largest settlement in south Bohemia and one of the most important administrative centres in the country. It is known for its vast, arcade-bordered square, said to be the second largest in Europe after St Mark's in Venice, but perhaps most of all as the home of the original Budweiser beer, called Budvar in Czech. Another fine beer, Samson, is also produced in the city, and brewing has been a key feature of the town's way of life since the 13th century. A trip to

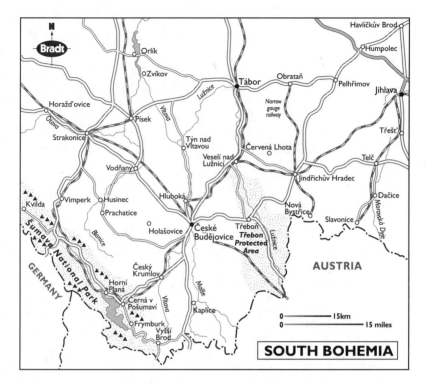

Budweis (the German for Budějovice, hence the name of the world-famous beer) is not complete without tasting some original local brew in one of the town's numerous pubs and bars.

Budějovice is the best place to base yourself for a holiday in south Bohemia. The town enjoys all the services of a large town and Budějovice hotels can be a good option when nearby Český Krumlov is booked up.

History

The main square in Budějovice is named after the town's founder, Czech King Přemysl Otakar II, who in 1265 created a settlement to consolidate his power in south Bohemia. The town soon grew fat on trade and by the turn of the 13th century already boasted two large churches and sturdy town walls. These proved invaluable during the Hussite wars, when the Hussite warlord, Jan Žižka, considered them so strong, he did not even attempt to take staunchly Catholic Budějovice.

Throughout the 16th century the town continued to prosper thanks to silver mining, brewing, fishing and the salt trade. Several of the best-known landmarks were added at this time, such as the town hall and the Black Tower. Budějovice stayed loyal to the emperor during the revolt of the estates and the ensuing Thirty Years War. The town was considered so impregnable that for a time during the troubled 17th century the Czech crown jewels were kept in a church within the walls.

Although wars hardly touched the town, a fire in 1641 destroyed more than half its houses. Several significant landmarks were added during the subsequent Baroque reconstruction, such as the Samson Fountain. The late 18th century saw Budějovice

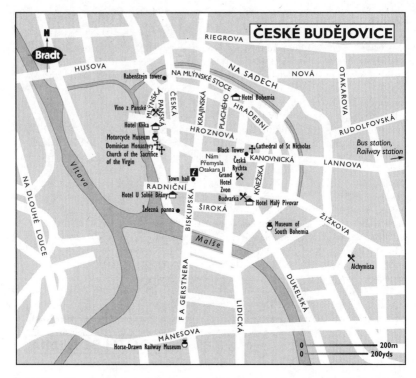

become regional capital, and the arrival of the Piarist order, who founded a school here in 1762. In 1785, the bishopric of České Budějovice was created.

The 19th century saw the construction of the horse-drawn railway to Linz in Austria, and the growth of industries including pencil production (still going today in the Koh-i-noor factory), and the founding of the world famous brewery.

České Budějovice last hit the news during the floods of August 2002. Due to its location on the confluence of two rivers, one of those being the Vltava, the town was hit by a deluge, which flooded almost the entire historical centre, damaging many buildings. Most of the bridges around the centre were swept away and have been replaced. Look out for the small plaques indicating the highest level the flood waters reached in those dreadful days.

Getting there and away

Bus and train are both options when travelling to České Budějovice from the capital. **Coaches** leave Roztyly metro station (red line C), Florenc main coach station and the Na Knížecí station (Anděl metro station, yellow line B) at regular intervals throughout the day (2½ hours, 120Kč). The **train** journey is around the same length but costs 204Kč. Trains leave Prague's main station every one or two hours. České Budějovice is one of the country's most important centres and has direct connections to all parts of the country including Moravia and west Bohemia.

The bus and railway stations are next to one another on Nádražní Street. From there it is no more than 15 minutes' walk along Lannova třída to the historical centre. Within the city an excellent trolleybus service runs 24 hours a day. Tickets are bought from machines at stops (8Kč = 10 minutes, 10Kč = 20 minutes).

Where to stay

Grand Hotel Zvon nám Přemysla Otakara II 28; ℩ 387 311 384; f 387 311 385; www.hotel-zvon.cz. Visitors to the town have been staying at the Zvon (which means 'the Bell') allegedly since 1533. It is the place to stay in České Budějovice, right on the main square, with 70 3- and 4-star rooms, all attractively fitted out and with bathroom and TV etc. Room rates start at 1,150Kč for a sgl in low season, to 4,030Kč for a dbl in summer.

Hotel Malý Pivovar Karla IV 8–10; ℩ 386 360 471–3; f 386 360 474; www.malypivovar.cz. Just off the main square on the corner of Karla IV and Kněžská this 4-star hotel is located in a former brewery and is still the property of the Budvar Brewery. It has 28 spacious rooms with en-suite facilities, TV etc. Sgls cost 2,150Kč and dbls 3,100Kč with prices falling in the low season.

Hotel Bohemia Hradební 20; ℩/f 386 360 691; www.hotel-bohemia-cb.cz. On the corner of Hradební and Plachého streets about 200m from Přemysla Otakara II Square, this is a lovely place to stay in a tranquil part of the historical centre. The 16 rooms are light and airy and all have en-suite facilities. 3-star sgls with breakfast cost 1,490Kč, dbls 1,790Kč, breakfast included. Prices come down a few hundred crowns in winter.

Hotel Klika Hroznová 25; ℩ 387 318 171; f 387 222 775; www.hotelklika.cz. By a meander of the river Malše, next to the Dominican Monastery, the Klika has 26 tastefully renovated, quiet rooms of varying sizes and styles, and a restaurant with views of the river. Sgls cost around 1,300Kč, dbls 1,700Kč.

Hotel U Solné Brány Radniční 11; ℩ 386 354 121; f 386 354 120; www.hsb.cz. This inviting little hotel is tucked away in Radniční Street, 500m from the square. It has 12 quality rooms to choose from, some slightly on the snug side, but with their own balcony. A sgl with bathroom and breakfast here will cost you approximately 1,200Kč, a dbl around 1,600Kč.

Where to eat

Many may have recommended you eat at the town's best-known restaurant and a Budějovice institution, the Masné krámy. This rather touristy beer hall was damaged to such an extent by the floods of 2002 that it never reopened. The following is a selection of the best eateries, and those with most character.

Víno z Panské Panská 14; ℩ 387 318 511. This tiny restaurant is perched above a wine shop in one of the town's oldest houses in picturesque Panská Street. The name means 'Wine from Panská Street', and they serve a large selection of fine wines from all over the Czech Republic, not only Moravia. Czech main dishes cost a very reasonable 70–250Kč and the original interior, crammed with medieval character, is thrown in for free. A gem of a place, highly recommended.

Budvarka Karla IV 8–10; ℩ 386 360 471. This long thin beer hall, around 100m off the main square along Karla IV Street, stretches back a long way from the street. It is one of the best places to enjoy the local brew and fish (especially carp) from south Bohemia's famous lakes. The food is mainly Czech and mains cost 70–150Kč.

Česká Rychta nám Přemysla Otakara II 28; ℩ 387 311 384. This large Czech beer hall-cum-restaurant, with its dark wood panelling and vaulted ceiling, is conveniently situated on the main square and is one of the best places to seek refreshment in České Budějovice. Diners can enjoy main courses for 100–300Kč and Urquell beer.

Alchymista U Tří lvů; ℩ 386 356 545. Another great place to eat and enjoy the interior, this time under brick arches of a cellar in U Tří lvů Street, just outside the historical centre. At the 'Alchemist' they cook up traditional medieval Czech food for 100–350Kč, there are several vegetarian dishes on the menu and Krušovice and Urquell beer.

What to see and do

The municipal **information centre** (*nám Přemysla Otakara II 2;* ↘*386 801 413;* f *386 359 480; www.c-budejovice.cz*), as opposed to another centre across the square which is little more than a map shop, is housed in the building of the **town hall**, which gained its current appearance (huge protruding bronze gargoyles and all) thanks to a Baroque makeover in the 1720s. It stands on the **Square of Přemysl Otakar II**, one of the largest in Europe and truly square in measuring 133m by 133m with arcading on all sides. It is centred around the **Samson Fountain**, also from the 1720s. To the northeast rises the majestic, 72m-tall **Black Tower** (Černá věž) dating from the mid 16th century and until recently the highest structure in the town. From April to October it is possible to climb this former lookout and bell tower (*admission 20Kč*). Next to the tower stands the Baroque **Cathedral of St Nicholas**. Remodelled several times over the years, a church has stood on this site since the foundation of the town in 1265.

To the northwest of the square lies the medieval **Piaristické náměstí** (Piarist Square) where the oldest-surviving buildings in the town can be found. The first of these is the **Church of the Sacrifice of the Virgin**, a dirty white Gothic church also dating from 1265. Joined to the church is the **Dominican Monastery** dating from the 14th century but unfortunately not open to the public, though the church can be entered via the Gothic cloisters. From Piarist Square head up medieval Panská Street, which follows the line of the old town walls, to the **Rabenštejn Tower** (Rabenštejnská věž) built in the 14th century as part of the town walls. From there follow the arm of the Malše south past remnants of the walls to another tower, the so-called **Železná panna** (or Iron Maiden Tower), which used to house a torture chamber.

Museums

The **Museum of South Bohemia** (Jihočeské Muzeum) can be found just outside the historical centre and southwest of the square at Dukelská 1 in purpose-built premises from 1903. There are permanent exhibitions on the flora and fauna of south Bohemia, prehistory and the medieval period, Baroque and Renaissance art and interesting temporary exhibitions held year round (*admission 80/35Kč, open Tue–Sun*).

The **Horse-drawn Railway Museum** (Muzeum Koněspřežky, *admission 10Kč, open Apr–Oct, Tue–Sun*) is in fact part of the Museum of South Bohemia but is located in Mánesova Street, a five-minute walk south of the centre. The horse-drawn railway linking Budějovice with Linz in Austria, built in 1825–32, was the first such railway in Europe, had a total length of over 120km, and was in operation for over 40 years. The tour of the museum includes a film on the railway. The town council are planning to build a replica of the horse-drawn railway which will run through the town centre to the main square. Work on the project should have started by the time you read this.

The **Motorcycle Museum** (*admission 40Kč, open Mar–Oct*) is situated in the old salthouse on Piarist Square. The small but interesting museum has two floors of vintage motorcycles, the oldest from 1899.

Around České Budějovice
Hluboká

The romantic, eye-catching chateau at Hluboká, to the north of Budějovice, is one of the most popular and remarkable in the Czech Republic, and a must-see for any visitor to the region. The grounds, the chalky-white neo-Gothic façades and the breathtakingly handsome interiors all make this the perfect day trip. The Schwarzenbergs, the last private owners, gave the chateau its current appearance in the mid 19th century, remodelling it to resemble an English stately home and the likeness to Windsor Castle is no accident (*admission 90/50Kč for a tour in Czech and 160/80Kč in a foreign language, open Apr–Oct daily except Mon*).

Hluboká is 10km north of Budějovice on the Vltava. Local buses (20 minutes, 10Kč) leave Budějovice for Hluboká every half an hour on weekdays. Most trains heading north also stop there (10 minutes, 16Kč), including many of the expresses bound for Prague. Another option is on foot or by bicycle along the Vltava, a very pleasant, gentle route with the chateau coming dramatically into view on a distant hillside as you pass through the northern suburbs of Budějovice.

Holašovice

The tiny village of Holašovice lies peacefully undisturbed 15km west of České Budějovice. In 1998, the green was added to the UNESCO list of world heritage sites for its unique and perfectly preserved examples of south Bohemian folk Baroque architectural style from the 18th and 19th centuries. UNESCO decided it was worth this lofty status as it is 'an outstanding example of traditional rural settlement in central Europe'. Holašovice has a perfect little village green, encircled with pretty houses with pleasing bell-shaped gables. By far the best time to come is for the village festival at the end of July.

The only places to eat are two pubs which face each other across the green where the UNESCO plaque and column are located. Both have simple pub food. There are seven buses a day on weekdays from the main bus station in České Budějovice. Getting back can be tricky and you may have to walk 4km to Záboří to catch a bus.

ČESKÝ KRUMLOV

Picture a town with crooked, cobbled medieval streets, where every Baroque and Renaissance façade bears stunning testimony to the skill and judgement of master builders of centuries gone by; a town with a fairy-tale castle hugging the brow of the surrounding hills; a unique settlement not touched by the ravages of war, the forces of nature or the bulldozers of enterprise for over five centuries. All this is Český Krumlov, truly one of Europe's, if not the world's most beautiful and well-preserved medieval towns, a must for anyone venturing out of the capital.

Český Krumlov's unique townscape and its magnificent chateau, the second largest in the country after Prague Castle, have not gone unnoticed by UNESCO, who declared the town a World Heritage Site in 1992, thus guaranteeing its status and ensuring that no major development will violate the historical centre.

The medieval town starts at the chateau, which entirely dominates the skyline. From the last courtyard the Latrán twists its way down to the Lazebnický Bridge over the meandering river Vltava, whose swift currents all but encircle the historical core, centred around Svornosti Square. The colossal chateau, views of the town below, the quaint Svornosti Square and the rather perplexing maze of irregular, winding medieval lanes and alleys running off it, are what attract so many visitors to this corner of south Bohemia. The people of Český Krumlov have responded to this interest by creating tasteful pensions, medieval-style restaurants, cosy hotels and intriguing boutiques and shops in harmony with the atmosphere and historical backdrop the town provides.

The one slight downside to Český Krumlov is its popularity. From May to September the narrow streets are a crush of tourists from around the globe with legions of German and Austrian pensioners shuffling their way cautiously over the treacherous cobbles, and coaches weighed down with day trippers from Prague disgorging their human cargo on to a town which some now rather cynically call 'Czech Venice'. To get the most from your visit, come in April or October when the tourist crowds are at their thinnest, but the chateau is open.

History

Český Krumlov straddles a double bend in the river Vltava, slowly meandering its way from the Šumava to České Budějovice, and giving the town its name derived from the German 'Krumme Aue', translated as 'crooked meadow'. The town is first mentioned in 1253, when there was already a castle on the hill belonging to the Vítkovci family. The town budded below the castle along the Latrán and the main square, inhabited by Czechs and Germans from the outset. In 1302 the Vítkovci died out and Český Krumlov came into the ownership of the powerful south Bohemian Rožmberk family of five-petalled red rose fame who brought prosperity to the town which thrived on trade and brewing. During the 14th century the noble family added the Church of St Vitus, the Church of St Jošt and contributed significantly to the appearance of the town. Český Krumlov survived the Hussite wars unscathed thanks to the Rožmberks' crafty policy of switching sides whenever convenient and advantageous. However, their rule came to an end at the beginning of the 17th century when they were forced to sell up to Rudolf II to pay off debts. The town did not fare well during the Thirty Years War and was occupied by both the emperor and the Swedish. Emperor Ferdinand II gave Krumlov to the Eggenberg family in 1622 in gratitude for their financial support during the war. When they died out at the beginning of the 18th century, the new lords of the manor were the illustrious Schwarzenbergs, another powerful noble family who left an indelible mark on south Bohemia.

By the mid 19th century the economically asphyxiating town walls had gone and Český Krumlov became a flourishing town with 5,000 inhabitants and many local industries. Tensions arose between the town's German and Czech ethnic groups and the 1918 declaration of the Czechoslovak Republic had to be enforced here by the military. The town survived World War II unscathed and was liberated from Nazi occupation by the US Army in 1945. Český Krumlov's German inhabitants were driven out soon after.

Český Krumlov was not allowed to crumble away into the Vltava during the communist era thanks to the town's status from 1963 as a Historical Urban Reservation. The post-communist 1990s brought tourists and enterprise to the twisting streets, but the town also came under UNESCO's wing, protecting it from any unwanted excesses of capitalism. Český Krumlov was badly affected by the flood of August 2002, but you would not know it today.

Getting there and away

Český Krumlov lies 170km south of Prague and is not feasible as a day trip from the capital unless you join a special coach trip. **Bus** is the only realistic way to reach the town from Prague with regular services leaving Florenc coach station, Roztyly metro station (red line C) and Na Knížecí station (Anděl metro station, yellow line B) in the morning and in the afternoon after 15.00 (3 hours 20 minutes, 140Kč). Local buses (45 minutes, 26Kč) ply the route between Český Krumlov and České Budějovice every half-hour. **Trains** run far less frequently.

From the railway station follow třída Míru downhill for around 15–20 minutes until you reach the Latrán on the left. The bus station is just east of the chateau.

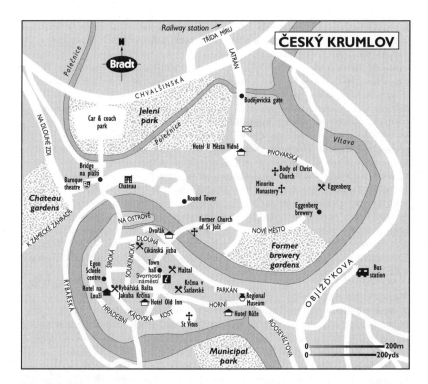

ČESKÝ KRUMLOV

Tourist information

The information centre (*nám Svornosti 2;* ☏ *380 704 622–3;* f *380 704 619;*
www.ckrumlov.cz) is one of the most professional and efficient in the country.
Their exceptionally meticulous website (laudably translated in its entirety into
English) provides an invaluable source of information before you arrive, and the
office on the main square has heaps of information, an accommodation booking
service, a left-luggage service, internet (1Kč per minute), fax, audio guides to the
town and much more.

Where to stay

Český Krumlov is crammed with pensions and hotels, but finding a bed in
summer, and other times regarded as high season, can still be a headache. And do
not expect anything you do find to be cheap. The information centre can supply
you with an accommodation list, and even book rooms for a small fee. Prices
come down by around a third in low season.

Hotel Růže Horní 154; ☏ 380 772 100, 380 713 146; www.hotelruze.cz. Not only the
best hotel in Český Krumlov, but one of the best in the entire republic. Housed in the
Renaissance former Jesuit College, it would be hard to find a hotel with more historical
character and style. The 71 rooms and hotel facilities are everything you would expect
from a 5-star establishment with prices to match. A sgl/dbl in high season will set you back
a whopping 4,200/5,200Kč, though this falls to a most agreeable 2,400/3,400Kč off
season. If money is no object, why not go for the de luxe apartment at 8,000Kč a night?
Hotel Dvořák Radniční 101; ☏ 380 711 020; f 380 711 024;
www.dvorakck.genea2000.cz. The Dvořák has unrivalled views of the castle and river as

it stands guard over the Lazebnický Bridge. Its 22 spacious rooms are elegantly fitted out and come for 3,000Kč for a sgl and 3,700Kč for a dbl. Why not splash out on the presidential suite at a very reasonable 5,900Kč?

Hotel U Města Vídně Latrán 77; ☎ 380 720 111; f 380 720 119; www.hmv.cz. This is a new hotel in an old building on a bend in the Latrán heading away from the chateau, a short walk from all the major sights, and quieter than down in the thick of things. The 'City of Vienna', as the name translates, is one of the town's better hotels with absolutely immaculate and stylish sgls and dbls for 2,420Kč and 2,790Kč respectively.

Hotel Old Inn nám Svornosti 12–14; ☎ 380 772 500; f 380 772 550; www.hoteloldinn.cz. The 4-star Old Inn is Krumlov's best-situated hotel, located on the main square. It has 52 snug rooms with all mod cons, and prices ranging from 3,200Kč for a sgl to 3,800Kč for a dbl. Expect a discount of almost 50% in low season.

Hotel na Louži Kájovská 66; ☎/f 380 711 280; www.nalouzi.cz. The Hotel na Louži is something a bit different from the above, and slightly less punishing to the wallet. Situated just off the square it has 11 rooms of varying shapes and sizes, most containing chunky traditional rural Czech furniture and décor. Each room has a name and 7 are dbls costing 1,350Kč, 3 are triples for 1,700Kč and 1 room, 'Kateřina', has 4 beds on 2 levels and costs 2,300Kč a night. A real gem of a place and highly recommended along with the pub of the same name below.

Where to eat

Krčma v Šatlavské Horní 157; ☎ 380 713 344. Although the address of this place is Horní Street, the entrance is actually up Šatlavská Street, which leaves the square a few metres east of the information centre. This is a medieval gem with low vaulted ceilings, an enormous hearth lit by the staff each evening, various cosy candlelit rooms, medievally attired staff and the fragrance of burning logs and roasting meat on the air. This quite well-known and popular place has Czech medieval meat dishes for 100–200Kč, Budvar beer and a choice of wines.

Rybářská bašta Jakuba Krčína Kajovská 54; ☎ 777 776 256. Jakub Krčín was responsible for the creation of many of the region's artificial lakes and therefore the fish industry. This fish restaurant named after him on Na Louži Square, facing back down Kajovská Street, has a slightly threadbare interior, but is probably the best place in town for local fish costing 140–250Kč a time. They also have a large selection of Moravian wines. Look out for the stuffed animals and fish in the window, but if you do not like fish, go elsewhere.

Restaurace Maštal nám Svornosti; ☎ 380 713 770. This great place is along an alley by the side of the information centre. Maštal is an old Czech word for stable and the restaurant is situated in 3 cosy cellars, once used for keeping horses, hence the décor of bridles, horseshoes etc. Giant portions, very reasonable prices, vegetarian options and Budvar and local Eggenberg beer make this one of the best places to eat in town. Czech mains cost 100–200Kč.

Restaurace Eggenberg Pivovar, Pivovarská ulice; ☎ 380 711 426. The Eggenberg brewery, like most others in the country, has its own pub and restaurant. The pub is downstairs with the cavernous restaurant-cum-beer hall on the first floor. It has a stage for live music, Czech food for 100–300Kč, and every type of beer the brewery produces.

Restaurace Cikánská jizba Dlouhá 31; ☎ 380 717 585. A Gypsy restaurant that anyone can enter is a rarity in the Czech Republic, and is something a little different. The 2 simple rooms make a change from dark Czech cellars, and Fri and Sat nights feature live Gypsy music. The menu is a mix of Czech, Gypsy and Slovak fare plus pizzas, all for a very reasonable 50–200Kč. Local Eggenberg brew is on tap as is Urquell from Pilsen.

Hospoda Na Louži Kájovská 66; ⤬ 380 717 446. For me this is the best place in town to try some real south Bohemian carp and down a local Eggenberg. This small, no-nonsense, old-style Czech pub serves up south Bohemian specialities for less than 160Kč.

What to see and do
Chateau
The vast complex of buildings, which make up the castle, traverses the length of a huge promontory of solid rock, towering above the town and the Vltava below, whose low hum resounds off the huge edifice. A total of 40 structures within the grounds make this the second-largest castle in the country after Prague Castle, its magnificent richly painted Round Tower (Válcová věž) dominating the skyline and visible from everywhere in town. (*Open Apr–Oct; closed Mon.*)

Viewed from below, the castle grounds start at the sprawling gardens, where the famous open-air revolving theatre is situated, the future of which looks rather uncertain. In the corner of the gardens we find the Castle riding school, now a restaurant. Leaving the gardens we enter the Renaissance part of the castle which connects to the Baroque theatre, one of only two in Europe preserved with its original stage technology intact and one of the most fascinating parts of the castle. The original dates from 1680, but gained its present almost over-elaborate appearance in 1765. Crossing over the Renaissance bridge called 'na plášti' or 'on the cloak' built slowly but surely during the 18th century, we reach the Upper Castle, the original Gothic structure, enclosing the third and fourth courtyards. The castle then opens out into the second courtyard surrounded by the Mint and the New Burgrave's House. In the southeast corner is the so-called Little Castle and the Round Tower. The huge first courtyard is surrounded by a jumble of Renaissance outbuildings which used to house the brewery, the salt house, the stables and the smithy. At the far end is the Red Gate, the entrance most visitors will use to access the castle.

Guided tours
The only way to see the exquisite interiors of the castle is by taking a guided tour. The ticket office is situated on the 2nd courtyard. There are two main tours and tickets can also be bought for other parts of the castle not included in these. Seeing everything costs 535Kč. Tour 1 and a visit to the Baroque theatre amount to the best combination in my opinion.

Tour 1 100Kč in Czech, 160Kč in a foreign language (*concessions 50/80Kč*). Includes Renaissance and Baroque chambers, the Golden Carriage and the Masquerade Hall. Length: 60 minutes.
Tour 2 80Kč in Czech, 140Kč in a foreign language (*concessions 50/70Kč*). Includes the Schwarzenberg interiors from the 19th century. Length: 60 minutes.
Baroque Theatre 110Kč in Czech, 180Kč in a foreign language (*concessions 50/90Kč*)
Round Tower 35Kč, concessions 20Kč (*no guided tour*)
Castle Lapidarium 20Kč, concessions 10Kč (*no guided tour*)
Castle Gardens Free

Latrán
At the top of the Latrán just before it crosses the Polečnice Stream stands the **Budějovická Gate** (1598–1602), which those arriving by rail will pass through on their way from the station. Along Pivovarská Street we find the **Eggenberg Brewery**, a complex of huge solid red-brick and plaster buildings, some from the

Renaissance period, others from the 19th and 20th centuries. Tours of the brewery cost 100Kč, 130Kč with a beer-tasting session at the end. The five types of beer produced from Žatec hops can be sampled in pubs and restaurants throughout the town. Another street, Klášterní, leads you to the gates of the **Minorite Monastery** (*admission 40/20Kč, open Apr–Nov*) and the apparently derelict **Body of Christ Church**. Heading downhill along the Latrán to the Lazebnický Bridge, we pass the **Former Church of St Jošt** from 1334.

Inner Town (Vnitřní město)

The bridge across the fast-flowing Vltava takes you into the Inner Town centred around **Svornosti Square** with its plague column erected (1714–16) in remembrance of the epidemic that ravaged the town in the 1680s. The Renaissance façade resting on six Gothic arches on the northeast side is the **town hall**, a single Renaissance front concealing three Gothic town houses. Another building dominating the Český Krumlov skyline is the Gothic **Church of St Vitus**, established sometime in the early 14th century and occasionally used for atmospheric concerts of classical music. The colossal white Renaissance façade in Široká Street (No 70–72) is the **Egon Schiele Centre**. Born near Vienna in 1890, Egon Schiele's mother hailed from Český Krumlov, a place which inspired the artist. Having decided that the town was the place for him, he was driven out by the townspeople, who did not appreciate his use of local young girls as models (a peek of his pictures from the time explains all). The 4,000m² of exhibition space at the centre is taken up with exhibitions of Czech and international modern art as well as a section on Schiele's life and work and a temporary exhibition space (*admission 180/105Kč, open daily, year round*).

Heading east out of the square along Horní Street, visitors arrive at the former **Jesuit College** and the **Regional Museum** which face each other across the cobbles. The impressive Renaissance sgraffito-covered edifice of the Jesuit College dates from 1586 to 1588 and now accommodates the plush five-star Hotel Růže. The museum houses interesting exhibits from the region (*admission 50/25Kč, open Mar–Oct*).

PRACHATICE

This small town of 12,000 souls just outside the Šumava National Park represents the Czech Republic at its best and most satisfying. A blend of 16th-century architecture, narrow medieval cobbled alleyways, low prices and the friendliest locals you will meet in the country combine with tourist-free streets to make Prachatice one of Bohemia's best-kept secrets.

Prachatice was built from scratch at the beginning of the 14th century and the newly established town soon grew rich thanks to the Zlatá stezka or Golden Path, a salt trade route from Bohemia to Passau. Soon churches and fortifications went up to protect the burghers' wealth but their prosperity was rudely interrupted by the Hussite wars. Jan Žižka attacked the town twice, the second time massacring 85 men in a church! In 1501, the Rožmberk family took possession of Prachatice, and following a great fire in 1507 the town was rebuilt, gaining its richly decorated Renaissance façades. Prachatice was again experiencing great prosperity from the salt trade and the 16th century could be described as its golden age. Steady economic decline from the beginning of the 17th century caused by war and the end of the salt trade meant that the town's appearance has changed little since. The townspeople hold a raucous medieval festival every year at the end of June to celebrate the trade route that put their town on the map. This also serves as a reminder of what an important commodity salt was in

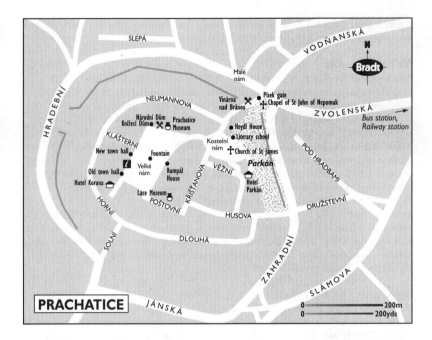

medieval society, and the Czech saying *sůl nad zlato*, 'salt is more precious than gold', hints at why the trade route was called the Golden Path.

Getting there and away

There are seven direct **buses** (2½ hours, 110Kč) a day from Prague via Písek to Prachatice, all departing from Na Knížecí station (Anděl metro station, yellow line B). Travelling by **train** is not really an option. To and from České Budějovice there is a half-hourly bus service (1 hour, 40Kč) and services to Strakonice and towns in the Šumava such as Lenora and Vimperk.

Prachatice is on a branch line extending into the Šumava and there are trains to Volary throughout the day where you can change on to the picturesque trans-Šumava line.

On arrival in Prachatice follow Nádražní from the adjacent bus and railway stations, go straight on at the crossroads and follow Zvolenská to the Lower Gate and the historical centre.

Tourist information

Prachatice's excellent tourist information centre is situated in the Rumpál House (*Velké náměstí 1; \/f 388 312 563; www.prachatice.cz*).

Where to stay

Hotel Parkán Věžní 51; \/f 388 311 868; www.hotelparkan.cz. The family-run Parkán is quite difficult to find along quaint Věžní alleyway behind the church. The owners take a personal approach and you will soon feel welcome. The 17 en-suite rooms are a touch cramped but still a good deal at 490–690Kč for a sgl and 790–990Kč for a dbl including breakfast. The pleasant restaurant is open in summer only.

Hotel Koruna Velké náměstí 48; \/f 388 310 177; www.pthotel.cz. Like the Parkán, some of the 24 rooms at the Koruna are on the small side though better furnished.

There is a flat year-round rate of 950Kč per room including breakfast and the hotel has a restaurant (see below) and an moody Gothic wine cellar.

Where to eat

Vinárna nad bránou Kostelní náměstí 19; ✆ 388 319 071. Situated actually inside the second gate as one enters the old historical town, this is a superb place to eat. Surrounded by history, diners can choose from 2 floors (no smoking upstairs) and from a wide-ranging menu with south Bohemian specialities for 100–200Kč. A large selection of wines is on offer as well as Pilsner Urquell and black Budvar. The service is as good as the location.
Hotel Koruna Velké náměstí 48; ✆/f 388 310 177. The restaurant in the hotel of the same name is the most upmarket of Prachatice's eateries, though the service leaves something to be desired. There is a wide range of meals on offer including numerous vegetarian options and not just the usual 5 takes on fried cheese. Expect to pay 60–200Kč for a main course. There is a good selection of beers.
Národní dům Velké náměstí 10; ✆ 608 111 481–2. The main square's basic Czech restaurant, where little has changed since 1989, is the place to come for a cheap meal and a beer or 5. The menu features fish, game and Chinese (probably brought from the Chinese restaurant upstairs) as well as other Czech staples and there is Radegast beer on tap. Mains come for a reasonable 50–170Kč.

What to see and do
From the Písek Gate to Velké náměstí

Visitors arriving on foot from the stations are greeted by the tiny **Chapel of St John of Nepomuk** on the left followed by the hefty double towers of the **Lower** or **Písek Gate** (Dolní or Písecká brána) with a fading mural of Vilém of Rožmberk on horseback greeting visitors. The second part of the gate now houses a restaurant (see above). Passing through the gate one comes to the crooked Heydl House on the left, now rather ominously leaning out over the narrow street and one of the town's finest sgraffitoed façades dating back to 1557. Why the Heydl family commissioned violent scenes of men clubbing each other to death on the side of their house is anybody's guess. Immediately behind that is the **Literary School** which, it is commonly believed, was attended by the young Jan Žižka and Jan Hus. The building with its Renaissance turrets is best viewed from the **Parkán**, a peaceful park, the entrance to which is between the two halves of the Písek Gate. A few paces from the Heydl House brings you to the Gothic **Church of St James** (kostel sv Jakuba) founded along with the town in the early 14th century. The triple-nave interior is quite impressive with delicate Gothic ribbed vaulting and a gaudy Baroque altar sporting chunky vine-wreathed barley-sugar columns.

Velké náměstí

The **New Town Hall** dominates the eastern side of the main square (simply called 'Big Square'). It was built in 1902–03 by Viennese architect Antonín Schurda in the neo-Renaissance style, somewhat inevitably some may say considering its neighbours. The sgraffito decoration depicts the import of salt along the Zlatá stezka, above which rises an elaborate clock tower. Despite being severely damaged in a fire in 1832 the **Old Town Hall** dating from 1570 on the same side of the square is probably the town's most attractive building and one of the finest examples of Renaissance architecture in the Czech lands with its incredibly intricate chiaroscuro decoration.

The **Prachatice Museum** (*admission 40/15Kč*) occupies three floors of the ornate Sitrův dům. The creator of the beautiful façade was inspired by the town hall. Look out for the paintings of ten Czech kings (from Václav IV to Rudolf II) and the two white lions rampant, a Czech national symbol. Inside there is an interesting exhibition on the Zlatá stezka.

Of the other decorated façades on the square, look out for the Knížecí dům at No 169 which hides a sgraffito elephant around the corner. On the eastern side of the square one cannot fail to notice house No 41, the Renaissance **Rumpál House**. The former brewery sports highly detailed brown and cream sgraffito battle scenes. House No 71, the so-called Hus House, is allegedly Hus's former dwelling, though there is no evidence that the Czechs' most prominent religious figure ever set foot in the place. A few steps across the square, in the midst of the cobbles plays a gurgling **fountain** with four spouts of water falling into a pool, often the loudest noise on the square. Atop stands a small statue representing justice holding a pair of scales which swing gently in the Šumava breeze.

Other places of interest
Halfway along Poštovní Street at the southern end of the main square is a tiny **Lace Museum** (*Muzeum krajky, admission 60/40Kč*) housed in a listed Renaissance building from the early 16th century, expertly restored by the owners. Lace from all over Europe, all kinds of bobbins, folk costumes and pin cushions are on display, and the expert guide will provide you with enthusiastic explanations. The oldest exhibit is a piece of Belgian lace from 1600. Notice the newly created Renaissance-style wooden ceiling in the end room crafted by experts and containing 64 Renaissance-style motifs relating to the town and the lace industry.

Prachatice is almost unique in the Czech lands for having spared its **town walls** from demolition in the 19th century. While other towns happily tore down the ring of stone, considered to be slowly strangling economic growth, Prachatice felt no need to do so, and its town fortifications stand to this day with only the odd break in places. Visitors can walk full circle around the walls and information boards in English (starting at the Lower Gate) guide you round as well as adding a little historical spice.

STRAKONICE
What do bagpipes, fezzes and Jawa motorcycles have in common? As all self-respecting Strakonice citizens know, this odd selection of items represents the industrial output of their town, and forms the core of the museum collection housed in the colossal castle, the principal reason for stopping off here. Other than the castle Strakonice has little of interest, and could be visited as a summer day trip from Písek or České Budějovice. The only time there is an influx of visitors is during the International Bagpipe Festival, held every other year in mid August in the castle courtyard and inevitably graced by pipers from Scotland.

Strakonice brews a delicious beer rather aptly called Nektar, not widely available outside of the Strakonice region.

Getting there and away
Strakonice has an unexpectedly good **bus** service (3 hours, 80Kč) to and from the capital with up to 17 services a day departing from Na Knížecí station (Anděl metro station, yellow line B). There are also services to and from České Budějovice (1½ hours, 50Kč), Písek (40 minutes, 22Kč), and Tábor (1½ hours, 60Kč).

Rail is the best option when heading from Pilsen with hourly services making the one- to two-hour trip. Tickets cost 98Kč. There is also a frequent service to České Budějovice (1 hour, 76Kč) and Volary in the Šumava (2½ hours, 98Kč).

The bus and rail stations are a five- to ten-minute walk from the castle. From the Billa supermarket which divides the two, take Nádražní Street to the traffic lights, continue along Alfonse Šťastného then take the first right into Bezděkovská which leads to the castle.

Tourist information
The town's official municipal information centre is located on the main square (*Velké náměstí 2;* ✆ *383 700 700–1;* f *383 700 702; www.strakonice.net*). The centre inside the entrance to the castle is a privately run map centre and travel agent which can help with accommodation and has limited information on the town's sights.

Where to stay
Amber Hotel Bavor Na Ohradě 31; ✆ 383 321 300; f 383 321 299. Housed in a tower block by the river the Bavor has 77 business-standard rooms costing around 1,200Kč including breakfast. Try to get a room with a view of the castle.
Fontána Lidická 203; ✆ 383 321 440; f 383 321 494. The Fontána is actually just a few basic rooms above a restaurant just off the square but it does the job. Sgl occupancy will cost you 550–800Kč and a dbl comes for 800–1,200Kč including breakfast.

Where to eat
U Madly Velké náměstí 53; ✆ 383 323 158. Set back off the square in red-brick cellar-like rooms at U Madly you can enjoy Bohemian specialities as well as fish, pasta and several vegetarian dishes all for around 100Kč. The friendly staff also pull a refreshing Staropramen.
U Papeže Velké náměstí 45; ✆ 607 835 308. Modern and popular, the restaurant 'At the Pope's' serves a wide selection of Czech and international fare including venison, wild boar and pizzas all in the region of 100–200Kč. There is outdoor seating to the rear.

What to see and do
Castle and museum
Strakonice's only tourist sight stands in a strategic location at the confluence of the Volyňka and Otava rivers. The huge original 13th-century castle, added to over the centuries, now houses the town's museum (*admission 50/25Kč, open May–Oct*). While wandering through the historical rooms of the castle, look out for exhibitions on fezzes, which at the beginning of the 20th century Strakonice supplied to the whole of the Islamic world, and Jawa and ČZ motorbikes, still seen across the former communist world from Cheb to Vladivostok. Apart from these and other interesting exhibitions on honey and wax production, ČZ firearms and Strakonice in the 19th century, a large room is devoted to local bagpipes (*dudy* in Czech) as well as examples from around Europe, including Northumbrian pipes. An interactive touch-screen allows visitors to see and hear pipers from the 15 countries represented at the annual International Bagpipe Festival. It quickly becomes obvious to the listener that the local pipes emit a much more pleasant, less whining sound than their Scottish cousins. The instrument also differs physically with some locally crafted pipes even possessing a small set of miniature bellows. Round off your visit with a climb up the extremely narrow steps to the top of the pigeon-inhabited Rumpál Tower, a superb vantage point from which to view the town and the dark wooded hills surrounding it.

Town centre
Strakonice's main piazza called Velké náměstí has a couple of interesting façades, most notably the **former butchers' stalls** (Masné krámy) sporting a Baroque

front with a naïve stucco relief of a butcher slaughtering a bull. The fancy façades
of the neo-Renaissance Savings Bank (spořitelna) and former town hall (now a
school) face one another across the cobbles, competing pompously for attention.

ŠUMAVA
Occasionally called the Green Roof of Europe, this very sparsely populated area
of deep pine forests, peat bogs, alpine meadows, fast-flowing streams and ancient
rounded mountains extends for roughly 130km in the southwest of the country
creating a natural border between the Czech Republic and its German-speaking
neighbours. The area derives its name from the Czech word *šum* meaning
'murmur', the sound the vast forests make in the breeze. It is part of a larger
region known as the Böhmerwald on the other side of the mountains, one of the
last remaining true wildernesses in central Europe. No significant industry within
100km, the absence of acid rain and 40 years of proximity to the Iron Curtain
have combined to preserve this corner of Europe in pristine condition,
undoubtedly its key asset.

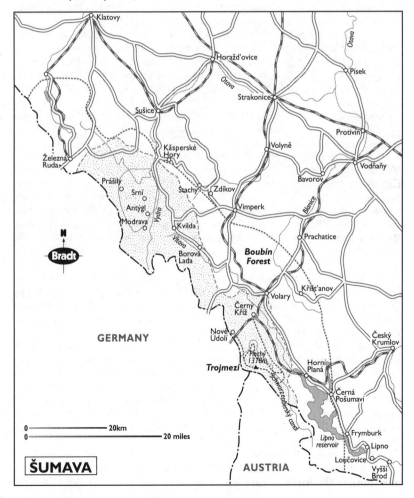

HIKING IN THE ŠUMAVA

Before starting out into the wilds of the Šumava it is vital to get hold of some adequate maps. The unsurpassed VKÚ-KČT maps 64 *Šumava Železnorudsko*, 65 *Šumava Povydří*, 66 *Šumava Trojmezí* and 67 *Šumava Lipno* provide more than enough detail, and illustrate all the region's marked walking trails. With over 1,500km of trails it is easy to plan an itinerary of any length and for any ability. There are a couple of long-distance trails, but generally linking together shorter trails of different colours is necessary. Wild camping and fires are officially not permitted and remember – take only photographs, leave only footprints!
Suggested itineraries:

1 **Along the Otava and Vydra rivers** (60km) – Starting in Sušice catch a bus south to Kašperské Hory, an old German mining town and the beginning of the hike. From there take the blue trail south to Rejštejn, then continue on the red trail along the Otava River to Čeňkova Pila where the Otava becomes the Vydra. *Vydra* means 'otter' in Czech and the river once teemed with the animals; alas no more. This is one of the best sections of trail in the Šumava, picking its way along the winding, boulder-strewn river surrounded by forested slopes of dense pine. The hamlet of Antýgl with its examples of typical Šumava architecture is the next stop on the red trail which then carries on west along the Roklánský Stream through the Javoří peat bogs to Prášily via Poledník Mountain (1,315m). From Prášily a green trail will take you back through the forest to the Otava and on to Rejštejn and Kasperské Hory. Three days is ideal for the hike, breaking at Antýgl and Prášily where there are campsites and food.

2 **The Bear Trail – Medvědí stezka** (14km) – The starting point for this one-day hike is the railway station at Černý Kříž on the trans-Šumava line. This is the area's oldest trail. Starting at the station, take the yellow trail called the Rudolfova cesta (Rudolf's Trail) to the site where the last bear to inhabit the Šumava was shot in 1856, hence the trail's name. From there take the 1km dead-end branch to the top of Jelenská Mountain (1,068m). Back down on the Bear Trail negotiate the rugged Jelení vrchy to reach the

The Šumava National Park (*www.npsumava.cz*), created in 1991, stretches from Lipno reservoir in the south to Železná Ruda in the north and is surrounded by the Šumava Protected Landscape Area forming the largest protected chunk of territory in the country measuring 163,000ha. Some 81% of the national park is carpeted in dense forest and only 9% is used for agriculture resulting in great hiking and cycling possibilities. The one drawback is the climate which tends to be wetter and cooler than the rest of the country, and frequent showers in summer are a common occurrence. In winter expect heavy snowfalls which paralyse transport links and leave many areas cut off. Hiking is the best way to see the region though the trans-Šumava railway from Český Krumlov to Vimperk comes a close second. The scenic line forms the backbone of the region's transport infrastructure and a lifeline for the few thousand people who inhabit this ruggedly picturesque landscape.

The Šumava remained virtually uninhabited until the 17th and 18th centuries when the glass and timber industries attracted largely German-speaking colonists. The Schwarzenberg family lorded it over the locals until 1945 when the steep climb to the top of Perník Mountain (1,048m) with its curious rock formations. From there it is around a 3km hike to Ovesná railway station. Remember to take enough food and water to last a whole day.

3 **To Plechý Mountain (1,378m), Trojmezí and the Schwarzenberský Canal** (approx 40km) – This sometimes demanding hike takes walkers to the top of the highest mountain in the Šumava and to the meeting point of three countries' borders at Trojmezí. Starting at the railway station in Nová Pec on the trans-Šumava line, take the green trail all the way to the stunning Plešné Lake, a picture-postcard alpine lake with the forest defining its banks. From the lake a yellow trail winds its way to the top of Plechý, the highest peak in the Šumava and located on the border between the Czech Republic and Austria. Two kilometres west along the red trail which hugs the border is Trojmezí where the Czech Republic, Austria and Germany converge. Continue on to Třístoličník Mountain (1,311m) where you can end your hike 3km away at Nové Údolí railway station or carry on along a blue trail which follows the Schwarzenberský Canal, built in 1789–1822 to transport timber to the Danube. Hikers can leave the trail where it joins the Bear Trail at Jelení or further on where a green trail peels off towards Nová Pec and the railway line. Check the weather forecast before you set off into the mountains in spring and autumn and take all necessary equipment. Two days are ideal for this hike, breaking at the Berggasthof Dreisessel mountain hotel on the German side of the Třístoličník.

4 **Boubín Forest – Boubínský prales** (15km) – The Boubín Forest was declared a protected area as far back as 1858 making it one of the oldest in the world. Almost 670ha of virgin forest containing some trees estimated to be over 400 years old form the reservation, some of which is out of bounds to the public. From Lenora on the trans-Šumava rail line take the blue marked trail via Zátoň village to the Boubín Lake (Boubínské jezero), ideal for a rest and a picnic. From there continue around the perimeter of the protected forest to the top of Boubín Mountain (1,362m). From there it is around 4km to Kubova Huť which boasts the highest railway station in the Czech Republic.

population was greatly reduced following the expulsion of almost all the ethnic Germans. Despite incentives throughout the communist decades few Czechs have arrived to rejuvenate the Šumava and the population continues to fall. During the Cold War the remoteness and loneliness of the forests and mountains made this a frequented route for those fleeing from the regime to the West despite the heavily guarded border.

Getting there and away

The towns of Sušice, Vimperk, Prachatice and to a lesser extent Český Krumlov are all gateways to the Šumava. **Buses** leave Prague's Na Knížecí station (metro line B, Anděl station) for Sušice six times daily (2½ hours, 110Kč). There is also one direct early-morning **train** service a day from the main railway station (3 hours 40 minutes, 224Kč) otherwise the rail journey is tedious. Buses also depart Na Knížecí for Vimperk five times a day (2¼ hours, 100Kč). For information on getting to and from Prachatice and Český Krumlov see pages 223 and 218.

Getting around

The trans-Šumava railway line provides a scenic way of getting from one end of the region to the other. Line 194 follows the course of the Vltava from České Budějovice to Volary (3 hours) via Český Krumlov, Černá v Pošumaví, Horní Planá and Černý Kříž. Seven trains a day brave the route whatever the weather and a ticket for the whole stretch costs 120Kč. At Volary the tracks divide with line 208 snaking its way north to Strakonice (2½ hours, 98Kč) via Lenora and Vimperk while line 197 heads northeast to Prachatice (40 minutes, 40Kč). Slow and infrequent services require patience and stamina from the traveller!

PÍSEK

Founded in the mid 13th century by Václav I, the town of Písek (which means 'sand' in Czech) sits on the river Otava, traversed by the town's most famous landmark, the medieval Stone Bridge, older than Prague's Charles Bridge and the oldest in Bohemia. Gold put Písek on the map and the town derives its name from the sand from which the gold was panned. The 13th century saw the town's biggest gold rush though in the 1990s the industry was almost revived before environmentalists stepped in to avoid the area's waterways suffering devastating cyanide pollution.

Rich, prosperous and privileged under the Přemyslid dynasty, Písek took the side of the Hussites in 1419 and grew even richer after the Hussite wars as a virtual independent city state. All that ended in the mid 16th century when first a fire put paid to half the town then Ferdinand I punished the inhabitants for their support of the estates against the Habsburgs in 1547 by confiscating property and withdrawing privileges. The town, which supported the estates again at the Battle of the White Mountain, hit its lowest point in 1620 when, after a ferocious attack by imperial forces led by Count Buquoy only the women, children and 13 men were left alive. Písek never regained its former glory, but had it continued in its prosperity it may have grown into a major Czech city.

Getting there and away

Písek lies approximately 100km south of Prague and 50km north of České Budějovice. There are regular **buses** to Písek from Prague's Na Knížecí station (1½ hours, 80Kč). There are up to 14 buses a day between Písek and České Budějovice. The journey from Prague can be done by **train** but takes an hour longer. The *Otava* service, named after the river flowing through Písek, takes 2½ hours to complete the journey. Otherwise a change in Zdice on the Prague–Pilsen main line on to southbound services is required. There are reasonably frequent direct rail services to Tábor, and one a day to Pilsen.

The bus and railway stations are a few hundred metres away from each other. From both simply follow Nádražní Street to the centre, 15 minutes on foot.

Tourist information

The information centre (*Heydukova 97;* ╲/f *382 213 592*) has comprehensive information on the town and the region, public internet access for 30Kč per half-hour, sells maps, guides and souvenirs, and can help with timetables, tickets, accommodation and tour guides.

Where to stay

Hotel Bílá Růže Fráni Šrámka 169; ╲ 382 214 931; f 382 219 002. Fráni Šrámka Street runs off Velké Square to the south of the Church of the Holy Cross. The Bílá Růže (White Rose) is one of the town's most popular hotels offering accommodation in 25 reasonably well-furnished en-suite rooms, some with nice views of the river below. It also has a large restaurant and beer hall. Sgl with breakfast costs around 800Kč, dbl around 1,100Kč.

Hotel Pod Skalou Podkalí 158; \/f 382 214 753; www.hotelpodskalou.cz. This small 16-room hotel is situated by the river beneath the town walls (the name means 'Hotel under the cliff'). To reach it, follow Fráni Šrámka Street to the end then turn back on yourself heading to the river on the left. Comfortable sgls here without breakfast cost 420Kč, dbls 840Kč.

City Hotel Alšovo náměstí 35; \ 382 215 634; f 382 215 192; www.cityhotel.cz. The 3-star City has 19 reasonable rooms with TV, minibar and bathroom for 850Kč for a sgl and 1,330Kč for dbl with a slight reduction off season.

Where to eat

Restaurace U Reinerů Heydukova 98; \ 382 213 484. To the right of the information centre take the passage leading to Palackého sady park. The restaurant U Reinerů is immediately to your left. For my money this is probably the best place to get a bite to eat and down a beer. Czech traditional dishes for 100–170Kč are served in the large wood-panelled dining space, very lively when full. Outdoor seating in summer and Pilsner Urquell beer on tap.

Jihočeská restaurace Komenského 56; \ 382 212 861. *Jihočeská* means 'south Bohemian' but there is nothing really traditional about this place, not to say it is not one of the best places to eat in town. Situated in the former Hotel Otava on the corner of Komenského and Chelčického streets, main courses are served for 80–230Kč and pizzas for around 100Kč under the high ceilings of this stylish late 19th-century building.

Restaurace U Přemysla Otakara II Velké náměstí 114; \ 382 212 132. Those who search for this establishment on the square will do so in vain, as it is tucked away in the courtyard of the castle behind the town hall. For a restaurant at a tourist sight it has very reasonable prices (all main courses for around 110Kč except beef dishes which cost double that) and has a cosy, quite stylish dining space in a historical setting.

What to see and do

The large white **Church of the Virgin Mary** is the first sight of note you will see on arriving in the historical centre from the bus and railway stations. Dating from the mid 13th century it is a fine example of the early Gothic style. The interior with its low arches and simple vaulted ceiling is worth a look. The 70m-high tower dates from 1489. Písek's Baroque **town hall** is the large yellow building on Velké Square. Built between 1740 and 1767, it is also the entrance to the secluded courtyard of **Písek Castle** and the superb **Prácheňské Museum**. The castle, like many of Písek's sites, has its origins in the 13th century, and was built for King Přemysl Otakar II. It originally had three towers and four wings, only one of which has survived to the museum (*admission 30/10Kč*). Písek should be held up to all other towns in the Czech Republic as an example of what a regional museum should look like, with one criticism: none of the exhibits is marked in English. Peruse the collections on gold panning, the south Bohemian fish industry complete with aquaria containing fish from the region, prehistory until the break-up of Czechoslovakia including Nazi and communist exhibits, flora and fauna of the region and heaps more.

Along from the town hall on Velké Square is the **Church of the Holy Cross**, once part of a Dominican monastery, razed to the ground in 1419 by the Hussites, enraged at the local priest's refusal to give them Holy Communion *sub utraque specie*. The monastery was reinstated during the Counter-Reformation but then abolished under Austrian Emperor Joseph II. The church's impressive Renaissance sgraffito-etched façade dates from the time the building served as a salt house. The interior is a simple affair with a small Baroque altar. Behind the church the **town walls** (accessible from Fráni Šrámka Street) drop down to the Otava River, on the banks of which stands the town's first power station, now converted into a **Technical Museum**.

Follow the river north to Písek's best-known landmark, the **Stone Bridge** (Kamenný most, the original name for Charles Bridge too) which has connected the banks of the Otava for over eight centuries, making it the oldest bridge in Bohemia. It may be older than Prague's most celebrated bridge but Charles Bridge it is not. This very modest, simple structure boasts a mere four statues, but does have a flock of swans bobbing under its arches like its more illustrious cousin.

North of Písek

The Otava joins the Vltava just north of Písek to form the Orlík reservoir. Two dramatic castles can be found here – **Zvíkov**, 15km north of Písek, and **Orlík**, 8km further upriver. Gothic Zvíkov, built on a rocky crag which used to be high above the river, has kept its medieval appearance while Orlík underwent the usual neo-Gothic rebuild in the 19th century. Both are open April–October. Zvíkovské podhradí can be reached by bus from Písek (30 minutes, 18Kč) but only five buses a day go to Orlík and a day trip can be difficult. Between the two castles walking (14km), cycling or boat in summer are all options.

TÁBOR

If untouched medieval towns steeped in history are what you are in search of in the Czech Republic, then Tábor, south Bohemia's second city, is the place for you. This Hussite fortress town built high on a mountain above the river Lužnice has a remarkable history, and can be visited in a day from Prague. Its foundation was linked to one of the most turbulent times in Czech history, and its very existence is testament to the strength of the Hussite movement in the Czech lands. One could spend hours exploring the narrow, medieval streets of the old town designed especially with protruding houses to hinder the progress of potential enemies and make it easier to defend. Almost every building is a fine example of the dominant architectural styles in the Czech lands since the 15th century.

History

This hill above the River Lužnice had always been a natural place of human settlement even before the Hussites decided to turn it into their power base. There is evidence of a Celtic settlement here, and in the 13th century Přemysl Otakar II founded the castle and town of Hradiště. Kotnov Castle, of which only the tower remains, was built here by the Vítek family in the 14th century.

The town of Tábor we see today was founded by followers of Jan Hus in 1420, five years after he had died at the hands of the Church Council in Constance. Hus's ideas had wide acceptance in south Bohemia, and he had written some of his major works at places in the area. The hill on which the town stands had the biblical name Tábor, and all of these factors, plus its strategic and easily defendable location made it the ideal place for the radical Hussites to found a community where they could live according to the Bible, and transform their vision of society into reality.

At the end of the Hussite revolution the town was granted royal status by none other than the arch enemy of the Hussites, King Zikmund. However, Tábor went on rejecting the power of the Czech kings until it was conquered by Jiří of Poděbrady in 1452. The end of the 15th century brought peace and normality to Tábor, as the town shed its role as a fortress, and a town hall and the Church of the Lord's Conversion on Mount Tábor were added. In 1492, the oldest artificial

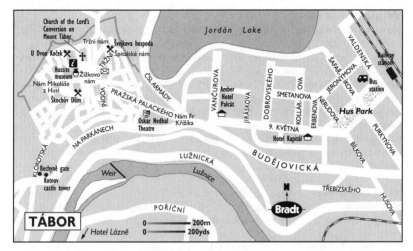

lake in central Europe was created by damming the Tisemnický Stream. It also bears a biblical name, Jordán, and provided the town with drinking water. The town suffered two huge fires in 1532 and 1559 which destroyed the many wooden structures, but these were replaced by sgraffito-decorated Renaissance buildings, many of which can still be admired today in all their glory. The subterranean passageways burrowing a few metres under the main square and used to store beer, ammunition and food, were begun in the 15th century.

In accordance with its tradition of defiance of Catholic Europe, the town refused to swear allegiance to the Habsburgs in 1618, but this proved costly as the town was pillaged by imperial troops in 1621. The Swedish did likewise during the Thirty Years War. The end of the 17th and beginning of the 18th century brought peace, recovery and relative prosperity.

During the Czech National Revival interest in the Hussites was reawakened, and in 1878 a museum was created in Tábor devoted solely to the period, a neglected part of Czech history up until then. Interest continued after the founding of the independent Czechoslovak state as the Czechs continued to rediscover their past. Tábor was not left untouched by the Nazi occupation with the persecution of its Jewish inhabitants, the destruction of the Jewish cemetery and the execution of 156 people in the town.

Getting there and away

Day trippers from Prague can use several direct **train** services a day from the main station (1½ hours, 130Kč). Probably the slightly better option to Tábor is the **bus**, with services departing Florenc coach station around once an hour (1½ hours, 70Kč). Tábor is also an hour or so away from České Budějovice by train; buses take slightly longer.

The bus and railway stations are next to each other. Walk the length of Hus Park and veer right along 9 května Street until you reach Palackého and Pražská streets, and eventually the main Žižkovo Square.

Tourist information

The information centre (Žižkovo nám 2; ☏ +381 486 230; f +381 486 239) is the essential place to start. The obliging staff have heaps of information on Tábor, the Tábor region and south Bohemia. They can also book accommodation.

Where to stay

Hotel Lázně Čelkovice 44; ↘ 381 202 511; f 381 202 513; www.lazne.genea2000.cz. By the river Lužnice this is one of only 2 4-star establishments in town. It is a bit of a hike to the historical centre though. It has 15 comfortable rooms and prices range from 2,000–2,500Kč for sgls and dbls alike.

Amber Hotel Palcát tř 9 května 2471; ↘ 381 252 901; f 381 252 905. This hotel looks about as appealing as the Hussite mace it is named after, but the rooms are of a good standard and prices start from a very reasonable 570Kč for a sgl and 960Kč for a dbl.

Hotel Kapitál tř 9 května 617; ↘ 381 256 096; f 381 252 411. Further along 9 května from the Palcát, heading out of town this place looks and feels better. It has 26 reasonably spacious rooms, and represents good value at 900Kč for a sgl with breakfast, and 1,200Kč for a dbl.

Where to eat

Škochův dům Žižkovo nám 22; ↘ 381 251 221 This recently opened place is next to the museum, and has a wide-ranging menu with dishes from 90–240Kč. Enjoy your food outside in summer on the main square or under the Gothic vaulting inside.

Restaurace U Dvou Koček Svatošova 310; ↘ 381 256 802. More food and Gothic vaulting can be found here, with hearty Czech favourites from 50–200Kč washed down with Pilsner Urquell beer.

Švejkova hospoda Špitalské nám 509; ↘ 381 257 733. For the kitschy Czech pub experience, seek out this typical theme pub where you will pay 60–200Kč for main dishes. They also pull a delicious Gambrinus.

What to see and do
Žižkovo Square

A Renaissance fountain dating from 1568 and the statue of Jan Žižka adorn the main square. The original statue by Myslbek dating from 1884 had to be replaced by the one we see now. On every side the square is bordered by fine Gothic, Baroque and Renaissance houses. Next to the information centre stands the late Gothic town hall housing the Hussite Museum.

Church of the Lord's Conversion on Mount Tábor

The church bearing the name recalling this biblical event stands in the corner of Žižkovo Square to the right of the information centre. It was originally a wooden structure but was rebuilt in the 1480s in the late Gothic style, to which Renaissance and Baroque elements were added over the centuries. One can peer into the church for free, though most of it is roped off. Fit and adventurous visitors can climb the 200 steps to the top of the 84m-high **church tower** (*20/10Kč*). The enormous Václav bell blocks the way halfway up (not the one that chimes, it must be added), and stooping under it is quite a feat.

Hussite Museum

If you do not have a particular interest in the subject, the Hussite Museum (*admission 60/30Kč*) may be a let-down, though it does have some interesting individual exhibits. The ten rooms trace the development of the Hussite movement from its origins to its significance in the Czech National Revival. The Hussite weapons and a scale model of the town, illustrating just how difficult it must have been to take by force, are some of the highlights. Next to the ticket booth stands a replica of a primitive early tank invented by the Hussite military genius Jan Žižka, the *hejtman* of Tábor, possibly the first ever used in battle.

Approximately once every half-hour in summer, less often out of season, a tour leaves for the **underground cellars and passageways**. There are an estimated 12–14km of subterranean spaces under Tábor's historical centre, but the tour covers a comfortable 650m of them. The temperature underground is a constant 7–8°C so take a jacket or sweater (*admission 40/20Kč*).

Other places of interest

The **Bechyně Gate** and **Kotnov Castle Tower** are about ten minutes' walk from Žižkovo Square. The Gothic gate is the only one remaining in Tábor, and houses an exhibition of Life and Work in Medieval Society. The tower is the only remaining part of Kotnov Castle which over time was gradually pulled down wing by wing to make way for a brewery. For 20/10Kč you can climb to the top for views of the river Lužnice and surrounding countryside. As can be seen in the Hussite Museum the whole of Tábor used to be ringed by town walls constructed by the Hussites and, it is claimed, the most impenetrable in central Europe. Most of them were knocked down in the 19th century, but parts remain around the Žižka Bastion in the northwest corner of the historical centre.

TŘEBOŇ

Lying halfway between Jindřichův Hradec and České Budějovice in a lowland region called the Třeboň Basin, peppered with scenic artificial lakes and ponds, the town of Třeboň remains deeply involved in its traditional industries of fishing, brewing and forestry, as well as serving as a relaxing spa. Nowhere else in the country has man altered the natural surroundings to such an extent as here, with huge fishponds covering a large percentage of the region and providing leisure, a living for the local people, fish at Christmas and for the restaurants of the town, and a unique UNESCO biosphere reserve. Add to this a town brimming with fine examples of historical architecture, a pretty square, an unexpected castle and delicious local Regent beer, and Třeboň becomes a place worthy of any visitor's attention.

In the 12th century a small settlement existed here sheltered by thick forest and owned by the eminent nobleman, Vítek of Prčice, along with vast swathes of south Bohemia. By 1300, it was a walled town and in 1366 it came into the possession of the Rožmberk clan, under whose rule it prospered. Its strong walls, castle, moat and the surrounding marshlands halted even the marauding Hussites during the 15th century. The second half of that century witnessed the creation of the first lakes and the naissance of fish farming, ushering in Třeboň's golden era, overseen by Rožmberk estate manager, Jakub Krčín of Jelčany, the father of the lakes. His monument looks proudly out over Svět Lake south of the town. As in Jindřichův Hradec, the Rožmberks were eventually replaced by the Schwarzenbergs, the last owners of the estate, who left a neo-Gothic mausoleum in parkland south of the town, one of Třeboň's highlights. The town's appearance dates mostly from the end of the 18th century, rebuilt after the last major fire in 1781.

Getting there and away

A single **bus** a day travels from Prague to Třeboň leaving Florenc at 14.30 and arriving three hours later. The **train** is slightly quicker, but involves a change in Veselí nad Lužnicí. Tickets cost 184Kč. Třeboň is equidistant from České Budějovice and Jindřichův Hradec, and bus is the best way to travel to and from both towns (30 minutes in both directions, 20–40Kč).

Třeboň has two railway stations, Třeboň and Třeboň lázně (spa). Both are on a branch line running from Veselí nad Lužnicí to the border with Austria. The Třeboň lázně stop is closer to the historical centre. The bus station is roughly 1½km from Masarykovo Square along Táboritská Street, Palackého Square and Sokolská Street.

Tourist information
The small municipal information centre (*Masarykovo náměstí 103;* ↘ *+384 721;* f *384 721 356; www.trebon-mesto.cz*) is next to the town hall and produces helpful guides to the town as well as accommodation lists.

Where to stay
Hotel Bílý Koníček Masarykovo nám 97; ↘/f 384 721 213; www.hotelbilykonicek.cz. The 'White Horse', as the name translates, is housed in the turreted Renaissance sugar cube at the corner of Masarykovo Square and Petra Voka Street. Its 23 en-suite rooms represent good value and are light and airy. The restaurant downstairs is a touch pub-like, and there are better places in town. Sgls without breakfast are 600–800Kč, dbls 800–1,000Kč.
Hotel Zlatá Hvězda Masarykovo nám 107; ↘ 384 757 111; f 384 757 300; www.zhvezda.cz. Třeboň's top hotel has 48 4-star rooms spread throughout the Baroque interiors of 3 town houses. It has some simply gorgeous rooms and suites, well worth the price. A sgl is 1,620Kč, a dbl 1,980Kč. Rates drop by around a third in low season.
Pension U Míšků Husova 11; ↘ 384 721 698; f 384 723 917; www.misek.cz. Behind the double folk Baroque façade of the Pension U Míšků, near the Church of St Giles, hide 6 modern rooms, an intimate restaurant and a petite swimming pool and sauna. It is a truly charming place to stay, and very reasonable at 1,200Kč for a sgl and 1,650Kč for a dbl.

Where to eat
Malá Bašta Masarykovo nám 87; ↘ 384 722 563. This small, no-nonsense restaurant specialising in local fish and game dishes is located at the chateau end of the square. Enjoy your meal out on the square, weather permitting. Local fish feature heavily on the menu, and mains cost 90–300Kč. Local Regent beer is on tap.
Bílý Jednorožec Žižkovo nám 46; ↘ 384 701 723; www.bilyjednorozec.crnet.cz. The name of this smallish restaurant translates as 'White Unicorn' and can be found along an alley next to the Svinenská Gate. Again the menu is heavy on local fish which can be washed down with the local Regent brew. The friendly waiters will gladly serve hungry diners mains for a very reasonable 80–140Kč in the modern dining space, or outside in the small yard.
Šupina Valy 155; ↘ 384 721 149; www.supina.cz. Across the road from the Regent Brewery is this modern eatery, whose name has a fishy association, translating as 'Fish Scale'. The interior is draped in fish nets, shells etc. It is probably the best place in town for local fish dishes and Regent beer, which does not have far to travel. The service is first-rate and mains are 100–300Kč.

What to see and do
Chateau
Třeboň's ostentatious Renaissance chateau occupies a large share of the southwest corner of the historical centre, giving on to both the square and the Chateau Park (*open Apr–Oct; closed Mon*). Though a fort of some kind had stood here before the arrival of the Rožmberks, a great fire in 1562 provided an

opportune moment to rebuild it into the proud structure we see today. The rebirth of the chateau is usually credited to Petr Vok, the last of the Rožmberks, but it was begun by his brother Vilém. Petr Vok is famous for his reckless and flamboyant character, selling off Český Krumlov to Rudolf II to pay his debts.

Třeboň's premier tourist attraction is open for business April–October. The only way to see the chateau is to join one of three guided tours:

Route A Rožmberks' Renaissance interiors, 50/25Kč in Czech, 90/50Kč in English
Route B Schwarzenbergs' private apartments, 60/30Kč in Czech, 120/60Kč in English
Route C Part of route A and all of route B, 70/35Kč in Czech, 140/70Kč in English

Route A focuses on the history of Třeboň, the Rožmberks' fixation with fishponds, and the Renaissance chateau built by Petr Vok and his brother. Route B leads visitors through the 19th-century private living quarters of the Schwarzenberg family, which they used as their Christmas residence. The guides acquaint visitors with the history of the family and last private owners of the chateau, focusing on some of the most notable personalities of the 19th and 20th centuries. Route C offers the broadest overview.

Historical centre

Třeboň's intimate **Masarykovo Square** is one of the most pleasing to the eye in the country. A jumble of pallid Renaissance and Baroque gables and interrupted arcading surround a miniature plague column in the centre which could easily be overlooked. Dominating the square is the 31m-tall tower of the former town hall. Třeboň is a rarity in having three surviving **town gates**, all still serving their original purpose. The **Budějovická Gate** forms the only entrance to the centre from Sokolská Street and the Chateau Park. The **Novohradská Gate** stands superfluously behind the **Svinenská Gate** near the **Regent Brewery** to the south, home of Regent beer since 1379, one of the country's best brews but hardly obtainable outside of south Bohemia.

From the chateau end of the square follow Březanova Street to the neat Gothic **Church of St Giles** (Kostel sv Jiljí). Built sometime before 1280, it has tall cream façades, conservative flying buttresses and a Baroque interior including an impressive Baroque altar which fills the back wall of the sanctuary. You can peek inside year round. The **Augustine Monastery**, founded in 1367 by the Rožmberks, lurks behind the church.

Outside Třeboň

Leave the historical centre via the Novohradská and Svinenská gates and you will arrive at the Svět Lake. Created by Jakub of Jelčany, it met with protests from townspeople, afraid of flooding should the dyke just outside the town walls burst. Because of widespread hatred for the lake, it was at first christened 'Nevděk' meaning 'Ingratitude' but later renamed. The townspeople's fears became a reality, but not until 1890. Turn left at the dyke and skirt around the lake past the fishery to the park containing the ghoulish neo-Gothic **Schwarzenberg Mausoleum**, dating from the 1870s (*open Apr–Oct*). A guided tour takes visitors down into the crypt of this strangely out-of-the-way display of Schwarzenberg wealth and power. It will come as no surprise that the Schwarzenberg's chief architect, Deworetzký, creator of the mausoleum, also worked on the neo-Gothic transformation of Hluboká.

The Třeboň region is pockmarked with manmade lakes and ponds, and Rožmberk a few kilometres north of the town is the largest in the Czech Republic, measuring a massive 489ha. Literally hundreds of smaller lakes stretch from Veselí nad Lužnicí in the north to the Austrian border and form the CHKO Třeboňsko, the Třeboň protected area.

JINDŘICHŮV HRADEC

Picturesque Jindřichův Hradec is a small town with a large castle, the chief motive for travelling there. The town is flanked to the west by the Nežárka River, to the east by the Vajgar Lake, which feeds the castle moat. The castle mirrored in the tranquil waters of the lake on a balmy summer evening can be one of the prettiest panoramas in the region. The town also has an attractive central square, and some interesting churches.

The town's double-barrelled name means 'Henry's Castle', referring to Vítek of Prčice's eldest son Jindřich (translates as Henry), who had a Gothic castle built where an original Slavic fort had stood. Vítek of Prčice was an important 12th century nobleman who, it is said, divided his estate between his five sons, thus creating the most powerful noble families in south Bohemia – the Vítkovci, who were the lords of Landštejn, Stráž, Ústí, Rožmberk and Hradec. Each of these branches has a five-petalled rose of a different colour in their coat of arms, making south Bohemia the land of the rose.

The best-known legend tied to the town concerns the White Lady (Bílá paní), said to roam the castle, warning of forthcoming events by donning different-coloured gloves, red prophesying fire, black an unfortunate event, and white a happy event such as a birth or marriage. The whole story is based around a real person, Perchta of Rožmberk, who was unhappily married to Jindřich of Hradec, a violent, unpleasant man. After his death she continued to live in the castle, and do good deeds such as cooking up a sweet gruel to give to the poor of the town on Maundy Thursday. Her ghost is said to appear when this is not done. She is a good ghost and nothing to be afraid of, should you catch sight of her. It must be added that there are several versions of the above story and the White Lady is said to have appeared in several other castles in the five-petalled rose towns.

Getting there and away

Jindřichův Hradec is situated around 120km south of Prague and 50km east of České Budějovice on the main road linking Brno with south Bohemia, and the railway line between the junction at Veselí nad Lušnicí and Jihlava. From the capital five **buses** a day make the journey via Tábor (2½ hours,86Kč). There are direct buses to and from České Budějovice (hourly, 38Kč), but to and from Jihlava the **train** is the better choice with services running up to once an hour (1 hour 20 minutes, 88Kč). The three-hour journey to Brno is best done by bus as this is the cheapest option (approximately once every 2 hours, 130Kč). Jindřichův Hradec is linked to villages to the north and south by a narrow-gauge railway which runs erratically throughout the day. The service north ends in Obrataň on the Pelhřimov–Tábor line.

The bus and railway stations are next to each other approximately 15–20 minutes' walk from the historical centre.

Tourist information

The municipal information centre (*Panská 136;* ℡ *384 363 546; www.jh.cz*) provides information on the region, helps with accommodation, guides and timetables, and sells tickets for local events.

Where to stay
Hotel Grand nám Míru 165; ☏ 384 361 252; f 384 361 251; www.grand-jh.cz. The Grand stands on the main square opposite the town hall. It has 26 respectable 3-star-standard rooms with bathrooms, some perhaps on the cramped side. Sgls cost from 850Kč, dbls from 990Kč. The hotel also offers a range of relaxation and wellness procedures.
Hotel Vajgar nám Míru 162; ☏ 384 361 271; f 384 361 270; www.hotel-vajgar.cz. A hotel since the 19th century, it is named after the lake to its rear. There are 21 OK rooms, with sgls for as little as 360Kč without bathroom, rising to around 700Kč for a dbl with bathroom.
Hotel Concertino nám Míru 141; ☏ 384 362 320–2; f 384 362 323; www.concertino.cz. By far the most luxurious hotel in town, the Concertino, run by the Orea chain (like the Grand) is also on the main square. It has 37 immaculate, discerningly furnished en-suite rooms. Expect to pay around 1,000–1,500Kč for a sgl with breakfast in high season, 1,700–2,500Kč for a dbl.

Where to eat
Restaurants are rather thin on the ground in Jindřichův Hradec and most probably find themselves in the slightly pricey hotel restaurants on the square.

Krčma U Jáchyma Dobrovského 1; ☏ 384 363 462; www. krcmaujachyma.unas.cz. You will find this medium-sized eatery in the first courtyard of the chateau on the left as you enter. Once an outbuilding belonging to the chateau it has an arched roof and modern décor. Mains come for a rather steep 110–300Kč and Urquell beer is on tap. From the menu try the White Lady's Gruel, apparently prepared according to the original recipe. You have to try it to find out what is in it, but the White Lady herself cooked it up from an appetising mixture of semolina, warm beer, honey and poppy seed oil!
Grand Hotel nám Míru 165; ☏ 384 361 252. The most acceptable of the hotel restaurants on the main square, this is not at all a bad place with a wide selection of international staples for up to 160Kč, pizzas for 100Kč, vegetarian dishes and Urquell beer.
Hostinec Měšťan Panská 102; ☏ 384 364 262. Something of a Hradec institution, the Měšťan was getting a facelift at the time of writing. It is outside the historical centre on the busy Panská shopping street. Apparently it was and will be a great place to eat and drink.
Kaštánek Masarykovo nám 168. If it is just a quick coffee and a cream cake you are after, try this modern *cukrárna* at the junction of Masaryk Square and Klášterská Street. Czech prices and traditional tooth-rotters are the norm here.

What to see and do
Castle
The principal reason for travelling to Jindřichův Hradec is to visit the castle, the third largest in the country after Prague and Český Krumlov. The stern façades of the building give away little of the exquisite interiors, with 320 rooms housing over 10,000 works of art. Three noble families owned the chateau over seven centuries. Before that a Slav fortress stood on the site. The Černín family lost the chateau in 1945 when Evžen Alfons Černín, the last owner, was accused of collaboration with the Nazis. The chateau gained its Renaissance appearance in 1560, but was almost completely destroyed in a fire in 1773. It took many years and 120 million Czech crowns to restore it to its former glory, a process completed in 1993, since which time it has been welcoming visitors from April until September.

There are three guided tours on offer:

Route A The Renaissance castle
Route B The Gothic castle
Route C 18th and 19th centuries

All tours cost 70/35Kč in Czech, 140/70Kč in a foreign language. To take all three tours costs 360/180Kč.

Other places of interest

The town's central plaza is **náměstí Míru**, with its fine Renaissance town houses behind 18th- and 19th-century pastel façades, and the immense, chunky Baroque **Trinity Column**, topped with a radiating Baroque sun. House No 88 is the **Old Town Hall**, rebuilt in 1801 after a fire. Note the stucco coat of arms of the town above the entrance with two lions bearing a rose and the 'W' of Vladislav Jagelonský, added in 1483. The black-and-white sgraffito-scored house Nos 138 and 139 is the **Langrův dům**. One of the oldest houses in town, it is adorned with scenes from the Old Testament, and reposes on the only arcading on the square.

Heading northeast along Svatojánská Street, one arrives at the **Church of John the Baptist** and the **Minorite Monastery**. The church is the oldest in Jindřichův Hradec, almost certainly founded in 1320 on the arrival of the Minorite order, but evidence exists of a Romanesque church on the site prior to this. It is open to be viewed in July and August only.

The **Church of the Ascension of our Lady** can be located by passing under the coat of arms on the town hall and continuing uphill for around 50m. The Gothic church dates from the second half of the 14th century, and sits directly on the 15°E line of longitude. The lords of the manor, mainly from the Hradec family, are buried in the crypt and its lofty tower can be climbed in summer. You can sneak into the church for a peek when a service is taking place but otherwise it is locked up. Across Balbínovo Square is the former Jesuit Seminary, where the famous 17th-century historian Bohuslav Balbín taught from 1655 to 1661, which now houses the **Regional Museum** (*admission 40/20Kč*). Apart from exhibits on archaeology, clocks, historical painted targets and the parlour of the opera singer, Ema Destinnová, who lived in the nearby village of Stráž nad Nežárkou, the museum's pride and joy is a mechanical Nativity scene (Krýzovy jesličky). A local, Tomáš Krýza, whiled away an incredible 60 years crafting the 60m² scene, involving 1,398 figures of which 133 come to life, earning it an entry in the *Guinness Book of Records*. Next to the museum along Nežárecká Street stands the town's last remaining gate, the **Nežárecká Gate**. Pass through this and take a left into a winding cobbled medieval street to view the last remnants of the town walls. Continue along the street to the lock that holds the Malý Vajgar Lake in place.

Heading out of town towards the railway station at the top of Klášterská Street is the bulky red-and-cream early Baroque **Monastery of St Catherine** (not open to the public) dating from 1479, with a curious bridge arching over a side street into the former Franciscan monastery, now the town court.

Around Jindřichův Hradec
Červená Lhota

Like a red sugar cube about to sink into a lake-sized tea cup, the Renaissance chateau of Červená Lhota 20km north of Jindřichův Hradec is the tourist brochure-designer's dream and one of the most popular images from the country.

NARROW-GAUGE RAILWAY
Those with a soft spot for anything that runs along tracks will be fascinated by the Jindřichohradecké místní dráhy, JHMD for short, a narrow-gauge railway running north of the town to Obrataň (46km) and south to Nová Bystřice (33km) on the border with Austria. It is the only working narrow-gauge railway in the country. Although pint-size steam trains ply the lines once a day in summer, this is by no means a tourist attraction, but a real, year-round, functioning railway, with services throughout the day. The narrow-gauge station in Jindřichův Hradec is in front of the main station to the right. Timetables can be found at www.vlak.cz.

Unfortunately it is so hard to reach by public transport and so disappointing close up that your only sight of this red chateau, built on a rock in the middle of a lake may be from the glossy tourist bumf.

SLAVONICE
Squeezed tight up against the border with Austria, the small, provincial town of Slavonice is another of the Czech Republic's practically undiscovered treasures. Unlike Telč 25km to the north, Slavonice was hardly Baroque-ified and sports more elaborate Renaissance sgraffito work and original 16th-century architectural features than its more frequented neighbour, so much so, that it is a candidate to be added to UNESCO's world heritage list. To my mind Slavonice is a touch more pleasing to the eye than Telč, as it has undergone less renovation, and has a used, lived-in ambience. This is one of my personal favourites and I strongly recommend taking the trouble to reach this extremity of the Czech lands.

The 2,000 inhabitants of today's Slavonice owe the beauty of their town to an economic boom in the mid 16th century thanks to its position at the halfway point on the post road between Prague and Vienna. In its prime the town had 156 houses and 11,000 inhabitants. But as one tourist brochure reads: 'In the last 350 years Slavonice has seen marked decline – thanks goodness …'. To explain, a series of events from the Thirty Years War to the rerouting of the post road, and more recently the expulsion of most of the inhabitants (ethnic Germans) in 1945 and the unwelcome proximity of the Iron Curtain isolating it from Austria just 1½ km away have put the town's development on ice for 300 years. The result is an almost perfectly preserved Gothic-Renaissance centre, undoubtedly one of the finest in central Europe.

Getting there and away
Connections are abysmal in this part of the country, and Slavonice is no exception. The tiny **railway** station is end of the line as far as Czech Railways go. Despite the railway station in the village of Fratres on the Austrian side of the border, an ongoing legacy of the Cold War is the absence of any rail link from Slavonice. Slavonice is at the end of a branch line (Telč–Slavonice) which runs from another branch line (Kostelec u Jihlavy–Telč) making for a slow, patience-testing journey. **Bus** connections between the two towns are even worse as a change is necessary in Dačice, and the journey takes up to two hours! Take the train, but plan ahead.

The railway station is five minutes' walk past the cemetery from the main square. The bus station is on the other side of the town down a passageway next to the town hall.

Tourist information

The superb information centre (*Náměstí Míru 480;* ☎ *384 493 320; www.slavonice-mesto.cz*) is on the main square above the Cukrárna Šárka. Check out the murals on the walls of the office and the amazing Renaissance diamond vaulting at the foot of the stairs.

Where to stay

Hotel Arkáda nám Míru 466; ☎ 384 408 408; f 384 408 401; www.hotelarkada.cz. The pink and white façade of the Arkáda is right in the thick of things on the main square, surrounded by the town's architectural wealth. The 19 en-suite 3-star rooms are a touch basic but comfortable enough. Prices range from 380Kč per person for a dbl in winter to 620Kč for a sgl in summer. The more nights you stay, the cheaper the room. Breakfast costs an extra 70kč.

Hotel U Růže nám Míru 452; ☎ 384 493 004; f 384 493 987; www.dumuruze.cz. The 'House at the Rose' stands at the thin end of the main square. The rooms are of a higher standard than the Arkáda's, but are more expensive. Sgls cost 900–1,100Kč, dbls 1,200–1,500Kč. Breakfast is an extra 100Kč. The room rate includes free use of the sauna, solarium and pool and cycle hire.

Where to eat

Apetito nám Míru 478; ☎ 384 493 438. Apetito is a basic Czech eatery on the first floor of house No 478 across the square from the Arkáda Hotel. Despite the indifferent staff the dining room has a cosy feel, and the wide selection of mainly Czech mains are cheap at 75–160Kč. There is Slovak Zlatý bažant and Gambrinus on tap.

Besídka Horní nám 52; ☎ 384 493 293. The trendy, arty Besídka is just off the main square heading towards the Jemnická Gate. The 2 rooms are a pleasant mix of snack bar, restaurant and gallery. Admire the works of art as you tuck into mains for around 100Kč washed down with one of a selection of beers. There is a garden and on-square seating in summer and you can even stay the night here in one of the 11 dbls for around 1,000Kč.

What to see and do

The best of Slavonice's Renaissance architecture can be found on the main square **náměstí Míru** and the adjoining **Horní náměstí**. The rows of perfectly preserved 16th-century town houses sporting intricately etched sgrafitto, wonderfully shaped symmetrical gables and chunky diamond vaulting inside are a truly amazing sight. The most endearing thing about the buildings is that this is no deserted tourist reserve, and life still goes on behind the sgrafitto – TVs babble, babies cry, children play and the townsfolk sit outside on warm summer evenings and chat.

Of Slavonice's tourist sights, perhaps the best known is the **Lutheran prayer room** (*admission 20Kč, short tours with guide*) at Horní náměstí No 517 which inexplicably survived the Counter-Reformation. The frescoes from 1559 pre-date the hall's use as a prayer room by nine years, and are surprisingly bright and clear considering they have never been renovated. The room is cluttered with an exhibition of old agricultural tools, and you can even stay the night in five rooms above the prayer room.

Of the town's three 13th-century gates, two survive. The **Dačická Gate** with its simple sgrafitto and Baroque spire stands at the end of Dačická Street north of the main square while the hefty **Jemnická Gate** still patrols traffic entering Horní náměstí. Fragments of Slavonice's **town walls** can be found in many places surrounding the squares. If you are feeling adventurous, ask at the information centre about descending into the town's **underground passages** (*admission: 130m short tour – 40/30Kč, 380m long tour – 70/40Kč*). Dating from the time of the original Gothic town, flooded cellars were linked together to flush out the water, thus creating a network of subterranean passageways. Slavonice's underground experience is like no other in the Czech lands. Visitors must don high waterproof rubber boots and wade through some wet, dank places; quite an exciting experience.

The small **museum** at house No 476 (*open May and Sep weekends, Jun–Aug Tue–Sun*) has archaeological finds from the nearby village of Pfaffenschlag that did not survive the Hussite wars, as well as other temporary exhibitions. The **Municipal Tower** next to the church hidden behind the old town hall, was built in the first half of the 16th century, and can be climbed (*open May and Sep weekends, Jun–Aug daily*) for those wishing to admire Slavonice in its entirety from above.

Artists' studios

The town's beauty and quaint atmosphere has attracted numerous artists and craftsmen to set up their studios and workshops in its narrow streets, many of which are open to visitors to come and try their hand at various crafts. Ceramic painting, textile printing and pottery are just some of the activities you can try. Ask at the information centre for details.

Border crossing into Austria

A short walk along Wolkerova from the railway station brings you to the Slavonice–Fratres pedestrian border crossing into Austria. Open 06.00–22.00, it can only be used by those not requiring a visa for either country. Fratres is a tiny village on the Austrian side with very limited connections to the rest of Austria.

Stone pine

The Highlands Region

Most visitors to the Czech Republic only glimpse the Highlands Region from an express train or a bus as it bounces its way over the concrete panels of the D1 motorway. In fact a mere 1% of all foreign tourists in the country spend a night in the region which extends roughly from Pelhřimov in the west and almost to Brno in the east. Harsh in winter, soothing in summer, the Highlands is one of the least visited, least explored and most undiscovered regions of the Czech Republic. Poor and sparsely populated it is a picturesque area of rounded wooded hills, fast-flowing rivers and winding country roads, ideal for cycling. However, it is not all countryside, and towns such as Jihlava and Třebíč have some fascinating and under-visited sights. Pretty Telč is the exception when it comes to visitor numbers, drawing coach parties and Austrian day trippers in ever increasing numbers. Up until 2001 the Highlands were divided administratively between Bohemia and Moravia and today it is even less obvious where towns such as Jihlava and Pelhřimov belong. My guess is that the region will create its own individual identity free of the wine-versus- beer stereotypes and rivalry.

GETTING AROUND

The D1 motorway bisects the Highlands and forms the principal route through the region. South of the D1, bus is the better option with all roads leading to Jihlava and many journeys requiring a change at its large bus station. North of the D1 train connections are better as the main Prague–Brno line passes through Žďár nad Sázavou.

JIHLAVA

Surrounded by a land of hills, forests and lakes, the town of Jihlava is the administrative capital of the Czech-Moravian Highlands Region. Until 1945, the town had a large German population who knew it as Igel, the German for hedgehog, hence the small prickly animal's presence on the town's coat of arms, and the name of the local brew. It came by the name as countless hedgehogs had to be evicted when the town and town walls were being built. Jihlava is a large town by Czech standards with over 50,000 inhabitants, a schizophrenic bunch, unable to agree on whether they are Czech or Moravian. Some say they take the best of both.

Jihlava owes its birth to a similar mid 13th-century silver rush as took place in Kutná Hora in the same century. From almost nothing, one of the most powerful royal towns appeared within a couple of decades, protected behind bulky impenetrable town walls encircling a vast square lined with stone houses. Its three churches, begun during this period, are testament to its wealth. The short-lived

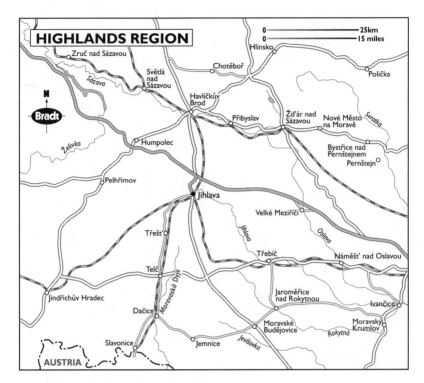

and flood-prone silver mines may have virtually run dry in the 14th century, but Jihlava continued to be a significant centre, turning to cloth to make its living, and becoming the second-largest producer in the Austrian Empire. The single most important historical event to take place in Jihlava was the declaration of the *Compactata* in 1436, bringing to an end the Hussite wars.

Jihlava may not have the largest square in the country, but its impressive cobbled expanse certainly must come close. Try not to let the carbuncle of a department store in the middle of the square, added by insensitive communist councillors, spoil your overall impression. One recent suggestion was to cover it in mirrors to reflect the surrounding historical buildings. I have another suggestion: pull it down. One interesting aspect of the square is its old flagstones, which remain thanks to the underground catacombs which carry all pipes and cables etc, meaning they never have to be dug up.

Getting there and away

The swiftest and simplest way to reach Jihlava is definitely by **bus** ($1^{3}/_{4}$ hours, 100Kč). Departures are from Florenc coach station and occasionally from Roztyly (metro line C southbound) approximately once every half-hour. Some long-distance coaches to Slovakia stop in Jihlava, and owing to its position just off the major D1 motorway there are also very regular bus connections to Brno. You can get to Jihlava from Prague by **rail** if you really want to, changing in Havlíčkův Brod en route, but the trip takes about an hour longer than the bus journey and is twice as expensive at just over 200Kč. There are also four direct trains a day between Jihlava and České Budějovice which take $2^{1}/_{2}$ hours to reach the capital of south Bohemia, with a single ticket costing 162Kč.

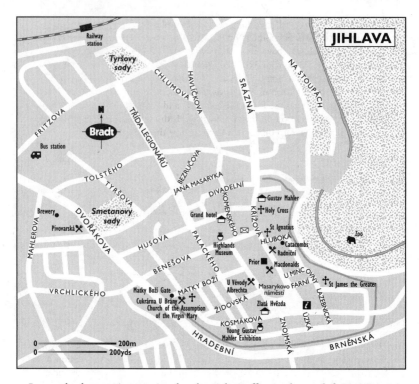

Leave the bus station passing by the ticket office and veer left into Fritzova Street then immediately left again into Dvořákova Street. The historical centre starts on the left opposite the brewery after around five minutes on foot. Jihlava has two railway stations, Jihlava město (Jihlava Town) and Jihlava hlavní (Jihlava Main Station). From Jihlava město head straight out of the building on to třída Legionářů Street which will lead you to the centre in about five minutes. The main railway station is quite a distance from Jihlava's historical centre, but trolleybuses run regularly from there to Masaryk Square.

Tourist information

Most of Jihlava's sites are in and around Masaryk Square as is the information centre (*Masarykovo nám 19;* \ *567 167 158–9;* f *567 308 034; www.jihlava.cz*). This must be one of the best centres in the country as the helpful staff seem very knowledgeable about their town and have produced comprehensive leaflets on all its features. They are also not distracted by having to sell things.

Where to stay

Grand Hotel Husova 1; \ 567 303 541; f 567 310 199; www.grandjihlava.cz. The Grand reminds guests of what a holiday to Czechoslovakia used to be like. It has many reminders of pre-revolution days, but is by no means unpleasant, and its 27 rooms are comfortable despite the nostalgia-inducing décor. Sgls come at 440Kč and dbls from 640Kč, though the very cheapest rooms do not have en-suite facilities.

Hotel Gustav Mahler Kříšová 4; \ 567 320 501; f 567 320 507; www.hotelgmahler.cz. This very pleasant hotel is housed in the former Dominican cloister and named after the town's most illustrious citizen. It boasts perfectly renovated interiors including a huge hall used for balls and classical music concerts, a stylish restaurant and 36 rooms. Sgls come at 520Kč and dbls from 810Kč though again, the very cheapest rooms do not have en-suite facilities.

Zlatá Hvězda Masarykovo nám 32; ☎ 567 309 421; f 567 309 496; www.zlatahvezda.cz. Situated at the lower end of the main square across from the information centre, this 18-room, 3-star hotel has reasonable rooms starting at 750Kč for a dbl with bathroom for sgl use including breakfast, and 950Kč for a dbl for 2 people. A tavern of some kind has stood on this site since the 14th century and the façade boasts the only Renaissance sgraffito on the square to survive the ravages of time.

Where to eat

While Jihlava is not bursting at the seams with excellent eateries, there are a couple of interesting places to dine. The Pivovarská restaurace in particular has bags of character, and if Czech pubs have taken your fancy, make sure you do not miss this one. Perhaps rather surprisingly for a Czech town of this size, Jihlava has a McDonald's (corner of the Prior department store), so if you cannot face another *knedlík*, retreat to the golden 'M' (unless they have come up with the McKnedlík by then).

U Vévody Albrechta Masarykovo nám 40/41; ☎ 567 308 074. This Jihlava favourite is actually quite hard to track down as it shares a building with several other businesses. Climb up to the first floor and follow the signs. Eat your food (70–300Kč) under dark wood beams at dark wood tables either downstairs or on the upper floor. They serve Gambrinus beer.

Radniční restaurace Masarykovo nám 66/67; ☎ 567 303 556. Almost every town in the country has a restaurant in or under its town hall and Jihlava is no exception. Czech and international standards (70–200Kč) are served in the superb dining space under Gothic vaulting daubed in medieval murals. This is a pleasant place but would have more character without the bar and the radio in the background. There is also a disco in the same building so Saturday nights may not be the time to reserve.

Pivovarská restaurace Vrchlického 2; ☎ 567 164 263. This is a gem and should not be missed by pub lovers. It is situated in the grounds of the brewery which makes the local *Ježek* (hedgehog) brand of beer. Do not worry; they do not actually brew it from the spiky creatures. It has a huge beer hall and a large beer garden outside, great in summer. With its high ceilings, murals of old Czech pub scenes and its 'sit down and drink!' kind of staff, this is how Czech public houses should be. Mains cost 55–250Kč.

Grand Hotel Husova 1; ☎ 567 303 541. The restaurant at the Grand Hotel is not a bad place to eat. It has a few obvious reminders of pre-revolution hospitality, but is pleasant nonetheless. Czech and international main courses can be consumed for 70–180Kč.

Cukrárna U Brány Matky Boží 37; ☎ 567 303 256. This is a cosy little coffee and cakes place next to the U Matky Boží Gate with a wide range of desserts, gateaux and other assorted tooth-rotters.

What to see and do
Around Masaryk Square

The huge Masaryk Square is one of the largest in the country and would also be one of the most attractive were it not for the inexplicable eyesore, the Prior department store dumped right in the middle. It must be one of the most incongruous buildings in the Czech Republic, and is an excellent illustration of the communist authorities' insensitivity towards the delicate historical character of towns and cities in Czechoslovakia. The **Highlands Museum** can be found at the top of the main square in two Renaissance houses, Nos 57/58. Only 30Kč will gain you admittance to the second-largest museum in Moravia housing interesting exhibitions on the Czech-Moravian Highlands, the history of Jihlava, silver mining and the protected area around Jihlava. Unfortunately there are no explanations in English, but I was assured they are working on it. When entering the square from the north, the first building you will notice (apart from the hideous department store) is the early Baroque **Church of St Ignatius**, built by the Jesuits in the late 17th century. Concerts are held in the church thanks to its fine acoustics. By the side of the church is the entrance to **Jihlava's catacombs**, a labyrinth of underground tunnels, passageways and storerooms, reaching four floors down in places. It is the largest underground network of its kind in the Czech Republic at 25km long, with some older sources putting the total length at an amazing 56km (*admission 40/20Kč, open Apr–Sep, tour lasts 30 minutes*). Take a sweater.

Just off the square along Farní Street stands the Gothic **Church of St James the Greater** begun in 1250. This is a beautiful building with a lovingly preserved Gothic exterior and packed with exquisite works of art inside. You may have to hunt down someone with a key if you want to take a look inside. If you call ahead to the information centre, you can arrange to be taken up to the top of the 63m-high tower for spectacular views of the town and surrounding hills (*admission is 10Kč, open May–Aug Mon–Fri*).

Other places of interest

From the lower end of the square turn right into Kosmákova Street where you will find the **Young Gustav Mahler exhibition** that charts the childhood and formative years which the world-famous composer spent in Jihlava. Back to the square and right into Znojemská Street is house No 4 where he lived from 1860 to 1875. The **Church of the Assumption of the Virgin Mary** sits in Matky Boží Street between the square and the Matky Boží Gate. The Baroque façade conceals one of Jihlava's oldest buildings, founded in 1221 by Přemysl Otakar I. Originally a Romanesque structure, it was rebuilt in the Gothic style in 1353. The remains of Gothic frescoes can be seen on the walls and pillars and the Baroque altar dates from 1745. The interior is a typical combination of Gothic and Baroque and is well worth a peek inside. The church is open and there is no admission fee.

The **Matky Boží Gate**, Jihlava's only remaining gate, makes its last stand at the end of the street bearing the same name. It was built at the same time as the town walls and renovated in 1853 when it acquired its clock. In 1999, the gate was opened up to the public. Inside you can see various exhibitions and peer out at the town below (*admission 15/10Kč, open year round*).

Next to the Hotel Gustav Mahler stands the **Church of the Holy Cross**, originally dating from the 13th century but rebuilt in the 16th century in the Renaissance style. From 1871 until 1947 it was used by the army as a store and much of the church's interior was lost. It is now used by the Czechoslovak Hussite Church.

Jihlava's zoo spreads out beneath the town walls by the river.

PELHŘIMOV

Quaintly picturesque Pelhřimov is a drowsy town of 17,000 souls on the tiny Bělá River, encircled by the dark hills of the Highlands covered in spruce, pine and birch. It can be used as a base to explore the surrounding hills, which is excellent cycling country. The town itself is centred around a handsome little square with appealing pastel Baroque and Renaissance façades and a fountain.

There is an assortment of sights and museums dotted around the historical centre, representing about half a day's exploration.

Pelhřimov awakes from its slumber once a year in mid June to host the International Festival of Records and Curiosities, and is often dubbed 'Pelhřimov, the Town of Records'. The festival consists of numerous attempts to break or set bizarre and amusing records, such as the most people on a motorcycle, the biggest X-shaped cake or the largest book made of gingerbread and countless other such frivolous enterprises which often make their way into the *Guinness Book of Records*. The festival draws huge crowds to the town, and is followed closely by the media. The 'Dobrý den' agency, the festival organisers, runs the small Museum of Records and Curiosities in the town's Jihlava Gate.

Getting there and away

As Pelhřimov lies just off the main D1 Prague–Brno motorway, **bus** is the optimal choice from the capital, a journey of around 120km. Services depart from Roztyly metro station in southern Prague (red line C) and Florenc main coach station. The bumpy ride across the western reaches of the Czech-Moravian Highlands takes around two hours, and costs 80Kč. From the station follow Nádražní Street into the town centre.

Pelhřimov lies on a branch line connecting Tábor with the important rail junction at Horní Cerekev where you can change on to **trains** heading northeast to Jihlava, or southwest to České Budějovice.

Where to stay

Pelhřimov has very few accommodation options. If the following are full in summer, ask at the information centre (*Masarykovo nám 10;* \ *565 326 924; www.pelhrimovsko.cz*) about private rooms.

Hotel Slávie Masarykovo nám 29; \ 565 321 540; f 565 321 857; www.hotelslavie.web.tiscali.cz. The 9-room, 3-star Slávie is housed in the sole Art Nouveau building on the main square, where it enjoys a monopoly as far as accommodation goes. Reasonable sgls and dbls with breakfast and bathroom are good value at 600Kč and 900Kč respectively. The friendly owner can also arrange cycle hire and other services plus activities in and around the town.

Hotel Rekrea Slovanského bratrství 1664; \ 565 350 111; f 565 325 357; www.hotel.cz/rekrea_pelhrimov. Standing at a busy crossroads, 100m east of the Jihlavská Gate, the Rekrea will transport you back to the glum days of communism, at least as far as the décor and the building's exterior are concerned. The rooms are a throwback to the 1980s and the hotel looks like a typical uninviting Czech tower block. The only advantages to this place are its 55 rooms, making it easily the largest hotel far and wide, and the room rates, 610Kč for a sgl and 650Kč for a dbl. There is a large restaurant on the ground floor with Czech and international standards for 70–150Kč.

Where to eat

Hotel Slávie Masarykovo nám 29; \ 565 321 540. The Slávie has a restaurant looking out on to the square and a pizzeria on the first floor. The high-ceilinged, Art Deco dining room downstairs is a bit pub-like, but is agreeable enough with mainly Czech food for 50–125Kč and Gambrinus and Urquell beers. There are views of the cute main square, and people-watching prospects from the large windows. The Pizzeria is less smoky, has fewer beer drinkers and satisfactory pizzas for 45–105Kč.

Restaurace Na Náměstí Masarykovo nám 4; \ 565 323 959. This is a no-nonsense eating place for Czechs on their lunch breaks. The menu is heavy with Czech dishes (60–150Kč), there is Budvar on tap, and a large selection of wines. *Closed Sun.*

Cukrárna u Radnice Masarykovo nám 2; ☎ 603 281 635. A few metres along from the Restaurace Na Náměstí, hidden under the arcading, this is the place to go on the square if you are just after a cup of coffee and some delicious Czech cream cakes. As is the rule in these little places, it has a modern interior, the standard choice of goodies and low Czech prices.

What to see and do

Masaryk Square, with its gurgling central fountain, has arcading on two sides, several Renaissance façades, most notably house Nos 17 and 22, and Baroque town houses facing the Hotel Slávie. Notice the Cubist **Farův dům** at No 13, built by the famous Czech Cubist architect, Pavel Janák in 1913–14. The plague column is conspicuous by its absence. The **Museum of Ghosts and Ghouls** (Muzeum strašidel) can be found under house No 17. A series of cellars, full of traditional Czech ghosts and other supernatural beings reproduced in wax, is a good place to frighten the kids (*admission 25/15Kč*). Most of the town's historical sites are located in the northwest corner of the square.

In the same building as the information centre you will find the **Highlands Museum in Pelhřimov** (Muzeum Vysočiny Pelhřimov) which has permanent exhibitions on the history of the town, the Hussite period and life in the 19th century. The admission fee of 30/15Kč also gains visitors entrance to the small red chateau behind the main building, housing various works of art, a torture chamber and historical cells. The chateau dates from 1550, but was used from 1582 until 1850 as the town hall. To the right of the museum stands the curious Church of St Bartholomew with its Gothic skeleton, Baroque inventory and blazing red and white Renaissance panel façades. The observation tower next to the church can be ascended from May until September for views of the square and the surrounding hills.

Two of Pelhřimov's robust Gothic gates have survived. South of the square sits the Rynárecká (or Horní) Gate and northeast along Palackého Street is the Jihlavská (or Dolní) Gate housing the **Museum of Records and Curiosities**. The museum is open at weekends (*admission 40Kč*); during the week visitors must call 563 321 228 to get someone to let them in. The five floors are full of the weird and wonderful from the world of record breaking, including a 3m-long toothbrush, the largest pair of pyjamas in the world, a model of Masaryk Square made entirely from pasta and many other curious objects and photographs.

ŽĎÁR NAD SÁZAVOU

The gritty industrial town of Žďár nad Sázavou would be quite justifiably well away from the beaten track were it not for the UNESCO-listed Church of St John of Nepomuk and the adjacent chateau a few kilometres north of the town centre. The town seems intent on preserving its run-down communist-era appearance, arguably worth seeing in itself. The area around the bus and rail stations is particularly gloomy.

Getting there and away

Because of its location on the main line between Prague and Brno, **rail** is the best option for getting to Žďár nad Sázavou from both places. Trains depart around every two hours from Prague main station and occasionally from Smíchov and Holešovice stations (2–2½ hours, 204Kč). From Žďár nad Sázavou you can carry on to Brno (1 hour–1 hour 40 minutes, 110Kč) with very frequent connections, as on top of the expresses, slower *osobní* services make the run too. As there are so many trains, travelling by **bus** to or from the town is just making life difficult for yourself.

Getting around
The monastery and Church of St John of Nepomuk are roughly 3km north of the stations. Take bus 2A heading for Pilská nádrž, alighting at the Zámek stop. Otherwise follow Nádražní Street to the main square and then head north along Bezručova for around 15 minutes.

Tourist information
Santini tour (*nám Republiky, Stará Radnice;* \/f *566 625 808; www.santinitour.cz*) is a privately run company which takes care of tourist information. They have nothing for free, but are open at weekends during summer. They also have around 70 cottages in the Highlands Region for rent.

Where to stay and eat
If you really must stay the night, try the 16-room **Hotel U Labutě** (*nám Republiky 70;* \ *566 622 949;* f *566 629 620; www.oxigen.cz/u-labute*), a one-stop shop at the top end of the main square. All rooms have en-suite facilities and TV. Singles are 500Kč, doubles 700Kč. The restaurant is a traditional, basic Czech eatery one finds away from the tourist sights with main courses for 60–150Kč and Staropramen beer on tap. Another decent dining option is the **Radniční Restaurant** (*nám Republiky 24;* \ *566 623 188*) in several converted cellars under the town hall which serves all sorts of dishes (100–200Kč) including Czech and Highland specialities.

What to see and do
Having made your way from town, the best place to start is the ticket office at the chateau. Here you can buy one ticket for 140/70Kč covering all the sites, including the Church of the Assumption, the Santini exhibition, the exhibition of old pianos, the Kinsky Gallery and the Church of St John of Nepomuk (but not the Book Museum). Alas, one must join a rather tedious guided tour, but thankfully the guides can be shaken off at the Church of St John of Nepomuk, and replaced with a livelier English text.

The chateau started life as a **Cistercian Monastery**, founded by Přibyslav z Křižanova in the early 13th century. Burnt down by the Hussites in 1422, reconstruction work began in 1638. The monastery's glory days came during the time of Abbot Václav Vejmluva in the early 18th century, who employed the architect Santini-Aichl to rebuild the monastery church and construct the Church of St John of Nepomuk, one of the most outlandish buildings of the period, on a hill opposite. Žďár nad Sázavou was not spared in the 1782 abolition of the monasteries, and the whole complex came into the ownership of the nobility. The Kinsky family lost it in 1945, but regained it through restitution in the early 1990s. In 1994, the Church of St John of Nepomuk became a UNESCO-listed building.

The definite highlight of the tour of the monastery is the **Church of the Assumption**, a three-aisled Gothic church given the Santini Gothic Baroque treatment in the early 18th century. Now suffering from a chronic case of damp, it is still an impressive sight. Notice the Baroque organ which was moved from the rear of the church to specially built arches at the front. The magnificent altar is by Gregor Thény who gave one of the cherubs the face of his recently deceased wife.

Apart from exhibitions on Santini and old pianos (undergoing reinstallation at the time of writing) the only other place of real interest at the monastery is the large **Book Museum** (*admission 30/15Kč, open Apr–Aug*), a far-flung outpost of the National Museum. Charting the development of writing, printing and books from ancient Egypt to the present day, it is well worth visiting. There are some English explanations provided.

UNESCO-listed Church of St John of Nepomuk

The real reason for travelling to Žďár nad Sázavou is to inspect Santini's zany Gothic Baroque Church of St John of Nepomuk, a five-minute uphill walk from the monastery heading back towards town. When one compares the building with others constructed in the same period, one appreciates just how daring and outrageous it must have seemed at the time. Personally it vaguely reminds me of Prague's Cubist architecture of two centuries later.

Sitting on top of Zelená Hora (Green Mountain) the church is built in the shape of a five-pointed star and surrounded by a decagonal cloister. The legend goes that John of Nepomuk was cast from Charles Bridge by Václav IV in 1393 for refusing to divulge the confessional secrets of the queen. Five stars are said to have appeared above the Vltava after his death, and the tongue (which he held) became his symbol. In reality he was almost certainly murdered for political reasons, but nevertheless his cult quickly spread across the Catholic world, and he was canonised in 1729. The church was begun in 1719 to commemorate the rediscovery of the saint's miraculously preserved tongue and the 500th anniversary of the founding of the monastery. The interior is full of representations of tongues, stars and the number 5 linking together the legend of St John of Nepomuk with the anniversary. The six-pointed stars represent the Virgin Mary. Regarded as the pinnacle of Santini's work, the church has loftiness about it, and inventively links ground-breaking architecture of the day with symbolism. Notice the odd-shaped windows and Santini's original main altar.

End your visit by walking full circle around the cloister (best seen from the air) then head back down the hill for a stroll round the picturesque lake and a picnic.

Around Žďár nad Sázavou
Žďárské vrchy

The sparsely inhabited Žďár Hills protected area is 700km^2 of wooded knolls, rivers and lakes to the north of the town. The terrain is superb for gentle hiking and mountain biking and is riddled with marked walking trails. The area is covered by VKÚ-KČT map 48.

Pernštejn Castle

Equidistant from Žďár nad Sázavou and Brno, one of the finest Gothic castles in the Czech Republic stands colossal, imposing but picturesque above the small town of Nedvědice, surrounded by a sea of trees. A visit to the archetypal medieval stronghold makes a rewarding day trip from either Žďár nad Sázavou or Brno, and despite the relative remoteness of the location, is easy to reach.

The castle was built in the first half of the 13th century, and originally belonged to the powerful Pernštejn noble family. The building was added to over the centuries, and changed hands several times during the 17th and 18th centuries until in 1818 it came into the possession of the Mitrovský family. The castle's current appearance is partly down to the Mitrovský family's reluctance to succumb to the fashion among the nobility and rebuild in the Romantic throwback styles of the 19th century, and partly thanks to the castle never having suffered at an enemy's hands. It has been suggested that the exterior of the castle looks the same as the day the Mitrovskýs bought it, although this cannot be said of the interiors. They eventually relinquished their noble seat to the Czech state in 1945, in whose care it remains to this day.

The classic tour (*65Kč*, quite physically demanding) follows the development of the architecture of the interior from original Gothic to 19th-century Classic and provides visitors with dramatic views out across the forested hills. There is a second tour (*160Kč*) which focuses solely on the Mitrovský family's 19th-century rooms. The castle is open for business weekends in April and October and daily except Mondays May–September.

Pernštejn is on a branch line which snakes its way from Žďár nad Sázavou down to Tišnov. The nearest stop to the castle is the village of Nedvědice 2km away, and hourly trains from Žďár nad Sázavou (1 hour 20 minutes, 64Kč) make a halt there. If travelling from Brno, a change in Tišnov is required, but the journey is slightly shorter. On alighting at Nedvědice, the castle is clearly visible and easy to reach along the road or yellow marked trail.

TŘEBÍČ

The somewhat overlooked town of Třebíč, 60km west of Brno, received a huge boost in 2003 when UNESCO listed the Basilica of St Prokop and the Jewish Zámostí Quarter as cultural heritage sites. Since then, interest in this out-of-the-way former industrial town of 40,000 has grown, though it does not receive as many visitors as it deserves. Perhaps this fact makes Třebíč one of the friendliest towns in the Czech Republic that welcomes visitors with unfeigned enthusiasm.

Třebíč grew around a Benedictine monastery founded in 1101 by Přemyslid princes and soon became an important centre of trade and commerce. Today's Karlovo Square ranked among the largest marketplaces in the country in the 13th century. In 1335, the town reached the height of its importance when it was granted wide-ranging privileges by the Margrave of Moravia, none other than the future Holy Roman Emperor and King of Bohemia Charles IV. However, decline followed after the town fell to the Hussites in the early 15th century setting it on a collision course with more powerful towns in the region such as Znojmo and Brno and eventually with Matyáš Korvín, who laid siege to Třebíč in 1468, when the son of the Hussite King Jiří z Poděbrad was given refuge in the monastery which was destroyed along with much of the town. Třebíč still has a strong Hussite tradition.

The monks were driven out in 1525, and the town came into the ownership of the nobility, a state of affairs which lasted until 1945. The last owners were the Valdštejns who had held the estate since 1614. Despite emerging unscathed from the Thirty Years War, fire, plague and poor harvests meant the town's importance waned until the arrival of the railway in 1886 and the development of industries such as tanning and shoe production. Throughout Třebíč's history from at least 1410 the left bank of the river Jihlava was occupied by a large Jewish community, the largest in Moravia at the beginning of the 19th century. Many Jews moved out of the cramped Jewish Quarter of Zámostí even before World War II, and of the 281 remaining Jews sent to concentration camps by the Nazis, only ten returned, which along with the expulsion of the German population in 1945, marked the end of Třebíč's multi-ethnic character.

Getting there and away

Třebíč is not the simplest place to get to from Prague, and you should allow at least half a day for the journey. **Buses** leave Florenc coach station around once every two to three hours (2 hours 40 minutes, 130Kč). Changing in Jihlava draws the journey out even more. If you are travelling from Brno approximately 60km to the east things are much easier with regular bus and **train** connections trundling between the two places (1 hour, 56Kč). Třebíč is a stop on the branch

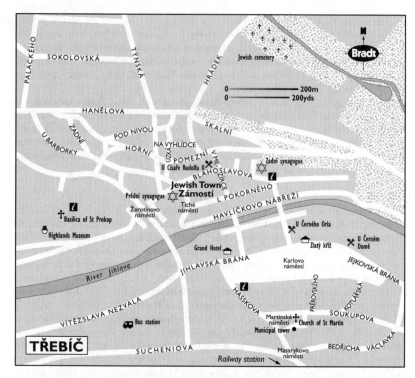

line between Brno and Jihlava and the slow *osobní*-type trains do the journey in 1½ hours, though there are some *spěšný*-type services which manage it in just over an hour. Whichever type of train you use, a ticket will cost 88Kč.

The bus station is five minutes' walk west of Karlovo Square, the railway station ten minutes to the south.

Tourist information
Třebíč has three official municipal tourist information centres situated in Karlovo Square, the Zadní Synagogue and at the Basilica of St Prokop; overkill some might say for a town that receives only a trickle of visitors at the best of times. But long may this situation last as an example to other towns. The main centre (*Karlovo náměstí 53;* ◆ *568 847 070; www.kviztrebic.cz*) on Karlovo Square is housed in the Renaissance-sgraffitoed building on the corner as you enter from the bus station.

Where to stay
Grand Hotel Karlovo nám 5; ◆ 568 848 560; f 568 848 540; www.hotel-cz.moonface.cz. The Grand does not look much from the outside but the 65 rooms are surprisingly trendy in décor and cheap with a flat rate of 1,100Kč.

Hotel Zlatý kříž Karlovo nám 19; ◆ 568 821 157 or mobile 602 326 182; www.pumax.cz. Though bland and very basic the 'Golden Cross' is friendly, clean and cheap and is situated on the main square on the third floor of a building containing a restaurant as well as other businesses. It must be the only hotel in the world to have a reception which doubles up as a sock shop (ground floor). Sgls are 390Kč, dbls 700Kč (with TV and shower, without breakfast), and make sure they explain the system of keys for getting in and out of the building when it is closed.

Where to eat

U Černého orla Karlovo nám 17; ℡ 568 840 477; www.cerny-orel.com. Down the passageway leading to the Jewish Quarter, the 'Red Eagle' has international and Moravian nosh for 100–150Kč and beer from Pilsen and Havlíčkův Brod. It is pretty ordinary inside and the outdoor seating has even less appeal.

V Černém domě Karlovo nám 16; ℡ 568 844 455. The popular 'Black House' restaurant can also be found just off the main square along a passageway at house No 16 sporting black sgraffito. Not a place for a quiet meal, but the Czech and Moravian food (50–200Kč) is cheap, and they have some interesting beers such as Guinness-like Kelt and Černá Hora.

U Císaře Rudolfa II Blahoslavova 19; ℡ 731 576 144. Probably the best place for food and entertainment in Zámostí, it has a cosy, no-smoking dining room as well as a small garden and a wine bar with weekend live music. Czech and Jewish specialities are 70–130Kč, and there is Krušovice beer on tap. The Jewish food is not kosher.

What to see and do

The cucumber-shaped **Karlovo náměstí**, Třebíč's bustling focal point, could compete with its namesake in Prague as far as size goes, and is allegedly the third-largest square in the country. It must also be the only square in the country not to boast any of its town's tourist sights, and most visitors only come back to it in the evening to eat and sleep.

The **Church of St Martin** and adjoining **Municipal Tower** loom above the roofs just off Karlovo Square and dominate the Třebíč skyline. The fabulously chunky 75m-tall, white Gothic tower with its huge clockface (rather incredibly the largest in Europe), built as part of the town's defences, can be climbed in summer for a bird's-eye view of the surroundings (*admission 20/10Kč*). This remarkable building has had a turbulent history (fires, wars etc) but has proven virtually indestructible throughout. Amazingly the widow of the last town crier left the tower only in 1956.

Basilica of St Prokop

The UNESCO-listed late Romano-Gothic basilica on the left bank of the river is truly one of the most architecturally interesting buildings in the country. Built by masons from France in 1240–60 for the Benedictine Monastery, it is a superb example of the transition between the Romanesque and Gothic building styles. Matyáš Korvín burnt it down in 1468, and subsequent noble owners of the estate used it as a store and the Romanesque crypt as a brewery. Several renovations followed, the last carried out in the inter-war years.

The highlights of the informative guided tour (*40/20Kč, tickets from the information office opposite*) are the crypt and a side chapel whose walls are adorned with the second-oldest frescoes in the country.

Housed in the chateau adjacent to the basilica is the Třebíč branch of the **Highlands Museum** (*admission 20/10Kč, English texts*). The definite highlight of this reasonably large collection is the amazing Cecil B De Mille-style Nativity scenes with throngs of cut-out Holy Land extras, animals and palm trees spreading out from Mary, Joseph and the infant Jesus in the centre.

Třebíč's UNESCO-listed Jewish sites

The reason most people now make the trip to Třebíč is to wander the narrow, crooked streets of the perfectly preserved Jewish town, and to visit the two synagogues and Jewish cemetery. It is astonishing to think that in 1975 the whole historical left bank was earmarked for demolition to make way for blocks of flats! Thankfully by the 1980s the significance of the Zámostí Quarter (meaning literally 'over the bridge') had been realised, and since 1990 the whole area has undergone renovation and rejuvenation, culminating in recognition by UNESCO in 2003. It is the only solely Jewish site outside of Israel to be afforded the honour. Stroll through the quiet streets, visit a gallery, take a look at the synagogues and end your visit at one of the pleasant restaurants or cafés.

To get to Zámostí from Karlovo Square, pass down an innocuous passageway at house No 18, pass by the U Černého orla restaurant and cross the footbridge. The Zadní Synagogue is up the hill to the left.

Two synagogues have survived in Zámostí, the **Přední synagoga** (Front Synagogue) and **Zadní synagoga** (Rear Synagogue). The Renaissance Front Synagogue is the elder of the two, probably built in the 15th century. It now serves as a Czechoslovak Hussite church, apparently the fate of many synagogues in the Czech lands following World War II. The Front Synagogue dates from the 16th century and was a place of worship only until World War I. Used as a storehouse for most of the 20th century it was renovated in the 1990s, and is now open to the public (admission 40/20Kã). As well as boasting lovingly restored Hebrew murals, it also houses an informative exhibition on the Třebíč Jewish community. The small collection of photos, artefacts, religious items and documents provides a peek into a lost world. At the back of the synagogue there is a small monument to the town's Jews murdered during World War II. The rest of Zámostí is a series of crooked streets, alleyways and steep steps dotted with other Jewish buildings such as the rabbi's house, the town hall, the school and the poorhouse. Ask at the information centre for a map to guide you round.

Ten minutes' walk up the hill following Hrádek Street, there is the Jewish Cemetery founded in the early 17th century and one of the largest in the country. A total of 11,000 graves and 3,000 tightly packed, crooked gravestones etched with Hebrew characters and draped with ivy create a wonderfully eerie scene among the pine trees.

Around Třebíč
Jaroměřice nad Rokytnou
One of the largest Baroque chateaux in the country (and indeed Europe) dominates the small, drowsy town of Jaroměřice 14km due south of Třebíč. The massive red and white Baroque residence was built by an ambitious nobleman Jan Adam Questenberk in the early 18th century in a bid to create his very own Versailles and the whole complex took almost 40 years to complete. The adjoining Church of St Margaret (chrám sv Markéty) with its huge dome and frescoes was built at the same time. Take the long guided tour (*admission 50/25Kč or 30/15Kč for short tour, church 30/15Kč, open Apr–Oct*).

When travelling from Brno, six buses a day (1 hour 45 minutes, 48–68Kč) stop in Jaroměřice near the end of their journey to Moravské Budějovice, though some continue on to destinations in south Bohemia. From Třebíč climb aboard any local bus headed for Moravské Budějovice, all of which call at Jaroměřice (20 minutes, 20Kč).

Náměšť' nad Oslavou
Tongue-twisting Náměšť' straddling the busy highway east to Brno lives in the shadow of a huge Renaissance chateau, built by the Žerotín clan in the 16th century. The interior (*admission 50/30Kč, open Apr–Oct*) is mildly disappointing but the priceless collection of 16th–18th-century French tapestries makes up for it as does the Baroque library. The handsome statue-lined bridge down in the town gracefully spanning the Oslava River dates from 1744 making it the third

oldest in the Czech lands after those in Písek and Prague. As recently as 1986 it was the sole bridge uniting both banks of the river! Locals are as proud of the bridge as they are of the chateau, dubbing it the 'Moravian Charles Bridge'.

Lying roughly equidistant from Třebíč and Brno, Náměšť is easy to reach from both by rail, as both Třebíč and Náměšť sit astride the main Brno–Jihlava line. An average of two trains an hour (45 minute–1 hour 15 minutes, 64Kč) travel from Brno to Náměšť, and the service is equally as frequent from Třebíč (30 minutes, 28Kč).

TELČ

Tiny tranquil Telč, midway between Jihlava to the north and the border with Austria to the south, must be one of the most enchanting places in the whole republic. With its long square lined with almost uninterrupted arcading, its two chunky gates, town walls, moats and surrounding protective lakes, it resembles an open-air museum of 16th-century architecture and town planning, and is unquestionably one of the highlights of any visit to the region.

The town was founded by the Hradec clan sometime in the mid 14th century, but the most celebrated lord of the manor was one Zachariáš z Hradce in the mid 16th century. On inheriting the estate he quickly set about transforming the Gothic castle into a Renaissance residence, and also helped the townsfolk replace fire-prone wooden houses along the square and surrounding streets with stone buildings, which have remained virtually unaltered to this day. Zachariáš died without an heir (Telč was inherited by his sister, married to Vilem Slavata, one of the governors famously defenestrated at Prague Castle in 1618) and it is as though at that moment the town was dunked in formaldehyde, preserved in all its 15th-century glory to this day, except for the odd Baroque addition. The long stretches of arcading, the brightly coloured gables and the slightly crooked houses, no two the same, provide one of the most recognisable sights in the Czech lands outside Prague. The historical centre was listed by UNESCO as early as 1992, one of the first places to receive the honour, underlining its significance.

Getting there and away

Telč is a relatively fair way from Prague in Czech terms and **buses** from Florenc coach station take between three and 4½ hours to reach the provincial town in the south of the country. The fare should not come to more than 125Kč, and services depart every hour or so. Many buses continue on to Dačice. Services from České Budějovice to Brno stop in Telč five times a day. As far as **rail** travel is concerned, Telč is on a branch line from Kostelec u Jihlavy to the Austrian border, so is reachable, but the journey is somewhat tedious. Slavonice is 50 slow minutes further down the branch line and tickets cost 40Kč. There are frequent bus connections from Jihlava (30–50 minutes, 25–40Kč). The bus and railway stations lie southeast of the historical centre around ten minutes' walk along Masarykova Street.

Tourist information

The information centre is at nám Zachariáše z Hradce 10 (\ 567 112 407; f 567 112 403; www.telc-etc.cz).

Where to stay

Černý orel nám Zachariáše z Hradce 7; \ 567 243 222; f 567 243 221; www.cernyorel.cz. Situated in the heart of Telč, the stylish 'Black Eagle' is one of the best places to stay in town. The immaculate rooms cost 850–1,150Kč for a sgl and 1,250–1,650Kč depending on the time of year. Of the 33 rooms, 28 are en suite and the room rate includes a buffet breakfast. The restaurant is also recommended.

Hotel Celerin nám Zachariáše z Hradce 43; ☎ 567 243 477; f 567 213 581; www.hotelcelerin.cz. Tucked away in a southeast nook of the main square the Celerin has 12 decent, 3-star-standard rooms for 1,000Kč for sgl use and 1,600Kč for a dbl including breakfast. Rates rise around 10% in summer and the Černý orel may be the slightly better option.

Hotel Telč Na Můstku 37; ☎ 567 243 109; f 567 223 887; www.hoteltelc.cz. The quaint, 3-star, 19-bed Telč has a good location just off the square and very comfortable en-suite rooms for 900Kč for a sgl out of season, rising to 1,800Kč for a large dbl in season.

Hotel pod Kaštany Štěpnická 409; ☎ 567 213 042; f 567 223 065. Those on a budget should head straight for the 'Hotel under the Horsechestnuts'. The 25 communist-era rooms are basic but reasonable enough, as is the price at 400Kč for a sgl and 660Kč for a dbl with breakfast. There is also a cheap restaurant.

Where to eat

U Marušky Palackého 28; ☎ 567 223 866. There is a lively, friendly Czech pub atmosphere at U Marušky at the foot of the tower. An odd collection of furniture and antique objects decorate the place. Czech and international main courses come for 50–160Kč and they pull Slovak Zlatý bažant and Moravian Starobrno beer.

Šenk pod věží Palackého 116; ☎ 567 243 889. U Marušky has a greater claim to be 'pod věží' (under the tower) but the Šenk pod věží is right next door. In the snug dining space and outside on the terrace overlooking the former moat they serve pizzas for 70–100Kč and Czech and international staples for 50–150Kč. The menu is in English; however, they close 15.00–18.00.

What to see and do
Square of Zachariáš z Hradce and around

Telč's most impressive sight is the two rows of gaily coloured façades resting on unbroken arcading which face each other across what is probably the Czech Republic's most photogenic piazza. Not a single modern housefront breaks the jumbled chain of 16th-century irregular gables, with the much-photographed northern side perhaps the most striking. Some of the houses sport simple pastel façades, while others are decorated with complicated sgrafitto work, a couple in full colour. The plague column at the southern end, though dating from 1717, blends in well with the older houses. The whole ensemble is testament to the skill and imagination of 16th-century craftsmen and has somehow miraculously survived intact to this day. The only downsides are the hordes of Austrian day trippers after cheap salami, and Vietnamese shopkeepers hanging their wares from the arcading.

Leave the square to the northeast through a narrow lane and the **Malá brána** (Lesser Gate) on the other side of which is Štěpnický Lake, just one of three which surround the historical centre. The other two, the Ulický and Staroměstský lakes, can be seen by heading south through the **Velká brána** (Greater Gate) and down on to Na Hrázi. The surrounding banks and parks are lovely places for picnics and summer evening strolls.

Chateau

At the northeast end of the square stands the **chateau** (*www.zamek-telc.cz, admission 70/35Kč, 140Kč in foreign language per tour, open Apr–Sep*) which started life as a Gothic castle, but then underwent a Renaissance transformation under Zachariáš z Hradce, carried out by Italian architects Antonio Vlach and Baldassare

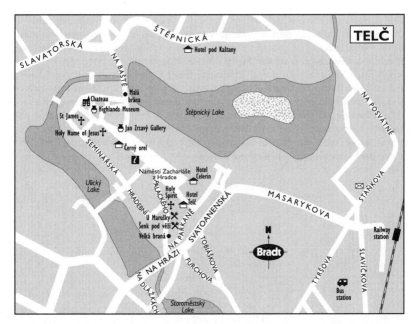

Maggi between 1553 and 1568. The chateau changed hands several times over the following centuries until 1945 when it was confiscated from the Liechtenstein-Podstatský family by the state, in whose hands it remains today. Before buying your ticket, take a peek into the **All Saints' Chapel** opposite the ticket office. Built in 1850 it sports incredibly detailed Rococo stucco work and houses the tomb of Zachariáš z Hradce and his wife Kateřina z Valdštejna.

There are two guided tours, A and B. Tour A takes visitors through the bulk of the Renaissance chateau, taking in several exquisite halls with their original wooden ceilings and floors and sgrafitto décor, as well as the Gothic parts of the original castle such as the Knights Hall (Rytířský sál) and the Golden Hall (Zlatý sál). You may be lucky enough to catch a glimpse of the White Lady who appears from time to time here as she does at most of the chateaux in the region (ie: Třeboň, Jindřichův Hradec). The residence of the last owners is the theme of Tour B with richly decorated rooms full of 19th- and 20th-century furniture, paintings and everyday household items. Tour A is the more interesting of the two.

If you have time to kill before your guide appears, why not visit the **Museum Vysočiny** (*admission 20/10Kč*) in the courtyard where you will find interesting exhibits on life in Telč, a scale model of the town from the end of the 19th century and examples of local folk costume. In a corner of the beautifully kept, tranquil chateau gardens visitors will also find the small but excellent **Jan Zrzavý Gallery** (Galerie Jana Zrzavého, *admission 30/15Kč*). In 1966, the artist Jan Zrzavý visited Telč and expressed a desire for his work to be exhibited at the chateau one day. His wish came true 11 years after his death when this gallery was opened in 1988. He is perhaps best known for his sparse, chilly Breton harbour scenes, a part of the world he visited many times. His love of simplicity is evident in much of his work.

Telč's churches
Next to the chateau in its own private square stands the Gothic **Church of St James the Elderly** (kostel sv Jakuba), rebuilt in the mid 15th century following

one of the town's many fires. The plain interior has some painted Gothic vaulting and there are two impressive ceramic war memorials in the passageway leading to the entrance. The double steeples of the ubiquitous piece of Baroque meringue, the **Church of the Holy Name of Jesus** (kostel Jména Ješíše), stand side on to the main square and adjoin the Jesuit College. Built in the mid 17th century the interior is relatively sober for the Baroque era and represents one of the few incursions into the 16th-century appearance of Telč's historical core. The **Church of the Holy Spirit** (kostel sv Ducha) at the other end of the square is most interesting for visitors thanks to its 60m-high tower with its five green neo-Gothic spires, which can be climbed for bird's-eye views across the town and surroundings (*admission 15/10Kč*).

South Moravia

For every Czech the south of Moravia evokes romantic visions of pretty villages among fertile fields, traditional folk architecture, girls in colourful local costume dancing to the faintly oriental chimes of the *cimbál*, crisp whites in cool wine cellars, feasts of fresh local produce, wild folk festivals and locally distilled *slivovice*. All this plus a gentle landscape, welcoming laid-back locals and a slightly warmer climate make this one of the most appealing areas of the country and most visitors quickly succumb to its charms.

There is so much to see and do in south Moravia you will be spoilt for choice. Brno is the country's second city, drawing visitors to its museums and galleries. The south of the region is strong with the sweet smell of fermenting wine and wine-growing towns such as Znojmo and Mikulov are also rich in historical sights and picturesque views of the surrounding countryside. Alternatively spend some time in the Slovácko region with its folk festivals and the picturesque spa at Luhačovice. Whatever you do here, end the day at one of the region's excellent restaurants where the locally grown fresh produce arrives at your table for much less than in the capital.

GETTING AROUND
Trains and buses serve most regions and travel poses no great difficulties except perhaps in the Slovácko region where services are few and far between. Brno is the obvious transport hub though many towns in the region are linked directly.

BRNO
Poking fun at the capital I have heard Moravians say cheekily that 'Prague is the Brno of Bohemia'. Alas, Brno is not the Prague of Moravia. Visitors who imagine the Czech Republic's second city will be anything like its first, are in for a disappointment. Brno has very few sights comparable to the capital's, and an analogy with Birmingham and London comes to mind. Tour buses miss it out, tourists avoid it, and the only time the city sees any swell in visitor numbers is during the motorcycle Grand Prix and major trade fairs, of which Brno is the Czech capital. That is not to say Brno's 390,000 inhabitants have nothing to be proud of. The city has a number of interesting sights such as Špilberk Castle, the Cathedral of SS Peter and Paul and the UNESCO-protected Villa Tugendhat, a few worthwhile museums and galleries and some lively nightlife and busy shops, though it never feels like a city of almost half a million. Base yourself in Brno to explore the south Moravia region, as it has excellent transport links, though accommodation is on the dear side.

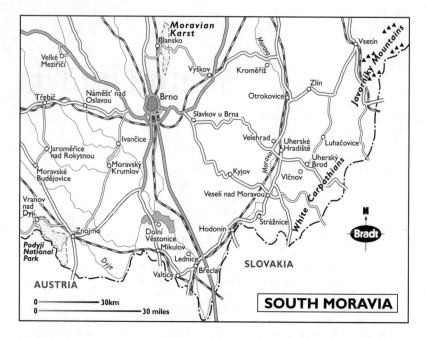

History

The site of today's city has been inhabited since prehistoric times and by the time of the Great Moravian Empire there was some kind of settlement at a ford across the Svratka River. From the 11th century a Přemyslid castle stood on Petrov Hill around which a small town began to form. Various ethnic groups (Germans, Jews) moved in, and in 1243 Václav I granted the town certain privileges. Town walls went up, churches were built and Špilberk Castle was remodelled in the Gothic style. By this time Brno was a relatively large settlement with a population of 11,000.

Brno sided with King Zikmund against the Hussites who consequently tried, and failed, to take the town by siege in 1428 and 1430. Even after the Hussite hostilities had died down, rigidly Catholic Brno preferred Matyás Korvín as king over Jiří of Poděbrady. However, by the mid 16th century a transformation had taken place with Brno displaying distinct Protestant leanings, eventually taking the side of the estates in their dispute with Habsburg Emperor Ferdinand I. During the ensuing Thirty Years War Brno was the only Moravian town not to fall to the Swedish despite a long siege. Brno became the capital of Moravia, and its reputation for steadfast resistance was proved yet again when it repulsed another invading army, this time the Prussians in 1742. Brno became a bishopric in 1777.

Brno saw widespread and swift industrial development in the 18th and 19th centuries, especially in textile production and engineering. The arrival of the rail link to Vienna in 1839 signalled yet more expansion, and the town spilled out of its town walls. Špilberk Castle was turned into an infamous prison for the Austrian Empire's political prisoners. This was Czechoslovakia's second city during the ill-fated First Republic, which saw municipal administration taken out of German hands. The population rocketed from 210,000 in 1921 to 300,000 in 1937. Masaryk University and the famous exhibition grounds were also founded at this time. During World War II Špilberk was used as a Nazi prison and all industry was forced to contribute to the Nazi war effort. The Red Army liberated the town on 26 April 1945, and the large German population was expelled the same year. Brno was a key industrial centre for the communists, focusing on machine production, and subsequently the population grew even more, creating a need for housing. The acres of ugly tower blocks surrounding the city are the legacy of this population boom.

Getting there and away

Czech Airlines advertise **flights** from Prague to Brno, but in reality this is a coach service from Prague Ruzyně Airport. The coach is almost certainly faster than flying anyway, when you take into account check-in time etc, taking 2¾ hours to travel the 200km along the D1 motorway to Brno. Passengers alight at the main bus station in the city. The coach runs four times a day in both directions including handy night-time departures from Brno to catch early flights from Prague. A return ticket, however, costs a steep 1,200Kč, considerably more than regular coach services. Ryanair operates direct flights from Stansted to Brno's tiny Tuřany Airport. Local buses run from there into the centre of town around 8km away.

From Prague's Florenc **coach** station there are several departures an hour at certain times of the day. Various coach companies run services between the Czech Republic's two major cities and tickets cost in the region of 130–200Kč. Reservations are essential. Student Agency has hourly departures and modern comfortable coaches with stewardesses and refreshments. Tickets for these services are bought from special yellow booths at departure points. The coach station in Brno is called 'Zvonařka' and is situated southeast of the historical centre though many buses to Prague (including Student Agency services) leave from opposite the Grandhotel Brno, a much more convenient spot.

A total of 15 **trains** a day leave Prague's main railway station heading for Brno, making it one of the easiest places to reach from the capital (2 hours 40 minutes to 3 hours 40 minutes, 130Kč). Travelling on east from Brno, Bratislava is a mere two hours away by train and there are also direct services to Austria, Hungary and other points east.

Getting around

Tickets for Brno's trams, buses and trolleybuses are bought from yellow ticket machines at stops. A ten-minute ticket costs 8Kč, and tickets valid for 40 minutes cost 13Kč. Punch your ticket immediately you board.

Tourist information

A rather Spartan information centre can be found in the **Old Town Hall** (*Radnická 8;* ↘ *542 221 450; www.ticbrno.cz*). The affable staff can help with accommodation and sell maps and guides. Unfortunately their praiseworthy website is in Czech only! The Old Town Hall tower is climbable and for 30Kč visitors can be taken on a guided tour of the elaborate interior. The entrance to the town hall always captures visitors' attention. The wobbly looking Gothic pinnacle above the gateway on Radnická is said to have been created deliberately by Anton Pilgrim in reprisal for not being paid enough by tight-fisted town councillors. For an explanation of the crocodile and the wheel both suspended inside the gateway see boxed text *Three Brno Tales*, page 266.

Where to stay

Brno has no shortage of decent accommodation, except, that is, when there is a trade fair in town when hotels are booked to bursting point and rates double.

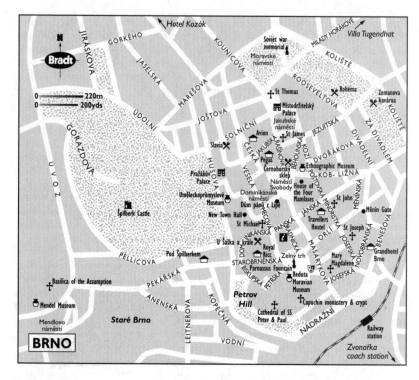

Luxury

Grandhotel Brno Benešova 18/20; ☎ 542 518 111; f 542 210 345;
www.grandhotelbrno.cz. The business traveller-orientated Grand, part of the Austria
Hotels International group, was founded in 1870 and is still going strong. The 110
reasonably luxurious high-ceilinged rooms have every facility possible including bath,
but even so are a touch overpriced at €75–150 for a sgl and €110–180 for a dbl.

Royal Ricc Starobrněnská 10; ☎ 542 219 262; f 542 219 265; www.romantichotels.cz.
Located in a narrow, picturesque street just off Zelný trh, the Ricc is a truly enchanting
place to stay. Occupying a Renaissance town house, the 30 rooms ooze historical style.
Some even have real fire stoves, but all have the necessary modern facilities too. You
may find cheaper, but you will not find better. Sgls cost 3,300–3,700Kč, dbls
3,700–4,200Kč and the hotel has a superb restaurant.

Mid range

Hotel Pegas Jakubská 4; ☎ 542 210 104; f 542 214 314; www.hotelpegas.cz. Located
in a quiet street in the heart of the city centre, the Pegas sits atop a microbrewery and
great *pivnice*. The 14 rooms are of a reasonable standard if a touch bare and prices
range from 1,000–1,500Kč per night including breakfast. These rates almost double
during big trade fairs.

Hotel Pod Špilberkem Pekařská 10; ☎ 543 235 003; f 543 235 066;
www.hotelpodspilberkem.cz. The 3-star, 50-bed 'Hotel Under Špilberk' can be found
on the busy road leading to the Basilica of the Assumption. The basic rooms are quite a
good deal at 1,100Kč for sgls and 1,450Kč for dbls, but again beware the 'trade fair
prices', precisely double the standard rate. Prices include breakfast.

Hotel Avion Česká 20; ☎ 542 215 016; f 542 214 055; www.iqnet.cz/avion. The

Avion is housed in one of Brno's First Republic functionalist structures, built by architect Bohuslav Fuchs in 1928 on bustling Česká Street. Some of the 31 rooms are spacious affairs with large windows, others are somewhat cramped. Sgls come for 800–2,200Kč, dbls for 900–2,800Kč depending on time of year, trade fair bookings etc.

Tighter budgets
Hotel Kozák Horova 30; \/f 541 210 330; www.hotelkozak.cz. This budget hotel is located 3½km northwest of the city centre in Žabovřesky district. The 24 comfortable rooms are a great deal, with sgls as low as 390Kč and dbls as cheap as 560Kč with breakfast included. The cheaper rooms are not en suite. To get there take trams 3 or 11 to Burianovo náměstí; the hotel is 3 mins on foot along Horova.
Travellers' Hostel Jánská 22; \ 542 213 573; www.travellers.cz. This friendly, basic hostel has dorm beds for 290Kč a night and is very centrally situated just off náměstí Svobody. *Open Jul–Aug only.*

Where to eat
Černohorský sklep nám Svobody 5; \ 542 210 987. The Czechs' (and Moravians') love of subterranean dining is satisfied in this large, surprisingly light and airy cellar pub-cum-restaurant buried deep beneath Svobody Square. Czech/Moravian staples arrive at your table for 80–200Kč and can be washed down with Černá Hora beer brewed in the Moravian town of Blansko.
U Šaška a krále Dominikánská 7; \ 543 235 015. The name of this merry eatery behind the Church of St Michael which translates as 'The Jester and King' refers to the owner, the well-known Czech actor Bolek Polívka, a comedian and self-proclaimed King of Wallachia! Stills and posters from his films line the walls of this fun, down-to-earth pubby restaurant where mains with comical names (lost on those who do not speak Czech) cost around 150Kč. Starobrno and Slovak Zlatý bažant beers are on tap and the service is agreeable.
Restaurace Slavia Solniční 15; \ 542 321 249; www.slaviabrno.cz. The Slavia is a real throwback to pre-revolution days but has preserved the best features of socialist hospitality such as monster portions, attentive old-world service, table linen and fresh flowers. Mains cost 50–250Kč and there is a large selection of wines and Starobrno beer on tap.
Bohéma Rooseveltova 1; \ 542 210 315; www.bohema.cz. A restaurant, *kavárna* and canteen all in one, this interesting and modern place can be found beneath the huge Janáčkovo Theatre. The international menu features a variety of salads, fish and meat dishes for 60–200Kč and the Starobrno is as good as anywhere in town.
Zemanova kavárna Jezuitská 6; \ 542 218 096; www.1926-zemanovakavarna.cz. A replica of a Bohuslav Fuchs's functionalist coffee house (see Hotel Avion) stands in the Koliště Park. Built in 1926 it bears a resemblance to the Mánes Building in Prague. The original was demolished to make way for the Janáčkovo Theatre. The huge windows and airy interior packed with small café tables transport visitors to the chic, confident 1920s. However, you will be brought rudely back to the less glamorous present when you see the prices plus the cover charges on everything, very rare in the Czech lands. Choose from the vast selection of coffees and desserts, but eat elsewhere.

What to see and do
Around Zelný trh
Irregular, sloping **Zelný trh** (literally 'Cabbage Market') is Brno's most picturesque square, surrounded by a jumble of historical buildings and crowned with the equally misshapen, unattractive grotto of the Baroque **Parnassus Fountain**, crawling with mythological beasts. Around the fountain a daily

vegetable market extends across the cobbles, its stalls laden with wholesome south Moravian produce. Looking up the square, the white block on the left at No 4 is the **Reduta** (in an endless state of renovation) where Mozart performed in 1767. Beyond that is the **Capuchin Monastery and Crypt** (*admission 40/20Kč*), Brno's most gory and ghoulish tourist attraction housing the mummified bodies of monks and members of the nobility, some in glass cases, some simply laid out in rows on the earth floor – not recommended for the squeamish. The remains were preserved in this state due to a complicated airflow system which prevented the bodies from rotting.

At the very top of Zelný trh stands the **Moravian Museum** (*www.mzm.cz, admission 20/10Kč*) housing the standard dusty, lacklustre collection of rocks, bones and fossils on the first floor, and a fairly interesting exhibition on prehistoric Moravia and the Great Moravian Empire on the second, though there is not a word of English to be found. The highlight of the collection is the authentic Venus of Věstonice displayed alongside an array of similar swollen fertility figures. Many finds from Staré Město (see *Uherské Hradiště*, page 287) are also exhibited here. The museum's home since 1923 has been the Dietrichstein Palace, Brno's largest noble residence built in 1614–19.

From the museum continue up Petrská to the top of Petrov Hill where the double needle-thin spires of the **Cathedral of SS Peter and Paul** rise majestically above the city. Before you arrive, get a preview of the cathedral by looking at the Czech 10Kč coin. The hill is a natural place of worship and may have been a pagan ritual site. A church was established here sometime before the 13th century, rebuilt in the 14th and 15th centuries in the Gothic style but burnt down during the Swedish siege in the mid 17th century. Promoted to cathedral in 1777 it remained spireless until the 19th century when it received a neo-Gothic makeover. The Baroque interior is surprisingly tame. For 15Kč visitors can climb the 400 steps to the top of one of the spires for the best views of Brno and the surrounding countryside, and the crypt is also accessible.

THREE BRNO TALES

The **Brno dragon** legend starts with a nobleman who brings a dragon's egg back from a crusade in the Holy Land. The egg hatched and the dragon grew so large it devoured all the noble's farm animals and then one of his staff. The nobleman was forced to leave it tied to a tree but it escaped and began to terrorise the locals. They managed to stuff its mouth with lime so when it slid back into the Svratka it met a fizzy death, after which it was stuffed and suspended in the entrance to the town hall. One look at the dragon is enough to ascertain that it is, in fact, a crocodile.

A wheelwright bet the locals 12 pieces of silver he could fell a tree, make a **cartwheel** and wheel it to Brno before the town gates closed in the evening. The wheelwright was in league with the devil, won the bet but died a pauper when the suspicious locals boycotted his business. The cartwheel also hangs in the entrance to the town hall.

In 1645, impatient Swedish general Torstenson was growing tired of the siege of Brno and declared that if the city was not taken by noon next day, the troops would have to give up and forfeit their dose of looting and pillage. Torstenson's ultimatum was leaked to the city defenders who rang the noon **bell** an hour early, saving the city from the marauding Swedes. The bells of the cathedral still ring noon at 11.00.

Špilberk Castle

Brno's best-known landmark sits atop a wooded hill to the west of the historical centre. Originally a Gothic stronghold it was completely rebuilt in the 17th and 18th centuries into a Baroque fortress, later transformed into the Habsburgs' most feared prison where numerous individuals, perceived as threats to imperial power (Italian nationalists, Polish revolutionaries), were left to rot. The prison closed in 1857 and served as a garrison until the arrival of the Gestapo in 1939, who once again utilised it as a place of gruesome incarceration. The end of World War II saw the end of Špilberk's dark history, and since 1961 it has been home to a vast museum on the castle and the city of Brno.

There is a huge amount to see and do at Špilberk and you should allow yourself at least an entire morning or afternoon to see everything. The place is vast and comfortable shoes are a must. A ticket to all places of interest (the museum, viewing tower, casemates) costs 110/55Kč *(family tickets are 230Kč)*.

The **museum** is divided into five sections spread over three floors. The first two parts deal with the history of the castle itself and its development from Gothic fort to Habsburg prison. Section three contains colourful exhibits on the history of Brno and the best works of art held by the museum are displayed in section four. Section five may be of interest only to architecture buffs as it deals with Brno's First Republic building boom and the bold architects behind it.

The short ascent up the **tower** is worth it for the sweeping views over the historical centre and the less attractive communist era suburbs lining the surrounding hillsides. Make sure the staff give you the free map before entering the **casemates** or you may never find your way out of this labyrinth of dank cellars, cramped cells and creepy passageways within the fortress walls. The map guides you round the interesting, if rather bare spaces used down the centuries as a prison and store.

Southeast corner

There seems to be a church in every street in Brno and nowhere is this truer than in the southeast corner of the historical centre. Usually the first historical building that those arriving by train see is the large yellow façade of the **Church of Mary Magdelene** in Masarykova Street with a Minorite monastery, founded in 1451. Follow crooked Františkánská Street to pedestrianised Josefská where you will find the sorry-looking **Church of St Joseph**, closed to the public and in need of a lick of paint. Take the first right into Orlí Street to have a quick look at the **Měnín Gate**, obviously once a typical bulky Gothic entrance to the city but extensively altered over the centuries and possibly the least-preserved gate of this kind in the country. Double back to Josefská, turn right into Minoritská and continue to the Baroque **Church of St John**, so immense it can hardly be appreciated from the narrow street outside. Brno's best Baroque interior awaits you inside, as well as a Loreto Chapel equipped with Black Madonna. It is also a regular classical music concert venue.

Around Náměstí Svobody

Brno's oldest and largest square, triangular Náměstí Svobody, is certainly not its prettiest. Its relatively small area reflects Brno's late arrival as a major centre (compare the square with Prague's Wenceslas or Charles squares or the squares of Olomouc or Jihlava) and the whole place has a slightly dilapidated, neglected feel, especially since the once-convenient trams ceased to run across it (the tracks remain). Even the plague column is a modest affair. Nevertheless the square does boast some attractive architecture such as the elaborate *fin de siècle* **House of the**

Four Mamlases (Dům U Čtyř mamlasů) with four large slaves in loincloths holding up the façade, or the Renaissance, sgrafitto-decorated **Dům pánů z Lipé** with a roof café providing vistas over the city.

At the corner of Koblišná and Běhounská you will find the **Ethnographic Museum** (*admission 30/18Kč*) housed in the Baroque Palác Šlechtičen. Due to a lack of funds the permanent exhibit is taking years to reinstall but there are always good temporary shows. Head north along Běhounská Street to view another of Brno's gargantuan churches, this time dedicated to **St James** (kostel sv Jakuba). Established originally by German colonists in the early 13th century, it was completely rebuilt in the 14th and 15th centuries in the late Gothic style. Look out for the small figure on the corner of the tower allegedly mooning at the (Czech) cathedral across town (interpretations vary!). Inside the nave is a forest of Gothic columns, the ceiling a web of vaulting and the high narrow Gothic windows uncorrupted with stained glass. All of this comes together to form one of Moravia's finest Gothic church interiors. You will also find the tomb of Luis Raduit de Souches, a French Protestant who died defending the city from the Swedish in 1645.

Dominikánské náměstí
Dominican Square, a few steps off Náměstí Svobody now seems to serve merely as a car park for municipal officials from the huge, newly renovated **New Town Hall** which dominates the western flank. Yet another huge piece of Baroque wedding cake, the **Church of St Michael**, towers to the left, guarded by a statue-lined balustrade. Regrettably, it is usually closed to the public.

Other places of interest
The colossal, Baroque **Church of St Thomas** at the end of Joštova Street was originally founded in 1350 by the brother of Charles IV, Jindřich, and was intended to serve as a mausoleum for the Luxembourg family. However, only Jindřich and his son are buried there. It was given its Baroque visage after sustaining considerable damage at the hands of the Swedish. Compared with other churches of the Baroque period this is a relatively subdued affair though it does have an impressive mock marble altar. Just behind the church at the crossroads on Moravské náměstí stands a huge, well-maintained **Soviet War Memorial**, one of the largest in the Czech lands.

The **Moravian Gallery** (*www.moravska-galerie.cz, admission 40/20Kč or 50/25Kč per site, open Wed–Sun year round*) is accommodated at three sites. The **Místodržitelský palác** (Governor's Palace) on Moravské náměstí, stuck on to the Church of St Thomas, houses the collection of paintings from the 14th to 19th centuries as well as temporary exhibitions. The **Pražákův palác** (Pražák Palace) in the shadow of Špilberk Castle on Husova Street is where you will find Brno's modern art collection with fine works by Procházka, Čapek, Špála, Štýrský and Toyen as well as some pieces of furniture by architect Josef Gočár. In the same street stands the **Uměleckoprůmyslové muzeum** housing a collection of applied arts and cutting-edge temporary shows.

Outside the city centre
The **Basilica of the Assumption** lies southwest of the centre, a 15-minute walk along Pekářská Street or a short tram ride (5, 6, 7 from Moravské náměstí, alighting at Mendlovo náměstí). An 11th-century rotunda stood on this site before it was rebuilt into a full-blown Gothic church in the early 13th century when the Augustine Abbey of St Thomas was founded next door by Eliška

Rejčka, the Polish widow of King Václav II. The Basilica became her final resting place in 1335 and her grave is marked with an 'E'. Visitors must join a guided tour to visit the basilica and abbey (*admission 60Kč, open May–Oct Mon–Fri, tours at 10.00 and 15.00, 10.00 only at weekends*). However, the abbey is best known for something quite different altogether. In the mid 19th century Gregor Mendel, a monk at the abbey, began experimenting with peas in a small garden, crossbreeding them and noting down the results of the various combinations. Unbeknown to the humble monk (who was also a keen meteorologist), he had stumbled upon the basis of the revolutionary modern science of genetics. The fresh new **Mendel Museum** (*admission 80/40Kč, open year round, Apr–Nov Wed and Sun only*) tells the story in a modern, captivating way combining historical artefacts with the latest technology. Strange to think that the world of genetic science began on a small patch of earth in an unlikely suburb of Brno.

The UNESCO-listed **Villa Tugendhat** (*www.tugendhat-villa.cz, admission 80/40Kč, open Wed–Fri*), northeast of the centre, can be reached by trams 3, 5 and 11 from Moravské náměstí, alighting at Dětská nemocnice stop. From there it is five minutes on foot up Černopolní. Built by German architect Ludwig Mies van der Rohe for the young Tugendhat couple from rich Jewish textile families just before their wedding in 1929, the open-plan house was designed to 'create spatial continuity without definite borders' made possible by new building materials, a revolutionary concept at the time. The interior was also packed full of cutting-edge furniture and the latest mod cons, much of which the couple took with them when forced to flee from the Nazis in 1938. Some of the furnishings and fittings have been returned, others are replicas, some made by the same companies who produced the 1920s' originals. The villa's UNESCO listing in 2001 was unique for a modern structure. Tours leave every hour, but calling ahead (❧ 545 212 118) is recommended just to make sure the place is open.

Around Brno
Slavkov u Brna
While most will not have heard of Slavkov, many may know it by its German name – Austerlitz. While London has Waterloo, Paris in turn has the Gare d'Austerlitz in celebration of a battle which took place on a muddy field near Brno on 2 December 1802 between Napoleon's forces and a joint Russo-Austrian army. In what some regard as Napoleon's greatest tactical victory, outnumbered French forces thrashed the opposing army of over 89,000 troops employing nifty manoeuvres to fool the Russo-Austrian army who were soon on the run. The French lost 9,000 men, the Russians and Austrians 24,000 and their defeat led to the signing of the Treaty of Pressburg which ceded territory to the French. The Czechs sometimes inaccurately refer to the events of the day as the 'Battle of the Three Emperors'; Napoleon and Tsar Alexander I directed their troops in the field but Austrian Emperor Franz II was safe and warm in Vienna. The battlefield itself is 8km west of Slavkov at Pracký Hill marked by the 36m-high Art Nouveau **Mohyla Míru** (Peace Monument) erected a century after the battle. A small museum nearby houses exhibits from the battle and a miniature reconstruction. Every year military enthusiasts and Napoleon buffs gather on surrounding muddy (or frozen) fields to take part in a re-enactment of the battle.

Back in Slavkov itself, the main attraction is the Baroque **chateau** built by Italian architect Domenico Martinelli at the beginning of the 18th century. The highlight of the guided tour (*admission 60/40Kč, 105/45Kč in English, open Apr–Oct Tue–Sun*) is the dome of the Sál předků with its amazing acoustics. The

tourist information centre is next to the chateau (*Palackého náměstí 1;* ✆ *544 220 988;* f *544 220 988*) and should you wish to spend the night why not stay at the **Hotel Stará pošta** (*Rousínov 109;* ✆/f *517 375 985; www.staraposta.cz*) where Napoleon slept after the battle and where he received the Austrian envoy to agree on the Austrian surrender?

Slavkov lies some 20km east of Brno and there are very frequent bus and train services to the town. Both take in the region of 30 minutes (40Kč for the train, 24Kč for the bus). The Peace Monument is more difficult to reach without your own transport. The nearby village of Prace is 8km west of Slavkov and is served by just one bus a day from Brno. Alternatively take the train to Ponětovice from where it is a short 2km walk along a road that runs southeast to Prace.

Moravian Karst (Moravský kras)

The best day trip you can make from Brno is to the Moravian Karst, a network of around 1,000 caves 25km to the north. Millennia of rainwater dripping through the topsoil on to the limestone rock base have formed the caves and the process continues. Some of the dank, watery caverns have amazing stalactite and stalagmite formations but take warm clothing as it is cold down there even in summer.

The best way to approach the area by public transport is via the town of Blansko. Very infrequent buses run from there to Skalní mlýn where the ticket office and information centre is located and it is probably better to walk the 5km green marked trail to the caves. Only four are open to the public. The **Punkevní Cave** and the **Macocha abyss**, an incredible 138m-deep opening in the earth's surface are the highlights of the area. The tour of the Punkevní Cave is on foot and by small boat along the underground Punkva River. The two gargantuan subterranean chambers of the nearby **Kateřinská Cave** should also not be missed. The other two caves, **Balcarka** and **Sloupsko-Šošuvské**, are smaller and difficult to reach. Entrance fees range from 40–100Kč depending on the cave. Punkevní Cave is open year-round, the others close over winter.

Moravský Krumlov

This unexciting provincial town of 6,000 souls deep in the south Moravian countryside 30km southwest of Brno would receive next to no visitors were it not for the *Slovanská epopej* or Slav Epic, a unique series of 20 oversize canvases by Alfons Mucha which hang in the town's almost derelict Renaissance chateau. Mucha was born 10km to the north in Ivančice, and the canvases, which belong to the National Gallery in Prague, were brought here after World War II on the understanding that they would return to Prague once a suitable exhibition space had been built to accommodate them. In 2005, the contract which has kept the works in Moravský Krumlov for over 30 years ran out, and the fate of the exhibition hangs in the balance.

To locate the chateau, follow Zámecká out of the square for 300m. The huge oils hang in two large halls (*admission 60/30Kč, English texts, open Apr–Oct, no photography*). Alfons Mucha (see box opposite) is known in the West primarily for the Art Nouveau posters of Sarah Bernhardt he produced while working in Paris. However, few know that Mucha later dismissed this period of his work as too commercial and had been toying with the idea of a Slav Epic while still in Paris. In 1910, he returned to Prague and in 1912 began work on the giant canvases with financial backing from Charles Crane, a wealthy donor he had met in the USA. They took 16 years to complete (Mucha managed to design the fledgling republic's banknotes and stamps in between) and the complete set was exhibited for the first time at Prague's Veletržní palác in 1928 (half of them were exhibited

ALFONS MUCHA

Alfons Mucha was born in 1860 in the small industrial town of Ivančice near Brno. Denied a place at the Prague Art Academy, he left for Paris (via a short engagement designing theatre decorations in Vienna), where he worked for seven years before being asked to design a poster for a new play starring Sarah Bernhardt. More posters and similar work followed and soon he became famous. Parisians talked of the 'Le styl Mucha', but the artist was restless, and soon found himself working in America. He married a former student Marie Chytilová in 1906, and returned to Prague in 1910. Soon afterwards he started work on the Slav Epic, an undertaking which occupied the next 16 years of his life. Mucha died following interrogation by the Gestapo in 1939.

in the USA in 1920). Mucha, almost 70 when he finished the last painting, dedicated the works to the Czech nation, and the National Gallery, not possessing an exhibition space large enough, lent the Slav Epic to the chateau in Moravský Krumlov after World War II.

Monumental events in the turbulent history of Slavdom (naturally with a Czech bias), semi-mythical and actual, are depicted on canvases so large they were originally intended as ship sails. The Slavs being driven from their original homeland, battles between the Balkan Slavs and the Turks, the last sermon of Jan Hus under the Gothic vaulting of Bethlehem Chapel, Methodius's return to the Great Moravian Empire, Hus's forerunner Jan Milíč z Kroměříže converting Prague's prostitutes, storm clouds brewing in Bohemia after the burning of Jan Hus in 1415, a proud, rather oriental-looking King Přemysl Otakar II, an elderly Komenský sitting gloomily on the shore in Holland, Jan Žižka victorious at the Battle of Vítkov, a fiery George of Poděbrady defying the pope and many other momentous scenes are depicted on the 20 breathtaking, larger-than-life canvases. They are better than any history book and really bring the events and figures to life, essential viewing for anyone with an interest in the history of the Slavic peoples. There is also a small display of the beautiful Czechoslovak banknotes and stamps Mucha designed in the 1920s. The 500Kč note is particularly striking.

To reach Moravský Krumlov from Brno, hop on one of the hourly local trains which ply the branch line south to Hrušovany nad Jevišovkou (50 minutes, 46Kč). Buses from Brno's Zvonařka coach station are also an option with very frequent departures during the week, but at the weekend reward the train with your custom for operating a service. The railway station lies almost 3km beyond the town, but trains are met by local buses that whisk you to the main Masarykovo Square for 5Kč (tickets from the driver, simply ask for náměstí). Buses return to the railway station from stop number 1.

ZNOJMO

The sweet fragrance of maturing grapes, warm south-facing slopes, gentle rolling hills and cosy traditional wine cellars come to the mind of every Czech on hearing the name Znojmo. The town is an ideal stopping-off point on the way from Prague to Vienna, and it is a joy to explore its web of medieval streets and soak up its relaxed atmosphere. Its 36,000 inhabitants are a friendly crowd who welcome foreign visitors with genuine enthusiasm. Znojmo is also the best launch pad to explore the tiny but strikingly beautiful Podyjí National Park which starts at the edge of town near the castle. The best-known sight in town

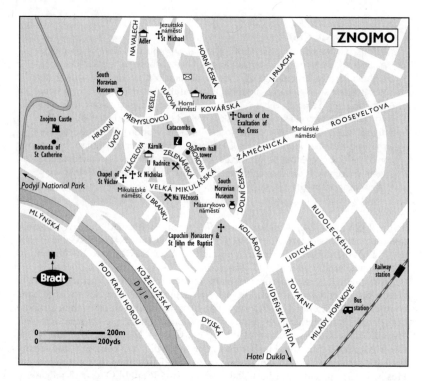

is the 11th-century Romanesque Rotunda of St Catherine, famous for its well-preserved Přemyslid frescoes, a must for any visitor to the region.

History

A stronghold at Znojmo belonged to the Great Moravian Empire in the 9th century. Břetislav I raised a Přemyslid castle at another site nearby in 1030, building the Romanesque Rotunda of St Catherine in the process. King Přemysl Otakar I raised Znojmo to royal town status in 1226, sparking an influx of German and Jewish settlers. After his death at the Battle of Marchfeld in 1278, the great King Přemysl Otakar II was temporarily buried in the Minorite Monastery (now housing the museum) until 1297, when his remains were moved to Prague.

Znojmo sided with Emperor Zikmund during the Hussite wars and Zikmund actually died in the town in 1437. A particularly destructive fire in 1490 handed the people of Znojmo an opportunity to give the town a Renaissance revamp during the 16th century. The 17th century saw Znojmo's darkest times, suffering occupation by the Swedes in 1645, skirmishes with the Turks in 1663 and a plague in 1679–80. More foreign armies, the Russians and Napoleon's forces, briefly occupied the town in 1799 and 1805 respectively.

The industrial revolution overlooked this part of Moravia, which continued to develop as a fruit- and wine-producing region, regarded as traditional industries since as far back as the 12th century. Ethnic tensions erupted between Czechs and Germans after the declaration of an independent Czechoslovakia in 1918, and the fledgling state's authority had to be enforced by the military. Znojmo was annexed by the Third Reich in 1938, but on liberation, the Germans were banished over the border for good.

Getting there and away

Znojmo lies around 60km southwest of Brno and less than 10km from the border with Austria. On weekdays from Brno there are several **coach** departures an hour at certain times of the day (1 hour, 70Kč). There is only one direct **train** a day so usually a change in Hrušovany nad Jevišovkou is necessary (110Kč). Eleven trains a day link Znojmo with Břeclav (1½ hours, 88Kč) to the east via Mikulov and Valtice. There are also nine services to Retz over the border in Austria with four trains continuing on to Vienna.

Znojmo is quite well connected to Prague by bus with up to eight departures daily (3 hours, 162Kč) generally passing through Jihlava en route.

Tourist information

The somewhat Spartan information centre (*Obroková 10; \/f 515 222 552*) under the Town Hall Tower can assist with accommodation, inform you about the town's tourist attractions and sell tickets for cultural and sporting events. The staff can also point you in the direction of the best places to sample the region's delicious wines.

Where to stay

Hotel Adler Na Valech 1556; \ 515 220 307; f 515 220 895; www.znojman.cz/hotel-adler. The 22-bed Adler is a renovated villa, below the Church of St Michael, accessible by steps from Jezuitské Square. The unremarkable but comfortable rooms are a good deal at 750Kč for a sgl and 1,200Kč for a dbl. Rooms at the front enjoy views of the Podyjí National Park.

Hotel Dukla Holandská 5; \ 515 227 320; f 515 227 322; www.hotel-dukla.cz. The Dukla is 2½km south of the historical centre. The only advantage of staying this far out is the price (sgls 520Kč, dbls 640Kč, breakfast extra). Otherwise the 154-room tower block has little going for it.

Hotel Kárník Zelenářská 25; \ 515 226 826; www.hotelkarnik.net. Situated in the heart of the historical centre this is one of the best places to stay in town. Comfortable basic rooms cost 750Kč without breakfast, and there is a great restaurant and wine cellar downstairs.

Hotel Morava Horní náměstí 16; \ 515 224 147; www.znojman.cz/morava. 2 huge airy rooms full of ageing Czech furniture, but with modern bathrooms above the restaurant of the same name, sleep 8. They represent good value at 700Kč for sgl occupancy including breakfast. There is no reception, just ask the friendly waiters in the restaurant.

Where to eat

Na Věčnosti Velká Mikulášská 11; \ 515 221 811. Take a refreshing break from meat and *knedlíky* at this unexpected vegetarian restaurant. Inevitably the menu is heavy on fried cheese (13 kinds!), but there is a wide selection of salads, rice dishes, mushroom-based meals and *halušky* from Slovakia. The atmosphere is quiet, relaxed and a couple of tables just have cushions strewn around them hippy style. No meal costs over 100Kč.

Hotel Morava Horní náměstí 16; \ 515 224 147. Thanks to the warm climate and fertile soil south Moravians are used to a better standard of food than in the rest of the country and the modest Morava strives not to disappoint. Choose from a wide range of Moravian and international meals (100–200Kč) washed down with an excellent local wine or Pilsen beer.

U Radnice Zelenářská 11; \ 515 241 194. Perhaps not up to the standard of the previous 2 eateries, but a good place for a quick lunch with office workers from the town centre. The half medieval, half modern décor is unimpressive but the food is cheap (50–100Kč) and there is Krušovice beer on tap.

What to see and do

After visiting the information centre you will find yourself directly below the slender **Town Hall Tower** with its huge green copper roof. The 15th-century tower is all that remains of the old town hall which was burnt down by the retreating Nazis in 1945. Climb to the top (*admission 20/10Kč*) to admire the view for miles around over into Austria and along the river Dyje. Perhaps this is a good place to start just to get your bearings as Znojmo can be difficult to navigate at first with narrow streets shooting off in every direction from numerous picturesque squares. A short walk down Obrokova brings you to the sloping main **Masarykovo Square** with its distinctive pink and white plague column at the top and the rather dilapidated **Capuchin Monastery and Church of St John the Baptist** at the lower end. There is a small daily fruit and vegetable market at the bottom end outside the monastery where you can buy mouth-watering fresh produce from the hundreds of smallholdings surrounding the town. The only blemish on an otherwise agreeable square is the huge concrete communist-era supermarket, which may be a candidate for the most poorly planned and incongruous building in the Czech lands.

Heading back north on to Slepičí trh you will find the entrance to the **Znojmo Catacombs** (*admission 40/20Kč, open Apr–Oct*) at house No 2 where visitors can explore roughly 1km of the interconnected cellars and stores. This is only a fraction of the kilometres of underground passageways which were previously used as stores for vegetables and, rather predictably, wine. One block east of Slepičí trh stands the immense Baroque **Church of the Exaltation of the Cross** which has had a turbid history. A church was established here as early as 1243 but lay in ruins for over a century following a fire in 1400. Another fire destroyed the rebuilt church in 1555. Having survived Emperor Josef II's reforms in the early 1780s it was put to work as a hospital during the Napoleonic Wars and as a barracks by the Prussians in 1866. Even the communists gave the adjoining Dominican Monastery a rough time in 1950 and for 40 years the monastery was used by border officials. The monastery and the church were returned to the Dominican order in 1990. The interior is modestly simple except for the Baroque side altars linked by archways, the organ crawling with instrument-wielding cherubs celebrating the Counter-Reformation and extraordinary stucco work above the entrance. Another church of interest is the **Church of St Michael** at the northern edge of the historical centre on Jezuitské Square which looks like a Baroque church consuming an earlier Gothic one.

Back across town set high above the river Dyje are the town's best attractions. On Mikulášské Square rises the Gothic **Church of St Nicholas,** under extensive renovation at the time of research. Side on to the church is the fascinating little Gothic **Chapel of St Václav** which sits on top of an earlier Romanesque church. The chapel is rented by the Eastern Orthodox Church and the very enthusiastic verger (he is not a priest as many presume) will give you an extensive tour of the building including the Romanesque church, the former ossuary and the balcony running round the chapel with sensational views down the Dyje Valley into the Podyjí National Park.

Rotunda of St Catherine and Znojmo Castle

Znojmo's premier tourist attraction sits high above the river Dyje providing truly magnificent views of the valley and the beginning of the national park. To get to the castle and rotunda, follow the special path beginning by the gate to the Hostan Brewery on Přemyslovců Street, which wafts a distracting musty fragrance across the path. The **rotunda** is the primary motive for coming here and it does not disappoint. After buying your 90Kč ticket (*no concessions, open May–Sep*) you will be taken ceremoniously to the small rotunda perched on a small outcrop of rock, and given a Walkman with a spoken text about the building and frescoes. The hourly tours are done this way as voice vibrations and moisture from the guides' breath could cause damage. Every possible surface of the interior is adorned with frescoes dating from the late 11th century. Biblical scenes, Czech legendary figures such as Libuše and Přemysl and most significantly the depiction of 19 Přemyslid rulers cover the interior in four horizontal bands, astonishingly clear after 900 years.

The nearby **castle** serves as a branch of the **South Moravian Museum** (*admission 40/20Kč*) and houses exhibitions on Znojmo's past, local ceramics (very similar to Wedgwood) and historical weapons. Other branches can be found in the Minorite Monastery on Přemyslovců Street (archaeology, oriental weapons) and in the Dům umění on Masarykovo Square (Gothic and Baroque art). Admission to each is 20/10Kč.

Around Znojmo
Podyjí National Park
At just 63km² the Podyjí National Park is the smallest in the country, extending from Znojmo in the east to Vranov nad Dyjí in the west and following the line of the river Dyje and the Austrian border all the way. The densely wooded meandering river valley reaches a depth of 220m in some places creating a breathtaking landscape and countless microclimates in which rare species thrive. Some 77 of these are protected varieties including 18 types of orchid. The park is also home to 65 species of mammal and an amazing 152 types of bird, quite incredible for such a relatively small area. The untouched nature of the Podyjí is partly down to the Iron Curtain defined by the river Dyje for over 40 years, then strictly out of bounds to the populace and tourists.

A red marked trail starts in Znojmo and winds its way the length of the park avoiding the ecologically sensitive areas. Disappointingly one hardly sees the river at all. Two dead-end trails leave the red trail en route, one to Nový Hrádek, a castle ruin high above the valley and the other to the Hardecká Tower in close proximity to the Austrian border affording views into Austria and across the park. VKÚ-KČT map 81 *Podyjí-Vranovská přehrada* covers the area though you are unlikely to really need it just for the national park.

Some 35km later at the end of the Podyjí National Park and the red marked trail is the castle at **Vranov nad Dyjí**, perched impressively on a rocky spur above the Dyje. Once a Přemyslid Gothic castle guarding the border, it was rebuilt in 1687 into a grand Baroque residence by master architect Johann Bernard Fischer von Erlach for the lords of the manor, the Althan family. The highlight of the guided tour (*admission 70/40Kč, open Apr–Oct*) is the awesome **Sál předků** (Ancestors' Hall) with its high dome, frescoes celebrating the Althan family and oval windows. The chapel (*admission 25/15Kč*) is also worth a look for its superb frescoes.

From Znojmo there are hourly buses to Vranov (30 minutes, 20Kč). An interesting way to reach the village is to catch a train from Znojmo to Šumná and walk the 5km using the green trail via the reservoir. Of course the most interesting way is to hike from Znojmo through the national park.

MIKULOV
Tight up against the Austrian border, Mikulov is synonymous in the Czech lands with wine, and most Czechs will assume foreign tourists are heading this way to

imbibe some of the local fermentation introduced to the area by the Romans. Wine certainly is the biggest attraction (staying sober in this town can pose a problem!), but Mikulov also has a picturesque Baroque chateau, and is set in a stunning landscape of towering limestone bluffs and rolling vineyards, the UNESCO-protected Pálava region.

Getting there and away

Up to one **bus** an hour (1 hour 20 minutes, 50Kč) makes the 54km journey due south from Brno to Mikulov. A change in Břeclav is necessary when travelling by **train**, making the trip a touch longer and considerably more expensive (1 hour 40, 170Kč). There are 11 trains a day to Znojmo (1 hour, 64Kč). Two buses a day call at Mikulov on their way from Brno to Vienna (2 hours, 230Kč).

Tourist information

The municipal tourist information centre (*Náměstí 30;* ↘/f *519 510 855; www.mikulov.cz*) assists with transport, accommodation and information enquiries, and can arrange wine-tasting sessions in local cellars. Should you be heading this way in September, ask about the wine harvest festival which takes place towards the end of the month.

Where to stay

Hotel Rohatý krokodýl Husova 8; ↘ 519 510 692; f 519 511 695; www.rohatykrokodyl.cz. The 14-room hotel over the restaurant of the same name is a safe option with decent if a little characterless rooms for 700–1,300Kč. The staff can organise wine tasting.

Hotel Réva Česká 2; ↘/f 519 512 076. Well situated just off the main square the Réva is a touch better and cheaper than the Crocodile with dbls going for 700–800Kč a night without breakfast.

Where to eat

Alfa Náměstí 27; ↘ 519 510 877. Situated in the sgraffito-decorated Renaissance house U Rytířů on the main square, the Alfa has mains for 100–200Kč and a selection of beers. To the right is a more pub-like area, to the left a pleasant, quieter dining space.

Rohatý krokodýl Husova 8; ↘ 519 510 692. Housed in the former rabbi's dwelling and the place the artist Alfons Mucha stayed from 1881–83, the 'Horned Crocodile' gets my vote in Mikulov for its huge portions of Moravian fare (all around 100Kč) and, of course, wine.

What to see and do
Chateau

The lofty chateau, visible for miles around, is Mikulov's most obvious historical attraction. Built up by the Liechtensteins, and then owned by the Dietrichstein family from 1575 until 1945, it was burnt down by the Gestapo at the end of World War II, and rebuilt in the 1950s as a museum. Today the upper floors house an exhibition on lifestyles through the ages and some rather lacklustre rooms on the Dietrichstein family. The admission fee of 60Kč is worth it just for the views from the windows. A separate exhibition on winemaking can be found in the cellars, the highlight of which is the colossal wine barrel made in 1643 and allegedly the second largest in central Europe. Weighing 26 tonnes and capable of swallowing 100,000 litres of wine, it was in fact hardly ever used to store the beverage, and has always served as a kind of tourist curiosity.

Dietrichstein Mausoleum

At the lower end of the square (simply called 'Náměstí') stands an impressive neo-Classical façade, behind which you will discover the final resting place of eminent members of the Dietrichstein family. The site has had a turbulent history, beginning life as the Church of St Anne containing a Santa Casa (see page 98 for explanation) complete with Black Madonna, and founded by the most illustrious Dietrichstein, Cardinal Franz Josef Dietrichstein, Bishop of Olomouc in the early 17th century. Generations of the family were buried in the church until 1784 when it burnt down, Santa Casa and all. The coffins were taken to the **Church of St Wenceslas** along with the Black Madonna which was saved from the flames. It remains there to this day. The Church of St Anne was rebuilt as a mausoleum in 1845–52 and the coffins returned. The guided tour (*admission 35/15Kč*) takes visitors round the newly renovated mausoleum with the dusty wrought-iron coffins lined up in rows on both sides and contrasting starkly with the newly whitewashed walls. A statue of Franz Josef stands on the site of the former Santa Casa.

Jewish Mikulov

At the end of the 19th century Jews constituted 40% of Mikulov's population, and the town was one of the major Jewish centres in Moravia. Probably the best-known Jewish figure from the Czech lands, Rabbi Löw, the creator of the Golem legend, hailed from Mikulov, and the town was the see of the main rabbi for the whole of Moravia. The Jewish quarter was concentrated around Husova Street west of the chateau though all that remains there now is the **Synagogue** at No 13 (*admission 20Kč, open May–Sep Tue–Sun*), one of an original 12 in the town. The most visited part of the old **Jewish Cemetery** to the north is the Rabbi's Hill (Rabínský vršek) where rabbis were buried from the mid 16th to the 20th century. The last burial in the cemetery as a whole, which has over 4,000 graves, took place in 1938 just prior to the Nazi occupation.

Svatý kopeček and Kozí Hrádek

Svatý kopeček or 'Sacred Hill', the huge barren limestone mound east of the chateau, was an old pagan ritual site until the arrival of Christianity. On the first Sunday in September a procession of boys and girls in folk costume make a pilgrimage to the top ceremoniously carrying the Black Madonna with them. Do likewise, following the series of chapels to the top, from which there are incredible views in all directions. Atop another limestone crag to the north stand the ruins of the 15th-century Kozí Hrádek, providing dramatic vistas over the Pavlovské vrchy.

Around Mikulov
Wine cellars

One of the main reasons for travelling to Mikulov is to sample some of the incredibly good wine produced in the area. There is archaeological evidence that the Romans produced wine in the area, a custom today's natives apply themselves to with fervour. Mikulov has some great cellars, but for the real experience travel to one of the outlying villages such as Dolní Dunajovice, Novosedly, Klentnice, Perná, Březí or Sedlec where you will find row upon row of tiny, privately owned cellars. The proud owners will be more than happy to let you taste some of their superb wines, all produced from grapes from nearby slopes. The dark, fragrant cellars, the ritual of drawing the wine from the barrels, the deep emotional relationship of the locals to the wine, the tasting and the banter around the whole process are truly magic. Organise a tasting session from Mikulov, or just wander from cellar to cellar and village to village and see what you discover. Fragrant whites are superior to the sometimes pale reds, but if wine is not your tipple, ask to try some of the superb plum or apricot brandy instead.

Pálava

The Pálava region around Mikulov is a UNESCO-listed biosphere reserve thanks to the flora and fauna which thrive in its various microclimates and unique habitats. There are various marked walks through the area. Ask at the information centre for details.

An archaeological dig near the village of **Dolní Věstonice** on the banks of the Nové Mlýny Reservoir 7km north of Mikulov rendered the famous **Venus of Věstonice** (see *History*, page 5). A copy can be seen at the small exhibition in the village hall.

LEDNICE AND VALTICE

The two noble chateaux in the villages of Lednice and Valtice and the scenic woodland, lakes and vineyards between them, dotted with 19th-century follies, make up the Lednicko-valtický areál, listed by UNESCO in 1996. The villages, which lie 7km apart, are connected by an arrow-straight country road lined with lime trees, built specially for the former lords of the manor, the Liechtenstein family, owners of vast tracts of land in central Europe until 1945, to quicken the journey between their two residences. The Liechtensteins are responsible for the creation of this magical landscape including the watery Chateau Gardens in Lednice boasting a 60m minaret!

Some visitors may limit themselves to guided tours of the chateaux with a bus ride in between, others may prefer to don walking gear and take in the sights along the gentle walking trail linking the two villages. The region prides itself on some of the best vines in the country and whatever you choose to do during the day, you could do worse than to end it with a bottle of the fine local red.

Getting there and away

Valtice straddles the main Znojmo–Břeclav **railway** line with regular services in both directions (1½ hours, 76Kč from Znojmo; 12 minutes, 22Kč from Břeclav). You should alight at the Valtice-město station; the centre is a ten-minute walk past the Hotel Apollon.

There are regular local **buses** between Valtice and Lednice (15 minutes, 12Kč), though as mentioned earlier, hiking is an option. The roughly 15km red trail takes in almost all the follies en route.

Lednice has local **bus** connections to both Valtice and Břeclav (15 minutes, 12Kč). Special summer **trains** also run between Lednice and Břeclav (20 minutes, 22Kč). The service operates from April to September at weekends and every day except Mondays in June, and is made up of historical rolling stock (not steam).

Tourist information

Valtice náměstí Svobody 4; ⅃/f +420 519 352 978; www.radnice-valtice.cz
Lednice Zámecké náměstí 68; ⅃/f +420 519 340 986; www.lednice.cz (abysmal website)

Where to stay and eat

Neither village has an abundance of places to eat and sleep, and many choose to transfer around 10km east to the large industrial town of Břeclav, which also has

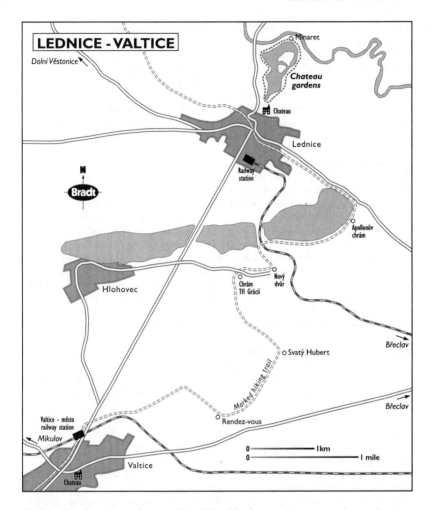

the benefit of a major railway station. Dire Břeclav receives no tourists on its own merit, making accommodation and restaurants cheap and friendly. Connections to both villages are excellent. Břeclav's efficient little **information centre** in the town hall (*náměstí T G Masaryka 3;* ✆/f *519 326 900; www.breclav.org*) can provide accommodation lists.

In Lednice
My Hotel 21. dubna 657; ✆ 519 340 130; f 519 340 166; www.myhotel.cz. The large My Hotel has a stranglehold on accommodation in Lednice and could do with some competition to force its out-of-control prices down a little. The 44 very comfortable dbls cost in the region of 2,000Kč including breakfast, and there is a respectable restaurant. Reservations are recommended in summer.

In Valtice
Hotel Apollon P Bezruče 720; ✆ 519 352 625; f 519 352 009; www.genea2000.cz. The 3-star Apollon is Valtice's best hotel, and can be found on the main road leading

from the railway station to the village green. The 22 rooms are modern and spotless, if hopelessly unstylish, with sgls and dbls for around 1,000Kč and 1,400Kč respectively. Part of the hotel is a very pleasant restaurant, and the staff can arrange wine tasting. **Valtická rychta** Mikulovská 165; ⟍ 519 352 366. The place to go in Valtice for food and wine stands 200m from the village green on the main road heading northwest. The interior has a traditional theme with folksy timber furniture, rural whitewash décor and fresh flowers on the tables. Excellent Moravian main dishes come for 100–200Kč, the service cannot be faulted and naturally there is a large selection of the superb local *víno*.

What to see and do
Valtice

Thanks to its superior transport links, most visitors start in **Valtice**. The star attraction is the huge Baroque **chateau**, just behind the quaint village green, the Liechtensteins' principal residence from 1560. Given a major Baroque remodelling in the 17th century, Valtice Chateau is now regarded as one of the finest buildings of that period in the country. Tours lasting 40 minutes (*admission 50/30Kč, open Apr and Oct weekends, May–Aug daily except Mon*) guide visitors through the elegantly decorated halls and representative rooms, left somewhat bare in 1945 when the Liechtensteins carted their precious contents off to Liechtenstein. Behind the chateau extends a large, rather unkempt English park. In the chateau cellars sample the local wine at the Národní salón vín (National Wine Show) where an unsupervised tasting of any of the wines costs 350Kč.

The trail from Valtice to Lednice and the follies

To my mind, the best way to spend a day in the Lednice–Valtice area is to hike the approximately 15km between the two villages through the **Bořf Woods** via many of the follies created for the Liechtensteins in the 19th century. VKÚ–KČT map 88 *Pavlovské vrchy* covers the area as does Shocart's *Břeclavsko-Pálava* map. Heading north from Valtice, the first place of interest the trail arrives at is **Rendezvous** from 1813, a mock temple to Diana, the Roman goddess of hunting, where hunt breakfasts used to take place. Further into the forest stands the **Chapel of St Hubert** the patron saint of the hunt. After a further 2km comes the **Tři Grácie**, a gracefully curving colonnade with neo-Classical statues of the gods. **Nový Dvůr**, a few hundred metres away, is a fine example of Empire-style architecture and was used originally to breed plants and animals. The trail then skirts around the Mlýnský Lake to the **Apollonův chrám** (Apollo's Temple) from 1819 and then joins the Břeclav road into Lednice.

Lednice

The **chateau** in Lednice is fast becoming one of the most popular in the country, and a few minutes of the guided tour (*admission 80/40Kč, English texts available, open Apr–Oct*) are enough to tell you why. Nowhere in the country is there a finer example of 19th-century English neo-Gothic restyling, and some of the carved oak ceilings, doorways, staircases and panelling are truly awe-inspiring. I would vote this the Czech Republic's most exquisite chateau interior, and if Lednice was anywhere near Prague, you would have trouble getting in. The tour includes the draughty neo-Gothic halls lined with hunting trophies, the Liechtensteins' living quarters in the late Empire style, stunning Japanese and Chinese rooms and then moves on into the plush pseudo-medieval halls including the Knights Hall, the Turquoise and Red rooms with their amazing colour schemes, and the library containing the highlight of the chateau, the famous intricately carved oak spiral staircase rising up into the gallery, which took five years to make, and which is fashioned from a single tree.

The curious wrought-iron and bottle-glass structure which looks like a capsized ship adjoining the chateau is actually a **greenhouse** (*skleník, admission 50/25Kč*) crammed full of exotic plants and flowers. If that does not take your fancy, take a wander into the Chateau Gardens which expand for acres behind the chateau. A substantial portion is occupied by artificial lakes making it possible to take a boat (the walk takes 30 minutes) to the 60m-high **minaret** (*admission 20/10Kč*) dating from 1802, the last word in superfluous aristocratic architecture. It is claimed this is the largest minaret outside the Arab world, but the plain, draughty, fashion statement is as fake as an eight-dollar bill, and has never had any religious use. That said, the view from the top back across the lakes, woods and lawns towards the chateau is the best you will see anywhere in the world and testament to the Liechtensteins' taste and imagination.

KROMĚŘÍŽ

Situated on the fertile plain of the river Morava bang in the middle of Moravia, the site of today's Kroměříž has been inhabited since humans first arrived in the area and developed around a staging post and market where trade routes crossed. The turning point in Kroměříž's history came in 1260 when the Bishop of Olomouc chose the then village as the site of his residence. This developed from Gothic castle to Renaissance chateau and after the Thirty Years War was transformed into an exquisite Baroque residence by bishop Karel Liechtenstein-Kastelkorn. Hundreds of thousands now travel to Kroměříž annually to visit the Archbishop's Palace and the beautiful gardens, all under UNESCO's wing since 1998.

Getting there and away

Kroměříž is awkward to reach by **train** as a change is required when coming from both north and south. From Brno change at nearby Kojetín (1¼ hours, 98Kč) and from Olomouc change at Hulín (1½ hours, 64Kč). There are regular **buses** from both places throughout the day, and Kroměříž is relatively well connected to Prague with up to six buses a day making the 280km journey (4 hours, 190Kč).

The bus and railway stations are next to one another on the opposite side of the river from the historical centre, ten minutes on foot.

Tourist information

The tourist information centre (*Velké náměstí 50/45;* \/f *573 331 473; www.mesto-kromeriz.cz*) is helpful and friendly and has lots of free information and maps. They can book accommodation and tours of the Archbishop's Palace at any time of year.

Where to stay

Hotel Bouček Velké náměstí 108; \/f 573 342 777; www.hotelboucek.cz. The 11-room Bouček is the town's most prestigious hotel, perfectly situated slap bang on Velké náměstí. However, it is a touch overpriced and is a disappointment as, with a little more care and attention, it could be such a great little place. That said, the staff are very friendly, and the rooms are of a decent standard. Rooms cost from 800–1,700Kč. Breakfast is an additional 100Kč.

Pension Na Octárně Tovačovského 318; \ 573 515 555; f 573 515 615; www.octarna.cz. Housed in a former Franciscan monastery east of Velké náměstí this is a

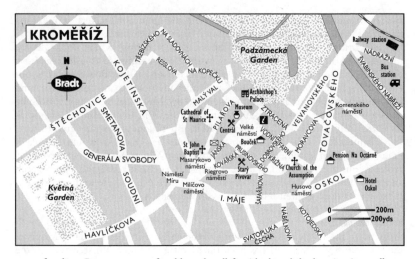

gem of a place. Rooms are comfortable and well furnished, and the location is excellent. Rooms range in price from 800–3,000Kč including breakfast.

Hotel Oskol Oskol 3203; \ 573 341 240; f 573 341 180; www.hoteloskol.wz.cz. The communist-era Oskol is housed in an unwelcoming tower block 10 minutes off Velké náměstí. The en-suite rooms are basic but adequate, and are a good deal at 500Kč for a sgl and 600Kč for a dbl. Definitely for those on a tight budget.

Where to eat
Centrál Velké náměstí 37; \ 573 337 788. Possible Kroměříž's best eatery is situated on the main square. It has bags of First Republic character (high ceilings, wood panelling, dark timber furniture) as well as hearty Czech main dishes for 60–140Kč and Pilsen beer.
Starý pivovar Prusinovského 114; \ 573 342 441. For a cheap, filling meal and a beer look no further than 'The Old Brewery' a few steps off the main square. The principal pastime of most of the regulars in this smoky beer hall is downing as much Starobrno as possible, but you can also get your daily dose of meat and *knedlíky* here for 50–120Kč.
Hotel Bouček Velké náměstí 108; \/f 573 342 777. The Bouček has a respectable restaurant with some outdoor seating under the arcading, huge servings, Pilsen beer, but alas rather unexciting early 1990s décor. Main courses arrive at your table for 100–250Kč.

What to see and do
Historical centre
All roads in Kroměříž lead to the heart of the town, sloping **Velké náměstí**, with one corner dominated by the tower of the Archbishop's Palace. Some arcading has survived in places. On the same side as the information centre next to house No 37/46 there is a narrow medieval alleyway with an interesting name – Lennonova, Lennon Street! Kroměříž's **museum** (*admission 60/30Kč*) can be found at No. 38, but has second-rate exhibits on local archaeology and wildlife etc, plus a section on painter Max Švábinský who was born in the town. Not surprisingly for a town full of bishops, Kroměříž has three grand churches, each just off the square. The Gothic **Cathedral of St Maurice** on Pilařova Street near the palace was established in the late 13th century. Despite the unwanted attentions of the Hussites who inflicted huge damage on it, the cathedral survives to this day as one of Kroměříž's oldest buildings. The interior is simple and

impressive despite some neo-Gothic alterations. The huge dome further along Pilařova belongs to the Baroque **Church of St John the Baptist** commissioned by the Piarist order and built by architect Cyrani von Bolleshaus in 1737 on the site of an older Romanesque church. The imitation marble interior is considered one of the finest of the 18th century in Moravia. Kroměříž's third grand place of worship is the **Church of the Assumption** on Farní Street, also the work of Cyrani von Bolleshaus and housing paintings by Maulbertsche whose work can also be admired in the Archbishop's Palace.

UNESCO sites

Kroměříž's main attraction, the **Archbishop's Palace** (*Admission: Historical Rooms 90/50Kč; Gallery 50/25Kč; Tower 40/20Kč; Sala Terrena 20/10Kč*) stands a few metres off the square. Tours are with a guide, and the main Historical Rooms tour takes around 1½ hours. The large gallery, the peculiar Sala Terrena and the tower are also worth seeing, so allow at least a whole morning or afternoon to do everything. Tours are in Czech but English texts are available.

As already mentioned, the bishop's residence started life as a Gothic fortress built on the site of a raised fort from the Great Moravian Empire era. This was rebuilt in the early 16th century into a Renaissance residence, but was razed by the Swedish during the Thirty Years War. Bishop Karel Liechtenstein-Kastelkorn (1664–95) is responsible for the grand Baroque palace we see today, the work of Italian architects from the Viennese court, Filiberto Lucchese and Giovanni Pietro Tencalla. They also rebuilt parts of the town, similarly wreaked havoc upon by the Protestant forces. After its rebirth, the palace was used only as a summer residence by the bishops and archbishops until 1950 when it was 'nationalised' by the communist authorities. It remains in state ownership today, and has been a UNESCO site since 1998.

The interesting guided tour takes visitors shuffling comically over the polished floors in huge red felt slippers through the richly decorated and furnished rooms of the palace, packed with priceless portraits, crystal chandeliers, statues, furniture and countless other precious objects. Without doubt the highlight is the incredible **Sněmovní sál** (Assembly Hall) the backdrop for some scenes in Miloš Forman's film *Amadeus*. The lofty 16m-high ceilings, delicate gold stucco on cream walls, huge mirrors and enormous crystal chandeliers, which before electrification held 440 candles, combine to form the finest Rococo interior in the Czech lands. The truly stunning space was originally called the Great Dining Hall until 1848, when for five fleeting months Kroměříž became the provisional capital of the entire Habsburg Empire following the revolutionary events of that year. The tour also includes the archbishop's private quarters and the library.

The **gallery**, explored without a guide, houses paintings from the 15th to 18th centuries and includes works by Van Dyck (portrait of King Charles I of England and wife Henrietta), Cranach, Titian, Veronese and Pagani. The collection was founded by Bishop Karel Liechtenstein-Kastelkorn, and is second only to the National Gallery. Away from the main tour be sure not to miss the **Sala Terrena** with its curious grotto and mock silver mine and the dominant feature of the palace, the 84m-high **tower**, the only part to have preserved some of the original Gothic and Renaissance architecture. It was badly damaged by the retreating Nazis in 1945.

Other must-sees in Kroměříž are the UNESCO-listed gardens. The extensive **Podzámecká Garden** established by the Chotek family, archbishops in the 1830s, stretches out from the rear of the Archbishop's Palace to the river Morava and is dotted with lakes and pavilions, an aviary and a menagerie. The tamer, more formal **Květná Garden**, ten minutes' walk from the palace, was created by the Liechtensteins in 1665–75. A white, statue-lined colonnade borders one side while the focal point amid the well-pruned hedges is the octagonal rotunda. Note that both gardens are open year round but close during wet weather.

ZLÍN

Those travelling to the Czech lands in search of medieval grandeur and history should steer well clear of Zlín. This industrial town of 90,000 which sprawls out along the Dřevnice Stream is more interesting for its meteoric rise as a centre for Baťa (pronounced *Batya*) shoe production than for today's reality. In sharp contrast to the vast majority of towns in south Moravia, Zlín is busy, pricey and in the process of wholeheartedly embracing capitalism. The business-orientated population has been doing its best since the revolution to revive Baťa's overdeveloped spirit of enterprise.

Zlín reminds me personally of towns in the former USSR; a confusing layout of ugly utilitarian architecture, wide thundering boulevards like race tracks for vehicles of every kind and scattered with untidy parks, ad hoc markets and kiosks. A plethora of post-communist advertising hoardings fixed loosely to overambitious budget 1920s and '30s industrial architecture, interspersed with communist additions is not a combination I would recommend. Like an island of north Moravia in south Moravia, it is certainly a candidate for the region's ugliest town.

The unlikely duo of Tom Stoppard, born Thomas Straussler in 1937, son of a shoe factory worker (nothing strange in these parts), and Ivana Trump, neé Zelníčková, were born in Zlín.

Getting there and away

Reflecting its former dimensions, Zlín is a mere **rail** halt on a branch line between the village of Vizovice to the east and Otrokovice to the west where travellers can change on to services heading north and south on the Břeclav–Přerov main line. Regular services make the run to Otrokovice throughout the day.

All this means that **bus** is the superior option. Several buses an hour make the 100km trip from Brno's Zvonařka coach station on weekdays (2 hours, 70–100Kč) and from Olomouc there are nine direct services a day (1½ hours, 65Kč). You can also reach Zlín directly from the capital with a total of nine coaches stopping a day at Zlín (4–5 hours, around 200Kč).

The bus station and Zlín střed railway station are beside one another roughly 300m west of the main square, náměstí Míru.

Tourist information

The reasonably helpful information centre (*nám Míru 12;* ↘ *577 630 270–3;* f *577 630 274; www.cityzlin.cz, www.mestozlin.cz*) can be found on the main square.

Where to stay

Zlín is enjoying an entrepreneurial boom and is popular with business travellers, making accommodation sometimes difficult to come by. Walk-in prospects are not good, and booking ahead is advised.

Hotel Moskva nám Práce 2512; ↘ 577 561 111; f 577 560 111; www.moskva-zlin.cz. The 10-storey Moskva built in typical steel frame and red brick in 1932 is Zlín's most

THE BAŤA STORY

The son of the village cobbler, Tomáš Baťa, founded his own modest business in 1894 in Zlín, a village of 3,000 at the time. Showing early ambition, Baťa supplied the Austro-Hungarian army with 50,000 boots during World War I, a nifty deal which made him his fortune. He invested heavily in buildings and machinery and his 120 employees in 1900 had grown to a workforce of 42,000 by 1930. This meteoric rise was because of the cheap, low-cost shoes he was producing, affordable to all if never very fashionable. He was ahead of his time in exploiting the easyJet business philosophy of cutting out middlemen (he even built his own rubber plant, power station and film studios to shoot adverts) and providing a no-frills product. In 1923, he became mayor of Zlín (slight conflict of interests if ever there was one) and by the end of the decade had become the largest footwear manufacturer in the world with outlets across the globe. The town underwent a construction boom unsurpassed in Czech history with hundreds of steel-frame and red-brick buildings sprouting up quickly and cheaply along the valley. Alas, Baťa tragically died in an air crash in nearby Otrokovice in 1932 and his brother Jan Antonín Baťa took the reins. With storm clouds gathering in central Europe Baťa's son (also called Tomáš) decided to flee to Canada in 1938 taking machinery and expertise with him. The Baťa factories were nationalised in 1945, Zlín rechristened Gottwaldov in 1949 after the first workers' president Klement Gottwald and the Baťa brand name changed to Svit. The town's name reverted back to Zlín in 1990 but Svit has stayed, as Tomáš Baťa was not returned a jot in the restitution process because of his uncle's alleged co-operation with the Nazis.

prominent (and visible) hotel. The 135 smallish business-standard rooms are quite run of the mill with sgls for 1,000Kč and dbls for 1,200Kč. Breakfast is an extra 90Kč. Despite its size the Moskva is very often fully booked.

Hotel Garni nám T G Masaryka 1335; ↘ 577 212 074; f 577 436 660; www.hotelgarnizlin.cz. The Garni occupies another of Zlín's typical Baťa-era buildings next door to the Hotel Moskva. Same rooms and prices as the Moskva with reductions at weekends and booking ahead is recommended.

Hotel Ondráš Kvítkova 4323; ↘/f 577 210 178; www.ondras.zlin.cz. Housed in an ugly *panelák* just off Míru Square, the Ondráš has 26 basic rooms for the less well-heeled business traveller. Sgls are a reasonable 750Kč, dbls come for 850Kč and breakfast is an extra 80Kč.

Where to eat

Valtická hospůdka Třída T Bati 200; ↘ 577 220 393. Valtice, a village in south Moravia is synonymous with wine and you will find lots of south Moravia's favourite beverage on the menu of this intimate wine bar-cum-restaurant. Meals cost 100–200Kč and Krušovice beer is on tap.

Zámecká restaurace Zámek; ↘ 577 202 201. This stylish oasis in and beneath the Zámek is one of Zlín's premier dining spots. The interior is tastefully decorated, the tables beautifully laid and the service flawless. The underground cellars are fragrant with traditional wine but sport cutting-edge décor. Come and relax here with a smooth glass of Moravian wine or over a delicious meal (100–200Kč) and rest your senses, weary from the shoebox architecture outside. There is live music every Friday evening down in the cellars. Reservations strongly recommended.

Záložna nám Míru 174; ↘ 577 019 343. Primarily for office workers on their lunch break, this is a large, busy, modern, fast-moving place on Míru Square, cheap and cheerful with Moravian and international mains for 60–150Kč and Litovel beer.

What to see and do
Shoe Museum
Playwright George Bernard Shaw once said that if a complete museum of footwear were to be put together, the result would illustrate the history of culture from its simple beginnings, through complex errors and perversions, to the purposefulness of modern times. Judge for yourself at Zlín's only real tourist sight, the fascinating **Shoe Museum** (Obuvnické museum, *admission 30/20Kč, open Apr–Oct Tue–Sun*) at the foot of the former Baťa headquarters, a 1920s skyscraper now housing offices of the regional authority. The collection, which brings together footwear from around the world and all periods of history, is a foot fetishist's heaven. Among the hundreds of pairs of shoes on display look out for the mammoth Hussite riding boots, sexy geisha sandals and a pair of women's slippers from 1912 made from a whole hamster. An interesting film in English relates the Baťa story.

Chateau Museum and Gallery
Sitting almost forgotten under the trees of shady Sad Svobody between the bus station and the main square is an island of piece and quiet in the shape of the chateau, one of the town's few pre-Baťa buildings. Apart from an excellent restaurant the modest building also houses a rather uninteresting museum (*admission 20/10Kč*) and a superb little art gallery (*admission 20/10Kč*) containing a collection of Czech 20th-century art including Cubist works by Čapek, Kubišta and Filla and paintings by Toyen and Zrzavý. Some of the works belonged to Baťa's own private collection.

Zlín's architecture
The one aspect of Zlín which strikes visitors most is its architecture. Those who have visited Prague and other Czech historical towns will have become used to the Czech lands as a country of pastel façades and red-tiled roofs. Zlín's buildings of red brick inserted into a concrete shoebox-shape frame come as something of a shock. Baťa had the same attitude towards the buildings he had built as towards the shoes he made: cheap, mass produced and accessible to all. The result is a unique townscape of planned, purpose-built structures, all quickly and efficiently erected in a uniform style by the best architects of the day: Karfík, Gahura, Kotěra, Lorenc and even Le Corbusier. Allied bombing and subsequent communist-era additions have obscured the town's planned layout considerably, but some of the best examples of Baťa-era construction are the **former company headquarters** at Tomáše Bati Street 21, one of the first skyscrapers to be built in Europe, put up in an incredible eight months; Karlík and Lorenz's huge **Hotel Moskva**; Karfík's **Obchodní dům** on the same hillside; Gahura's **Dům umění** at the top of Masaryk Square; and the **Velké kino** (Great Cinema) by the same architect next to the Hotel Moskva, the largest picturehouse in the country, capable of seating over 1,000 people. There are also hundreds of other office blocks, factory buildings and perhaps most notably colonies of low red-brick workers' houses and other facilities such as schools and hospitals built by Baťa for his employees under the slogan 'work collectively, live individually'.

UHERSKÉ HRADIŠTĚ
The busy town of Uherské Hradiště on the Morava River is perhaps not worth a detour, but is a transport hub, and in the course of exploring the Slovácko region you may well find yourself there sooner or later. The town has two good museums (though one is a fair way out of the town centre) as well as a picturesque main square.

Getting there and away
There are up to six **buses** a day to Uherské Hradiště from Zlín (30 minutes–1 hour, 30Kč) and up to nine from Brno (1½ hours, 80Kč). Main line **rail** services from Břeclav and Přerov and beyond arrive at Staré Město, a suburb 2km northwest of the town centre. The station in the town centre is on a branch line from there and local trains are flexible in meeting expresses at Staré Město. Even if you do not arrive by train go and take a look at the town's railway station, 200m southwest of Masarykovo Square, wonderfully bedecked in folk motifs, an ideal alternative to the soulless modernity which Czech railways now prefer. The bus station is 200m northeast of the square.

Tourist information
The municipal information centre (*Masarykovo nám 21;* ✆ *572 525 525–6;* f *572 525 527; www.mic.uh.cz*) housed in the former Jesuit College on the main square can supply visitors with maps and information on the town and Slovácko region.

Where to stay
Hotel Slunce Masarykovo náměstí 155; ✆ 572 432 640; f 572 432 668; www.synothotels.com. The stylish Renaissance building of the Slunce, conveniently situated on Masarykovo Square, contains 21 4-star rooms and has few rivals in town. The décor is simple but elegant and all rooms have AC, TV and telephone. Sgls are available for a very reasonable 1,500Kč, dbls for 2,400Kč.
Hotel Grand Palackého náměstí 349; ✆ 572 551 511; f 572 552 119; www.grand-uh.cz. For those on a tighter budget, the 54-room Grand, situated 100m east of Masarykovo Square, is an excellent option with surprisingly good en-suite sgls for 830Kč and dbls for 1,230Kč including breakfast.

Where to eat
Pivnice Koruna Tyršovo náměstí 113; ✆ 603 552 114. Although called a *pivnice* (beer hall) the 'Crown', a short walk north of the main square on the way to the Památník Velké Moravy, is really a typical Czech restaurant and a great place to get your fill of beer and *knedlíky*. Moravian specialities go for 50–150Kč, and this is *the* place to sample the local Janáček beer, declared beer of the year in 2004.
Hotel Slunce Masarykovo náměstí 155; ✆ 572 432 640. Probably the most upmarket establishment in town, the restaurant in the hotel of the same name serves up Slovácko specialities and local wine in a modern, prim environment. All meals cost in the region of 150Kč and the service is impeccable. Notice the glass floor in the centre of the dining space revealing Gothic foundations.

What to see and do
Five minutes' walk northeast of the railway station **Masarykovo Square** will be your first stop in Uherské Hradiště. The pleasant symmetrical, tree-lined square is dominated by the late Baroque Church of St Francis Xavier. The information centre can be found on the same side as the church.
In Smetanovy Sady, a five-minute walk east of Masarykovo Square, stands the

superb ethnographic **Slovácko Museum** (*admission 20/10Kč, English text available*), one of the few places visitors can get an idea of the richness of local traditions and folk costumes any time of year without attending a folk festival. The first part of the collection is devoted to folk handicrafts in the Czech Republic including beautiful examples of traditional pottery, *kraslice* (intricately decorated eggs), wicker and straw weaving, wood carving, leather, traditional rustic kitchenware, gingerbread, lace and fabric printing. All exhibits are examples of things still produced in the country and are recent creations. The second part on the Slovácko region highlights the wealth, colour and variety of regional folk costume, and does a lot to inspire visitors to get out into the countryside to experience one of the region's many folk festivals.

Uherské Hradiště's other, slightly less inspiring museum, the **Památník Velké Moravy** (Monument to the Great Moravian Empire, *admission 20/10Kč, open Apr–Oct*), is a 20–25-minute walk north across the river Morava in Staré Město, officially a separate town, but usually regarded as a suburb. The site is now generally considered as the location of Veligrad (as opposed to the more logical choice of nearby Velehrad), the lost capital of the 9th-century Great Moravian Empire, though debate and excavation are ongoing. A modern building erected over the foundations of a church and burial site contains some of the archaeological finds made here and in the surrounding area since 1948. An English text is available, but foreign visitors may be slightly disappointed by the dusty remains. Ask the friendly English-speaking curator to show you round. The most precious object found here (now in a museum in Brno) is a brooch which adorns the Czech 2Kč coin.

Around Uherské Hradiště
Velehrad
Some 8km northwest of Uherské Hradiště stands one of the most important traditional pilgrimage sites in Moravia, Velehrad. Originally thought to be the place Cyril and Methodius practised the Slavic liturgy during the days of the Great Moravian Empire, the first Cistercian monastery in Moravia was founded here in 1204. Originally a late Romanesque and early Gothic structure it was rebuilt in the Baroque style in the 17th and 18th centuries, and is one of the best-known Counter-Reformation-era buildings in the country. The Cistercians were served their notice in 1784 by Emperor Josef II, but the monastery was restored under the Jesuits in the mid 19th century. The communists evicted them in 1950 but the monks returned during the 1990s just in time to receive Pope John Paul II on his first visit to Czechoslovakia. Despite archaeological evidence that the original Veligrad of the Great Moravian Empire was situated in nearby Staré Město, Velehrad continues to celebrate the traditions of Cyril and Methodius and a pilgrimage takes place each year on 5 July to honour the apostles of the Slavs, a colourful mixture of religious service and procession in full local costume.

The highlight of any visit to Velehrad is the **Basilica of the Virgin Mary and SS Cyril and Methodius** (bazilika Panny Marie a sv Cyrila a Metoděje), the largest Baroque church in the country. The gargantuan interior of the church is a truly impressive sight and well worth the trip. Underneath is a Lapidarium (*admission 15/10Kč*) where you can see the original 13th-century Romanesque foundations.

There are almost hourly local **buses** from Uherské Hradiště to Velehrad throughout the day (20 minutes, 14Kč) calling at Staré Město railway station en route.

Slovácko region

The Slovácko region stretches from Břeclav in the south to Uherské Hradiště in the north and eastwards over the border into Slovakia. Rich in folk traditions it is regarded as a transition zone, not really Czech but not completely Slovak either. By far the best time to visit is during the summer festival season, to enjoy colourful events with much music, dancing and merry-making fuelled by the local wines. As well as wine the most elaborate folk costumes come from this region. Traditions are kept alive by both young and old, fiercely proud of their heritage. The two best events to attend to sample the full flavour of the region are the folk festival in Strážnice and the 'Ride of the Kings' in Vlčnov.

The festival in **Strážnice** is the best known in the country attracting thousands of visitors every year. The festival is held in late June and booking accommodation early is essential. Contact the **information centre** (IRRA, *Předměstí 399;* ✎ *518 332 184;* f *518 332 067;* e *irra@irra.cz*) for details. Strážnice also has a chateau now housing a museum with exhibits of local costume and folk traditions and a small open-air museum of folk architecture.

Almost every village in Moravia used to hold an annual *Jízda králů*, the Ride of the Kings, but the only place this colourful folk tradition has survived is **Vlčnov**, 10km to the southeast of Uherské Hradiště. Every year a young boy of ten to 12 years of age is elected as king, and over a weekend in late May he rides through the village dressed in women's folk costume on a horse almost lost under layers of ribbons and accompanied by a procession. This is followed by three days of raucous folk celebrations, music, song and dance, mostly oiled with large quantities of local wine. A folk ensemble in full swing, dressed in traditional, elaborately decorated red, black and white costume, is a sight you will not forget.

The exact origins of the tradition have been lost in the mists of time, but the Ride of the Kings has become associated with the struggle between King George of Poděbrady and Matyáš Korvín in the mid 15th century. What *is* known, is that the celebrations have been held uninterrupted for almost 200 years. During World War II the men of the village riskily travelled to the Gestapo headquarters in Zlín to request permission to hold the *Jízda králů*, demonstrating the importance of the event to the local people. For more information and photographs, visit Vlčnov's website at www.jizdakralu.cz.

Getting there and away

Close to the border with Slovakia, Strážnice is a halt on a branch line running from Veselí nad Moravou to the northeast and Hodonín to the southwest. There are 11 **trains** to Hodonín (30 minutes, 28Kč) and 17 to Veselí nad Moravou (12 minutes, 16Kč). Veselí nad Moravou has services to Brno, while Hodonín has departures to both Prague and Bratislava.

The nearest you will get to Vlčnov by train is Uherský Brod, 5km away on a branch line heading east from Uherské Hradiště to the border with Slovakia. Local **bus** from Uherské Hradiště is better with services around every two hours on weekdays (25 minutes, 17Kč).

LUHAČOVICE

The small town of Luhačovice, halfway between Zlín and the border with Slovakia, is Moravia's biggest and best-known spa town but nevertheless a rather low-key affair, no match for the grand spas of west Bohemia. Quiet, out-of-the-way Luhačovice is a place for rest and relaxation among the picturesque wooded foothills of the White Carpathians which form the border between the Czech

Republic and Slovakia. It is also known for its tasty *oplatky* (spa wafers), and is the home of the Vincentka Spring available in bottled form across the country.

Although the curative properties of the spring water in Luhačovice had been known for centuries, it was not until Dr František Veselý joined forces with the owner of the estate, Count Otto Serenyi, in 1902 that things really began to happen. Dr Veselý saw Luhačovice's potential, and in an effort to develop the spa he brought in a Slovak architect, Dušan Jurkovič, who gave the town a rather attractive, traditional, half-timbered character with elements of Wallachian rural architecture perfectly suited to the forest backcloth. The finest example of his work is the Jurkovičův dům on Lázeňské Square. Thanks to the newly built railway soon spa guests were flocking to Luhačovice which has not looked back since.

Getting there and away
Luhačovice is at least a 2¼-hour **bus** ride from Brno. Six buses a day make the 100km trip (90–130Kč). One lone bus a day makes the journey at weekends. Several local buses an hour (40 minutes, 23–33Kč) depart from Zlín on weekdays. Travelling anywhere locally by **train** from Luhačovice is a tedious affair as the spa lies at the end of a little-frequented branch line off another sleepy branch line. Take the bus.

As Luhačovice enjoys a nationwide reputation as a spa, it has direct bus and rail links to Prague. Three coaches a day (5–6 hours, 240Kč) leave Prague's Florenc coach station on weekdays only. The one train connection a day (424Kč) heads out from Prague's main railway station at 08.10 and arrives 5½ hours later, stopping at Olomouc and Uherské Hradiště en route.

The bus and railway stations are next to each other, ten minutes' walk from the spa district along Masarykova and Dr Veselého.

Tourist information
The town's information centre (*Masarykova 950;* \ *577 133 980;* f *577 133 980; www.mesto-luhacovice.cz*) is pretty useless and has nothing for free (they even charge 5Kč for a hotel list!). They sell maps and guides.

Where to stay
Luhačovice has no shortage of accommodation though things can get busy in summer. All hotels charge a 15Kč per night spa tax.

Hotel Praha L Janáčka 379; \ 577 131 102–3; f 577 132 754; www.volny.cz/anna.keblova. The 100-bed Praha is a very cheap spa house with small, basic rooms for 350–500Kč and all kinds of spa treatments on offer. It is situated north of the spa district.
Pension Pomněnka Příční 292; \ 577 113 211; f 577 113 212; www.penzionpomnenka.cz. The Pomněnka (which translates as 'Forget-me-not') can be found 2 mins on foot from the stations along the main Masarykova Street. Excellent value, tastefully fitted-out rooms go for 600–750Kč for sgl occupancy with breakfast and 900–1,300Kč for dbl occupancy.

Where to eat
Most hotels in Luhačovice have decent-standard restaurants. Other suggested eateries include the modern **Elektra** behind the information centre where mains for around 100Kč can be washed down with Černá Hora beer from Slovakia. For superb pastries head for the **Merkur Cukrárna and bakery at** 28 října Square.

Continuing on into the spa district join the Czechs for lunch at the self-service **Samoobslužná restaurace** at Dr Veselého 195 (*open 10.30–14.00 only*), a modern take on the old communist-era canteens with large portions of filling Czech stodge with dumplings and nothing costing over 70Kč. In the spa district head for the **Lázeňská cukrárna**, a coffee and cakes joint with a waiter service and huge windows looking out on to Lázeňské Square. At the end of the Colonnade the popular **Kavárna a Restaurace v lázních** has pleasant outdoor seating.

What to see and do

All of the town's places of interest are on or within walking distance of **Lázeňské náměstí**, a sandy square with a fountain, next to which stands a statue of the father of modern-day Luhačovice, Dr Veselý. The first building you will notice as you enter the square heading from the railway and bus stations is the technicolour **Jurkovičův dům** (Jurkovič House), the finest and most visible example of Jurkovič's work. The carved flourishes, turrets and traditional shapes with just a hint of Art Nouveau are very pleasing to the eye. Alas, later contributors to the town's appearance were less sensitive to the rural setting, seen all too clearly to the left of the Jurkovičův dům in the form of the **Colonnade**, a curving, bleak concrete structure resembling a desolate bus station. It houses a couple of shops and at the far end you will find the **Vincentka Spring**, from which spits the town's best-known mineral water, a somewhat salty *aqua mineralis* but not unpleasant. Interestingly, one of its many beneficial uses is as a hangover remedy! Across from the Colonnade the forest provides a dramatic backdrop for the white functionalist **Společenský dům** in front of which you may be lucky enough to catch a free concert of brass band music in summer.

Across the Šťavnice Stream next to the tennis courts on the side of the hill stands the tiny yellow building of the Vila Lipová containing a quaint **museum** (*admission 20/10Kč*). The collection includes a small but informative exhibition on the history of the spa and traditional folk items from the villages of the surrounding Luhačovické Zálesí area. Look out for the intricately carved wooden blocks used to print traditional patterns on textiles and the black decorated Easter eggs called *kraslice*. Turn left out of the museum to reach the **Ottovka spring** gurgling under a small pavilion.

Beyond Lázeňské Square heading along the Šťavnice Stream the valley opens out into relaxing parkland where you will find more of Jurkovič's idiosyncratic creations such as the **Jestřábí dům** and the **Vodoléčebné lázně**.

North Moravia

While parts of north Moravia certainly live up to their
reputation as scenes of sad, post-industrial decay
complete with mass unemployment, rusting
factories, soot-smeared buildings and choking
pollution, this is not the whole story. While
Ostrava and many other towns and communities
struggle to recuperate from communist industrial
policies and face perhaps the even greater challenge of their collapse, the Jeseníky
Mountains in the northwest and the Beskydy range to the southeast are as
tranquil, unspoilt and traditional as ever, creating a contrast few ever get this far
to appreciate. The glowing exception to the industrial nightmare of the region's
towns is resplendent Olomouc, hardly touched by industrialisation and the only
city in Moravia to mirror some of Prague's historical sights. Other highlights
include the wonderful open-air museums in Rožnov pod Radhoštěm and
Ostrava's modern architecture and thriving nightlife scene.

A large percentage of the region is occupied by an area known as Silesia, a strip
of territory extending from the Jeseníky Mountains to the border with Slovakia.
This is just a fraction of Silesia in its entirety, most of which can be found over
the border in Poland. The historical capital of Czech Silesia is Opava, though
Ostrava is the administrative centre of north Moravia as a whole. Until the mid
18th century the rest of Silesia was part of the Czech lands (or the Austrian
Empire depending on how you see it), but was lost to Prussia in the War of
Austrian Accession. A mere 15% remained in the Austrian Empire and was only
united with Moravia in 1849. Until 1945, Czech speakers were outnumbered by
both Germans and Poles. The Germans were expelled, but the language of the
region still retains a Polish feel reflected in the heavy accent and lopsided
intonation. A certain percentage of the population still claim to be ethnic Poles.

GETTING AROUND

Excellent bus and rail connections throughout the region mean reaching even
the most far-flung places in the mountains does not generally pose a problem.

OSTRAVA

Sprawling Ostrava is the Czech Republic's third-largest city, tucked away in the
northeast corner of the country not too distant from the borders with Poland and
Slovakia. Most Czechs would think you were slightly mad to head off to this
extremity of the country as its reputation is one of the least enviable in the region.

Ostrava was the heart of Czechoslovakia's mining and steel industries, both a
curse and a blessing for the town's inhabitants throughout the communist era.
The curse came in the form of pollution which blanketed the town in a daily
layer of carcinogenic grime for four decades, and had a devastating effect on

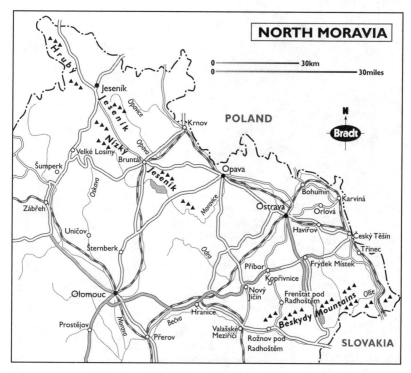

health and the environment. The blessing was the status of the miners in communist society who were rewarded for their devotion to the cause with well-supplied shops, higher wages and regular holidays to Bulgaria and Yugoslavia. The Velvet Revolution brought everything to an end. The last coal was mined in 1994 and the steelworks in Vítkovice closed in 1998. Now Ostrava is a rather neutered town with next to no industry, the once-proud workforce shunted off into service industries, the dole queue or the *pivnice* and the city centre cleaned up for tourists who will never arrive. Nostalgia inevitably abounds and this is reflected in the ongoing popularity of the communist party in the region. Although the communists are perceived as having been good to Ostrava, people have been quick to forget the pollution which plagued people's lives for 40 years, now mercifully a thing of the past.

Like all mining communities that lose their *raison d'être* Ostrava faces the task of redefining itself. Today there seems to be a fountain in every square, most façades are being pastelised, new office blocks are going up and there is a vibrant, young atmosphere on its pedestrianised shopping streets. However, one look to the horizon at the rusting works which ring the city reminds visitors of the city's polluted heyday.

Getting there and away

Ostrava is just far enough away from Prague to make overnight **rail** travel a possibility. The Františkovy Lázně–Košice overnight express arrives in Prague at 23.45, leaves at 00.45, and arrives in Ostrava at just after 06.00. A seat ticket costs 424Kč, but a few hundred crowns extra buys a berth in a compartment, or a full-blown bed with washbasin in a sleeping car. Otherwise there are a total of 15

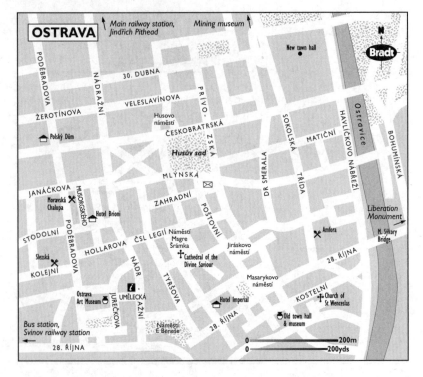

trains throughout the day from Prague to Ostrava, most with a journey time of around five hours.

Bus travel is a bad option to Ostrava, its only virtue being a ticket price of 250Kč. There are few services, and coaches can take over seven hours to inch their way across the republic.

Ostrava is a large city and therefore has good connections to virtually anywhere in Moravia. There are frequent buses and trains to Brno (bus, 3–4 hours, 140–180Kč; train, 2–3 hours, 204Kč) and Olomouc (bus, 2 hours or less, 110Kč; train 1–3 hours, 190Kč). For those travelling on to Poland there are three trains a day to Kraków (around 3 hours) and three to Katowice, all departing in the dead of night.

Naturally the quickest way to reach north Moravia is a one-hour hop from Prague by **plane**. Czech Airlines operates up to four flights daily. Prices start at around 1,000Kč excluding taxes, though expect to pay more in the region of 2,500Kč one way. Ostrava's tiny airport, Mošnov, is located 20km southwest of the city.

Tourist information

The main municipal information centre is situated by the Elektra tram stop (*Nádražní 7;* \f *596 123 913; www.ostravainfo.cz*). There are other branches in the tower of the town hall, the main railway station and Ostrava–Svinov railway station.

Getting around

Ostrava's bus and rail stations are sufficiently far from the city centre to make using public transport unavoidable. Tickets are purchased from yellow machines at stops and must be punched as soon as you get on. A 15-minute ticket costs 8Kč, a 45-minute ticket 12Kč. You are unlikely to need any other type.

From the main railway station hop on any tram and alight at the Elektra stop outside the information centre. To or from the bus station take tram 1 or 2 to or from náměstí Republiky. Should your train leave from Ostrava–Svinov railway station to the west of the city centre take tram 4 or 8 from outside the information centre on Nádražní Street and alight at Svinov mosty. The journey takes 15 minutes so a 12Kč ticket is recommended.

Where to stay

Hotel Brioni Stodolní 8; ↘ 599 500 000; www.hotelbrioni.cz. The Brioni, in the thick of things on Stodolní Street, represents excellent value for money. The 47 very comfortable 4-star-standard rooms come for 3-star prices, and there is a restaurant downstairs. Sgls with breakfast cost from 850Kč, dbls from 1,600Kč.

Hotel Imperial Tyršova 6; ↘ 599 099 099; f 599 099 599; www.imperial.cz. Situated at the southern end of the city centre the 154-room, 4-star Imperial is perhaps Ostrava's top hotel. Luxury sgls start at 56, dbls at 86.

Polský dům Poděbradova 53; ↘ 596 122 001; f 596 125 062; www.polskydum.cz. The 46-bed 'Polish House' can be found one block west of Nádražní Street in the city centre. The rooms are basic but comfortable with sgls going for 850Kč and dbls for 1,200Kč.

Where to eat

Moravská chalupa Musorgského 9; ↘ 596 124 937; www.moravskachalupa.cz. The 'Moravian Cottage' located in the popular club and restaurant district centred around Stodolní Street serves up overpriced Czech and Moravian favourites (180–260Kč) in a large, rustic setting. There is Pilsen beer on tap and of course lots of quality Moravian wine. The service is first rate.

Amfora Sokolská 6; ↘ 595 136 830. The smart Amfora is an oasis of tranquillity and style in Ostrava's busy city centre. Housed in an attractive red-brick building on Sokolská Street it has attractively laid tables, outdoor seating in a yard with a fountain, all sorts of food including some vegetarian dishes for 70–200Kč and Pilsen beer. Reservations are recommended at weekends.

Restaurace Slezská Kolejní 2; ↘ 732 564 615. A block south of Stodolní sits Ostrava's largest pub. The Czech and international menu holds no surprises (mains 100–200Kč) and there is Pilsen beer on tap. The outdoor seating is in a rather unattractive spot and the interior was under reconstruction at time of writing.

Stodolní Street www.stodolni.cz. 'The street that never sleeps' is fast becoming Ostrava's number-one attraction. Some 70 pubs, clubs and restaurants line this and surrounding streets. Those weary of meat and *knedlíky* will find a refreshing selection of Mexican, Turkish, Spanish, Cuban restaurants and many others including several Irish pubs.

What to see and do

Ostrava's places of interest are scattered around the city centre starting at the red-brick **Jindřich Pithead** dating from 1913, on the left as you come from the main railway station. It is all that remains of a mine and now rises bizarrely over the communist *paneláky*.

A few blocks east of Nádražní Street soars Ostrava's most architecturally engaging structure, the functionalist **New Town Hall** (Nová radnice), the largest in the Czech Republic and built by architects V Fischer, V Kolář and J Ruby from 1925 to 1930. Four large statues representing mining, commerce, science and metallurgy (some more relevant than others in today's Ostrava) stand on plinths at the top of the facade. The building is dominated by an 86m-high green clock tower which can be ascended by lift (*admission 20Kč*). From the 73m viewing platform there are astonishing views across the surprisingly green city, one of the highlights of any visit to Ostrava. Vítkovice's steelworks and pitheads set against the dark Beskydy Mountains are an impressive sight. One can also see into Poland and west to the Jeseníky. The large football stadium to the northeast belongs to Baník Ostrava, Czech league champions in 2004.

In contrast to the proud, modern New Town Hall, the Baroque and neo-Classical **Old Town Hall** (Stará radnice) on Masarykovo Square is the oldest building in Ostrava and home to the **Ostrava Museum** (*admission 30/20Kč*). The collection is currently in a state of flux, but a permanent exhibition on the city's history is planned. Some 100m east of the square stands the recently renovated **Church of St Wenceslas** (Kostel sv Václava) with its clearly Romanesque forms incorporated into later Gothic and Baroque reconstructions. The interior is modestly plain. From the church head east across the river Ostravice to see the **Liberation Monument** commemorating the Czech Tank Brigade in the USSR and the Red Army who liberated the city at the end of World War II. Atop the well-kept monument still defiantly sporting its hammer and sickle sits a real tank. Head 100m west of Masarykovo Square and you will find the huge neo-Renaissance **Cathedral of the Divine Saviour** (Katedrála božského spasitele) blocking your way. The enormous grubby red-brick and beige house of worship dating from 1883 with its double spires and simple interior is the second-largest church in Moravia after Velehrad and can seat 4,000, a rather redundant statistic in Europe's most atheist country.

One block west of Nádražní behind the information centre, take a few moments to visit **Ostrava Art Museum** (*admission 50/20Kč*) in the Dům umění. The ground floor hosts temporary shows while the permanent exhibition is on the first floor. The collection includes works by Cubists Špála, Čapek, Kubišta and Filla as well as paintings by Toyen, Zrzavý (his well-known Ostrava slag heaps), Mánes, Klimt and Munch with the exhibition changing approximately every two years.

You have to leave the city centre and travel out to the suburb of Petřkovice to reach the **Mining Museum** (Hornické muzeum, *admission 30–90Kč depending on tour; trams 1, 2, 8, 12 to Muglinovská stop then buses 34, 52, 67, 68, 70 or 73 to the Hornické muzeum stop*). Here you can inspect artefacts from Ostrava's mining past, travel down the mine to see the coal face and learn about the history of the underground rescue service.

ROŽNOV POD RADHOŠTĚM

The once entirely wooden town of Rožnov pod Radhoštěm around 40km south of Ostrava is overshadowed by Radošť Mountain, part of the Beskydy range. The main reason for travelling to the town is to visit the fascinating open-air museum and as a starting point for the marked hiking trails which disappear off into the Beskydy Mountains in almost every direction. Until 1960 Rožnov was a spa town, though not the classic spring water and radioactive mud affair. The spa procedures here involved lots of fresh air and the imbibing of large quantities of sheep's milk!

Getting there and away

From Ostrava bus station there are half-hourly **buses** at some times of the day on weekdays, journeying through Ostrava's industrial suburbs then out into the picturesque Wallach region (1½ hours, 60Kč). Travel from Brno is more complicated. There are a couple of direct buses a day otherwise a change in any of Přerov, Kroměříž, Valašské Meziříčí or Prostějov is necessary. Rožnov's **railway** station is the last stop on a sleepy branch line from Valašské Meziříčí to the west. There are up to 13 services a day.

On arrival, the bus and railway stations are next to one another on the opposite side of the Rožnovská Bečva River to the main square and the open-air museum.

Tourist information
The information centre of the 'Wallachian Kingdom' (*Palackého 484;* ↘ *571 655 196;* ↘/f *571 619 444; www.valasske-kralovstvi.cz*) is quite difficult to find and does not sport the usual white 'i' on a green background sign on account of its proximity to the open-air museum. Internet access here costs less than 1Kč a minute.

Where to stay
Hotel Eroplán Horní Paseky 451; ↘ 571 648 014–5; f 571 648 222; www.eroplan.cz. You cannot miss the Eroplán as you arrive by bus from the north as it stands at the main crossroads as you enter the town. The 40 rooms offer 4-star comfort and the location is ideal for the museum. Sgls with breakfast cost 1,400Kč, dbls 1,600Kč. Rates come down to around 1,000Kč for all rooms at weekends and there is 10% off for stays of 5 days or more.
Hotel Relax Lesní 1689; ↘ 571 648 100–4; f 571 648 106; www.hotelrelax.cz. The modern, 178-bed Relax is situated around 1km north of the open-air museum not far from the Eroplán. Its main attraction is a large open-air swimming pool which guests can use free of charge. Rooms are of a good standard and dbls with breakfast range from 960Kč to 1,400Kč and sgls from 850Kč to 1,110Kč.

Where to eat
Rožnovský rynek Palackého 487; ↘ 571 666 089; www.spolak.cz. Located in the long building of the former spa house in the park next to the Wooden Town Museum this is without doubt the best place to eat in Rožnov. The wooden rustic interior on 2 levels imitates the buildings of the open-air museum and each table is situated in its own mock Wallachian dwelling. The menu features Wallachian specialities and international mainstays for a reasonable 100–180Kč, and there is Pilsen beer on tap.
Na Posledním groši Dřevěné městečko, part of the Wallachian Open Air Museum. This traditional Wallachian restaurant is situated in the Wooden Town Museum. Rustic timber benches, waiters in traditional garb and local folk music on the CD player make this an ideal place to round off a visit to the museum. They serve exclusively traditional Wallachian food here for 100–200Kč and it can get full in summer. Unfortunately it is open only when the museum is.

The **Albert supermarket** on the main Masarykovo Square is the place to stock up on supplies before hikes into the mountains.

What to see and do
Wallachian Open Air Museum (Valašské muzeum v přírodě)
The museum (*www.vmp.cz*) has three parts and admission to all of them costs 120/100Kč. Tickets to each of the individual sites cost 50/40Kč and there is a 50% reduction for ISIC card holders. The place to start is the **Wooden Town** (Dřevěné městečko, *open year round except Nov*), the original site founded in 1925

by Bohumír Jaroněk and his brother Alois and sister Julie, making this the oldest open-air museum in central Europe. Bohumír, a local artist, was inspired by a similar museum in Stockholm at Skansen in 1909. The word *skanzen* is sometimes used to describe any outdoor museum in the Czech lands though the guides in Rožnov prefer not to use this inaccurate term. The Jaroněks moved some of the original wooden buildings which lined Rožnov's square and rebuilt them here in the wooden town. Others such as the church and pubs were added later (the last wooden structure was removed from the square in 1969). Some of the buildings are originals, some are copies, but all recreate traditional ways of life inside using original furniture and household items. It is a fascinating place to explore and enthusiastic guides are on hand at every site ready to provide interesting explanations. A feature of the wooden town is the so-called **Valašský Slavín**, the cemetery encircling the church where you will find the modest grave of Emil Zátopek, the legendary Czech long-distance runner and winner of three gold medals at the Helsinki Olympics in 1952. Almost every summer weekend sees an event at the Wooden Town and some of the best times to come are Easter and Christmas.

From the Wooden Town visitors then usually move on to the newest and perhaps most interesting part of the museum, the **Mill Valley** (Mlýnská dolina, *open May–Sep*) just across the road. This is the only part of the museum where visitors must join a 45-minute-long guided tour which leave at least once an hour (*English texts available*). The Mill Valley contains replicas of a water- powered woollen mill (*valcha*), flour mill (*mlýn*), sawmill (*pila*), oil press (*lisovna oleje*, not water powered) and a smithy (*hamr*) and concludes with a tour of a newly opened exhibition of original local horse-drawn vehicles. All the machinery is functional and the aim of the exhibition is to demonstrate how processes vital to everyday life such as flour grinding or knife sharpening were carried out before the arrival of steam and electricity. The water-powered mills are particularly awe-inspiring. When the miller opens the mill race and the machinery grinds into motion the buildings shake, and the raw power produced by water and gravity is quite incredible. Visitors leave with an appreciation of how ingenious and in tune with nature our not-so-distant ancestors used to be.

The largest of the three sites is the **Wallachian Village** (Valašská dědina, *open May–Sep and Dec*), scattered across the hillside behind the Mill Valley. The wooden buildings dotted around the hillside are an attempt to recreate a typical Wallachian highland community. The barns, dairy, windmill, tiny smithy and many other cottages and houses take about 1½ hours to get round. During the summer demonstrations of local crafts, domestic chores and agricultural work take place, animals are bred here and fruit is harvested by the 'locals' in authentic rustic costume.

Masarykovo náměstí

Away from the museum, there is not much to see in Rožnov. The main Masarykovo Square has a fine statue of T G Masaryk. These days it is hard to imagine the square's buildings were once made entirely of wood.

Walks into the Beskydy Mountains

Rožnov is as good a place as any to strike out into the steep-sided valleys, high wooded peaks and alpine meadows of the Beskydy Mountains, an extension of the Carpathians which run from the Polish border, along the Czech–Slovak border and across to Vsetín and Valašské Meziříčí. VKÚ-KČT maps 96 *Moravskoslezské Beskydy* and 97 *Slezské Beskydy a Jablunkovsko* cover a region interlaced with marked walking trails providing some of the best hiking in the country. For those not up to long-distance slogs, why not walk the easy 9km red trail to the top of Radhošť, at 1,129m the highest peak near Rožnov.

Other places of interest in the region
North of the Beskydy protected area between the towns of Nový Jičín and Frýdek–Místek are four interesting places worth a few hours if you happen to be in the region.

Hukvaldy
The best known of the four, the village of Hukvaldy is the birthplace of Moravian composer Leoš Janáček. There is a small museum dedicated to him and the annual Janáčkovy Hukvaldy music festival is held at the small castle in July and August.

Kopřivnice
Ten kilometres east of Nový Jičín lies the ugly industrial town of Kopřivnice. The only reason to venture here is to visit the *Technické museum Tatra Kopřivnice* to see the huge luxury Tatra limousines produced in the town, the car of choice for Communist Party bigwigs. In the grounds of the museum stands the 'Slovenská střela', an oddly shaped locomotive from 1935 which could cover the 400km from Prague to Bratislava in less than five hours.

Štramberk
Unlike the buildings in the museum in Rožnov, people still inhabit the wooden cottages in Štramberk, a short walk west of Kopřivnice. It is tourist free and there is no admission fee!

Příbor
Few Czechs will be aware that Sigmund Freud was born in a small town in the northeast of their country. This is Příbor's (only) claim to fame. A few rooms of the local museum are devoted to the town's most famous son and the square bears his name. Příbor is 5km north of Kopřivnice.

OLOMOUC
For those seeking Moravia's real answer to Prague, Olomouc (pronounced *Olo-moh-ts*) is the place to see. This city of 105,000 souls, the fifth largest in the republic, has a wealth of architecture, cobbled squares and a historical atmosphere to compare to parts of the capital, but thankfully there the similarity ends. Unlike Prague, Olomouc is a laid-back, cheap, friendly, student city that has the ambience of a town one-fifth the size. Unhurried locals still have time for foreigners, unlike their tourist-weary Prague counterparts, and service here comes with a genuine smile. Less has changed in this corner of Moravia since the fall of communism, and there is a decidedly less commercial atmosphere, fewer advertising hoardings and less development. It is the perfect antidote to some of the country's tourist traps, and why the town receives only a trickle of foreign tourists is quite inexplicable.

History
The three hills of Olomouc, which rise out of the Morava floodplain, have formed a naturally strategic site for human habitation for possibly the last 8,000 years. Early settlers, the Romans, Celts, Germanic and Slavic tribes, the Great

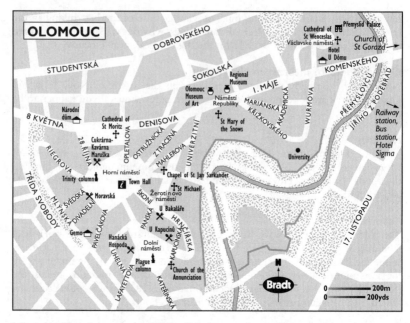

Moravian Empire and the Přemyslid dynasty have all made it an important stronghold, helped by its position on a trans-European trade route which followed the fertile plain of the Morava River. By the 11th century the town had become an important seat of administrative and religious power, a bishopric from 1063 and the capital of Moravia from the 12th century until the Thirty Years War, when it was occupied by the Swedes. The capital was shifted south to more secure Brno, and Olomouc's significance waned slightly, though it was promoted to the seat of the Moravian archbishopric in 1777. Industrialisation and economic development, choked by redundant fortifications, was slow to get off the ground in the 19th century, but the city soon made up for it in the early 20th century.

Getting there and away
Though in deepest Moravia, Olomouc is easier and quicker to reach from Prague than from some parts of Moravia itself. The **train** has a time advantage over the bus thanks to the main line east running through the city and numerous trains zip to Olomouc in just over three hours (354Kč). **Buses** from Florenc coach station take up to four hours, but are cheaper at around 170Kč. Bus is best for travelling down to Brno (1½ hours, 80Kč), but train is the better option to Opava as there is a more frequent service (2–3 hours, 140Kč).

Olomouc bus station is 500m east of the railway station which boasts pure 1950s communist-era architecture. Check out the 1960s' sgrafitto mural of workers and country folk enjoying a socialist utopia above the departures board. On arrival buy an 8Kč tram ticket from the yellow machines at the station and board trams 2, 4 or 6 to make the approximately 2km journey to the city centre, alighting at náměstí Republiky. Services peter out circa 23.00.

Tourist information
The municipal information centre can be found next to the astronomical clock at the town hall (*Horní náměstí – podloubí radnice;* \/f *585 203 790–1;*

www.olomouc-tourism.cz). The information centre at the railway station belongs to Czech Railways but has maps and other information.

Where to stay
Olomouc has little need for a hotel in every street and accommodation is decidedly thin on the ground. Private rooms are apparently difficult to find. The following are some of the cheapest and best options in town.

Hotel U Dómu Dómská 4; ☏ 585 220 502; f 585 220 501; www.udomu.360-panorama.net. Situated in a quiet street leading from busy 1. máje Street to the Cathedral of St Wenceslas, this friendly 6-room pension is one of the best options in the historical centre. Rooms come for 1,200Kč for sgl occupancy rising to 1,800Kč for 2 people sharing. The room rate includes a 'breakfast fit for a king' as the friendly staff will proudly tell you.

Gemo Pavelčákova 22; ☏ 585 222 115; f 585 231 730; www.hotel-gemo.cz. Olomouc's top hotel lies just outside the historical centre. Accommodation is in 33 4-star-standard light, airy, tastefully decorated rooms. Expect to pay 2,000–2,500Kč for a sgl and around 3,000Kč for a dbl.

Hotel Sigma Jeremenkova 36; ☏ 585 232 076–9; f 585 231 725; www.sigmahotel.cz. The Sigma is housed in an unattractive tower block opposite the railway station. However, things improve inside and the basic rooms represent good value at as little as 630Kč for a sgl and 1,000Kč for a dbl with breakfast.

Národní dům 8. května 21; ☏ 585 224 806–7; f 585 224 983; www.tady.cz/hotelnarodnidum. The large Národní dům is well situated and cheap, but may be just too basic for most people. Nothing has changed here since 1989 (not even the signs in Russian) and some of the rooms look like mock-ups of communist-era hotel rooms complete with chunky Tesla colour TV, net curtains and obligatory bottle opener. Sgl occupancy is 570Kč, dbl occupancy 770Kč.

Where to eat
Hanácká hospoda Dolní náměstí 38; ☏ 585 237 186. Staff in Haná folk costume, live music on Fridays, monster helpings, reasonable prices (70–200Kč), 4 types of Pilsen beer and a wide selection of Moravian wines make this place, housed in the historical Hauenschild House where the young Mozart stayed with his family in 1767, the best place to eat in Olomouc. If only they would turn the radio down…

Moravská restaurace Horní náměstí 23; ☏ 585 222 868; f 585 224 327; www.moravskarestaurace.cz. Another great place with a traditional local atmosphere is the Moravian restaurant a few strides from the Trinity Column. The menu is heavy with international staples as well as Moravian specialities such as rabbit, pheasant and veal (*danč*) for 125–200Kč (some specialities more). The dining space is done out like a traditional Moravian village cottage with hefty timber tables and chairs and ample decoration and even the staff are dressed appropriately. The usual annoying FM commercial radio is replaced by Moravian folk music in this small, intimate and popular eatery.

Restaurace U Bakaláře Žerotínovo náměstí 3; ☏ 585 226 786. This unbelievably cheap place is hidden at the end of Žerotínovo Square. In 2 rooms of tightly packed benches, ideal for getting to know the locals, Czech and international standards can be consumed for 25–120Kč.

U Kapucínů Dolní náměstí 23; ☏ 585 222 700. Without knowing that the entrance is actually in Kapucínská Street you would never find this place. Light and airy and spread out over 3 rooms, this is dinner-break territory for local office workers. Czech and international staples come for 60–200Kč, there is Gambrinus on tap and the staff are friendly, as they seem to be throughout Olomouc.

Cukrárna-Kavárna Maruška 28. října 2. If it is coffee and cakes you are after, try Maruška next to the Prior department store, a modern *cukrárna* with a popular coffee shop upstairs, both open until 22.00 every day. They have a huge selection of cream cakes for Czech prices.

What to see and do
Around Václavské náměstí
For those coming on foot from the station, a cluster of sites huddled around miniature Václavské náměstí, serve as an hors d'oeuvre to the historical main course of the city centre. Built around a Romanesque basilica, the twin spires of the **Cathedral of St Wenceslas** (Dóm sv Václava) attract most attention, and the recently sandblasted exterior has doubtlessly never looked better since its construction in the mid 13th century and its neo-Gothic facelift in the mid 19th century. Only Pilsen's Cathedral of St Bartholomew can boast a higher spire. As is the case across less tourist-infested Moravia, the cathedral can be wandered at will, and rewards visitors with a light, airy interior full of stained glass, exquisite lofty Gothic vaulting and painted pillars. It also houses the tomb of St Jan Sarkander (see page 303). A plaque at the entrance to the cathedral commemorates the visit of Pope John Paul II in 1995. Adjoining the cathedral is the erroneously named **Přemyslid Palace** (Přemyslovský palác, *admission 60/30Kč, open Apr–Oct*), once thought to have served the Přemyslid dynasty, but now known to have been built by Bishop Jindřich Zdík in the mid 12th century (the Přemyslid princes probably lived next door in a palace where the deanery now stands and where the last Přemyslid ruler, Václav III, was murdered in 1306). The remains of this gem of European Romanesque residential architecture are toured with an English text and highlights include 15th- and 16th-century frescoes in the cloister, the purely Romanesque bishop's rooms and the Chapel of St John the Baptist.

Around náměstí Republiky
From Václavské náměstí continue along 1 máje Street to náměstí Republiky and the Baroque **Church of St Mary of the Snows** (Kostel Panny Marie Sněžné), built by the Jesuits in 1712 and originally part of a college complex which evolved into today's Palacký University. The architect Michael Josef Klen z Nisy was clearly inspired by the Church of St Nicholas in Prague's Malá Strana though the interior falls way short of anything the Dientzenhofers created. Opposite the church seek out the **Olomouc Museum of Art** (*admission 20/10Kč, free every Wed*) which hosts changing exhibitions year round. Next to that is the large **Regional Museum** (*admission 40/20Kč*) which dusty rocks, moth-eaten stuffed animals and overbearing attendants aside, has an intriguing exhibition on Olomouc's astronomical clock including fragments of the original, carved figures from past reincarnations and photos of the clock's glory days before it received a direct hit from a shell on 7 May 1945.

Around Horní náměstí
Irregular **Horní náměstí** is where it happens in Olomouc and is the focal point of the city. Several attractions interrupt its cobbled span, starting with the **town hall** accommodating the information centre. The original, constructed entirely of wood, went up in 1378 then went up again in 1417, this time in flames. Today's town hall dates from the mid 15th century but has been tinkered with considerably since. The climbable tower dates from 1607 and measures 75m. The main attraction on the north-facing façade of the building is the **Astronomical**

Clock (*orloj*), very obviously not the work of a medieval craftsman and resembling an elaborate, oversize gas meter. The damaged original was ripped out after World War II and replaced with a more proletariat-friendly version. On the hour figures representing the workers twirl pitifully around at the top and the whole thing is encased in a typical communist-era mosaic which would look more at home at a railway station. While the *orloj* may be a let-down, the huge **Trinity Column** (Sloup Nejsvětější Trojice), by far the bulkiest in the Czech lands, is not. The blackened sculptures of the column, so big it has a chapel inside, has adorned the square since 1754, making it one of the last to be built in the country. The 35m-high monument, crowned with a riot of gilt figures, is the work of Moravian sculptor Ondřej Zahner and in 2000 became one of the Czech Republic's numerous UNESCO sites.

To the north of Horní náměstí soars the uninviting, fortress-like late Gothic **Cathedral of St Moritz** (Kostel sv Mořice). In stark contrast to the bare, plain stone of the exterior, the interior with its curious peaches-and-cream colour scheme is a surprise. There are touches of Baroque and neo-Gothic 'improvements' here and there and the church boasts the largest organ in the country with some of the tubes resembling chunky Czech tin drainpipes. The 46m-high bell tower can be scaled in summer (*admission 15/10Kč*) for views across the steeples of Olomouc. The only blot in Olomouc's copybook is the adjacent Prior supermarket, a candidate for worst-located building in the Czech Republic.

Around Dolní náměstí

Linked to Horní náměstí by a narrow pedestrian thoroughfare, Dolní náměstí is a much less grand, low-key affair. The only sights of note are the **plague column** erected in 1716–23 in memory of victims of the pestilence which struck Olomouc in 1713–15, and the characteristically sober Capuchin **Church of the Annunciation** from 1661.

Around Žerotínovo náměstí

Elongated Žerotínovo náměstí, east of Horní náměstí and accessed via some picturesque alleyways from both squares, is home to two interesting churches. The triple-domed **Church of St Michael** with its subdued Baroque interior and intricately decorated, illuminated altar also has a *Křížová chodba*, a kind of enclosed courtyard where you will find a free exhibition of images of Olomouc from the air as well as 18th-century sculpture. Anyone can wander in and take a look around (and, seemingly, one of the statues too as there is no-one around). One can also climb the rickety tower though health and safety may be a serious issue here! The large building next door is a former Dominican monastery.

Further along Žerotínovo náměstí stands the tiny rotund **Chapel of St Jan Sarkander**. Sarkander was a priest in the Moravian town of Holešov put on trial

OLOMOUC'S BAROQUE FOUNTAINS

Name	Place	Year created
Caesar's Fountain (Caesarova kašna)	Horní náměstí	1724
Hercules's Fountain (Herkulova kašna)	Horní náměstí	1688
Mercury's Fountain (Merkurova kašna)	Ulice 8 května	1727
Triton's Fountain (Kašna Tritonů)	náměstí Republiky	1709
Jupiter's Fountain (Jupiterova kašna)	Dolní náměstí	1735
Neptune's Fountain (Neptunova kašna)	Dolní náměstí	1683

for treason and conspiracy against the estates in 1620 during their uprising against Emperor Ferdinand II. He professed his innocence throughout, even under torture which eventually cost him his life. The chapel to the martyr was built in 1909 on the site of the prison where he was kept. Jan Sarkander had to wait over 370 years for beatification which came in 1993, with his canonisation taking place two years later in Olomouc in the presence of Pope John Paul II.

Other places of interest
On Gorazdovo Square across the Morava River stands the small Orthodox **Church of St Gorazd** dating from 1939, worth seeing just for its striking pink, white and green exterior and three gold onion domes. If it happens to be open, take a peek inside at the icon-filled interior.

Around Olomouc
Šternberk
Some 15km north of Olomouc stands the Castle of Šternberk in a town of the same name. Built in the second half of the 13th century it was given a Renaissance facelift in the 16th century, a Baroque reconstruction was never fully realised, and the whole lot was given a typical 19th-century Romantic makeover leaving an interesting jumble of styles. The Gothic and Baroque interiors (*admission 60/30Kč, open Apr–Oct*) host an exhibition on sculpture and art from the Gothic era to Baroque, and there is also a museum of historical timepieces. The very impressive Baroque Church of the Annunciation of Our Lord with its grand façade and 60m-high towers also merits a perusal.

The town can be visited on a leisurely outing from Olomouc with frequent trains and buses making the trip which takes around 20 minutes.

PROSTĚJOV
Many a Czech businessman, state official and ball-goer has the name of this town rubbing against the back of his neck! The Prostějov brand of clothing is the Czechs' answer to Armani, and the town is proud of its thriving textile and clothing industries. Perhaps not worth a visit on its own, stop off here on your way to or from Brno or Olomouc, if only to see the extraordinary Art Nouveau Národní dům by one of the best-known Czech architects of the early 20th century, Jan Kotěra. Apart from clothing generations of Czechs, Prostějov's other major contribution to life on the planet is as the birthplace of Otto Wichterle (1913–98), the inventor of soft contact lenses.

Getting there and away
Prostějov lies on the main Brno–Olomouc **railway** line making the rail journey fast and easy from both cities. Brno is just over an hour away (98Kč) while Olomouc can be reached in less than 30 minutes, though some *osobní* category of train take considerably longer.

There is also a very frequent **bus** service between Brno and Olomouc (40–60 minutes, 44–70Kč), though train is the better option from Olomouc.

The bus and rail stations are next to one another at the end of Svatoplukova Street which leads to the main T G Masaryka Square, ten minutes away on foot.

Tourist information
The friendly but rather frugal information centre (*nám T G Masaryka 12;* ↘ *582 329 722–3;* f *582 342 338; www.mestopv.cz*) has basic information on the town including hotel and restaurant lists and maps of the centre.

Where to stay
Hotel Avion nám E Husserla 15; ℄ 582 344 561; f 582 330 513;
www.avion.prostejov.cz. This characterless building lurks in a corner of E Husserla
Square, a quiet and convenient location. The 23 rooms are acceptable, clean and each
has TV and shower. About the only thing going for the place is the price with sgl rooms
for 550Kč and dbls for 900Kč without breakfast.
Grandhotel Palackého 3–5; ℄ 582 332 311; f 582 332 323; www.grandhotel.cz. The
green marble Art Nouveau building of Prostějov's best hotel stands on busy Palackého
Street. The 39 en-suite rooms are comfortable and well furnished and the hotel has a
sound restaurant. Sgls go for 1,340Kč, dbls for 2,110Kč.

Where to eat
Národní dům Vojáčkovo nám 1; ℄ 582 336 840; www.narodni-dum.cz. Prostějov has
the usual selection of smoky, pub-like Czech restaurants with blaring FM radio and
nonchalant staff, but the restaurant in the Národní dům (see *What to see and do* section) is
something a bit special. Apart from the large portions of food (60–150Kč) and Bernard
beer, the Art Nouveau interiors, unaltered since they were created almost 100 years ago,
are one of the reasons to eat here. The high ceilings, huge windows, period fittings and
gentle murmur of fellow diners takes one back to a more elegant time. The restaurant
also trains waiters and other staff, always a guarantee that things are done in a more 'old
world' sort of way.

What to see and do
The best place to start in town is **Náměstí T G Masaryka**, Prostějov's main
piazza. A hybrid between a square and a park it is a pleasant place to relax on a
bench and admire the dominant work of architecture, the towering **New Town
Hall**. Built in 1911–14 by Karel Hugo Kepka on the site of a former barracks it
would be even more impressive had the right wing been completed as planned,
and is irritatingly asymmetrical as if it has lost a limb. The 66m-high oversize
tower sporting an astronomical clock would not look out of place in a town five
times the size of Prostějov. Ask at the information centre next door about tours
of the plush, richly decorated Art Nouveau interiors, each room a work of art.
Standing side on to the New Town Hall is a bronze statue of a glum-looking T
G Masaryk in his customary raincoat.
  The New Town Hall (logically) replaced the Renaissance **Old Town Hall** at
the opposite end of the square, now home to the **Prostějov Museum** (*admission
20/10Kč, open Tue–Sun*). Apart from the usual faded collection of rocks and
minerals there is an interesting display of clocks and a few examples of folk
costumes and rural furniture from the Haná region. One room is devoted to
Czech poet Jiří Wolker (1900–24), another of the town's famous sons. Behind
the museum hides the **Church of the Ascension of the Holy Cross**, a Gothic
structure with a Baroque tower. Unfortunately it is generally closed to visitors,
but the key can be procured from the adjacent vicarage to view the Baroque altar
and furnishings as well as the *Stations of the Cross* carved by František Bílek.

Other places
Northwest of Náměstí T G Masaryka stands Prostějov's dilapidated Renaissance
chateau. Visitors can still admire its sgraffito decoration by Jan Kohler, but that
is about all that can be said for this crumbling hulk which appears to be inhabited
and has a *pivnice* in the basement. It reminds me of the state of many historical
buildings after 1989. Most underwent renovation, but this poor *zámek* seems to
have slipped through the net and gone to seed. From the chateau head east

through Smetanovy sady which has a long stretch of the town's original walls still intact along one side, ending in a bastion which houses an art gallery and which served as a prison in the 19th century. Behind that is Vojáčkovo náměstí dominated by the Art Nouveau **Národní dům**, built by the famous architect Jan Kotěra in 1905–07, and commissioned by a Czech town council eager to have a prestigious venue where Czech culture and social life could thrive. It houses a large theatre, a lecture hall, several smaller meeting rooms, a restaurant and a café, all virtually untouched since the day they were built and considered one of the best examples of Kotěra's work and Art Nouveau in the region.

On your way to or from the stations veer off Svatoplukova on to náměstí Padlých hrdinů to see the curious **Kovaříkova Villa**, built in 1911 by the architect E Králík and now housing an Indian tearoom. The only remaining evidence of Prostějov's once-thriving Jewish community is the **synagogue** on náměstí svat Čecha, now used by the Hussite Church, and a forgotten Hebrew plaque in adjacent Demelova Street.

OPAVA

With the Opava flood plain to the east, the Jeseníky Mountains to the west and the Polish border immediately to the north, Opava with its 60,000 inhabitants is perhaps not worth an excursion in itself, but could provide an hour or two of distraction between trains when heading from Ostrava to the Jeseníky Mountains.

Opava is one of the oldest towns in the Czech lands. Established around a ford in the river Opava before the 12th century the town was a staging post on a trade route linking the Baltic with the Adriatic, the so-called Amber Route. Opava was a seat of Přemyslid power and even had its own mint from the 13th century. Its wealth and importance waned only after the Thirty Years War when the Habsburgs centralised their power in Vienna. The ethnic make-up also changed, and by the 1720s the vast majority of the townsfolk were German. After the division of Silesia between Prussia and Austria during the reign of Empress Maria Theresa, Opava became the capital of Austrian Silesia and many of the grand palaces we see today date from that period. The town's importance was underlined in 1820 when the Opava Conference, attended by the rulers of Austria, Russia and Prussia, took place there. Throughout the 19th century it was an important centre of the textile industry. Because of the high percentage of Germans in the town, Opava suffered an uneasy first half of the 20th century. In 1918, the authority of the Czechoslovak state had to be enforced militarily, and in the 1930s the disgruntled Germans were in favour of uniting Silesia with Hitler's Third Reich. After liberation in late April 1945 (during which a third of the town was destroyed) the Germans were driven out

Getting there and away

Lying approximately halfway between Ostrava to the southeast and Krnov to the northwest, it is easy to reach Opava from both on a **railway** line which hugs the Polish border. Hourly departures from Ostrava–Svinov railway station get travellers to Opava in around 45 minutes for 40Kč, while **buses** set off from the main coach station several times an hour on weekdays, taking just short of an hour with similar ticket prices. Train is better to and from the mountainous regions of the northeast with hourly services to and from Krnov (40 minutes, 40Kč) where you can change on to trains to Jeseník, Velké Losiny and Šumperk. The railway station (Opava-východ) is ten minutes' walk from Horní Square. The bus station is around 15 minutes on foot along Těšínská Street.

Tourist information
The very obliging municipal information centre can be found next to the Hláska (*Horní náměstí 67;* ↘ *553 756 143; www.opava-city.cz, www.infocentrum.opava.cz*).

Where to stay
Hotel Koruna nám Republiky 17; ↘ 553 621 132; f 553 621 900; www.hotelkoruna.cz. The Koruna's maroon vinyl 1980s exterior may be off-putting, but the 3-star interior is decent enough. The 85 rooms are clean and basic and all are en suite. A sgl without breakfast can be had for as little as 790Kč, a luxury dbl with breakfast costs 1,700Kč. There is also a very acceptable restaurant on the premises.
Hotel Opava Žižkova 8; ↘ 553 759 340; www.hotel-opava.cz. Situated approximately 3km northwest of the town centre along Krnovská St the peaceful Opava's spick-and-span 4-star rooms are a superb deal at 1,200–1,600Kč for a dbl with breakfast. Each guest is also entitled to a free taxi ride to the centre and back and there is 20% off weekend room rates.

Where to eat
U Krbu Masařská 3; ↘ 553 613 488; www.aoc.cz/ukrbu. Just off Horní Square behind the Hláska, the restaurant 'By the Hearth' has dark, snug timber cubicles, a huge selection of mainly Czech dishes (100–160Kč) and Pilsen, Velvet and Kelt beers.
Kavárna čas Matiční 2a; ↘ 553 611 655. Roughly 200m along Matiční Street from the cathedral, this tiny eatery has 2 cosy wallpapered dining areas and a garden at the rear. Most meals are under 100Kč and there is Krušovice beer on tap. Vegetarian options are limited to the usual takes on fried cheese. The service is curt and the rooms may be a tad smoky for some people's liking.

What to see and do
Most of the town's sights are within easy walking distance of **Horní náměstí**, Opava's central square. Once a proud historical centrepiece, now two chunks of classic communist-era architecture line two sides. The very 1990s fountain in the centre does little to improve things. The dominant building is the **Hláska**, currently Opava's town hall, but originally the centre of trade in the town which housed stores, the town's official scales, the court and the council chambers. The tower dates from 1618 and the building underwent reconstruction in 1803 after which it served as a museum until 1888. Facing the Hláska across the square stands the **Slezské divadlo** (Silesian Theatre) built in 1804.

Obscured by the socialist-era shopping mall the **Cathedral of the Assumption** is an example of the Silesian brick Gothic style. A church was founded on the site in the 13th century by the Order of the Teutonic Knights. Its current appearance dates from the 14th century with some Baroque alterations. The cavernous interior sports hefty columns, a huge Baroque altar and is lined with false marble Baroque side altars. The Chapel of the Holy Trinity to the right of the side entrance houses a precious panel painting from 1452. Opava's newest place of worship dating from 1933–38, the **Church of St Hedvika** is ten minutes' walk from Horní Square along busy Krnovská then left into Hany Kvapilové Street. This dark grey and white compact example of functionalist architecture is possibly Opava's best-kept secret. A church dedicated to Hedvika, the patron saint of Silesia, had been planned from 1894 when a local professor donated 5,000 gold pieces to finance the project. The new church, built on the site of the town's defunct cemetery, was not begun until 1933, but was immediately used by the Nazis from 1938 and subsequently by the communists as a storehouse. The church opened its doors properly in 1993 almost 100 years after the idea to build it was conceived. The tower has some Cubist elements and inside look out for the frescoes depicting Silesian miners, foundry workers and other professions.

Back over on the other side of town the **Slezské zemské muzeum** (*www.szmo.cz, admission 30/15Kč*) in Smetanovy sady with its collections of local folk art and folk costumes is worth a stopover, as is the **Minorite Monastery and Church of the Holy Spirit** on attractive, palace-lined Masarykova třída. The church is the venue for the International Organ Music Festival held annually in May.

THE JESENÍKY MOUNTAINS

The highest mountains in Moravia rise up in the isolated northwest of the region, their green slopes a stark contrast to the industrial landscape to the east. This is a remote, sparsely populated region dotted with tiny spa towns and a great place to escape from tourists and people in general, as these are the republic's least-visited highlands. Comprising two distinct ranges, the Hrubý Jeseník with its rugged terrain with peaks over 1,000m high and the Nízký Jeseník, low hills barely reaching 700m, the entire area is great for hiking in summer and cross-country skiing in winter, though acid rain damage due to decades of industrial pollution wafting in from Poland occasionally spoil the vistas. Praděd is the highest mountain in Moravia at a touch over 1,490m.

Getting there and around

The towns of **Šumperk** and **Jeseník** are the best starting points for exploring the mountains. To reach Šumperk from Prague take trains heading east to Olomouc and change at Zábřeh na Moravě (3 hours, 250Kč). There are two direct buses a day (4½ hours, 200Kč) but one arrives at 02.00. To Jeseník there is one direct train a day from Prague (5½ hours, 300Kč) and two direct buses (4½ hours, 180Kč) otherwise change in Zábřeh na Moravě on the east–west main line.

Rail forms the backbone of the Jeseníky transport infrastructure. The main artery is line 292 linking Šumperk with Jeseník with several branch lines snaking off into the mountains at various points. Another line heads north from Šumperk to Kouty nad Desnou, a trailhead for hikes to Praděd. Buses also ply the frantically twisting mountain roads and the journey from Šumperk to Jeseník should not take more than 1½ hours.

Hiking in the Jeseníky Mountains

VKÚ-KČT maps 54 *Rychlebské hory a Lázně Jeseník*, 55 *Hrubý Jeseník* and 56 *Nízký Jeseník* are the best maps to study before setting off. There are enough marked trails crisscrossing the mountains for you to plan itineraries of any length and difficulty. I recommend the following routes:

Kouty nad Desnou–Karlova Studánka (approx 30km). From the railway station in Kouty nad Desnou take the yellow trail up to Červenohorské sedlo, a mountain pass on the Jeseník–Šumperk highway. From there it's a hard slog to the top of Praděd on a red trail, but hikers are rewarded with fine views of the surrounding mountainous terrain. Another 12km or so along the green trail will bring you to Karlova Studánka where there are pensions and food. Fit hikers could manage this hike in a long day.

Jeseník–Červenohorské sedlo–Jeseník (approx 30km). From Jeseník catch the early-morning bus to Červenohorské sedlo (25 minutes, 20Kč). From there select the red trail heading northwest leading to the top of Keprník Mountain

(1,424m) with breathtaking views from the top. From there it is around 20km along the red trail then on a yellow trail back into Jeseník. Another long day of strenuous walking but worth every step. For both of these hikes check the weather before starting out in spring and autumn.

Jeseník

This spa town of 14,000 souls nestled among forested hills is on the whole pretty unremarkable. Its foremost claim to fame is as the location of the world's first hydrotherapeutic spa, founded by one Vincenz Priessnitz in the 19th century. The large spa complex still sits on a hillside above the town. Jeseník has several hotels and pensions away from the spa district making it a good base for exploring the mountains. Ask at the **information centre** (*Masarykovo náměstí 167/1;* ⟍ *584 498 155;* f *584 498 156*).

Velké Losiny

One of the most interesting towns in the Jeseníky region is the tiny spa town of Velké Losiny, 10km north of Šumperk on the Jeseník road. From 1496 to 1802 the exquisite Renaissance **chateau** with its striking three-tiered loggia (*admission 50/30Kž, open Apr–Oct*) was the residence of the Žerotín family, powerful Moravian nobles who gained notoriety for their insane witch hunts in the 17th and 18th centuries, the subject of a sinister Czech film, *Kladivo na čarodějnice*. Even more interesting is the **Handmade Paper Museum** (Ruční papírna, *admission 60/30Kč*) where visitors can watch the engrossing paper-making process, visit an exhibition on the history of the paper mill and buy some of the beautiful, thick, luxurious produce in all shapes and sizes. The mill was established by the Žerotíns at the end of the 16th century and the much sought-after paper has been used by the central European nobility and governments for centuries.

Getting there and away

Velké Losiny is served by both bus (18 minutes, 13Kč) and train (20 minutes, 12Kč) from Šumperk.

European hedgehog

Appendix 1

LANGUAGE
Pronunciation

The following is a very rough guide to Czech pronunciation which should enable you to tackle any word you come across. The golden rule is that Czech pronunciation is 95% regular and position in the word does not have an effect on the sound of the letter. Each letter is pronounced clearly and crisply and there is no aspiration (a short burst of air after a letter) or reduction ('swallowing' half the word, dropping 'h' and 't') as is common in English.

a	as the 'u' in 'sh<u>u</u>t'
á	as the 'a' in 'f<u>a</u>ther'
b	as the 'b' in '<u>b</u>ed'
c	as the 'ts' in 'ca<u>ts</u>'
č	as the 'ch' in '<u>ch</u>at'
d	as the 'd' in '<u>d</u>og'
ď	as the 'd y' in 'foole<u>d you</u>'
e	as the 'e' in 'l<u>e</u>t'
é	as the 'e' in 'wh<u>e</u>re'
ě	as the 'ye' in '<u>ye</u>s' except after 'm' when it becomes '<u>nye</u>'. *Město* (town) = '*mnyesto*'
f	as the 'f' in '<u>f</u>an', never as in 'of'
g	as the 'g' in '<u>g</u>ot', never as in 'page'
h	as the 'h' in '<u>h</u>alt' but very pronounced, as 'ch' in 'lo<u>ch</u>' at the end of a word – *tah* (pull) = '*tach*'
i	as the 'i' in 'm<u>i</u>nt'
í	as the 'ee' in 't<u>ee</u>n'
j	as the 'y' in '<u>y</u>ell', never as 'j' in 'jelly'
k	as the 'k' in '<u>k</u>ill'
l	as the 'l' in '<u>l</u>ot'
m	as the 'm' in '<u>m</u>other'
n	as the 'n' in '<u>n</u>ever'
ň	as the 'ny' in 'ca<u>ny</u>on'
o	as the 'o' in 'n<u>o</u>t'
ó	as the 'aw' in 'p<u>aw</u>'
p	as the 'p' in '<u>p</u>en'
q	there is no letter 'q' in Czech.
r	always rolled, no matter where it falls in a word
ř	no equivalent sound in English. Try saying 'rž' together very quickly.
s	as the 's' in '<u>s</u>in', never as in 'nose'
š	as the 'sh' in '<u>sh</u>ell'
t	as the 't' in '<u>t</u>ell'
ť	as the 't' in '<u>t</u>utor'

311

u	as the 'u' in 'f<u>u</u>ll'
ú, ů	as the 'oo' in 'm<u>oo</u>n'
v	as the 'v' in '<u>v</u>et', as the 'f' in '<u>f</u>an' at the end of a word, hence Bítov = 'Beetof'
w	pronounced in the same way as 'v'; only occurs in words of foreign origin. Never as 'w' in 'wet'
x	as the 'ks' in 'boo<u>ks</u>' even at the beginning of a word
y	as the 'i' in 'm<u>i</u>nt', never as the 'y' in 'silly'
ý	as the 'ee' in 't<u>ee</u>n'
z	as the 'z' in '<u>z</u>oo'
ž	as the 's' in 'plea<u>s</u>ure'
ou	as the '<u>oa</u>' in 'throat', never as 'oo' in 'moon' or 'ou' in 'house'
eu	as the 'o' in a posh-sounding 'n<u>o</u>'
au	as the 'ow' in 'n<u>ow</u>', never as 'au' in 'automatic'
dž	as the 'dg' in 'fu<u>dg</u>e'

Basic everyday phrases

English	*Czech*
Hello	*Dobrý den* (formal), *ahoj* (informal)
Goodbye	*Na shledanou* (formal), *ahoj* (informal)
Good morning	*Dobré ráno*
Good evening	*Dobrý večer*
Good night	*Dobrou noc*
Yes	*Ano*
No	*Ne*
Please	*Prosím*
Thank you	*Děkuji, díky*
You are welcome	*Není zač*
Excuse me	*Promiň*(+te = formal)
What is your name?	*Jak se jmenujete?*
My name is...	*Jmenuji se...*
Pleased to meet you	*Těší mě*
How are you?	*Jak se máte?*
I am fine	*Mám se dobře*
Not so good	*Mám se špatně*
Look out	*Pozor*
Help!	*Pomoc!*
Help me!	*Pomozte mi!*
I like	*Mám rád, ráda for a female*
I do not like	*Nemám rád, ráda for a female*

Asking

Do you speak...?	*Mluvíte...?*	I understand	*Rozumím*
English	*anglicky*	I do not understand	*Nerozumím*
Czech	*česky*	Could you repeat	*Mohl byste to*
German	*německy*	that?	*zopakovat*
French	*francouzsky*	What?	*Co?*
Polish	*polsky*	Where?	*Kde?*
Hungarian	*maďarsky*	Why?	*Proč*
Slovak	*slovensky*	How?	*Jak?*
Do you understand?	*Rozumíte?*	Who?	*Kdo?*

Asking directions

Where is the...?	Kde je...?	here	tady, tu, zde
square	náměstí	there	tam
railway station	vlakové nádraží	near	blízko
bus station	autobusové nádraží	far	daleko
ticket office	pokladna,	Is it far?	Je to daleko?
	výdejna jízdenek	How far is it?	Jak je to daleko?
church	kostel	on the left	nalevo
town hall	radnice	on the right	napravo
information centre	infocentrum	straight on	rovně
toilet	WC		
food shop	potraviny		
chateau	zámek		
hospital	nemocnice		
chemists	lékárna		

Buying

How much is it?	Kolik to stojí?	money	peníze
expensive	drahý	credit card	kreditní karta
cheap	levný	Do you take credit	Berete kreditní
checkout	pokladna	cards?	karty?
small change	drobné	sale	sleva/akce

Needs

I want...	Chci...	to eat	jíst
I would like...	Chtěl bych...	to drink	pít
I need...	Potřebuji...	to go	jít
May I...?	Mohu...?	to pay	zaplatit
to sleep	spát	to find	najít
to buy	koupit		

Food and drink

bread	chléb (chleba in	fried	smažený
	spoken Czech)	fruit	ovoce
cheese	sýr	ice cream	zmrzlina
meat	maso	dessert	zákusek
pork	vepřové	vegetarian	vegetarián
beef	hovězí	water	voda
chicken	kuřecí, kuře	milk	mléko
fish	ryba	juice	džus
side dish	příloha	tea	čaj
dumplings	knedlíky	coffee	káva
chips	hranolky	sugar	cukr
rice	rýže	beer	pivo
vegetables	zelenina	wine	víno
potatoes	brambory		

Other useful words

book	kniha	train	vlak
map	mapa, plán	bus	autobus
ticket	jízdenka, lístek,	room	pokoj
	vstupenka	key	klíč

bed	*postel*	rain	*déšť*
north	*sever*	sun	*slunce*
south	*jih*	mountain	*hora*
east	*východ*	hill	*kopec*
west	*západ*	lake	*jezero*
entrance	*vchod*	river	*řeka*
exit	*východ*	tree	*strom*
restaurant	*restaurace*	forest	*les*
pub	*hospoda*	field	*pole*
stop (bus, tram)	*zastávka*		

Adjectives

big/small	*velký/malý*	nice	*hezký*
cold/hot	*studený/horký*	important	*důležitý*
new/old	*nový/starý*	beautiful	*krásný*
good/bad	*dobrý/špatný*		

Numbers

1	*jeden*	50	*padesát*
2	*dva*	60	*šedesát*
3	*tři*	70	*sedmdesát*
4	*čtyři*	80	*osmdesát*
5	*pět*	90	*devadesát*
6	*šest*	100	*sto*
7	*sedm*	200	*dvě stě*
8	*osm*	300	*tři sta*
9	*devět*	400	*čtyři sta*
10	*deset*	500	*pět set*
11	*jedenáct*	600	*šest set*
12	*dvanáct*	700	*sedm set*
13	*třináct*	800	*osm set*
14	*čtrnáct*	900	*devět set*
15	*patnáct*	1,000	*tisíc* (pronounced
16	*šestnáct*		'tyiseets')
17	*sedmnáct*	2,000	*dva tisíce*
18	*osmnáct*	3,000	*tři tisíce*
19	*devatenáct*	4,000	*čtyři tisíce*
20	*dvacet*	5,000	*pět tisíc*
21	*dvacet jedna*	6,000	*šest tisíc*
22	*dvacet dva*	7,000	*sedm tisíc*
30	*třicet*	8,000	*osm tisíc*
40	*čtyřicet*	9,000	*devět tisíc*

Days and time

today	*dnes*	Monday	*pondělí*
yesterday	*včera*	Tuesday	*úterý*
tomorrow	*zítra*	Wednesday	*středa*
the day after		Thursday	*čtvrtek*
tomorrow	*pozítří*	Friday	*pátek*
		Saturday	*sobota*
		Sunday	*neděle*

What time is it?	*Kolik je hodin?*	clock	*hodiny*
now	*teď, nyní*	watch	*hodinky*
hour	*hodina*	at 5 o'clock	*V pět hodin*
minute	*minuta*		

Appendix

FURTHER INFORMATION
Books
History

Banville, John *Prague Pictues: Portrait of a City* Bloomsbury, 2003. Traces the history of Prague.

Demetz, Peter *Prague in Black and Gold* Penguin, 1998. A deep insight into the history of the city – occasionally too dry and academic for the casual reader.

Englund, Terje *The Czechs in a Nutshell* Baset, 2004. A witty, tongue-in-cheek look at the quirkier aspects of the Czech national character.

Innes, Abby *Czechoslovakia – The Short Goodbye* Yale University Press, 2001. An account of the so-called Velvet Divorce, the peaceful break-up of Czechoslovakia in 1992.

Kaplan, Jan *A Traveller's Companion to Prague* Constable and Robinson, 2005. The creative power of the city through letters, diaries, memoirs and anecdotes of famous people who have lived in or visited the city.

Klima, Ivan *The Spirit of Prague* Granta Books, 1998. A collection of essays charting the events of five critical decades of 20th-century Czechoslovakia.

Sayer, Derek *The Coasts of Bohemia* Princeton University Press, 1998. Put the history of the Czech lands at the heart of European history.

Architecture

Knox, Derek *The Architecture of Prague and Bohemia* Faber and Faber, 1962. A wonderful overview of Czech architecture and its creators. Hard to get hold of.

Sedláková, Radomíra *Prague: An Architectural Guide* Arsenale, 1997. Pocket guidebook to the architectural treasures of Prague.

General

James, Hilary *Prague My Love* Archangel, 1993. The hidden corners, myths and legends of Prague.

Lee, W R *Teach Yourself Czech* Teach Yourself, 2003. For my money still the best Czech textbook in English.

Randle, Dave *The True Story of Škoda* Sutton Publishing, 2002. A sometimes humorous look at this once much-ridiculed brand name

Trnka, Peter *The Best of Czech Cooking* Hippocrene Books, 2000. A Czech recipe book.

Art and photography

Kaplan, Jan *Prague* Konemann, 1997. Historical photographs, prints and other images from the Czech capital.

Mucha, Sarah *Alphonse Mucha* Frances Lincoln Publishers, 2005. A coffee-table book of Mucha's work.

Fiction

Fermor, Patrick Leigh *A Time of Gifts* John Murray, 2004

Hrabal, Bohumil *Closely Observed Trains* Abacus, 1990. A tale of sexual frustration, suicide and Czech resistance during World War II against the backdrop of a rural railway station. Made into an Oscar-winning film in 1966.

Jirásek, Alois *Old Czech Tales* UNESCO, 1992. The definitive collection of Czech myths and legends with a 19th-century romantic, nationalist flavour. Difficult to find.

Neruda, Jan *Prague Tales* Central European University Press, 2000. Tales of everyday folk from Prague's Malá Strana district.

Useful websites
Travel
www.czechtourism.com CzechTourism
www.pis.cz Prague Information Service
www.vlak.cz Rail and bus timetables
www.mapy.cz Maps of Czech towns and cities
www.airport-ruzyne.cz Prague Ruzyně Airport
www.csa.cz Czech Airlines
www.cdrail.cz Czech Railways
www.czecot.com CZeCOT tourist server
www.pamatky.cz Details on tourist sights around the Czech Republic

Internet
www.seznam.cz Seznam internet portal

Culture
www.czechcentres.cz Czech cultural centres worldwide
www.musica.cz Czech music news
www.czechmania.com Cutting-edge Czech design

Media
www.praguepost.cz *Prague Post*
www.radio.cz/english Radio Prague
www.ceskenoviny.cz Latest news from the Czech Republic in English
www.ctk.cz/english Official Czech news agency website
www.cbw.cz *Czech Business Weekly*

Miscellaneous
www.squaremeal.cz Prague restaurant guide
www.wordbook.cz Online Czech-English-Czech dictionary
www.czech.cz Ministry of Foreign Affairs website in English
www.czech-language.cz Everything to do with the Czech language

Bradt Travel Guides

www.bradtguides.com

Africa

Africa Overland	£15.99
Benin	£14.99
Botswana: Okavango, Chobe, Northern Kalahari	£14.95
Burkina Faso	£14.99
Cameroon	£13.95
Cape Verde Islands	£13.99
Eritrea	£12.95
Ethiopia	£15.99
Gabon, São Tomé, Príncipe	£13.95
Gambia, The	£12.95
Ghana	£13.95
Kenya	£14.95
Madagascar	£14.95
Malawi	£12.95
Mali	£13.95
Mauritius, Rodrigues & Réunion	£12.95
Mozambique	£12.95
Namibia	£14.95
Niger	£14.99
Nigeria	£15.99
Rwanda	£13.95
Seychelles	£14.99
Sudan	£13.95
Tanzania	£16.99
Tanzania, Northern	£13.99
Uganda	£13.95
Zambia	£15.95
Zanzibar	£12.99

Americas and Caribbean

Amazon, The	£14.95
Argentina	£15.99
Bolivia	£13.99
Cayman Islands	£12.95
Chile	£16.95
Chile & Argentina: Trekking	£12.95
Costa Rica	£13.99
Eccentric America	£13.95
Eccentric California	£13.99
Ecuador: Climbing & Hiking	£13.95
Falkland Islands	£13.95
Panama	£13.95
Peru & Bolivia: Backpacking and Trekking	£12.95
USA by Rail	£13.99
Venezuela	£14.95

Britain and Europe

Albania	£13.99
Armenia, with Nagorno Karabagh	£13.95
Azores	£12.95
Baltic Capitals: Tallinn, Riga, Vilnius, Kaliningrad	£12.99
Belgrade	£6.99
Bosnia & Herzegovina	£13.95
Bratislava	£6.99
Budapest	£7.95
Canary Islands	£13.95
Cork	£6.95
Croatia	£12.95

Cyprus see North Cyprus	
Czech Republic	£13.99
Dubrovnik	£6.95
Eccentric Britain	£13.99
Eccentric Edinburgh	£5.95
Eccentric France	£12.95
Eccentric London	£12.95
Eccentric Oxford	£5.95
Estonia	£12.95
Faroe Islands	£13.95
Georgia	£13.95
Hungary	£14.99
Kiev	£7.95
Latvia	£13.99
Lille	£6.99
Lithuania	£13.99
Ljubljana	£6.99
Macedonia	£13.95
Montenegro	£13.99
North Cyprus	£12.95
Paris, Lille & Brussels	£11.95
Riga	£6.95
River Thames, In the Footsteps of the Famous	£10.95
St Helena, Ascension, Tristan da Cunha	£14.95
Serbia	£13.99
Slovenia	£12.99
Spitsbergen	£14.99
Switzerland: Rail, Road, Lake	£13.99
Tallinn	£6.95
Ukraine	£13.95
Vilnius	£6.99

Middle East, Asia and Australasia

China: Yunnan Province	£13.99
Great Wall of China	£13.99
Iran	£14.99
Iraq	£14.95
Kabul	£9.95
Maldives	£13.99
Mongolia	£14.95
North Korea	£13.95
Oman	£13.99
Palestine, with Jerusalem	£12.95
Sri Lanka	£13.99
Syria	£13.99
Tasmania	£12.95
Tibet	£12.95
Turkmenistan	£14.99

Wildlife

Antarctica: Guide to the Wildlife	£14.95
Arctic: Guide to Coastal Wildlife	£14.95
British Isles: Wildlife of Coastal Waters	£14.95
Galápagos Wildlife	£15.99
Madagascar Wildlife	£14.95
Southern African Wildlife	£18.95

Health

Your Child Abroad: A Travel Health Guide	£10.95

WIN £100 CASH!

READER QUESTIONNAIRE

Send in your completed questionnaire for the chance to win £100 in our regular cash draw

All respondents may order a Bradt guide at half the UK retail price – please complete the order form overleaf.

(Entries may be posted or faxed to us, or scanned and emailed.)

We are interested in getting feedback from our readers to help us plan future Bradt guides. Please answer ALL the questions below and return the form to us in order to qualify for an entry in our regular draw.

Have you used any other Bradt guides? If so, which titles? . . . .
. . . .

What other publishers' travel guides do you use regularly? . . . .
. . . .

Where did you buy this guidebook? . . . .

What was the main purpose of your trip to the Czech Republic (or for what other reason did you read our guide)? eg: holiday/business/charity, etc. . . . .
. . . .

What other destinations would you like to see covered by a Bradt guide?
. . . .

Would you like to receive our catalogue/newsletters?

YES / NO (If yes, please complete details on reverse)

If yes – by post or email? . . . .

Age (circle relevant category) 16–25   26–45   46–60   60+

Male/Female (delete as appropriate)

Home country . . . .

Please send us any comments about our guide to the Czech Republic or other Bradt Travel Guides. . . . .
. . . .
. . . .
. . . .

Bradt Travel Guides/CZE

23 High Street, Chalfont St Peter, Bucks SL9 9QE, UK
☎ +44 1753 893444 f +44 1753 892333
e info@bradtguides.com
www.bradtguides.com

CLAIM YOUR HALF-PRICE BRADT GUIDE!

Order Form

To order your half-price copy of a Bradt guide, and to enter our prize draw to win £100 (see overleaf), please fill in the order form below, complete the questionnaire overleaf, and send it to Bradt Travel Guides by post, fax or email.

Please send me one copy of the following guide at half the UK retail price

Title	*Retail price*	*Half price*

Please send the following additional guides at full UK retail price

No	*Title*	*Retail price*	*Total*
...	....	....	....
...	....	....	....
...	....	....	....

	Sub total	......
	Post & packing	......
(£1 per book UK; £2 per book Europe; £3 per book rest of world)		
	Total	......

Name ....

Address...

Tel .... Email ....

☐ I enclose a cheque for £ .... made payable to Bradt Travel Guides Ltd

☐ I would like to pay by credit card. Number: ....

Expiry date ... / ... 3-digit security code (on reverse of card) .....

☐ Please add my name to your catalogue mailing list.

☐ I would be happy for you to use my name and comments in Bradt marketing material.

Send your order on this form, with the completed questionnaire, to:

Bradt Travel Guides/CZE
23 High Street, Chalfont St Peter, Bucks SL9 9QE
✆ +44 1753 893444 f +44 1753 892333
e info@bradtguides.com
www.bradtguides.com

NOTES

NOTES

NOTES

NOTES

Index

*Page numbers in bold indicate major entries;
those in italics indicate maps*